PRENTICE HALL

SCIENCE EXPLORER

Life Science

Prentice
Hall

Needham, Massachusetts
Upper Saddle River, New Jersey
Glenview, Illinois

Life Science

Print Resources

Student Edition
Annotated Teacher's Edition
Unit Resource Books, including:
- Chapter Project Support
- Lesson Plans
- Section Summaries
- Review and Reinforce Worksheets
- Enrich Worksheets
- Student Edition Lab Worksheets
- Complete Answer Keys

Chapter and Unit Tests
Performance Assessment
Standardized Test Preparation Book
Laboratory Manual, Student Edition
Laboratory Manual, Teacher's Edition
Inquiry Skills Activity Book
Student-Centered Science Activity Books
Guided Study Workbook
Reading in the Content Area with Literature Connections
Science Explorer Interdisciplinary Explorations
Prentice Hall Interdisciplinary Explorations series
Product Testing Activities by Consumer Reports™
How to Manage Instruction in the Block
How to Assess Student Work

Media and Technology

Interactive Student Tutorial CD-ROM
Computer Test Bank with Dial-A-Test®
Resource Pro® (Lesson Plans and Teaching Resources on CD-ROM)
Science Explorer Activity Videos
Internet Site at www.phschool.com (includes www.PlanetDiary.com)
Color Transparencies
Section Summaries Audio CD Library
Spanish Section Summaries Audio CD Library and Book
Videotape Library
Spanish Videotape Library
Videodisc Library (English/Spanish)
Odyssey of Discovery (CD-ROMs for Life and Earth Science)
Mindscape CD-ROMs
A.D.A.M. CD-ROM
Interactive Earth CD-ROM
Interactive Physics Software

Materials Kits

Consumable Materials Kit
Nonconsumable Materials Kit
Materials List CD-ROM

Acknowledgments

Excerpt on page 178 from *James Herriot's Dog Stories.* Copyright © 1986 by James Herriot. Published by St. Martin's Press.

Excerpt on pages 466–467 from *Dragons and Dynasties: An Introduction to Chinese Mythology* by Yuan Ke, selected and translated by Kim Echlin and Nie Zhixong, published by Penguin Books, 1993. First published in the People's Republic of China by Foreign Languages Press, Beijing, 1991. Copyright © Foreign Languages Press, 1991, 1992, 1993. Reprinted by permission of Penguin UK.

Excerpt on page 784 from *The Amateur Naturalist* by Gerald Durrell. Copyright © 1982 by Dorling Kindersley Ltd., London. Reprinted by permission of Alfred A. Knopf, Inc.

ISBN 0-13-050621-4
2 3 4 5 6 7 8 9 10   05 04 03 02 01 00

Prentice
Hall

Cover: A brilliantly colored macaw flies gracefully through the sky.

Program Authors

Michael J. Padilla, Ph.D.
Professor
Department of Science Education
University of Georgia
Athens, Georgia

Michael Padilla is a leader in middle school science education. He has served as an editor and elected officer for the National Science Teachers Association. He has been principal investigator of several National Science Foundation and Eisenhower grants and served as a writer of the National Science Education Standards.

As lead author of *Science Explorer,* Mike has inspired the team in developing a program that meets the needs of middle grades students, promotes science inquiry, and is aligned with the National Science Education Standards.

Ioannis Miaoulis, Ph.D.
Dean of Engineering
College of Engineering
Tufts University
Medford, Massachusetts

Martha Cyr, Ph.D.
Director, Engineering
 Educational Outreach
College of Engineering
Tufts University
Medford, Massachusetts

Science Explorer was created in collaboration with the College of Engineering at Tufts University. Tufts has an extensive engineering outreach program that uses engineering design and construction to excite and motivate students and teachers in science and technology education.

Faculty from Tufts University participated in the development of *Science Explorer* chapter projects, reviewed the student books for content accuracy, and helped coordinate field testing.

Book Authors

Elizabeth Coolidge-Stoltz, M.D.
Medical Writer
North Reading, Massachusetts

Donald Cronkite, Ph.D.
Professor of Biology
Hope College
Holland, Michigan

Dawn Graff-Haight, Ph.D., CHES
Associate Professor, Health
 Education
Linfield College
McMinnville, Oregon

Fred Holtzclaw
Science Teacher
Oak Ridge High School
Oak Ridge, Tennessee

Jan Jenner, Ph.D.
Science Writer
Talladega, Alabama

Linda Cronin Jones, Ph.D.
College of Education
University of Florida
Gainesville, Florida

Contributing Writers

Douglas E. Bowman
Health/Physical Education Teacher
Welches Middle School
Welches, Oregon

James Robert Kaczynski, Jr.
Science Teacher
Barrington Middle School
Barrington, Rhode Island

Evan P. Silberstein
Science Teacher
Spring Valley High School
Spring Valley, New York

Patricia M. Doran
Science Teacher
Rondout Valley Junior High School
Stone Ridge, New York

Susan Offner
Biology Teacher
Milton High School
Milton, Massachusetts

Joseph Stukey, Ph.D.
Department of Biology
Hope College
Holland, Michigan

Theresa Holtzclaw
Former Science Teacher
Clinton, Tennessee

Warren Phillips
Science Teacher
Plymouth Community
    Intermediate School
Plymouth, Massachusetts

Thomas R. Wellnitz
Science Teacher
The Paideia School
Atlanta, Georgia

Jorie Hunken
Science Consultant
Woodstock, Connecticut

Reading Consultant

Bonnie B. Armbruster, Ph.D.
Department of Curriculum
    and Instruction
University of Illinois
Champaign, Illinois

Interdisciplinary Consultant

Heidi Hayes Jacobs, Ed.D.
Teacher's College
Columbia University
New York, New York

Safety Consultants

W. H. Breazeale, Ph.D.
Department of Chemistry
College of Charleston
Charleston, South Carolina

Ruth Hathaway, Ph.D.
Hathaway Consulting
Cape Girardeau, Missouri

Content Reviewers

Tufts University Program Reviewers

Behrouz Abedian, Ph.D.
Department of Mechanical
    Engineering

Wayne Chudyk, Ph.D.
Department of Civil and
    Environmental Engineering

Eliana De Bernardez-Clark, Ph.D.
Department of Chemical
    Engineering

Anne Marie Desmarais, Ph.D.
Department of Civil and
    Environmental Engineering

David L. Kaplan, Ph.D.
Department of Chemical
    Engineering

Paul Kelley, Ph.D.
Department of Electro-Optics

George S. Mumford, Ph.D.
Professor of Astronomy, Emeritus

Jan A. Pechenik, Ph.D.
Department of Biology

Livia Racz, Ph.D.
Department of Mechanical
    Engineering

Robert Rifkin, M.D.
School of Medicine

Jack Ridge, Ph.D.
Department of Geology

Chris Swan, Ph.D.
Department of Civil and
    Environmental Engineering

Peter Y. Wong, Ph.D.
Department of Mechanical
    Engineering

Teacher Reviewers

Stephanie Anderson
Sierra Vista Junior
    High School
Canyon Country,
    California

John W. Anson
Mesa Intermediate School
Palmdale, California

Pamela Arline
Lake Taylor Middle School
Norfolk, Virginia

Lynn Beason
College Station Junior
    High School
College Station, Texas

Richard Bothmer
Hollis School District
Hollis, New Hampshire

Jeffrey C. Callister
Newburgh Free Academy
Newburgh, New York

Judy D'Albert
Harvard Day School
Corona Del Mar,
    California

Betty Scott Dean
Guilford County Schools
McLeansville,
    North Carolina

Sarah C. Duff
Baltimore City Public
    Schools
Baltimore, Maryland

Melody Law Ewey
Holmes Junior High
    School
Davis, California

Sherry L. Fisher
Lake Zurich Middle
    School North
Lake Zurich, Illinois

Melissa Gibbons
Fort Worth ISD
Fort Worth, Texas

Debra J. Goodding
Kraemer Middle School
Placentia, California

Jack Grande
Weber Middle School
Port Washington,
    New York

Steve Hills
Riverside Middle School
Grand Rapids, Michigan

Sandra M. Justin
Swift Junior High School
Oakville Connecticut

Carol Ann Lionello
Kraemer Middle School
Placentia, California

Jaime A. Morales
Henry T. Gage Middle
    School
Huntington Park,
    California

Patsy Partin
Cameron Middle School
Nashville, Tennessee

Deedra H. Robinson
Newport News Public
    Schools
Newport News, Virginia

Bonnie Scott
Clack Middle School
Abilene, Texas

Charles M. Sears
Belzer Middle School
Indianapolis, Indiana

Barbara M. Strange
Ferndale Middle School
High Point,
    North Carolina

Jackie Louise Ulfig
Ford Middle School
Allen, Texas

Kathy Usina
Belzer Middle School
Indianapolis, Indiana

Heidi M. von Oetinger
L'Anse Creuse Public
    School
Harrison Township,
    Michigan

Pam Watson
Hill Country Middle
    School
Austin, Texas

Activity Field Testers

Nicki Bibbo
Russell Street School
Littleton, Massachusetts

Connie Boone
Fletcher Middle School
Jacksonville Beach, Florida

Rose-Marie Botting
Broward County School District
Fort Lauderdale, Florida

Colleen Campos
Laredo Middle School
Aurora, Colorado

Elizabeth Chait
W. L. Chenery Middle School
Belmont, Massachusetts

Holly Estes
Hale Middle School
Stow, Massachusetts

Laura Hapgood
Plymouth Community
   Intermediate School
Plymouth, Massachusetts

Sandra M. Harris
Winman Junior High School
Warwick, Rhode Island

Jason Ho
Walter Reed Middle School
Los Angeles, California

Joanne Jackson
Winman Junior High School
Warwick, Rhode Island

Mary F. Lavin
Plymouth Community
   Intermediate School
Plymouth, Massachusetts

James MacNeil, Ph.D.
Concord Public Schools
Concord, Massachusetts

Lauren Magruder
St. Michael's Country
   Day School
Newport, Rhode Island

Jeanne Maurand
Glen Urquhart School
Beverly Farms, Massachusetts

Warren Phillips
Plymouth Community
   Intermediate School
Plymouth, Massachusetts

Carol Pirtle
Hale Middle School
Stow, Massachusetts

Kathleen M. Poe
Kirby-Smith Middle School
Jacksonville, Florida

Cynthia B. Pope
Ruffner Middle School
Norfolk, Virginia

Anne Scammell
Geneva Middle School
Geneva, New York

Karen Riley Sievers
Callanan Middle School
Des Moines, Iowa

David M. Smith
Howard A. Eyer Middle School
Macungie, Pennsylvania

Derek Strohschneider
Plymouth Community
   Intermediate School
Plymouth, Massachusetts

Sallie Teames
Rosemont Middle School
Fort Worth, Texas

Gene Vitale
Parkland Middle School
McHenry, Illinois

Zenovia Young
Meyer Levin Junior
   High School (IS 285)
Brooklyn, New York

Contents

Life Science

Introduction to Life Science ....**xxii**

Unit 1 Cells and Heredity

Chapter 1 **Cells: The Building Blocks of Life** **16**
1 What Is Life? 18
2 Discovering Cells 27
3 Looking Inside Cells 34
4 Integrating Earth Science: The Origin of Life 44

Chapter 2 **Cell Processes and Energy** **50**
1 Integrating Chemistry: Chemical Compounds in Cells 52
2 The Cell in Its Environment 56
3 Photosynthesis 61
4 Respiration 66
5 Cell Division 72

Chapter 3 **Genetics: The Science of Heredity** **84**
1 Mendel's Work 86
2 Integrating Mathematics: Probability and Genetics 94
3 The Cell and Inheritance 102
4 The DNA Connection 107

Chapter 4 **Modern Genetics**..............................**116**
1 Human Inheritance 118
2 Human Genetic Disorders 125
3 Integrating Technology: Advances in Genetics 132

Chapter 5 **Changes Over Time** **144**
1 Darwin's Voyage 146
2 Integrating Earth Science: The Fossil Record 157
3 Other Evidence for Evolution 165

Interdisciplinary Exploration:
   Dogs—Loyal Companions **174**

Unit 2 From Bacteria to Plants

Chapter 6 Bacteria and Viruses **180**
1 Classifying Organisms 182
2 The Six Kingdoms 189
3 Bacteria 192
4 Integrating Health: Viruses 204

Chapter 7 Protists and Fungi **216**
1 Protists 218
2 Integrating Environmental Science: Algal Blooms 228
3 Fungi 233

Chapter 8 Introduction to Plants **246**
1 The Plant Kingdom 248
2 Mosses, Liverworts, and Hornworts 256
3 Ferns and Their Relatives 261
4 Integrating Technology: Feeding the World 266

Chapter 9 Seed Plants **272**
1 The Characteristics of Seed Plants 274
2 Gymnosperms 284
3 Angiosperms 289
4 Integrating Chemistry: Plant Responses and Growth 297

Nature of Science:
From Plants to Chemicals **304**

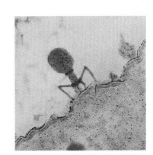

Unit 3 Animals

Chapter 10 **Sponges, Cnidarians, and Worms** **308**
    1 What Is an Animal? 310
    2 Integrating Mathematics: Symmetry 315
    3 Sponges and Cnidarians 320
    4 Worms 327

Chapter 11 **Mollusks, Arthropods, and Echinoderms** . . .**338**
    1 Mollusks 340
    2 Arthropods 346
    3 Insects 354
    4 Integrating Chemistry:
      The Chemistry of Communication 362
    5 Echinoderms 365

Chapter 12 **Fishes, Amphibians, and Reptiles** **372**
    1 Integrating Earth Science: Evolution of Vertebrates 374
    2 Fishes 381
    3 Amphibians 389
    4 Reptiles 395

Chapter 13 **Birds and Mammals** **408**
   1 Birds 410
   2 Integrating Physics: The Physics of Bird Flight 420
   3 What Is a Mammal? 423
   4 Diversity of Mammals 431

Chapter 14 **Animal Behavior** **440**
   1 Integrating Psychology:
     Why Do Animals Behave As They Do? 442
   2 Patterns of Behavior 450

Interdisciplinary Exploration: The Secret of Silk **462**

PRENTICE HALL
SCIENCE
EXPLORER
LIFE SCIENCE

Unit 4 Human Biology and Health

Chapter 15 Bones, Muscles, and Skin 470
  1 Integrating Health:
    Body Organization and Homeostasis 472
  2 The Skeletal System 480
  3 The Muscular System 488
  4 The Skin 494

Chapter 16 Food and Digestion **504**
  1 Integrating Chemistry: Food and Energy 506
  2 The Digestive Process Begins 518
  3 Final Digestion and Absorption 526

Chapter 17 Circulation **534**
  1 The Body's Transportation System 536
  2 A Closer Look at Blood Vessels 543
  3 Blood and Lymph 549
  4 Integrating Health: Cardiovascular Health 556

Chapter 18 Respiration and Excretion **564**
  1 The Respiratory System 566
  2 Integrating Health: Smoking and Your Health 576
  3 The Excretory System 581

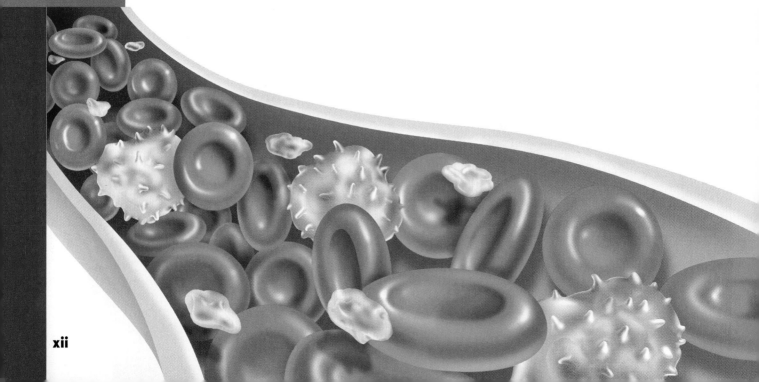

Chapter 19 **Fighting Disease** **590**
    1 Infectious Disease 592
    2 The Body's Defenses 596
    3 Integrating Health: Preventing Infectious Disease 605
    4 Noninfectious Disease 612

Chapter 20 **The Nervous System** **620**
    1 How the Nervous System Works 622
    2 Divisions of the Nervous System 628
    3 The Senses 636
    4 Integrating Health: Alcohol and Other Drugs 644

Chapter 21 **The Endocrine System and Reproduction** . . .**656**
    1 The Endocrine System 658
    2 The Male and Female Reproductive Systems 663
    3 Integrating Health: The Human Life Cycle 669

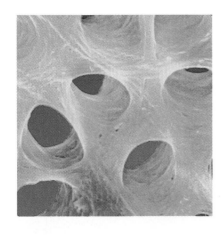

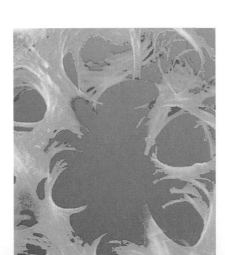

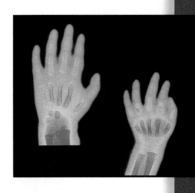

Unit 5 Ecology

Nature of Science: Protecting Desert Wildlife **682**

Chapter 22 **Populations and Communities** **686**
    1 Living Things and the Environment 688
    2 Integrating Mathematics: Studying Populations 695
    3 Interactions Among Living Things 703

Chapter 23 **Ecosystems and Biomes** **714**
    1 Energy Flow in Ecosystems 716
    2 Integrating Chemistry: Cycles of Matter 723
    3 Biogeography 728
    4 Earth's Biomes 734
    5 Succession 748

Chapter 24 **Living Resources** **754**
    1 Integrating Environmental Science: Environmental Issues ..756
    2 Forests and Fisheries 762
    3 Biodiversity 768

Interdisciplinary Exploration: African Rain Forests....**780**

Reference Section
    Skills Handbook **786**
        Think Like a Scientist 786
        Making Measurements 788
        Conducting a Scientific Investigation 790
        Thinking Critically 792
        Organizing Information 794
        Creating Data Tables and Graphs 796
    Appendix A: Laboratory Safety **799**
    Appendix B: Using the Microscope **802**
    Glossary **804**
    Index **818**
    Acknowledgments **830**

Activities

Inquiry Activities

CHAPTER PROJECT

Opportunities for long-term inquiry

Chapter 1: Mystery Object 17
Chapter 2: Egg-speriment With a Cell 51
Chapter 3: All in the Family 85
Chapter 4: A Family Portrait 117
Chapter 5: Life's Long Calendar 145
Chapter 6: Be a Disease Detective 181
Chapter 7: A Mushroom Farm 217
Chapter 8: Become a Moss Expert 247
Chapter 9: Cycle of a Lifetime 273
Chapter 10: Alive and Well 309
Chapter 11: Going Through Changes 339
Chapter 12: Animal Adaptations 373
Chapter 13: Bird Watch 409
Chapter 14: Learning New Tricks 441
Chapter 15: On the Move 471
Chapter 16: What's on Your Menu? 505
Chapter 17: Travels of a Red Blood Cell 535
Chapter 18: Get the Message Out 565
Chapter 19: Stop the Invasion 591
Chapter 20: Tricks and Illusions 621
Chapter 21: A Precious Bundle 657
Chapter 22: What's a Crowd? 687
Chapter 23: Breaking It Down 715
Chapter 24: Variety Show 755

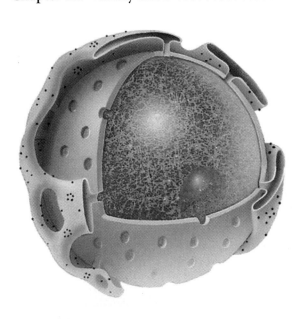

DISCOVER

Exploration and inquiry before reading

Is It Living or Nonliving? 17
Is Seeing Believing? 27
How Large Are Cells? 34
How Can the Composition of Air Change? ...44
What Is a Compound? 52
How Do Molecules Move? 56
Where Does the Energy Come From? 61
What Is a Product of Respiration? 66
What Are the Cells Doing? 72
What Does the Father Look Like? 86
What's the Chance? 94
Which Chromosome is Which? 102
Can You Crack the Code? 107
How Tall Is Tall? 118
How Many Chromosomes? 125
What Do Fingerprints Reveal? 132

DISCOVER

continued

How Do Living Things Vary? 146
What Can Fossils Tell You? 157
How Can You Classify Species? 165
Can You Organize a Junk Drawer? 182
Which Organism Goes Where? 189
How Fast Do Bacteria Multiply? 192
Can You Cure a Cold? 204
What Lives in a Drop of Water? 218
How Can Algal Growth Affect Pond Life? . . .228
Do All Molds Look Alike? 233
What Do Leaves Reveal About Plants? 248
Will Mosses Absorb Water? 256
How Quickly Can Water Move Upward? 261
Will There Be Enough to Eat? 266
Which Plant Part Is It? 274
Are All Leaves Alike? 284
What Is a Fruit? 289
Can a Plant Respond to Touch? 297
Is It an Animal? 310
How Many Ways Can You Fold It? 315
How Do Natural and Synthetic Sponges
    Compare? 320
What Can You See in a Worm? 327
How Can You Classify Shells? 340
Will It Bend and Move? 346
What Kinds of Appendages
    Do Insects Have? 354
Can You Match the Scents? 362
How Do Sea Stars Hold On? 365
How Is an Umbrella Like a Skeleton? 374
How Does Water Flow Over a Fish's Gills? . .381
What's the Advantage of Being Green? 389
How Do Snakes Feed? 395

What Are Feathers Like? 410
What Lifts Airplanes and Birds
    Into the Air? 420
What Are Mammals' Teeth Like? 423
How Is a Thumb Useful? 431
What Can You Observe About a
    Vertebrate's Behavior? 442
What Can You Express Without Words? 450
How Do You Lift Books? 472
Hard as a Rock? 480
How Do Muscles Work? 488
What Can You Observe About Skin? 494
Food Claims—Fact or Fiction? 506
How Can You Speed Up Digestion? 518
Which Surface Is Larger? 526
How Hard Does Your Heart Work? 536
How Does Pressure Affect the
    Flow of Blood? 543
What Kinds of Cells Are in Blood? 549
Which Foods Are "Heart Healthy"? 556
How Big Can You Blow Up a Balloon? 566
What Are the Dangers of Smoking? 576
How Does Filtering a Liquid Change
    What Is in It? 581
How Does a Disease Spread? 592
Which Pieces Fit Together? 596
What Substances Can Kill Pathogens? 605
What Happens When Airflow Is
    Restricted? 612
How Simple Is a Simple Task? 622
How Does Your Knee React? 628
What's in the Bag? 636
How Can You Best Say No? 644
What's the Signal? 658
What's the Big Difference? 663
How Many Ways Does a Child Grow? 669
What's in the Scene? 688
What's the Bean Population? 695
How Well Can You Hide a Butterfly? 703
Where Did Your Dinner Come From? 716
Are You Part of a Cycle? 723
How Can You Move a Seed? 728
How Much Rain Is That? 734
What Happened Here? 748
How Do You Decide? 756
What Happened to the Tuna? 762
How Much Variety Is There? 768

Sharpen your *Skills*

Practice of specific science inquiry skills

Designing an Experiment 24
Observing 32
Inferring 63
Interpreting Data 75
Predicting 109
Communicating 137
Inferring 151
Calculating 160
Drawing Conclusions 166
Observing 186
Graphing 195
Predicting 225
Interpreting Data .249
Calculating 280
Inferring 313
Communicating 331
Observing 332
Classifying 342
Graphing 356
Communicating 382
Drawing Conclusions 403
Classifying 427
Predicting 444
Classifying 484
Predicting 508

Creating Data Tables 546
Calculating 579
Posing Questions .594
Drawing Conclusions 613
Controlling Variables 630
Designing Experiments 642
Communicating 646
Graphing 667
Calculating 696
Classifying 709
Observing 718
Developing Hypotheses 724
Inferring 739
Interpreting Data .741
Calculating 765
Communicating 774

TRY THIS

Reinforcement of key concepts

React 20
Gelatin Cell 40
What's That Taste? 54
Diffusion in Action 58
Modeling Mitosis 74
Coin Crosses 97
The Eyes Have It 120
Girl or Boy? 122
Bird Beak Adaptations 149
Preservation in Ice 159
Bacteria for Breakfast 197
Modeling a Virus 207
Feeding Paramecia 222
Making Spore Prints 235
Spreading Spores 236
Examining a Fern 262
The In-Seed Story 276
The Scoop on Cones 286
Hydra Doing? 324
Pill Bugs—Wet or Dry? 350
Bead-y Bones 376
Webbing Through Water 392
Eggs-amination 417
It's Plane to See 421
Insulated Mammals 425
Line Them Up 447
Worker Bees 453

How Is a Book Organized? 473
Soft Bones? 482
Get a Grip 490
Sweaty Skin 497
Modeling Peristalsis 521
Break Up! 527
Caught in the Web .552
Blocking the Flow 557
Do You Exhale Carbon Dioxide? 571
Stuck Together 603
Why Do You Need Two Eyes? 637
Tick! Tick! Tick! 640
Way to Grow! 671
With or Without Salt? 690
Elbow Room 699
Weaving a Food Web 721
Desert Survival 737

Skills Lab

In-depth practice of inquiry skills

Keeping Flowers Fresh 10
Please Pass the Bread! 26
A Magnified View of Life 43
Multiplying by Dividing 80
Take a Class Survey .92
Make the Right Call 100
Nature at Work 152
Telltale Molecules 170
How Many Viruses Fit on a Pin? 212
What's for Lunch? 238
Eye on Photosynthesis 254
Masses of Mosses 260
Which Way Is Up? .300
Earthworm Responses 334
A Snail's Pace 345
Soaking Up Those Rays 400
Looking at an Owl's Leftovers 414
Become a Learning Detective 449
A Look Beneath the Skin 493
As the Stomach Churns 524
Heart Beat, Health Beat 548
A Breath of Fresh Air 575
Causes of Death, Then and Now 610
Ready or Not 627
Growing Up 678
A World in a Bottle 694
Change in a Tiny Community 746
Tree Cookie Tales 767

Real-World Lab

Everyday application of science concepts

Gases in Balance 71
Family Puzzles 130
Guilty or Innocent? 140
Do Disinfectants Work? 202
An Explosion of Life 231
A Close Look at Flowers 294
A Tale Told By Tracks 318
What's Living in the Soil? 360
Home Sweet Home 388
Keeping Warm 429
One For All 458
Sun Safety 498
Iron for Breakfast .517
Do You Know Your A-B-O's? 555
Clues About Health 584
The Skin as a Barrier 598
With Caffeine or Without? 648
Counting Turtles 701
Biomes in Miniature 732
Is Paper a Renewable Resource? 761

Science at Home

Family involvement in science exploration

Building Blocks 42
Organic Compounds in Food 55
Fermentation in Bread 70
The Guessing Game 99
Grocery Genetics .138
Make Your Mark 164
Kitchen Classification 188
Helpful Bacteria 201
Kitchen Algae 227
State Flowers 253
Seed Germination 283
Front-End Advantages 317
Edible Mollusks 344
Chemicals and Insect Pests 364
Focus on Backbones 380
Mammals' Milk 428
Exercising Safely .487
Protection From the Sun 500
Healthy Hearts 560
Modeling Alveoli .574
Vaccination History 609
Stimulus and Response 626
Word Estimates 700
Sock Walk 731
Succession 750
Renewable Survey 766

Interdisciplinary Activities

Science and History
The Microscope—Improvements Over Time . .30
Bacteria and Foods of the World 198
Discovering Vertebrate Fossils 378
Cardiovascular Advances in the
    Twentieth Century 558
Fighting Infectious Disease 606
Making a Difference 758

Science and Society
Who Should Have Access to Genetic
    Test Results? 139
Eutrophication—The Threat to Clear,
    Clean Water 232
Coral Reefs in Danger 326
Animals and Medical Research 430
Advertising and Nutrition 530
Should People Be Required to Wear
    Bicycle Helmets? .635
Animal Overpopulation: How Can
    People Help? 702

Math Toolbox
Calculating Probability 95
Calculating Percent .509
Pulse Rate 544
Inequalities 698

Connection

Language Arts 36
Social Studies 69
Language Arts 88
Social Studies 127
Social Studies 154
Language Arts 184
Language Arts 241
Social Studies 258
Visual Arts 291
Language Arts 322
Social Studies 358
Language Arts 391
Visual Arts 411
Social Studies 456
Language Arts 478
Visual Arts 486
Social Studies 510
Language Arts 540
Social Studies 572
Social Studies 600
Visual Arts 631
Social Studies 676
Language Arts 692
Social Studies 730
Social Studies 763

EXPLORING

Visual exploration of concepts

Careers in Life Science 12
The Experiments of Redi and Pasteur 22
Plant and Animal Cells 38
The Cell Cycle 76
Meiosis 105
Protein Synthesis .110
A Pedigree 124
Genetic Engineering 135
Life's History 162
How Viruses Multiply 208
Protozoans 220
Plant Adaptations 250
A Leaf 279
The Life Cycle of a Gymnosperm 287
The Life Cycle of an Angiosperm 292
A Sponge 321
The Life Cycle of a Dog Tapeworm 329
A Snail 343
A Crayfish 351
Insect Metamorphosis 357
A Sea Star 367
A Bony Fish 385
A Frog 393
A Lizard 398
A Bird 413
Birds 418
Placental Mammals 434
A Honeybee Society 455
Movable Joints 485
The Food Guide Pyramid 514
The Heart 539
Blood Cells 550
The Respiratory System 569
A Kidney 582
The Immune Response 602
The Path of a Nerve Impulse 625
The Effects of Alcohol 651
The Endocrine System 660
Defense Strategies 706
A Food Web 720
Endangered Species 772

DISEASE DETECTIVE SOLVES
MYSTERY

**The Colorado Health Department
had a problem.**

**Seven children had become sick with diarrhea,
stomach cramps, fever, and vomiting.**

**Within days, another 43 people
had the same symptoms.**

Tests indicated that they all had become infected with salmonella. Salmonella are bacteria that are usually transmitted through foods such as contaminated meat or eggs.

How did these children become infected with salmonella? To find the answer, Colorado health officials called in Dr. Cindy Friedman. Dr. Friedman works at the Centers for Disease Control and Prevention (CDC), a United States government agency that tracks down and studies the transmission of diseases throughout the world.

Cindy Friedman studies outbreaks of diseases in groups of people rather than in individuals. Her specialty is infectious diseases, illnesses that spread from one organism to another. She has investigated outbreaks of disease in such places as rural Bolivia in South America, the Cape Verde Islands off the coast of Africa, and a Vermont farm.

Dr. Cindy Friedman is a physician and investigator in the Foodborne and Diarrheal Diseases Branch of the Centers for Disease Control and Prevention (CDC). The youngest of three sisters, Dr. Friedman is originally from Brooklyn, New York. In her spare time she enjoys horseback riding.

An Interview With Dr. Cindy Friedman

Q *How did you get started in science?*

A When I was young, we always had pets around the house and a lot of books about medicine and science. I wanted to be a veterinarian. In college I decided that I loved animals but didn't want to practice medicine on them. I'd rather keep them as a hobby and devote my career to human medicine.

Q *How did you come to specialize in infectious diseases?*

A Out of all the subjects I studied in medical school, I liked microbiology the best—learning about different viruses and bacteria. Then, when I did my medical training in New Jersey, we had a lot of patients from Latin America. So I saw quite a few tropical and exotic diseases, which further heightened my interest.

Q *What do you enjoy about your job?*

A I really like being able to help more than one patient at a time. We do this by figuring out the risk factors for a disease and how to prevent people from getting it. Sometimes the answer is complicated, like adding chlorine to the water. Sometimes it's simple measures, like washing your hands or cooking your food thoroughly.

Q *What clues did you have in the Colorado case?*

A At first, state investigators thought the bacteria came from some contaminated food. But when they questioned the children, they couldn't identify one place where they had all eaten.

Q *How did you find out what experiences the children had in common?*

A The investigators did a second set of interviews and learned that the children had all visited the zoo the week before they got sick. They didn't eat the same food at the zoo. But they all went to a special exhibit at the reptile house.

How did the children get infected?

Did the salmonella come from infected food?

What common place had the children visited?

Q *Did you think the exhibit might be a new clue?*

A Yes. It was a clue because reptiles frequently carry the salmonella bacteria without becoming ill. In the special exhibit, there were four baby Komodo dragons, meat-eating lizards from the island of Komodo in Indonesia. They were displayed in a pen filled with mulch, surrounded by a wooden barrier about two feet high. We tested the Komodo dragons and found that one of them had salmonella bacteria. But it wasn't a petting exhibit, so I couldn't understand how the children got infected.

Q *How did you gather new data?*

A I questioned the children who became ill and compared their answers with those of children who didn't become ill. I asked about their behavior at the exhibit—where they stood, what they touched, and whether they had anything to eat or drink there. I also asked all the children if they washed their hands after visiting the exhibit. Those who did destroyed the bacteria. It was only the children who didn't wash their hands who became ill.

Q *How did you figure out the source of contamination?*

A I found that anyone who touched the wooden barrier was much more likely to have gotten sick. Children would go up to the barrier and put their hands on it. Then some of them would put their hands in their mouth or would eat without washing their hands first. Those were the children who became infected with salmonella.

Could reptiles provide the clue?

Why did some children get infected and not others?

The Komodo dragon is the largest lizard species in existence. It is found on Komodo Island in Indonesia, and is ~~nearly~~ extinct.

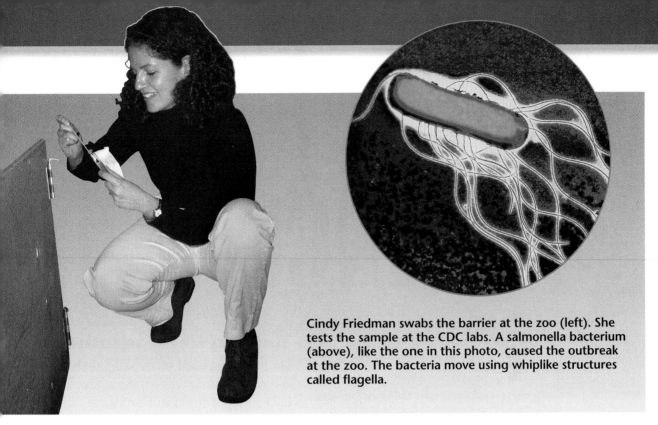

Cindy Friedman swabs the barrier at the zoo (left). She tests the sample at the CDC labs. A salmonella bacterium (above), like the one in this photo, caused the outbreak at the zoo. The bacteria move using whiplike structures called flagella.

Q *How did you test your hypothesis?*

A We took cultures—swabs from the top of the barrier where the children put their hands. When we tested those cultures in the lab, we found salmonella bacteria.

Q *What did you conclude about the bacteria on the barrier?*

A The infected Komodo dragon left its droppings in the mulch and the animals walked in it. Then they would stand on their hind legs, bracing themselves by putting their front paws on top of the barrier.

Q *What recommendations did you make?*

A We didn't want to tell zoos not to have reptile exhibits, because they're a good thing. And children should be able to get close to the animals. But at this particular exhibit, the outbreak could have been prevented with a double barrier system, so that the reptiles and the children couldn't touch the same barrier. And hand-washing is really important. Zoos should have signs instructing people to wash their hands after going to that kind of exhibit. In homes and schools with pet reptiles, hand-washing is very important, too.

Q *What's it like being a disease detective?*

A It's more the old-fashioned idea of medicine. What I do is examine the patients and listen to the stories they tell—where they've traveled, what they ate, and what they were exposed to. Then I try to figure out what caused their illness.

How can the zoo prevent future infections?

In Your Journal

Review the scientific process that Dr. Friedman used to solve the case of salmonella infections. What makes her a disease detective? Write a paragraph or two about the skills and character traits that Cindy Friedman needs to track down the source of an infectious disease.

What is SCIENCE ?

GUIDE FOR READING

◆ What skills do scientists use to find answers and solve problems?

◆ What are the general rules of laboratory safety?

Reading Tip
As you read, write a definition, in your own words, of each boldfaced term you encounter.

You might think of Dr. Friedman as a detective trying to piece together clues in a mystery. You might think of her as a problem solver, coming up with solutions to help people. Or you might think of her as a biologist, a scientist who studies living things. Which is correct? All of them are! In her job Dr. Friedman plays all of these roles. Dr. Friedman is a scientist.

Science is a way of learning about the natural world. Science also includes all of the knowledge gained through the process of exploring the natural world. This body of knowledge is always growing and changing as scientists ask new questions and explore new ideas.

Another term for the diverse ways in which scientists study the natural world is **scientific inquiry.** Scientific inquiry is used every day by people studying plants and animals, by physicians, and by many others. You may not realize it, but you use this process too, whether you're trying to help a sick pet feel better or to find the best place to plant flowers. Science, as you'll learn, is everywhere.

Thinking Like a Scientist

Dr. Friedman used many skills as she solved the salmonella mystery. You have probably used some of these same skills, while others may be new to you. **Some of the skills that scientists use are posing questions, making observations and inferences, developing hypotheses, designing experiments, making measurements and collecting data, interpreting data, drawing conclusions, and communicating.** Scientists do not always use all of these skills in every investigation.

Figure 1 In studying this pond, these students are using many of the same skills that scientists use.

Posing Questions Scientific inquiry often begins with a question or a problem. In Dr. Friedman's case, the problem she faced was: What caused the children to get sick?

You can probably think of a question or problem that you would like to investigate further. For example, if you have ever had a garden, you may have wondered whether fertilizer would help your tomato plants grow. Your investigation would begin with the following question: Does adding fertilizer to tomato plants help them grow larger?

Making Observations and Inferences Dr. Friedman used the skill of observation to gather information about the children and the zoo. The skill of **observation** involves using one or more of your senses—sight, hearing, touch, smell, and sometimes taste—to gather information and collect data. **Data** are the facts, figures, and other evidence gathered through observations. Dr. Friedman collected data on such things as the number of children who became infected and the types of animals in the zoo.

Often, a scientist's observations and data lead to an **inference,** which is an interpretation of an observation that is based on evidence or prior knowledge. Some scientists working with Dr. Friedman inferred that the children got sick from eating contaminated food. This inference was based on their knowledge that contaminated food was the cause of salmonella outbreaks they had seen before.

Because an inference is only one of many possible interpretations, it is not a fact. In this case the scientists' inference turned out to be wrong.

Figure 2 Have you ever wondered if fertilizer can help the plants in a garden grow faster? This question can be answered using scientific inquiry.

Like a scientist, you also draw inferences from observations you make. For example, you may notice that plants in your neighbor's garden are growing unusually tall and looking healthy. Because you observed your neighbor applying fertilizer to her plants, you may infer that fertilizer makes tomato plants grow taller. Your inference could prove to be true. Or maybe your neighbor's plants are getting more water and sunlight.

✓ *Checkpoint* *What senses can the skill of observation involve?*

Figure 3 Imagine that you are a scientist studying these dolphins. *Observing List five observations that you can make about the dolphins.*

Developing Hypotheses The next step is to develop a **hypothesis,** which is a possible explanation for a set of observations or answer to a scientific question. In science, a hypothesis must be something that can be tested. A hypothesis can be worded as an *If…then…* statement. For example, you could develop the following hypothesis:

> *If fertilizer is added to the soil surrounding a tomato plant, then the plant will grow taller.*

When a hypothesis is worded in this way, the phrase that begins with the word *If* can serve as a rough outline of your experiment. The phrase that begins with the word *then* suggests a possible outcome of the experiment.

A hypothesis can either be supported or disproved by an experiment. If an experiment supports a hypothesis, many more trials are needed before a hypothesis can be accepted as true.

Designing an Experiment to Test a Hypothesis After you have stated your hypothesis, you are ready to plan an experiment to test it. You know that you will need to grow a tomato plant, give it fertilizer, and observe its growth. But how will you know how tall it would have grown if you hadn't given it fertilizer? To answer this question, you will need another plant to compare it to.

You will need to grow two identical plants under the exact same conditions, except for the amount of fertilizer the plants receive. All other **variables,** or factors that can change in an experiment, need to be the same for both plants. Some other variables are the amounts of water, sunlight, and soil. By keeping all of these variables the same, you will know that any difference in plant growth must be due to the fertilizer alone.

Figure 4 A hypothesis is a possible explanation for a set of observations or answer to a scientific question. *Developing Hypotheses Suppose that the salmon population in an area dwindled. Write a hypothesis about how the grizzly bear population might be affected.*

Figure 5 The tomato plant experiment is an example of a controlled experiment. The two plants received the same amounts of water and sunlight.
Applying Concepts What is the manipulated variable in this experiment?

The one variable that is changed to test a hypothesis is called the **manipulated variable** (sometimes called the independent variable). In your experiment, the manipulated variable would be the fertilizer.

The factor that changes because of the manipulated variable is called the **responding variable** (sometimes called the dependent variable). The height of the tomato plant is the responding variable.

An experiment in which all of the variables except for one remain the same is a **controlled experiment.** You would plant two similar tomato plants in identical pots. You would then add fertilizer to the soil around one tomato plant while leaving the soil around the other tomato plant unfertilized. Both plants would receive the same amounts of water and sunlight throughout the experiment.

☑ *Checkpoint* *What is meant by a controlled experiment?*

Making Measurements and Collecting Data As you observe the tomato plants growing, how will you determine how much each plant has grown? You could measure the height of both plants daily. Or you could select a frequency, such as once a week, to collect your data.

Scientists have developed a standard system of measurement, called the International System of Units, which is abbreviated as SI (for the French, *Système International d'Unités).* SI is based on the metric system of measurement, which is used in many countries of the world. By using SI, scientists from all over the world can communicate their detailed findings with one another.

Can you imagine what it would be like if everyone in the world spoke one language? It would make communication much easier. That's what it's like for scientists using SI. Before you conduct any experiments, review Making Measurements on pages 788–789 of the Skills Handbook.

Figure 6 This scientist is using an instrument called calipers to measure the length of a Virginia rail's beak. By using SI to make scientific measurements, scientists all over the world have a standard "language" of measurement.

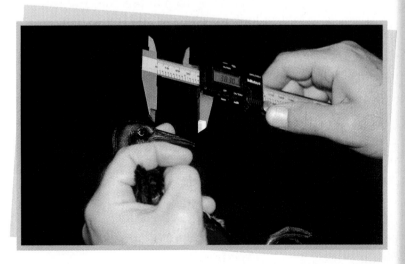

Day	Height of Tomato Plants (cm)	
	Unfertilized plant	Fertilized plant
Day 0	30	30
Day 3	30	30
Day 6	31	31
Day 9	32	33
Day 12	33	35
Day 15	34	38
Day 18	35	40
Day 21	36	42

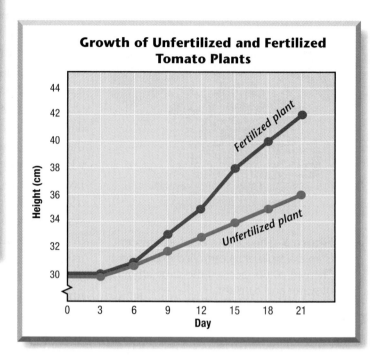

Figure 7 The data table shows the height of the two tomato plants over a three-week period. A graph was created using this data. *Interpreting Graphs How does the growth of the fertilized plant compare with the growth of the unfertilized plant?*

Interpreting Data After all of the data are collected, they need to be interpreted. Interpreting data that you have collected in an experiment means arranging the results in an organized way.

Look at Figure 7 to see how graphing data helps you visualize and organize your findings. By organizing data in this way, you can look for patterns and trends. For example, you can see that the two tomato plants were the same height through the first six days of the experiment. The fertilized plant then grew faster than the unfertilized plant over the next fifteen days. To learn more about data tables and graphs, look at pages 796–798 in the Skills Handbook.

☑ *Checkpoint* *Why is it necessary to organize the data collected in an experiment?*

Drawing Conclusions After you have organized and interpreted your data, the next step is to draw a conclusion, which means summing up what you learned from the investigation. To draw a conclusion, you need to decide whether or not the data support your original hypothesis.

In the tomato experiment, the data showed that fertilizer did help the tomato plant grow taller. You could say that the evidence supports your hypothesis.

Evidence can either support a hypothesis or prove it to be false. Even if you conclude that your hypothesis was false, you will have learned something important from your experiment. You may have new questions that you want to investigate further. Conclusions often lead to new questions, which lead to new experiments.

Communicating in Science

For scientists, an important step in the inquiry process is communicating their results and conclusions to other scientists. Communication is the sharing of ideas and experimental findings with others through writing and speaking.

Scientists share their conclusions with one another by writing articles in scientific journals, by attending scientific meetings, and by using the Internet. The Internet is very useful to scientists in communicating with one another and with nonscientists.

When scientists communicate their conclusions to nonscientists, it is important that they use nontechnical terms that can be easily understood. In life science, communicating with nonscientists is especially important. Many experimental findings directly affect the health and safety of people. In these cases, findings must be communicated clearly and quickly.

Communication with the public was very important in Dr. Friedman's work. Once she discovered the source of the salmonella, Dr. Friedman communicated the need for double railings and the importance of hand washing. Her communication skills may have helped prevent future salmonella infections.

Scientific Theories

Often a set of experiments is repeated by many scientists, who all arrive at the same conclusions. This can lead to the development of a scientific theory. A **scientific theory** is a well-tested concept that explains a wide range of observations. You will learn about many important theories in life science as you read this book.

Although a theory is based on thousands of experiments done by different scientists, future testing can still prove a theory to be incorrect. In that case, scientists may revise the theory or abandon it.

Figure 8 Scientists must communicate their findings to other scientists and to the public. These two scientists are discussing a computer model of a chemical that can be used to fight disease.

Designing Experiments

KEEPING FLOWERS FRESH

You have just been given a bouquet of cut flowers. A friend tells you that the flowers will stay fresh for longer if you add sugar to the water in the vase. You decide to put your friend's idea to the test.

Problem

Do cut flowers stay fresher for a longer time if sugar is added to the water?

Suggested Materials

plastic cups	cut flowers	spoon
water	sugar	

Design a Plan

1. Write a hypothesis for an experiment you could perform to find out whether your friend's advice is correct.
2. Working with a partner, design a controlled experiment to test your hypothesis. Brainstorm a list of all of the variables you will need to control. Discuss how you will control each of the variables. Also decide what data you will need to collect. For example, you could count the number of petals each flower drops. Decide how often you will collect the data. Then write out a detailed experimental plan for your teacher to review.
3. If necessary, revise your plan according to your teacher's instructions. Then set up your experiment and begin collecting your data. Remember to keep careful, accurate records of the data you collect.

Analyze and Conclude

1. What was the manipulated variable in the experiment you performed? What was the responding variable? What variables were kept constant?
2. Use the data you collected to create one or more graphs of your experimental results. (See pages 796–798 of the Skills Handbook for directions on creating graphs.) What patterns or trends do your graphs reveal?
3. Based on your graphs, what conclusion can you draw about sugar and cut flowers? Do your results support your hypothesis? Why or why not?
4. Make a list of some additional questions that you would like to investigate about how to keep cut flowers fresh.
5. **Think About It** What aspects of your experimental plan were difficult to carry out? Were any variables hard to control? Was it difficult to collect accurate data? What changes could you make to improve your experimental plan?

Design an Experiment

Choose one of the questions you listed in response to Question 4 above. Write a hypothesis and design a controlled experiment to test your hypothesis. Obtain your teacher's approval before carrying out the experiment.

Laboratory Safety

What do you think is the most important part of a scientific experiment? Careful observation? Accurate measurements? Clear communication? All of these skills are very important. But the most important skill in any experiment is following safe laboratory practices.

In general, laboratory safety means following your teacher's instructions and making sure you understand all laboratory procedures before you begin. Laboratory safety also means showing respect and courtesy to your teacher and classmates, wearing proper safety equipment, being careful with lab materials, and keeping your work area neat and clean.

Safe laboratory practices will not only protect you and your classmates from injury, they will also help make your experiments more successful. Before you conduct any experiments, review the laboratory safety symbols and rules in Appendix A on pages 799–801.

☑ *Checkpoint* *Why is laboratory safety important?*

Branches of Life Science

In this book you will explore tiny life forms such as bacteria and larger forms such as plants, reptiles, and mammals. You will learn about the microscopic structures that make up living things and how living things interact with one another and with their environment.

You will also learn about many scientists who have made important

Figure 9 Following safe laboratory practices keeps scientists safe and makes experiments more successful. *Observing What things have these students done to protect themselves while carrying out this experiment?*

discoveries in life science. You will read about biologists such as Cindy Friedman, who are at work today in laboratories, hospitals, jungles, and other places all over the world. Look at *Exploring Careers in Life Science* on the next page to see just some of the things that life scientists do. This year, you too will be a life scientist— thinking like a scientist, carrying out experiments, and gaining new understandings about the living world around you.

EXPLORING Careers in Life Science

Life scientists study many things—from the workings of tiny particles inside cells to the interactions of thousands of organisms in a forest. You can find life scientists at work in such diverse places as hospitals, laboratories, tropical rain forests, and national parks.

Physician ▶

Some physicians, such as the one in this photo, examine patients and diagnose illnesses and injuries. They may also design health programs to help patients prevent illness. Other physicians do research to try to find cures for diseases, such as cancer.

◀ Botanist

Botanists study plants. Many botanists, such as the one shown here, work outdoors, studying plants growing in their natural environment. Other botanists work with farmers to identify ways to increase crop yields. Still others study the relationship between plants and the environment.

Marine ▶ Biologist

Marine biologists study organisms that live in the oceans—from microscopic plankton to giant whales. Many marine biologists spend a lot of time in the water, observing marine animals such as the Florida manatee shown here.

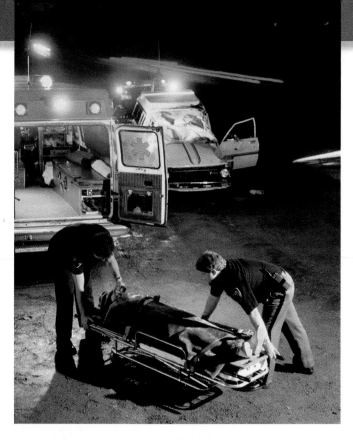

▲ Emergency Medical Technician (EMT)

EMTs play an important role in keeping the public healthy and safe. They ride in ambulances and fire engines, where they provide medical help for sick and injured people. EMTs may transport patients to the hospital by ambulance or helicopter in cases of severe injury.

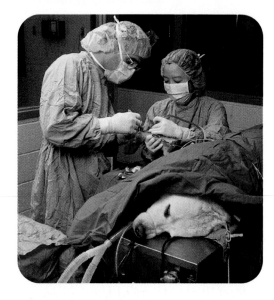

Veterinarian ▲

Veterinarians are animal doctors. Some veterinarians perform surgery on household pets, or on farm and zoo animals. They also perform routine checkups and care for sick and injured animals. Many veterinarians also provide advice to pet owners on animal behavior.

Park Ranger ▲

Park rangers work in government parks. Some rangers record data on animal habitats, populations, and migration. The rangers in this photo are tagging a bird so they can track its migration pattern. Other rangers lead tours for park visitors, educating them about protecting the environment.

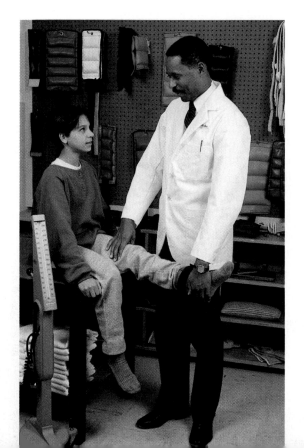

◀ Physical Therapist

Physical therapists help people regain their strength and coordination after serious illness or injury. Physical therapists use massage, weight training, and stretching exercises to help a patient recover. The work of physical therapists also helps patients prevent future injuries.

Study Guide

Key Ideas

◆ Science is a way of learning about the natural world and the knowledge gained through that process. Another term for the diverse ways in which scientists study the natural world is scientific inquiry.

◆ Some of the skills that scientists use are posing questions, making observations and inferences, developing hypotheses, designing experiments, making measurements and collecting data, interpreting data, drawing conclusions, and communicating.

◆ The International System of Units (SI) is the standard system of measurement in science.

◆ A scientific theory is a well-tested concept that explains a wide range of observations.

◆ Laboratory safety means following your teacher's instructions and making sure you understand all laboratory procedures before you begin.

Key Terms

science	variable
scientific inquiry	manipulated variable
observation	responding variable
data	controlled experiment
inference	scientific theory
hypothesis	

Reviewing Content

 For more review of key concepts, see the Interactive Student Tutorial CD-ROM.

Multiple Choice

Choose the letter of the best answer.

1. The diverse ways in which scientists study the natural world is called
   a. scientific inquiry. b. observation.
   c. data. d. communication.
2. The facts, figures, and other evidence gathered through observations are called
   a. inferences. b. data.
   c. hypotheses. d. variables.
3. A possible explanation for a set of observations or answer to a scientific question is a(n)
   a. variable. b. controlled experiment.
   c. scientific theory. d. hypothesis.
4. The factors that can change in an experiment are called
   a. variables. b. inferences.
   c. hypotheses. d. scientific theories.
5. A well-tested concept that explains a wide range of observations is a
   a. variable.
   b. scientific theory.
   c. hypothesis.
   d. controlled experiment.

True or False

If the statement is true, write true. If it is false, change the underlined word or words to make the statement true.

6. The skill of <u>laboratory safety</u> involves using one or more of the senses to gather information and collect data.
7. An <u>inference</u> is an interpretation of an observation that is based on evidence or prior knowledge.
8. The standard system of measurement used in science is called <u>SI</u>.
9. <u>Observation</u> is the sharing of ideas and experimental findings with others.
10. The most important skill in any experiment is <u>laboratory safety</u>.

Checking Concepts

11. What is scientific inquiry?

12. What is a hypothesis? Give an example of a hypothesis. Describe how the hypothesis can be tested.

13. What makes a controlled experiment different from other types of experiments?

14. What are some of the methods that scientists use to communicate their findings with one another?

15. Writing to Learn You probably use the same route to travel home from school each day. The next time you make the trip, write down directions home from school. Also, record at least ten things that you observe. Then write a letter to a friend or relative in another town detailing exactly how you get home from school and what you notice along the way.

Thinking Critically

16. Applying Concepts Suppose you would like to find out which dog food your dog likes best. What variables would you need to control in your experiment?

17. Making Judgments Scientists often perform experiments and make new discoveries. Other scientists must then repeat the experiments and arrive at the same conclusions before the discoveries are widely accepted. Explain how controlled experiments are important in ensuring that experiments are repeatable.

18. Inferring While walking by the nurse's office, you notice a student in gym clothes with an ice pack on his arm. What inference could you draw? Explain how your inference differs from an observation.

Use the information to answer Questions 19–21. Three students conducted a controlled experiment to find out how walking and running affected their heart rates. Their data are found in the table below.

Effect of Activity on Heart Rate (in beats per minute)			
Student	Heart Rate (at rest)	Heart Rate (walking)	Heart Rate (running)
Student One	70	90	115
Student Two	72	80	110
Student Three	80	100	120

19. Which factor is the manipulated variable in this experiment?
   a. heart rate
   b. breathing rate
   c. the activity the person is doing
   d. the students' ages

20. Which of the following statements would be a good hypothesis for this experiment?
   a. If a person's heart rate increases, then he or she will run.
   b. If a person runs or walks, then his or her heart rate will increase.
   c. If a person's heart rate increases, then he or she is in good shape.
   d. If a person runs or walks, then he or she is in good shape.

21. Based on the data in the table, which statement is true?
   a. Every student's heart rate increased while walking and running.
   b. Heart rates increased while running but not while walking.
   c. Student One's heart rate increased while running, but Student Two's did not.
   d. Student Three's running heart rate was 110.

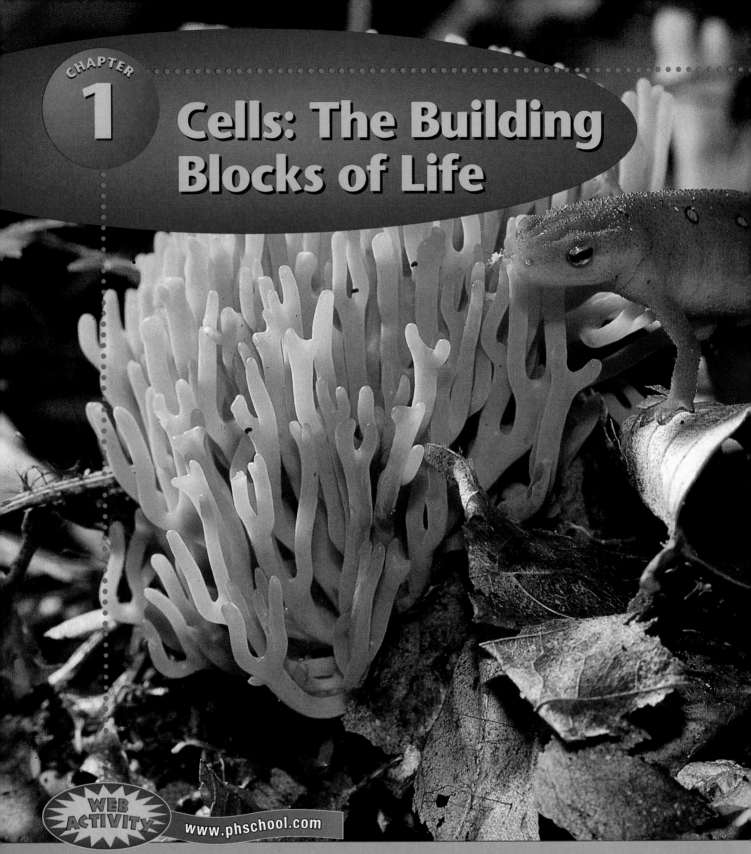

1

Cells: The Building Blocks of Life

WEB ACTIVITY www.phschool.com

1 What Is Life?

Discover **Is It Living or Nonliving?**
Try This **React!**
Sharpen Your Skills **Designing an Experiment**
Skills Lab **Please Pass the Bread!**

2 Discovering Cells

Discover **Is Seeing Believing?**
Sharpen Your Skills **Observing**

3 Looking Inside Cells

Discover **How Large Are Cells?**
Try This **Gelatin Cell**
Science at Home **Building Blocks**
Skills Lab **A Magnified View of Life**

Mystery Object

Suppose that you visited a location like the one in this scene. Imagine yourself standing perfectly still, all your senses alert to the things around you. You wonder which of the things around you are alive. The newt clearly is, but what about the rest? Is the pink thing alive? Are the other things living or nonliving?

In this chapter, you will learn that it is not always easy to determine whether something is alive. This is because living things share some characteristics with nonliving things. To explore this idea firsthand, you will be given a mystery object to observe. How can you determine if your object is a living thing? What signs of life will you look for?

Your Goal To study an object for several days to determine whether or not it is alive.

To complete this project successfully, you must
◆ care for your object following your teacher's instructions
◆ observe your object each day, and record your data
◆ determine whether your object is alive
◆ follow the safety guidelines in Appendix A

Get Started With a few classmates, brainstorm a list of characteristics that living things share. Can you think of any nonliving things that share some of these characteristics? Which characteristics on your list can help you conclude whether or not your mystery object is alive?

Check Your Progress You'll be working on this project as you study this chapter. To keep your project on track, look for Check Your Progress boxes at the following points.
Section 1 Review, page 25: Carry out your tests.
Section 2 Review, page 33: Record your observations daily.
Section 4 Review, page 46: Classify the object as living or nonliving.

Present Your Project At the end of the chapter (page 49), you will display your object and present evidence for whether or not it is alive. Be prepared to answer questions from your classmates.

Both the beautiful pink coral fungus and the newt sitting beside it are alive.

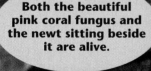

SECTION 4
Integrating Earth Science
The Origin of Life

Discover How Can the Composition of Air Change?

Is It Living or Nonliving?

1. Your teacher will give you and a partner a wind-up toy.

2. With your partner, decide who will find evidence that the toy is alive and who will find evidence that the toy is not alive.

3. Observe the wind-up toy. Record the characteristics of the toy that support your position about whether or not the toy is alive.

4. Share your lists of living and nonliving characteristics with your classmates.

Think It Over

Forming Operational Definitions Based on what you learned from the activity, create a list of characteristics that living things share.

GUIDE FOR READING

◆ What characteristics do all living things share?

◆ What do living things need to survive?

Reading Tip As you read, use the headings to make an outline of the characteristics and needs of living things.

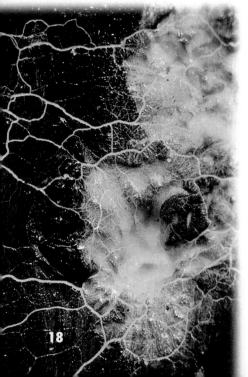

Looking like the slimy creatures that star in horror movies, the "blobs" appeared in towns near Dallas, Texas, in the summer of 1973. Jellylike masses, like the ones in Figure 1, overran yards and porches all over the towns. The glistening blobs oozed slowly along the ground. Terrified homeowners didn't know what the blobs were. Some people thought that they were life forms from another planet. People around Dallas were worried until biologists, scientists who study living things, put their minds at ease. The blobs were slime molds—living things usually found on damp, decaying material on a forest floor. The unusually wet weather around Dallas that year provided ideal conditions for the slime molds to grow in people's yards.

The Characteristics of Living Things

If you were asked to name some living things, or **organisms,** you might name yourself, a pet, and maybe some insects or plants. But you would probably not mention a moss growing in a shady spot, the mildew on bathroom tiles, or the slime molds that oozed across the lawns in towns near Dallas. But all of these things are also organisms that share six important characteristics

Figure 1 Slime molds similar to these grew in yards and porches in towns near Dallas, Texas.

◀ Animal cells

◀ Plant cells

with all other living things. **All living things have a cellular organization, contain similar chemicals, use energy, grow and develop, respond to their surroundings, and reproduce.**

Cellular Organization All organisms are made of small building blocks called cells. A **cell** is the basic unit of structure and function in an organism. The smallest cells are so tiny that you could fit over a million of them on the period at the end of this sentence. To see most cells, you need a microscope—a tool that uses lenses, like those in eyeglasses, to magnify small objects.

Organisms may be composed of only one cell or of many cells. **Unicellular,** or single-celled organisms, include bacteria (bak TEER ee uh), the most numerous organisms on Earth. A bacterial cell carries out all of the functions necessary for the organism to stay alive. **Multicellular** organisms are composed of many cells. The cells of many multicellular organisms are specialized to do certain tasks. For example, you are made of trillions of cells. Specialized cells in your body, such as muscle and nerve cells, work together to keep you alive. Nerve cells carry messages from your surroundings to your brain. Other nerve cells then carry messages to your muscle cells, making your body move.

The Chemicals of Life The cells of all living things are composed of chemicals. The most abundant chemical in cells is water. Other chemicals called carbohydrates (kahr boh HY drayt) are a cell's energy source. Two other chemicals, proteins (PROH teenz) and lipids (LIP idz), are the building materials of cells, much like wood and bricks are the building materials of houses. Finally, nucleic (noo KLEE ik) acids are the genetic material—the chemical instructions that direct the cell's activities.

Figure 2 Like all living things, the butterfly and the leaf are made of cells. Although the cells of different organisms are not identical, they share important characteristics. *Making Generalizations In what ways are cells similar?*

Figure 3 Over time, a tiny acorn develops into a giant oak tree. A great deal of energy is needed to produce the trillions of cells that make up the body of an oak tree.
Comparing and Contrasting In what way does the seedling resemble the oak tree? In what ways is it different?

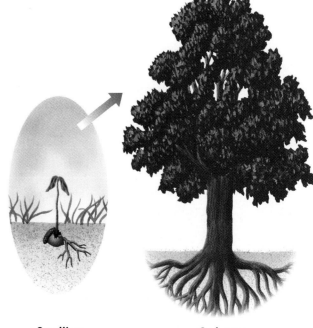
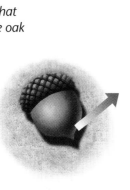

Acorn   Seedling   Oak tree

React!

ACTIVITY

In this activity, you will test your responses to three different stimuli.

1. Have a partner clap his or her hands together about six inches in front of your face. Describe how you react.

2. Look at one of your eyes in a mirror. Cover the eye with your hand for a minute. While looking in the mirror, remove your hand. Observe how the size of your pupil changes.

3. Bring a slice of lemon close to your nose and mouth. Describe what happens.

Classifying For each action performed, name the stimulus and the response.

Energy Use The cells of organisms use energy to do what living things must do, such as grow and repair injured parts. An organism's cells are always hard at work. For example, as you read this paragraph, not only are your eye and brain cells busy, but most of your other cells are working, too. The cells of your stomach and intestine are digesting food. Your blood cells are moving chemicals around your body. If you've hurt yourself, some of your cells are repairing the damage.

Growth and Development Another characteristic of living things is that they grow and develop. Growth is the process of becoming larger. **Development** is the process of change that occurs during an organism's life to produce a more complex organism. For example, as multicellular organisms develop, their cells differentiate, or become specialized. To grow and develop, organisms use energy to create new cells. Look at Figure 3 to see how an acorn develops as it grows into an oak tree.

You may argue that some nonliving things grow and change as they age. For example, a pickup truck rusts as it ages. Icicles grow longer as more water freezes on their tips. But pickup trucks and icicles do not use energy to change and grow. They also don't become more complex over time.

Response to Surroundings If you've ever seen a plant in a sunny window, you may have observed that the plant's stems have bent so that the leaves face the sun. Like a plant bending toward the light, all organisms react to changes in their environment. A change in an organism's surroundings that causes the organism to react is called a **stimulus** (plural *stimuli*). Stimuli include changes in temperature, light, sound, and other factors.

An organism reacts to a stimulus with a **response**—an action or change in behavior. For example, has someone ever leapt out at you from behind a door? If so, it's likely that you jumped or screamed. Your friend's sudden motion was the stimulus that caused your startled response. Nonliving things, such as rocks, do not react to stimuli as living things do.

Reproduction Another characteristic of organisms is the ability to **reproduce,** or produce offspring that are similar to the parents. Robins lay eggs that develop into young robins that closely resemble their parents. Sunflowers produce seeds that develop into sunflower plants, which in turn make more seeds. Bacteria produce other bacteria exactly like themselves.

☑ *Checkpoint* *How do growth and development differ?*

Life Comes From Life

Today, when people observe young plants in a garden or see a litter of puppies, they know that these new organisms are the result of reproduction. Four hundred years ago, however, people believed that life could appear suddenly from nonliving material. For example, when people saw flies swarming around decaying meat, they concluded that flies could arise from rotting meat. When frogs appeared in muddy puddles after heavy rains, people concluded that frogs could sprout from the mud in ponds. The mistaken idea that living things arise from nonliving sources is called **spontaneous generation.**

It took hundreds of years of experiments to convince people that spontaneous generation does not occur. One scientist who did some of these experiments was an Italian doctor, Francesco Redi. In the mid-1600s, Redi designed a controlled experiment to show that flies do not spontaneously arise from decaying meat. In a **controlled experiment,** a scientist carries out two tests that are identical in every respect except for one factor. The one factor that the scientist changes is called the **variable.** The scientist can conclude that any differences in the results of the two tests must be due to the variable.

Even after Redi's work, many people continued to believe that spontaneous generation occurred in bacteria. In the mid-1800s,

Figure 4 All organisms respond to changes in their surroundings. This willow ptarmigan's feathers have turned white in response to its snowy surroundings. This Alaskan bird's plumage will remain white until spring.

the French chemist Louis Pasteur designed some controlled experiments that finally disproved spontaneous generation. The controlled experiments of Francesco Redi and Louis Pasteur helped to convince people that living things do not arise from nonliving material. Look at *Exploring the Experiments of Redi and Pasteur* to learn more about the experiments they performed.

☑ *Checkpoint* *What is a controlled experiment?*

The Needs of Living Things

Imagine yourself biking through a park on a warm spring day. As you ride by a tree, you see a squirrel running up the tree trunk. Although it may seem that squirrels and trees do not have the

EXPLORING the Experiments of Redi and Pasteur

Redi designed one of the first controlled experiments. By Pasteur's time, controlled experiments were standard procedure. As you explore, identify the variable in each experiment.

FRANCESCO REDI

REDI'S EXPERIMENT

1 Redi placed meat in two identical jars. He left one jar uncovered. He covered the other jar with a cloth that let in air.

2 After a few days, Redi saw maggots (young flies) on the decaying meat in the open jar. There were no maggots on the meat in the covered jar.

3 Redi reasoned that flies had laid eggs on the meat in the open jar. The eggs hatched into maggots. Because flies could not lay eggs on the meat in the covered jar, there were no maggots there. Therefore, Redi concluded that the decaying meat did not produce maggots.

same basic needs as you, they do. All organisms need four things to stay alive. **Living things must satisfy their basic needs for energy, water, living space, and stable internal conditions.**

Energy You read earlier that organisms need a source of energy to live. They use food as their energy source. Organisms differ in the ways they obtain their energy. Some organisms, such as plants, capture the sun's energy and use it along with carbon dioxide, a gas found in Earth's atmosphere, and water to make their own food. Organisms that make their own food are called **autotrophs** (AW tuh trawfs). *Auto-* means "self" and *-troph* means "feeder." Autotrophs use the food they make as an energy source to carry out their life functions.

PASTEUR'S EXPERIMENT

LOUIS PASTEUR

1 In one experiment, Pasteur put clear broth into two flasks with curved necks. The necks would let in oxygen but keep out bacteria from the air. Pasteur boiled the broth in one flask to kill any bacteria in the broth. He did not boil the broth in the other flask.

2 In a few days, the unboiled broth became cloudy, showing that new bacteria were growing. The boiled broth remained clear. Pasteur concluded that bacteria do not spontaneously arise from the broth. New bacteria appeared only when living bacteria were already present.

Later, Pasteur took the curve-necked flask containing the broth that had remained clear and broke its long neck. Bacteria from the air could now enter the flask. In a few days, the broth became cloudy. This evidence confirmed Pasteur's conclusion that new bacteria appear only when they are produced by existing bacteria.

Figure 5 All organisms need a source of energy to live. **A.** *Volvox* is an autotroph that lives in fresh water, where it uses the sun's energy to make its own food. **B.** This American lobster, a heterotroph, is feeding on a herring it has caught. *Applying Concepts How do heterotrophs depend on autotrophs for energy?*

Organisms that cannot make their own food are called **heterotrophs** (HET uh roh trawfs). *Hetero-* means "other." A heterotroph's energy source is also the sun—but in an indirect way. Heterotrophs either eat autotrophs and obtain the energy in the autotroph's stored food, or they consume other heterotrophs that eat autotrophs. Animals, mushrooms, and slime molds are examples of heterotrophs.

Water All living things need water to survive—in fact, most organisms can live for only a few days without water. Organisms need water to do things such as obtain chemicals from their surroundings, break down food, grow, move substances within their bodies, and reproduce.

INTEGRATING CHEMISTRY One important property of water that is vital to living things is its ability to dissolve more chemicals than any other substance on Earth. In your body, for example, water makes up 92 percent of the liquid part of your blood. The oxygen and food that your cells need dissolve in the blood and are transported throughout your body. Carbon dioxide and other waste also dissolve in the blood. Your body's cells also provide a watery environment in which chemicals are dissolved. In a sense, you can think of yourself as a person-shaped sack of water in which other substances are dissolved. Fortunately, your body contains some substances that do not dissolve in water, so you hold your shape.

Sharpen your Skills

Designing an Experiment ACTIVITY

Your teacher will give you a slice of potato. Predict what percentage of the potato's mass is water. Then come up with a plan to test your prediction. For materials, you will be given a hairdryer and a balance. Obtain your teacher's approval before carrying out your plan. How does your result compare with your prediction?

Living Space All organisms need a place to live—a place to get food and water and find shelter. Because there is a limited amount of living space on Earth, some organisms may compete for space. Plants, for example, occupy a fixed living space. Above the ground, their branches and leaves compete for living space with those of other plants. Below ground, their roots compete for water and minerals. Unlike plants, organisms such as animals move around. They may either share living space with others or compete for living space.

Stable Internal Conditions Because conditions in their surroundings can change significantly, organisms must be able to keep the conditions inside their bodies constant. The maintenance of stable internal conditions despite changes in the surroundings is called **homeostasis** (hoh mee oh STAY sis). You know that when you are healthy your body temperature stays constant despite temperature changes in your surroundings. Your body's regulation of temperature is an example of homeostasis.

Other organisms have different mechanisms for maintaining homeostasis. For example, imagine that you are a barnacle attached to a rock at the edge of the ocean. At high tide, the ocean water covers you. At low tide, however, your watery surroundings disappear, and you are exposed to hours of sun and wind. Without a way to keep water in your cells, you'd die. Fortunately, a barnacle can close up its hard outer plates, trapping droplets of water inside. In this way, the barnacle can keep its body moist until the next high tide.

Figure 6 A tree trunk provides these mushrooms with food, water, and shelter.

Section 1 Review

1. Name six characteristics that you have in common with a tree.
2. List the four things that all organisms need to stay alive.
3. How did Pasteur's experiment show that bacteria do not arise spontaneously in broth?
4. **Thinking Critically** **Applying Concepts** You see a crowd of gulls fighting over an object on the wet sand at the ocean's edge. You investigate. The object is a pink blob about as round as a dinner plate. How will you decide if it is a living thing?

Check Your Progress
At this point, you should be ready to carry out your tests for signs of life following your teacher's directions. Before you start, examine your mystery object carefully, and record your observations. Also, decide whether you need to revise the list of life characteristics you prepared earlier. (Hint: Do not be fooled by the object's appearance—some organisms appear dead during a certain stage of their life.)

Please Pass the Bread!

In this lab, you will control variables in an investigation into the needs of living things.

Problem

What factors are necessary for bread molds to grow?

Materials

paper plates
plastic dropper
bread without preservatives
sealable plastic bags
tap water
packing tape

Procedure

1. Brainstorm with others to predict which factors might affect the growth of bread mold. Record your ideas.
2. To test the effect of moisture on bread mold growth, place two slices of bread of the same size and thickness on separate, clean plates.
3. Add drops of tap water to one bread slice until the whole slice is moist. Keep the other slice dry. Expose both slices to the air for 1 hour.
4. Put each slice into its own sealable bag. Press the outside of each bag to remove the air. Seal the bags. Then use packing tape to seal the bags again. Store the bags in a warm, dark place.
5. Copy the data table into your notebook.

6. Every day for at least 5 days, briefly remove the sealed bags from their storage place. Record whether any mold has grown. Estimate the area of the bread where mold is present. **CAUTION:** *Do not unseal the bags. At the end of the experiment, give the sealed bags to your teacher.*
7. Choose another factor that may affect mold growth, such as temperature or the amount of light. Set up an experiment to test the factor you choose. Remember to keep all conditions the same except for the one you are testing.

Analyze and Conclude

1. What conclusions can you draw from each of your experiments?
2. What was the variable in the first experiment? In the second experiment?
3. What basic needs of living things were demonstrated in this lab? Explain.
4. **Think About It** What is meant by "controlling variables"? Why is it necessary to control variables in an experiment?

Design an Experiment

Suppose that you lived in Redi's time. A friend tells you that molds just suddenly appear on bread. Design an experiment to show that the new mold comes from existing mold. Consult your teacher before performing the experiment.

DATA TABLE				
	Moistened Bread Slice		Unmoistened Bread Slice	
	Mold Present?	Area with Mold	Mold Present?	Area with Mold
Day 1				
Day 2				

SECTION
②Discovering Cells

Is Seeing Believing?

1. ✂ Cut a black-and-white photograph out of a page in a newspaper. With your eyes alone, closely examine the photo. Record your observations.

2. Examine the same photo with a hand lens. Record your observations.

3. Place the photo on the stage of a microscope. Use the clips to hold the photo in place. Shine a light down on the photo. Focus the microscope on part of the photo. (See Appendix B for instructions on using the microscope.) Record your observations.

Think It Over
Observing What did you see in the photo with the hand lens and the microscope that you could not see with your eyes alone?

A majestic oak tree shades you on a sunny day at the park. A lumbering rhinoceros wanders over to look at you at the zoo. After a rain storm, mushrooms sprout in the damp woods. What do you think an oak tree, a rhinoceros, and a mushroom have in common? You might say that they are all living things. What makes all of these living things alike? If you said that they are made of cells, you are correct.

Cells are the basic units of structure and function in living things. Just as bricks are the building blocks of a house or school, cells are the building blocks of life. Since you are alive, you are made of cells, too. Look closely at the skin on your arm. No

GUIDE FOR READING

◆ How did the invention of the microscope contribute to scientists' understanding of living things?

◆ What is the cell theory?

◆ How does a lens magnify an object?

Reading Tip As you read, make a flowchart showing how the contributions of several scientists led to the development of the cell theory.

Figure 7 This building is made up of individual bricks. Similarly, all living things are made up of individual cells.

matter how hard you look with your eyes alone, you won't be able to see individual skin cells. The reason is that cells are very small. In fact, one square centimeter of your skin's surface contains over 100,000 cells.

First Sightings of Cells

Until the late 1500s there was no way to see cells. No one even knew that cells existed. Around 1590, the invention of the microscope enabled people to look at very small objects. **The invention of the microscope made it possible for people to discover and learn about cells.**

A **microscope** is an instrument that makes small objects look larger. Some microscopes do this by using lenses to focus light. The lenses used in light microscopes are similar to the clear curved pieces of glass used in eyeglasses. A simple microscope contains only one lens. A hand lens is an example of a simple microscope. A light microscope that has more than one lens is called a **compound microscope.**

Robert Hooke One of the first people to observe cells was the English scientist and inventor Robert Hooke. In 1663, Hooke observed the structure of a thin slice of cork using a compound microscope he had built himself. Cork, the bark of the cork oak tree, is made up of cells that are no longer alive. To Hooke, the cork looked like tiny rectangular rooms, which he called *cells.* Hooke described his observations this way: "These pores, or cells, were not very deep...." You can see Hooke's drawings of cork cells in Figure 8. What most amazed Hooke was how many cells the cork contained. He calculated that in a cubic inch there were about 1.2 billion cells—a number he described as "most incredible."

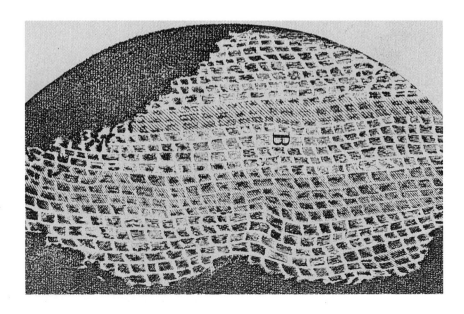

Figure 8 Robert Hooke made this drawing of dead cork cells that he saw through his microscope. Hooke called these structures *cells* because they reminded him of tiny rooms. *Comparing and Contrasting How are cells similar to the bricks in a building? How are they different?*

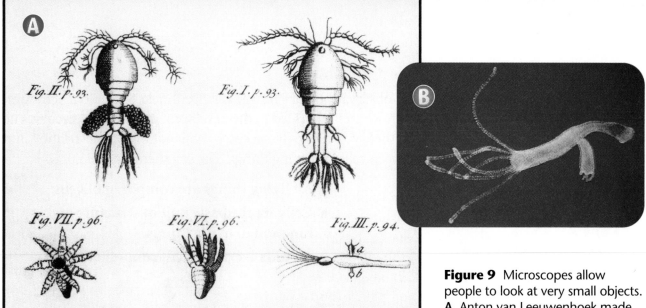

Figure 9 Microscopes allow people to look at very small objects. **A.** Anton van Leeuwenhoek made these drawings of organisms in the late 1600s after looking through a simple microscope. **B.** This is a hydra, a tiny water organism, as seen through a modern microscope. Compare this hydra to the one Leeuwenhoek drew, which is labeled Fig. III.

Anton van Leeuwenhoek   At about the same time that Robert Hooke made his discovery, Anton van Leeuwenhoek (LAY vun hook) also began to observe tiny objects with microscopes. Leeuwenhoek was a Dutch businessman and amateur scientist who made his own lenses. He then used the lenses to construct simple microscopes.

One of the things Leeuwenhoek looked at was water from a pond. He was surprised to see one-celled organisms, which he called *animalcules* (an uh MAL kyoolz), meaning "little animals."

Leeuwenhoek looked at many other specimens, including scrapings from teeth. When Leeuwenhoek looked at the scrapings, he became the first person to see the tiny single-celled organisms that are now called bacteria. Leeuwenhoek's many discoveries caught the attention of other researchers. Many other people began to use microscopes to see what secrets they could uncover about cells.

Matthais Schleiden and Theodor Schwann   Over the years, scientists have continued to use and improve the microscope. They have discovered that all kinds of living things are made up of cells. In 1838, a German scientist named Matthais Schleiden (SHLY dun) concluded that all plants are made of cells. He based this conclusion on his own research and on the research of others before him. The next year, another German scientist, Theodor Schwann, concluded that all animals are also made up of cells. Thus, stated Schwann, all living things are made up of cells.

Schleiden and Schwann had made an important discovery about living things. However, they didn't understand where cells came from. Until their time, most people thought that living things could come from nonliving matter. In 1855, a German doctor, Rudolf Virchow (FUR koh) proposed that new cells are formed only from existing cells. "All cells come from cells," wrote Virchow.

Checkpoint *What did Schleiden and Schwann conclude about cells?*

The Cell Theory

The observations of Hooke, Leeuwenhoek, Schleiden, Schwann, Virchow, and others led to the development of the **cell theory**. The cell theory is a widely accepted explanation of the relationship between cells and living things. **The cell theory states:**

◆ **All living things are composed of cells.**

◆ **Cells are the basic unit of structure and function in living things.**

◆ **All cells are produced from other cells.**

SCIENCE & History

The Microscope — Improvements Over Time

The discovery of cells would not have been possible without the microscope. Microscopes have been improved in many ways over the last 400 years.

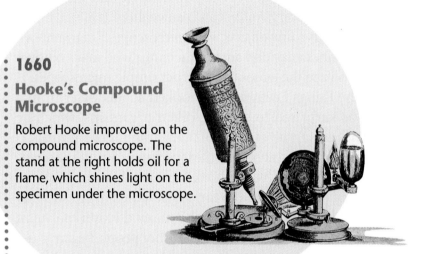

1660
Hooke's Compound Microscope

Robert Hooke improved on the compound microscope. The stand at the right holds oil for a flame, which shines light on the specimen under the microscope.

1600   **1750**

1590
First Compound Microscope

Hans Janssen and his son Zacharias, Dutch eyeglass makers, made one of the first compound microscopes. Their microscope was simply a tube with a lens at each end.

1683
Leeuwenhoek's Simple Microscope

Although Leeuwenhoek's simple microscope used only one tiny lens, it could magnify a specimen up to 266 times. Leeuwenhoek was the first person to see many one-celled organisms, including bacteria.

The cell theory holds true for all living things, no matter how big or small, or how simple or complex. Since cells are common to all living things, they can provide information about all life. And because all cells come from other cells, scientists can study cells to learn about growth, reproduction, and all other functions that living things perform. By learning about cells and how they function, you can learn about all types of living things.

☑ *Checkpoint* **Which scientists contributed to the development of the cell theory?**

In Your Journal

Choose one of the microscopes. Write an advertisement for it that might appear in a popular science magazine. Be creative. Emphasize the microscope's usefulness or describe the wonders that can be seen with it.

1933
Transmission Electron Microscope (TEM)

The German physicist Ernst Ruska created the first electron microscope. TEMs make images by sending electrons through a very thinly sliced specimen. They can only examine dead specimens, but are very useful for viewing internal cell structures. TEMs can magnify a specimen up to 500,000 times.

1981
Scanning Tunneling Microscope (STM)

A STM measures electrons that leak, or "tunnel," from the surface of a specimen. With a STM, scientists can see individual molecules on the outer layer of a cell. STMs can magnify a specimen up to 1,000,000 times.

1900

2050

1886
Modern Compound Light Microscope

German scientists Ernst Abbé and Carl Zeiss made a compound light microscope similar to this one. The horseshoe stand helps keep the microscope steady. The mirror at the bottom focuses light up through the specimen. Modern compound light microscopes can magnify a specimen up to 1,000 times.

1965
Scanning Electron Microscope (SEM)

The first commercial SEM is produced. This microscope sends a beam of electrons over the surface of a specimen, rather than through it. The result is a detailed three-dimensional image of the specimen's surface. SEMs can magnify a specimen up to 150,000 times.

Observing

1. Place a prepared slide of a thin slice of cork on the stage of a microscope.

2. Observe the slide under low power. Draw what you see.

3. Place a few drops of pond water on another slide and cover it with a coverslip.

4. Observe the slide under low power. Draw what you see. Wash your hands after handling pond water.

Observing How does your drawing in Step 2 compare to Hooke's drawing in Figure 8? Based on your observations in Step 4, why did Leeuwenhoek call the organisms he saw "little animals"?

How a Light Microscope Works

INTEGRATING PHYSICS Microscopes use lenses to make small objects look larger. But simply enlarging a small object is not useful unless you can see the details clearly. For a microscope to be useful to a scientist, it must combine two important properties—magnification and resolution.

Magnification The first property, **magnification,** is the ability to make things look larger than they are. **The lens or lenses in a light microscope magnify an object by bending the light that passes through them.** If you examine a hand lens, you will see that the glass lens is curved, not flat. The center of the lens is thicker than the edges. A lens with this curved shape is called a **convex lens.** Look at Figure 10 to see how light is bent by a convex lens. The light passing through the sides of the lens bends inward. When this light hits the eye, the eye sees the object as larger than it really is.

Because a compound microscope uses more than one lens, it can magnify an object even more. Light passes through a specimen and then through two lenses. Figure 10 also shows the path that light takes through a compound microscope. The first lens near the specimen magnifies the object. Then a second lens near the eye further magnifies the enlarged image. The total magnification of the microscope is equal to the magnifications of the two lenses multiplied together. For example, if the first lens has a magnification of 10 and the second lens has a magnification of 40, then the total magnification of the microscope is 400.

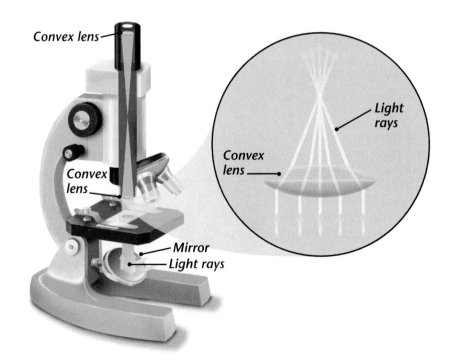

Figure 10 Microscopes use lenses to make objects look larger. A compound microscope has two convex lenses. Each convex lens bends light, making the image larger. *Calculating If one lens had a magnification of 10, and the other lens had a magnification of 50, what would the total magnification be?*

Resolution To create a useful image, a microscope must also help you see individual parts clearly. The ability to clearly distinguish the individual parts of an object is called **resolution.** Resolution is another term for the sharpness of an image.

For example, when you use your eyes to look at a photo printed in a newspaper, it looks like a complete picture from one side to the other. That picture, however, is really made up of a collection of small dots. To the unaided eye, two tiny dots close together appear as one. If you put the photo under a microscope, however, you can see the dots. You see the dots not only because they are magnified but also because the microscope improves resolution. Good resolution—being able to see fine detail—is not needed when you are reading the newspaper. But it is just what you need when you study cells.

Electron Microscopes

The microscopes used by Hooke, Leeuwenhoek, and other early researchers were all light microscopes. Since the 1930s, scientists have developed a different type of microscope called an electron microscope. Electron microscopes use a beam of electrons instead of light to examine a specimen. Electrons are tiny particles that are smaller than atoms. The resolution of electron microscopes is much higher than the resolution of light microscopes. As the technology of microscopes keeps improving, scientists will continue to learn more about the structure and function of cells.

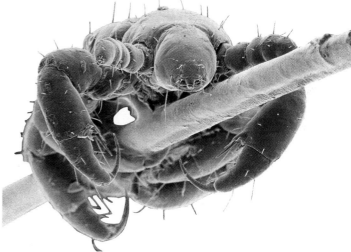

Figure 11 This head louse, shown clinging to a human hair, was photographed through a scanning electron microscope. It has been magnified to about 80 times its actual size.

Section 2 Review

1. How did the invention of the microscope affect scientists' understanding of living things?
2. Explain the three main ideas of the cell theory.
3. How does a compound microscope use lenses to magnify an object?
4. Explain why both magnification and resolution are important when viewing a small object with a microscope.
5. **Thinking Critically Applying Concepts** Why do scientists learn more about cells each time the microscope is improved?

Check Your Progress
CHAPTER PROJECT
Observe your object at least once a day. Record your observations in a data table. Draw accurate diagrams. (*Hint:* Measuring provides important information. Take measurements of your object regularly. If you cannot measure it directly, make estimates.)

Looking Inside Cells

How Large Are Cells?

1. Look at the organism in the photo. The organism is an ameba, a large single-celled organism. This type of ameba is about 1 millimeter (mm) long.

2. Multiply your height in meters by 1,000 to get your height in millimeters. How many amebas would you have to stack end-to-end to equal your height?

3. Many of the cells in your body are about 0.01 mm long—one hundredth the size of an ameba. How many body cells would you have to stack end-to-end to equal your height?

Think It Over

Inferring Look at a metric ruler to see how small 1 mm is. Now imagine a distance one-hundredth as long, or 0.01 mm. Why can't you see your body's cells without the aid of a microscope?

GUIDE FOR READING

◆ What role do the cell membrane and nucleus play in the cell?

◆ What functions do other organelles in the cell perform?

◆ How do bacterial cells differ from plant and animal cells?

Reading Tip Before you read, preview *Exploring Plant and Animal Cells* on pages 38–39. Make a list of any unfamiliar terms. As you read, write a definition for each term.

A giant redwood tree ▶

Imagine you're in California standing next to a giant redwood tree. You have to bend your head way back to see the top of the tree. Some of these trees are over 110 meters tall and more than 10 meters in circumference! How do redwoods grow so large? How do they carry out all the functions necessary to stay alive?

To answer these questions, and to learn many other things about living things, you are about to take an imaginary journey. It will be quite an unusual trip. You will be traveling inside a living redwood tree, visiting its tiny cells. On your trip you will observe some of the structures found in plant cells. You will also learn about some of the differences between plant and animal cells.

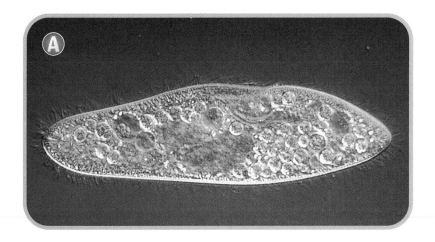

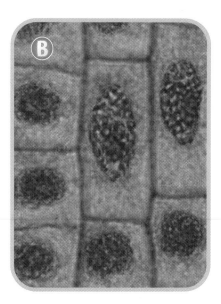

Figure 12 All cells have cell membranes, but not all cells have cell walls. **A.** The cell membrane of this single-celled paramecium controls what substances enter and leave the cell. **B.** The cell walls of these onion root cells have been stained green so you can see them clearly. Cell walls protect and support plant cells.

As you will discover on your journey, cells themselves contain even smaller structures. These tiny cell structures, called **organelles,** carry out specific functions within the cell. Just as your stomach, lungs, and heart have different functions in your body, each organelle has a different function within the cell. You can see the organelles found in plant and animal cells in *Exploring Plant and Animal Cells* on pages 38 and 39. Now it's time to hop aboard your imaginary ship and prepare to enter a typical plant cell.

Cell Wall

Entering a plant's cell is a bit difficult. First you must pass through the cell wall. The **cell wall** is a rigid layer of nonliving material that surrounds the cells of plants and some other organisms. The cell wall is made of a tough, yet flexible, material called cellulose. If you think of a wooden desk, you will have a good idea of what cellulose is. Wood contains a lot of cellulose.

The cells of plants and some other organisms have cell walls. In contrast, the cells of animals and some other organisms lack cell walls. A plant's cell wall helps to protect and support the cell. In woody plants, the cell walls are very rigid. This is why giant redwood trees can stand so tall. Each cell wall in the tree adds strength to the tree. Although the cell wall is stiff, many materials, including water and oxygen, can pass through the cell wall quite easily. So sail on through the cell wall and enter the cell.

✓ *Checkpoint* *What is the function of the cell wall?*

Cell Membrane

After you pass through the cell wall, the next structure you encounter is the **cell membrane.** All cells have cell membranes. In cells with cell walls, the cell membrane is located just inside the cell wall. In other cells, the cell membrane forms the outside boundary that separates the cell from its environment.

As your ship nears the edge of the cell membrane, you notice that there are tiny openings, or pores, in the cell membrane. You steer toward an opening. Suddenly, your ship narrowly misses being stuck by a chunk of waste material passing out of the cell. **You have discovered one of the cell membrane's main functions: the cell membrane controls what substances come into and out of a cell.**

Everything the cell needs—from food to oxygen—enters the cell through the cell membrane. Harmful waste products leave the cell through the cell membrane. For a cell to survive, the cell membrane must allow these materials to pass into and out of the cell. In a sense, the cell membrane is like a window screen. The screen keeps insects out of a room. But holes in the screen allow air to enter and leave the room.

Nucleus

As you sail inside the cell, a large, oval structure comes into view. This structure, called the **nucleus** (NOO klee us), acts as the "brain" of the cell. **You can think of the nucleus as the cell's control center, directing all of the cell's activities.**

Nuclear Membrane Notice in Figure 13 that the nucleus is surrounded by a nuclear membrane. Just as the cell membrane protects the cell, the nuclear membrane protects the nucleus. Materials pass in and out of the nucleus through small openings, or pores, in the nuclear membrane. So aim for that pore just ahead and carefully glide into the nucleus.

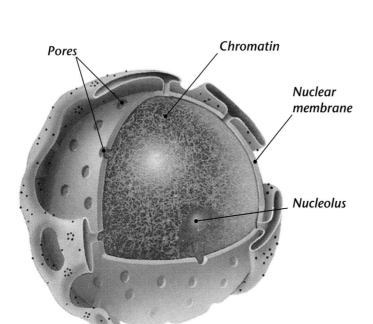

Pores

Chromatin

Nuclear membrane

Nucleolus

Figure 13 The nucleus is the cell's control center. The chromatin in the nucleus contains instructions for carrying out the cell's activities.

36

Chromatin You might wonder how the nucleus "knows" how to direct the cell. The answer lies in those thin strands floating directly ahead in the nucleus. These strands, called **chromatin,** contain the genetic material, the instructions that direct the functions of a cell. For example, the instructions in the chromatin ensure that leaf cells grow and divide to form more leaf cells. The genetic material is passed on to each new cell when an existing cell divides. You'll learn more about how cells divide in Chapter 2.

Nucleolus As you prepare to leave the nucleus, you spot a small object floating by. This structure, the nucleolus, is where ribosomes are made. Ribosomes are the organelles where proteins are produced.

☑ *Checkpoint* *Where in the nucleus is genetic material found?*

Organelles in the Cytoplasm

As you leave the nucleus, you find yourself in the **cytoplasm,** the region between the cell membrane and the nucleus. Your ship floats in a clear, thick, gel-like fluid. The fluid in the cytoplasm is constantly moving, so your ship does not need to propel itself. Many cell organelles are found in the cytoplasm. **The organelles function to produce energy, build and transport needed materials, and store and recycle wastes.**

Mitochondria As you pass into the cytoplasm, you see rod-shaped structures looming ahead. These organelles are called **mitochondria** (my tuh KAHN dree uh) (singular *mitochondrion*). Mitochondria are called the "powerhouses" of the cell because they produce most of the energy the cell needs to carry out its functions. Muscle cells and other very active cells have large numbers of mitochondria.

Figure 14 The mitochondria produce most of the cell's energy. *Predicting* *In what types of cells would you expect to find a lot of mitochondria?*

EXPLORING Plant and Animal Cells

On these pages, you can compare structures found in two kinds of cells: plant cells and animal cells. As you study these cells, remember that they are generalized cells. In living organisms, cells vary somewhat in shape and structure.

PLANT CELL

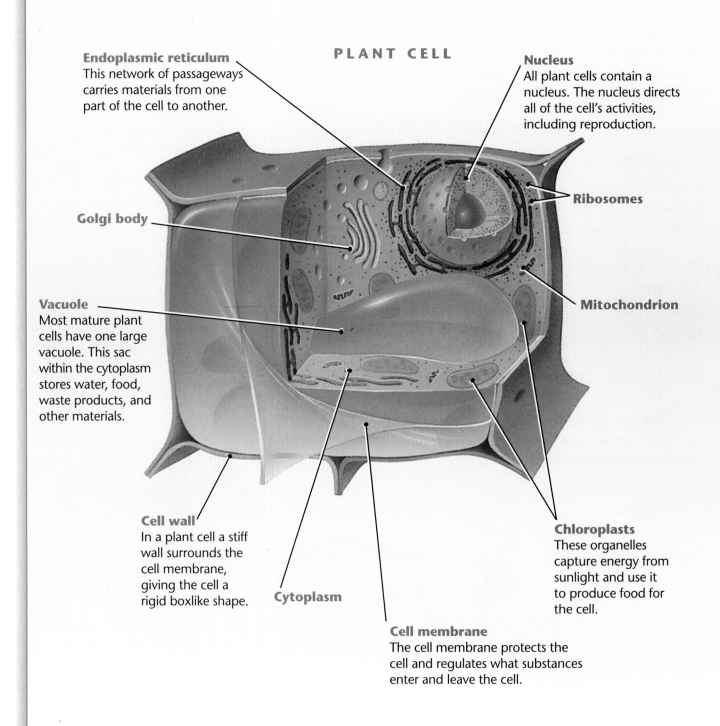

Endoplasmic reticulum
This network of passageways carries materials from one part of the cell to another.

Nucleus
All plant cells contain a nucleus. The nucleus directs all of the cell's activities, including reproduction.

Ribosomes

Golgi body

Mitochondrion

Vacuole
Most mature plant cells have one large vacuole. This sac within the cytoplasm stores water, food, waste products, and other materials.

Cell wall
In a plant cell a stiff wall surrounds the cell membrane, giving the cell a rigid boxlike shape.

Cytoplasm

Chloroplasts
These organelles capture energy from sunlight and use it to produce food for the cell.

Cell membrane
The cell membrane protects the cell and regulates what substances enter and leave the cell.

Vacuole
Some animal cells have
vacuoles that store food, water,
wastes, and other materials.

ANIMAL CELL

Golgi body
The Golgi bodies receive
materials from the
endoplasmic reticulum
and send them to other parts
of the cell. They also release
materials outside the cell.

Ribosomes
These small structures function
as factories to produce proteins.
Ribosomes may be attached to
the outer surfaces of the
endoplasmic reticulum, or they
may float free in the cytoplasm.

Cytoplasm
The cytoplasm is
the area between
the cell membrane
and the nucleus. It
contains a gel-like
fluid in which
many different
organelles are
found.

**Endoplasmic
reticulum**

Nucleus
Almost all animal
cells contain a
nucleus. The nucleus
directs all of the cell's
activities, including
reproduction.

Mitochondria
Most of the cell's energy
is produced within these
rod-shaped organelles.

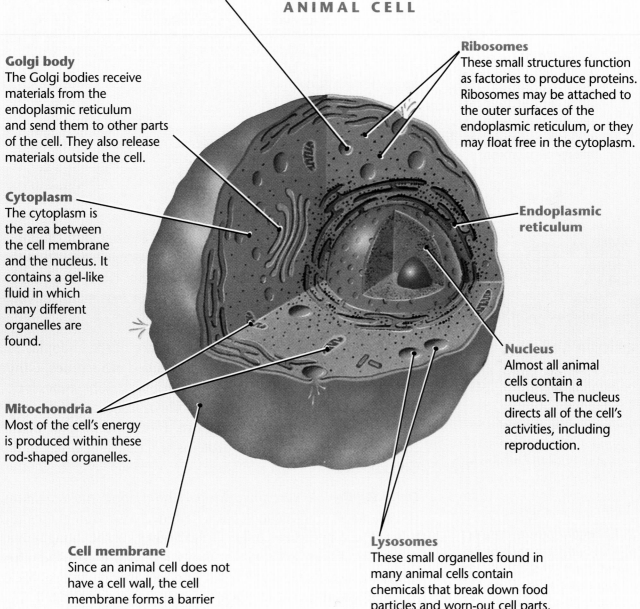

Cell membrane
Since an animal cell does not
have a cell wall, the cell
membrane forms a barrier
between the cytoplasm and the
environment outside the cell.

Lysosomes
These small organelles found in
many animal cells contain
chemicals that break down food
particles and worn-out cell parts.

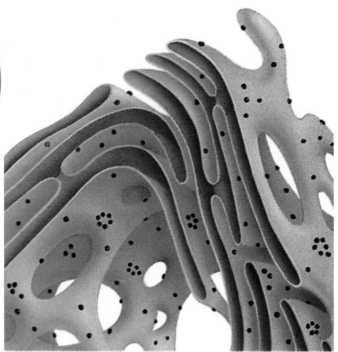

Figure 15 The endoplasmic reticulum is a passageway through which proteins and other materials move within the cell. The spots on the outside of the endoplasmic reticulum are ribosomes, structures that produce proteins.

Endoplasmic Reticulum As you sail farther into the cytoplasm, you find yourself in a maze of passageways called the **endoplasmic reticulum** (en duh PLAZ mik rih TIK yuh lum). These passageways carry proteins and other materials from one part of the cell to another.

Ribosomes Attached to the outer surface of the endoplasmic reticulum are small grainlike bodies called **ribosomes.** Other ribosomes are found floating in the cytoplasm. Ribosomes function as factories to produce proteins. The ribosomes pass the proteins to the endoplasmic reticulum. From the interior of the endoplasmic reticulum, the proteins will be transported to the Golgi bodies.

Golgi Bodies As you move through the endoplasmic reticulum, you see structures that look like a flattened collection of sacs and tubes. These structures, called **Golgi bodies,** can be thought of as the cell's mailroom. The Golgi bodies receive proteins and other newly formed materials from the endoplasmic reticulum, package them, and distribute them to other parts of the cell. The Golgi bodies also release materials outside the cell.

Chloroplasts Have you noticed the many large green structures floating in the cytoplasm? Only the cells of plants and some other organisms have these structures. These organelles, called **chloroplasts,** capture energy from sunlight and use it to produce food for the cell. It is the chloroplasts that give plants their green color. You will learn more about chloroplasts in Chapter 2.

Vacuoles Steer past the chloroplasts and head for that large, round, water-filled sac floating in the cytoplasm. This sac, called a **vacuole** (VAK yoo ohl), is the storage area of the cell. Most plant cells have one large vacuole. Some animal cells do not have vacuoles; others do.

Vacuoles store food and other materials needed by the cell. Vacuoles can also store waste products. Most of the water in plant cells is stored in vacuoles. When the vacuoles are full of water, they make the cell plump and firm. Without much water in the vacuoles, the plant wilts.

Lysosomes Your journey through the cell is almost over. Before you leave, take another look around you. If you carefully swing your ship around the vacuole, you may be lucky enough to see a lysosome. **Lysosomes** (LY suh sohmz) are small round structures that contain chemicals that break down large food particles into smaller ones. Lysosomes also break down old cell parts and release the substances so they can be used again. In this sense, you can think of the lysosomes as the cell's cleanup crew. Lysosomes are found in both animal cells and plant cells.

Although lysosomes contain powerful chemicals, you need not worry about your ship's safety. The membrane around a lysosome keeps these harsh chemicals from escaping and breaking down the rest of the cell.

Bacterial Cells

The plant and animal cells that you just learned about are very different from the bacterial cell you see in Figure 16. First, bacterial cells are usually smaller than plant or animal cells. A human skin cell, for example, is about 10 times as large as an average bacterial cell.

There are several other ways in which bacterial cells are different from plant and animal cells. **While a bacterial cell does have a cell wall and a cell membrane, it does not contain a nucleus.** Organisms whose cells lack a nucleus are called **prokaryotes** (proh KAR ee ohtz). The bacterial cell's genetic material, which looks like a thick, tangled string, is found in the cytoplasm. Bacterial cells contain ribosomes, but none of the other organelles found in plant or animal cells. Organisms whose cells contain a nucleus and many of the organelles you just read about are called **eukaryotes** (yoo KAR ee ohtz).

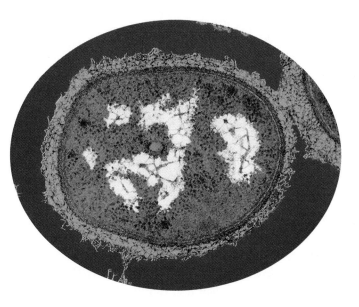

Figure 16 This single-celled organism is a type of bacteria. Bacterial cells lack a nucleus and some other organelles.
Applying Concepts Where is the genetic material in a bacterial cell found?

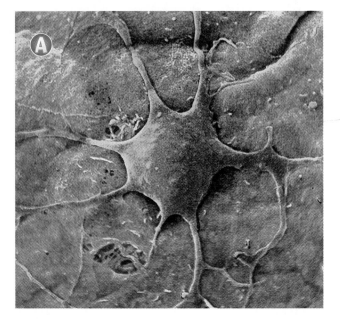
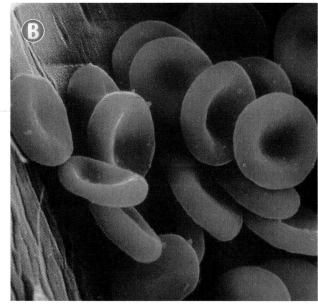

Figure 17 Your body contains a variety of different types of cells. **A.** Nerve cells have long projections through which messages are sent throughout the body. **B.** Red blood cells are thin and flexible, which allows them to fit through tiny blood vessels.

Specialized Cells

Unlike bacteria and other single-celled organisms, plants, animals (including yourself), and other organisms contain many cells. In a many-celled organism, the cells often vary greatly in size and structure. Think of the different parts of your body. You have skin, bones, muscles, blood, a brain, a liver, a stomach, and so on. Each of these body parts carries out a very different function. Yet all of these body parts are made up of cells.

Figure 17 shows two examples of different kinds of cells in your body—nerve cells and red blood cells. The structure of each kind of cell is suited to the unique function it carries out within the organism.

Section 3 Review

1. What is the function of the cell membrane?
2. Why is the nucleus sometimes called the control center of the cell?
3. Name two plant cell parts that are not found in animal cells. What is the function of each part?
4. How do the cells of bacteria differ from those of other organisms?
5. **Thinking Critically Comparing and Contrasting** Compare the functions of the cell wall in a plant cell and the cell membrane in an animal cell. How are the functions of the two structures similar and different?

Science at Home

Building Blocks Ask family members to help you find five items in your house that are made of smaller things. Make a list of the items and identify as many of their building blocks as you can. Be sure to look at prepared foods, furniture, and books. Discuss with your family how these building blocks come together to make up the larger objects. Do these objects or their building blocks possess any characteristics of living things?

A Magnified View of Life

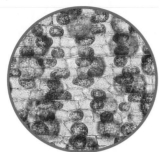

I n this lab, you will use your observation skills to compare plant and animal cells.

Problem

How are plant and animal cells alike and different?

Materials

plastic dropper
water
microscope slide
microscope
colored pencils
prepared slide of animal cells

Elodea leaf
forceps
coverslip

Procedure

1. Before you start this lab, read *Using the Microscope* (Appendix B) on pages 802–803. Be sure you know how to use a microscope correctly and safely.

Part 1 Observing Plant Cells

2. Use a plastic dropper to place a drop of water in the center of a slide. **CAUTION:** *Slides and coverslips are fragile. Handle them carefully. Do not touch broken glass.*

3. With forceps, remove a leaf from an *Elodea* plant. Place the leaf in the drop of water on the slide. Make sure that the leaf is flat. If it is folded, straighten it with the forceps.

4. Holding a coverslip by its edges, slowly lower it onto the drop of water and *Elodea* leaf. If any air bubbles form, tap the slide gently to get rid of them.

5. Use a microscope to examine the *Elodea* leaf under low power. Then, carefully switch to high power.

6. Observe the cells of the *Elodea* leaf. Draw and label what you see, including the colors of the cell parts. Record the magnification.

7. Discard the *Elodea* leaf as directed by your teacher. Carefully clean and dry your slide and coverslip. Wash your hands thoroughly.

Part 2 Observing Animals Cells

8. Obtain a prepared slide of animal cells. The cells on the slide have been stained with an artificial color.

9. Observe the animal cells with a microscope under both low and high power. Draw and label the cell parts that you see. Record the magnification.

Analyze and Conclude

1. How are plant and animal cells alike?
2. How are plant and animal cells different?
3. What natural color appeared in the plant cells? What structures give the plant cells this color?
4. **Think About It** Why is it important to record your observations while you are examining a specimen?

More to Explore

Observe other prepared slides of animal cells. Look for ways that animal cells differ from each other. Obtain your teacher's permission before carrying out these observations.

SECTION 4 The Origin of Life

DISCOVER
ACTIVITY

How Can the Composition of Air Change?

1.  Your teacher will give you two covered plastic jars. One contains a plant and one contains an animal.

2. Observe the organisms in each jar. Talk with a partner about how you think each organism affects the composition of the air in its jar.

3. Write a prediction about how the amount of oxygen in each jar would change over time if left undisturbed.

4. Return the jars to your teacher.

Think It Over

Inferring Scientists hypothesize that Earth's early atmosphere was different from today's atmosphere. What role might early organisms have played in bringing about those changes?

GUIDE FOR READING

◆ How was the atmosphere of early Earth different from today's atmosphere?

◆ How do scientists hypothesize that life arose on early Earth?

Reading Tip Before you read, write a paragraph stating what you already know about early life on Earth. As you read this section, make changes and additions to your paragraph.

You stare out the window of your time machine. You have traveled back to Earth as it was 3.6 billion years ago. The landscape is rugged, with bare, jagged rocks and little soil. You search for a hint of green, but there is none. You see only blacks, browns, and grays. Lightning flashes all around you. You hear the rumble of thunder, howling winds, and waves pounding the shore.

You neither see nor hear any living things. However, you know that this is the time period when scientists think that early life forms arose on Earth. You decide to explore. To be safe, you put on your oxygen mask. Stepping outside, you wonder what kinds of organisms could ever live in such a place.

Earth's Early Atmosphere

You were smart to put on your oxygen mask before exploring early Earth. Scientists think that early Earth had a different atmosphere than it has today. **Nitrogen, water vapor, carbon dioxide, and methane were probably the most abundant gases in Earth's atmosphere 3.6 billion years ago. Although all these gases are still found in the atmosphere today, the major gases are nitrogen and oxygen.** You, like most of today's organisms, could not have lived on Earth 3.6 billion years ago, because there was no oxygen in the air. Scientists think, however, that the first forms of life on Earth appeared at that time.

No one can ever be sure what the first life forms were like, but scientists have formed hypotheses about them. First, early life forms did not need oxygen to survive. Second, they were probably unicellular organisms. Third, they probably lived in the oceans. Many scientists think that the first organisms resembled the bacteria that live today in places without oxygen, such as the polar ice caps, hot springs, or the mud of the ocean bottoms. These bacteria survive in extreme environments—surroundings where temperatures are often above 100°C or below 0°C, or where the water pressure is extremely high.

Life's Chemicals

One of the most intriguing questions that scientists face is explaining how early life forms arose. Although Redi and Pasteur demonstrated that living things do not spontaneously arise on today's Earth, scientists reason that the first life forms probably did arise from nonliving materials.

Two American scientists, Harold Urey and Stanley Miller, provided the first clue as to how organisms might have arisen on Earth. In 1953, they designed an experiment in which they re-created the conditions of early Earth in their laboratory. They placed water (to represent the ocean), and a mixture of the gases thought to compose Earth's early atmosphere into a flask. They were careful to keep oxygen and unicellular organisms out of the mixture. Then, they sent an electric current through the mixture to simulate lightning. Within a week, the mixture darkened. In the dark fluid, Miller and Urey found some small chemical units that, if joined together, could form proteins—one of the building blocks of life.

✓ *Checkpoint* *What did Harold Urey and Stanley Miller model in their experiment?*

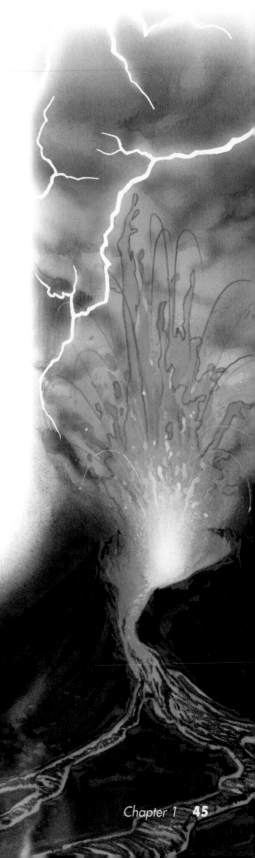

Figure 18 The atmosphere of early Earth had little oxygen. There were frequent volcanic eruptions, earthquakes, and violent weather.
Inferring *What conditions on early Earth would have made it impossible for modern organisms to survive?*

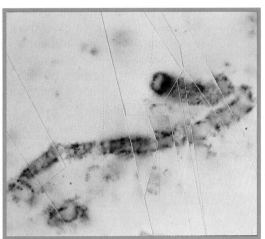

Figure 19 This fossil of bacteria-like cells was found in western Australia. It is the oldest fossil known—about 3.5 billion years old.

The First Cells

In experiments similar to Miller and Urey's, other scientists succeeded in producing chemical units that make up carbohydrates and nucleic acids. **From the results of these experiments, scientists hypothesized that the small chemical units of life formed gradually over millions of years in Earth's waters.** Some of these units joined to form the large chemical building blocks that are found in cells. Eventually, some of these large chemicals accumulated and became the forerunners of the first cells.

These hypotheses are consistent with evidence from fossils. **Fossils** are traces of ancient organisms that have been preserved in rock or other substances. The fossils in Figure 19 are of bacteria-like organisms that were determined to be between 3.4 and 3.5 billion years old. Scientists think that these ancient cells may be evidence of Earth's earliest life forms.

The first cells could not have needed oxygen to survive. They probably were heterotrophs that used the chemicals in their surroundings for energy. As they grew and reproduced, their numbers increased. In turn, the amount of chemicals available to them decreased. At some point, some of the cells may have developed the ability to make their own food. These early ancestors of today's autotrophs had an important effect on the atmosphere. As they made their own food, they produced oxygen as a waste product. As the autotrophs thrived, oxygen accumulated in Earth's atmosphere. Over many, many millions of years, the amount of oxygen increased to its current level.

No one will ever know for certain how life first appeared on Earth. However, scientists will continue to ask questions, construct models, and look for both experimental and fossil evidence about the origin of life on Earth.

Section 4 Review

1. Explain why you could not have survived in the atmosphere of early Earth.
2. Describe how scientists think that life could have arisen on Earth.
3. Describe Urey and Miller's experiment.
4. **Thinking Critically** Inferring How is the existence of organisms in hot springs today consistent with the scientific hypothesis of how life forms arose on Earth?

Check Your Progress CHAPTER PROJECT
Now that you have completed your observations, analyze your data. Arrange your data in a chart or diagram. Find another object that is familiar to you and similar to your mystery object. Compare the two objects. Conclude whether your object is alive.

SECTION 1 What Is Life?

Key Ideas
◆ All living things are made of cells, contain similar chemicals, use energy, grow and develop, respond to their surroundings, and reproduce.
◆ All living things must satisfy their basic needs for energy, water, living space, and stable internal conditions.

Key Terms
organism	response	variable
cell	reproduce	autotroph
unicellular	spontaneous	heterotroph
multicellular	generation	homeostasis
development	controlled	
stimulus	experiment	

SECTION 2 Discovering Cells

Key Ideas
◆ The invention of the microscope made the discovery of the cell possible.
◆ The cell theory explains the relationship between cells and living things.

Key Terms
microscope	magnification
compound microscope	convex lens
cell theory	resolution

SECTION 3 Looking Inside Cells

Key Ideas
◆ The cell membrane protects the cell and controls what substances enter and leave it.
◆ The nucleus is the cell's control center.
◆ Organelles in the cytoplasm perform many different vital functions.

Key Terms
organelle	mitochondrion	chloroplast
cell wall	endoplasmic	vacuole
cell membrane	reticulum	lysosome
nucleus	ribosome	prokaryote
chromatin	Golgi body	eukaryote
cytoplasm		

SECTION 4 The Origin of Life

INTEGRATING EARTH SCIENCE

Key Ideas
◆ Nitrogen, water vapor, carbon dioxide, and methane were probably the most abundant gases in Earth's atmosphere 3.6 billion years ago. Today the major gases are nitrogen and oxygen.
◆ Scientists hypothesize that over millions of years, the small chemical units of life formed in Earth's oceans. Over time, some of these units joined to form the large chemical building blocks found in cells.

Key Term
fossil

Organizing Information

Concept Map Copy the concept map about the needs of organisms onto a separate sheet of paper. Then complete it and add a title. (For more on concept maps, see the Skills Handbook.)

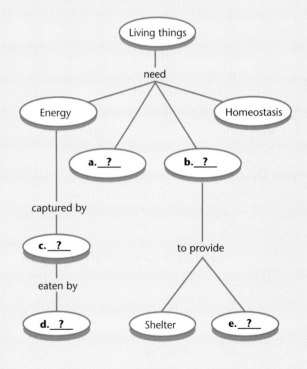

Reviewing Content

 For more review of key concepts, see the Interactive Student Tutorial CD-ROM.

Multiple Choice
Choose the letter of the best answer.

1. The idea that life could spring from nonliving matter is called
   a. development.
   b. spontaneous generation.
   c. homeostasis.
   d. evolution.

2. The ability of microscopes to distinguish fine details is called
   a. resolution.
   b. bending.
   c. magnification.
   d. active transport.

3. In plant and animal cells, the control center of the cell is the
   a. chloroplast.
   b. ribosome.
   c. nucleus.
   d. Golgi body.

4. The storage compartment of a cell is the
   a. cell wall.
   b. lysosome.
   c. endoplasmic reticulum.
   d. vacuole.

5. Which gas was not part of Earth's atmosphere 3.6 billion years ago?
   a. methane   b. nitrogen
   c. oxygen   d. water vapor

True or False
If the statement is true, write true. If it is false, change the underlined word or words to make the statement true.

6. When you eat salad, you are acting like an <u>autotroph</u>.

7. Cells were discovered using <u>electron</u> microscopes.

8. <u>Vacuoles</u> are the "powerhouses" of the cell.

9. Bacterial cells differ from the cells of plants and animals in that they lack a <u>nucleus</u>.

10. The first organisms on Earth were probably <u>heterotrophs</u>.

Checking Concepts

11. Your friend thinks that plants are not alive because they do not move. How would you respond to your friend?

12. What role did the microscope play in the development of the cell theory?

13. Describe the function of the cell wall in the cells that have these structures.

14. Describe where Earth's early organisms lived, and how they obtained food.

15. **Writing to Learn** Suppose you had been a reporter assigned to cover early scientists' discoveries about cells. Write a brief article for your daily newspaper that explains one scientist's discoveries. Be sure to explain both how the discoveries were made and why they are important.

Thinking Critically

16. **Classifying** How do you know that a robot is not alive?

17. **Relating Cause and Effect** When people believed that spontaneous generation occurred, there was a recipe for making mice: Place a dirty shirt and a few wheat grains in an open pot; wait three weeks. List the reasons why this recipe might have worked. How could you demonstrate that spontaneous generation was not responsible for the appearance of mice?

18. **Applying Concepts** Explain how the cell theory applies to a dog.

19. **Predicting** Could a cell survive without a cell membrane? Give reasons to support your answer.

20. **Comparing and Contrasting** How are plant and animal cells similar? How are they different? To answer these questions, make a list of the different organelles in each cell. Explain how each organelle is vital to the life and function of a plant or animal.

Applying Skills

A student designed an experiment to test how light affects the growth of plants. Refer to the illustrations below to answer Questions 21–24.

21. Controlling Variables Is this a controlled experiment? If not, why not? If so, identify the manipulated variable.

22. Developing Hypotheses What hypothesis might this experiment be testing?

23. Predicting Based on what you know about plants, predict how each plant will have changed after two weeks.

24. Designing Experiments Design a controlled experiment to determine whether the amount of water that a plant receives affects its growth.

Performance ▼ CHAPTER PROJECT Assessment

Present Your Project Prepare a display presenting your conclusion about your mystery object. Describe the observations that helped you reach your conclusion. Compare your ideas with those of other students. If necessary, defend your work.

Reflect and Record Make a list of the characteristics of life that you observed in your mystery object. Which were hard to study? Explain in your journal why some characteristics were hard to investigate.

Test Preparation

Use these questions to prepare for standardized tests.

Study the table. Then answer Questions 25–29.

Cell	Nucleus	Cell Wall	Cell Membrane
Cell A	Yes	Yes	Yes
Cell B	Yes	No	Yes
Cell C	No	Yes	Yes

25. Which cell is probably an animal cell?
  a. cell A   **b.** cell B
  c. cell C   **d.** none of the above

26. Which cell is probably a plant cell?
  a. cell A   **b.** cell B
  c. cell C   **d.** none of the above

27. Which cell is a prokaryote?
  a. cell A   **b.** cell B
  c. cell C   **d.** none of the above

28. In Cell B, where would the genetic material be found?
  a. in the mitochondria
  b. in the vacuoles
  c. in the nucleus
  d. in the cell membrane

29. Which cell(s) would most likely contain chloroplasts?
  a. cell A   **b.** cell B
  c. cell C   **d.** cell B and cell C

WEB ACTIVITY www.phschool.com

 Integrating Chemistry
SECTION **1** **Chemical Compounds in Cells**

Discover **What Is a Compound?**
Try This **What's That Taste?**
Science at Home **Organic Compounds in Food**

SECTION **2** **The Cell in Its Environment**

Discover **How Do Molecules Move?**
Try This **Diffusion in Action**

SECTION **3** **Photosynthesis**

Discover **Where Does the Energy Come From?**
Sharpen Your Skills **Inferring**

Egg-speriment With a Cell

Did you ever wonder how a baby chick can breathe when it's still inside the egg? The shell of the egg allows air to reach the developing chick inside, while it keeps most other substances outside. Just as an egg needs to control which substances can enter it, so too does every cell in your body.

In this chapter, you'll learn more about cells and how they carry out the essential functions of life. You'll learn how cells make and use energy and how they grow and divide. You can start your discoveries right away by studying an everyday object that can serve as a model of a cell: an uncooked egg.

Your Goal To observe how various materials enter or leave a cell, using an egg as a model of the cell.

To complete this project, you will
- ◆ observe what happens when you soak an uncooked egg in vinegar, then in water, food coloring, salt water, and finally in a liquid of your choice
- ◆ measure the circumference of the egg every day, and graph your results
- ◆ explain the changes that your egg underwent
- ◆ follow the safety guidelines in Appendix A

Get Started Predict what might happen when you put an uncooked egg in vinegar for two days. How might other liquids affect an egg? Find a place where you can leave your egg undisturbed. Then begin your egg-speriment!

Check Your Progress You will be working on this project as you study this chapter. To keep your project on track, look for Check Your Progress boxes at the following points.

Section 2 Review, page 60: Make measurements and record data.
Section 3 Review, page 65: Experiment with different liquids.
Section 5 Review, page 79: Graph your data and draw conclusions.

Present Your Project At the end of the chapter (page 83), you will display your egg and share your results.

The thin shells of these eggs control what substances reach the developing chick inside.

SECTION 4 Respiration

Discover **What Is a Product of Respiration?**
Science at Home **Fermentation in Bread**
Real-World Lab **Gases in Balance**

SECTION 5 Cell Division

Discover **What Are the Cells Doing?**
Try This **Modeling Mitosis**
Sharpen Your Skills **Interpreting Data**
Skills Lab **Multiplying by Dividing**

1 Chemical Compounds in Cells

DISCOVER ·· ACTIVITY····

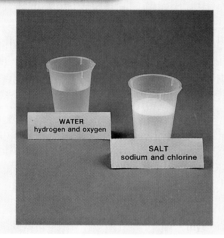

WATER
hydrogen and oxygen

SALT
sodium and chlorine

What Is a Compound?

1. Your teacher will provide you with containers filled with various substances. All of the substances are chemical compounds.

2. Examine each substance. Read the label on each container to learn what each substance is made of.

Think It Over

Forming Operational Definitions Write a definition of what you think a chemical compound is.

GUIDE FOR READING

◆ What are the four main kinds of organic molecules in living things?

◆ How is water important to the function of cells?

Reading Tip As you read, make a table of the main types of organic molecules and where in the cell each one is found.

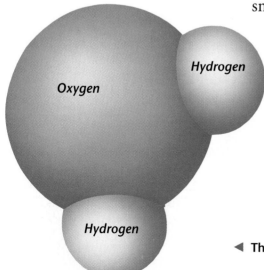

Oxygen

Hydrogen

Hydrogen

◀ The structure of a water molecule

If cells are the basic building blocks of living things, then what substances are the basic building blocks of cells? In what ways are the basic building blocks of cells similar to those that make up other things around you? In this section you will explore how the substances that make up living cells differ from those that make up nonliving things.

Elements and Compounds

Think about the air around you. You probably know that air is a mixture of gases, including oxygen and nitrogen. Oxygen and nitrogen are examples of elements. An **element** is any substance that cannot be broken down into simpler substances. The smallest unit of an element is called an **atom.** An element is made up of only one kind of atom. The most common elements in living things, including you, are carbon, oxygen, hydrogen, and nitrogen.

When two or more elements combine chemically they form a **compound.** Water, for example, is a compound made up of the elements hydrogen and oxygen. The smallest unit of most compounds is called a **molecule.** Each water molecule is made up of two hydrogen atoms and one oxygen atom.

Organic and Inorganic Compounds

Many of the compounds found in living things contain the element carbon, which is usually combined with other elements. Most compounds that contain carbon are called **organic compounds.**

The most important groups of organic compounds found in living things are proteins, carbohydrates, lipids, and nucleic acids. As you may know, many of these compounds are found in the foods you eat. This is not surprising, since the foods you eat come from living things.

Compounds that don't contain the element carbon are called **inorganic compounds.** One exception to this definition is carbon dioxide. Although carbon dioxide contains carbon, it is classified as an inorganic compound. Other inorganic compounds include water and sodium chloride, or table salt.

Proteins

What do a bird's feathers, a spider's web, and your fingernails have in common? All of these substances are made mainly of proteins. **Proteins** are large organic molecules made of carbon, hydrogen, oxygen, nitrogen, and, in some cases, sulfur. Foods that are high in protein include meat, eggs, fish, nuts, and beans.

Cells use proteins for many different things. For instance, proteins form parts of cell membranes. Proteins also make up many of the organelles within the cell. Certain cells in your body use proteins to build body structures such as muscles.

Protein Structure Protein molecules are made up of smaller molecules called **amino acids.** Although there are only 20 common amino acids, cells can combine them in different ways to form thousands of different proteins. The kinds of amino acids and the order in which they link together determine the type of protein that forms.

You can think of the 20 amino acids as being like the 26 letters of the alphabet. Those 26 letters can form thousands of words. The letters you use and their order determine the words you form. Even a change in one letter, for example, from *rice* to *mice,* creates a new word. Similarly, changes in the type or order of amino acids result in a different protein.

Figure 1 This peacock's feathers are made up mainly of proteins. Proteins are important components of the cell membrane and many of the cell's organelles.

Enzymes An **enzyme** is a type of protein that speeds up a chemical reaction in a living thing. Without enzymes, many chemical reactions that are necessary for life would either take too long or not occur at all. For example, enzymes in your saliva speed up the digestion of food by breaking down starches into sugars in your mouth.

Carbohydrates

A **carbohydrate** is an energy-rich organic compound made of the elements carbon, hydrogen, and oxygen. Sugars and starches are examples of carbohydrates.

Sugars are produced during the food-making process that takes place in plants. Foods such as fruits and some vegetables are high in sugar content. Sugar molecules can combine, forming large molecules called starches. Plant cells store excess energy in molecules of starch.

Carbohydrates are important components of some cell parts. The cellulose found in the cell walls of plants is a type of carbohydrate. Carbohydrates are also found in cell membranes.

Lipids

Have you ever seen a cook trim the fat from a piece of meat before cooking it? The cook is trimming away a lipid. Fats, oils, and waxes are all **lipids.** Like carbohydrates, lipids are energy-rich, organic compounds made of carbon, hydrogen, and oxygen.

Lipids contain even more energy than carbohydrates. Cells store energy in lipids for later use. For example, during winter a dormant bear lives on the energy stored as fat within its cells.

Figure 2 These potatoes contain large amounts of starch, a type of carbohydrate. The blue grains you see in the close-up are starch granules in a potato. The grains have been colored blue to make them easier to see. *Classifying What types of carbohydrates combine to form starches?*

Nucleic Acids

Nucleic acids are very large organic molecules made of carbon, oxygen, hydrogen, nitrogen, and phosphorus. Nucleic acids contain the instructions that cells need to carry out all the functions of life.

There are two kinds of nucleic acids. Deoxyribonucleic acid (dee ahk see ry boh noo KLEE ik), or **DNA,** is the genetic material that carries information about an organism that is passed from parent to offspring. The information in DNA also directs all of the cell's functions. Most of the DNA in a cell is found in the chromatin in the nucleus. Ribonucleic acid (ry boh noo KLEE ik), or **RNA,** plays an important role in the production of proteins. RNA is found in the cytoplasm, as well as in the nucleus.

Water and Living Things

Did you know that water makes up about two thirds of your body? Water plays many vital roles in cells. For example, most chemical reactions that take place in cells can occur only when substances are dissolved in water. **Without water, most chemical reactions within cells could not take place.** Also, water molecules themselves take part in many chemical reactions in cells.

Water also helps cells keep their size and shape. In fact, a cell without water would be like a balloon without air. In addition, because water changes temperature slowly, it helps keep the temperature of a cell from changing rapidly.

Figure 3 Water is essential for all living things to survive. The cells of these tulips need water to function.

Section 1 Review

1. Name the four main groups of organic molecules in living things. Describe the function of each type of molecule.
2. What roles does water play in cells?
3. How are elements related to compounds?
4. **Thinking Critically Predicting** Suppose a cell did not have a supply of amino acids and could not produce them. What effect might this have on the cell?

Science at Home

Organic Compounds in Food With family members, look at the "Nutrition Facts" labels on a variety of food products. Identify foods that contain large amounts of the following organic compounds: carbohydrates, proteins, and fats. Discuss with your family what elements each of these compounds are made of and what roles they play in cells and in your body.

② The Cell in Its Environment

How Do Molecules Move?

1. With your classmates, stand so that you are evenly spaced throughout the classroom.

2. Your teacher will spray an air freshener into the room. When you first begin to smell the air freshener, raise your hand.

3. Note how long it takes for other students in the classroom to smell the scent.

Think It Over

Developing Hypotheses How was each student's distance from the teacher related to when he or she smelled the air freshener? Develop a hypothesis about why this pattern occurred.

GUIDE FOR READING

◆ By what three methods do materials move into and out of cells?

◆ What is the difference between passive transport and active transport?

Reading Tip Before you read, use the headings to make an outline about how materials move into and out of cells. As you read, make notes about each process.

▼ The *Mir* space station

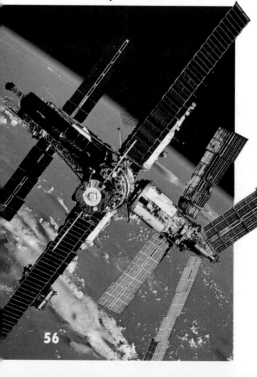

How is a cell like a space station? The walls of a space station protect the astronauts inside from the airless vacuum of space. Food, water, and other supplies must be brought to the space station by shuttles from Earth. In addition, the space station needs to be able to get rid of wastes. The doors of the space station allow the astronauts to bring materials in and move wastes out into the shuttle to be returned to Earth.

Like space stations, cells also have structures that protect them from the outside environment. As you learned, all cells are surrounded by a cell membrane that separates the cell from the outside environment. Just like the space station, the cell also has to take in needed materials and get rid of wastes. It is the cell membrane that controls what materials move into and out of the cell.

The Cell Membrane as Gatekeeper

The cell membrane is **selectively permeable,** which means that some substances can pass through it while others cannot. The term *permeable* comes from a Latin word that means "to pass through." You can think of the cell membrane as being like a gatekeeper at an ancient castle. It was the gatekeeper's job to decide when to open the gate to allow people to pass into and out of the castle. The gatekeeper made the castle wall "selectively permeable"—it was permeable to friendly folks but not to enemies.

A cell membrane is usually permeable to substances such as oxygen, water, and carbon dioxide. On the other hand, the cell membrane is usually not permeable to some large molecules and salts. **Substances that can move into and out of a cell do so by one of three methods: diffusion, osmosis, or active transport.**

Diffusion—Molecules in Motion

The main method by which small molecules move into and out of cells is diffusion. **Diffusion** (dih FYOO zhun) is the process by which molecules tend to move from an area of higher concentration to an area of lower concentration. The concentration of a substance is the amount of the substance in a given volume.

If you did the Discover activity, you observed diffusion in action. The area where the air freshener was sprayed had many molecules of freshener. The molecules gradually moved from this area of higher concentration to the other parts of the classroom, where there were few molecules of freshener, and thus a lower concentration.

What Causes Diffusion? Molecules are always moving. As they move, the molecules bump into one another. The more molecules there are in an area, the more collisions there will be. Collisions cause molecules to push away from one another. Over time, the molecules of a substance will continue to spread out. Eventually they will be spread evenly throughout the area.

INTEGRATING CHEMISTRY

Diffusion in Cells Have you ever used a microscope to observe one-celled organisms in pond water? These organisms obtain the oxygen they need to survive from the water around them. Luckily for them, there are many more molecules of oxygen in the water outside the cell than there are inside the cell. In other words, there is a higher concentration of oxygen molecules in the water than inside the cell. Remember that the cell membrane is permeable to oxygen molecules. The oxygen molecules diffuse from the area of higher concentration—the pond water—through the cell membrane to the area of lower concentration—the inside of the cell.

Figure 4 Molecules move by diffusion from an area of higher concentration to an area of lower concentration. **A.** There is a higher concentration of molecules outside the cell than inside. **B.** The molecules diffuse into the cell. Eventually, there is an equal concentration of molecules inside and outside the cell.
Predicting What would happen if the concentration of the molecules outside the cell was lower than the concentration inside?

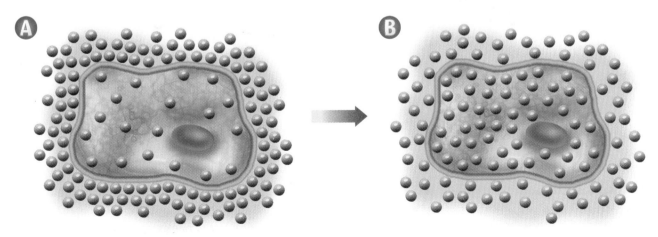

Here's how you can observe the effects of diffusion.

1. Fill a small clear plastic cup with cold water. Place the cup on a table and allow it to sit until there is no movement in the water.

2. Use a plastic dropper to add one large drop of food coloring to the water.

3. Observe the water every minute. Note any changes that take place. Continue to observe until you can no longer see any changes.

Inferring What role did diffusion play in the changes you observed?

Osmosis—The Diffusion of Water Molecules

Like oxygen, water passes easily into and out of cells through the cell membrane. The diffusion of water molecules through a selectively permeable membrane is called **osmosis.** Osmosis is important to cells because cells cannot function properly without adequate water.

Remember that molecules tend to move from an area of higher concentration to an area of lower concentration. In osmosis, water molecules move by diffusion from an area where they are highly concentrated through the cell membrane to an area where they are less concentrated. This can have important consequences for the cell.

Look at Figure 5 to see the effect of osmosis on cells. In Figure 5A, red blood cells are bathed in a solution in which the concentration of water is the same as it is inside the cells. This is the normal shape of a red blood cell.

Now look at Figure 5B. The red blood cells are floating in water that contains a lot of salt. The concentration of water molecules outside the cells is lower than the concentration of water molecules inside the cells. This is because the salt takes up space in the salt water, so there are fewer water molecules. As a result, water moves out of the cells by osmosis, and the cells shrink.

Finally, consider Figure 5C. The red blood cells are floating in water that contains a very small amount of salt. The water inside the cells contains more salt than the solution they are floating in. Thus, the concentration of water outside the cell is greater than it is inside the cell. The water moves into the cell, causing it to swell.

☑ *Checkpoint* *How is osmosis related to diffusion?*

Figure 5 Osmosis is the diffusion of water molecules through a selectively permeable membrane.

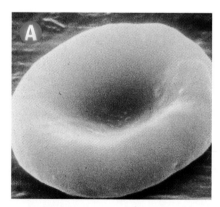

A. This is the normal shape of a red blood cell.

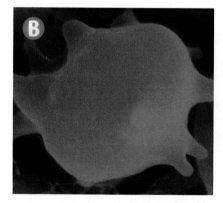

B. This cell has shrunk because water moved out of it by osmosis.

C. This cell is swollen with water that has moved into it by osmosis.

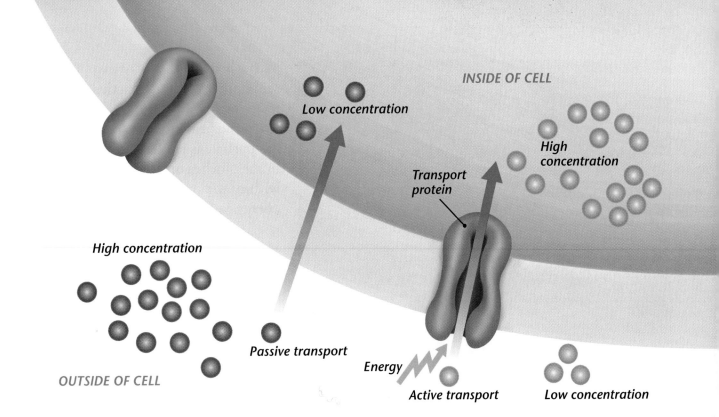

INSIDE OF CELL

Low concentration

High concentration

Transport protein

High concentration

Passive transport

OUTSIDE OF CELL

Energy

Active transport

Low concentration

Active Transport

If you have ever ridden a bicycle down a long hill, you know that it doesn't take any of your energy to go fast. But pedaling back up the hill does take energy. For a cell, moving materials through the cell membrane by diffusion and osmosis is like cycling downhill. These processes do not require the cell to use any energy. The movement of materials through a cell membrane without using energy is called **passive transport.**

What if a cell needs to take in a substance that is in higher concentration inside the cell than outside? The cell would have to move the molecules in the opposite direction than they naturally move by diffusion. Cells can do this, but they have to use energy—just as you would use energy to pedal back up the hill. **Active transport** is the movement of materials through a cell membrane using energy. **The main difference between passive transport and active transport is that active transport requires the cell to use energy while passive transport does not.**

Transport Proteins A cell has several ways of moving materials by active transport. In one method, transport proteins in the cell membrane "pick up" molecules outside the cell and carry them in, using energy in the process. Transport proteins also carry molecules out of cells in a similar way. Some substances that are carried into and out of cells in this way include calcium, potassium, and sodium.

Figure 6 Diffusion and osmosis are forms of passive transport. These processes do not require the cell to use any energy. Active transport, on the other hand, requires the use of energy.
Interpreting Diagrams How are passive and active transport related to the concentrations of the molecules inside and outside the cell?

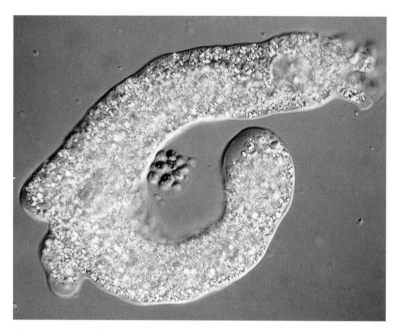

Figure 7 A cell can move some materials into the cell by engulfing them. This single-celled ameba is engulfing a smaller single-celled organism. *Applying Concepts How does this process differ from passive transport?*

Transport by Engulfing You can see another method of active transport in Figure 7. First the cell membrane surrounds, or engulfs, a particle. Once the particle is engulfed, the cell membrane pinches off and forms a vacuole within the cell. The cell must use energy in this process.

Why Are Cells Small?

As you know, most cells are so small that you cannot see them without a microscope. Have you ever wondered why cells are so small? One reason is related to how materials move into and out of cells.

As a cell's size increases, more of its cytoplasm is located farther from the cell membrane. Once a molecule enters a cell, it is carried to its destination by a stream of moving cytoplasm, somewhat like the way currents of water in the ocean move a raft. But in a very large cell, the streams of cytoplasm must travel farther to bring materials to all parts of the cell. It would take much longer for a molecule to reach the center of a very large cell than it would in a small cell. Likewise, it would take a long time for wastes to be removed. If a cell grew too large, it could not function well enough to survive. When a cell reaches a certain size, it divides into two new cells. You will learn more about cell division later in this chapter.

Section 2 Review

1. Describe three methods by which substances can move into and out of cells.
2. How are passive transport and active transport similar? How do they differ?
3. Why is small size an advantage to a cell?
4. **Thinking Critically Predicting** A single-celled organism is transferred from a tank of fresh water into a tank of salt water. How will the cell change? Explain.

Check Your Progress CHAPTER PROJECT
By now you should have started your egg-speriment by soaking an uncooked egg in vinegar. Leave your egg in the vinegar for at least two days. Each day, rinse your egg in water and measure its circumference. Record all of your observations. (*Hint:* Handle the egg gently. If your egg breaks, don't give up or throw away your data. Simply start again with another egg and keep investigating.)

DISCOVER

ACTIVITY

Where Does the Energy Come From?

1. Obtain a solar-powered calculator that does not use batteries. Place the calculator in direct light.

2. Cover the solar cells with your finger. Note how your action affects the number display.

3. Uncover the solar cells. What happens to the number display?

4. Now cover all but one of the solar cells. How does that affect the number display?

Think It Over

Inferring From your observations, what can you infer about the energy that powers the calculator?

I t's a beautiful summer afternoon—a perfect day for a picnic in the park. The aroma of chicken cooking on the grill fills the air. Your dog is busy chasing sticks under a nearby tree. Up above, blue jays swoop down from the tree's branches, hunting for food. "Let's go for a bike ride before lunch," suggests your cousin. "Great idea," you say, and you ride off down the path.

Dogs running, birds flying, people biking—all of these activities require energy. Where do you think this energy comes from? Believe it or not, all the energy used to perform such activities comes from the sun. In fact, the sun provides almost all the energy used by living things on Earth.

GUIDE FOR READING

◆ What happens during the process of photosynthesis?

◆ How does the sun supply living things with the energy they need?

Reading Tip As you read, create a flowchart that shows the steps involved in the process of photosynthesis.

What Is Photosynthesis?

Every living thing needs energy. All cells need energy to carry out their functions, such as making proteins and transporting substances into and out of the cell. Your picnic lunch supplies your cells with the energy they need. But plants and other organisms, such as algae and some bacteria, obtain their energy in a different way. These organisms use the energy in sunlight to make their own food.

The process by which a cell captures the energy in sunlight and uses it to make food is called **photosynthesis** (foh toh SIN thuh sis). The term *photosynthesis* comes from the root words *photo,* which means "light," and *synthesis,* which means "putting together." Photosynthesis means using light to make food.

A Two-Stage Process

Photosynthesis is a very complicated process. **During photosynthesis, plants and some other organisms use energy from the sun to convert carbon dioxide and water into oxygen and sugars, including glucose.** You can think of photosynthesis as taking place in two stages: capturing the sun's energy and producing sugars. You're probably familiar with many two-stage processes. To make a cake, for example, the first stage is to combine the ingredients to make the batter. The second stage is to bake the batter in an oven. To get the desired result—the cake—both stages must occur in the correct order.

Capturing the Sun's Energy The first stage of photosynthesis involves capturing the energy in sunlight. In plants, this energy-capturing process occurs in the leaves and other green parts of the plant. Recall from Chapter 1 that chloroplasts are green organelles inside plant cells. In most plants, leaf cells contain more chloroplasts than do cells in other parts of the plant.

Figure 8 Photosynthesis occurs inside chloroplasts in the cells of plants and some other organisms. The chloroplasts are the green structures in the cell in the inset. *Applying Concepts Where in a plant are cells with many chloroplasts found?*

The chloroplasts in plant cells give plants their green color. The green color comes from **pigments,** colored chemical compounds that absorb light. The main pigment found in the chloroplasts of plants is **chlorophyll.** Chloroplasts may also contain yellow and orange pigments, but they are usually masked by the green color of chlorophyll.

Chlorophyll and the other pigments function in a manner similar to that of the solar "cells" in a solar-powered calculator. Solar cells capture the energy in light and use it to power the calculator. Similarly, the pigments capture light energy and use it to power the second stage of photosynthesis.

Using Energy to Make Food In the second stage of photosynthesis, the cell uses the captured energy to produce sugars. The cell needs two raw materials for this stage: water (H_2O) and carbon dioxide (CO_2). In plants, the roots absorb water from the soil. The water then moves up through the plant's stem to the leaves. Carbon dioxide is one of the gases in the air. Carbon dioxide enters the plant through small openings on the undersides of the leaves called **stomata** (STOH muh tuh)(singular *stoma*). Once in the leaves, the water and carbon dioxide move into the chloroplasts.

Inside the chloroplasts, the water and carbon dioxide undergo a complex series of chemical reactions. The reactions are powered by the energy captured in the first stage. One of the products of the reactions is oxygen (O_2). The other products are sugars, including glucose ($C_6H_{12}O_6$). Recall from Section 1 that sugars are a type of carbohydrate. Cells can use the energy in the sugars to carry out important cell functions.

☑ *Checkpoint* *Why are plants green?*

Figure 9 Stomata are small openings on the undersides of leaves. Stomata can open (left) or close (right) to control the movement of carbon dioxide, oxygen, and water vapor.

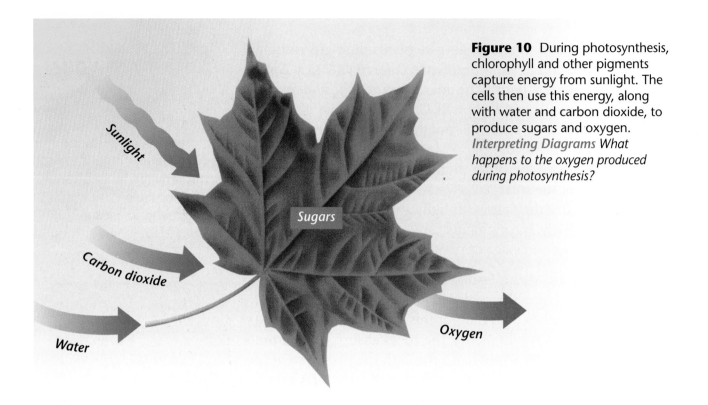

Figure 10 During photosynthesis, chlorophyll and other pigments capture energy from sunlight. The cells then use this energy, along with water and carbon dioxide, to produce sugars and oxygen. *Interpreting Diagrams What happens to the oxygen produced during photosynthesis?*

The Photosynthesis Equation

The events of photosynthesis can be summed up by the following chemical equation:

$$6\,CO_2 + 6\,H_2O \xrightarrow{\text{light energy}} C_6H_{12}O_6 + 6\,O_2$$

carbon dioxide   water   glucose   oxygen

INTEGRATING CHEMISTRY Notice that the raw materials—six molecules of carbon dioxide and six molecules of water—are on the left side of the equation. The products—one molecule of glucose and six molecules of oxygen—are on the right side of the equation. An arrow, which is read as "yields," connects the raw materials to the products. Light energy, which is necessary for the chemical reaction to occur, is written above the arrow.

What happens to the products of photosynthesis? Plant cells use some of the sugar for food. The cells break down the sugar molecules to release the energy they contain. This energy can then be used to carry out the plant's functions. Some sugar molecules are converted into other compounds, such as cellulose. Other sugar molecules may be stored in the plant's cells for later use. When you eat food from plants, such as potatoes or carrots, you are eating the plant's stored food.

The other product of photosynthesis is oxygen. Most of the oxygen passes out of the plant through the stomata and into the air. All organisms that carry out photosynthesis release oxygen.

Photosynthesis and Life

INTEGRATING ENVIRONMENTAL SCIENCE If you were a caterpillar, you might be sitting on a plant chewing on a leaf. The plant is an autotroph, an organism that makes its own food. The plant's leaves contain sugars made during photosynthesis. Leaves also contain starches, cellulose, and other compounds made from sugars. The energy in these compounds originally came from the sun.

The caterpillar is a heterotroph, an organism that cannot make its own food. To live, grow, and perform other caterpillar functions, it needs the energy in the plant's sugars. By eating plants, the caterpillar gets its energy from the sun, although in an indirect way.

Watch out—there's a bird! The bird, a heterotroph, gets its energy by eating caterpillars. Since the energy in caterpillars indirectly comes from the sun, the bird too is living off the sun's energy. **Nearly all living things obtain energy either directly or indirectly from the energy of sunlight captured during photosynthesis.**

Photosynthesis is also essential for the air you breathe. Most living things need oxygen to survive. About 21% of Earth's atmosphere is oxygen—thanks to plants and other organisms that carry out photosynthesis. Almost all the oxygen in Earth's atmosphere was produced by living things through the process of photosynthesis.

Figure 11 Both the caterpillar and the western bluebird obtain their energy indirectly from the sun.

Section 3 Review

1. What are the raw materials needed for photosynthesis? What are the products?
2. How do plants get energy? How do animals get energy?
3. What role does chlorophyll play in photosynthesis? Where is chlorophyll found?
4. **Thinking Critically Applying Concepts** List three ways that autotrophs were important to you today.

Check Your Progress CHAPTER PROJECT
At this point, you should soak your egg for one or two days in water, then in water with food coloring, then in salt water, and finally in another liquid of your choice. Continue to rinse your egg and measure and record its circumference every day. Your egg should be going through some amazing changes in appearance.

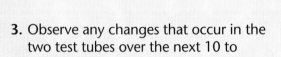

What Is a Product of Respiration?

1. Put on your goggles. Fill two test tubes half full of warm water. Add 5 milliliters of sugar to one of the test tubes. Put the tubes in a test tube rack.

2. Add 0.5 milliliter of dried yeast (a single-celled organism) to each tube. Stir the contents of each tube with a straw. Place a stopper snugly in the top of each tube.

3. Observe any changes that occur in the two test tubes over the next 10 to 15 minutes.

Think It Over

Observing What changes occurred in each test tube? How can you account for any differences that you observed?

GUIDE FOR READING

◆ What events occur during respiration?

◆ How are photosynthesis and respiration related?

◆ What is fermentation?

Reading Tip Before you read, write a definition of *respiration*. After reading this section, revise your definition to include what you've learned.

Your friend stops along the trail ahead of you and calls out, "Let's eat!" He looks around for a flat rock to sit on. You're ready for lunch. You didn't have much breakfast this morning, and you've been hiking for the past hour. As you look around you, you see that the steepest part of the trail is still ahead of you. You'll need a lot of energy to make it to the top.

Everyone knows that food provides energy. But not everyone knows *how* food provides energy. The food you eat does not provide your body with energy immediately after you eat it. First, the food must pass through your digestive system. There, the food is broken down into small molecules. These small molecules can then pass out of the digestive system and into your bloodstream. Next, the molecules travel through the bloodstream to the cells of your body. Inside the cells, the energy in the molecules is released. In this section, you'll learn how your body's cells obtain energy from the food you eat.

Figure 12 All organisms need energy to live. **A.** Although these mushrooms don't move, they still need a continuous supply of energy to grow and reproduce. **B.** This leopard frog uses the energy stored in carbohydrates to leap great distances.
Applying Concepts What is the name of the process by which cells obtain the energy they need?

Storing and Releasing Energy

To understand how cells use energy, think about how people save money in a bank. You might, for example, put some money in a savings account. Then, when you want to buy something, you withdraw some of the money. Cells store and use energy in a similar way. During photosynthesis, plants capture the energy from sunlight and "save" it in the form of carbohydrates, including sugars and starches. When the cells need energy, they "withdraw" it by breaking down the carbohydrates. This process releases energy. Similarly, when you eat a meal, you add to your body's energy savings account. When your cells need energy, they make a withdrawal and break down the food to release energy.

Respiration

After you eat a meal, your body converts the carbohydrates in the food into glucose, a type of sugar. When cells need energy, they "withdraw" energy from glucose in a process called **respiration. During respiration, cells break down simple food molecules such as glucose and release the energy they contain.** Because living things need a continuous supply of energy, the cells of all living things carry out respiration continuously.

The term *respiration* might be confusing. You have probably used it to mean breathing, that is, moving air in and out of your lungs. Because of this confusion, the respiration process that takes place inside cells is sometimes called *cellular respiration.*

The double use of the term *respiration* does point out a connection that you should keep in mind. Breathing brings oxygen into your lungs, and oxygen is necessary for cellular respiration to occur in most cells. The most efficient means of obtaining energy from glucose requires the presence of oxygen. Some cells, however, can obtain energy from glucose without using oxygen.

The Respiration Equation Although respiration occurs in a series of complex steps, the overall process can be summarized in the following equation:

$$C_6H_{12}O_6 + 6\,O_2 \longrightarrow 6\,CO_2 + 6\,H_2O + energy$$

glucose   oxygen   carbon dioxide water

Notice that the raw materials for respiration are glucose and oxygen. Plants and other organisms that undergo photosynthesis make their own glucose. The glucose in the cells of animals and other organisms comes from the food they consume. The oxygen comes from the air or water surrounding the organism.

The Two Stages of Respiration Like photosynthesis, respiration is a two-stage process. The first stage takes place in the cytoplasm of the organism's cells. There, glucose molecules are broken down into smaller molecules. Oxygen is not involved in this stage of respiration. Only a small amount of the energy in glucose is released during this stage.

The second stage of respiration takes place in the mitochondria. There, the small molecules are broken down into even smaller molecules. These chemical reactions require oxygen, and a great deal of energy is released. This is why the mitochondria are sometimes called the "powerhouses" of the cell.

Figure 13 summarizes the process of respiration. If you trace the steps in the breakdown of glucose, you'll see that energy is released in both stages. Two other products of respiration are carbon dioxide and water. These products diffuse out of the cell. In animals, the carbon dioxide and some water leave the body when they breathe out. Thus, when you breathe in, you take in oxygen, a raw material for respiration. When you breathe out, you release carbon dioxide and water, products of respiration.

Checkpoint *What are the raw materials for respiration?*

Figure 13 The first stage of respiration, which takes place in the cytoplasm, releases a small amount of energy. The second stage takes place in the mitochondria. A large amount of energy is released at this stage.

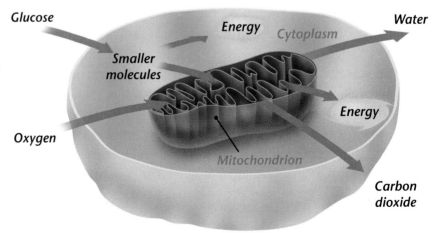

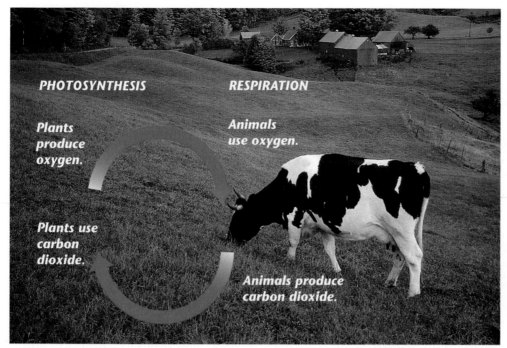

Figure 14 Photosynthesis and respiration can be thought of as opposite processes. *Interpreting Photographs How do these two processes keep the levels of oxygen and carbon dioxide in the atmosphere fairly constant?*

Comparing Photosynthesis and Respiration

Do you notice anything familiar about the equation for respiration? You are quite right if you said it is the opposite of the equation for photosynthesis. This is an important point to remember. During photosynthesis, carbon dioxide and water are used to produce sugars and oxygen. During respiration, glucose (a sugar) and oxygen are used to produce carbon dioxide and water. **Photosynthesis and respiration can be thought of as opposite processes.** Together, these two processes form a cycle that keeps the levels of oxygen and carbon dioxide fairly constant in the atmosphere. As you can see in Figure 14, living things use both gases over and over again.

Fermentation

Some cells are able to obtain energy from food without using oxygen. For example, some single-celled organisms live where there is no oxygen, such as deep in the ocean or in the mud of lakes or swamps. These organisms obtain their energy through **fermentation,** an energy-releasing process that does not require oxygen. **Fermentation provides energy for cells without using oxygen.** The amount of energy released from each sugar molecule during fermentation, however, is much lower than the amount released during respiration.

Alcoholic Fermentation One type of fermentation occurs in yeast and some other single-celled organisms. This process is sometimes called alcoholic fermentation because alcohol is one of the products made when these organisms break down sugars. The other products are carbon dioxide and a small amount of energy.

The products of alcoholic fermentation are important to bakers and brewers. The carbon dioxide produced by yeast causes dough to rise, and it creates the air pockets you see in bread. Carbon dioxide is also the source of bubbles in alcoholic drinks such as beer and sparkling wine.

Lactic-Acid Fermentation Another type of **INTEGRATING HEALTH** fermentation takes place at times in your body, and you've probably felt its effects. Think of a time when you've run as fast as you could for as long as you could. Your leg muscles were pushing hard against the pavement, and you were breathing quickly. Eventually, however, your legs became tired and you couldn't run any more.

No matter how hard you breathed, your muscle cells used up the oxygen faster than it could be replaced. Because your cells lacked oxygen, they used the process of fermentation to produce energy. One by-product of this type of fermentation is a substance known as lactic acid. When lactic acid builds up, your muscles feel weak, tired, and sore.

Figure 15 When an athlete's muscles run out of oxygen, lactic-acid fermentation occurs. The athlete's muscles feel tired and sore. *Inferring Which muscles in this runner were producing the most lactic acid?*

Section 4 Review

1. Why is respiration important for a cell?
2. Explain the relationship between photosynthesis and respiration.
3. Which raw material is *not* needed for fermentation to occur?
4. How do plants and animals maintain the level of oxygen in the atmosphere?
5. **Thinking Critically** **Applying Concepts** Do plant cells need to carry out respiration? Explain.

Science at Home

Fermentation in Bread With an adult family member, follow a recipe in a cookbook to make a loaf of bread using yeast. Explain to your family what causes the dough to rise. After you bake the bread, observe a slice and look for evidence that fermentation occurred.

70

Gases in Balance

Problem

How are photosynthesis and respiration related?

Skills Focus

controlling variables, interpreting data

Materials

marking pens
2 *Elodea* plants
plastic graduated cylinder, 100-mL
bromthymol blue solution
3 flasks with stoppers, 250-mL
straws
light source

Procedure

1. Bromthymol blue can be used to test for carbon dioxide. To see how this dye works, pour 100 mL of bromthymol blue solution into a flask. Record its color. **CAUTION:** *Bromthymol blue can stain skin and clothing. Avoid spilling or splashing it on yourself.*

2. Provide a supply of carbon dioxide by gently blowing into the solution through a straw until the dye changes color. Record the new color. **CAUTION:** *Do not inhale any of the solution through the straw.*

3. Copy the data table into your notebook. Add 100 mL of bromthymol blue to the other flasks. Then blow through clean straws into each solution until the color changes.

4. Now you will test to see what gas is used by a plant in the presence of light. Obtain two *Elodea* plants of about the same size.

5. Place one plant into the first flask. Label the flask "L" for light. Place the other plant in the second flask. Label the flask "D" for darkness. Label the third flask "C" for control. Put stoppers in all three flasks.

DATA TABLE

Flask	Color of Solution	
	Day 1	Day 2
L (light)		
D (dark)		
C (control)		

6. Record the colors of the three solutions under Day 1 in your data table.

7. Place the flasks labeled L and C in a lighted location as directed by your teacher. Place the flask labeled D in a dark location as directed by your teacher. Wash your hands thoroughly when you have finished.

8. On Day 2, examine the flasks and record the colors of the solutions in your data table.

Analyze and Conclude

1. Explain why the color of each solution did or did not change from Day 1 to Day 2.

2. Why was it important to include the flask labeled C as part of this experiment?

3. Predict what would happen if you blew into the flask labeled L after you completed Step 8. Explain your prediction.

4. **Apply** How does this lab show that photosynthesis and respiration are opposite processes? Why are both processes necessary to maintain an environment suitable for living things?

More to Explore

Suppose you were to put an *Elodea* plant and a small fish in a stoppered flask. Predict what would happen to the levels of oxygen and carbon dioxide in the flask. Explain your prediction.

What Are the Cells Doing?

1. Use a plastic dropper to transfer some yeast cells from a yeast culture to a microscope slide. Your teacher has prepared the slide by drying methylene blue stain onto it. Add a cover-slip and place the slide under a microscope.

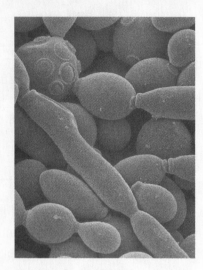

2. Examine the cells on the slide. Use low power first, then high power. Look for what appears to be two cells attached to each other. One cell may be larger than the other. Draw what you see.

Think It Over

Developing Hypotheses What process do you think the "double cells" are undergoing? Develop a hypothesis that might explain what you see.

GUIDE FOR READING

◆ What events take place during the three stages of the cell cycle?

◆ What is the role of DNA replication?

Reading Tip Before you read, use the headings to outline the process of cell division. As you read, draw pictures to help you understand the process.

In the early autumn, many local fairs run pumpkin contests. Proud growers enter their largest pumpkins, hoping to win a prize. If you've never seen these prize-winning pumpkins, you would be amazed. Some have masses close to 400 kilograms and can be as big as a doghouse. What's even more amazing is that these giant pumpkins began as small flowers on pumpkin plants. How did the pumpkins grow so big?

A pumpkin grows in size by increasing both the size and the number of its cells. A single cell divides, forming two cells. Then two cells divide, forming four, and so on. This process of cell division does not occur only in pumpkins, though. In fact, many cells in your body are undergoing cell division as you read this page.

The Cell Cycle

Think about the cells you learned about in Chapter 1. Each cell contains many different structures, including a cell membrane, a nucleus, mitochondria, and ribosomes. To divide into two equal parts, the cell would need to either duplicate the structures or divide them equally between the two new cells. Both cells would then contain everything they need in order to survive and carry out their life functions.

The regular sequence of growth and division that cells undergo is known as the **cell cycle.** You can see details of the cell cycle in *Exploring the Cell Cycle* on pages 76 and 77. Notice that the cell cycle is divided into three main stages. As you read about each stage, follow the events that occur as one "parent" cell divides to form two identical "daughter" cells.

Figure 16 The cells that make up this young monkey are the same size as those that make up its mother. However, the adult has many more cells in its body. *Applying Concepts What is the name of the regular sequence of growth and division that a cell undergoes?*

Stage 1: Interphase

The first stage of the cell cycle is called **interphase.** Interphase is the period before cell division occurs. Even though it is not dividing, the cell is quite active during this stage. **During interphase, the cell grows to its mature size, makes a copy of its DNA, and prepares to divide into two cells.**

Growth During the first part of interphase, the cell doubles in size and produces all the structures needed to carry out its functions. For example, the cell enlarges its endoplasmic reticulum, makes new ribosomes, and produces enzymes. Both mitochondria and chloroplasts make copies of themselves during the growth stage. The cell matures to its full size and structure.

DNA Replication After a cell has grown to its mature size, the next part of interphase begins. The cell makes a copy of the DNA in its nucleus in a process called **replication.** Recall that DNA is a nucleic acid found in the chromatin in a cell's nucleus. DNA holds all the information that the cell needs to carry out its functions. The replication of a cell's DNA is very important, since each daughter cell must have a complete set of DNA to survive. At the end of DNA replication, the cell contains two identical sets of DNA. One set will be distributed to each daughter cell. You will learn the details of DNA replication later in this section.

Centromere

Chromatids

Figure 17 During mitosis, the chromatin condenses to form rodlike chromosomes. Each chromosome consists of two identical strands, or chromatids. *Interpreting Diagrams What is the name of the structure that holds the chromatids together?*

Modeling Mitosis

Refer to *Exploring the Cell Cycle* as you carry out this activity.

ACTIVITY

1. Construct a model of a cell that has three chromosomes. Use a piece of construction paper to represent the cell. Use different colored pipe cleaners to represent the chromosomes. Make sure that the chromosomes look like double rods.

2. Position the chromosomes in the cell where they would be during prophase.

3. Repeat Step 2 for metaphase, anaphase, and telophase.

Making Models How did the model help you understand the events of mitosis?

Preparation for Division Once the cell's DNA has replicated, preparation for cell division begins. The cell produces structures that it will use to divide during the rest of the cell cycle. At the end of interphase, the cell is ready to divide.

Stage 2: Mitosis

Once interphase is complete, the second stage of the cell cycle begins. **Mitosis** (my TOH sis) is the stage during which the cell's nucleus divides into two new nuclei. **During mitosis, one copy of the DNA is distributed into each of the two daughter cells.**

Scientists divide mitosis into four parts, or phases: prophase, metaphase, anaphase, and telophase. During prophase, the threadlike chromatin in the cell's nucleus begins to condense and coil, like fishing line wrapping around a ball. Under a light microscope, the condensed chromatin looks like tiny rods, as you can see in Figure 17. Since the cell's DNA has replicated, each rod has doubled. Each is an exact copy of the other. Scientists call each doubled rod of condensed chromatin a **chromosome.** Each identical rod, or strand, of the chromosome is called a **chromatid.** The two strands are held together by a structure called a centromere.

As the cell progresses through metaphase, anaphase, and telophase, the chromatids separate from each other and move to opposite ends of the cell. Then two nuclei form around the chromatids at the two ends of the cell. You can follow this process in *Exploring the Cell Cycle.*

Checkpoint During which stage of mitosis does the chromatin condense to form rodlike structures?

Stage 3: Cytokinesis

After mitosis, the final stage of the cell cycle, called **cytokinesis** (sy toh kih NEE sis), completes the process of cell division. **During cytokinesis, the cytoplasm divides, distributing the organelles into each of the two new cells.** Cytokinesis usually starts at about the same time as telophase.

During cytokinesis in animal cells, the cell membrane squeezes together around the middle of the cell. The cytoplasm pinches into two cells with about half of the organelles in each daughter cell.

Cytokinesis is somewhat different in plant cells. A plant cell's rigid cell wall cannot squeeze together in the same way that a cell membrane can. Instead, a structure called a cell plate forms across the middle of the cell. The cell plate gradually develops into new cell membranes between the two daughter cells. New cell walls then form around the cell membranes.

There are many variations of the basic pattern of cytokinesis. For example, yeast cells divide, though not equally. A small daughter cell, or bud, pinches off of the parent cell. The bud then grows into a full-sized yeast cell.

Cytokinesis marks the end of the cell cycle. Two new cells have formed. Each daughter cell has the same number of chromosomes as the original parent cell. At the end of cytokinesis, each cell enters interphase, and the cycle begins again.

☑ *Checkpoint* *When in the cell cycle does cytokinesis begin?*

Length of the Cell Cycle

How long does it take for a cell to go through one cell cycle? The answer depends on the type of cell. In a young sea urchin, for example, one cell cycle takes about 2 hours. In contrast, a human liver cell completes one cell cycle in about 22 hours, as shown in Figure 18. The length of each stage in the cell cycle also varies greatly from cell to cell. Some cells, such as human brain cells, never divide—they remain in the first part of interphase for as long as they live.

Interpreting Data

Use the circle graph shown in Figure 18 to answer the following questions.

1. How long is the cell cycle shown in the graph?
2. Which stage of the cell cycle would you expect more of the cells to be in at any given time—interphase, mitosis, or cytokinesis? Explain.

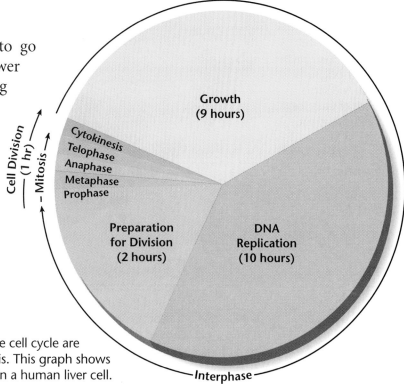

Figure 18 The main stages of the cell cycle are interphase, mitosis, and cytokinesis. This graph shows the average length of each stage in a human liver cell.

EXPLORING the Cell Cycle

Cells undergo an orderly sequence of events as they grow and divide. The sequence shown here is a typical cell cycle in an animal cell. Plant cells have somewhat different cell cycles.

1 INTERPHASE
The cell grows to its mature size, makes a copy of its DNA, and prepares to divide into two cells.

3 CYTOKINESIS
The cell membrane pinches in around the middle of the cell. Eventually, the cell pinches in two. Each daughter cell ends up with the same number of identical chromosomes and about half the organelles and cytoplasm.

2 D MITOSIS: Telophase
The chromosomes begin to stretch out and lose their rodlike appearance. This occurs in the two regions at the ends of the cell. A new nuclear membrane forms around each region of chromosomes.

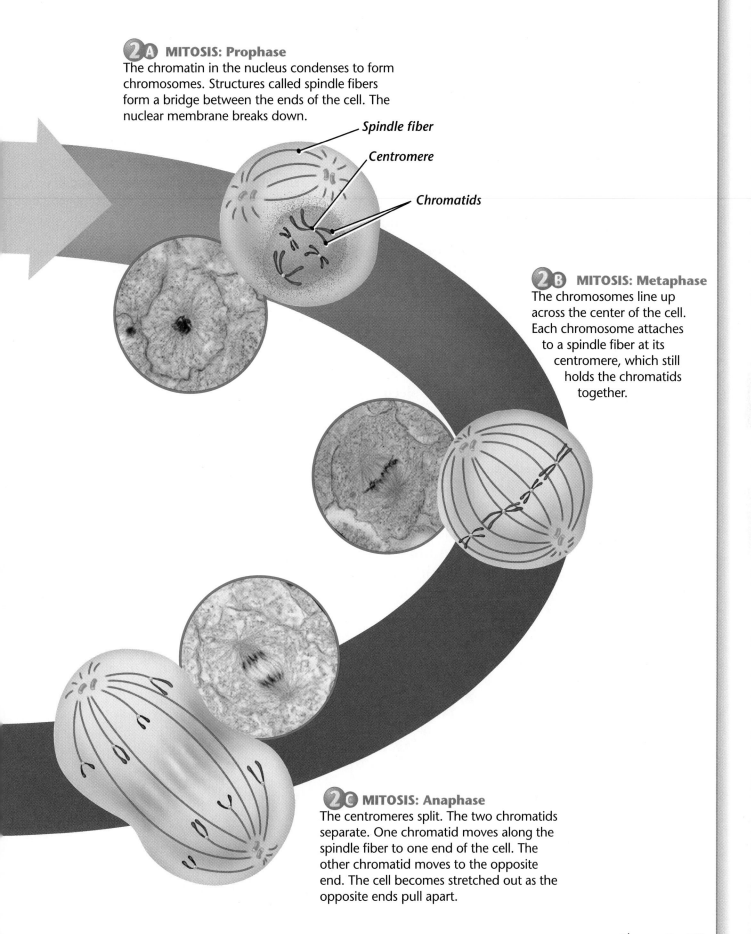

2A MITOSIS: Prophase
The chromatin in the nucleus condenses to form chromosomes. Structures called spindle fibers form a bridge between the ends of the cell. The nuclear membrane breaks down.

Spindle fiber

Centromere

Chromatids

2B MITOSIS: Metaphase
The chromosomes line up across the center of the cell. Each chromosome attaches to a spindle fiber at its centromere, which still holds the chromatids together.

2C MITOSIS: Anaphase
The centromeres split. The two chromatids separate. One chromatid moves along the spindle fiber to one end of the cell. The other chromatid moves to the opposite end. The cell becomes stretched out as the opposite ends pull apart.

Figure 19 A DNA molecule is shaped like a twisted ladder. The sides are made up of sugar and phosphate molecules. The rungs are formed by pairs of nitrogen bases. *Classifying Which base always pairs with adenine?*

DNA Replication

A cell makes a copy of its DNA before mitosis occurs. **DNA replication ensures that each daughter cell will have all of the genetic information it needs to carry out its activities.**

Only in the last 50 years have scientists understood the importance of DNA. By the early 1950s, the work of several scientists showed that DNA carries all of the cell's instructions. They also learned that DNA is passed from a parent cell to its daughter cells. In 1953, two scientists, James Watson and Francis Crick, figured out the structure of DNA. Their discovery revealed important information about how DNA copies itself.

The Structure of DNA Notice in Figure 19 that a DNA molecule looks like a twisted ladder, or spiral staircase. Because of its shape, a DNA molecule is often called a "double helix." A helix is a shape that twists like the threads of a screw.

The two sides of the DNA ladder are made up of molecules of a sugar called deoxyribose, alternating with molecules known as phosphates. Each rung of the DNA ladder is made up of a pair of molecules called nitrogen bases. Nitrogen bases are molecules that combine the element nitrogen with other elements. There are four kinds of nitrogen bases: adenine (AD uh neen), thymine (THY meen), guanine (GWAH neen), and cytosine (SY tuh seen). The capital letters A, T, G, and C are used to represent the four bases.

Look closely at Figure 19. Notice that the bases on one side of the ladder match up in a specific way with the bases on the other side. Adenine (A) only pairs with thymine (T), while guanine (G) only pairs with cytosine (C). This pairing pattern is the key to understanding how DNA replication occurs.

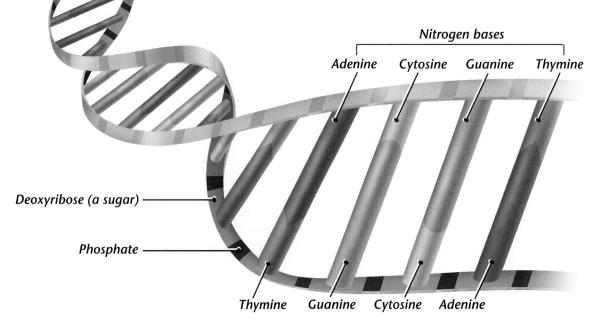

Nitrogen bases

Adenine   Cytosine   Guanine   Thymine

Deoxyribose (a sugar)

Phosphate

Thymine   Guanine   Cytosine   Adenine

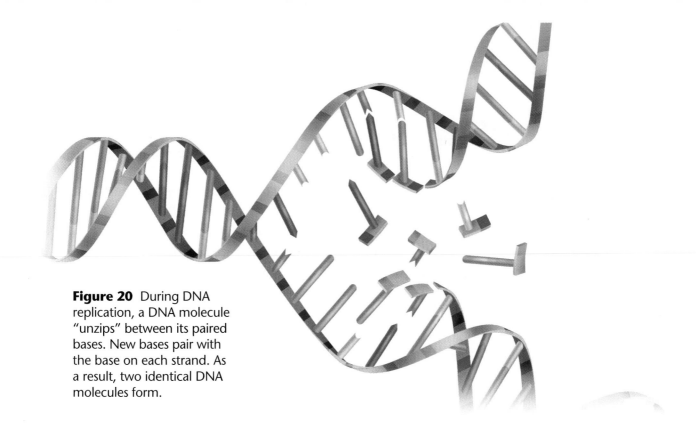

Figure 20 During DNA replication, a DNA molecule "unzips" between its paired bases. New bases pair with the base on each strand. As a result, two identical DNA molecules form.

The Replication Process DNA replication begins when the two sides of the DNA molecule unwind and separate, like a zipper unzipping. As you can see in Figure 20, the molecule separates between the paired nitrogen bases on each rung. Next, nitrogen bases that are floating in the nucleus pair up with the bases on each half of the DNA molecule. Remember that the pairing of bases follows definite rules: A always pairs with T, while G always pairs with C. Once the new bases are attached, two new DNA molecules are formed. The order of the bases in each new DNA molecule will exactly match the order in the original DNA molecule.

Section 5 Review

1. What are the three main stages of the cell cycle? Briefly describe the events that occur at each stage.
2. Why must the DNA in a cell replicate before the cell divides?
3. How does cytokinesis differ in plant and animal cells?
4. **Thinking Critically** **Predicting** Suppose that during anaphase, the centromeres did not split, and the chromatids did not separate. Predict the results.

Check Your Progress

CHAPTER PROJECT

Begin to think about why the egg changed as it did at each stage of the project. Consider how each of the different substances affected your egg. (*Hint:* Water plays a crucial role in the activities of a cell. How has water been involved in your investigation?) Organize your results into a report and make a graph of your egg's changing circumference. You may want to include diagrams to explain the processes that took place.

Multiplying by Dividing

Skills Lab

Problem

How long do the stages of the cell cycle take?

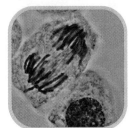

Materials

microscope
colored pencils
calculator (optional)
prepared slides of onion root tip cells
  undergoing cell division

Procedure

1. Place the slide on the stage of a microscope. Use low power to locate a cell in interphase. Then switch to high power, and make a labeled drawing of the cell. **CAUTION:** *Slides and coverslips break easily. Do not allow the objective to touch the slide. If the slide breaks, notify your teacher. Do not touch broken glass.*

2. Repeat Step 1 to find cells in prophase, metaphase, anaphase, and telophase. Then copy the data table into your notebook.

3. Return to low power. Find an area of the slide with many cells undergoing cell division. Switch to the magnification that lets you see about 50 cells at once (for example, 100 ×).

4. Examine the cells row by row, and count the cells that are in interphase. Record that number in the data table under *First Sample.*

5. Examine the cells row-by-row four more times to count the cells in prophase, metaphase, anaphase, and telophase. Record the results.

6. Move to a new area on the slide. Repeat Steps 3–5 and record your counts in the column labeled *Second Sample.*

7. Fill in the column labeled *Total Number* by adding the numbers across each row in your data table.

8. Add the totals for the five stages to find the total number of cells counted.

Analyze and Conclude

1. Which stage of the cell cycle did you observe most often?

2. The cell cycle for onion root tips takes about 720 minutes (12 hours). Use your data and the formula below to find the number of minutes each stage takes.

$$\text{Time for each stage} = \frac{\text{Number of cells at each stage}}{\text{Total number of cells counted}} \times 720 \text{ min}$$

3. **Think About It** Use the data to compare the amount of time spent in mitosis with the total time for the whole cell cycle.

More to Explore

Examine prepared slides of animal cells undergoing cell division. Use drawings and descriptions to compare plant and animal mitosis.

DATA TABLE

Stage of Cell Cycle	First Sample	Second Sample	Total Number
Interphase			
Mitosis: Prophase			
Metaphase			
Anaphase			
Telophase			
Total number of cells counted			

SECTION 1 **Chemical Compounds in Cells**

INTEGRATING CHEMISTRY

Key Ideas

◆ When two or more elements combine chemically, they form a compound.

◆ Organic compounds in living things include proteins, carbohydrates, lipids, and nucleic acids.

◆ Without water, most chemical reactions within cells could not take place.

Key Terms

element	protein	lipid
atom	amino acid	nucleic acid
compound	enzyme	DNA
molecule	carbohydrate	RNA
organic compound		
inorganic compound		

 SECTION 2 **The Cell in Its Environment**

Key Ideas

◆ Substances can move into and out of a cell by diffusion, osmosis, or active transport.

◆ Active transport requires the cell to use energy while passive transport does not.

Key Terms

selectively permeable	passive transport
diffusion	active transport
osmosis	

 SECTION 3 **Photosynthesis**

Key Ideas

◆ During photosynthesis, plants use energy from the sun to convert carbon dioxide and water into oxygen and sugars.

◆ Chlorophyll and other plant pigments capture energy from sunlight. Cells use the energy to produce sugars from carbon dioxide and water.

◆ Most living things obtain the energy they need either directly or indirectly from the sun.

Key Terms

photosynthesis	chlorophyll	stomata
pigment		

 SECTION 4 **Respiration**

Key Ideas

◆ Respiration is a process in which cells break down simple food substances, such as glucose, and release the energy they contain.

◆ During respiration, glucose and oxygen are converted into carbon dioxide and water.

Key Terms

respiration	fermentation

 SECTION 5 **Cell Division**

Key Ideas

◆ Cells go through a regular cycle of growth and division called the cell cycle.

◆ The major phases of the cell cycle are interphase, mitosis, and cytokinesis.

Key Terms

cell cycle	mitosis	chromatid
interphase	chromosome	cytokinesis
replication		

Organizing Information

Cycle Diagram Copy the cycle diagram about the cell cycle onto a separate sheet of paper. Then complete it and add a title. (For more on cycle diagrams, see the Skills Handbook.)

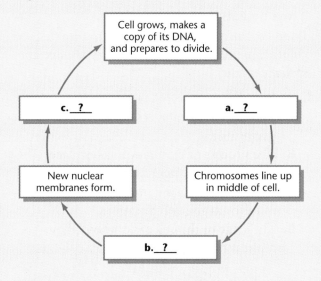

Reviewing Content

 For more review of key concepts, see the Interactive Student Tutorial CD-ROM.

Multiple Choice

Choose the letter of the best answer.

 1. Starch is an example of a
   a. nucleic acid.
   b. protein.
   c. lipid.
   d. carbohydrate.

2. The process by which water moves across a cell membrane is called
   a. osmosis.
   b. active transport.
   c. diffusion.
   d. resolution.

3. What process is responsible for producing most of Earth's oxygen?
   a. photosynthesis
   b. replication
   c. mutation
   d. respiration

4. The process in which a cell makes an exact copy of its DNA is called
   a. fermentation.
   b. respiration.
   c. replication.
   d. reproduction.

5. Chromatids are held together by a
   a. spindle.   **b.** chloroplast.
   c. centromere.   **d.** cell membrane.

True or False

If the statement is true, write true. If it is false, change the underlined word or words to make the statement true.

 6. Both DNA and RNA are <u>proteins</u>.

7. The <u>cell membrane</u> is selectively permeable.

8. The process of respiration takes place mainly in the <u>mitochondria</u>.

9. An energy-releasing process that does not require oxygen is <u>replication</u>.

10. The stage of the cell cycle when DNA replication occurs is <u>telophase</u>.

Checking Concepts

 11. How are enzymes important to living things?

12. What is diffusion? What role does diffusion play in the cell?

13. Briefly explain what happens to energy from the sun during photosynthesis.

14. Explain how heterotrophs depend on the sun for energy.

15. Why do organisms need to carry out the process of respiration?

16. How do the events of the cell cycle ensure that the daughter cells will be identical to the parent cell?

17. Writing to Learn Write a paragraph comparing and contrasting photosynthesis and respiration. Be sure to discuss how the two processes maintain the oxygen and carbon dioxide balance in the atmosphere.

Thinking Critically

18. Making Generalizations Why is the study of chemistry important to the understanding of living things?

19. Predicting Suppose a volcano spewed so much ash into the air that it blocked most of the sunlight that usually strikes Earth. How might this affect the ability of animals to obtain the energy they need to live?

20. Applying Concepts Explain the relationship between the processes of breathing and respiration.

21. Inferring Suppose one strand of a DNA molecule contained the following bases: A C G T C T G. What would the bases on the other strand be?

22. Problem Solving Explain why it is important that the cell cycle results in daughter cells that are identical to the parent cell.

Applying Skills

Use the table below to answer Questions 23–25.

Percentages of Nitrogen Bases In the DNA of Various Organisms

Nitrogen Base	Human	Wheat	E. coli bacterium
Adenine	30%	27%	24%
Guanine	20%	23%	26%
Thymine	30%	27%	24%
Cytosine	20%	23%	26%

23. Graphing For each organism, draw a bar graph to show the percentages of each nitrogen base in its DNA.

24. Interpreting Data What is the relationship between the amounts of adenine and thymine in the DNA of each organism? Between the amounts of guanine and cytosine?

25. Inferring Based on your answer to Question 20, what can you infer about the structure of DNA in these three organisms?

CHAPTER PROJECT

Performance ▼ Assessment

Present Your Project Bring in your egg, your graph, and any diagrams you made. As a class or in groups, discuss your results and conclusions. Then, as a group, try to agree on answers to these questions: What happened to the eggshell? What process took place at each stage of the experiment?

Reflect and Record In your notebook, describe what you learned from doing this egg-speriment. Which part of the project was the most surprising? Why? When did you begin to understand what was happening to the egg? If you did the project again, what would you do differently? Why?

Test Preparation

Use these questions to prepare for standardized tests.

Study the equations. Then answer Questions 26–28.

Photosynthesis

$$6\,CO_2 + 6\,H_2O \xrightarrow{\text{light energy}} C_6H_{12}O_6 + 6\,O_2$$

Respiration

$$C_6H_{12}O_6 + 6\,O_2 \rightarrow 6\,CO_2 + 6\,H_2O + \text{energy}$$

26. What products are produced during photosynthesis?
a. carbon dioxide and water
b. light energy and carbon dioxide
c. carbon dioxide and sugar
d. sugar and oxygen

27. What raw materials are needed for respiration to occur?
a. energy and water
b. carbon dioxide, water, and energy
c. sugar and oxygen
d. sugar and carbon dioxide

28. Why are the words "light energy" written above the arrow in the photosynthesis equation?
a. Light energy is necessary for the reaction to occur.
b. Light energy is produced during the reaction.
c. Oxygen can exist only in the presence of light.
d. Sugar can exist only in the presence of light.

Genetics: The Science of Heredity

WEB ACTIVITY
www.phschool.com

SECTION
1 Mendel's Work

Discover What Does the Father Look
Like?
Skills Lab Take a Class Survey

SECTION
2
Integrating Mathematics
Probability and
Genetics

Discover What's the Chance?
Try This Coin Crosses
Science at Home The Guessing Game
Skills Lab Make the Right Call!

SECTION
3 The Cell and
Inheritance

Discover Which Chromosome Is Which?

All in the Family

Did you ever wonder why some offspring resemble their parents while others do not? In this chapter, you'll learn how offspring come to have traits similar to those of their parents. In this project, you'll create a family of "paper pets" to explore how traits pass from parents to offspring.

Your Goal To create a "paper pet" that will be crossed with a pet belonging to a classmate, and to determine what traits the offspring will have.

To complete this project successfully, you must
- create your own unique paper pet with five different traits
- cross your pet with another pet to produce six offspring
- determine what traits the offspring will have, and explain how they came to have those traits

Get Started Cut out your pet from either blue or yellow construction paper. Choose other traits for your pet from this list: female or male; square eyes or round eyes; oval nose or triangular nose; pointed teeth or square teeth. Then create your pet using materials of your choice.

Check Your Progress You'll be working on this project as you study this chapter. To keep your project on track, look for Check Your Progress boxes at the following points.
> **Section 1 Review,** page 91: Identify your pet's genotype.
> **Section 3 Review,** page 106: Determine what traits your pet's offspring have.
> **Section 4 Review,** page 112: Make a display of your pet's family.

Present Your Project At the end of the chapter (page 115), you and your partner will display your pet's family and analyze the inheritance patterns.

These boxer puppies and their mother resemble each other in many ways. However, there are also noticeable differences between one dog and the next.

SECTION
4 The DNA Connection

Discover **Can You Crack the Code?**
Sharpen Your Skills **Predicting**

SECTION
1 Mendel's Work

DISCOVER

What Does the Father Look Like?

1. Observe the colors of each kitten in the photo. Record each kitten's coat colors and patterns. Include as many details as you can.

2. Observe the mother cat in the photo. Record her coat color and pattern.

Think It Over

Inferring Based on your observations, describe what you think the kittens' father might look like. Identify the evidence on which you based your inference.

GUIDE FOR READING

◆ What factors control the inheritance of traits in organisms?

Reading Tip Before you read, preview the section and make a list of the boldfaced terms. As you read, write a definition for each term in your own words.

Gregor Mendel in the monastery garden ▼

The year was 1851. Gregor Mendel, a young priest from a monastery in Central Europe, entered the University of Vienna to study mathematics and science. Two years later, Mendel returned to the monastery and began teaching at a nearby high school.

Mendel also cared for the monastery's garden, where he grew hundreds of pea plants. He became curious about why some of the plants had different physical characteristics, or **traits.** Some pea plants grew tall while others were short. Some plants produced green seeds, while others had yellow seeds.

Mendel observed that the pea plants' traits were often similar to those of their parents. Sometimes, however, the pea plants had different traits than their parents. The passing of traits from parents to offspring is called **heredity.** For more than ten years, Mendel experimented with thousands of pea plants to understand the process of heredity. Mendel's work formed the foundation of **genetics,** the scientific study of heredity.

Mendel's Peas

Mendel made a wise decision when he chose to study peas rather than other plants in the monastery garden. Pea plants are easy to study because they have many traits that exist in only two forms. For example, pea plant stems are either tall or short, but not medium height. Also, garden peas produce a large number of offspring in one generation. Thus, it is easy to collect large amounts of data to analyze.

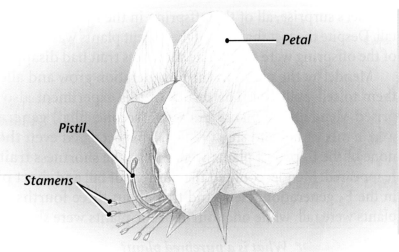

Petal

Pistil

Stamens

Figure 1 Garden peas usually reproduce by self-pollination. Pollen from a flower's stamens lands on the pistil of the same flower. Plants that result from self-pollination inherit all of their characteristics from the single parent plant. *Relating Cause and Effect Why was it important for Mendel to prevent his pea plants from self-pollinating?*

Figure 1 shows a flowering pea plant. Notice that the flower's petals surround the pistil and the stamens. The pistil produces female sex cells, or eggs, while the stamens produce pollen, which contains the male sex cells.

In nature, pea plants are usually self-pollinating. This means that pollen from one flower lands on the pistil of the same flower. Mendel developed a method by which he could cross-pollinate, or "cross," pea plants. To cross two plants, he removed pollen from a flower on one plant and brushed it onto a flower on a second plant. To prevent the pea plants from self-pollinating, he carefully removed the stamens from the flowers on the second plant.

Mendel's Experiments

Suppose you had a garden full of pea plants, and you wanted to study the inheritance of traits. What would you do? Mendel decided to cross plants with opposite forms of a trait, for example, tall plants and short plants. He started his experiments with purebred plants. A **purebred** plant is one that always produces offspring with the same form of a trait as the parent. For example, purebred short pea plants always produce short offspring. Purebred tall pea plants always produce tall offspring. To produce purebred plants, Mendel allowed peas with one particular trait to self-pollinate for many generations. By using purebred plants, Mendel knew that the offspring's trait would always be identical to that of the parents.

In his first experiment, Mendel crossed purebred tall plants with purebred short plants. He called these parent plants the parental generation, or P generation. He called the offspring from this cross the first filial (FIL ee ul) generation, or the F_1 generation. The word *filial* means "son" in Latin.

WEB ACTIVITY
www.phschool.com

SECTION **1** **Human Inheritance**

Discover How Tall Is Tall?
Try This The Eyes Have It
Try This Girl or Boy?

SECTION **2** **Human Genetic Disorders**

Discover How Many Chromosomes?
Real-World Lab Family Puzzles

Integrating Technology

SECTION **3** **Advances in Genetics**

Discover What Do Fingerprints Reveal?
Sharpen Your Skills Communicating
Science at Home Grocery Genetics
Real-World Lab Guilty or Innocent?

A Family Portrait

A pedigree, or family tree, is a branched drawing that shows many generations of a family. In some cases, a pedigree may show centuries of a family's history.

In genetics, pedigrees are used to show how traits are passed from one generation to the next. In this project, you will create a genetic pedigree for an imaginary family. Although the family will be imaginary, your pedigree must show how real human traits are passed from parents to children.

Your Goal To create a pedigree for an imaginary family that shows the transfer of genetic traits from one generation to the next.

To complete the project you will
◆ choose two different genetic traits, and identify all the possible genotypes and phenotypes
◆ create pedigrees that trace each trait through three generations of your imaginary family
◆ prepare a family "photo" album to show what each family member looks like

Get Started With a partner, review the human traits described on page 92 in Chapter 3. List what you already know about human inheritance. For example, which human traits are controlled by dominant alleles? Which are controlled by recessive alleles? Then preview Section 1 of this chapter, and list the traits you'll be studying. Choose two traits that you would like to focus on in your project.

Check Your Progress You'll be working on this project as you study this chapter. To keep your project on track, look for Check Your Progress boxes at the following points.

Section 1 Review, page 124: Create a pedigree for the first trait you chose.

Section 2 Review, page 129: Create the second pedigree, and begin your family album.

Present Your Project At the end of the chapter (page 143), you will present your family's pedigrees and "photo" album to the class.

The children in this family have some traits like their mother's and some traits like their father's.

1 Human Inheritance

How Tall Is Tall?

1. Choose a partner. Measure each other's height to the nearest 5 centimeters. Record your measurements on the chalkboard.

2. Create a bar graph showing the number of students at each height. Plot the heights on the horizontal axis and the number of students on the vertical axis.

Think It Over

Inferring If Gregor Mendel had graphed the heights of his pea plants, the graph would have had two bars—one for tall stems and one for short stems. Do you think height in humans is controlled by a single gene, as it is in peas? Explain your answer.

GUIDE FOR READING

◆ Why do some human traits show a large variety of phenotypes?

◆ Why are some sex-linked traits more common in males than in females?

◆ How do geneticists use pedigrees?

Reading Tip Before you read, rewrite the headings in this section as *how, why,* or *what* questions. As you read, write answers to the questions.

Have you ever heard someone say "He's the spitting image of his dad" or "She has her mother's eyes"? Children often resemble their parents. The reason for this is that alleles for eye color, hair color, and thousands of other traits are passed from parents to their children. People inherit some alleles from their mother and some from their father. This is why most people look a little like their mother and a little like their father.

Traits Controlled by Single Genes

In Chapter 3, you learned that many traits in peas and other organisms are controlled by a single gene with two alleles. Often one allele is dominant, while the other is recessive. Many human traits are also controlled by a single gene with one dominant allele and one recessive allele. As with tall and short pea plants, these human traits have two distinctly different phenotypes, or physical appearances.

For example, a widow's peak is a hairline that comes to a point in the middle of the forehead. The allele for a widow's peak is dominant over the allele for a straight hairline. The Punnett square in Figure 1 illustrates a cross between two parents who are heterozygous for a widow's peak. Trace the possible combinations of alleles that a child may inherit. Notice that each child has a 3 in 4, or 75 percent, probability of having a widow's peak. There is only a 1 in 4, or 25 percent, probability that a child will have a straight hairline. Recall from Chapter 3 that when Mendel crossed peas that were heterozygous for a trait, he obtained similar percentages in the offspring.

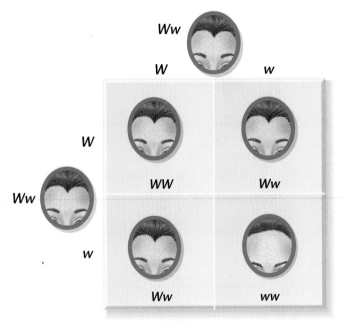

Figure 1 This Punnett square shows a cross between two parents with widow's peaks. *Interpreting Diagrams What are the possible genotypes of the offspring? What percent of the offspring will have each genotype?*

Do you have dimples when you smile? If so, then you have the dominant allele for this trait. Like having a widow's peak, having smile dimples is controlled by a single gene. People who have two recessive alleles do not have smile dimples.

Multiple Alleles

Some human traits are controlled by a single gene that has more than two alleles. Such a gene is said to have **multiple alleles**—three or more forms of a gene that code for a single trait. You can think of multiple alleles as being like flavors of pudding. Pudding usually comes in more flavors than just chocolate and vanilla!

Even though a gene may have multiple alleles, a person can carry only two of those alleles. This is because chromosomes exist in pairs. Each chromosome in a pair carries only one allele for each gene.

One human trait that is controlled by a gene with multiple alleles is blood type. There are four main blood types—A, B, AB, and O. Three alleles control the inheritance of blood types. The allele for blood type A and the allele for blood type B are codominant. The codominant alleles are written as capital letters with superscripts—I^A for blood type A and I^B for blood type B. The allele for blood type O—written i—is recessive. Recall that when two codominant alleles are inherited, neither allele is masked. A person who inherits an I^A allele from one parent and an I^B allele from the other parent will have type AB blood. Figure 2 shows the allele combinations that result in each blood type. Notice that only people who inherit two i alleles have type O blood.

Checkpoint If a gene has multiple alleles, why can a person only have two of the alleles for the gene?

Blood Types	
Blood Type	**Combination of Alleles**
A	$I^A I^A$ or $I^A i$
B	$I^B I^B$ or $I^B i$
AB	$I^A I^B$
O	ii

Figure 2 Blood type is determined by a single gene with three alleles. This chart shows which combinations of alleles result in each blood type.

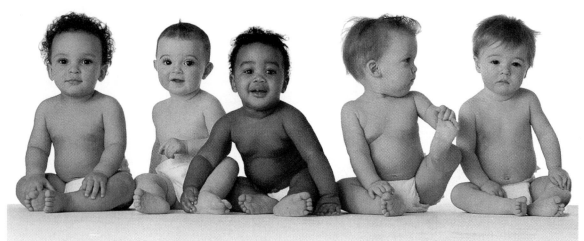

Figure 3 Skin color in humans is determined by three or more genes. Different combinations of alleles at each of the genes result in a wide range of possible skin colors.

The Eyes Have It

One inherited trait is eye dominance—the tendency to use one eye more than the other. Here's how you can test yourself for this trait.

1. Hold your hand out in front of you at arm's length. Point your finger at an object across the room.

2. Close your right eye. With only your left eye open, observe how far your finger appears to move.

3. Repeat Step 2 with the right eye open. With which eye did your finger seem to remain closer to the object? That eye is dominant.

Designing Experiments Is eye dominance related to hand dominance—whether a person is right-handed or left-handed? Design an experiment to find out. Obtain your teacher's permission before carrying out your experiment.

Traits Controlled by Many Genes

If you did the Discover activity, you observed that height in humans has more than two distinct phenotypes. In fact, there is an enormous variety of phenotypes for height. What causes this wide range of phenotypes? **Some human traits show a large number of phenotypes because the traits are controlled by many genes. The genes act together as a group to produce a single trait.** At least four genes control height in humans, so there are many possible combinations of genes and alleles.

Like height, skin color is determined by many genes. Human skin color ranges from almost white to nearly black, with many shades in between. Skin color is controlled by at least three genes. Each gene, in turn, has at least two possible alleles. Various combinations of alleles at each of the genes determine the amount of pigment that a person's skin cells produce. Thus, a wide variety of skin colors is possible.

The Effect of Environment

The effects of genes are often altered by the environment—the organism's surroundings. For example, people's diets can affect their height. A diet lacking in protein, minerals, and vitamins can prevent a person from growing to his or her potential maximum height. Since the late 1800s, the average height of adults in the United States has increased by almost 10 centimeters. During that time, American diets have become more healthful. Other environmental factors, such as medical care and living conditions, have also improved since the late 1800s.

Checkpoint How can environmental factors affect a person's height?

Male or Female?

"Congratulations, Mr. and Mrs. Gonzales. It's a baby girl!" What factors determine whether a baby is a boy or a girl? As with other traits, the sex of a baby is determined by genes on chromosomes. Among the 23 pairs of chromosomes in each body cell is a single pair of chromosomes called the sex chromosomes. The sex chromosomes determine whether a person is male or female.

The sex chromosomes are the only pair of chromosomes that do not always match. If you are female, your two sex chromosomes match. The two chromosomes are called X chromosomes. If you are male, your sex chromosomes do not match. One of your sex chromosomes is an X chromosome. The other chromosome is a Y chromosome. The Y chromosome is much smaller than the X chromosome.

What happens to the sex chromosomes when egg and sperm cells form? As you know, each egg and sperm cell has only one chromosome from each pair. Since both of a female's sex chromosomes are X chromosomes, all eggs carry one X chromosome. Males, however, have two different sex chromosomes. This means that half of a male's sperm cells carry an X chromosome, while half carry a Y chromosome.

When a sperm cell with an X chromosome fertilizes an egg, the egg has two X chromosomes. The fertilized egg will develop into a girl. When a sperm with a Y chromosome fertilizes an egg, the egg has one X chromosome and one Y chromosome. The fertilized egg will develop into a boy. Thus it is the sperm that determines the sex of the child, as you can see in Figure 4.

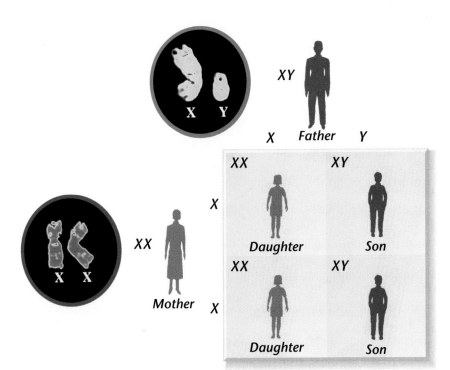

Figure 4 As this Punnett square shows, there is a 50 percent probability that a child will be a girl and a 50 percent probability that a child will be a boy.
Interpreting Diagrams What sex will the child be if a sperm with a Y chromosome fertilizes an egg?

You can model how the sex of an offspring is determined.

1. Label one paper bag "female." Label another paper bag "male."

2. Place two red marbles in the bag labeled "female." The red marbles represent X chromosomes.

3. Place one red marble and one white marble in the bag labeled "male." The white marble represents a Y chromosome.

4. Without looking, pick one marble from each bag. Two red marbles represent a female offspring. One red marble and one white marble represent a male offspring. Record the sex of the "offspring."

5. Put the marbles back in the correct bags. Repeat Step 4 nine more times.

Making Models How many males were produced? How many females? How close were your results to the expected probabilities for male and female offspring?

Sex-Linked Genes

Some human traits occur more often in one sex than the other. The genes for these traits are often carried on the sex chromosomes. Genes on the X and Y chromosomes are often called **sex-linked genes** because their alleles are passed from parent to child on a sex chromosome. Traits controlled by sex-linked genes are called sex-linked traits.

Like other genes, sex-linked genes can have dominant and recessive alleles. Recall that females have two X chromosomes, whereas males have one X chromosome and one Y chromosome. In females, a dominant allele on one X chromosome will mask a recessive allele on the other X chromosome. The situation is not the same in males, however. In males, there is no matching allele on the Y chromosome to mask, or hide, the allele on the X chromosome. As a result, any allele on the X chromosome—even a recessive allele—will produce the trait in a male who inherits it. **Because males have only one X chromosome, males are more likely than females to have a sex-linked trait that is controlled by a recessive allele.**

One example of a sex-linked trait that is controlled by a recessive allele is red-green colorblindness. A person with red-green colorblindness cannot distinguish between red and green.

Many more males than females have red-green colorblindness. You can understand why this is the case by examining the Punnett square in Figure 6. Both parents in this example have normal color vision. Notice, however, that the mother is a carrier of colorblindness. A **carrier** is a person who has one recessive allele for a trait and one dominant allele. Although a carrier does not have the trait, the carrier can pass the recessive allele on to his or her offspring. In the case of sex-linked traits, only females can be carriers.

Figure 5 A person with red-green colorblindness cannot see the loop of red and pink dots in this test chart.

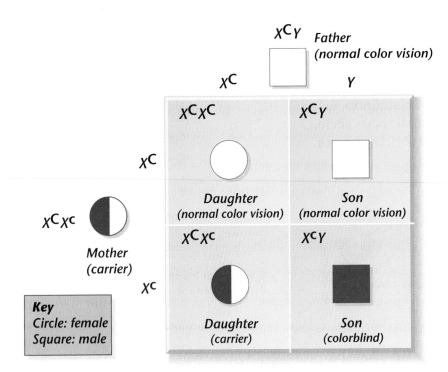

Father
(normal color vision) X^CY

Mother
(carrier) X^CX^c

X^CX^C
Daughter
(normal color vision)

X^CY
Son
(normal color vision)

X^CX^c
Daughter
(carrier)

X^cY
Son
(colorblind)

Key
Circle: female
Square: male

Figure 6 Red-green color-blindness is a sex-linked trait. A girl who receives only one recessive allele (written X^c) for red-green colorblindness will not have the trait. However, a boy who receives one recessive allele will be colorblind. *Applying Concepts What allele combination would a daughter need to inherit to be colorblind?*

As you can see in Figure 6, there is a 25 percent probability that this couple will have a colorblind child. Notice that none of the couple's daughters will be colorblind. On the other hand, the sons have a 50 percent probability of being colorblind. For a female to be colorblind, she must inherit two recessive alleles for colorblindness, one from each parent. A male needs to inherit only one recessive allele. This is because there is no gene for color vision on the Y chromosome. Thus, there is no allele that could mask the recessive allele on the X chromosome.

Pedigrees

Imagine that you are a geneticist interested in studying inheritance patterns in humans. What would you do? You can't set up crosses with people as Mendel did with peas. Instead, you would need to trace the inheritance of traits through many generations in a number of families.

One tool that geneticists use to trace the inheritance of traits in humans is a pedigree. A **pedigree** is a chart or "family tree" that tracks which members of a family have a particular trait. The trait recorded in a pedigree can be an ordinary trait such as the widow's peak, or it could be a sex-linked trait such as colorblindness. In *Exploring a Pedigree* on page 124, you can trace the inheritance of colorblindness through three generations of a family.

✓ *Checkpoint* How is a pedigree like a "family tree"?

EXPLORING *a Pedigree*

This pedigree traces the occurrence of colorblindness in three generations of a family. Colorblindness is a sex-linked trait that is controlled by a recessive allele. Notice that specific symbols are used in pedigrees to communicate genetic information.

A circle represents a female.

A square represents a male.

A horizontal line connecting a male and female represents a marriage.

A vertical line and a bracket connect the parents to their children.

A half-shaded circle or square indicates that a person is a carrier of the trait.

A completely shaded circle or square indicates that a person has the trait.

A circle or square that is not shaded indicates that a person neither has the trait nor is a carrier of the trait.

Section 1 Review

1. Why do human traits such as height and skin color have many different phenotypes?
2. Explain why red-green colorblindness is more common in males than in females.
3. What is a pedigree? How are pedigrees used?
4. **Thinking Critically** **Predicting** Could two people with widow's peaks have a child with a straight hairline? Could two people with straight hairlines have a child with a widow's peak? Explain.

Check Your Progress

CHAPTER PROJECT

By now, you should be creating your pedigree for the first trait you chose. Start with one couple, and show two generations of offspring. The couple should have five children. It is up to you to decide how many children each of those children has. Use Punnett squares to make sure that your imaginary family's inheritance pattern follows the laws of genetics.

② Human Genetic Disorders

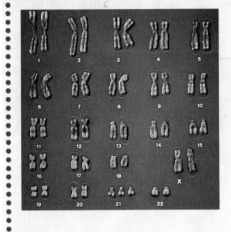

How Many Chromosomes?

The photo at the left shows the chromosomes from a cell of a person with Down syndrome, a genetic disorder. The chromosomes have been sorted into pairs.

1. Count the number of chromosomes in the photo.

2. How does the number of chromosomes compare to the usual number of chromosomes in human cells?

Think It Over

Inferring How do you think a cell could have ended up with this number of chromosomes? (*Hint:* Think about the events that occur during meiosis.)

The air inside the stadium was hot and still. The crowd cheered loudly as eight runners approached the starting blocks. The runners shook out their arms and legs to loosen up their muscles and calm their jitters. When the starter raised the gun, all eyes focused on the runners. At the crack of the starter's gun, the runners leaped into motion and sprinted down the track.

Seconds later, the race was over. The runners, bursting with pride, hugged each other and their coaches. It didn't matter where each of the runners placed. All that mattered was that they had finished the race and done their best. These athletes were running in the Special Olympics, a competition for people with disabilities.

Many of the athletes who compete in the Special Olympics have disabilities that result from genetic disorders. A **genetic disorder** is an abnormal condition that a person inherits through genes or chromosomes. **Genetic disorders are caused by mutations, or changes in a person's DNA.** In some cases, a mutation occurs when sex cells form during meiosis. In other cases, a mutation that is already present in a parent's cells is passed on to the offspring. In this section, you will learn about some common genetic disorders.

GUIDE FOR READING

◆ What causes genetic disorders?

◆ How are genetic disorders diagnosed?

Reading Tip As you read, make a list of different types of genetic disorders. Write a sentence about each disorder.

A runner at the Special Olympics ▶

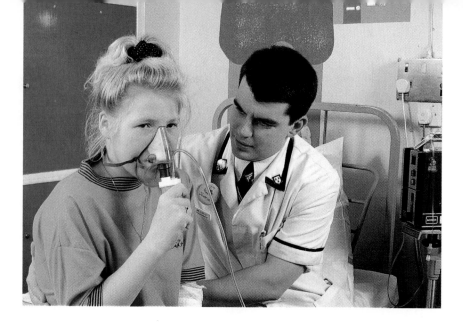

Figure 7 Cystic fibrosis is a genetic disorder that causes thick mucus to build up in a person's lungs and intestines. This patient is inhaling a fine mist that will help loosen the mucus in her lungs.

Cystic Fibrosis

Cystic fibrosis is a genetic disorder in which the body produces abnormally thick mucus in the lungs and intestines. The thick mucus fills the lungs, making it hard for the affected person to breathe. Bacteria that grow in the mucus can cause infections and, eventually, lung damage. In the intestines, the mucus makes it difficult for digestion to occur.

The mutation that leads to cystic fibrosis is carried on a recessive allele. The cystic fibrosis allele is most common among people whose ancestors are from Northern Europe. Every day in this country, four babies are born with cystic fibrosis.

Currently there is no cure for cystic fibrosis. Medical treatments include drugs to prevent infections and physical therapy to break up mucus in the lungs. Recent advances in scientists' understanding of the disease may lead to better treatments and longer lifespans for people with cystic fibrosis.

✓ *Checkpoint* *What are some symptoms of cystic fibrosis?*

Figure 8 Normally, red blood cells are shaped like round disks (top). In a person with sickle-cell disease, red blood cells can become sickle-shaped (bottom). *Relating Cause and Effect What combination of alleles leads to sickle-cell disease?*

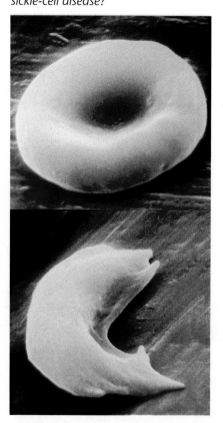

Sickle-Cell Disease

Sickle-cell disease is a genetic disorder that affects the blood. The mutation that causes the disorder affects the production of an important protein called hemoglobin. Hemoglobin is the protein in red blood cells that carries oxygen. People with sickle-cell disease produce an abnormal form of hemoglobin. When oxygen concentrations are low, their red blood cells have an unusual sickle shape, as you can see in Figure 8.

Sickle-shaped red blood cells cannot carry as much oxygen as normal-shaped cells. Because of their shape, the cells become stuck in narrow blood vessels, blocking them. People with sickle-cell disease suffer from lack of oxygen in the blood and experience pain and weakness.

The allele for the sickle-cell trait is most common in people of African ancestry. About 9 percent of African Americans carry the sickle-cell allele. The allele for the sickle-cell trait is codominant with the normal allele. A person with two sickle-cell alleles will have the disease. A person with one sickle-cell allele will produce both normal hemoglobin and abnormal hemoglobin. This person usually will not have symptoms of the disease.

Currently, there is no cure for sickle-cell disease. People with sickle-cell disease are given drugs to relieve their painful symptoms and to prevent blockages in blood vessels. As with cystic fibrosis, scientists are hopeful that new, successful treatments will soon be found.

Hemophilia

Hemophilia is a genetic disorder in which a person's blood clots very slowly or not at all. People with the disorder do not produce one of the proteins needed for normal blood clotting. A person with hemophilia can bleed to death from a minor cut or scrape. The danger of internal bleeding from small bumps and bruises is also very high.

Hemophilia is an example of a disorder that is caused by a recessive allele on the X chromosome. Because hemophilia is a sex-linked disorder, it occurs more frequently in males than in females. **INTEGRATING HEALTH** People with hemophilia must get regular doses of the missing clotting protein. In general, people with hemophilia can lead normal lives. However, they are advised to avoid contact sports and other activities that could cause internal injuries.

Social Studies
CONNECTION

Hemophilia has affected European history. Queen Victoria of England had a son and three grandsons with hemophilia. Victoria, at least two of her daughters, and four of her granddaughters were carriers of the disease.

As Victoria's descendants passed the hemophilia allele to their offspring, hemophilia spread through the royal families of Europe. For example, Empress Alexandra, Queen Victoria's grand-daughter, married the Russian Czar Nicholas II in 1894. Alexandra, a carrier of hemophilia, passed the disease to her son Alexis, who was heir to the throne.

A monk named Rasputin convinced Alexandra that he could cure Alexis. As a result of his control over Alexandra, Rasputin was able to control the Czar as well. The people's anger at Rasputin's influence may have played a part in the Russian Revolution of 1917, in which the Czar was overthrown.

In Your Journal

Imagine that you are Empress Alexandra. Write a diary entry expressing your feelings and unanswered questions about Alexis's condition.

Figure 9 Empress Alexandra of Russia (center row, left) passed the allele for hemophilia to her son Alexis (front).

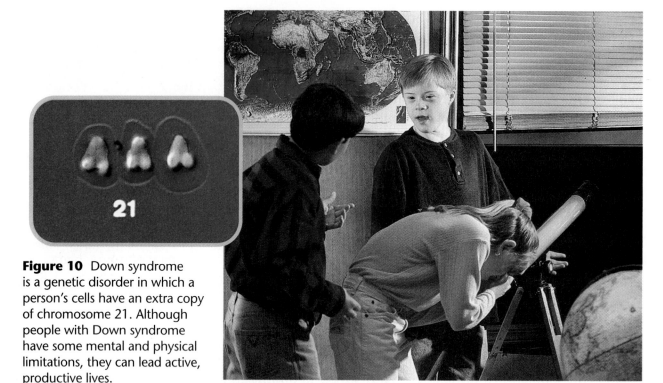

Figure 10 Down syndrome is a genetic disorder in which a person's cells have an extra copy of chromosome 21. Although people with Down syndrome have some mental and physical limitations, they can lead active, productive lives.

21

Down Syndrome

Some genetic disorders are the result of too many or too few chromosomes. In one such disorder, called Down syndrome, a person's cells have an extra copy of chromosome 21. The extra chromosome is the result of an error during meiosis. Recall that in meiosis, cells divide and chromosomes separate to produce sex cells with half the normal chromosome number. Down syndrome most often occurs when chromosomes fail to separate properly during meiosis.

People with Down syndrome have a distinctive physical appearance, and have some degree of mental retardation. Heart defects are also common, but can be treated. Despite their limitations, many people with Down syndrome lead full, active lives.

Diagnosing Genetic Disorders

INTEGRATING TECHNOLOGY Years ago, doctors had only Punnett squares and pedigrees to help them predict whether a child might have a genetic disorder. **Today doctors use tools such as amniocentesis and karyotypes to help detect genetic disorders.**

Before a baby is born, doctors can use a procedure called **amniocentesis** (am nee oh sen TEE sis) to determine whether the baby will have some genetic disorders. During amniocentesis, a doctor uses a very long needle to remove a small amount of the fluid that surrounds the developing baby. The fluid contains cells from the baby.

The doctor then examines the chromosomes from the cells. To do this, the doctor creates a karyotype. A **karyotype** (KA ree uh typ) is a picture of all the chromosomes in a cell. The chromosomes in a karyotype are arranged in pairs. A karyotype can reveal whether a developing baby has the correct number of chromosomes in its cells and whether it is a boy or a girl. If you did the Discover activity, you saw a karyotype from a girl with Down syndrome.

Genetic Counseling

A couple that has a family history or concern about a genetic disorder may turn to a genetic counselor for advice. Genetic counselors help couples understand their chances of having a child with a particular genetic disorder. Genetic counselors use tools such as karyotypes, pedigree charts, and Punnett squares to help them in their work.

Suppose, for example, that a husband and wife both have a history of cystic fibrosis in their families. If they are considering having children, they might seek the advice of a genetic counselor. The genetic counselor might order a test to determine whether they are carriers of the allele for cystic fibrosis. The genetic counselor would then apply the same principles of probability that you learned about in Chapter 3 to calculate the couple's chances of having a child with cystic fibrosis.

Figure 11 Couples may meet with a genetic counselor and their doctor in order to understand their chances of having a child with a genetic disorder.

Section 2 Review

1. Explain how genetic disorders occur in humans. Give two examples of genetic disorders.
2. Describe two tools that doctors use to detect genetic disorders.
3. How do the cells of people with Down syndrome differ from those of others? How might this difference arise?
4. **Thinking Critically Problem Solving** A couple with a family history of hemophilia is about to have a baby girl. What information about the parents would you want to know? How would this information help you determine whether the baby will have hemophilia?

Check Your Progress

CHAPTER PROJECT

At this point, you should begin to trace the inheritance of another trait through the same family members that are in your first pedigree. Also, start making your family "photo" album. Will you use drawings or some other method to show what the family members look like? (*Hint:* Photo albums show phenotypes. Remember that more than one genotype can have the same phenotype.)

Family Puzzles

I magine that you are a genetic counselor. Two couples come to you for advice. Their family histories are summarized in the boxes labeled *Case Study 1* and *Case Study 2*. They want to understand more about certain genetic disorders that run in their families. In this lab, you will find answers to their questions.

Problem

How can you investigate inheritance patterns in families?

Materials

12 index cards
scissors
marker

Procedure

Part 1 Investigating Case Study 1

1. Read over Case Study 1. In your notebook, draw a pedigree that shows all the family members. Use circles to represent the females, and squares to represent the males. Shade in the circles or squares representing the individuals who have cystic fibrosis.

Case Study 1: Joshua and Bella
- ◆ Joshua and Bella have a son named Ian. Ian has been diagnosed with cystic fibrosis.
- ◆ Joshua and Bella are both healthy.
- ◆ Bella's parents are both healthy.
- ◆ Joshua's parents are both healthy.
- ◆ Joshua's sister, Sara, has cystic fibrosis.

2. You know that cystic fibrosis is controlled by a recessive allele. To help you figure out Joshua and Bella's family pattern, create a set of cards to represent the alleles. Cut each of six index cards into four smaller cards. On 12 of the small cards, write *N* to represent the dominant normal allele. On the other 12 small cards, write *n* for the recessive allele.

3. Begin by using the cards to represent Ian's alleles. Since he has cystic fibrosis, what alleles must he have? Write in this genotype next to the pedigree symbol for Ian.

4. Joshua's sister, Sara, also has cystic fibrosis. What alleles does she have? Write in this genotype next to the pedigree symbol that represents Sara.

Case Study 2: Li and Mai

- ◆ The father, Li, has a skin condition. The mother, Mai, has normal skin.
- ◆ Li and Mai's first child, a girl named Gemma, has the same skin condition as Li.
- ◆ Mai's sister has a similar skin condition, but Mai's parents do not.
- ◆ Li has one brother whose skin is normal, and one sister who has the skin condition.
- ◆ Li's mother has the skin condition. His father does not.
- ◆ Li's family lives in a heavily wooded area. His family has always thought the skin condition was a type of allergy.

5. Now use the cards to figure out what genotypes Joshua and Bella must have. Write their genotypes next to their symbols in the pedigree.

6. Work with the cards to figure out the genotypes of all other family members. Fill in each person's genotype next to his or her symbol in the pedigree. If more than one genotype is possible, write in both genotypes.

Part 2 Investigating Case Study 2

7. Read over Case Study 2.

8. You suspect that Gemma and Li's skin condition is caused by an inherited recessive allele. Begin to investigate this possibility by drawing a family pedigree in your notebook. Use shading to indicate which individuals have the skin condition.

9. Fill in the genotype *ss* beside each individual who has the skin condition. Then use cards as you did in Case Study 1 to figure out each family member's genotype. If more than one genotype is possible, fill in both genotypes.

Analyze and Conclude

1. In Case Study 1, what were the genotypes of Joshua's parents? What were the genotypes of Bella's parents?

2. In Case Study 1, Joshua also has a brother. What is the probability that he has cystic fibrosis? Explain.

3. Can you conclude that the skin condition in Case Study 2 is most likely an inherited trait controlled by a recessive allele? Explain.

4. What is the probability that Mai and Li's next child will have the skin condition? Explain.

5. **Apply** Why do genetic counselors need information about many generations of a family in order to draw conclusions about a hereditary condition?

More to Explore

Review the two pedigrees that you just studied. What data suggests that the traits are not sex-linked? Explain.

SECTION 3 Advances in Genetics

DISCOVER · ACTIVITY · · · ·

What Do Fingerprints Reveal?

1. Label a sheet of paper with your name. Then roll one of your fingers from side to side on an ink pad. Make a fingerprint by carefully rolling your inked finger from side to side on the paper.

2. Divide into groups. Each group should choose one member to use the same finger to make a second fingerprint on a sheet of paper. Leave the paper unlabeled.

3. Exchange your group's fingerprints with those from another group. Compare each labeled fingerprint with the fingerprint on the unlabeled paper. Decide whose fingerprint it is.

4. Wash your hands after completing this activity.

Think It Over
Observing Why are fingerprints a useful tool for identifying people?

GUIDE FOR READING

◆ What are three ways in which an organism's traits can be altered?

◆ What is the goal of the Human Genome Project?

Reading Tip As you read, make a concept map of the methods used to produce organisms with desirable traits. Include at least one example of each technique.

In the summer of 1996, a lamb named Dolly was born in Scotland. Dolly was an ordinary lamb in every way except one. The fertilized cell that developed into Dolly was produced in a laboratory by geneticists using experimental techniques. You will learn more about the techniques used by the geneticists later in the section.

Although the techniques used to create Dolly are new, the idea of producing organisms with specific traits is not. For thousands of years, people have tried to produce plants and animals with desirable traits. **Three methods that people have used to develop organisms with desirable traits are selective breeding, cloning, and genetic engineering.**

Dolly ▼

Selective Breeding

More than 5,000 years ago, people living in what is now central Mexico discovered that a type of wild grass could be used as food. They saved the seeds from those plants that produced the best food, and planted them to grow new plants. By repeating this process over many generations of plants, they developed an early variety of the food crop we now call corn. The process of selecting a few organisms with desired traits to serve as parents of the next generation is called **selective breeding.**

People have used selective breeding with many different plants and animals. Breeding programs usually focus on increasing the value of the plant or animal to people. For

132

Figure 12 For thousands of years, people have used selective breeding to produce plants and animals with desirable traits.
Making Generalizations What are some traits for which corn may be bred?

example, dairy cows are bred to produce larger quantities of milk. Many varieties of fruits and vegetables are bred to resist diseases and insect pests.

Inbreeding One useful selective breeding technique is called inbreeding. **Inbreeding** involves crossing two individuals that have identical or similar sets of alleles. The organisms that result from inbreeding have alleles that are very similar to those of their parents. Mendel used inbreeding to produce purebred pea plants for his experiments.

One goal of inbreeding is to produce breeds of animals with specific traits. For example, by only crossing horses with exceptional speed, breeders can produce purebred horses that can run very fast. Purebred dogs, such as Labrador retrievers and German shepherds, were produced by inbreeding.

Unfortunately, because inbred organisms are genetically very similar, inbreeding reduces an offspring's chances of inheriting new allele combinations. Inbreeding also increases the probability that organisms may inherit alleles that lead to genetic disorders. For example, inherited hip problems are common in many breeds of dogs.

Hybridization Another selective breeding technique is called hybridization. In **hybridization** (hy brid ih ZAY shun), breeders cross two genetically different individuals. The hybrid organism that results is bred to have the best traits from both parents. For example, a farmer might cross corn that produces many kernels with corn that is resistant to disease. The result might be a hybrid corn plant with both of the desired traits. Today, most crops grown on farms and in gardens were produced by hybridization.

Figure 13 Plants can be easily cloned by making a cutting. Once the cutting has grown roots, it can be planted and will grow into a new plant. *Applying Concepts Why is the new plant considered to be a clone of the original plant?*

Cloning

One problem with selective breeding is that the breeder cannot control whether the desired allele will be passed from the parent to its offspring. This is because the transmission of alleles is determined by probability, as you learned in Chapter 3. For some organisms, another technique, called cloning, can be used to produce offspring with desired traits. A **clone** is an organism that is genetically identical to the organism from which it was produced. This means that a clone has exactly the same genes as the organism from which it was produced. Cloning can be done in plants and animals, as well as other organisms.

Cloning Plants One way to produce a clone of a plant is through a cutting. A cutting is a small part of a plant, such as a leaf or a stem, that is cut from the plant. The cutting can grow into an entire new plant. The new plant is genetically identical to the plant from which the cutting was taken.

Cloning Animals Producing a clone of an animal is much more difficult than producing a clone of a plant. It isn't possible to use a cutting from a cow to produce a new cow. However, scientists have been experimenting with various techniques to produce clones of animals. Remember Dolly, the lamb described at the beginning of this section? Dolly was the first clone of an adult mammal ever produced.

To create Dolly, researchers first removed an egg cell from one sheep. The cell's nucleus was replaced with the nucleus from a cell of a six-year-old sheep. The egg was then implanted into the uterus of a third sheep. Five months later, Dolly was born. Dolly is genetically identical to the six-year-old sheep that supplied the cell nucleus. Dolly is a clone of that sheep.

✓ *Checkpoint* How can a clone of a plant be produced?

Genetic Engineering

In the past few decades, geneticists have developed another powerful technique for producing organisms with desired traits. In this process, called **genetic engineering,** genes from one organism are transferred into the DNA of another organism. Genetic engineering is sometimes called "gene splicing" because a DNA molecule is cut open and a gene from another organism is spliced into it. Researchers use genetic engineering to produce medicines, to improve food crops, and to try to cure human genetic disorders.

EXPLORING Genetic Engineering

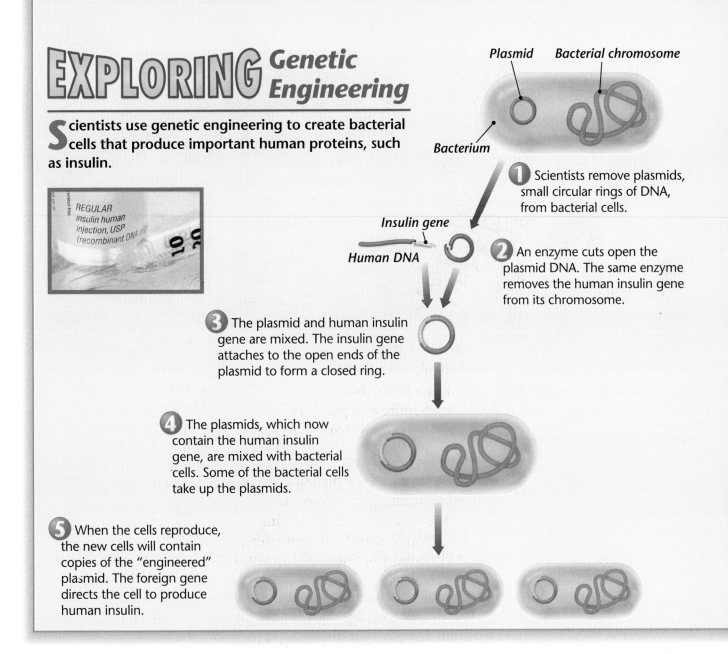

Scientists use genetic engineering to create bacterial cells that produce important human proteins, such as insulin.

REGULAR insulin human injection, USP (recombinant DNA ...)

Plasmid   **Bacterial chromosome**

Bacterium

Insulin gene

Human DNA

1 Scientists remove plasmids, small circular rings of DNA, from bacterial cells.

2 An enzyme cuts open the plasmid DNA. The same enzyme removes the human insulin gene from its chromosome.

3 The plasmid and human insulin gene are mixed. The insulin gene attaches to the open ends of the plasmid to form a closed ring.

4 The plasmids, which now contain the human insulin gene, are mixed with bacterial cells. Some of the bacterial cells take up the plasmids.

5 When the cells reproduce, the new cells will contain copies of the "engineered" plasmid. The foreign gene directs the cell to produce human insulin.

Genetic Engineering in Bacteria Researchers had their first successes with genetic engineering when they inserted DNA from other organisms into bacteria. Recall that the single DNA molecule of bacterial cells is found in the cytoplasm. Some bacterial cells also contain small circular pieces of DNA called plasmids.

In *Exploring Genetic Engineering,* you can see how scientists insert a human gene into the plasmid of a bacterium. Once the DNA is spliced into the plasmid, the bacterial cell and all its offspring will contain this human gene. As a result, the bacteria produce the protein that the human gene codes for, in this case insulin. Because bacteria reproduce quickly, large amounts of insulin can be produced in a short time. The insulin can be collected and used to treat people with diabetes, a disorder in which the body does not produce enough of this protein.

Figure 14 Scientists created this new variety of tomatoes using genetic engineering. The tomatoes taste better and keep longer than other varieties. *Making Judgments What other traits would be desirable in tomatoes?*

Today, many human proteins are produced in genetically engineered bacteria. For example, human growth hormone is a protein that controls the growth process in children. Children whose bodies do not produce enough human growth hormone can be given injections of the hormone. Today, an unlimited supply of the hormone exists, thanks to genetically engineered bacteria.

Genetic Engineering in Other Organisms Genetic engineering has also been used to insert genes into the cells of other organisms. Scientists have inserted genes from bacteria into the cells of tomatoes, wheat, rice, and other important crops. Some of the genes enable the plants to survive in colder temperatures or in poor soil conditions, and to resist insect pests.

Genetic engineering techniques can also be used to insert genes into animals, which then produce important medicines for humans. For example, scientists can insert human genes into the cells of cows. The cows then produce the human protein for which the gene codes. Scientists have used this technique to produce the blood clotting protein needed by people with hemophilia. The protein is produced in the cows' milk, and can easily be extracted and used to treat people with the disorder.

Gene Therapy Researchers are also using genetic engineering to try to correct some genetic disorders. This process, called **gene therapy,** involves inserting working copies of a gene directly into the cells of a person with a genetic disorder. For example, people with cystic fibrosis do not produce a protein that is needed for proper lung function. Both copies of the gene that codes for the protein are defective in these people.

Scientists can insert working copies of the gene into harmless viruses. The "engineered" viruses can then be sprayed into the lungs of patients with cystic fibrosis. The researchers hope that the working copies of the gene in the viruses will function in the patient to produce the protein. Gene therapy is still an experimental method for treating genetic disorders. Researchers are working hard to improve this promising technique.

DNA Fingerprinting

In courtrooms across the country, a genetic technique called DNA fingerprinting is being used to help solve crimes. If you did the Discover activity, you know that fingerprints can help to identify people. No two people have the same fingerprints. Detectives routinely use fingerprints found at a crime scene to help identify the person who committed the crime. In a similar way, DNA from samples of hair, skin, and blood can also be used to identify a person. No two people, except for identical twins, have the same DNA.

In DNA fingerprinting, enzymes are used to cut the DNA in the sample found at a crime scene into fragments. An electrical current then separates the fragments by size to form a pattern of bands, like the ones you see in Figure 15. Each person's pattern of DNA bands is unique. The DNA pattern can then be compared to the pattern produced by DNA taken from people suspected of committing the crime.

✓ *Checkpoint* **In what way is DNA like fingerprints?**

Sharpen your Skills

Communicating

Imagine that you are an **ACTIVITY** expert witness at a murder trial. You will be called to testify about the DNA evidence found in drops of blood at the crime scene. You will need to explain the process of DNA fingerprinting to the jury. Write a paragraph describing what you would say. How would you convince a jury that DNA fingerprinting is a reliable technique?

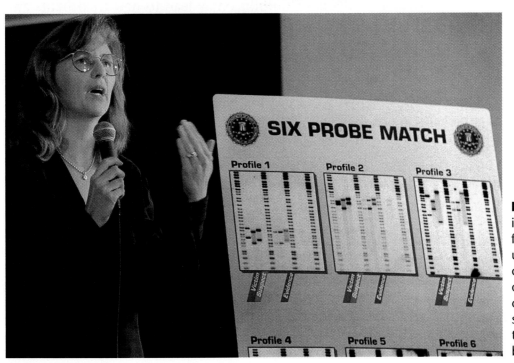

Figure 15 This scientist is explaining how DNA fingerprinting can be used to help solve crimes. DNA from blood or other substances collected at a crime scene can be compared to DNA from a suspect's blood.

Figure 16 The Human Genome Project is an attempt to identify the sequence of every DNA base pair in the human genome.

The Human Genome Project

Imagine trying to crack a code that is 3 billion characters long. Then imagine working with people all over the world to accomplish this task. That's exactly what scientists working on the Human Genome Project are doing. A **genome** is all the DNA in one cell of an organism. Researchers estimate that the 23 pairs of chromosomes that make up the human genome contain about 60,000 to 80,000 genes—or about 3 billion DNA base pairs.

The main goal of the Human Genome Project is to identify the DNA sequence of every gene in the human genome. When the Human Genome Project is completed, an encyclopedia of genetic information about humans will be available. Scientists will know the DNA sequence of every human gene, and thus the amino acid sequence of every protein.

With the information from the Human Genome Project, researchers may gain a better understanding of how humans develop from a fertilized egg to an adult. They may also learn what makes the body work, and what causes things to go wrong. New understandings may lead to new treatments and prevention strategies for many genetic disorders and for diseases such as cancer.

Section 3 Review

1. Name three techniques that people have used to produce organisms with desired traits.
2. Why do scientists want to identify the DNA sequence of every human gene?
3. What is genetic engineering? Describe three possible benefits of this technique.
4. Explain how a DNA fingerprint is produced. What information can a DNA fingerprint reveal?
5. **Thinking Critically Making Judgments** Do you think there should be any limitations on genetic engineering? Give reasons to support your position.

Science at Home

Grocery Genetics With a parent or other adult family member, go to a grocery store. Look at the different varieties of potatoes, apples, and other fruits and vegetables. Discuss how these varieties were created by selective breeding. Then choose one type of fruit or vegetable and make a list of different varieties. If possible, find out what traits each variety was bred for.

Who Should Have Access to Genetic Test Results?

Scientists working on the Human Genome Project have identified many alleles that put people at risk for certain diseases, such as breast cancer and Alzheimer's disease. Through techniques known as genetic testing, people can have their DNA analyzed to find out whether they have any of these alleles. If they do, they may be able to take steps to prevent the illness or to seek early treatment.

Some health insurance companies and employers want access to this type of genetic information. However, many people believe that genetic testing results should be kept private.

The Issues

Why Do Insurance Companies Want Genetic Information? Health insurance companies set their rates based on a person's risk of health problems. To determine a person's insurance rate, insurance companies often require that a person have a physical examination. If the examination reveals a condition such as high blood pressure, the company may charge that person more for an insurance policy. This is because he or she would be more likely to need expensive medical care.

Insurance companies view genetic testing as an additional way to gather information about a person's health status. Insurers argue that if they were unable to gather this information, they would need to raise rates for everyone. This would be unfair to people who are in good health.

Why Do Employers Want Genetic Information? Federal laws forbid employers with 15 or more workers from choosing job applicants based on their health status. These laws do not apply to smaller companies, however. Employers may not want to hire employees with health problems because they often miss more work time than other employees. In addition, employers who hire people with health problems may be charged higher health insurance rates. Many small companies cannot afford to pay these higher rates.

Should Genetic Information Be Kept Private? Some people think that the government should prohibit all access to genetic information. Today, some people fear that they will be discriminated against as a result of genetic test results. Because of this fear, some people avoid genetic testing—even though testing might allow them to seek early treatment for a disorder. These people want tighter control of genetic information. They want to be sure that insurers and employers will not have access to genetic test results.

You Decide

1. Identify the Problem

In your own words, explain the problem of deciding who should have access to genetic test results.

2. Analyze the Options

Examine the pros and cons of keeping genetic test results private. List reasons to maintain privacy. List reasons why test results should be shared.

3. Find a Solution

Create a list of rules to control access to genetic information. Who should have access, and under what circumstances? Explain your reasoning.

You Solve the Mystery

Guilty or Innocent?

In this lab, you will investigate how DNA fingerprinting can be used to provide evidence related to a crime.

Problem

How can DNA be used to identify individuals?

Skills Focus

observing, making models, drawing conclusions

Materials

4–6 bar codes

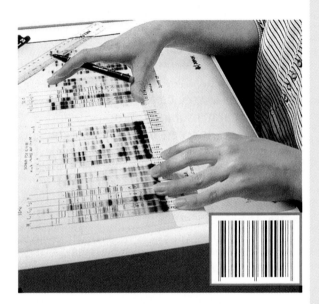

Procedure

1. Look at the photograph of DNA band patterns shown at right. Each person's DNA produces a unique pattern of these bands.
2. Now look at the Universal Product Code, also called a bar code, shown below the DNA bands. A bar code can be used as a model of a DNA band pattern. Compare the bar code with the DNA bands to see what they have in common. Record your observations.
3. Suppose that a burglary has taken place, and you're the detective leading the investigation. Your teacher will give you a bar code that represents DNA from blood found at the crime scene. You arrange to have DNA samples taken from several suspects. Write a sentence describing what you will look for as you try to match each suspect's DNA to the DNA sample from the crime scene.
4. You will now be given bar codes representing DNA samples taken from the suspects. Compare those bar codes with the bar code that represents DNA from the crime scene.

5. Use your comparisons to determine whether any of the suspects was present at the crime scene.

Analyze and Conclude

1. Based on your findings, were any of the suspects present at the crime scene? Support your conclusion with specific evidence.
2. Why do people's DNA patterns differ so greatly?
3. How would your conclusions be affected if you learned that the suspect whose DNA matched the evidence had an identical twin?
4. **Apply** In everyday life, do you think that DNA evidence is enough to determine that a suspect committed the crime? Explain.

More to Explore

Do you think the DNA fingerprints of a parent and a child would show any similarities? Draw what you think they would look like. Then explain your thinking.

SECTION 1 — Human Inheritance

Key Ideas

◆ Some human traits are controlled by a single gene that has multiple alleles—three or more forms.

◆ Some human traits show a wide range of phenotypes because these traits are controlled by many genes. The genes act together as a group to produce a single trait.

◆ Traits are often influenced by the organism's environment.

◆ Males have one X chromosome and one Y chromosome. Females have two X chromosomes. Males are more likely than females to have a sex-linked trait controlled by a recessive allele.

◆ Geneticists use pedigrees to trace the inheritance pattern of a particular trait through a number of generations of a family.

Key Terms

multiple alleles	carrier
sex-linked gene	pedigree

SECTION 2 — Human Genetic Disorders

Key Ideas

◆ Genetic disorders are abnormal conditions that are caused by mutations, or DNA changes, in genes or chromosomes.

◆ Common genetic disorders include cystic fibrosis, sickle-cell disease, hemophilia, and Down syndrome.

◆ Amniocentesis and karyotypes are tools used to diagnose genetic disorders.

◆ Genetic counselors help couples understand their chances of having a child with a genetic disorder.

Key Terms

genetic disorder	karyotype
amniocentesis	

SECTION 3 — Advances in Genetics

INTEGRATING TECHNOLOGY

Key Ideas

◆ Selective breeding is the process of selecting a few organisms with desired traits to serve as parents of the next generation.

◆ Cloning is a technique used to produce genetically identical organisms.

◆ Genetic engineering can be used to produce medicines and to improve food crops. Researchers are also using genetic engineering to try to cure human genetic disorders.

◆ DNA fingerprinting can be used to help determine whether material found at a crime scene came from a particular suspect.

◆ The goal of the Human Genome Project is to identify the DNA sequence of every gene in the human genome.

Key Terms

selective breeding	genetic engineering
inbreeding	gene therapy
hybridization	genome
clone	

Organizing Information

Concept Map Copy the concept map about human traits onto a separate sheet of paper. Then complete it and add a title. (For more on concept maps, see the Skills Handbook.)

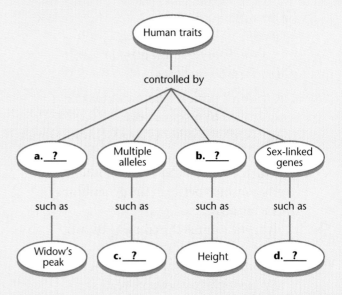

Reviewing Content

 For more review of key concepts, see the Interactive Student Tutorial CD-ROM.

Multiple Choice

Choose the letter of the best answer.

1. A human trait that is controlled by multiple alleles is
   a. dimples.   b. blood type.
   c. height.   d. skin color.
2. A genetic disorder caused by a sex-linked gene is
   a. cystic fibrosis.
   b. sickle-cell disease.
   c. hemophilia.
   d. Down syndrome.
3. Sickle-cell disease is characterized by
   a. abnormally shaped red blood cells.
   b. abnormally thick body fluids.
   c. abnormal blood clotting.
   d. an extra copy of chromosome 21.
4. Inserting a human gene into a bacterial plasmid is an example of
   a. inbreeding.
   b. selective breeding.
   c. DNA fingerprinting.
   d. genetic engineering.
5. DNA fingerprinting is a way to
   a. clone organisms.
   b. breed organisms with desirable traits.
   c. identify people.
   d. map and sequence human genes.

True or False

If the statement is true, write true. If it is false, change the underlined word or words to make the statement true.

6. A <u>widow's peak</u> is a human trait that is controlled by a single gene.
7. A person who inherits two X chromosomes will be <u>male</u>.
8. A <u>karyotype</u> is a chart that shows the relationships between the generations of a family.
9. <u>Hybridization</u> is the crossing of two genetically similar organisms.
10. A <u>clone</u> is an organism that is genetically identical to another organism.

Checking Concepts

11. Explain how both genes and the environment determine how tall a person will be.
12. Explain why traits controlled by recessive alleles on the X chromosome are more common in males than in females.
13. What is sickle-cell disease? How is this disorder inherited?
14. How can amniocentesis be used to detect a disorder such as Down syndrome?
15. Explain how a horse breeder might use selective breeding to produce horses that have golden coats.
16. Describe how gene therapy might be used in the future to treat a person with hemophilia.
17. **Writing to Learn** As the webmaster for a national genetics foundation, you must create a Web site to inform the public about genetic disorders. Choose one human genetic disorder discussed in this chapter. Write a description of the disorder that you will use for the Web site.

Thinking Critically

18. **Applying Concepts** Why can a person be a carrier of a trait caused by a recessive allele but not of a trait caused by a dominant allele?
19. **Problem Solving** A woman with normal color vision has a colorblind daughter. What are the genotypes and phenotypes of both parents?
20. **Calculating** If a mother is a carrier of hemophilia, what is the probability that her son will have the trait? Explain your answer.
21. **Inferring** How could ancient people selectively breed corn if they didn't know about genes and inheritance?
22. **Comparing and Contrasting** How are selective breeding and genetic engineering different? How are they similar?

Applying Skills

Use the information below to answer Questions 23–25.

◆ Bob and Helen have three children.

◆ Bob and Helen have one son who has albinism, an inherited condition in which the skin does not have brown pigments.

◆ Bob and Helen have two daughters who do not have albinism.

◆ Neither Bob nor Helen has albinism.

◆ Albinism is neither sex-linked nor codominant.

23. **Interpreting Data** Use the information to construct a pedigree. If you don't know whether someone is a carrier, leave their symbol empty. If you decide later that a person is a carrier, change your pedigree.

24. **Drawing Conclusions** Is albinism controlled by a dominant allele or by a recessive allele? Explain your answer.

25. **Predicting** Suppose Bob and Helen were to have another child. What is the probability that the child will have albinism? Explain.

Performance Assessment
CHAPTER PROJECT

Present Your Project Before displaying your project, exchange it with another group to check each other's work. Make any necessary corrections, and then display your materials to the class. Be ready to explain the inheritance patterns shown in your pedigrees.

Reflect and Record In your journal, describe what you learned by creating the pedigrees. What questions do you have as a result of the project?

Test Preparation

Use these questions to prepare for standardized tests.

Use the information to answer Questions 26–29. The Punnett square below shows how muscular dystrophy, a sex-linked recessive disorder, is inherited.

Key	Father (normal) $X^M Y$	
X^M = normal allele	X^M	Y
X^m = muscular dystrophy allele		

	Father (normal) $X^M Y$	
	X^M	Y
Mother $X^M X^m$ (carrier) — X^M	$X^M X^M$	$X^M Y$
X^m	$X^M X^m$	$X^m Y$

26. What is the probability that a daughter of these parents will have muscular dystrophy?
   a. 0% b. 25%
   c. 50% d. 100%

27. What is the probability that a son of these parents will have muscular dystrophy?
   a. 0% b. 25%
   c. 50% d. 100%

28. What is the probability that a daughter of these parents will be a carrier of the disease?
   a. 0% b. 25%
   c. 50% d. 100%

29. Which of the following statements is true of muscular dystrophy?
   a. More men than women have muscular dystrophy.
   b. More women than men have muscular dystrophy.
   c. More men than women are carriers of muscular dystrophy.
   d. No women can have muscular dystrophy.

WEB ACTIVITY
www.phschool.com

Integrating Earth Science

SECTION **1** **Darwin's Voyage**

Discover **How Do Living Things Vary?**
Try This **Bird Beak Adaptations**
Sharpen Your Skills **Inferring**
Skills Lab **Nature at Work**

SECTION **2** **The Fossil Record**

Discover **What Can Fossils Tell You?**
Try This **Preservation in Ice**
Sharpen Your Skills **Calculating**
Science at Home **Make Your Mark**

SECTION **3** **Other Evidence for Evolution**

Discover **How Can You Classify Species?**
Sharpen Your Skills **Drawing Conclusions**
Skills Lab **Telltale Molecules**

Life's Long Calendar

How far back in your life can you remember? How far can the adults you know remember? Think of how life has changed in the last ten, fifty, or one hundred years. This chapter looks back in time as well. But instead of looking back hundreds of years, you'll explore millions, hundreds of millions, and even billions of years.

The time frame of Earth's history is so large that it can be overwhelming. This chapter project will help you understand it. In this project, you'll find a way to convert enormous time periods into a more familiar scale.

Your Goal To use a familiar measurement scale to create two time lines for Earth's history.

To complete the project you will
◆ represent Earth's history using a familiar scale, such as hours on a clock, months on a calendar, or yards on a football field
◆ use your chosen scale twice, once to plot out 5 billion years of history, and then to focus on the past 600 million years
◆ include markers on both scales to show important events in the history of life

Get Started Preview *Exploring Life's History* on pages 162–163 to see what events occurred during the two time periods. In a small group, discuss some familiar scales you might use for your time lines. You could select a time interval such as a year or a day. Alternatively, you could choose a distance interval such as the length of your schoolyard or the walls in your classroom. Decide on the kind of time lines you will make.

Check Your Progress You will be working on this project as you study this chapter. To keep your project on track, look for Check Your Progress boxes at the following points.
Section 1 Review, page 156: Plan your time lines.
Section 3 Review, page 169: Construct your time lines.

Present Your Project At the end of the chapter (page 173), you'll display your time lines for the class.

This *Triceratops* lived in western North America about 70 million years ago. It used its sharp horns to defend itself against predators.

SECTION 1 Darwin's Voyage

DISCOVER ⋯⋯⋯⋯⋯⋯⋯⋯⋯⋯⋯⋯ ACTIVITY ⋯

How Do Living Things Vary?

1. Use a metric ruler to measure the length and width of 10 sunflower seeds. Record each measurement.

2. Now use a hand lens to carefully examine each seed. Record each seed's shape, color, and number of stripes.

Think It Over

Classifying In what ways are the seeds in your sample different from one another? In what ways are they similar? How could you group the seeds based on their similarities and differences?

GUIDE FOR READING

◆ How did Darwin explain the differences between species on the Galapagos Islands and on mainland South America?

◆ How does natural selection lead to evolution?

◆ How do new species form?

Reading Tip As you read, make a list of main ideas and supporting details about evolution.

In December 1831, the British naval ship HMS *Beagle* set sail from England on a five-year-long trip around the world. On board was a 22-year-old named Charles Darwin. Darwin eventually became the ship's naturalist—a person who studies the natural world. His job was to learn as much as he could about the living things he saw on the voyage.

During the voyage, Darwin observed plants and animals he had never seen before. He wondered why they were so different from those in England. Darwin's observations led him to develop one of the most important scientific theories of all time: the theory of evolution by natural selection.

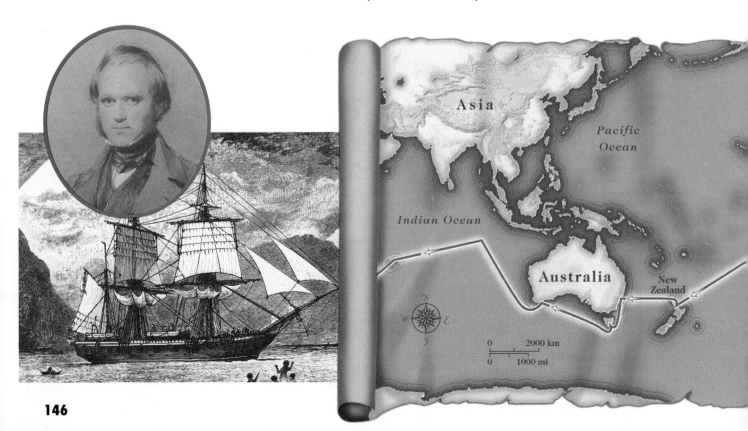

Darwin's Observations

One of the *Beagle's* first stops was the coast of South America. In Brazil, Darwin saw insects that looked like flowers, and ants that marched across the forest floor like huge armies. In Argentina, he saw armadillos—burrowing animals covered with small, bony plates. He also saw sloths, animals that moved very slowly and spent much of their time hanging upside down in trees.

Darwin was amazed by the tremendous diversity, or variety, of living things he saw. Today scientists know that living things are even more diverse than Darwin could ever have imagined. Scientists have identified more than 1.7 million species of organisms on Earth. A **species** is a group of similar organisms that can mate with each other and produce fertile offspring.

Darwin saw something else in Argentina that puzzled him: the bones of animals that had died long ago. From the bones, Darwin inferred that the animals had looked like the sloths he had seen. However, the bones were much larger than those of the living sloths. He wondered why only smaller sloths were alive today. What had happened to the giant creatures from the past?

In 1835, the *Beagle* reached the Galapagos Islands, a group of small islands in the Pacific Ocean off the west coast of South America. It was on the Galapagos Islands that Darwin observed some of the greatest diversity of life forms. The giant tortoises, or land turtles, he saw were so tall that they could look him in the eye. There were also seals covered with fur, and lizards that ate nothing but tough, prickly cactus plants.

Figure 1 Charles Darwin sailed on HMS *Beagle* from England to South America and then to the Galapagos Islands. He saw many unusual organisms on the Galapagos Islands.

Galapagos hawk ▼

▲ *Giant tortoise*

▲ *Sally light-foot crab*

◀ *Blue-footed booby*

Similarities and Differences

Darwin was surprised that many of the plants and animals on the Galapagos Islands were similar to organisms on mainland South America. For example, many of the birds on the islands, including hawks, mockingbirds, and finches, resembled those on the mainland. Many of the plants were also similar to plants Darwin had collected on the mainland.

However, there were also important differences between the organisms on the islands and those on the mainland. Large sea birds called cormorants, for example, lived in both places. The cormorants on the mainland were able to fly, while those on the Galapagos Islands were unable to fly. The iguanas on the Galapagos Islands had large claws that allowed them to keep their grip on slippery rocks, where they fed on seaweed. The iguanas on the mainland had smaller claws. Smaller claws allowed the mainland iguanas to climb trees, where they ate leaves.

From his observations, Darwin inferred that a small number of different plant and animal species had come to the Galapagos Islands from the mainland. They might have been blown out to sea during a storm or set adrift on a fallen log. Once the plants and animals reached the islands, they reproduced. Eventually, their offspring became different from their mainland relatives.

Darwin also noticed many differences among similar organisms as he traveled from one Galapagos island to the next. For example, the tortoises on one island had dome-shaped shells. Those on another island had saddle-shaped shells. The governor of one of the islands told Darwin that he could tell which island a tortoise came from just by looking at its shell.

☑ *Checkpoint* How did Darwin think plants and animals had originally come to the Galapagos Islands?

Figure 2 Darwin observed many differences between organisms in South America and similar organisms on the Galapagos Islands. For example, green iguanas (left) live in South America. Marine iguanas (right) live on the Galapagos Islands. *Comparing and Contrasting How are the two species similar? How are they different?*

Figure 3 Darwin made these drawings of four species of Galapagos finches. The beak of each finch is adapted to the type of food it eats.

Adaptations

Like the tortoises, the finches on the Galapagos Islands were noticeably different from one island to another. The most obvious differences were the varied sizes and shapes of the birds' beaks. As Darwin studied the different finches, he noticed that each species was well suited to the life it led. Finches that ate insects had sharp, needlelike beaks. Finches that ate seeds had strong, wide beaks. Beak shape is an example of an **adaptation,** a trait that helps an organism survive and reproduce.

Evolution

After he returned home to England, Darwin continued to think about what he had seen during his voyage on the *Beagle*. Darwin spent the next 20 years consulting with many other scientists, gathering more information, and thinking through his ideas. He especially wanted to understand how the variety of organisms with different adaptations arose on the Galapagos Islands.

Darwin reasoned that plants or animals that arrived on one of the Galapagos Islands faced conditions that were different from those on the mainland. **Perhaps, Darwin thought, the species gradually changed over many generations and became better adapted to the new conditions.** The gradual change in a species over time is called **evolution.**

Darwin's ideas are often referred to as the theory of evolution. A **scientific theory** is a well-tested concept that explains a wide range of observations.

It was clear to Darwin that evolution had occurred on the Galapagos Islands. He did not know, however, how this process had occurred. Darwin had to draw on other examples of changes in living things to help him understand how evolution occurs.

Bird Beak Adaptations

Use this activity to explore adaptations in birds.

1. Scatter a small amount of bird seed on a paper plate. Scatter 20 raisins on the plate to represent insects.

2. Obtain a variety of objects such as tweezers, hair clips, clothes pins, and hairpins. Pick one object to use as a "beak."

3. See how many seeds you can pick up and drop into a cup in 10 seconds.

4. Now see how many "insects" you can pick up and drop into a cup in 10 seconds.

5. Use a different "beak" and repeat Steps 3 and 4.

Inferring What type of beak worked well for seeds? For insects? How are different-shaped beaks useful for eating different foods?

Darwin knew that people used selective breeding to produce organisms with desired traits. For example, English farmers used selective breeding to produce sheep with fine wool. Darwin himself had bred pigeons with large, fan-shaped tails. By repeatedly allowing only those pigeons with many tail feathers to mate, Darwin produced pigeons with two or three times the usual number of tail feathers. Darwin thought that a process similar to selective breeding must happen in nature. But he wondered why certain traits were selected for, and how.

☑ *Checkpoint* **What observations led Darwin to propose his theory of evolution?**

Natural Selection

In 1858, Darwin and another British biologist, Alfred Russel Wallace, proposed an explanation for how evolution occurs. The next year, Darwin described this mechanism in a book entitled *The Origin of Species.* In his book, Darwin explained that evolution occurs by means of natural selection. **Natural selection** is the process by which individuals that are better adapted to their environment are more likely to survive and reproduce than other members of the same species. Darwin identified a number of factors that affect the process of natural selection: overproduction, competition, and variations.

Overproduction Most species produce far more offspring than can possibly survive. In many species, so many offspring are produced that there are not enough resources—food, water, and living space—for all of them. For example, each year a female sea turtle may lay more than 100 eggs. If all the young turtles survived, the sea would soon be full of turtles. Darwin knew that this doesn't happen. Why not?

Figure 4 Most newborn loggerhead sea turtles will not survive to adulthood.
Making Generalizations
What factors limit the number of young that survive?

150

Figure 5 The walruses lying on this rocky beach in Alaska must compete for resources. All organisms compete for limited resources such as food.

Competition Since food and other resources are limited, the offspring must compete with each other to survive. Competition does not usually involve direct physical fights between members of a species. Instead, competition is usually indirect. For example, some turtles may fail to find enough to eat. Others may not be able to escape from predators. Only a few turtles will survive long enough to reproduce.

Variations As you learned in your study of genetics, members of a species differ from one another in many of their traits. Any difference between individuals of the same species is called a **variation.** For example, some newly hatched turtles are able to swim faster than other turtles.

Selection Some variations make certain individuals better adapted to their environment. Those individuals are more likely to survive and reproduce. When those individuals reproduce, their offspring may inherit the allele for the helpful trait. The offspring, in turn, will be more likely to survive and reproduce, and thus pass on the allele to their offspring. After many generations, more members of the species will have the helpful trait. In effect, the environment has "selected" organisms with helpful traits to be the parents of the next generation—hence the term "natural selection." **Over a long period of time, natural selection can lead to evolution. Helpful variations gradually accumulate in a species, while unfavorable ones disappear.**

For example, suppose a new fast-swimming predator moves into the turtles' habitat. Turtles that are able to swim faster would be more likely to escape from the new predator. The faster turtles would thus be more likely to survive and reproduce. Over time, more and more turtles in the species would have the "fast-swimmer" trait.

Sharpen your Skills

Inferring ACTIVITY

Scatter 15 black buttons and 15 white buttons on a sheet of white paper. Have a partner time you to see how many buttons you can pick up in 10 seconds. Pick up the buttons one at a time.

Did you collect more buttons of one color than the other? Why? How can a variation such as color affect the process of natural selection?

Nature at Work

In this lab, you will investigate how natural selection can lead to changes in a species over time. You'll explore how both genetic and environmental factors play a part in natural selection.

Problem

How do species change over time?

Materials

scissors
marking pen
construction paper, 2 colors

Procedure

1. Work on this lab with two other students. One student should choose construction paper of one color and make the team's 50 "mouse" cards, as described in Table 1. The second student should choose a different color construction paper and make the team's 25 "event" cards, as described in Table 2. The third student should copy the data table and record all the data.

Part 1 A White Sand Environment

2. Mix up the mouse cards.
3. Begin by using the cards to model what might happen to a group of mice in an environment of white sand dunes. Choose two mouse cards. Allele pairs *WW* and *Ww* produce a white mouse. Allele pair *ww* produces a brown mouse. Record the color of the mouse with a tally mark in the data table.

4. Choose an event card. An "S" card means the mouse survives. A "D" or a "P" card means the mouse dies. A "C" card means the mouse dies if its color contrasts with the white sand dunes. (Only brown mice will die when a "C" card is drawn.) Record each death with a tally mark in the data table.
5. If the mouse lives, put the two mouse cards in a "live mice" pile. If the mouse dies, put the cards in a "dead mice" pile. Put the event card at the bottom of its pack.
6. Repeat Steps 3 through 5 with the remaining mouse cards to study the first generation of mice. Record your results.
7. Leave the dead mice cards untouched. Mix up the cards from the live mice pile. Mix up the events cards.
8. Repeat Steps 3 through 7 for the second generation. Then repeat Steps 3 through 6 for the third generation.

Table 1: "Mouse" Cards		
Number	**Label**	**Meaning**
25	*W*	Dominant allele for white fur
25	*w*	Recessive allele for brown fur

Table 2: "Event" Cards		
Number	**Label**	**Meaning**
5	S	Mouse survives.
1	D	Disease kills mouse.
1	P	Predator kills mice of all colors.
18	C	Predator kills mice that contrast with the environment.

DATA TABLE

Type of Environment:

Generation	White Mice	Brown Mice	Deaths	
			White Mice	Brown Mice
1				
2				
3				

Part 2 A Forest Floor Environment

9. How would the data differ if the mice in this model lived on a dark brown forest floor? Record your prediction in your notebook.

10. Make a new copy of the data table. Then use the cards to test your prediction. Remember that a "C" card now means that any mouse with white fur will die.

Analyze and Conclude

1. In Part 1, how many white mice were there in each generation? How many brown mice? In each generation, which color mouse had the higher death rate? (*Hint:* To calculate the death rate for white mice, divide the number of white mice that died by the total number of white mice, then multiply by 100%.)

2. If the events in Part 1 occurred in nature, how would the group of mice change over time?

3. How did the results in Part 2 differ from those in Part 1?

4. What are some ways in which this investigation models natural selection? What are some ways in which natural selection differs from this model?

5. **Think About It** How would it affect your model if you increased the number of "C" cards? If you decreased the number?

Design an Experiment

Choose a different species with a trait that interests you. Make a set of cards similar to these cards to investigate how natural selection might bring about the evolution of that species.

The case of the English peppered moth is an example of how human actions can affect natural selection. In the late 1700s, most English peppered moths were light gray in color. The light-colored moths had an advantage over black peppered moths because birds could not see them against the light-gray trees. Natural selection favored the light-colored moths over the black moths.

The Industrial Revolution began in England in the late 1700s. People built factories to make cloth and other goods. Over time, smoke from the factories blackened the trunks of the trees. Now the light-colored moths were easier to see than the black ones. As a result, birds caught more light-colored moths. Natural selection favored the black moths. By about 1850, almost all the peppered moths were black.

In Your Journal

Since the 1950s, strict pollution laws have reduced the amount of smoke released into the air in England. Predict how this has affected the trees and the moths.

The Role of Genes in Evolution

Without variations, all the members of a species would have the same traits. Evolution by natural selection would not occur because all individuals would have an equal chance of surviving and reproducing. But where do variations come from? How are they passed on from parents to offspring? Darwin could not answer these questions.

Darwin did not know anything about genes or mutations. It is not surprising that he could not explain what caused variations or how they were passed on. As scientists later learned, variations can result from mutations in genes or from the shuffling of alleles during meiosis. Only genes are passed from parents to their offspring. Because of this, only traits that are inherited, or controlled by genes, can be acted upon by natural selection.

Evolution in Action

Since Darwin published his book, scientists have observed many examples of evolution in action. In a 1977 study of the finches on Daphne Major, one of the Galapagos Islands, scientists observed that beak size could change very quickly by natural selection. That year, little rain fell on the island—only 25 millimeters instead of the usual 130 millimeters or so. Because of the lack of rain, many plants died. Fewer of the seeds that the finches usually ate were available. Instead, the birds had to eat large seeds that were enclosed in tough, thorny seed pods.

Finches with larger and stronger beaks were better able to open the tough pods than were finches with smaller, weaker beaks. Many of the finches with smaller beaks did not survive the drought. The next year, more finches on the island had larger and stronger beaks. Evolution by natural selection had occurred in just one year.

Figure 6 The Industrial Revolution affected natural selection in peppered moths in England. As pollution blackened the tree trunks, black moths became more likely to survive and reproduce.

How Do New Species Form?

Darwin's theory of evolution by natural selection explains how variations can lead to changes in a species. But how does an entirely new species evolve? Since Darwin's time, scientists have come to understand that geographic isolation is one of the main ways that new species form. Isolation, or complete separation, occurs when some members of a species become cut off from the rest of the species.

Sometimes a group is separated from the rest of its species by a river, volcano, or mountain range. Even an ocean wave can separate a few individuals from the rest of their species by sweeping them out to sea and later washing them ashore on an island. This may have happened on the Galapagos Islands. Once a group becomes isolated, members of the isolated group can no longer mate with members of the rest of the species.

A new species can form when a group of individuals remains separated from the rest of its species long enough to evolve different traits. The longer the group remains isolated from the rest of the species, the more likely it is to evolve into a new species. For example, the Abert squirrel and the Kaibab squirrel live in forests in the Southwest. About 10,000 years ago both types of squirrels were members of the same species. About that time, however, a small group of squirrels became isolated in a forest on the north side of the Grand Canyon in Arizona. Over time, this group evolved into the Kaibab squirrel, which has a distinctive black belly. Scientists are not sure whether the Kaibab squirrel has become different enough from the Abert squirrel to be considered a separate species.

☑ *Checkpoint* How did geographic isolation affect the Kaibab squirrel?

Figure 7 About 10,000 years ago, a group of squirrels became isolated from the rest of the species. As a result, the Kaibab squirrel (left) has evolved to become different from the Abert squirrel (right). *Interpreting Maps* What geographic feature separates the range of the Kaibab squirrel from that of the Abert squirrel?

Continental Drift

Geographic isolation has also occurred on a world-wide scale. For example, hundreds of millions of years ago all of Earth's landmasses were connected as one landmass. It formed a supercontinent called Pangaea. Organisms could migrate from one part of the supercontinent to another. Over millions of years, Pangaea gradually split apart in a process called continental drift. As the continents separated, species became isolated from one another and began to evolve independently.

Perhaps the most striking example of how continental drift affected the evolution of species is on the continent of Australia. The organisms living in Australia have been isolated from all other organisms on Earth for millions of years. Because of this, unique organisms have evolved in Australia. For example, most mammals in Australia belong to the group known as marsupials. Unlike other mammals, a marsupial gives birth to very small young that continue to develop in a pouch on the mother's body. Figure 8 shows two of the many marsupial species that exist in Australia. In contrast, few species of marsupials exist on other continents.

Figure 8 As a result of continental drift, many species of marsupials evolved in Australia. Australian marsupials include the numbat (top) and the spotted cuscus (bottom).

Section 1 Review

1. What is evolution? What did Darwin observe on the Galapagos Islands that he thought was the result of evolution?
2. Explain why variations are needed for natural selection to occur.
3. Describe how geographic isolation can result in the formation of a new species.
4. **Thinking Critically** Applying **Concepts** Some insects look just like sticks. How could this be an advantage to the insects? How could this trait have evolved through natural selection?

CHAPTER PROJECT

Check Your Progress

You should now be ready to submit your plans for your time lines to your teacher. Include a list of the major events you will include on your time lines. Remember, you want to emphasize the life forms that were present at each period. When your plans are approved, begin to construct your time lines. (*Hint:* You will need to divide your time lines into equal-sized intervals. For example, if you use a 12-month calendar to represent 5 billion years, calculate how many months will represent 1 billion years.)

SECTION 2 The Fossil Record

What Can Fossils Tell You?

1. Look at the fossil in the photograph. Describe the fossil's characteristics in as much detail as you can.

2. From your description in Step 1, try to figure out how the organism lived. How did it move? Where did it live?

Think It Over

Inferring What type of present-day organism do you think is related to the fossil? Why?

A crime has been committed. You and another detective arrive at the crime scene after the burglar has fled. To piece together what happened, you begin searching for clues. First you notice a broken first-floor window. Leading up to the window are footprints in the mud. From the prints, you can infer the size and type of shoes the burglar wore. As you gather these and other clues, you slowly piece together a picture of what happened and who the burglar might be.

To understand events that occurred long ago, scientists act like detectives. Some of the most important clues to Earth's past are fossils. A **fossil** is the preserved remains or traces of an organism that lived in the past. A fossil can be formed from a bone, tooth, shell, or other part of an organism. Other fossils can be traces of the organism, such as footprints or worm burrows left in mud that later turned to stone.

How Do Fossils Form?

Very few fossils are of complete organisms. Often when an animal dies, the soft parts of its body either decay or are eaten before a fossil can form. Usually only the hard parts of the animal, such as the bones or shells, remain. Plants also form fossils. The parts of plants that are most often preserved as fossils include leaves, stems, roots, and seeds.

The formation of any fossil is a rare event. The conditions must be just right for a fossil to form. **Most fossils form when organisms that die become buried in sediments.** Sediments are

◆ How do most fossils form?

◆ How can scientists determine a fossil's age?

Reading Tip As you read, write four multiple-choice questions about the content in this section. Exchange questions with a partner and answer each other's questions.

A fossilized shark tooth ▼

1. Two dinosaurs are buried by ash from an erupting volcano.

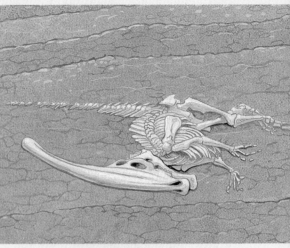

2. Minerals gradually replace the remains. Over millions of years, the fossils become buried by sediments.

Figure 9 Fossils are the preserved remains or traces of organisms that lived in the past. Fossils can form when organisms that die become buried in sediments.
Interpreting Diagrams What is one way in which a buried fossil can become uncovered?

particles of soil and rock. When a river flows into a lake or ocean, the sediments carried by the river settle to the bottom. Layers of sediments build up and cover the dead organisms. Over millions of years, the layers harden to become **sedimentary rock.**

Petrified Fossils Some remains that become buried in sediments are actually changed to rock. Minerals dissolved in the water soak into the buried remains. Gradually, the minerals replace the remains, changing them into rock. Fossils that form in this way are called **petrified fossils.**

Molds and Casts Sometimes shells or other hard parts buried by sediments are gradually dissolved. An empty space remains in the place the part once occupied. A hollow space in sediment in the shape of an organism or part of an organism is called a **mold.**

Sometimes a mold becomes filled in with hardened minerals, forming a **cast.** A cast is a copy of the shape of the organism that made the mold. If you have ever made a gelatin dessert in a plastic mold, then you can understand how a cast forms.

Preserved Remains Organisms can also be preserved in substances other than sediments. Entire organisms, such as the huge elephant-like mammoths that lived thousands of years ago, have been preserved in ice. The low temperatures preserved the mammoths' soft parts.

The bones and teeth of other ancient animals have been preserved in tar pits. Tar is a dark, sticky form of oil. Tar pits formed when tar seeped up from under the ground to the surface. The tar pits were often covered with water. Animals that came to drink the water became stuck in the tar.

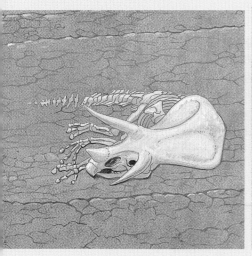
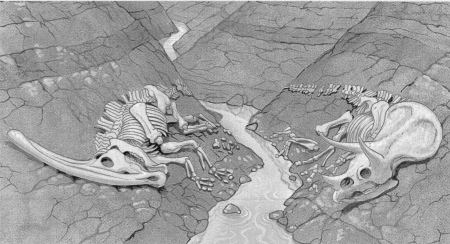

3. Running water cuts through the sedimentary rock layers, exposing the fossils.

Insects and some other organisms can become stuck in the sticky sap that some evergreen trees produce. The sap then hardens, forming amber. The amber protects the organism's body from decay.

Determining a Fossil's Age

To understand how living things have changed through time, scientists need to be able to determine the ages of fossils. They can then determine the sequence in which past events occurred. This information can be used to reconstruct the history of life on Earth. **Scientists can determine a fossil's age in two ways: relative dating and absolute dating.**

Relative Dating   Scientists use **relative dating** to determine which of two fossils is older. To understand how relative dating works, imagine that a river has cut down through layers of sedimentary rock to form a canyon. If you look at the canyon walls, you can see the layers of sedimentary rock piled up one on top of another. The layers near the top of the canyon were formed most recently. These layers are the youngest rock layers. The lower down the canyon wall you go, the older the layers are. Therefore, fossils found in layers near the top of the canyon are younger than fossils found near the bottom of the canyon.

Relative dating can only be used when the rock layers have been preserved in their original sequence. Relative dating can help scientists determine whether one fossil is older than another. However, relative dating does not tell scientists the fossil's actual age.

☑ *Checkpoint* *Which rock layers contain younger fossils?*

Preservation in Ice

1. Place fresh fruit, such as apple slices, strawberries, and blueberries, in an open plastic container.

2. Completely cover the fruit with water. Put the container in a freezer.

3. Place the same type and amount of fresh fruit in another open container. Leave it somewhere where no one will disturb it.

4. After three days, observe the fruit in both containers.

Inferring Use your observations to explain why fossils preserved in ice are more likely to include soft, fleshy body parts.

Figure 10 The half-life of potassium-40, a radioactive element, is 1.3 billion years. This means that half of the potassium-40 in a sample will break down into argon-40 every 1.3 billion years. *Interpreting Charts If a sample contains one fourth of the original amount of potassium-40, how old is the sample?*

Decay of Potassium-40 (Half-life = 1.3 billion years)		
Time	**Amount of Potassium-40**	**Amount of Argon-40**
2.6 billion years ago	1 g	0 g
1.3 billion years ago	0.5 g	0.5 g
Present	0.25 g	0.75 g

Absolute Dating Another technique, called **absolute dating,** allows scientists to determine the actual age of fossils. The rocks that fossils are found near contain **radioactive elements,** unstable elements that decay, or break down, into different elements. The **half-life** of a radioactive element is the time it takes for half of the atoms in a sample to decay. Figure 10 shows how a sample of potassium-40, a radioactive element, breaks down into argon-40 over time.

INTEGRATING CHEMISTRY

Scientists can compare the amount of a radioactive element in a sample to the amount of the element into which it breaks down. As you can see in Figure 10, this information can be used to calculate the age of the rock, and thus the age of the fossil.

✓ *Checkpoint What is a half-life?*

What Do Fossils Reveal?

Like pieces in a jigsaw puzzle, fossils help scientists piece together information about Earth's past. The millions of fossils that scientists have collected are called the **fossil record.** The fossil record, however, is incomplete. Many organisms die without leaving fossils behind. Despite gaps in the fossil record, it has given scientists a lot of important information about past life on Earth.

Almost all of the species preserved as fossils are now extinct. A species is **extinct** if no members of that species are still alive. Most of what scientists know about extinct species is based on the fossil record. Scientists use fossils of bones and teeth to build models of extinct animals. Fossil footprints provide clues about how fast an animal could move and how tall it was.

Sharpen your Skills

Calculating

ACTIVITY

A radioactive element has a half-life of 713 million years. After 2,139 million years, how many half-lives will have gone by?

Calculate how much of a 16-gram sample of the element will remain after 2,139 million years.

The fossil record also provides clues about how and when new groups of organisms evolved. The first animals appeared in the seas about 540 million years ago. These animals included worms, sponges, and other invertebrates—animals without backbones. About 500 million years ago, fishes evolved. These early fishes were the first vertebrates—animals with backbones.

The first land plants, which were similar to mosses, evolved around 410 million years ago. Land plants gradually evolved strong stems that held them upright. These plants were similar to modern ferns and cone-bearing trees. Look at *Exploring Life's History* on pages 162 and 163 to see when other groups of organisms evolved.

The Geologic Time Scale

Using absolute dating, scientists have calculated the ages of many different fossils and rocks. From this information, scientists have created a "calendar" of Earth's history that spans more than 4.6 billion years. Scientists have divided this large time period into smaller units called eras and periods. This calendar of Earth's history is sometimes called the Geologic Time Scale.

The largest span of time in the Geologic Time Scale is Precambrian Time. This span of time is sometimes referred to simply as the Precambrian (pree KAM bree un). It covers the first 4 billion years of Earth's history. Scientists know very little about the Precambrian because there are few fossils from these ancient times. After the Precambrian, the Geologic Time Scale is divided into three major blocks of time, or eras. Each era is further divided into shorter periods. In *Exploring Life's History,* you can see the events that occurred during each time period.

Figure 11 Complete skeletons of animals that lived thousands of years ago have been found in the Rancho La Brea tar pits in Los Angeles, California. The photo shows a model of an elephant-like animal. Scientists created the model based on information learned from the fossils.

EXPLORING Life's History

Take a trip through time to see how life on Earth has changed.

PRECAMBRIAN TIME
The Precambrian covers about 87 percent of Earth's history.

4.6 billion years ago

PRE-CAMBRIAN

PALEOZOIC ERA
Millions of years ago

544	505	438	408	360

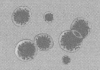

Early bacteria

Algae

Jellyfish-like animal

The formation of Earth marks the beginning of Precambrian Time. The first living things, which were bacteria, appeared in seas 3.5 billion years ago. Algae and fungi evolved 1 billion years ago. The earliest animals appeared 600 million years ago.

Cambrian Period

Opabinia

Sponges

Trilobite

Invertebrate sea animals such as sponges, snails, clams, and worms evolve.

Ordovician Period

Eumorphocystis

Jawless fish

The earliest fishes evolve. These were the first vertebrates. Although many new species of animals arise, many become extinct by the end of the period.

Silurian Period

Eurypterid

Arachnid

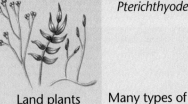

Land plants

Land plants and animals evolve. The plants are similar to present-day mosses. The animals resemble present-day insects and spiders.

Devonian Period

Shark

Pterichthyodes

Many types of fishes live in the seas. Early amphibians evolve. They are fish-like animals that have legs and can breathe air. The first ferns and cone-bearing plants grow on land.

Carboniferous Period

Tropical forest

Eryops

Cockroach

Tropical forests become widespread. Many different insects and amphibians evolve. The earliest reptiles appear.

| 544 million years ago | 245 million years ago | 66.4 million years ago |

MESOZOIC ERA

CENOZOIC ERA

| 286 | 245 | 208 | 144 | 66.4 | 1.6 |

| Permian Period | Triassic Period | Jurassic Period | Cretaceous Period | Tertiary Period | Quaternary Period |

Staurikosaurus

Haramiya

Magnolia

Saber-toothed cat

Megazostrodon

Coryphodon

Conifer

Stegosaurus

Crusafontia

Woolly mammoth

Dicynodon

Cycad

Mesohippus

Triceratops

Archaeopteryx

Homo sapiens

Seed plants become common. Insects and reptiles become widespread. Reptile-like mammals appear. At the end of the period, most sea animals and amphibians become extinct.

Reptiles such as turtles and crocodiles become common. The first dinosaurs evolve. Conifers and palmlike trees dominate forests.

Large dinosaurs roam the world. Mammals become more common and varied. The first birds appear.

The first flowering plants appear. There are more kinds of mammals than before. At the end of the period, dinosaurs become extinct.

New groups of mammals, including the first primates, appear. Flowering plants become the most common kind of plant.

Humans evolve. Later in the period, many large mammals, including woolly mammoths, become extinct.

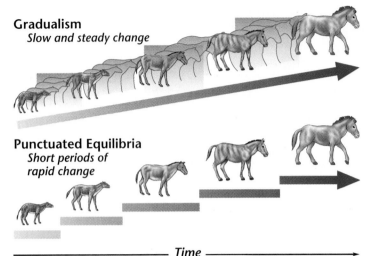

Gradualism
Slow and steady change

Punctuated Equilibria
*Short periods of
rapid change*

———— *Time* ————————→

Figure 12 According to the theory of gradualism, new species of horses evolved slowly and continuously. Intermediate forms were common. According to punctuated equilibria, new species evolved rapidly during short periods of time. Intermediate forms were rare.

How Fast Does Evolution Occur?

Because the fossil record is incomplete, many questions about evolution remain unanswered. For example, scientists cannot always tell from the fossil record how quickly a particular species evolved.

One theory, called **gradualism,** proposes that evolution occurs slowly but steadily. According to this theory, tiny changes in a species gradually add up to major changes over very long periods of time. This is how Darwin thought evolution occurred.

If the theory of gradualism is correct, intermediate forms of all species should have existed. However, the fossil record often shows no intermediate forms for long periods of time. Then, quite suddenly, fossils appear that are distinctly different. One possible explanation for the lack of intermediate forms is that the fossil record is incomplete. Scientists may eventually find more fossils to fill the gaps.

Rather than assuming that the fossil record is incomplete, two scientists, Stephen Jay Gould and Niles Eldridge, have developed a theory that agrees with the fossil data. According to the theory of **punctuated equilibria,** species evolve during short periods of rapid change. These periods of rapid change are separated by long periods of little or no change. According to this theory, species evolve quickly when groups become isolated and adapt to new environments.

Today most scientists think that evolution can occur gradually at some times and fairly rapidly at others. Both forms of evolution seem to have occurred during Earth's long history.

Section 2 Review

1. Describe how fossils form in sedimentary rock.
2. Explain the process of absolute dating.
3. What is the fossil record? What does the fossil record reveal about extinct species?
4. **Thinking Critically Comparing and Contrasting** How are the theories of gradualism and punctuated equilibria similar? How are they different?

Science at Home

Make Your Mark With a family member, spread some mud in a shallow flat-bottomed pan. Smooth the surface of the mud. Use your fingertips to make "footprints" across the mud. Let the mud dry and harden, so that the footprints become permanent. Explain to your family how this is similar to the way some fossils form.

SECTION 3 Other Evidence for Evolution

DISCOVER ⋯ ACTIVITY

How Can You Classify Species?

1. Collect six to eight different pens. Each pen will represent a different species of similar organisms.

2. Choose a trait that varies among your pen species, such as size or ink color. Using this trait, try to divide the pen species into two groups.

3. Now choose another trait. Divide each group into two smaller groups.

Think It Over

Classifying Which of the pen species share the most characteristics? What might the similarities suggest about how the pen species evolved?

Do you know anyone who has had their appendix out? The appendix is a tiny organ attached to the large intestine. You might think that having a part of the body removed would cause a problem. After all, you need your heart, lungs, stomach and other body parts to live. However, this is not the case with the appendix. In humans, the appendix does not seem to have much function. In some other species of mammals, though, the appendix is much larger and plays an important role in digestion. To scientists, this information about modern-day organisms provides clues about their ancestors and their relationships.

The appendix is just one example of how modern-day organisms can provide clues about evolution. By comparing organisms, scientists can infer how closely related the organisms are in an evolutionary sense. **Scientists compare body structures, development before birth, and DNA sequences to determine the evolutionary relationships among organisms.**

Similarities in Body Structure

Scientists long ago began to compare the body structures of living species to look for clues about evolution. In fact, this is how Darwin came to understand that evolution had occurred on the Galapagos Islands. An organism's body structure is its basic body plan, such as how its bones are arranged. Fishes, amphibians, reptiles, birds, and mammals, for example, all have a similar body

GUIDE FOR READING

◆ What evidence from modern-day organisms can help scientists determine evolutionary relationships among groups?

Reading Tip As you read, use the headings to make an outline about the different types of evidence for evolution.

Chapter 5 **165**

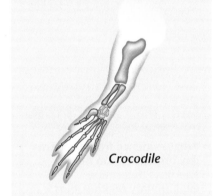
structure—an internal skeleton with a backbone. This is why scientists classify all five groups of animals together as vertebrates. Presumably, these groups all inherited these similarities in structure from an early vertebrate ancestor that they shared.

Look closely at the structure of the bones in the bird's wing, dolphin's flipper, and dog's leg shown in Figure 13. Notice that the bones in the forelimbs of these three animals are arranged in a similar way. These similarities provide evidence that these three organisms all evolved from a common ancestor. Similar structures that related species have inherited from a common ancestor are called **homologous structures** (hoh MAHL uh gus).

Sometimes scientists find fossil evidence that supports the evidence provided by homologous structures. For example, scientists have recently found fossils of ancient whale-like creatures. The fossils show that the ancestors of today's whales had legs and walked on land. This evidence supports other evidence that whales and humans share a common ancestor.

☑ *Checkpoint* *What information do homologous structures reveal?*

Similarities in Early Development

Scientists can also make inferences about evolutionary relationships by comparing the early development of different organisms. Suppose you were asked to compare an adult turtle, a chicken, and a rat. You would probably say they look quite different from each other. However, during early development, these three organisms go through similar stages, as you can see

Figure 13 A bird's wing, dolphin's flipper, and dog's leg are all adapted to performing different tasks. However, the structure of the bones in each forelimb is very similar. These homologous structures provide evidence that these animals evolved from a common ancestor. *Observing What similarities in structure do the three forelimbs share?*

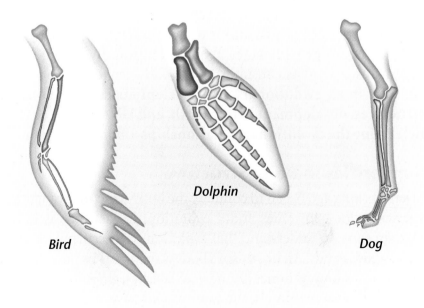

Bird

Dolphin

Dog

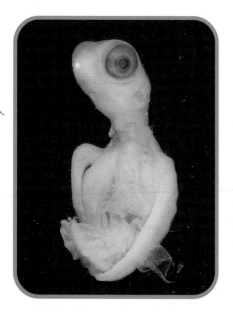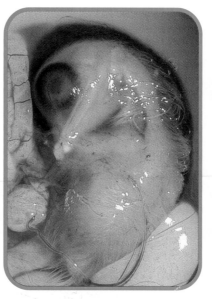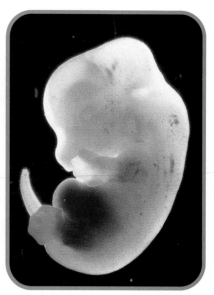

Figure 14 Turtles (left), chickens (center), and rats (right) look similar during the earliest stages of development. These similarities provide evidence that these three animals evolved from a common ancestor.

in Figure 14. For example, during the early stages of development all three organisms have a tail and tiny gill slits in their throats. These similarities suggest that these three vertebrate species are related and share a common ancestor.

When scientists study early development more closely, they notice that the turtle appears more similar to the chicken than it does to the rat. This evidence supports the conclusion that turtles are more closely related to chickens than they are to rats.

Similarities in DNA

Why do related species have similar body structures and development patterns? Scientists infer that the species inherited many of the same genes from a common ancestor. Recently, scientists have begun to compare the genes of different species to determine how closely related the species are.

Recall that genes are made of DNA. By comparing the sequence of nitrogen bases in the DNA of different species, scientists can infer how closely related the species are. The more similar the sequences, the more closely related the species are.

Recall also that the DNA bases along a gene specify what type of protein will be produced. Thus, scientists can also compare the order of amino acids in a protein to see how closely related two species are.

Sometimes DNA evidence does not confirm earlier conclusions about relationships between species. For example, aside from its long nose, the tiny elephant shrew looks very similar to rodents such as mice. Because of this, biologists used to think that the elephant shrew was closely related to rodents. But when scientists compared DNA from elephant shrews to that of both

Figure 15 Because of its appearance, the tiny elephant shrew was thought to be closely related to mice and other rodents. Surprisingly, DNA comparisons showed that the elephant shrew is actually more closely related to elephants.

rodents and elephants, they got a surprise. The elephant shrew's DNA was more similar to the elephant's DNA than it was to the rodent's DNA. Scientists now think that elephant shrews are more closely related to elephants than to rodents.

INTEGRATING TECHNOLOGY Recently, scientists have developed techniques that allow them to extract, or remove, DNA from fossils. Using these techniques, scientists have now extracted DNA from fossils of bones, teeth, and plants, and from insects trapped in amber. The DNA from fossils has provided scientists with new evidence about evolution.

Combining the Evidence

Scientists have combined evidence from fossils, body structures, early development, and DNA and protein sequences to determine the evolutionary relationships among species. In most cases, DNA and protein sequences have confirmed conclusions based on earlier evidence. For example, recent DNA comparisons show that dogs are more similar to wolves than they are to coyotes. Scientists had already reached this conclusion based on similarities in the structure and development of these three species.

Another example of how scientists combined evidence from different sources is shown in the branching tree in Figure 16. A **branching tree** is a diagram that shows how scientists think different groups of organisms are related. Based on similar body structures, lesser pandas were thought to be closely related to giant pandas. The two panda species also resemble both bears and raccoons. Until recently, scientists were not sure how these four groups were related. DNA analysis and other methods have shown that giant pandas and lesser pandas are not closely related. Instead, giant pandas are more closely related to bears, while lesser pandas are more closely related to raccoons.

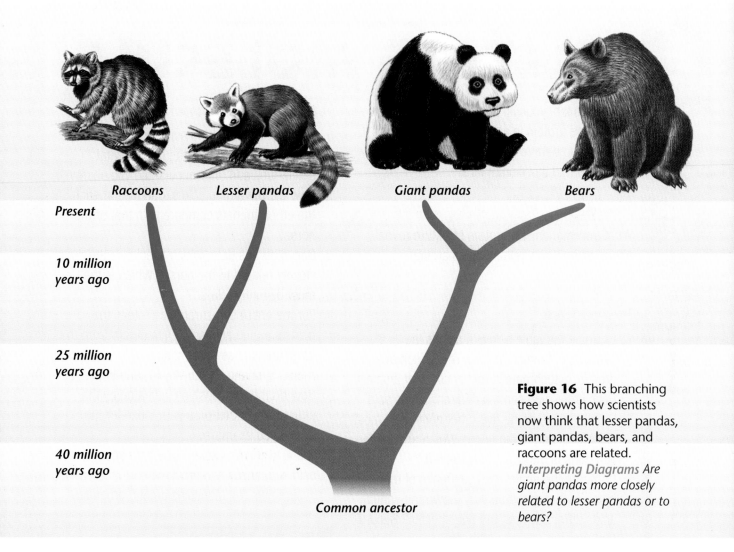

Raccoons Lesser pandas Giant pandas Bears

Present

10 million years ago

25 million years ago

40 million years ago

Common ancestor

Figure 16 This branching tree shows how scientists now think that lesser pandas, giant pandas, bears, and raccoons are related. *Interpreting Diagrams Are giant pandas more closely related to lesser pandas or to bears?*

 Section 3 Review

1. Name three types of evidence from modern-day organisms that scientists use to determine evolutionary relationships.

2. What are homologous structures?

3. What information did scientists learn by comparing the early developmental stages of turtles, chickens, and rats?

4. If two species are closely related, what would you expect a comparison of their DNA base sequences to reveal?

5. **Thinking Critically Making Judgments** Most scientists today consider similarities in DNA to be the best indicator of how closely two species are related. Why do you think this is the case?

Check Your Progress

CHAPTER PROJECT

You should be completing construction of the time line that covers 5 billion years. Now begin work on the time line showing 600 million years. This version is a magnified view of one part of the first time line. It will give you additional space to show what happened in the more recent years of Earth's history. (*Hint:* Prepare drawings to show how life forms on Earth were changing. Also, try to include three or more events not mentioned in the text.)

Skills Lab

TELLTALE MOLECULES

In this lab, you will compare the structure of one protein in a variety of animals. You'll use the data to draw conclusions about how closely related those animals are.

Problem

What information can protein structure reveal about evolutionary relationships among organisms?

Procedure

1. Examine the table below. It shows the sequence of amino acids in one region of a protein, cytochrome c, for six different animals. Each letter represents a different amino acid.
2. Predict which of the five other animals is most closely related to the horse. Which animal do you think is most distantly related?
3. Compare the amino acid sequence of the horse to that of the donkey. How many amino acids differ between the two species? Record that number in your notebook.
4. Compare the amino acid sequences of each of the other animals to that of the horse. Record the number of differences in your notebook.

Analyze and Conclude

1. Which animal's amino acid sequence was most similar to that of the horse? What similarities and difference(s) did you observe?
2. How did the amino acid sequences of each of the other animals compare with that of the horse?
3. Based on this data, which species is the most closely related to the horse? Which is the most distantly related?
4. For the entire cytochrome c protein, the horse's amino acid sequence differs from the other animals as follows: donkey, 1 difference; rabbit, 6; snake, 22; turtle, 11; and whale, 5. How do the relationships indicated by the entire protein compare with those for the region you examined?
5. **Think About It** Explain why data about amino acid sequences can provide information about evolutionary relationships among organisms.

More to Explore

Use the amino acid data to construct a branching tree that includes horses, donkeys, and snakes. The tree should show one way that the three species could have evolved from a common ancestor.

Section of Cytochrome c Protein in Animals														
	Amino Acid Position													
Animal	39	40	41	42	43	44	45	46	47	48	49	50	51	52	53
Horse	A	B	C	D	E	F	G	H	I	J	K	L	M	N	O
Donkey	A	B	C	D	E	F	G	H	Z	J	K	L	M	N	O
Rabbit	A	B	C	D	E	Y	G	H	Z	J	K	L	M	N	O
Snake	A	B	C	D	E	Y	G	H	Z	J	K	W	M	N	O
Turtle	A	B	C	D	E	V	G	H	Z	J	K	U	M	N	O
Whale	A	B	C	D	E	Y	G	H	Z	J	K	L	M	N	O

Fr...

About ...
have ...
may ...
than ...
came ...
in tu...
ate th...
stran...
dogs ...

O...
of hu...
the tr...
and h...
were ...
a kee...
dogs....
range...
Saint ...
fifty ...

To...
appea...
such ...
partic...

In Lab...
for da...
over t...

SECTION 1 — Darwin's Voyage

Key Ideas

◆ Darwin thought that species gradually changed over many generations as they became better adapted to new conditions. This process is called evolution.

◆ Darwin's observations led him to propose that evolution occurs through natural selection. Natural selection occurs due to overproduction, competition, and variations.

◆ Only traits controlled by genes can change over time as a result of natural selection.

◆ If a group of individuals remains separated from the rest of its species long enough to evolve different traits, a new species can form.

Key Terms

species	evolution	natural selection
adaptation	scientific theory	variation

SECTION 2 — The Fossil Record

INTEGRATING EARTH SCIENCE

Key Ideas

◆ Most fossils form when organisms die and sediments bury them. The sediments harden, preserving parts of the organisms.

◆ Relative dating determines which of two fossils is older and which is younger. Absolute dating determines the actual age of a fossil.

◆ Fossils help scientists understand how extinct organisms looked and evolved.

◆ The Geologic Time Scale shows when during Earth's 4.6-billion-year history major groups of organisms evolved.

◆ Evolution has occurred gradually at some times and fairly rapidly at other times.

Key Terms

fossil	radioactive element
sedimentary rock	half-life
petrified fossil	fossil record
mold	extinct
cast	gradualism
relative dating	punctuated equilibria
absolute dating	

SECTION 3 — Other Evidence for Evolution

Key Ideas

◆ By comparing modern-day organisms, scientists can infer how closely related they are in an evolutionary sense.

◆ Homologous structures can provide evidence of how species are related and of how they evolved from a common ancestor.

◆ Similarities in early developmental stages are evidence that species are related and shared a common ancestor.

◆ Scientists can compare DNA and protein sequences to determine more precisely how species are related.

◆ A branching tree is a diagram that shows how scientists think different groups of organisms are related.

Key Terms
homologous structure
branching tree

Organizing Information

Flowchart Copy the flowchart about natural selection onto a separate sheet of paper. Complete the flowchart by writing a sentence describing each factor that leads to natural selection. Then add a title. (For more on flowcharts, see the Skills Handbook.)

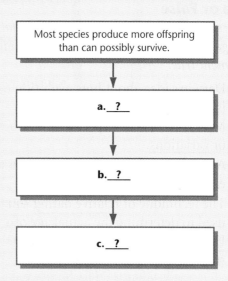

Most species produce more offspring than can possibly survive.

↓

a. ?

↓

b. ?

↓

c. ?

Golden Retriever
Great Britain, A.D. 1870s
Lord Tweedsmouth developed this breed to help hunters retrieve waterfowl and other small animals.

Border Collie
Great Britain, after A.D. 1100
This breed was developed in the counties near the border of England and Scotland for herding sheep. The Border collie's ancestors were cross-breeds of local sheepdogs and dogs brought to Scotland by the Vikings.

Dachshund
Germany, A.D. 1700s
These dogs were bred to catch badgers or rats. Their short legs and long body can fit into a badger's burrow. In fact, in German the word *Dachshund* means "badger dog."

Basset Hound
France, A.D. 1600s
Second only to the bloodhound at following a scent, the basset hound has short legs and a compact body that help it run through underbrush.

Greyhound
Egypt, 3500 B.C.
These speedy, slender hounds were bred for chasing prey. Today, greyhounds are famous as racers.

W
OF

✦ A
s

✦ A
C

✦ A
s

✦ A

✦ A

✦ A

Mo
ago
Egy
cha

Dogs and People

Over thousands of years, people have developed many different breeds of dogs. Each of the dogs shown on the map was bred for a purpose—hunting, herding, guarding, pulling sleds—as well as companionship. Every breed has its own story.

Siberian Husky
Siberia, 1000 B.C.
The Chukchi people of northeastern Siberia used these strong working dogs to pull sleds long distances across the snow.

Pekingese
China, A.D. 700s
These lapdogs were bred as pets in ancient China. One Chinese name for a Pekingese means "lion dog," which refers to the dog's long, golden mane.

Chow Chow
China, 150 B.C.
Chow chows, the working dogs of ancient China, worked as hunters, herders, and guard dogs.

Akita
Japan, A.D. 1600s
This breed was developed in the cold mountains of northern Japan as a guard dog and hunting dog. The Akita is able to hunt in deep snow and is also a powerful swimmer.

Lhasa Apso
Tibet, A.D. 1100
This breed has a long, thick coat to protect it from the cold air of the high Tibetan plateau. In spite of its small size, the Lhasa apso guarded homes and temples.

Social Studies Activity

Draw a time line that shows the approximate date of origin of different breeds of domestic dogs from 7000 B.C. to the present. Use the information on the map to fill out your time line. Include information about where each breed was developed.

Picking a Puppy

People look for different traits in the dogs they choose. Here is how one expert selected his dog based on good breeding and personality.

James Herriot, a veterinarian in England, had owned several dogs during his lifetime. But he had always wanted a Border terrier. These small, sturdy dogs are descendants of working terrier breeds that lived on the border of England and Scotland. For centuries they were used to hunt foxes, rats, and other small animals. In this story, Herriot and his wife Helen follow up on an advertisement for Border terrier puppies.

Language Arts Activity

James Herriot describes this scene using dialog and first-person narrative. The narrative describes Herriot's feelings about a memorable event—finally finding the dog he had wanted for so long. Write a first-person narrative describing a memorable event in your life. You might choose a childhood memory or a personal achievement at school. What emotions did you feel? How did you make your decision? If possible, use dialog in your writing.

Border terrier ▶

She [Helen, his wife] turned to me and spoke agitatedly, "I've got Mrs. Mason on the line now. There's only one pup left out of the litter and there are people coming from as far as eighty miles away to see it. We'll have to hurry. What a long time you've been out there!"

We bolted our lunch and Helen, Rosie, granddaughter Emma and I drove out to Bedale. Mrs. Mason led us into the kitchen and pointed to a tiny brindle creature twisting and writhing under the table.

"That's him," she said.

I reached down and lifted the puppy as he curled his little body round, apparently trying to touch his tail with his nose. But that tail wagged furiously and the pink tongue was busy at my hand. I knew he was ours before my quick examination for hernia and overshot jaw.

The deal was quickly struck and we went outside to inspect the puppy's relations. His mother and grandmother were out there. They lived in little barrels which served as kennels and both of them darted out and stood up at our legs, tails lashing, mouths panting in delight. I felt vastly reassured. With happy, healthy ancestors like those I knew we had every chance of a first rate dog.

As we drove home with the puppy in Emma's arms, the warm thought came to me. The wheel had indeed turned. After nearly fifty years I had my Border terrier.

James Herriot was a country veterinarian in Yorkshire, England. In several popular books published in the 1970s and 1980s, he wrote warm, humorous stories about the animals he cared for. His book *All Creatures Great and Small* was the basis for a television series.

Breed	1970	1980	1990	1997
Poodle	265,879	92,250	71,757	54,773
Labrador Retriever	25,667	52,398	99,776	158,366
Cocker Spaniel	21,811	76,113	105,642	41,439

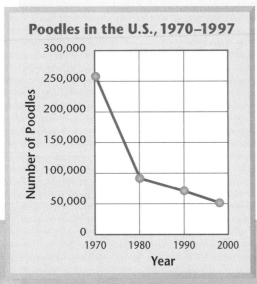

Poodles in the U.S., 1970–1997

Math Activity

The popularity of different breeds of dogs changes over time. For example, the line graph shows how the number of poodles registered with the American Kennel Club changed between 1970 and 1997. Use the table to create your own line graph for Labrador retrievers and cocker spaniels.

Which breed was more popular in 1980, Labrador retrievers or cocker spaniels? How has the number of Labrador retrievers changed from 1970 to 1997? How has the number of cocker spaniels changed over the same time?

Tie It Together

Best of Breed Show

In many places proud dog owners of all ages bring their animals to compete in dog shows. Organize your own dog show. With a partner, choose one specific breed of dog. Pick a breed shown on the map on pages 176–177, or use library resources to research another breed.

◆ Find out what the breed looks like, the time and place where it originated, and what traits it was first bred for.

◆ List your breed's characteristics, height, weight, and coloring.

◆ Research the breed's personality and behavior.

◆ Find out your breed's strengths. Learn what weakness may develop as a result of inbreeding.

◆ Make a poster for your breed. Include a drawing or photo and the information that you researched.

◆ With your class, organize the dog displays into categories of breeds, such as hunting dogs, herding dogs, and toy dogs.

If you've ever had chicken pox, this virus was responsible for your illness.

www.phschool.com

SECTION

1 Classifying Organisms

Discover **Can You Organize a Junk Drawer?**
Sharpen Your Skills **Observing**
Science at Home **Kitchen Classification**

SECTION

2 The Six Kingdoms

Discover **Which Organism Goes Where?**

SECTION

3 Bacteria

Discover **How Fast Do Bacteria Multiply?**
Sharpen Your Skills **Graphing**
Try This **Bacteria for Breakfast**
Science at Home **Helpful Bacteria**
Real-World Lab **Do Disinfectants Work?**

Be a Disease Detective

The virus pictured on this page may look harmless, but it's not. If you've ever had chicken pox, you've experienced it firsthand. Soon after the virus enters your body, red spots appear on your skin, and you begin to itch. As the virus reproduces inside your body, you become sick. But even though a virus can reproduce, scientists do not consider it a living thing. However, bacteria, which can also cause disease, are living things.

Not too long ago, catching viral and bacterial "childhood diseases" was a routine part of growing up. Those diseases included chicken pox, mumps, and pertussis (whooping cough). In this project, you will select a childhood disease to investigate. You'll then survey people to learn what they know about the disease.

Your Goal To survey people of different ages about a childhood disease.

To complete this project successfully, you must
- select and research one disease to learn more about it
- prepare a questionnaire to survey people about their knowledge and experience with the disease
- question a total of 30 people in different age groups, and report any patterns that you find

Get Started With classmates, make a list of childhood diseases. Choose one disease to research. Also list the steps involved in a survey. What questions will you need to ask? How will you select the people for your survey? Draft your questionnaire.

Check Your Progress You'll be working on this project as you study this chapter. To keep your project on track, look for Check Your Progress boxes at the following points.

Section 2 Review, page 191: Write your questionnaire, and identify the people to survey.

Section 4 Review, page 211: Analyze your survey results.

Present Your Project At the end of the chapter (page 215), you will present your survey results to your classmates.

SECTION 4 Integrating Health
Viruses

Discover **Can You Cure a Cold?**
Try This **Modeling a Virus**
Skills Lab **How Many Viruses Fit on a Pin?**

Classifying Organisms

Can You Organize a Junk Drawer?

1. Your teacher will give you some items that you might find in the junk drawer of a desk. Your job is to organize the items.

2. Examine the objects and decide on three groups into which you can sort them.

3. Place each object into one of the groups based on how the item's features match the characteristics of the group.

4. Compare your grouping system with those of your classmates.

Think It Over

Classifying Explain which grouping system seemed most useful.

GUIDE FOR READING

◆ Why do scientists organize living things into groups?

◆ What is the relationship between classification and evolution?

Reading Tip Before you read, make a list of the boldfaced vocabulary terms. As you read, write the meaning of each term in your own words.

Suppose you had only ten minutes to run into a supermarket to get what you need—milk and tomatoes. Could you do it? In most supermarkets this would be an easy task. First, you might go to the dairy aisle and find the milk. Then you'd go to the produce aisle and find the tomatoes. Finally, you'd pay for the items and leave the store.

Now imagine shopping for these same items in a market where the shelves were organized in a random manner. To find what you need, you'd have to search through boxes of cereal, cans of tuna, bins of apples, and much more. You could be there for a long time!

Why Do Scientists Classify?

Just as shopping can be a problem in a disorganized store, finding information about one of the millions of kinds of organisms can also be a problem. Today, scientists have identified at least 2.5 million kinds of organisms on Earth. This number includes all forms of life, from plants and animals to bacteria. It is important for biologists to have all these living things organized.

People organize a lot of things into groups. For example, if a friend asks you what kind of music you like, you might say that you like country or rock and roll music. Although you may not know it, you have grouped the music you like. **Classification** is the process of grouping things based on their similarities.

▼ Vegetables organized by type

Biologists use classification to organize living things into groups so that organisms are easier to study. The scientific study of how living things are classified is called **taxonomy** (tak SAHN uh mee). Taxonomy is useful because once an organism is classified, a scientist knows a lot about that organism. For example, if you know that crows are classified as birds, you know that crows have wings, feathers, and beaks.

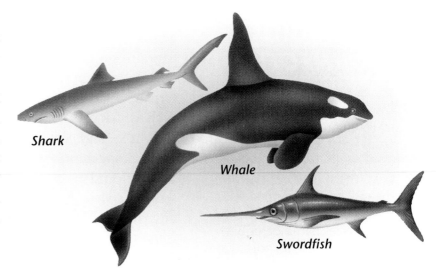

Shark

Whale

Swordfish

Figure 1 Aristotle would have classified this shark, whale, and swordfish together because they all swim. However, he would have separated them into subgroups because they differ from one another in many ways.
Classifying List two differences that would place these animals into separate subgroups.

Early Classification Systems

The first scientist to develop a classification system for organisms was the Greek scholar Aristotle. In the fourth century B.C., Aristotle observed many animals. He recorded each animal's appearance, behavior, and movement. Then he divided animals into three groups: those that fly, those that swim, and those that walk, crawl, or run.

Aristotle could see that even though all the organisms in a group moved in a similar way, they were different in many other ways. So he used their differences to further divide each group into subgroups—smaller groups of organisms that shared other similarities.

Aristotle's method of using careful observations as the basis for classification and his idea of creating subgroups are still used today. However, organisms are no longer classified into large groups on the basis of how they move or where they live.

✓ *Checkpoint* *What were the three major groups of animals in Aristotle's system of classification?*

The Classification System of Linnaeus

In the 1750s, a Swedish scientist named Carolus Linnaeus expanded on Aristotle's ideas of classification. Like Aristotle, Linnaeus used observations as the basis of his system. He wrote descriptions of organisms from his observations, and placed organisms in groups based on their observable features.

Linnaeus also used his observations to devise a naming system for organisms. In Linnaeus's naming system, called **binomial nomenclature** (by NOH mee ul NOH men klay chur), each organism is given a two-part name.

You don't have to understand Latin to know that you should avoid an organism named *Ursus horribilis. Ursus horribilis* is commonly known as a grizzly bear. The Latin word *ursus* means "bear" and *horribilis* means "horrible or feared."

A species name describes an organism like an adjective describes the noun it modifies. Some names describe a specific trait; others tell who discovered the organism. Other names tell you where the organism lives. Guess where you'd find the plant *Viola missouriensis.*

In Your Journal

Look up the meanings of these species names: *Musca domestica, Hirudo medicinalis,* and *Cornus florida.* Then find some English words derived from the Latin terms.

The first part of an organism's scientific name is its genus. A **genus** (JEE nus) (plural *genera*) is a classification grouping that contains similar, closely related organisms. For example, pumas, ocelots, and house cats are all classified in the genus *Felis.* Organisms that are classified in the genus *Felis* share features such as sharp, retractable claws and behaviors such as hunting.

The second part of an organism's scientific name is its species name. A **species** (SPEE sheez) is a group of similar organisms that can mate and produce fertile offspring in nature. A species name sets one species in a genus apart from another. The species name often describes a distinctive feature of an organism, such as where it lives or its color. For example, the scientific name for many pumas, or mountain lions, is *Felis concolor. Concolor* means "the same color" in Latin. The scientific name for some ocelots is *Felis pardalis.* The word *pardalis* means "spotted like a panther" in Latin. The scientific name for house cats is *Felis domesticus.* The species name *domesticus* means "of the house" in Latin.

Linnaeus's system might remind you of the way you are named because you, also, have a two-part name made up of your first name and your family name. Your two-part name distinguishes you from others. In a similar way, binomial nomenclature ensures that a combination of two names distinguishes one kind of organism from another. Together, a genus and a species name identify one kind of organism.

Figure 2 These animals belong to the genus *Felis.* Their species names distinguish them from one another. **A.** This puma's coat is one color, as indicated by its species name *concolor.* **B.** This ocelot has a spotted coat, described by its species name *pardalis.* **C.** The species name of this kitten is *domesticus,* which indicates that it is a house cat.

Notice that both the genus and species names are Latin words. Linnaeus used Latin words in his naming system because Latin was the language that scientists communicated in during that time. Notice also that a complete scientific name is written in italics. The genus is capitalized while the species name begins with a small letter.

Binomial nomenclature makes it easy for scientists to communicate about an organism because everyone uses the same name for the same organism. For example, people call the tree shown in Figure 3 by any one of a number of common names: loblolly pine, longstraw pine, or Indian pine. Fortunately, this tree has only one scientific name, *Pinus taeda*.

✓ *Checkpoint* *Which part of a scientific name is like your first name? Your family name?*

Classification Today

At the time that Linnaeus developed his classification system, people thought that species never change. They could see that some organisms were similar. They thought that these organisms had always been similar, yet distinct from each other.

The theory of evolution changed the way biologists think about classification. Today, scientists understand that certain organisms are similar because they share a common ancestor. When organisms share a common ancestor, they share an evolutionary history. Today's system of classification considers the history of a species when classifying the species. **Species with similar evolutionary histories are classified more closely together.**

Levels of Classification

The classification system that scientists use today is based on the contributions of both Aristotle and Linnaeus. But today's classification system uses a series of seven levels to classify organisms. To help you understand the levels in classification, imagine a room filled with everybody who lives in your state. First, all of the people who live in your *town* raise their hands. Next, those people who live in your *neighborhood* raise their hands. Then, those who live on your *street* raise their hands. Finally, those who live in your *house* raise their hands. Each time, fewer people raise their hands. But you would be in all of the groups. The most general group you belong to is the state. The most specific group is the house. The more levels you share with others, the more you have in common with them.

Figure 3 Although there are many common names for this tree, it has only one scientific name. *Making Generalizations What is the advantage of having scientific names for organisms?*

The Seven Levels of Classification Modern biologists classify organisms into the seven levels shown in Figure 4. Of course, organisms are not grouped by where they live but rather by their shared characteristics. First an organism is placed in a broad group, which in turn is divided into more specific groups.

A kingdom is the broadest level of organization. Within a kingdom, there are phyla (FY luh) (singular *phylum*). Within each phylum are classes. Each class is divided into orders. Each order contains families, and each family contains at least one genus. Finally, within a genus, there are species. The more classification levels that two organisms share, the more characteristics they have in common.

Classifying an Owl Take a closer look at Figure 4 to see how the levels of classification apply to the great horned owl, a member of the animal kingdom. Look at the top row of the figure. As you can see, a wide variety of organisms also belong to the animal kingdom. Now, look at the phylum, class, and order levels. Notice that as you move down the levels in the figure, there are fewer kinds of organisms in each group. More importantly, the organisms in each group look similar and have more in common with one another. For example, the class Aves includes all birds, while the order Strigiformes includes only owls. Different owls have more in common with each other than they do with other birds.

✓ *Checkpoint* List the seven levels of classification from the broadest to the most specific.

Using the Classification System

You may be wondering why you should care about taxonomy. Suppose you wake up and feel something tickling your ankle. You fling back the covers and stare at a tiny creature crouching in the sheets by your right foot. Although it's only the size of a small melon seed, you don't like the looks of its two claws waving at you. Then, in a flash, it's gone—darting off under the safety of your covers.

How could you learn the identity of the organism that woke you? One way to identify it would be to use a field guide. Field guides are books with illustrations that highlight differences between similar-looking organisms.

Another tool you could use to identify the organism is called a taxonomic key. A **taxonomic key** is a series of paired statements that describe the physical characteristics of different organisms.

Kingdom Animalia

Phylum Chordata

Class Aves

Order Strigiformes

Family Strygidae

Genus *Bubo*

Species *Bubo virginianus*

Figure 4 Scientists use seven levels to classify organisms such as the great horned owl. Notice that, as you move down the levels, the number of organisms decreases. The organisms at lower levels share more characteristics with each other. *Interpreting Diagrams How many levels do a robin and the great horned owl share?*

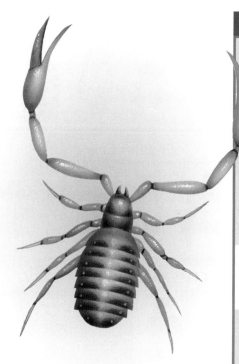

Taxonomic Key

Step 1

1a. Has 8 legs	Go to Step 2.
1b. Has more than 8 legs	Go to Step 3.

Step 2

2a. Has one oval-shaped body region	Go to Step 4.
2b. Has two body regions	Go to Step 5.

Step 3

3a. Has one pair of legs on each body segment	Centipede
3b. Has two pairs of legs on each body segment	Millipede

Step 4

4a. Is less than 1 millimeter long	Mite
4b. Is more than 1 millimeter long	Tick

Step 5

5a. Has clawlike pincers	Go to Step 6.
5b. Has no clawlike pincers	Spider

Step 6

6a. Has a long tail with a stinger	Scorpion
6b. Has no tail or stinger	Pseudoscorpion

Figure 5 A taxonomic key is a series of paired statements that describe the physical characteristics of different organisms. There are six pairs of statements in this key. *Drawing Conclusions What is the identity of the organism shown in the picture?*

The taxonomic key in Figure 5 can help you identify the organism in your bed. First, read the paired statements numbered 1a and 1b. Notice that the two statements are opposites. Decide which of the two statements applies to the organism. Then, follow the direction at the end of that statement. For example, if the organism has 8 legs, follow the direction at the end of statement 1a, which says "Go to Step 2." Continue this process until you learn the identity of the organism.

Section 1 Review

1. Why is it important for biologists to classify organisms into groups?
2. How is an organism's evolutionary history related to the way in which it is classified?
3. Explain Linnaeus's contribution to taxonomy.
4. **Thinking Critically Applying Concepts** Create a taxonomic key that could help identify a piece of fruit as either an apple, an orange, a strawberry, or a banana.

Science at Home

Kitchen Classification With a family member, go on a "classification hunt" in the kitchen. Look in your cabinets, refrigerator, and drawers to discover what classification systems your family uses to organize items. Discuss the advantages of organizing items in your kitchen in the way that you do. Then explain to your family member the importance of classification in biology.

DISCOVER ··· ACTIVITY

Which Organism Goes Where?

1. Your teacher will give you some organisms to observe. Two of the organisms are classified in the same kingdom.

2. Observe the organisms. Decide which organisms might belong in the same kingdom. Write the reasons for your decision. Wash your hands after handling the organisms.

3. Discuss your decision and reasoning with your classmates.

Think It Over
Forming Operational Definitions What characteristics do you think define the kingdom into which you placed the two organisms?

When Linnaeus developed his system of classification, there were two kingdoms: plant and animal. But, the use of the microscope led to the discovery of new organisms and the identification of differences among cells. A two-kingdom system was no longer useful. **Today, the system of classification includes six kingdoms: archaebacteria, eubacteria, protists, fungi, plants, and animals.** Organisms are placed into kingdoms based on their type of cells, their ability to make food, and the number of cells in their bodies.

GUIDE FOR READING

◆ What are the six kingdoms into which all organisms are grouped?

Reading Tip Before you read the section, make a list of the headings. As you read, list the characteristics of organisms in each kingdom.

Archaebacteria

In 1983, scientists took a water sample from a spot deep in the Pacific Ocean where hot gases and molten rock boiled into the ocean from Earth's interior. To their surprise, they discovered some unicellular organisms in the water sample. Today, scientists classify these tiny organisms in a kingdom called Archaebacteria (ahr kee bak TEER ee uh), which means "ancient bacteria." Archaebacteria already existed on Earth for billions of years before dinosaurs appeared. Scientists think that today's archaebacteria might resemble some of Earth's early life forms.

Figure 6 Heat-loving archaebacteria thrive in this hot spring in Yellowstone National Park.

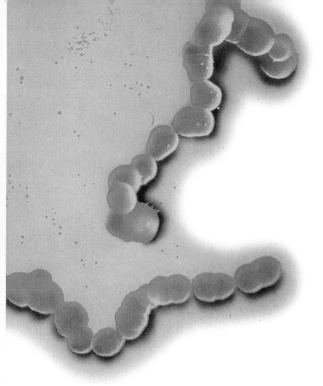

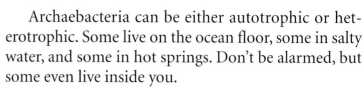

Figure 7 Most eubacteria are helpful. However, these eubacteria are *Streptococci*, which can give you strep throat! *Classifying What characteristics do eubacteria share?*

Archaebacteria can be either autotrophic or heterotrophic. Some live on the ocean floor, some in salty water, and some in hot springs. Don't be alarmed, but some even live inside you.

Archaebacteria are prokaryotes. As you read in Chapter 1, prokaryotes are organisms whose cells lack a nucleus. In prokaryotes, nucleic acids—the chemical instructions that direct the cell's activities—are not contained within a nucleus.

Eubacteria

What do the bacteria that produce yogurt have in common with the bacteria that give you strep throat? They both belong to the kingdom known as Eubacteria (yoo bak TEER ee uh). Like archaebacteria, eubacteria are unicellular prokaryotes. And like archaebacteria, some eubacteria are autotrophs while others are heterotrophs. Eubacteria are classified in their own kingdom, however, because their chemical makeup is different from that of archaebacteria. You will learn more about eubacteria in the next section.

✓ *Checkpoint* **How are eubacteria similar to archae-bacteria? How are they different?**

Protists

Have you ever walked along a beach scattered with dark clumps of seaweed? The tangled piles of seaweed are classified in the same kingdom as the unicellular organism in Figure 8. Both are protists (PROH tists). The protist kingdom is sometimes called the "odds and ends" kingdom because its organisms are very different from one another. For example, some protists are autotrophs, while others are heterotrophs. Also, although most protists are unicellular, some, such as the organisms that are commonly called seaweeds, are multicellular.

You may be wondering why those protists that are unicellular are not classified in one of the kingdoms of bacteria. It is because, unlike bacteria, protists are eukaryotes—organisms with cells that contain nuclei.

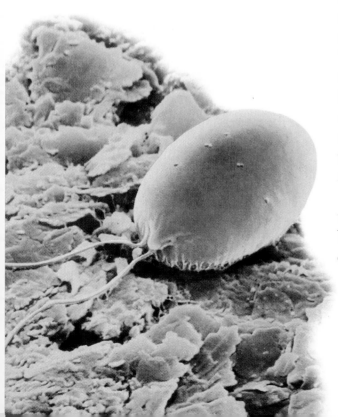

Figure 8 The protist kingdom contains diverse organisms. This unicellular green protist, which lives in fresh water, is called *Chlamydomonas.*

Fungi

If you have ever seen mushrooms, you have seen fungi (FUN jy). Mushrooms, molds, and mildew are all fungi. Most fungi are multicellular eukaryotes. A few, such as yeast, are unicellular eukaryotes. Fungi are found almost everywhere on land, but only a few live in fresh water. All fungi are heterotrophs. Most fungi feed on dead or decaying organisms. The cuplike fungus you see in Figure 9 obtains its food from the parts of plants that are decaying in the soil.

Plants

Dandelions on a lawn, mosses in a forest, and tomatoes in a garden are familiar kinds of plants. All plants are multicellular eukaryotes. In addition, plants are autotrophs that make their own food. Without plants, life on Earth would not exist. Plants feed almost all of the heterotrophs on Earth. The plant kingdom includes a variety of organisms. Some plants produce flowers, while others do not. Some plants, such as giant sequoia trees, can grow very tall. Others, like mosses, never grow taller than a few centimeters.

Animals

A dog, a flea on the dog's ear, and a rabbit the dog chases have much in common because all are animals. All animals are multicellular eukaryotes. In addition, all animals are heterotrophs. Animals have different adaptations that allow them to locate food, capture it, eat it, and digest it. You will learn more about these adaptations in Chapters 10 through 14 of this book. Members of the animal kingdom are found in diverse environments on Earth.

Figure 9 The animal you see peeking out of this cuplike fungus is a poison arrow frog. These organisms live in the forests of Central America.
Interpreting Photographs Which organisms in the photograph are heterotrophs?

Section 2 Review

1. List the six kingdoms into which all organisms are classified.
2. Which two kingdoms include only prokaryotes?
3. Which kingdoms include only heterotrophs?
4. **Thinking Critically Classifying** In a rain forest, you see an unfamiliar green organism. As you watch, an ant walks onto one of its cuplike leaves. The leaf closes and traps the ant. Do you have enough information to classify this organism? Why or why not?

Check Your Progress

CHAPTER PROJECT

By now, you should have a draft of the questions you will ask in your survey. Have your teacher review your questions. (*Hint*: Design the questionnaire so that you can easily record and tally the responses. Test your survey on a friend to make sure the questions are clear.)

SECTION 3 Bacteria

DISCOVER

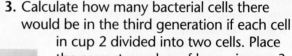

How Fast Do Bacteria Multiply?

1. Your teacher will give you some beans and paper cups. Number the cups 1 through 8. Each bean will represent a bacterial cell.

2. Put one bean into cup 1 to represent the first generation of bacteria. Approximately every 20 minutes, a bacterial cell reproduces by dividing into two cells. Put two beans into cup 2 to represent the second generation of bacteria.

3. Calculate how many bacterial cells there would be in the third generation if each cell in cup 2 divided into two cells. Place the correct number of beans in cup 3.

4. Repeat Step 3 five more times. All the cups should now contain beans. How many cells are in the eighth generation? How much time has elapsed since the first generation?

Think It Over

Inferring Based on this activity, explain why the number of bacteria can increase rapidly in a short period of time.

GUIDE FOR READING

◆ How are the cells of bacteria different from those of all other organisms?

◆ What roles do bacteria play in people's lives?

Reading Tip Before you read, make a list of the boldfaced vocabulary words in the section. Predict the meaning of each word. As you read, check your predictions.

You may not know it, but seconds after you were born, tiny organisms surrounded and invaded your body. Today, millions of these organisms coat your skin. As you read this page, they swarm inside your nose, throat, and mouth. In fact, there are more of these organisms living in your mouth than there are people who are living on Earth. You don't see or feel these organisms because they are very small. But you cannot escape them. They are found nearly everywhere on Earth—in soil, rocks, Arctic ice, volcanoes, and in all living things. These organisms are bacteria.

The Bacterial Cell

Although there are many bacteria on Earth, they were not discovered until the late 1600s. In Chapter 1 you read about Anton van Leeuwenhoek, who built microscopes as a hobby. One day, while he was using one of his microscopes to look at scrapings from his teeth, he saw some tiny organisms in the sample. However, because his microscopes were not very powerful, Leeuwenhoek could not see any details inside these tiny organisms.

◀ **Bacteria on the surface of a human tooth**

If Leeuwenhoek had owned one of the high-powered microscopes in use today, he would have seen the single-celled organisms that are known as **bacteria** (singular *bacterium*) in detail. As you learned in Section 2, the cells of bacteria differ from the cells of other organisms in many ways. **Bacteria are prokaryotes. The genetic material in their cells is not contained in a nucleus.** In addition to lacking a nucleus, the cells of prokaryotes also lack many other structures that are found in the cells of eukaryotes. However, regardless of the structure of their cells, prokaryotes accomplish all tasks necessary for life. That is, each bacterial cell uses energy, grows and develops, responds to its surroundings, and reproduces.

Cell Shapes If you were to look at bacterial cells under a microscope, you would notice that bacterial cells have one of three basic shapes: spherical, rodlike, or spiral shaped. The shape of a bacterial cell helps scientists identify the type of bacteria. For example, bacteria that cause strep throat are spherical. Figure 10 shows the different shapes of bacterial cells.

Cell Structures The shape of a bacterial cell is determined by the chemical makeup of its outermost structure—the cell wall. Cell walls surround most bacterial cells. A bacterium's rigid cell wall helps to protect the cell.

Bacterial cells contain many of the other structures you learned about in Chapter 1. Inside the cell wall is the cell membrane, which controls what materials pass into and out of the cell. Inside the cell membrane, the cytoplasm contains a gel-like material. Ribosomes, the sites where proteins are produced, are located in the cytoplasm. The cell's genetic material, which looks like a thick, tangled string, is also located in the cytoplasm. If you could untangle this genetic material, you would see that it forms a circular shape. The genetic material contains the instructions for all the cell's functions, such as how to produce proteins on the ribosomes.

Figure 10 Bacteria have three basic shapes. **A.** Like the bacteria that cause strep throat, these *Staphylococcus aureus* bacteria are spherical. They represent over 30 percent of the bacteria that live on your skin. **B.** *Escherichia coli* bacteria have rodlike shapes. These bacteria are found in your intestines. **C.** *Borrelia burgdorferi* bacteria, which cause Lyme disease, are spiral-shaped.

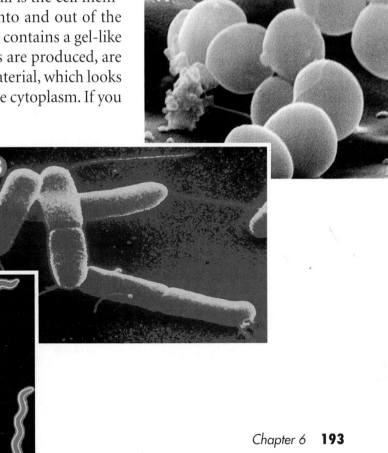

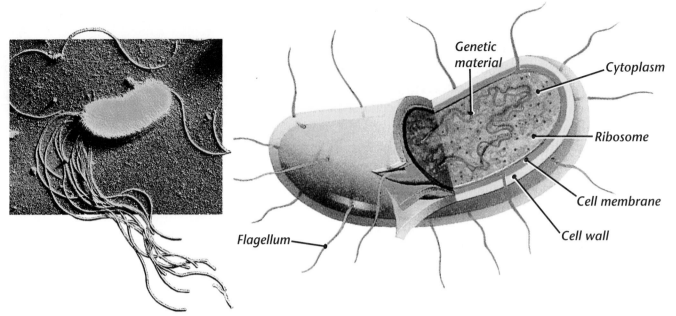

Genetic material

Cytoplasm

Ribosome

Cell membrane

Cell wall

Flagellum

Figure 11 The diagram shows the structures found in a typical bacterial cell. *Interpreting Photographs Which structures can you locate in the photograph of the bacterium? What roles do these structures play?*

You can see the cell wall, cytoplasm, ribosomes, and genetic material in the bacterial cell in Figure 11. Another structure you see is a flagellum. A **flagellum** (fluh JEL um) (plural *flagella*) is a long, whiplike structure that extends from the cell membrane and passes out through the cell wall. A flagellum helps a cell to move by spinning in place like a propeller. A bacterial cell can have many flagella, one, or none. Most bacteria that do not have flagella cannot move on their own. Instead, they depend on air, water currents, clothing, and other objects to carry them from one place to another.

☑ *Checkpoint* *What structure determines the shape of a bacterial cell?*

Two Kingdoms of Bacteria

Until recently, biologists grouped all bacteria together in a single kingdom on the basis of their similar cellular structure. However, although all bacteria look similar, some differ chemically. After analyzing the chemical differences, scientists have reclassified bacteria into two separate kingdoms—archaebacteria and eubacteria.

Archaebacteria Many archaebacteria live in extreme environments. Some thrive in hot springs, where the water can be as hot as 110°C. Others live in environments that are as acidic as lemon juice. Archaebacteria also live in the intestines of animals, the mud in swamps, and in sewage. These bacteria produce the foul odors that you may associate with these places.

Eubacteria Unlike archaebacteria, most eubacteria do not live in extreme environments. However, they live everywhere else. For example, millions of eubacteria live on and in your body. Eubacteria coat your skin and swarm in your nose. Don't be alarmed. Most of them are either useful or harmless to you.

 **INTEGRATING EARTH SCIENCE** Eubacteria help maintain some of Earth's physical conditions and thus help other organisms to survive. For example, some eubacteria are autotrophs that float near the surfaces of Earth's waters. These bacteria use the sun's energy to produce food and oxygen. Scientists think that billions of years ago autotrophic bacteria were responsible for adding oxygen to Earth's atmosphere. Today, the distant offspring of those bacteria help to keep Earth's current level of oxygen at about 20 percent.

Reproduction in Bacteria

When bacteria have plenty of food, the right temperature, and other suitable conditions, they thrive and reproduce frequently. Under these ideal conditions, some bacteria can reproduce as often as once every 20 minutes. Fortunately, growing conditions for bacteria are rarely ideal. Otherwise, there would soon be no room on Earth for other organisms!

Asexual Reproduction Bacteria reproduce by **binary fission**, a process in which one cell divides to form two identical cells. Binary fission is a form of **asexual reproduction.** Asexual reproduction is a reproductive process that involves only one parent and produces offspring that are identical to the parent. In binary fission, the cell first duplicates its genetic material and then divides into two separate cells. Each new cell gets its own complete copy of the parent cell's genetic material as well as some of the parent's ribosomes and cytoplasm. Figure 12 shows a parent cell forming two new cells by binary fission.

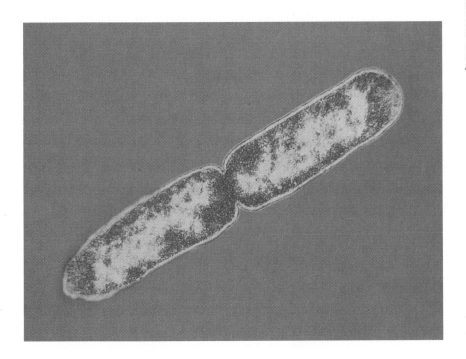

Figure 12 Bacteria, such as this *Escherichia coli,* reproduce by binary fission. Each new cell is identical to the parent cell.

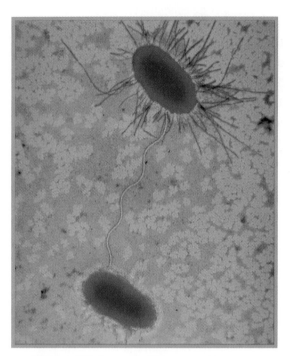

Figure 13 In conjugation, one bacterium transfers some of its genetic material into another bacterium. *Observing What structure allows the cells to transfer genetic material?*

Sexual Reproduction Some bacteria, such as the ones in Figure 13, may at times undergo a simple form of sexual reproduction called conjugation. **Sexual reproduction** involves two parents who combine their genetic material to produce a new organism, which differs from both parents. During **conjugation** (kahn juh GAY shun), one bacterium transfers some of its genetic material into another bacterial cell through a thin, threadlike bridge that joins the two cells. After the transfer, the cells separate.

Conjugation results in bacteria with new combinations of genetic material. When these bacteria divide by binary fission, the new genetic material passes to the new cells. Conjugation does not increase the number of bacteria. However, it does result in the production of new bacteria, which are genetically different than the parent cells.

Survival Needs

From the bacteria that live inside the craters of active volcanoes to those that live in the pores of your skin, all bacteria need certain things to survive. Bacteria must have a source of food, a way of breaking down the food to release the food's energy, and survival techniques when conditions in their surroundings become unfavorable.

Obtaining Food Some bacteria are autotrophs and make their own food. Autotrophic bacteria make food in one of two ways. Some autotrophic bacteria make food by capturing and using the sun's energy as plants do. Other autotrophic bacteria, such as those that live deep in the ocean, do not use the sun's energy. Instead, these bacteria use the energy from chemical substances in their environment to make their food.

Some bacteria are heterotrophs that obtain food by consuming autotrophs or other heterotrophs. Heterotrophic bacteria may consume a variety of foods—from milk and meat, which you might also eat, to the decaying leaves on a forest floor.

Respiration Like all organisms, bacteria need a constant supply of energy to carry out their functions. This energy comes from food. As you learned in Chapter 2, the process of breaking down food to release its energy is called respiration. Like many other organisms, most bacteria need oxygen to break down their food. But a few kinds of bacteria do not need oxygen for respiration. In fact, those bacteria die if oxygen is present in their surroundings. For them, oxygen is a poison that kills!

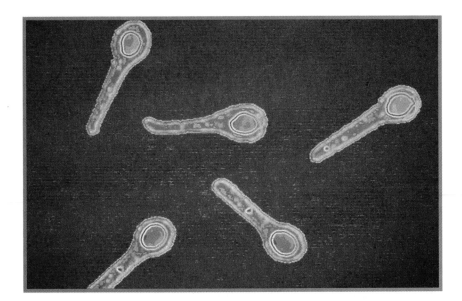

Figure 14 When conditions in the environment become unfavorable for growth, some bacteria form endospores. These endospores of *Clostridium tetani* can survive for years.

Endospore Formation Sometimes the conditions in the environment become unfavorable for the growth of bacteria. For example, food sources can disappear or wastes can poison the bacteria. Some bacteria can survive these harsh conditions by forming endospores like the ones you see in Figure 14. An **endospore** is a small, rounded, thick-walled, resting cell that forms inside a bacterial cell. It contains the cell's genetic material and some of its cytoplasm. Because endospores can resist freezing, heating, and drying, they can survive for many years. Endospores are also light—a breeze can lift and carry them to new places. If an endospore lands in a place where conditions are suitable, it opens up. Then the bacterium can begin to grow and multiply.

☑ *Checkpoint* *How do autotrophic bacteria obtain energy?*

Bacteria and The Living World

When you think about bacteria in your life, you might think of strep throat or ear infections before you think of cheese or fertile soil. But most of the ways that bacteria interact with living organisms are harmless or positive, not harmful. **Bacteria are involved in fuel and food production as well as in environmental recycling and cleanup. However, some bacteria do cause diseases and other harmful effects.**

Fuel The next time you use natural gas to boil an egg, grill a hamburger, or heat your house, think of archaebacteria. The archaebacteria that live in oxygen-free environments, such as the thick mud at the bottom of a lake or swamp, produce a gas called methane during respiration. The methane produced by archaebacteria that died millions of years ago is the major component in about 20 percent of Earth's deposits of natural gas.

Bacteria for Breakfast

In this activity, you will observe helpful bacteria in a common food.

1. Put on your apron. Add water to plain yogurt to make a thin mixture.
2. With a plastic dropper, place a drop of the mixture on a glass slide.
3. Use another plastic dropper to add one drop of methylene blue dye to the slide. **CAUTION:** *This dye can stain your skin.*
4. Put a coverslip on the slide.
5. Observe the slide under both the low and high power lenses of a microscope.

Observing Draw a diagram of what you see under high power. Label any cell structures that you see.

Food Do you like cheese, yogurt, and apple cider? What about olives and sauerkraut? The activities of helpful bacteria produce all of these foods and more. For example, bacteria that grow in a liquid poured around fresh cucumbers turn the cucumbers into pickles. Bacteria that grow in apple cider change the cider to vinegar. Bacteria that grow in milk produce dairy products such as buttermilk, sour cream, yogurt, and cheeses.

However, some bacteria cause food to spoil when they break down the food's chemicals. Spoiled food usually smells or tastes foul and can make you very sick. Since ancient times, people have

SCIENCE & History

Bacteria and Foods of the World

Ancient cultures lacked refrigeration and other modern methods of preventing food spoilage. People in these cultures developed ways to use bacteria to preserve foods. You may enjoy some of these foods today.

1000 B.C. China

The Chinese salted vegetables and packed them in containers. Naturally occurring bacteria fed on the vegetables and produced a sour taste. The salt pulled water out of the vegetables and left them crisp. These vegetables were part of the food rations given to workers who built the Great Wall of China.

3000 B.C.	2000 B.C.	1000 B.C.

2300 B.C. Egypt

Ancient Egyptians made cheese from milk. Cheesemaking begins when bacteria feed on the sugars in milk. The milk separates into solid curds and liquid whey. The curds are processed into cheeses, which keep longer than milk.

500 B.C. Mediterranean Sea Region

People who lived in the region around the Mediterranean Sea chopped meat, seasoned it with salt and spices, rolled it, and hung it to dry. Bacteria in the drying meat gave unusual flavors to the food. The rolled meat would keep for weeks in cool places.

developed ways to slow down food spoilage. They have used such methods as heating, refrigerating, drying, salting, or smoking foods. These methods help to preserve food by preventing the bacteria that cause spoiling from growing in the food.

Environmental Recycling Do you recycle plastic, glass, and other materials? If you do, you have something in common with some heterotrophic eubacteria. These bacteria, which live in the soil, are **decomposers**—organisms that break down large chemicals in dead organisms into small chemicals. Decomposers are

In Your Journal

Find out more about one of these ancient food production methods and the culture that developed it. Write a report about the importance of the food to the culture.

A.D. 1500

The West Indies

People in the West Indies mixed beans from the cocoa plant with bacteria and other microorganisms, then dried and roasted them. The roasted beans were then brewed to produce a beverage with a chocolate flavor. The drink was served cold with honey, spices, and vanilla.

A.D. 1   **A.D. 1000**   **A.D. 2000**

A.D. 500

China

The Chinese crushed soybeans with wheat, salt, bacteria, and other microorganisms. The microorganisms fed on the proteins in the wheat and soybeans. The salt pulled water out of the mixture. The protein-rich soy paste that remained was used to flavor foods. The soy sauce you may use today is made in a similar manner.

A.D. 1850

United States of America

Gold prospectors in California ate a bread called sourdough bread. The bacteria *Lactobacillus san francisco* gave the bread its sour taste. Each day before baking, cooks would set aside some dough that contained the bacteria to use in the next day's bread.

Figure 15 Bacteria live in the swellings on the roots of this soybean plant. The bacteria convert nitrogen from the air into substances the plant needs. *Applying Concepts Why might farmers plant soybeans in a field that is low in nitrogen?*

"nature's recyclers"—they return basic chemicals to the environment for other living things to reuse. For example, in the fall, the leaves of many trees die and fall to the ground. Decomposing bacteria spend the next months breaking down the chemicals in the dead leaves. The broken-down chemicals mix with the soil, and can then be absorbed by the roots of nearby plants.

Other recycling eubacteria live in swellings on the roots of some plants, such as peanuts and soybeans. There, they convert nitrogen gas from the air into nitrogen compounds that the plants need to grow. The plants cannot convert nitrogen from the air into the nitrogen compounds they need. The bacteria that live in the roots of plants help the plants to survive.

Environmental Cleanup   Some bacteria help to clean up

INTEGRATING
ENVIRONMENTAL SCIENCE

Earth's land and water. Can you imagine having a bowl of oil for dinner? Well, there are some bacteria that feast on oil. They convert the dangerous chemicals in oil into harmless substances. Scientists have put these bacteria to work cleaning up oil spills in oceans and gasoline leaks around gas stations.

Illness and Health   Most people have experienced a disease caused by bacteria, such as strep throat or food poisoning. These and many other diseases are called **infectious diseases**—illnesses that pass from one organism to another. Viruses can also cause infectious diseases, as you will read in Section 4.

Infectious diseases can spread in many ways. One way is direct contact, such as touching, hugging, or kissing an infected person. Indirect contact, such as inhaling the drops of moisture from an infected person's sneeze or sharing food and drink, can also spread disease. Some disease-causing bacteria are found naturally in the environment. An example is the bacterium *Clostridium tetani,* which lives in the soil. This bacterium can enter your body through an open wound. It produces a poison known as a **toxin,** which causes the disease tetanus.

Figure 16 Scientists use bacteria such as these *Ochrobactrum anthropi* to help clean up oil spills.

Bacterial Infectious Diseases

Disease	Symptoms	How Spread	Treatment	Prevention
Food poisoning	Vomiting; cramps; diarrhea; fever	Eating foods containing the bacteria	Antitoxin medicines; rest	Properly cook and store foods; avoid foods in rusted and swollen cans
Lyme disease	Rash at site of tick bite; chills; fever; body aches; joint swelling	Animal bite	Antibiotic	Tuck pants into socks; wear long-sleeved shirt; vaccine
Strep throat	Fever; sore throat; swollen glands	Inhale droplets; contact with infected object	Antibiotic	Avoid contact with infected people
Tetanus (lockjaw)	Stiff jaw and neck muscles; spasms; difficulty swallowing	Deep puncture wound	Antibiotic; opening and cleaning wound	Vaccine
Tuberculosis (TB)	Fatigue; mild fever; weight loss; night sweats; cough	Inhale droplets	Antibiotic	Vaccine (for those in high-risk occupations only)

Figure 17 This table lists some diseases caused by bacteria. *Interpreting Charts How can you avoid catching Lyme disease?*

Fortunately, many bacterial diseases can be cured with medications known as antibiotics. An **antibiotic** is a chemical that can kill bacteria without harming a person's own cells. Penicillin is a familiar antibiotic that works by weakening the cell walls of certain bacteria until the cells burst.

 INTEGRATING HEALTH You may find it hard to believe that many of the bacteria living in your body actually keep you healthy. In your digestive system, for example, your intestines teem with bacteria. This is a natural and healthy situation. Some of the bacteria help you digest your food. Some make vitamins that your body needs. Others compete for space with disease-causing organisms. They prevent the harmful bacteria from attaching to your intestines and making you sick.

Section 3 Review

1. How is a bacterial cell different from the cells of other kinds of organisms?
2. List four ways in which bacteria interact with people.
3. What happens during binary fission?
4. **Thinking Critically** **Applying Concepts** Why are some foods, such as milk, heated to high temperatures before they are bottled?

Science at Home

Helpful Bacteria With a family member, look around your kitchen for foods that are made using bacteria. Read the labels on the foods to see if the role of bacteria in the food's production is mentioned. Discuss with your family member the helpful roles that bacteria play in people's lives.

Do Disinfectants Work?

When your family goes shopping, you may buy cleaning products called disinfectants. Disinfectants kill micro-organisms such as bacteria, which may cause infection or decay. In this lab, you will compare the effects of two different disinfectants.

Problem

How well do disinfectants control the growth of bacteria?

Skills Focus

observing, inferring, drawing conclusions

Materials

clock
2 plastic droppers
2 household disinfectants
3 plastic petri dishes with sterile nutrient agar
wax pencil
transparent tape

Procedure

1. Copy the data table into your notebook.
2. Work with a partner. Obtain 3 petri dishes containing sterile agar. Without opening them, use a wax pencil to label the bottoms "A," "B," and "C." Write your initials beside each letter.

3. Wash your hands thoroughly with soap, then run a fingertip across the surface of your worktable. Your partner should hold open the cover of petri dish A while you run that fingertip gently across the agar in a zig-zag motion. Close the dish immediately.
4. Repeat Step 3 for dishes B and C.
5. Use a plastic dropper to transfer 2 drops of one disinfectant to the center of petri dish A. Open the cover just long enough to add the disinfectant to the dish. Close the cover immediately. Record the name of the disinfectant in your data table. **CAUTION:** *Do not inhale vapors from the disinfectant.*
6. Repeat Step 5 for dish B but add 2 drops of the second disinfectant. **CAUTION:** *Do not mix any disinfectants together.*
7. Do not add any disinfectant to dish C.
8. Tape down the covers of all 3 petri dishes so that they will remain tightly closed. Allow the 3 dishes to sit upright on your work surface for at least 5 minutes. **CAUTION:** *Do not open the petri dishes again.* Wash your hands with soap and water.
9. As directed by your teacher, store the petri dishes in a warm, dark place where they can remain for at least 3 days. Remove them only to make a brief examination each day.

DATA TABLE

Petri Dish	Disinfectant	Day 1	Day 2	Day 3
A				
B				
C				

10. After one day, observe the contents of each dish without removing the covers. Estimate the percentage of the agar surface that shows any changes. Record your observations. Return the dishes to their storage place when you have finished making your observations. Wash your hands with soap.

11. Repeat Step 10 after the second day and again after the third day.

12. After you and your partner have made your last observations, return the petri dishes to your teacher unopened.

Analyze and Conclude

1. How did the appearance of dish C change during the lab?

2. How did the appearance of dishes A and B compare with dish C? Explain any similarities or differences.

3. How did the appearance of dishes A and B compare with each other? How can you account for any differences?

4. Why was it important to set aside one petri dish that did not contain any disinfectant?

5. **Apply** Based on the results of this lab, what recommendation would you make to your family about the use of disinfectants? Where in the house do you think these products would be needed most?

Design an Experiment

Go to a store and look at soap products that claim to be "antibacterial" soaps. How do their ingredients differ from other soaps? How do their prices compare? Design an experiment to test how well these products control the growth of bacteria.

SECTION 4 Viruses

DISCOVER

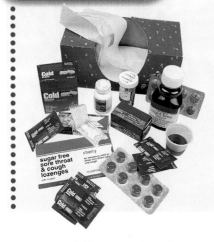

Can You Cure a Cold?

1. Look at the cold medications that your teacher displays. You may have used some of these products when you had a cold.

2. Read the ingredient labels on the products. Read the product claims.

3. Decide which medication you would use if you had a cold. Record the reasons for your choice of product.

Think It Over

Inferring Do medications cure colds? Explain your answer.

GUIDE FOR READING

◆ Why are viruses considered to be nonliving?

◆ What is the basic structure of a virus?

◆ How do viruses multiply?

Reading Tip As you read, use the headings to outline information about the characteristics of viruses.

It is a dark and quiet night. An enemy spy slips silently across the border. Invisible to the guards, the spy creeps cautiously along the edge of the road, heading toward the command center. Undetected, the spy sneaks by the center's security system and reaches the door. Breaking into the control room, the spy takes command of the central computer. The enemy is in control.

Moments later the command center's defenses finally activate. Depending on the enemy's strength and cunning, the defenses may squash the invasion before much damage is done. Otherwise the enemy will win and take over the territory.

What Is a Virus?

Although this spy story may read like a movie script, it describes events that can occur in your body. The spy acts very much like a virus invading an organism. A **virus** is a small, nonliving particle that invades and then reproduces inside a living cell.

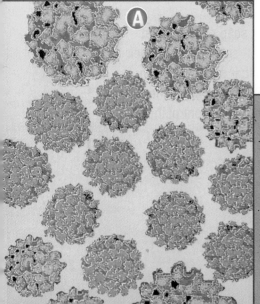

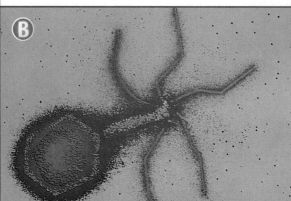

Biologists consider viruses to be nonliving because viruses are not cells. Viruses do not use energy to grow or to respond to their surroundings. Viruses also cannot make food, take in food, or produce wastes.

The only way in which viruses are like organisms is in their ability to multiply. But, although viruses can multiply, they do so differently than organisms. Viruses can only multiply when they are inside a living cell. The organism that a virus enters and multiplies inside is called a host. A **host** is a living thing that provides a source of energy for a virus or an organism. Organisms that live on or in a host and cause harm to the host are called **parasites** (PA ruh syts). Almost all viruses act like parasites because they destroy the cells in which they multiply.

No organisms are safe from viruses. Viruses can infect the organisms of all six kingdoms—archaebacteria, eubacteria, protists, fungi, plants, and animals. Each virus, however, can enter, or infect, only a few types of cells in a few specific species. For example, most cold viruses only infect cells in the nose and throat of humans. The tobacco mosaic virus only infects the leaf cells of tobacco plants.

Checkpoint *When you have a cold, are you the host or the parasite?*

Naming Viruses

Because viruses are not alive, scientists do not use binomial nomenclature to name them. Instead, scientists may name a virus, such as the polio virus, after the disease it causes. Other viruses are named for the organisms they infect, as is the case with the tomato mosaic virus, which infects tomato plants. Scientists named the Ebola virus after the place in Africa where it was first found. And scientists sometimes name viruses after people. The Epstein-Barr virus, for example, was named for the two scientists who first identified the virus that causes the disease known as infectious mononucleosis.

Figure 18 Viruses are tiny nonliving particles that invade and reproduce inside living cells. Viruses can infect the organisms of all six kingdoms. **A.** Papilloma viruses cause warts to form on human skin. **B.** This virus, called a bacteriophage, infects bacteria. **C.** Tobacco mosaic viruses infect tobacco plants. **D.** The rabies virus infects nerve cells in certain animals. **E.** The blue circles in this photo are viruses that cause German measles in humans.

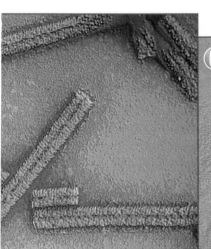

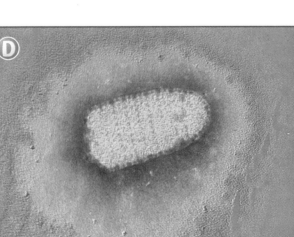

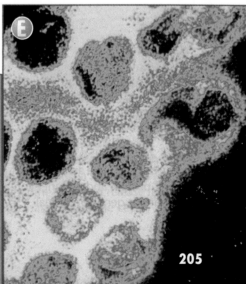

WEB ACTIVITY
www.phschool.com

SECTION
1 Protists

Discover **What Lives in a Drop of Water?**
Try This **Feeding Paramecia**
Sharpen Your Skills **Predicting**
Science at Home **Kitchen Algae**

SECTION
2 *Integrating Environmental Science*
Algal Blooms

Discover **How Can Algal Growth Affect Pond Life?**
Real-World Lab **An Explosion of Life**

SECTION
3 Fungi

Discover **Do All Molds Look Alike?**
Try This **Making Spore Prints**
Try This **Spreading Spores**
Skills Lab **What's for Lunch?**

216

A Mushroom Farm

Have you ever seen mushrooms growing in a local park or on a forest floor? Over the centuries, people have been curious about these organisms because they seem to sprout up without warning, often after a rainfall. Mushrooms are the most familiar type of fungi. In some ways, they resemble plants, often growing near or even on them like small umbrellas. But mushrooms are very different from plants in some important ways. In this project, you'll learn these differences.

As you read the chapter, you'll also learn about other fungi and about the diverse kingdom known as protists. You'll find out how these organisms carry out their life activities and how important they are to people and to the environment.

Your Goal To determine the conditions needed for mushrooms to grow.

To complete this project successfully, you must
◆ choose one variable, and design a way to test how it affects mushroom growth
◆ make daily observations, and record them in a data table
◆ prepare a poster that describes the results of your experiment
◆ follow the safety guidelines in Appendix A

Get Started With your partners, brainstorm possible hypotheses about the way variables such as light or moisture could affect the growth of mushrooms. Write your own hypothesis and the reasons why you chose it. Write out a plan for testing the variable that you chose. Then start growing your mushrooms!

Check Your Progress You'll be working on this project as you study the chapter. To keep your project on track, look for Check Your Progress boxes at the following points.
Section 2 Review, page 230: Make observations and collect data.
Section 3 Review, page 242: Plan a poster about your discoveries.

Present Your Project At the end of the chapter (page 245), you will display your poster that details what you learned about mushroom growth.

Although these scarlet waxy cap mushrooms are quite tasty, beware. There are poisonous mushrooms that look just like them.

SECTION
① Protists

DISCOVER •••••••••••••••••••••••••••••••••• **ACTIVITY**

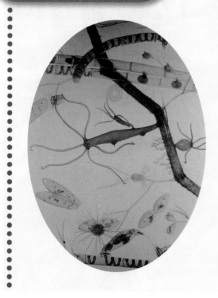

What Lives in a Drop of Water?

1. Use a plastic dropper to place a drop of pond water on a microscope slide.
2. Put the slide under your microscope's low-power lens. Focus on the objects you see.
3. Find at least three different objects that you think might be organisms. Observe them for a few minutes.
4. Draw the three organisms in your notebook. Below each sketch, describe the movements or behaviors of the organism. Wash your hands thoroughly when you have finished.

Think It Over

Observing What characteristics did you observe that made you think that each organism was alive?

GUIDE FOR READING

◆ What are the characteristics of animal-like, funguslike, and plantlike protists?

Reading Tip As you read, use the headings to make an outline of the different kinds of protists.

ook at the objects in Figure 1. What do they look like to you? Jewels? Stained glass windows? Crystal ornaments? You might be surprised to learn that these beautiful, delicate structures are the walls of unicellular organisms called diatoms. Diatoms live in both salt water and fresh water. These tiny organisms are at the base of the food web that provides food for some of Earth's largest organisms—whales.

What Is a Protist?

Diatoms are only one type of organism classified in the protist kingdom. Protists are so different from each other that you can think of this kingdom as the "junk drawer" kingdom. You may have a drawer in your room where you store ticket stubs, postcards, and other odds and ends. Just as these items don't really fit anywhere else in your room, protists don't really fit into any other biological kingdom. Protists do share some characteristics. They are all eukaryotes, or organisms that have cells with nuclei. In addition, all protists live in moist surroundings.

Despite these common characteristics, the word that best describes the protist kingdom is diversity. For example, most protists are unicellular like the diatoms. On the other hand, some

Figure 1 These delicate-looking diatoms are classified in the protist kingdom.

218

protists are multicellular. In fact, the protists known as giant kelps can be over 100 meters long. Protists also vary in how they obtain food—some are heterotrophs, some are autotrophs, and others are both. Some protists cannot move, while others zoom around their moist surroundings.

Because of the great variety of protists, scientists have proposed different ways of grouping these organisms. One useful way of grouping protists is to divide them into three categories: animal-like protists, funguslike protists, and plantlike protists.

☑ *Checkpoint* *What characteristics do all protists share?*

Animal-like Protists

What image pops into your head when you think of an animal? A tiger chasing its prey? A snake slithering onto a rock? Most people immediately associate animals with movement. In fact, movement is often involved with an important characteristic of animals—obtaining food. All animals are heterotrophs that must obtain food by consuming other organisms.

Like animals, animal-like protists are heterotrophs. And most animal-like protists, or **protozoans** (proh tuh ZOH unz), are able to move from place to place to obtain their food. Unlike animals, however, protozoans are unicellular. Some scientists distinguish between four types of protozoans based on the way these organisms move and live.

Figure 2 The protist kingdom includes animal-like, plantlike, and funguslike organisms. **A.** These shells contained unicellular, animal-like protists called foraminifera. **B.** This red alga is a multicellular, plantlike protist that lives on ocean floors. **C.** This yellow slime mold is a funguslike protist.
Comparing and Contrasting In what way are animal-like protists similar to animals? How do they differ?

Protozoans With Pseudopods The ameba in *Exploring Protozoans* on the next page belongs to the group of protozoans called sarcodines. Sarcodines move and feed by forming **pseudopods** (SOO doh pahdz)—temporary bulges of the cell membrane that fill with cytoplasm. The word *pseudopod* means "false foot." Pseudopods form when the cell membrane pushes outward in one location. The cytoplasm flows into the bulge and the rest of the organism follows. Pseudopods enable sarcodines to move in response to changes in the environment. For example, amebas use psuedopods to move away from bright light. Sarcodines also use pseudopods to trap food. The organism extends a pseudopod on each side of the food particle. The two pseudopods then join together, trapping the particle inside.

Organisms that live in fresh water, such as amebas, have a problem. Small particles, like those of water, pass easily through the cell membrane into the cytoplasm. If the excess water were to build up inside the cell, the ameba would burst. Fortunately, amebas have a **contractile vacuole** (kun TRAK til VAK yoo ohl), a structure that collects the extra water and then expels it from the cell.

EXPLORING *Protozoans*

Amebas are sarcodines that live either in water or soil. They feed on bacteria and smaller protists in the surroundings. Paramecia are ciliates that live mostly in fresh water. Like amebas, paramecia feed on bacteria and smaller protists.

AMEBA

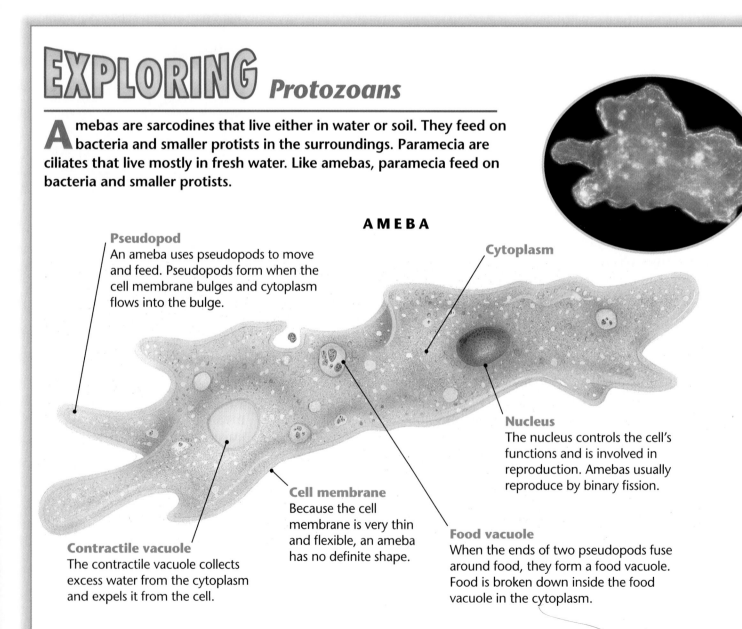

Pseudopod
An ameba uses pseudopods to move and feed. Pseudopods form when the cell membrane bulges and cytoplasm flows into the bulge.

Cytoplasm

Nucleus
The nucleus controls the cell's functions and is involved in reproduction. Amebas usually reproduce by binary fission.

Cell membrane
Because the cell membrane is very thin and flexible, an ameba has no definite shape.

Contractile vacuole
The contractile vacuole collects excess water from the cytoplasm and expels it from the cell.

Food vacuole
When the ends of two pseudopods fuse around food, they form a food vacuole. Food is broken down inside the food vacuole in the cytoplasm.

Protozoans With Cilia The second type of animal-like protist is the ciliate. Ciliates have structures called **cilia** (SIL ee uh) which are hairlike projections from cells that move with a wavelike pattern. They use cilia to move, obtain food, and sense the environment. Cilia act something like tiny oars to move a ciliate. Their movement also sweeps food into the organism.

Ciliates have complex cells. In *Exploring Protozoans*, you see a ciliate called a paramecium. Notice that the paramecium has two nuclei. The large nucleus controls the everyday tasks of the cell. The small nucleus functions in reproduction. Paramecia usually reproduce asexually by binary fission. Sometimes, they reproduce by conjugation. This occurs when two paramecia join together and exchange genetic material.

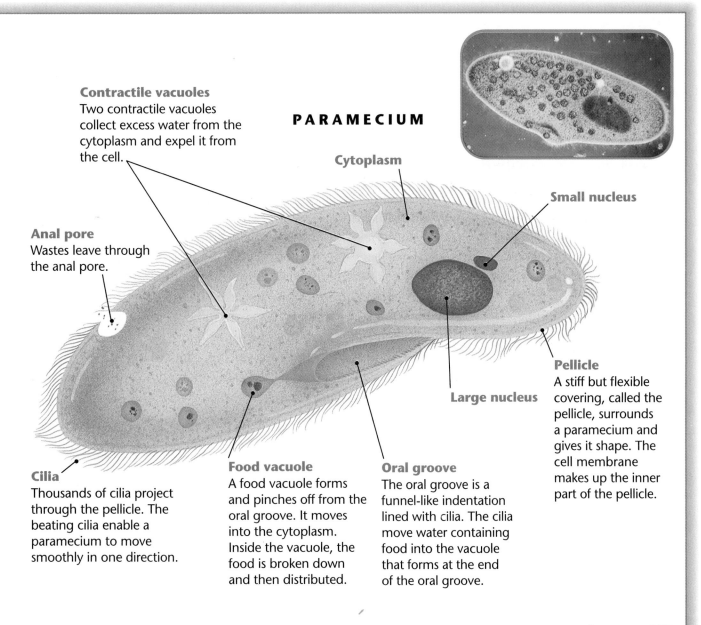

PARAMECIUM

Contractile vacuoles
Two contractile vacuoles collect excess water from the cytoplasm and expel it from the cell.

Cytoplasm

Small nucleus

Anal pore
Wastes leave through the anal pore.

Cilia
Thousands of cilia project through the pellicle. The beating cilia enable a paramecium to move smoothly in one direction.

Food vacuole
A food vacuole forms and pinches off from the oral groove. It moves into the cytoplasm. Inside the vacuole, the food is broken down and then distributed.

Oral groove
The oral groove is a funnel-like indentation lined with cilia. The cilia move water containing food into the vacuole that forms at the end of the oral groove.

Large nucleus

Pellicle
A stiff but flexible covering, called the pellicle, surrounds a paramecium and gives it shape. The cell membrane makes up the inner part of the pellicle.

Figure 3 When people drink from freshwater streams and lakes, they may become ill. Below you see the organism that makes them sick, a protozoan called *Giardia lamblia*.

Protozoans With Flagella The third type of protozoans are called zooflagellates (zoh uh FLAJ uh lits)—animal-like protists that use flagella to move. Most zooflagellates have one to eight long, whiplike flagella that help them move.

Many zooflagellates live inside the bodies of other organisms. For example, one type of zooflagellate lives in the intestines of termites. The zooflagellates digest the wood that the termites eat, producing sugars for themselves and for some termites. In turn, the termites protect the zooflagellates. The interaction between these two species is an example of **symbiosis** (sim bee OH sis)—a close relationship where at least one of the species benefits. When both partners benefit from living together, the relationship is a type of symbiosis called **mutualism.**

INTEGRATING HEALTH Sometimes a zooflagellate harms the animal in which it lives. In Figure 3 you see a zooflagellate called *Giardia*. This zooflagellate is a parasite in humans. When a person drinks water containing *Giardia*, the zooflagellates attach to the person's intestine, where they feed and reproduce. The person develops a serious intestinal condition. This can occur even in unpopulated areas where wild animals, such as beavers, deposit *Giardia* into streams, rivers, and lakes.

Other Protozoans The fourth type of protozoans, the sporozoans, are characterized more by the way they live than by the way they move. Sporozoans are parasites that feed on the cells and body fluids of their hosts. They move in a variety of ways. Some have flagella and some depend on hosts for transport. One even slides from place to place on a layer of slime that it produces.

Many sporozoans have more than one host. For example, *Plasmodium* is a sporozoan that causes malaria, a serious disease of the blood. Two hosts are involved in *Plasmodium's* life cycle—humans and a species of mosquitoes found in tropical areas. The disease spreads when a healthy mosquito bites a person with malaria, becomes infected, and then bites a healthy person. Symptoms of malaria include high fevers that alternate with severe chills. These symptoms can last for weeks, then disappear, only to reappear a few months later.

☑ *Checkpoint* *What structures do protozoans use to move?*

Funguslike Protists

The second group of protists are the funguslike protists. Recall from Chapter 6 that fungi include organisms such as mushrooms and yeast. Until you learn more about fungi in Section 3, you can think of fungi as the "sort of like" organisms. Fungi are "sort of like" animals because they are heterotrophs. They are "sort of like" plants because their cells have cell walls. In addition, most fungi use spores to reproduce. A **spore** is a tiny cell that is able to grow into a new organism.

Like fungi, funguslike protists are heterotrophs, have cell walls, and use spores to reproduce. Unlike fungi, however, all funguslike protists are able to move at some point in their lives. The three types of funguslike protists are water molds, downy mildews, and slime molds.

Water Molds and Downy Mildews Most water molds and downy mildews live in water or in moist places. These organisms grow as tiny threads that look like a fuzzy covering. Figure 5 shows a fish attacked by a water mold.

Water molds and downy mildews also attack food crops, such as potatoes, cabbages, corn, and grapes. A water mold destroyed the Irish potato crops in 1845 and 1846. The loss of these crops led to a famine that resulted in the deaths of over one million Irish people. Many others left Ireland and moved to other countries, such as Canada and the United States.

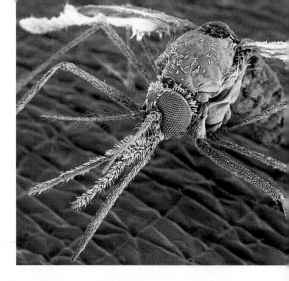

Figure 4 *Anopheles* mosquitoes can carry a sporozoan, *Plasmodium*, which causes malaria in people. *Relating Cause and Effect Why do you think it is difficult to control the spread of malaria?*

Figure 5 This threadlike water mold is a parasite that grows on fish. The water mold eventually kills the fish.

Figure 6 Slime molds, like the chocolate tube slime mold (left), feed on microorganisms on the surfaces of decaying materials. When food runs low, they grow stalks that produce spores (right).

Slime Molds Slime molds live in moist soil and on decaying plants and trees. Slime molds are often beautifully colored. Many are bright yellow, like the one in Figure 6. Their glistening bodies creep over fallen logs and dead leaves on shady, moist forest floors. They move in an amebalike way by forming pseudopods and oozing along the surfaces of decaying materials. Slime molds feed on bacteria and other microorganisms.

Some slime molds are large enough to be seen with the naked eye. Many, however, are so small that you need a microscope to see them. When the food supply decreases or other conditions change, some tiny slime molds creep together and form a multicellular mass. Spore-producing structures grow out of the mass and release spores, which can develop into a new generation of slime molds.

✓ *Checkpoint* *In what environments are slime molds found?*

Plantlike Protists

If you've ever seen seaweed at a beach, then you are familiar with a type of plantlike protist. Plantlike protists, which are commonly called **algae** (AL jee), are even more varied than the animal-like and funguslike protists. **The one characteristic that all algae share is that, like plants, they are autotrophs.**

Some algae live in the soil, others live on the barks of trees, and still others live in fresh water and salt water. Algae that live on the surface of ponds, lakes, and oceans are an important food source for other organisms in the water. In addition, most of the oxygen in Earth's atmosphere is made by these algae.

Algae range greatly in size. Some algae, such as diatoms, are unicellular. Others are groups of unicellular organisms that live together in colonies. Still others, such as seaweeds, are multicellular. Recall from Chapter 1 that a unicellular organism carries out all the functions necessary for life. But the cells of a multi-cellular organism are specialized to do certain tasks. When single-celled algae come together to form colonies, some of the cells may become specialized to perform certain functions, such as reproduction. However, most cells in a colony continue to carry out all functions. Colonies can contain from four up to thousands of cells.

Algae exist in a wide variety of colors because they contain many types of **pigments**—chemicals that produce color. Depending on their pigments, algae can be green, yellow, red, brown, orange, or even black. Read on to learn about the types of algae that live on Earth.

Euglenoids Euglenoids are green, unicellular algae that are found mostly in fresh water. Unlike other algae, euglenoids have one animal-like characteristic—they can be heterotrophs under certain conditions. When sunlight is available, euglenoids are autotrophs that produce their own food. However, when sunlight is not available, euglenoids will act like heterotrophs by finding and taking in food from their environment.

In Figure 7 you see a euglena, which is a common euglenoid. Notice the long whiplike flagellum that helps the organism move. Locate the eyespot near the flagellum. Although the eyespot is not really an eye, it contains pigments. These pigments are sensitive to light and help a euglena recognize the direction of a light source. You can imagine how important this response is to an organism that needs light to make food.

Sharpen your Skills

Predicting **ACTIVITY**

Predict what will happen when you pour a culture of euglenas into a petri dish, then cover half the dish with aluminum foil. Give a reason for your prediction.

Then carry out the experiment with a culture of euglenas in a plastic petri dish. Cover half the dish with aluminum foil as shown. After 10 minutes, uncover the dish. What do you observe? Was your prediction correct? Explain why euglenas behave this way.

Figure 7 Euglenas are unicellular algae that live in fresh water. In sunlight, euglenas make their own food. Without sunlight, they obtain food from their environment.
Interpreting Diagrams What structures help a euglena find and move toward light?

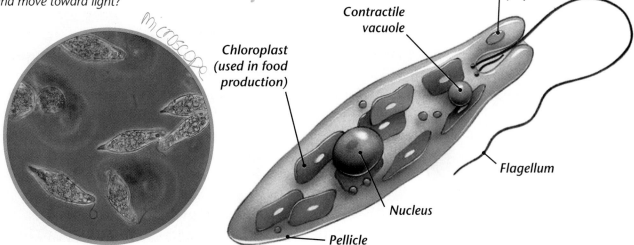

Chloroplast (used in food production)

Contractile vacuole

Eyespot

Flagellum

Nucleus

Pellicle

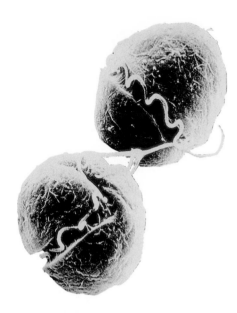

Figure 8 Dinoflagellates, such as these *Gonyaulax,* have rigid plates for protection. They use flagella to move through the water.

Dinoflagellates Dinoflagellates are unicellular algae covered by stiff plates that look like a suit of armor. Because they have different amounts of green, red, and other pigments, dinoflagellates exist in a variety of colors.

All dinoflagellates have two flagella held in grooves between their plates. When the flagella beat, the dinoflagellates twirl like toy tops through the water. Many glow in the dark and look like miniature fireflies dancing on the ocean's surface at night.

Diatoms Diatoms are unicellular protists with beautiful glasslike cell walls. Some float on the surface of freshwater and saltwater environments. Others attach to objects such as rocks in shallow water. Diatoms move by oozing slime out of slits in their cell walls. They then glide in the slime. Diatoms are a food source for heterotrophs in the water.

INTEGRATING TECHNOLOGY When diatoms die, their cell walls collect on the bottoms of oceans and lakes. Over time, they form layers of a coarse material called diatomaceous (dy uh tuh MAY shus) earth. This makes a good polishing agent. Manufacturers add diatomaceous earth to most toothpastes. Diatomaceous earth is also used in many household scouring products as well as in swimming pool filters. It is even used as an insecticide. The sharp edges puncture the bodies of insects.

Green Algae As their name suggests, all green algae contain green pigments. Otherwise, green algae are quite diverse, as you can see in Figure 9. Although most green algae are unicellular, some form colonies, and a few are multicellular. You might have seen multicellular green algae, or green seaweed, washed up on a beach. Most green algae live in either freshwater or saltwater surroundings. The few that live on land are found along the bases of trees or in moist soils.

Figure 9 Green algae range in size from unicellular organisms to multicellular seaweeds. **A.** The multicellular sea lettuce, *Ulva,* lives in oceans. **B.** This unicellular alga, *Closterium,* lives in fresh water.

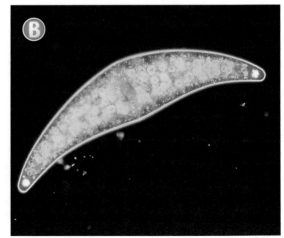

Red Algae Almost all red algae are multicellular seaweeds. Divers have found red algae growing at depths greater than 260 meters below the ocean's surface. Their red pigments are especially good at absorbing the small amount of light that enters deep ocean waters.

Red algae are used by humans in a variety of ways. Carrageenan (kar uh JEE nun), a substance extracted from red algae, is used in products such as ice creams and hair conditioners. For people in many Asians cultures, red algae is a nutrient-rich delicacy that is eaten fresh, dried, or toasted.

Brown Algae Many of the organisms that are commonly called seaweeds are brown algae. In addition to their brown pigment, brown algae also contain green, yellow, and orange pigments. As you can see in Figure 10, a typical brown alga has many plantlike structures. Holdfasts anchor the alga to rocks. Stalks support the blades, which are the leaflike structures of the alga. Brown algae also have gas-filled sacs called bladders that allow the algae to float upright in the water.

Brown algae flourish in cool, rocky waters. Brown algae called rockweed live along the Atlantic coast of North America. Giant kelps, which can grow to 100 meters in length, live in some Pacific coastal waters. The giant kelps form large underwater "forests" where many organisms, including sea otters and abalone, live. Some people eat brown algae for their nutrients. Substances called algins are extracted from brown algae and used as thickeners in foods such as puddings and salad dressings.

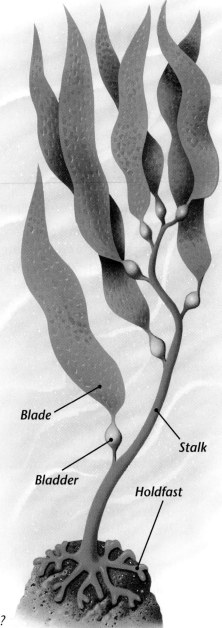

Figure 10 Giant kelps have many plantlike structures. *Applying Concepts* What plant structures do the holdfasts and blades resemble?

 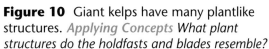
Section 1 Review

1. What characteristic do all protozoans share?
2. What are three characteristics of the funguslike protists?
3. What characteristic do algae share with plants?
4. **Thinking Critically Making Judgments** Would you classify a euglena as an animal-like protist or as a plantlike protist? Explain your answer.

Science at Home

Kitchen Algae Look through your kitchen with a family member to find products that contain substances made from algae. Look for both food and non-food items. First tell your family member that words such as diatomaceous earth, algin, and carrageenan are substances that come from algae. Make a list of the products and the algae-based ingredient they contain. Share your list with the class.

SECTION 2 Algal Blooms

DISCOVER ··· ACTIVITY

How Can Algal Growth Affect Pond Life?

1. Pour water into a plastic petri dish until the dish is half full. The petri dish will represent a pond.

2. Sprinkle a spoonful of green paper punches into the water in the petri dish to represent green algae growing in the pond water.

3. Sprinkle two more spoonfuls of paper punches into the water to represent one cycle of algae reproduction.

4. Sprinkle four more spoonfuls of paper punches into the water to represent the next reproduction cycle of the algae.

Think It Over

Predicting How might algae growing on the surface affect organisms living deep in a pond?

GUIDE FOR READING

◆ What makes red tides dangerous?

◆ How does the rapid growth of algae affect a pond or lake?

Reading Tip As you read, look for evidence of the dangers of algal blooms. Make a list of sentences from the text that provide this evidence.

Over a five week period one year, the bodies of 14 humpback whales washed up along beaches on Cape Cod, Massachusetts. The whales showed no outward signs of sickness. Their stomachs were full of food. Their bodies contained plenty of blubber to insulate them from changes in water temperature. What caused such healthy-looking animals to die?

When biologists examined the dead whales' tissues, they identified the cause of the puzzling deaths. The whales' cells contained a deadly toxin produced by a dinoflagellate called *Alexandrium tamarense*. For reasons that scientists don't fully understand, the population of these algae grew rapidly in the ocean waters through which the whales were migrating. When the whales fed on the toxin-producing algae or on fishes that had eaten the algae, the toxins reached a deadly level and killed the whales.

Algae are common in both saltwater and freshwater environments on Earth. They float on the surface of the waters and use sunlight to make food. The rapid growth of a population of algae is called an **algal bloom.** The deaths of the humpbacks is one example of the damage that an algal bloom can cause.

◀ A humpback whale

Saltwater Blooms

In Figure 11, you see an algal bloom in ocean water. Saltwater algal blooms are commonly called **red tides.** This is because the algae that grow rapidly often contain red pigments and turn the color of the water red. But red tides do not always look red. Some red tides are brown, green, or colorless depending on the species of algae that blooms. Dinoflagellates and diatoms are two algae that frequently bloom in red tides.

Scientists are not sure why some saltwater algal populations increase rapidly at times. But red tides occur most often when there is an increase in nutrients in the water. Increases in ocean temperature due to climate changes also affect the occurrence of red tides. Some red tides occur regularly in certain seasons. The cold bottom layers of the ocean contain a lot of nutrients. When the cold water mixes with the surface waters, more nutrients become available to surface organisms. With excess nutrients present in the surface waters, blooms of algae occur.

Red tides are dangerous when the toxins that the algae produce become concentrated in the bodies of organisms that consume the algae. Shellfish feed on large numbers of the algae and store the toxins in their cells. Fishes may also feed on the algae and store the toxins. When people or other large organisms eat these shellfish and fishes, it may lead to serious illness or even death. Public health officials close beaches in areas of red tides and prohibit people from gathering shellfish or fishing.

INTEGRATING TECHNOLOGY Red tides occur more frequently worldwide today than they did a decade ago. Scientists cannot yet predict when red tides will occur. They use images taken by satellites in space to track how red tides move with ocean currents. Satellite images can also detect increases in ocean temperatures, which may put an area at risk for red tide.

✓ *Checkpoint* *What gives red tides their color?*

Figure 12 Increased nutrient levels in lakes and ponds can lead to algal blooms. The thick layer of algae on the surface can threaten other organisms in the water. *Problem Solving Outline a series of steps that could help slow down the rapid growth of algae in a lake.*

Freshwater Blooms

Algal blooms also occur in bodies of fresh water. Have you ever seen a pond or lake that looked as if it was coated with a layer of green paint? The green layer of surface scum usually consists of huge numbers of unicellular green algae.

Lakes and ponds undergo natural processes of change over time. In a process called **eutrophication** (yoo troh fih KAY shun), nutrients such as nitrogen and phosphorus build up in a lake or pond over time, causing an increase in the growth of algae.

Certain natural events and human activities can increase the rate of eutrophication. For example, when farmers spread fertilizers on fields, some of these chemicals can run off into nearby lakes and ponds. In addition, poorly designed or aging septic systems can leak their contents into the soil. The nutrients make their way from the soil into water that leads into lakes and ponds. These events cause a rapid increase in algae growth.

The rapid growth of algae in a pond or lake triggers a series of events with serious consequences. First, the layer of algae prevents sunlight from reaching plants and other algae beneath the surface. Those organisms die and sink to the bottom. Then organisms, such as bacteria, which break down the bodies of the dead plants and algae, increase in number. Soon the bacteria use up the oxygen in the water. Fishes and other organisms in the water die without the oxygen they need to survive. About the only life that survives is the algae on the surface.

Algal blooms in fresh water can be easier to control than those in salt water because lakes and ponds have definite boundaries. To slow eutrophication, scientists first need to find the sources of the excess nutrients and then eliminate them. If the source can be eliminated and the nutrients used up, eutrophication slows to its natural rate.

Section 2 Review

1. Why are red tides dangerous?
2. What causes a freshwater bloom?
3. How does the death of bottom plants in a shallow pond affect the rest of the pond?
4. **Thinking Critically Problem Solving** A new housing development is to be built along a recreational lake. What factors should the developers consider to protect the lake from rapid eutrophication?

Check Your Progress

CHAPTER PROJECT

By now, you should have your teacher's approval for your plan, and you should have started growing your mushrooms. Make careful observations of growth every day. Include sketches and measurements as appropriate. Use a data table to organize the data you collect. (*Hint:* As you make your observations, be careful not to disturb the experiment or introduce any new variables.)

You and Your Environment

AN EXPLOSION OF LIFE

Living things are interconnected with their surroundings in many ways. In this lab, you will investigate how one change in a freshwater environment can affect everything that lives in that environment.

Problem

How does the amount of fertilizer affect algae growth?

Skills Focus

controlling variables, predicting, drawing conclusions

Materials

4 glass jars with lids
aged tap water
graduated cylinder
marking pen
aquarium water
liquid fertilizer

Procedure

1. Read through the steps in the procedure. Then write a prediction describing what you think will happen in each of the four jars.
2. Copy the data table into your notebook. Be sure to allow enough lines to make entries for a two-week period.
3. Label four jars A, B, C, and D. Fill each jar half full with aged tap water.
4. Add aquarium water to each jar until the jar is three-fourths full.
5. Add 3 mL of liquid fertilizer to jar B; 6 mL to jar C; and 12 mL to jar D. Do not add any fertilizer to jar A. Loosely screw the lid on each jar. Place all the jars in a sunny location where they will receive the same amount of direct sunlight.

DATA TABLE

Date	Observations			
	Jar A no fertilizer	Jar B 3 mL fertilizer	Jar C 6 mL fertilizer	Jar D 12 mL fertilizer
Day 1				
Day 2				

6. Observe the jars every day for two weeks. Compare the color of the water in the four jars. Record your observations in your data table.

Analyze and Conclude

1. How did the color in the four jars compare at the end of the two-week period? How can you account for any differences that you observed?
2. What was the purpose of jar A?
3. Describe the process that led to the overall color change in the water. What organisms were responsible for causing that color change?
4. Predict what would have happened if you placed the four jars in a dark location instead of in sunlight. Explain your prediction.
5. **Apply** What do you think might happen to fish and other living organisms when fertilizer gets into a body of fresh water? What are some ways that fertilizer might get into a body of water?

Design an Experiment

Some detergents contain phosphates, which are an ingredient in many kinds of fertilizer. Design an experiment to compare how regular detergent and low-phosphate detergent affect the growth of algae.

Eutrophication — The Threat to Clear, Clean Water

Weiss Lake, on the Georgia-Alabama border, is a popular vacation area. People come to this lake to fish, boat, and swim. But every year about two million pounds of phosphorus pour into Weiss Lake from rivers. These excess nutrients are threatening the lake's good fishing and clean, clear water.

Weiss Lake is just one of thousands of lakes and ponds in the United States threatened by eutrophication. The threat is not just to recreation. Drinking water for nearly 70 percent of Americans comes from lakes, reservoirs, and other surface water.

The Issues

Where Does the Pollution Come From?
The two main sources of excess nutrients are wastes and fertilizers from farms and wastewater from sewage treatment plants. When farmers fertilize crops, the plants absorb only some of these nutrients. The excess nutrients can be washed with soil into lakes and ponds. When wastewater from homes and factories is treated, large amounts of nutrients still remain in the water. For example, about 380 million liters of treated wastewater flow toward Weiss Lake daily. This treated wastewater still contains large amounts of phosphorus produced by many factories.

What Are the Costs of Eutrophication?
People who live near Weiss Lake depend on the lake for jobs and money. But as the fish die in the oxygen-poor waters, swimming and boating in the murky water become less appealing and possibly unsafe. Over 4,000 jobs and millions of dollars each year would be lost if Weiss Lake were to close down. But upgrading or building new water-treatment plants would cost millions of dollars in higher taxes to citizens.

What Can Be Done? Even as cities, farms, and factories grow, the amount of nutrients reaching lakes and ponds can be reduced. Factories can install water-treatment facilities that remove more nitrogen and phosphorus from their wastewater. Farmers can often reduce the use of fertilizers. People can plant trees along the banks of lakes to reduce the amount of soil entering the lake. These solutions can cost millions of dollars, but they can reverse the problem.

You Decide

1. Identify the Problem
In your own words, describe the eutrophication issues that affect Weiss Lake.

2. Analyze the Options
Make a chart of different ways to slow the eutrophication process. How would each work? What groups of people would be affected?

3. Find a Solution
Create a "prevention plan" advising town leaders how to reduce eutrophication in lakes and ponds.

ACTIVITY

Do All Molds Look Alike?

1. Your teacher will give you two sealed, clear plastic bags—one containing moldy bread and another containing moldy fruit. **CAUTION:** *Do not open the sealed bags at any time.*

2. Examine each mold. In your notebook, describe what you see.

3. Then, use a hand lens to examine each mold. Sketch each mold in your notebook and list its characteristics.

4. Return the sealed bags to your teacher. Wash your hands.

Think It Over

Observing How are the molds similar? How do they differ?

Unnoticed, a speck of dust lands on a cricket's back. But this is no ordinary dust—it is alive! Tiny glistening threads emerge from the dust and begin to grow into the cricket's moist body. As they grow, the threads release chemicals that slowly dissolve the cricket's living tissues. The threads continue to grow deeper into the cricket's body. Within a few days, the cricket's body is little more than a hollow shell filled with a tangle of the deadly threads. Then the threads begin to grow up and out of the dead cricket. They produce long stalks with knobs at their tips. When one of the knobs breaks open, it will release thousands of dustlike specks, which the wind can carry to new victims.

What Are Fungi?

The strange cricket-killing organism is a member of the fungi kingdom. Although you may not have heard of a cricket-killing fungus before, you are probably familiar with other kinds of fungi. For example, the molds that grow on stale bread or on decaying fruit are all fungi. Mushrooms that sprout in forests or yards are also fungi.

GUIDE FOR READING

◆ What characteristics do fungi share?

◆ How do fungi obtain food?

◆ What roles do fungi play in the living world?

Reading Tip Before you read, preview the headings. Record them in outline form, leaving space for writing notes.

▼ A bush cricket attacked by a killer fungus

Fungi vary in size from the unicellular yeasts to the multicellular fungi, such as mushrooms and the bracket fungi that look like shelves growing on tree trunks. **Most fungi share three important characteristics: They are eukaryotes, use spores to reproduce, and are heterotrophs that feed in a similar way.** In addition, fungi need moist, warm places in which to grow. They thrive on moist foods, damp tree barks, lawns coated with dew, damp forest floors, and even wet bathroom tiles.

Cell Structure

Except for yeast cells, which are unicellular, the cells of fungi are arranged in structures called hyphae. **Hyphae** (HY fee) (singular *hypha*) are the branching, threadlike tubes that make up the bodies of multicellular fungi. The hyphae of some fungi are continuous threads of cytoplasm that contain many nuclei. Substances move quickly and freely through the hyphae.

The appearance of a fungus depends on how its hyphae are arranged. In some fungi, the threadlike hyphae are loosely tangled. Fuzzy-looking molds that grow on old foods have loosely tangled hyphae. In other fungi, hyphae are packed tightly together. For example, the stalk and cap of the mushrooms in Figure 13 are made of hyphae packed so tightly that they appear solid. Underground, however, a mushroom's hyphae form a loose, threadlike maze in the soil.

☑ *Checkpoint* *What structures make up the bodies of multicellular fungi?*

Cap

Gills

Stalk

Hyphae

Underground
hyphae

Figure 13 The hyphae in the stalk and cap of a mushroom are packed tightly to form very firm structures. Underground hyphae, on the other hand, are arranged loosely. *Inferring* *What function do you think the underground hyphae perform?*

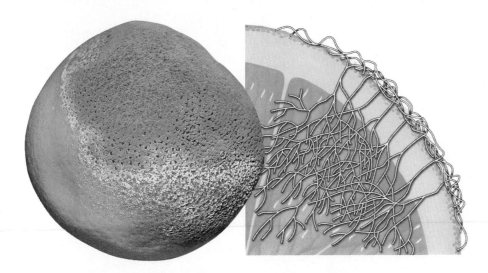

Figure 14 The mold *Penicillium* often grows on old fruits such as this orange. Notice that some hyphae grow deep inside the orange. These hyphae digest the food and absorb the smaller chemicals.

How Do Fungi Obtain Food?

Although fungi are heterotrophs, they do not take food into their bodies as you do. Instead fungi absorb food through hyphae that grow into the food source.

Look at Figure 14 to see how a fungus feeds. **First, the fungus grows hyphae into a food source. Then digestive chemicals ooze from the tips of the hyphae into the food. The digestive chemicals break down the food into small substances that can be absorbed by the hyphae.** Imagine yourself sinking your fingers down into a chocolate cake and dripping digestive chemicals out of your fingertips. Then imagine your fingers absorbing the digested particles of the cake. That's how a fungus feeds.

Some fungi feed on the remains of dead organisms. Other fungi are parasites that break down the chemicals in living organisms. For example, athlete's foot is a disease caused by a fungus that feeds on chemicals in a person's skin. Dutch elm disease is caused by a fungus that feeds on elm trees and eventually kills the trees.

Reproduction in Fungi

Like it or not, fungi are everywhere. The way they reproduce guarantees their survival and spread. Fungi usually reproduce by producing lightweight spores that are surrounded by a protective covering. Spores can be carried easily through air or water to new sites. Fungi produce many more spores than will ever grow into new fungi. Only a few of the thousands of spores that a fungus releases will fall where conditions are right for them to grow into new organisms.

Making Spore Prints

In this activity, you will examine the reproductive structures of a mushroom.

1. Place a fresh mushroom cap, gill side down, on a sheet of white paper. **CAUTION:** *Do not eat the mushroom.*

2. Cover the mushroom cap with a plastic container. Wash your hands with soap.

3. After two days, carefully remove the container and then the cap. You should find a spore print on the paper.

4. Examine the print with a hand lens. Then wash your hands with soap.

Predicting Use your spore print to estimate how many spores a mushroom could produce. Where would spores be most likely to grow into new mushrooms?

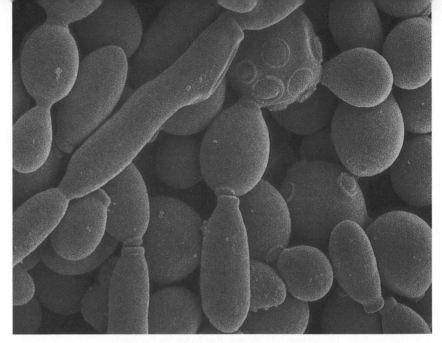

Figure 15 Budding is a form of asexual reproduction that occurs in yeast. The small yeast cell that grows from the body of a parent cell is identical to the parent.

Fungi produce spores in structures called **fruiting bodies,** which are reproductive hyphae that grow out of a fungus. The appearances of fruiting bodies vary from one type of fungus to another. For some fungi, such as mushrooms and puffballs, the part of the fungus that you see is the fruiting body. In other fungi, such as bread molds, the stalklike fruiting bodies grow upward from the hyphae on the surface of the bread. The knoblike structure, or spore case, at the tip of a stalk contains the spores.

Asexual Reproduction Most fungi reproduce both asexually and sexually. When there is adequate moisture and food, most fungi reproduce asexually by growing fruiting bodies that release thousands of spores.

Unicellular yeast cells undergo a form of asexual reproduction called **budding.** In budding, no spores are produced. Instead, a small yeast cell grows from the body of a large, well-fed parent cell in a way that might remind you of a bud forming on the branch of a tree. The new cell then breaks away and lives on its own.

Sexual Reproduction When growing conditions become unfavorable, fungi may reproduce sexually. In sexual reproduction, the hyphae of two fungi grow together and genetic material is exchanged. A new spore-producing structure grows from the joined hyphae. The new structure produces spores, which can develop into fungi that differ from either parent.

✓ *Checkpoint* *What is a fruiting body?*

Classification of Fungi

Fungi are classified into groups based on the shape of the spore-producing structures and on their ability to reproduce sexually. The four groups of fungi—the threadlike fungi, the sac fungi, the club fungi, and the imperfect fungi—are shown in Figure 16.

▲ **Threadlike Fungi**

This group contains about 600 different species of molds, including many common bread molds, such as this *Rhizopus*. These fungi produce spores in their threadlike hyphae.

▲ **Sac Fungi**

This group contains over 30,000 diverse species of fungi, including yeast, morels, truffles, and some fungi that cause plant diseases, such as Dutch elm disease. They are called sac fungi because they produce spores in structures that look like sacks. The sac fungi in the photo are called bird's nest fungi.

◀ **Club Fungi**

This group includes about 25,000 species of mushrooms, bracket fungi, plant parasites, and puffballs. Club fungi produce spores in structures that look like clubs. One of the puffballs in the photo is shooting out its spores.

▲ **Imperfect Fungi**

The 25,000 species in this group include this *Penicillium*, the source of an important antibiotic. The fungi in this group are not known to reproduce sexually.

Figure 16 The four groups of fungi differ in the appearance of their spore-producing structures and in how they reproduce. *Classifying* To which group do mushrooms belong?

What's for Lunch?

In this lab, you will draw conclusions about the effects of two substances on the activity of yeast.

Problem

How does the presence of sugar or salt affect the activity of yeast?

Materials

marking pen
5 plastic straws
salt
beaker
graduated cylinder
5 small narrow-necked bottles
5 round balloons
sugar
warm water (40–45°C)
dry powdered yeast

Procedure

1. Copy the data table into your notebook. Then read over the entire procedure to see how you will test the activity of the yeast cells in bottles A through E. Write a prediction about what will happen in each bottle.

2. Gently stretch each of the 5 balloons so that they will inflate easily.

3. Using the marking pen, label the bottles A, B, C, D, and E.

4. Use a beaker to fill each bottle with the same amount of warm water. **CAUTION:** *Glass is fragile. Handle the bottles and beaker gently to avoid breakage. Do not touch broken glass.*

5. Put 5 mL of salt into bottle B.

6. Put 5 mL of sugar into bottles C and E.

7. Put 30 mL of sugar into bottle D.

8. Put 2 mL of powdered yeast into bottle A, and stir the mixture with a clean straw. Remove the straw and discard it.

9. Immediately place a balloon over the opening of bottle A. Make sure that the balloon opening fits very tightly around the neck of the bottle.

10. Repeat Steps 8 and 9 for bottle B, bottle C, and bottle D.

DATA TABLE			
Bottle	Contents	Prediction	Observations
A	Yeast alone		
B	Yeast and 5 mL of salt		
C	Yeast and 5 mL of sugar		
D	Yeast and 30 mL of sugar		
E	No yeast and 5 mL of sugar		

11. Place a balloon over bottle E without adding yeast to the bottle.

12. Place the 5 bottles in a warm spot away from drafts. Observe and record what happens.

Analyze and Conclude

1. Which balloons changed in size during this lab? How did they change?

2. Explain why the balloon changed size in some bottles and not in others. What caused that change in size?

3. Do yeast cells use sugar as a food source? How do you know?

4. Do yeast cells use salt as a food source? How do you know?

5. What did the results from bottle C show, compared with the results from bottle D?

6. **Think About It** If you removed bottle E from your experiment, would you be able to conclude whether or not sugar is a food source for the yeast cells? Why or why not?

▶ Design an Experiment ◀

Develop a hypothesis about whether yeast cells need light to carry out their life activities. Then design an experiment to test your hypothesis. Obtain your teacher's permission before you carry out the experiment.

Fungi and the Living World

Fungi affect humans and other organisms in many ways. **Fungi play an important role as decomposers on Earth. In addition, many fungi provide foods for people. Some cause disease and some fight disease. Still other fungi live in symbiosis with other organisms.**

Environmental Recycling Like bacteria, many fungi are decomposers—organisms that break down the chemicals in dead organisms. For example, many fungi live in the soil and break down the chemicals in dead plant matter. This process returns important nutrients to the soil. Without fungi and bacteria, Earth would be buried under dead plants and animals.

Food and Fungi When you eat a slice of bread, you benefit from the work of yeast. Bakers add yeast to bread dough to make it rise. Yeast cells use the sugar in the dough for food and produce carbon dioxide gas as they feed. The gas forms bubbles, which cause the dough to rise. You see these bubbles as holes in a slice of bread. Without yeast, bread would be flat and solid. Yeast is also used to make wine from grapes. Yeast cells feed on the sugar in the grapes and produce carbon dioxide and alcohol.

Other fungi are also important sources of foods. Molds are used in the production of foods such as some cheeses. The blue streaks in blue cheese, for example, are actually growths of *Penicillium roqueforti*. People enjoy eating mushrooms in salads and soups and on pizza. Because some mushrooms are poisonous, however, you should never pick or eat wild mushrooms.

✓ *Checkpoint* *What are three foods that fungi help to produce?*

Disease-Causing Fungi Many fungi cause serious diseases in plants that result in huge crop losses every year. Corn smut and wheat rust are two club fungi that cause diseases in important food crops. Fungal plant diseases also affect other crops, including rice, cotton, and soybeans.

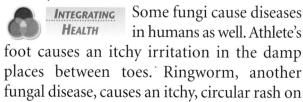

INTEGRATING HEALTH Some fungi cause diseases in humans as well. Athlete's foot causes an itchy irritation in the damp places between toes. Ringworm, another fungal disease, causes an itchy, circular rash on the skin. Because the fungi that cause these

Figure 17 Many food crops are lost each year due to fungal diseases. The ear of corn in the photo has been attacked by a fungus called corn smut. *Making Generalizations Why is the spread of fungal diseases difficult to control?*

diseases produce spores at the site of infection, the diseases can spread easily from person to person. Both diseases can be treated with antifungal medications.

Disease-Fighting Fungi In 1928 a Scottish biologist, Alexander Fleming, was examining petri dishes in which he was growing bacteria. To his surprise, Fleming noticed a spot of a bluish-green mold growing in one dish. Curiously, no bacteria were growing near the mold. Fleming hypothesized that the mold, a fungus named *Penicillium*, produced a substance that killed the bacteria growing near it. Fleming's work led to the development of the first antibiotic, penicillin. It has saved the lives of millions of people with bacterial infections. Since the discovery of penicillin, many additional antibiotics have been isolated from both fungi and eubacteria.

Fungus-Plant Root Associations Some fungi help plants grow larger and healthier when their hyphae grow among the plant's roots. The hyphae spread out underground and absorb water and nutrients from the soil for the plant. With more water and nutrients, the plant grows larger than it would have grown without its fungal partner. The plant is not the only partner that benefits. The fungi get to feed on the extra food that the plant makes and stores.

Many plants are so dependent on their fungal partners that they cannot survive well without them. For example, orchids cannot grow without their fungal partners.

Language Arts
CONNECTION

Folk tales are ancient stories that were passed down by word of mouth over many generations. Folk tales often involve magical elements, such as fairies—supernatural beings with powers to become invisible, change form, and affect the lives of people.

The circle of mushrooms in Figure 18 was often mentioned in folk tales. These circles were said to be the footprints of fairies who danced there at midnight. These mushroom circles were given the name "fairy rings"—a name that is still used today. People believed that the area inside a fairy ring was a magical location. Cutting down the tree inside a fairy ring was believed to bring bad luck.

In Your Journal

A type of mushroom called a toadstool is mentioned in some folk tales. Write a paragraph that could be part of a folk tale that reveals how toadstools got their name.

Figure 18 The fruiting bodies of these mushrooms have emerged in an almost perfect circular pattern. This pattern is called a fairy ring. The mushrooms share the same network of underground hyphae.

Figure 19 Lichens consist of a fungus living together with either algae or autotrophic bacteria. **A.** This lichen—a British soldier—probably gets its name from its scarlet red tops, which stand upright. **B.** The lichens covering these rocks are slowly breaking down the rocks to create soil.

Lichens A **lichen** (LY kun) consists of a fungus and either algae or autotrophic bacteria that also live together in a mutualistic relationship. You have probably seen some familiar lichens—irregular, flat, crusty patches that grow on tree barks or rocks. The fungus benefits from the food produced by the algae or bacteria. The algae or bacteria, in turn, obtain water and minerals from the fungus.

 *INTEGRATING EARTH SCIENCE* Lichens are often called "pioneer" organisms because they are the first organisms to appear on the bare rocks in an area after a volcano, fire, or rock slide has occurred. Over time, the lichens break down the rock into soil in which other organisms can grow. Lichens are also useful as indicators of air pollution. Many species of lichens are very sensitive to pollutants and die when pollution levels rise. By monitoring the growth of lichens, scientists can assess the air quality in an area.

 ## Section 3 Review

1. List three characteristics that fungi share.
2. Explain how a fungus feeds. What do fungi feed on?
3. Describe three roles that fungi play in the world.
4. **Thinking Critically Classifying** Explain why mushrooms are classified as fungi rather than as plants.

Check Your Progress

CHAPTER PROJECT

Continue to observe your mushrooms and collect data. Begin to review your data to see which conditions favored mushroom growth. How do your results compare with your hypothesis? Begin to plan your poster now. Think about how you can use graphs and diagrams to display your results. *(Hint: Draw a rough sketch of your poster, and show it to your teacher. Include a labeled drawing of a mushroom.)*

SECTION 1 — Protists

Key Ideas

◆ Animal-like protists, or protozoans, include sarcodines, ciliates, zooflagellates, and sporozoans. Like animals, these protists are heterotrophs. Most protozoans move by using pseudopods, cilia, or flagella.

◆ Funguslike protists include water molds, downy mildews, and slime molds. Like fungi, these protists are heterotrophs, have cell walls, and use spores to reproduce.

◆ Plantlike protists, or algae, include euglenoids, dinoflagellates, diatoms, green algae, red algae, and brown algae. Like plants, these organisms are autotrophs.

Key Terms

protozoan
pseudopod
contractile vacuole
cilia
symbiosis
mutualism
spore
algae
pigment

SECTION 2 — Algal Blooms

INTEGRATING ENVIRONMENTAL SCIENCE

Key Ideas

◆ Red tides occur when a population of algae increases quickly in ocean waters. Some algae can secrete toxins that poison animals.

◆ Nutrients in a lake or pond build up over time, causing an increase in the numbers of algae. An accelerated rate of eutrophication can lead to the deaths of many organisms in the lake or pond.

Key Terms

algal bloom   eutrophication
red tide

SECTION 3 — Fungi

Key Ideas

◆ Most fungi are eukaryotes, use spores to reproduce, and are heterotrophs.

◆ Most fungi feed by absorbing food through their hyphae. The hyphae secrete digestive chemicals into a food source, which is broken down into small substances that are absorbed by the hyphae.

◆ Fungi produce spores in fruiting bodies. Most fungi reproduce both asexually and sexually.

◆ Fungi are decomposers that recycle Earth's chemicals.

Key Terms

hypha   budding
fruiting body   lichen

Organizing Information

Flowchart Copy this flowchart about changes in a lake onto a separate sheet of paper. Then complete the flowchart and add a title. (For more on flowcharts, see the Skills Handbook.)

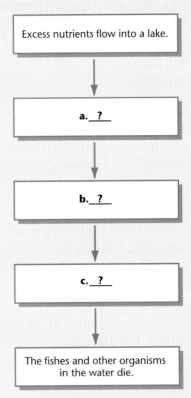

Excess nutrients flow into a lake.

↓

a. __?__

↓

b. __?__

↓

c. __?__

↓

The fishes and other organisms in the water die.

Reviewing Content

 For more review of key concepts, see the Interactive Student Tutorial CD-ROM.

Multiple Choice
Choose the letter of the best answer.

1. Which of the following characteristics describes *all* protists?
   a. They are unicellular.
   b. They can be seen with the unaided eye.
   c. Their cells have nuclei.
   d. They are unable to move on their own.

2. Which protist uses cilia to move?
   a. euglena
   b. ameba
   c. paramecium
   d. diatom

3. Which statement is true of slime molds?
   a. They are always unicellular.
   b. They are autotrophs.
   c. They are animal-like protists.
   d. They use spores to reproduce.

4. An overpopulation of saltwater algae is called a(n)
   a. pigment.
   b. lichen.
   c. red tide.
   d. eutrophication.

5. A lichen is a symbiotic association between which of the following?
   a. fungi and plant roots
   b. algae and fungi
   c. algae and bacteria
   d. protozoans and algae

True or False
If the statement is true, write true. If it is false, change the underlined word or words to make the statement true.

6. Sarcodines use <u>flagella</u> to move.

7. <u>Eutrophication</u> is the process by which nutrients in a lake build up over time, causing an increase in the growth of algae.

8. Most fungi are made up of threadlike structures called <u>hyphae</u>.

9. All mushrooms are classified as <u>sac</u> fungi.

10. Most fungi that live among the roots of plants are <u>beneficial</u> to the plants.

Checking Concepts

11. Describe the process by which an ameba obtains its food.

12. Describe the differences among algae in terms of their sizes.

13. Compare how animal-like, funguslike, and plantlike protists obtain food.

14. What problems can an algal bloom cause in an ocean? What problems can an algal bloom cause in a lake?

15. How does sexual reproduction occur in fungi?

16. Explain how both organisms that make up a lichen benefit from their symbiotic relationship.

17. **Writing to Learn** Imagine you are a spore inside a ripe puffball. An animal passing by brushes against the puffball and punctures the outer covering of your spore case. Write a description about what happens to you next.

Thinking Critically

18. **Comparing and Contrasting** Describe the ways in which amebas and paramecia are similar to one another. How are they different?

19. **Problem Solving** What are some actions that homeowners could take to discourage the growth of mildew in their basement? Explain why these actions might help solve the problem.

20. **Predicting** If all algae suddenly disappeared from Earth's waters, what would happen to living things on Earth? Explain your answer.

21. **Relating Cause and Effect** You see some green scumlike material growing on the walls of your freshwater aquarium at home. List some possible reasons why this growth has occurred.

Applying Skills

When yeast is added to bread dough, the yeast cells produce carbon dioxide, which causes the dough to rise. The graph below shows how temperature affects the amount of carbon dioxide that is produced. Use the graph to answer Questions 22–24.

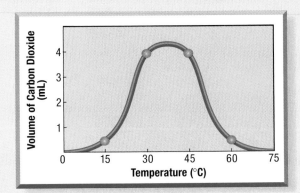

22. Interpreting Data Explain how temperature affects the amount of carbon dioxide that the yeast cells produce.

23. Inferring Use the graph to explain why yeast is dissolved in warm water rather than cold water when it is used to make bread.

24. Predicting Based on the graph, would you expect bread dough to continue to rise if it were placed in a refrigerator (about 2°–5°C)? Explain.

Performance ▼CHAPTER PROJECT▼ Assessment

Present Your Project Now it's time to finalize your poster. Include your hypothesis, and describe the conditions that produced the best mushroom growth. Make sure your graph is easy to understand. Check that your drawing of a mushroom is clearly labeled.

Reflect and Record What did you learn about mushrooms from this project? Did you encounter and solve any problems? Did the project raise new questions for you? If so, how could you answer those questions?

Test Preparation   *Use these questions to prepare for standardized tests.*

Study the graph. Then answer Questions 25–28.

25. What is the best title for this graph?
  a. The Growth Rates of Trees
  b. The Heights of Four Tree Species
  c. The Effect of Root-Associated Fungi on Tree Growth
  d. The Growth of Root-Associated Fungi

26. Which of the following statements is supported by the graph's data?
  a. All trees grew equally well.
  b. Trees with root-associated fungi grew taller than similar trees without such fungi.
  c. Yellow poplars are the tallest tree species.
  d. The data support none of the statements.

27. Based on the graph, which type of tree had the largest growth change with root-associated fungi?
  a. pine   **b.** sour orange
  c. avocado   **d.** yellow poplar

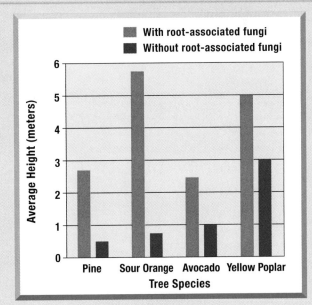

28. What is the average height difference between avocado trees that grew with root-associated fungi and those that grew without such fungi?
  a. 1.5 meters   **b.** 2.0 meters
  c. 2.25 meters   **d.** 5.0 meters

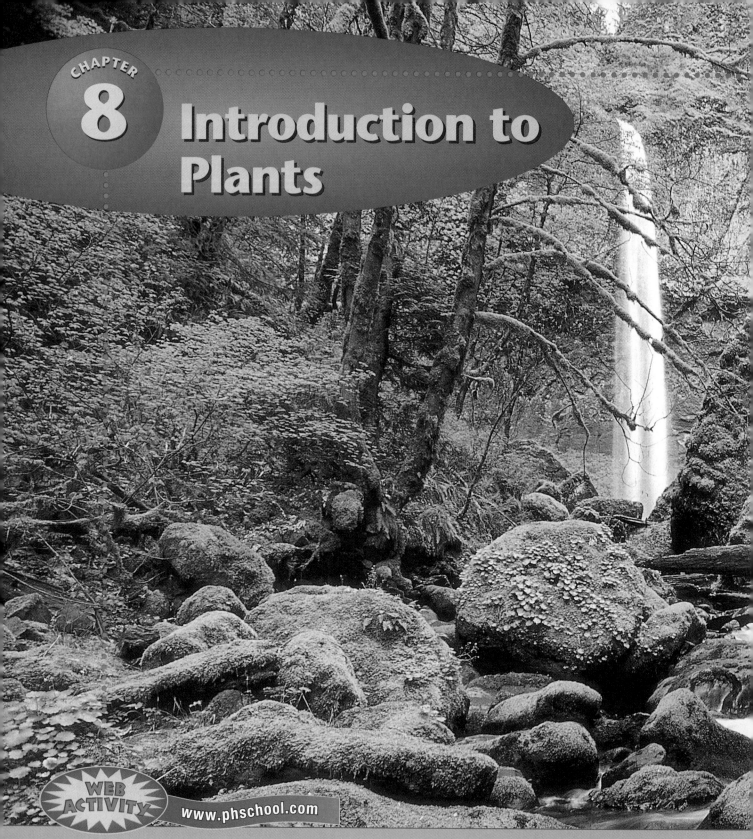

WEB ACTIVITY www.phschool.com

SECTION
1 The Plant Kingdom

Discover What Do Leaves Reveal About Plants?
Sharpen Your Skills Interpreting Data
Science at Home State Flowers
Skills Lab Eye on Photosynthesis

SECTION
2 Mosses, Liverworts, and Hornworts

Discover Will Mosses Absorb Water?
Skills Lab Masses of Mosses

SECTION
3 Ferns and Their Relatives

Discover How Quickly Can Water Move Upward?
Try This Examining a Fern

Become a Moss Expert

In a shady valley, mosses cover the banks of a stream. Overhead, trees stretch their branches toward the light. Each type of plant has its own requirements for growth. In this project, you'll care for one type of plant, a moss similar to the ones growing on these rocks. By the time you're finished, you'll be able to tell others what conditions are needed for mosses to grow.

Your Goal To create a brochure titled "How to Raise Mosses" to share with an audience of your choice.

To successfully complete this project you must
◆ grow moss in a terrarium you construct from a 2-liter bottle
◆ observe the moss daily, and keep a log of the amount of light, water, and other conditions you provide for it
◆ publish information about caring for mosses
◆ follow the safety guidelines in Appendix A

Get Started In a small group, create a list of places where you've seen mosses growing. Compare the list your group makes with those from other groups. What are some locations that many groups identified? What do you notice about the environments where mosses are found? List possible ways to create a similar environment in a terrarium. Start to write out a plan for making the terrarium.

Check Your Progress You'll be working on this project as you study this chapter. To keep your project on track, look for Check Your Progress boxes at the following points.
Section 2 Review, page 259: Plan your terrarium.
Section 3 Review, page 265: Provide the proper conditions as you care for your moss.
Section 4 Review, page 268: Plan and produce your brochure.

Present Your Project At the end of the chapter (page 271), you'll share your brochure about mosses with your audience.

Mosses carpet the rocks along this stream in Pennsylvania's Pocono Mountains.

Integrating Technology

SECTION 4 **Feeding the World**

Discover **Will There Be Enough to Eat?**

SECTION 1 The Plant Kingdom

What Do Leaves Reveal About Plants?

1. Your teacher will give you two leaves from plants that grow in two very different environments: a desert and an area with average rainfall.

2. Carefully observe the color, size, shape, and texture of the leaves. Touch the surfaces of each leaf. Examine each leaf with a hand lens. Record your observations in your notebook.

3. When you have finished, wash your hands thoroughly with soap and water.

Think It Over

Inferring Use your observations to determine which plant lives in the desert and which does not. Give at least one reason to support your inference.

GUIDE FOR READING

◆ What characteristics do all plants share?

◆ What do plants need to live successfully on land?

Reading Tip Before you read, list the boldfaced vocabulary words in your notebook. Leave space to add notes as you read.

I magine a forest where a thick growth of fungi, mosses, and ferns carpets the floor. Because there is no bare soil, seedlings start their lives on fallen logs. Ferns hang like curtains from the limbs of giant hemlock trees. Douglas fir trees grow taller than 20-story buildings. Other plants with strange names—vanilla leaf, self-heal, and licorice fern—also grow in the forest.

Such a forest exists on the western slopes of the Olympic Mountains in Washington State. Native Americans named the forest *Hoh*, which means "fast white water," after a river there. In some areas of the forest, over 300 centimeters of rain fall each year, which makes the area a rain forest.

What Is a Plant?

You would probably recognize many of the plants that grow in the Hoh rain forest. You encounter other familiar plants when you pick flowers, run across freshly cut grass, or eat vegetables such as peas.

▼ The Hoh rain forest

Members of the plant kingdom share some important characteristics. **All plants are eukaryotes that contain many cells. In addition, plants are autotrophs, which produce their own food.**

In Chapter 2, you learned that plants carry out the process called photosynthesis to make their food. During photosynthesis, a plant uses carbon dioxide gas and water to make food and oxygen. Sunlight provides the energy that powers the entire process.

Living on Land

Unlike algae, most plants live on land. How is living on land different from living in water? Imagine multicellular green algae floating in the ocean. Their bodies are held up toward the sunlight by the water around them. The algae obtain water and other materials directly from their watery surroundings. When algae reproduce, sperm cells swim to egg cells through the water.

On land, plants are not surrounded by water. **For plants to survive on land, they must have ways to obtain water and other materials from their surroundings, retain water, transport materials throughout the plant, support their bodies, and reproduce successfully.** In *Exploring Plant Adaptations* on the next page, you can see some of the ways in which plants are adapted to live on land.

Obtaining Water and Other Materials Recall that all organisms need water to survive. Obtaining water is easy for algae because water surrounds them. To live on land, though, plants need adaptations for obtaining water from the soil. Plants must also have ways of obtaining other nutrients from the soil.

Retaining Water Have you ever noticed that a puddle of rainwater gradually shrinks and then disappears after the rain stops? This happens because there is more water in the puddle than in the air. As a result, the water evaporates into the air. The same principle explains why a plant on land can dry out. Because there is more water in plant cells than in air, water evaporates into the air. Plants need adaptations to reduce water loss to the air. One common adaptation is a waxy, waterproof layer called the **cuticle** that covers the leaves of most plants.

Figure 1 Plants have adaptations that help them retain water. The shiny, waterproof cuticle on this leaf slows down evaporation.

EXPLORING *Plant Adaptations*

Today, plants are found in almost every environment on Earth—deserts, lakes, jungles, and even the polar regions. As you read about each plant, notice how it is adapted to living in its specific environment.

◄ Pasque Flower
Pasque flowers, such as this *Anemone patens,* often grow on cold, rocky mountain slopes. The flower's petals trap sunlight, keeping the flower up to 10° C warmer than the surrounding air. This feature enables the plant to survive in cold environments.

Staghorn Fern ►
Staghorn ferns do not grow in soil. Instead, they cling to the bark of trees in tropical areas. The leaves that hug the bark store water and nutrients. The leaves that hang down are involved in reproduction.

▲ Bristlecone Pine
Because the needles of bristlecone pines live more than 15 years, the trees survive long periods of drought. Bristlecone pine trees can live more than 4,000 years. This is because they grow slowly in high altitude areas where there are few harmful insects or other disease-causing organisims.

◄ Water Lily
Water lilies live only in fresh water. Large, flat leaves and sweet-smelling flowers float on the water's surface. The plants have long stems under the water. Roots anchor the plant in the mud at the bottom of the pond.

Rafflesia ▶
The rafflesia plant produces the largest flowers on Earth. This flower that grew in Borneo measures over 83 centimeters in diameter. Rafflesia flowers have a foul odor—something like rotting meat. The odor attracts insects that help the plant reproduce.

▲ Mangrove
Mangrove trees, such as these on Guadalcanal Island in the Pacific Ocean, grow in salt water in tropical areas. The tree's huge root system makes the tree appear as if it is on stilts. The roots trap soil and sand around them, providing a material in which to anchor as they grow.

◀ Date Palm
Date palms, such as these growing on a date farm in southern California, grow in warm climates. These flowering trees can grow up to 23 meters tall. The leaves are long and narrow, reducing the amount of surface area for evaporation. The female trees produce dates that hang from the stems in large clusters.

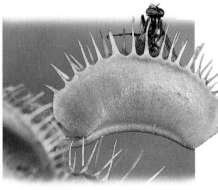

◀ Venus Fly Trap
The Venus fly trap can grow in soil that is low in nitrogen. This is because the plant obtains its nitrogen by digesting insects that it traps. When an insect touches sensitive hairs on the inner surface of a leaf, the two parts of the leaf quickly snap shut. It takes about ten days for the plant to digest an insect.

Figure 2 The vascular tissue in these tree ferns transports water and nutrients inside the plants. *Inferring What additional function might vascular tissue have in these tree ferns?*

Transporting Materials A plant needs to transport food, water, minerals, and other materials from one part of its body to another. In general, water and minerals are taken up by the bottom part of the plant. Food is made in the top part. But all the plant's cells need water, minerals, and food. To supply all cells with the materials they need, water and minerals must be transported up to the top of the plant. Then food must be transported throughout the plant.

Most plants that live on land have tissues that transport materials throughout their bodies. **Tissues** are groups of similar cells that perform a specific function in an organism. Some plants have transporting tissue called **vascular tissue.** Vascular tissue is an internal system of tubelike structures through which water and food move inside the plant. Plants that have vascular tissue are called vascular plants. Vascular plants can grow quite tall because they have an effective way of transporting substances to distant cells.

Support While algae are supported by the surrounding water, a plant on land must support its own body. Because plants need sunlight for photosynthesis, the food-making parts of the plant must be exposed to as much sunlight as possible. In vascular plants, vascular tissue strengthens and supports the large bodies of the plants.

Reproduction All plants undergo sexual reproduction that involves fertilization. **Fertilization** occurs when a sperm cell unites with an egg cell. The fertilized egg is called a **zygote.** For algae and some plants, fertilization can occur only if there is water in the environment. This is because sperm cells swim through the water to egg cells. Other plants, however, have an adaptation that make it possible for fertilization to occur in dry environments. You will learn more about this adaptation in the next chapter.

✓ *Checkpoint* *Why do plants need adaptations to prevent water loss?*

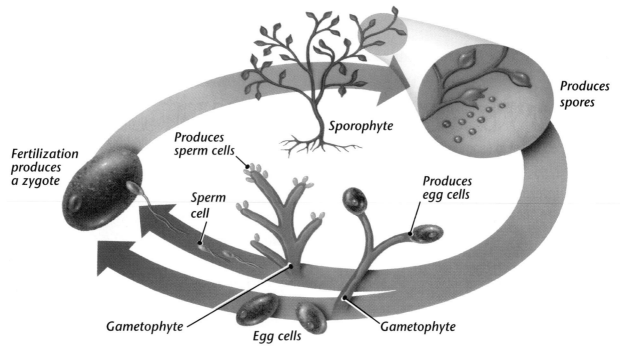

Fertilization produces a zygote

Produces sperm cells

Sporophyte

Produces spores

Sperm cell

Produces egg cells

Gametophyte

Egg cells

Gametophyte

Figure 3 Plants have complex life cycles that consist of two stages—the sporophyte stage and the gametophyte stage. *Interpreting Diagrams During which stage are sperm and egg cells produced?*

Complex Life Cycles

Unlike most animals, plants have complex life cycles that are made up of two different stages, or generations. In one stage, called the **sporophyte** (SPAWR uh fyt), the plant produces spores, the tiny cells that can grow into new organisms. A spore develops into the plant's other stage, called the gametophyte. In the **gametophyte** (guh MEE tuh fyt) stage, the plant produces two kinds of sex cells, or **gametes**—sperm cells and egg cells.

Figure 3 shows a typical plant life cycle. A sperm cell and egg cell join to form a zygote. The zygote then develops into a sporophyte. The sporophyte produces spores, which develop into the gameophyte. Then the gameophyte produces sperm cells and egg cells and the cycle starts again. The sporophyte of a plant usually looks quite different from the gametophyte.

Section 1 Review

1. List three characteristics that all plants share.
2. What are five adaptations that plants need to survive on land?
3. Distinguish between a sporophyte and a gametophyte.
4. **Thinking Critically** **Classifying** Suppose you found a tall plant living in the desert. Do you think it would be a vascular plant? Explain.

Science at Home

State Flowers Choose any state in the United States. With a family member, find out the name of the state's official plant. Research why that plant was chosen to represent the state. Then gather information about the plant. Make an illustrated poster to display in your school that includes the information you gather.

Mosses, Liverworts, and Hornworts

DISCOVER · ACTIVITY · · ·

Will Mosses Absorb Water?

1. Place 20 milliliters (mL) of sand into a plastic graduated cylinder. Place 20 mL of peat moss into a second plastic graduated cylinder.

2. Predict what would happen if you were to slowly pour 10 mL of water into each of the two graduated cylinders and then wait five minutes.

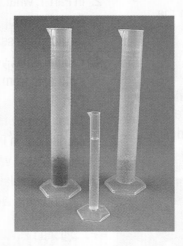

3. To test your prediction, use a third graduated cylinder to slowly add 10 mL of water to the sand. Then add 10 mL of water to the moss. After 5 minutes, record your observations.

Think It Over

Predicting How did your prediction compare with your results? What did you learn about moss from this investigation?

GUIDE FOR READING

◆ What characteristics do nonvascular plants share?

Reading Tip As you read, make a table comparing and contrasting mosses, liverworts, and hornworts.

If you enjoy gardening, you know that a garden requires time, effort, and knowledge. Before you start to plant your garden, you need to know how much water and sun your plants will need. You also need to know whether the soil in your garden can supply the plants with the water and nutrients they need.

Many gardeners add peat moss to the soil in their gardens. Peat moss improves the texture of soil and increases the soil's ability to hold water. When peat moss is added to claylike soil, it loosens the soil so that the plant's roots can easily grow through it. When peat moss is added to sandy soil, the soil stays moist for a longer time after it is watered.

Characteristics of Nonvascular Plants

Peat moss contains one type of **nonvascular plant.** Some other nonvascular plants are liverworts and hornworts. **All nonvascular plants are low-growing plants that lack vascular tissue.**

Nonvascular plants do not have vascular tissue—a system of tubelike structures that transport water and other materials. Nonvascular plants can only pass materials from one cell to the next. That means that the materials do not travel very far or very quickly. Also, these plants have only their rigid cell walls to provide support. With this type of structure, these plants cannot grow very wide or tall. As a result, nonvascular plants are small and grow low to the ground.

Like all plants, nonvascular plants require water to survive. These plants lack roots, but they can obtain water and minerals directly from their surroundings. Many nonvascular plants live where water is plentiful. But even nonvascular plants that live in drier areas need enough water to let the sperm cells swim to the egg cells during reproduction.

Mosses

Have you ever seen mosses growing in the crack of a sidewalk, on a tree trunk, or on rocks that are misted by waterfalls? With over 10,000 species, mosses are by far the most diverse group of nonvascular plants.

The Structure of a Moss If you were to look closely at a moss, you would see a plant that looks something like the one in Figure 4. The familiar green fuzzy moss is the gametophyte generation of the plant. Structures that look like tiny leaves grow off a small stemlike structure. Thin rootlike structures called **rhizoids** anchor the moss and absorb water and nutrients from the soil. The sporophyte generation grows out of the gametophyte. It consists of a slender stalk with a capsule at the end. The capsule contains spores.

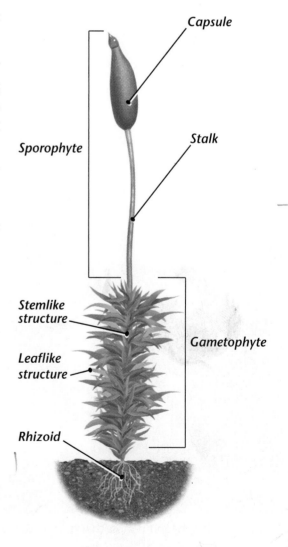

Figure 4 A moss gametophyte is low-growing and has structures that look like roots, stems, and leaves. The stalklike sporophyte generation remains attached to the gametophyte. *Interpreting Diagrams What structure anchors the gametophyte in the soil?*

Historians have found many items preserved in the acidic water of peat bogs. Weapons more than 1,600 years old have been recovered from bogs in northern Europe. In addition, about 700 human bodies have been found in bogs. Most of the bodies are as well preserved as the one that you see in the photo. This man, who lived 2,000 years ago, was found in a bog in Denmark.

In Your Journal

Imagine that you have just recovered an old wooden tool from a bog. Write a letter to a natural history museum explaining why the tool is so well preserved.

The Importance of Mosses Many people use peat moss in agriculture and gardening. The peat moss that gardeners use contains sphagnum (SFAG num) moss. Sphagnum moss grows in a type of wetland called a **bog.** The still water in a bog is so acidic that decomposing organisms cannot live in the water. Thus when the plants die, they do not decay. Instead, the dead plants accumulate at the bottom of the bog. Over time, the mosses become compressed into layers and form a blackish-brown material called **peat.** Large deposits of peat exist in North America, Europe, and Asia. In Europe and Asia, people use peat as a fuel to heat homes and to cook food.

INTEGRATING EARTH SCIENCE Like the lichens you learned about in Chapter 7, many mosses are pioneer plants. They are among the first organisms to grow in areas destroyed by volcanoes or in burnt-out forests. Like lichens, mosses trap wind-blown soil. Over time, enough soil accumulates to support the growth of other plants whose spores or seeds are blown there.

☑ *Checkpoint* *What does a moss sporophyte look like?*

Figure 5 The sphagnum moss that grew in this bog is being harvested as peat.

Figure 6 Like mosses, hornworts and liverworts are nonvascular plants. **A.** Hornworts grow only in soil and are often found growing among grasses. **B.** Liverworts grow flat along the ground on moist soil and rocks.

Liverworts and Hornworts

Figure 6 shows examples of two other groups of nonvascular plants—liverworts and hornworts. There are more than 8,000 species of liverworts. This group of plants is named for the shape of the plant's body, which looks somewhat like a human liver. *Wort* is an old English word for "plant." Liverworts are often found growing as a thick crust on moist rocks or soil along the sides of a stream. Unlike mosses, most liverworts grow flat along the ground. In Figure 6, you can see the gametophyte generation of one type of liverwort.

There are fewer than 100 species of hornworts. At first glance, these plants resemble liverworts. But if you look closely, you can see slender, curved structures that look like horns growing out of the gametophytes. These hornlike structures, which give these plants their names, are the sporophytes. Unlike mosses or liverworts, hornworts are seldom found on rocks or tree trunks. Instead, hornworts live in moist soil, often mixed in with grass plants.

Section 2 Review

1. Describe two characteristics that nonvascular plants share. Explain how the two characteristics are related.
2. Describe the structure of a moss plant.
3. How does peat form?
4. **Thinking Critically Comparing and Contrasting** In what ways are mosses, liverworts, and hornworts similar? How do they differ?

Check Your Progress CHAPTER PROJECT
At this point, your plan for creating a terrarium should be complete. On a sheet of paper, list the conditions that will affect moss growth. Explain how you'll provide those conditions in your terrarium. (*Hint:* Use a sketch to show what your bottle terrarium will look like.)

Masses of Mosses

I n this lab, you will look closely at some tiny members of the plant kingdom.

Problem

How is a moss plant adapted to carry out its life activities?

Materials

clump of moss   hand lens
metric ruler   toothpicks
plastic dropper   water

Procedure

1. Your teacher will give you a clump of moss. Examine the clump from all sides. Draw a diagram of what you see. Measure the size of the overall clump and the main parts of the clump. Record your observations.

2. Using toothpicks, gently separate five individual moss plants from the clump. Be sure to pull them totally apart so that you can observe each plant separately. If the moss plants appear to dry up as you are working, moisten them with a few drops of water.

3. Measure the length of the leaflike, stemlike, and rootlike structures on each plant. If brown stalks and capsules are present, measure them. Find the average length of each structure.

4. Make a life-size drawing of a moss plant. Label the parts, give their sizes, and record the color of each part. When you are finished observing the moss, return it to your teacher. Wash your hands thoroughly.

5. Obtain class averages for the sizes of the structures you measured in Step 3. Also, if the moss that you observed had brown stalks and capsules, share your observations about those structures.

Analyze and Conclude

1. Describe the typical size of the leaflike portion of moss plants, the typical height of the stemlike portion, and the typical length of the rootlike portion.

2. In which part(s) of the moss does photosynthesis occur? How do you know?

3. Why are mosses unable to grow very tall?

4. **Think About It** What did you learn by observing a moss up close and in detail?

More to Explore

Select a moss plant with stalks and capsules. Use toothpicks to release some of the spores, which can be as small as dust particles. Examine the spores under a microscope.

DISCOVER ···················ACTIVITY····

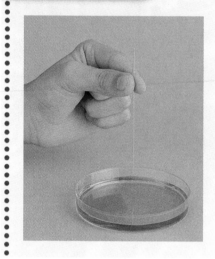

How Quickly Can Water Move Upward?

1. Put on your goggles. Your teacher will give you a plastic petri dish as well as a narrow glass tube that is open at both ends.

2. Fill the petri dish half full of water. Add a drop of food coloring to the water.

3. Stand the tube on end in the water and hold it upright. Observe what happens. Record your observations.

Think It Over

Inferring Why might it be an advantage for the transporting cells of plants to be arranged in a tubelike way?

The time is 340 million years ago—long before the dinosaurs lived. The place is somewhere in the forests that covered most of Earth's land. If you could have walked through one of these ancient forests, it would have looked very strange to you.

You might have recognized the mosses and liverworts that carpeted the moist soil. But overhead you would have seen odd-looking trees, some towering as high as 25 meters above the ground. Among the trees were ancient ferns—huge versions of the ferns you find in today's florist shops. Other trees resembled giant stick figures with leaves up to one meter long. The huge leaves hugged the branches, looking something like the scales that cover a fish.

GUIDE FOR READING

◆ What are the main characteristics of seedless vascular plants?

Reading Tip As you read, create a table comparing ferns, club mosses, and horsetails.

Figure 7 These fossils are from two plants that lived about 300 million years ago. The larger fossil is of a fern's leaf. The small star-shaped fossil is of a plant called a horsetail.

INTEGRATING EARTH SCIENCE As the trees and other plants died, they formed thick layers and partially decomposed. Over millions of years, the layers became compressed under the weight of the layers above them. Eventually, these layers became the coal deposits that we use for fuel today.

Characteristics of Seedless Vascular Plants

The odd-looking plants in the ancient forests were the ancestors of three groups of plants that are alive today—ferns, club mosses, and horsetails. **Ferns and their relatives share two characteristics. They have vascular tissue and use spores to reproduce.**

Vascular Tissue What adaptations allowed plants to grow very tall? Unlike the mosses, the ancient trees were **vascular plants**— plants that have vascular tissue. Vascular plants are better suited to life on land than are nonvascular plants. This is because vascular tissue solves the problems of support and transportation. Vascular tissue transports water quickly and efficiently throughout the plant's body. It also transports the food produced in the leaves to other parts of the plant, including the roots.

In addition, vascular tissue strengthens the plant's body. Imagine a handful of drinking straws bundled together with rubber bands. The bundle of straws would be stronger and more stable than a single straw would be. In a similar way, vascular tissue provides strength and stability to a plant.

Spores for Reproduction Ferns, club mosses, and horsetails still need to grow in moist surroundings. This is because the plants release spores into their surroundings, where they grow into gametophytes. When the gametophytes produce egg cells and sperm cells, there must be enough water available for fertilization to occur.

☑ *Checkpoint* *What adaptation allowed plants to grow tall?*

Ferns

Fossil records indicate that ferns first appeared on land about 400 million years ago. There are over 12,000 species of ferns alive today. They range in size from tiny plants about the size of this letter "M" to large tree ferns that grow up to 5 meters tall in moist, tropical areas.

The Structure of Ferns Like other vascular plants, ferns have true stems, roots, and leaves. The stems of most ferns are underground. Leaves grow upward from the top side of the stems, and roots grow downward from the bottom of the stems. Roots are structures that anchor the fern to the ground and absorb water and nutrients from the soil. These substances enter the root's vascular tissue and travel through the tissue into the stems and leaves. In Figure 8 you can see the fern's structure.

Figure 8 Most ferns have underground stems in addition to underground roots. The leaves, or fronds, grow above ground.

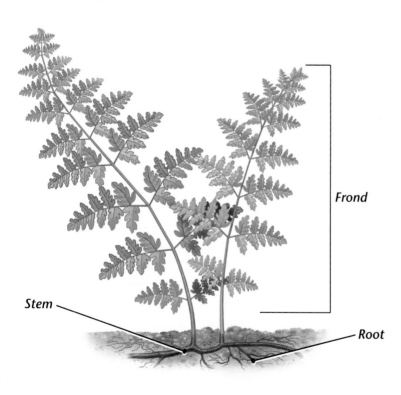

Frond

Stem

Root

Figure 9 Spores are produced on the undersides of mature fronds.
Applying Concepts What happens to spores that are released?

Look closely at the fern's leaves, or **fronds.** Notice that the frond is divided into many smaller parts that look like small leaves. Many other ferns have a similar divided-leaf structure. The upper surface of each frond is coated with a cuticle that helps the plant retain water. In many types of ferns, the developing leaves are coiled at first. Because they resemble the top of a violin, these young leaves are often called fiddleheads. As they mature, the fiddleheads uncurl.

Reproduction in Ferns The familiar fern with its visible fronds is the sporophyte stage of the plant. On the underside of mature fronds, spores develop in tiny spore cases. When the spores are released, wind and water can carry them great distances. If a spore lands in moist, shaded soil, it develops into a gametophyte. Fern gametophytes are tiny plants that grow low to the ground.

The Importance of Ferns Ferns are useful to people in many ways. They are popular houseplants because they are attractive and easy to grow. Ferns are also used to grow other kinds of houseplants. For example, orchids are often grown on the tangled masses of fern roots.

People eat some ferns. During the spring, fiddleheads are sold in supermarkets and farm stands. Fiddleheads make a nutritious vegetable dish. But because some ferns are not safe to eat, you should never gather wild fiddleheads for food.

In Southeast Asia, farmers grow a small aquatic fern alongside rice plants in their rice fields. Tiny pockets in the fern's leaves provide a home for some bacteria. The bacteria produce a natural fertilizer that helps the rice plants grow.

Figure 10 Fiddleheads are the developing leaves of a fern.

Club Mosses and Horsetails

Two other groups of seedless, vascular plants are the club mosses and horsetails. Like ferns, club mosses and horsetails have true leaves, stems, and roots. They also have a similar life cycle. However, there are relatively few species of club mosses and horsetails alive today.

Unlike their larger ancestors, today's club mosses are small. Do not be confused by the name *club mosses*. Unlike the true mosses, the club mosses have vascular tissue. You may be familiar with the club moss you see in Figure 11. The plant, which looks like the small branch of a pine tree, is sometimes called ground pine or princess pine. It grows in moist woodlands and near streams.

There are 30 species of horsetails on Earth today. As you can see in Figure 11, the stems of horsetails are jointed. Long, coarse, needlelike branches grow in a circle around each joint. Small leaves grow flat against the stem just above each joint. The stems contain silica, a gritty substance also found in sand. During colonial times, Americans called horsetails "scouring rushes" because they used the plants to scrub their pots and pans.

Figure 11 Horsetails and club mosses are other seedless vascular plants. **A.** These horsetail plants have jointed stems. Needle-like branches grow out of each joint. **B.** This club moss looks like a tiny pine tree.

Section 3 Review

1. What two characteristics do ferns, club mosses, and horsetails share? How do these characteristics differ from those of mosses?
2. Describe the structure of a fern plant. What do its leaves, stems, and roots look like?
3. List three ways that ferns are useful to people today.
4. **Thinking Critically Applying Concepts** Although ferns have vascular tissue, they still must live in moist, shady environments. Explain why this is true.

Check Your Progress
You should now be caring for your moss, and providing the best conditions for its survival and growth. Be sure to keep in mind how mosses differ from other familiar kinds of plants. (*Hint:* Keep your terrarium warm, but not hot, and make sure it remains moist.)

CHAPTER PROJECT

SECTION 4 Feeding the World

DISCOVER ·····················ACTIVITY···

Will There Be Enough to Eat?

1. Choose a numbered tag from the bag that your teacher provides. If you pick a tag with the number 1 on it, you're from a wealthy country. If you pick a tag with the number 2, you're from a middle-income country. If you pick a tag with the number 3, you're from a poor country.

2. Find classmates that have the same number on their tag. Sit down as a group.

3. Your teacher will serve your group a meal. The amount of food you receive will depend on the number on your tag.

4. As you eat, observe the people in your group and in the other groups. After you eat, record your observations. Also, record how you felt and what you were thinking during the meal.

Think It Over

Predicting Based on this activity, predict what effect an increase in the world's population would have on the world's food supply.

GUIDE FOR READING

◆ What methods may help farmers produce more crops?

Reading Tip As you read, make a list of the technologies being used to increase Earth's food supply.

Today, about six billion people live on Earth. Some scientists predict that by the year 2050 the population will grow to ten billion people. Think about how much additional food will be needed to feed the growing population. How will farmers be able to grow enough food?

Fortunately, both scientists and farmers are already hard at work trying to find answers to this question. **In laboratories, scientists are developing plants that are more resistant to insects, disease, and drought. They are also developing plants that produce more food per plant. On farms, new, efficient, "high-tech" farming practices are being used.**

Producing Better Plants

Wheat, corn, rice, and potatoes are the major sources of food for people on Earth today. To feed more people, then, the production, or yields, of these crops must be increased. This is not an easy task. One challenge facing farmers is that these crops grow only in certain climates. Another challenge is that the size and structure of these plants limit how much food they can produce.

Today scientists are using new technologies to address these challenges. Recall from Chapter 4 that scientists can manipulate the genetic material of certain bacteria to produce human insulin. The process that these scientists use is called genetic engineering. In genetic engineering, scientists alter an organism's genetic material to produce an organism with qualities that people find useful.

Scientists are using genetic engineering to produce plants that can grow in a wider range of climates. They are also engineering plants to be more resistant to damage from insects. For example, scientists have inserted genetic material from a bacterium into corn and tomato plants. The new genetic material enables the plants to produce substances that kill insects. Caterpillars or other insects that bite into the leaves of these plants are killed. Today, many kinds of genetically engineered plants are grown on experimental farms. Some of these plants may produce the crops of the future.

☑ *Checkpoint* *What are the four crops on which people depend?*

Figure 12 In this high-tech greenhouse, scientists control the environmental conditions as they develop new types of plants. *Applying Concepts How might new plant types lead to increased crop yields in the future?*

Improving the Efficiency of Farms

On the farms of the future, satellite images and computers will be just as important as tractors and harvesters. These new tools will allow farmers to practice "precision farming"—knowing just how much water and fertilizer different fields require. First, satellite images of the farmer's fields are taken. Then, a computer analyzes the images to determine the makeup of the soil in different fields on the farm. The computer uses the data to prepare a watering and fertilizing plan for each field. Precision farming benefits farmers because it saves time and money. It also increases crop yields by helping farmers maintain ideal conditions in all fields.

Figure 13 The map on the computer screen of this tractor shows the makeup of the soil in a farm's fields. The map was obtained by satellite imaging.

INTEGRATING ENVIRONMENTAL SCIENCE Precision farming also benefits the environment because farmers use only as much fertilizer as the soil needs. When less fertilizer is used, fewer nutrients wash off the land into lakes and rivers. As you read in Chapter 7, reducing the use of fertilizers is one way to prevent algal blooms from damaging bodies of water.

Hydroponics

In some areas of the world, poor soil does not support the growth of crops. For example, on some islands in the Pacific Ocean, the soil contains large amounts of salt from the surrounding ocean. Food crops will not grow in the salty soil.

On these islands, people can use hydroponics to grow food crops. **Hydroponics** (hy druh PAHN iks) is a method by which plants are grown in solutions of nutrients instead of in soil. Usually, the plants are grown in containers in which their roots are anchored in gravel or sand. The nutrient-rich water is pumped through the gravel or sand. Unfortunately, hydroponics is a costly method of growing food crops. But, the process allows people to grow crops in areas with poor farmland to help feed a growing population.

Section 4 Review

1. List three methods that farmers can use to increase crop yields.
2. Explain how genetic engineering may help farmers grow more food.
3. How does precision farming benefit farmers? How does it benefit the environment?
4. **Thinking Critically Applying Concepts** How are plants that are grown using hydroponics able to survive without soil?

CHAPTER PROJECT

Check Your Progress
Begin planning your brochure as you continue caring for your moss. What's the best way to give clear directions for making a terrarium? What must you say about the amount of light, water, and other conditions that mosses need to survive? (*Hint:* Be sure to include important information about mosses, such as how tall they grow and how they reproduce.)

1 The Plant Kingdom

Key Ideas

◆ Plants are multicellular eukaryotes and autotrophs.

◆ For plants to survive on land, they need ways to obtain water and other materials from their surroundings, retain moisture, support their bodies, transport materials throughout the plant, and reproduce successfully.

◆ All plants have complex life cycles. In the sporophyte stage, plants produce spores. In the gametophyte stage, plants produce sperm cells and egg cells.

Key Terms

cuticle   zygote
tissue   sporophyte
vascular tissue   gametophyte
fertilization   gamete

2 Mosses, Liverworts, and Hornworts

Key Ideas

◆ Nonvascular plants are small, low-growing plants that lack vascular tissue. Most nonvascular plants transport materials by passing them from one cell to the next.

◆ Mosses, liverworts, and hornworts are three types of nonvascular plants.

Key Terms

nonvascular plant   bog
rhizoid   peat

3 Ferns and Their Relatives

Key Ideas

◆ Seedless vascular plants have vascular tissue and use spores to reproduce. These plants include ferns, club mosses, and horsetails.

◆ Although seedless vascular plants grow taller than nonvascular plants, they still need to live in moist places. The plants' spores are released into the environment, where they grow into gametophytes.

Key Terms

vascular plant   frond

4 Feeding the World

INTEGRATING TECHNOLOGY

Key Idea

◆ Genetic engineering, precision farming, and hydroponics can help farmers produce more crops to feed the world's growing population.

Key Term

hydroponics

Organizing Information

Compare/Contrast Table Copy the table comparing mosses and ferns onto a separate sheet of paper. Complete the table by filling in the missing information. Then add a title. (For more on compare/contrast tables, see the Skills Handbook.)

Characteristic	Moss	Fern
Size	a. ?	Can be tall
Environment	Moist	b. ?
Body parts	Rootlike, stemlike, and leaflike	c. ?
Familiar generation	d. ?	sporophyte
Vascular tissue present?	e. ?	f. ?

Reviewing Content

 For more review of key concepts, see the Interactive Student Tutorial CD-ROM.

Multiple Choice
Choose the letter of the best answer.

1. The products of photosynthesis are
   a. food and carbon dioxide.
   b. food and water.
   c. food and oxygen.
   d. water and oxygen.
2. Mosses and ferns are both
   a. vascular plants.
   b. nonvascular plants.
   c. seed plants.
   d. plants.
3. The familiar green, fuzzy moss is the
   a. frond.
   b. rhizoid.
   c. gametophyte.
   d. sporophyte.
4. The leaves of ferns are called
   a. rhizoids.
   b. sporophytes.
   c. fronds.
   d. cuticles.
5. The process of growing crops in a nutrient solution is called
   a. genetic engineering.
   b. hydroponics.
   c. precision farming.
   d. satellite imaging.

True or False
If the statement is true, write true. If it is false, change the underlined word or words to make the statement true.

6. Plants are <u>autotrophs</u>.
7. <u>Tissues</u> are groups of similar cells that perform a specific function in an organism.
8. Mosses are <u>vascular</u> plants.
9. The young leaves of <u>liverworts</u> are known as fiddleheads.
10. The four basic food crops of the world are wheat, corn, rice, and <u>potatoes</u>.

Checking Concepts

11. Describe the process of photosynthesis. Explain why it is an important process for a plant.
12. In what two ways is vascular tissue important to a plant? Give an example of a plant that has vascular tissue.
13. Briefly describe the life cycle of a typical plant.
14. Explain why fern plants are found in moist areas.
15. In what ways do mosses and club mosses differ from each other? In what ways are they similar?
16. How can the use of hydroponics help increase the amount of food that can be grown on Earth?
17. **Writing to Learn** Suppose you are living in a farming community. Write a letter to the editor of the local newspaper that explains how precision farming can increase crop yields. Also explain the other benefits of precision farming to farmers and to the environment.

Thinking Critically

18. **Comparing and Contrasting** How does the sporophyte generation of a plant differ from the gametophyte generation?
19. **Applying Concepts** A friend tells you that he has seen moss plants that are about 2 meters tall. Is your friend correct? Explain your reasoning.
20. **Relating Cause and Effect** People have observed that mosses tend to grow on the north side of a tree rather than the south side. Why do you think this is so?
21. **Making Judgments** Suppose you were a scientist using genetic engineering to increase crop yields. What improvements would you try to introduce? How would they be beneficial?

Applying Skills

Some gardeners spread a protective layer of mulch—plant material such as wood chips, peat moss, or straw—on the soil around plants. The graph below compares how much moisture is retained by soil covered with mulch and by soil without mulch. Use the graph to answer Questions 22–24.

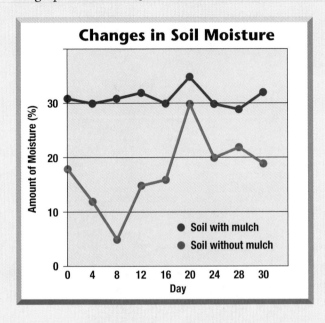

Changes in Soil Moisture

- ● Soil with mulch
- ● Soil without mulch

22. Comparing and Contrasting How does the amount of moisture in soil covered with mulch differ from the amount of moisture in the uncovered soil?

23. Inferring The amount of moisture in both soils increased greatly between days 16 and 20. Explain why this might have happened.

24. Drawing Conclusions If you were a gardener, would you grow your plants in soil covered with mulch or in soil that was uncovered? Explain.

CHAPTER PROJECT

Performance ▽ Assessment

Present Your Project It's time to share your "How to Raise Mosses" brochure with others. Be prepared to explain the information in your brochure. Ask other students about their work.

Reflect and Record What did you learn by keeping the terrarium and making the brochure? Did you discover new ideas from brochures made by others? If you were to repeat this project, how could you improve your work?

Test Preparation

Use these questions to prepare for standardized tests.

Use the information to answer Questions 25–27.
When bracken ferns grow, their underground stems grow outward and produce new plants. As the map below shows, the new ferns spread into nearby open areas. The bands of color indicate the areas where bracken ferns grew over a four-year period.

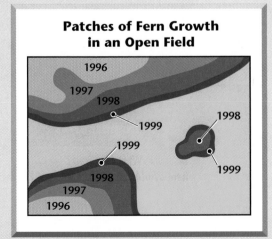

Patches of Fern Growth in an Open Field

1996
1997
1998
1999
1998
1999
1999
1998
1997
1996

25. During which year did the ferns grow most slowly?
  a. 1996   **b.** 1997
  c. 1998   **d.** 1999

26. In how many areas in the field were bracken ferns growing in 1997?
  a. one   **b.** two
  c. three   **d.** four

27. The underground stems of bracken ferns do not grow far before producing new plants. What is the most likely explanation for how bracken ferns began to grow in the middle of the field in 1998?
  a. It rained less than usual.
  b. The temperatures were higher than normal.
  c. The whole field was fertilized.
  d. Spores blew into a moist part of the field.

CHAPTER

9 Seed Plants

WEB ACTIVITY
www.phschool.com

SECTION
1 The Characteristics of Seed Plants

Discover Which Plant Part Is It?
Try This The In-Seed Story
Sharpen Your Skills Calculating
Science at Home Seed Germination

SECTION
2 Gymnosperms

Discover Are All Leaves Alike?
Try This The Scoop on Cones

SECTION
3 Angiosperms

Discover What Is a Fruit?
Real-World Lab A Close Look at Flowers

Cycle of a Lifetime

How long is a seed plant's life? Redwood trees can live for thousands of years. Tomato plants die after one growing season. Can organisms that seem so different have anything in common? In this chapter, you'll find out. Some answers will come from this chapter's project. In this project, you'll grow some seeds, then care for the plants until they, in turn, produce their own seeds.

Your Goal To care for and observe a plant throughout its life cycle. To complete this project successfully you must

◆ grow a plant from a seed
◆ observe and describe key parts of your plant's life cycle, such as seed germination and pollination
◆ harvest and plant the seeds that your growing plant produces
◆ follow the safety guidelines in Appendix A

Get Started Observe the seeds that your teacher gives you. In a small group, discuss what conditions the seeds might need to grow. What should you look for after you plant the seeds? What kinds of measurements could you make? Will it help to make drawings? When you are ready, plant your seeds.

Thistle plants depend on bees for pollination.

Check Your Progress You'll be working on this project as you study this chapter. To keep your project on track, look for Check Your Progress boxes at the following points.
Section 2 Review, page 288: Observe the developing seedlings.
Section 3 Review, page 296: Pollinate your flowers.
Section 4 Review, page 299: Collect the seeds from your plant and plant some of them.

Present Your Project At the end of the chapter (page 303), you'll present an exhibit showing the plant's life cycle.

Integrating Chemistry

SECTION 4

Plant Responses and Growth

Discover Can a Plant Respond to Touch?
Skills Lab Which Way Is Up?

The Characteristics of Seed Plants

Which Plant Part Is It?

1. With a partner, carefully observe the items of food your teacher gives you.

2. Make a list of the food items.

3. For each food item, write the name of the part of the plant—root, stem, or leaf—from which you think the food is obtained.

Think It Over

Classifying Classify the items into groups depending on the plant part from which the food is obtained. Compare your groupings with those of your classmates.

GUIDE FOR READING

◆ What characteristics do seed plants share?

◆ What are the main parts of a seed?

◆ What are the functions of leaves, stems, and roots?

Reading Tip As you read, make a list of the boldfaced terms. Write a definition for each term in your own words.

Chances are you've seen dandelions. But how much do you know about these common plants? For example, do you know that dandelion blossoms open only in sunlight? Or that each blossom is made up of hundreds of tube-shaped flowers? Do you know that a seed develops in each of these tiny flowers? And that, just like apple seeds, dandelion seeds are enclosed in structures that biologists call fruits?

The next time you see a dandelion's fluffy "seed head," examine it closely. It is made up of hundreds of individual fruits, each containing a seed. Each fruit has a hooklike structure at one end. Like tiny parachutes, the fruits ride in currents of air. When one hooks into moist soil, the seed inside can grow into a new dandelion plant.

What Is a Seed Plant?

Dandelions are seed plants. So are most of the other plants on Earth. In fact, seed plants outnumber seedless plants by more than ten to one. You eat many seed plants—rice, tomatoes, peas, and squash, for example. You may also eat the meat of animals that eat seed plants. You wear clothes made from seed plants, such as cotton and flax. You may even live in a home built from seed plants—oak, pine, or maple trees. In addition, seed plants produce much of the oxygen you breathe.

Figure 1 Some of these dandelions are releasing tiny parachute-like fruits, which carry the seeds inside to new areas.

Figure 2 Seed plants are diverse and live in many environments. **A.** Wheat is an important food for people. **B.** Organpipe cacti, here surrounded by other flowering plants, live in deserts. **C.** Lodgepole pines thrive in the mountains of the western United States.
Applying Concepts *What two roles does vascular tissue play in these plants?*

All seed plants share two characteristics. They have vascular tissue and use seeds to reproduce. In addition, they all have body plans that include leaves, stems, and roots. Like seedless plants, seed plants have complex life cycles that include the sporophyte and the gametophyte. In seed plants, the plants that you see are the sporophytes. The gametophytes are microscopic.

Vascular Tissue

Most seed plants live on land. Recall from Chapter 8 that land plants face many challenges, including standing upright and supplying all their cells with water and food. Like ferns, seed plants meet these two challenges with vascular tissue. The thick walls of the cells in the vascular tissue help support the plants. In addition, water, food, and nutrients are transported throughout the plants in vascular tissue.

There are two types of vascular tissue. **Phloem** (FLOH um) is the vascular tissue through which food moves. When food is made in the plant's leaves, it enters the phloem and travels to the plant's stems and roots. Water and nutrients, on the other hand, travel in the vascular tissue called **xylem** (ZY lum). The plant's roots absorb water and nutrients from the soil. These materials enter the root's xylem and move upward into the plant's stems and leaves.

☑ *Checkpoint* *What material travels in phloem? What materials travel in xylem?*

Seeds

One reason why seed plants are so numerous is that they produce seeds. **Seeds** are structures that contain a young plant inside a protective covering. As you learned in Chapter 8, seedless plants need water in the surroundings for fertilization to occur. Seed plants do not need water in the environment to reproduce. This is because the sperm cells are delivered directly to the regions near the eggs. After sperm cells fertilize the eggs, seeds develop and protect the young plant from drying out.

If you've ever planted seeds in a garden, you know that seeds look different from each other. Despite their differences, however, all seeds have a similar structure. **A seed has three important parts—an embryo, stored food, and a seed coat.**

The young plant that develops from the zygote, or fertilized egg, is called the **embryo.** The embryo already has the beginnings of roots, stems, and leaves. In the seeds of most plants, the embryo stops growing when it is quite small. When the embryo begins to grow again, it uses the food stored in the seed until it can make its food. In some plants, food is stored inside one or two seed leaves, or **cotyledons** (kaht uh LEED unz). You can see the cotyledons in the seeds in Figure 3.

The outer covering of a seed is called the seed coat. Some familiar seed coats are the "skins" on lima beans, peanuts, and peas. The seed coat acts like plastic wrap, protecting the embryo and its food from drying out. This allows a seed to remain inactive for a long time. For example, after finding some 10,000-year-old seeds in the Arctic, scientists placed them in warm water. Two days later, the seeds began to grow!

☑ *Checkpoint* *What is the function of the seed coat?*

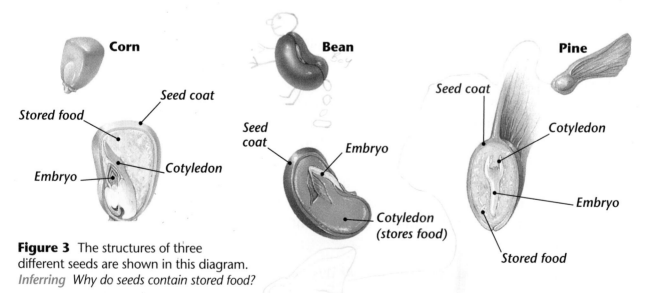

Figure 3 The structures of three different seeds are shown in this diagram. *Inferring* Why do seeds contain stored food?

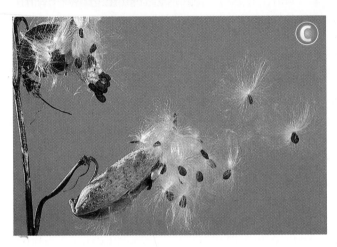

Figure 4 Plants have different ways of dispersing their seeds. **A.** Both grass seeds and spiny parsley seeds are hitching a ride on this dog's fur. **B.** Water transports coconut palm seeds to new areas. **C.** The wind carries milkweed seeds through the air. **D.** Witch hazel plants shoot out seeds when their pods explode.

Seed Dispersal

To develop into a new plant, a seed needs light, water, and nutrients. After seeds have formed, they are usually scattered, sometimes far from where they were produced. When seeds land in a suitable area, they can sprout, or begin to grow.

The scattering of seeds is called seed dispersal. Seeds, or the fruits that enclose the seeds, are dispersed in many ways. One method involves animals. Some animals eat fruits, such as cherries and grapes. The seeds inside pass through the animal's digestive system and are deposited in new areas. Other seeds are enclosed in barblike structures that hook onto an animal's fur or a person's clothes. The structures then fall off in a new area. Water disperses other seeds when the seeds float in oceans, rivers, and streams. The seeds inside coconuts, for example, are carried from one area to another by ocean currents.

A third dispersal method involves wind. Wind disperses lightweight seeds, such as those of milkweed plants and pine trees. Finally, some plants shoot out their seeds, in a way that might remind you of popping popcorn. For example, the seedpods of wisteria and impatiens plants burst suddenly. The force scatters the seeds away from the pods in many directions.

Figure 5 The embryo in this peanut seed uses stored food to germinate. **A.** The peanut's root is the first structure to begin growing. **B.** After the root anchors the germinating plant, the peanut's stem and first two leaves emerge from the seed.

Germination

After seeds are dispersed, they may remain inactive for a while, or they may begin to grow immediately. **Germination** (jur muh NAY shun) is the early growth stage of the embryo. Germination begins when the seed absorbs water from the environment. Then the embryo uses its stored food to begin to grow. First, the embryo's roots grow downward, then its leaves and stem grow upward.

Seeds that are dispersed far away from the parent have a better chance of survival. This is because these young plants do not have to compete with their parent for light, water, and nutrients as they begin to grow.

☑ *Checkpoint* *What must happen before germination can begin?*

Leaves

The most numerous parts on many plants are their leaves. Plant leaves vary greatly in size and shape. Pine trees, for example, have needle-shaped leaves. Birch trees have small rounded leaves with jagged edges. Yellow skunk cabbages, which grow in the northwestern United States, have oval leaves that can be more than one meter wide. No matter what their shape, leaves play an important role in a plant. **Leaves capture the sun's energy and carry out the food-making process of photosynthesis.**

The Structure of a Leaf If you were to cut through a leaf and look at the edge under a microscope, you would see the structures in *Exploring a Leaf.* The leaf's top and bottom surface layers protect the cells inside. Between the layers of cells inside the leaf are veins that contain xylem and phloem. The underside of the leaf has small openings, or pores, called **stomata** (STOH muh tuh) (singular *stoma*). The Greek word *stoma* means "mouth"—and stomata do look like tiny mouths. The stomata open and close to control when gases enter and leave the leaf. When the stomata are open, carbon dioxide enters the leaf and oxygen and water vapor exit.

The Leaf and Photosynthesis The structure of a leaf is ideal for carrying out photosynthesis. Recall from Chapter 2 that photosynthesis occurs in the chloroplasts of plant cells. The cells that contain the most chloroplasts are located near the leaf's upper surface, where they are exposed to the sun. The chlorophyll in the chloroplasts traps the sun's energy.

Carbon dioxide enters the leaf through open stomata. Water, which is absorbed by the plant's roots, travels up the stem to the leaf through the xylem. During photosynthesis, sugar and oxygen are produced from the carbon dioxide and water. Oxygen passes out of the leaf through the open stomata. The sugar enters the phloem and then travels throughout the plant.

EXPLORING a Leaf

A leaf is a well-adapted food factory. Each structure helps the leaf produce food.

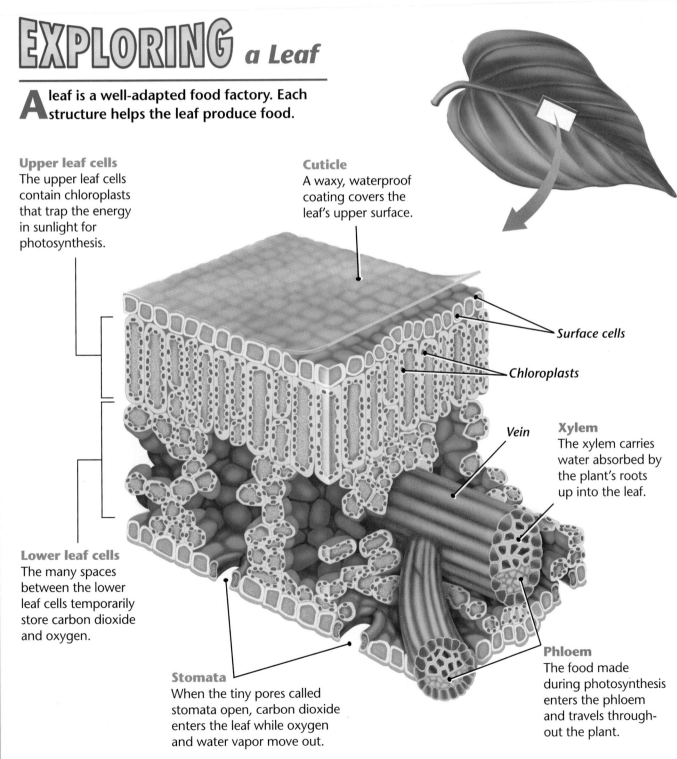

Upper leaf cells
The upper leaf cells contain chloroplasts that trap the energy in sunlight for photosynthesis.

Cuticle
A waxy, waterproof coating covers the leaf's upper surface.

Surface cells

Chloroplasts

Vein

Xylem
The xylem carries water absorbed by the plant's roots up into the leaf.

Lower leaf cells
The many spaces between the lower leaf cells temporarily store carbon dioxide and oxygen.

Stomata
When the tiny pores called stomata open, carbon dioxide enters the leaf while oxygen and water vapor move out.

Phloem
The food made during photosynthesis enters the phloem and travels through-out the plant.

Calculating ACTIVITY

In this activity you will calculate the speed at which fluid moves up a celery stalk.

1. Put on your apron. Fill a plastic container halfway with water. Stir in a drop of red food coloring.

2. Place the freshly cut end of a celery stalk in the water. Lean the stalk against the container's side.

3. After 20 minutes, remove the celery. Use a metric ruler to measure the height of the water in the stalk.

4. Use the measurement and the following formula to calculate how fast the water moved up the stalk.

$$\text{Speed} = \frac{\text{Height}}{\text{Time}}$$

Based on your calculation, predict how far the water would move in 2 hours. Then test your prediction.

Controlling Water Loss Because such a large area of a leaf is exposed to the air, water can quickly evaporate, or be lost, from a leaf into the air. The process by which water evaporates from a plant's leaves is called **transpiration.** A plant can lose a lot of water through transpiration. A corn plant, for example, can lose as much as 3.8 liters of water on a hot summer day. Without a way to slow down the process of transpiration, a plant would shrivel up and die.

Fortunately, plants have ways to slow down transpiration. One way that plants retain water is by closing the stomata. The stomata often close when the temperature is very hot.

☑ *Checkpoint* *How does carbon dioxide get into a leaf?*

Stems

The stem of a plant has two important functions. **The stem carries substances between the plant's roots and leaves. The stem also provides support for the plant and holds up the leaves so they are exposed to the sun.** In addition, some stems, such as those of asparagus, also store food.

Stems vary in size and shape. Some stems, like those of the baobab trees in Figure 6, are a prominent part of the plant. Other stems, like those of cabbages, are short and hidden.

The Structure of a Stem Stems can be either herbaceous (hur BAY shus) or woody. Herbaceous stems are soft. Dandelions, dahlias, peppers, and tomato plants have herbaceous stems.

Figure 6 This road in Madagascar is called Baobab Avenue. Tall, fat stems and stubby branches give baobab trees an unusual appearance.

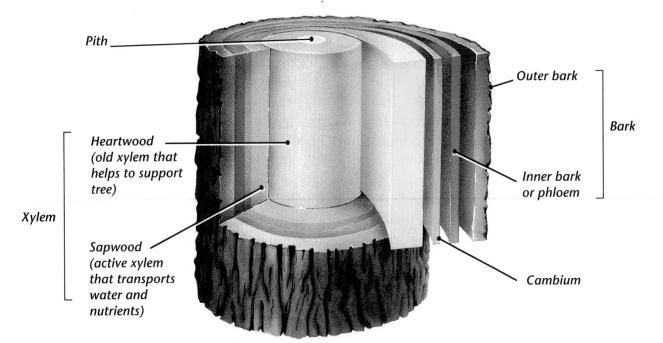

Pith

Outer bark

Bark

Heartwood
(old xylem that
helps to support
tree)

Inner bark
or phloem

Xylem

Sapwood
(active xylem
that transports
water and
nutrients)

Cambium

Figure 7 A typical woody stem is made up of many cell layers. *Interpreting Diagrams Where is the cambium located? What is the function of this layer of cells?*

In contrast, woody stems are hard and rigid. Maple trees, pine trees, and roses all have woody stems.

Herbaceous and woody stems consist of phloem and xylem tissue as well as many other supporting cells. However, unlike herbaceous stems, woody stems have an outer layer of material called bark, which helps protect the cells inside it, and inner layers of heartwood for additional support.

In Figure 7 you can see the inner structure of a woody stem. Bark covers the outer part of the stem. Just inside the outer bark layer is the phloem. Inside the phloem is a layer of cells called the **cambium** (KAM bee um). The cells of the cambium divide to produce new phloem and xylem. This process increases the stem's width. Just inside the cambium is a layer of active xylem that transports water and nutrients. Inside that layer is a layer of xylem cells that no longer carries water and nutrients. This layer, which is called heartwood, strengthens the stem, providing it with additional support. In the center of the stem is a material called the pith. In young trees, the pith stores food and water.

Annual Rings Have you ever looked at a tree stump and seen a pattern of circles that looks something like a target? These circles are called annual rings because they represent one year of a tree's growth. Annual rings are made of xylem. Xylem cells that form in the spring are large and have thin walls because they grow rapidly. They produce a wide, light brown ring. Xylem cells that form in the summer grow slowly and, therefore, are small and have thick walls. They produce a thin, dark ring. One pair of

Figure 8 Tree rings tell more than just the age of a tree. For example, thick rings that are far apart indicate years in which growing conditions were favorable.
Interpreting Photographs What was the weather like during the early years of this locust tree's life?

light and dark rings represents one year's growth. You can estimate a tree's age by counting its annual rings.

INTEGRATING EARTH SCIENCE The width of a tree's annual rings can provide important clues about past weather conditions, such as rainfall. In rainy years, more xylem is produced, so the tree's annual rings are wide. In dry years, rings are narrow. By examining a tree's annual rings, scientists can make inferences about the weather conditions during the tree's life. For example, when scientists examined annual rings from trees in the southwestern United States, they inferred that severe droughts occurred in the years 840, 1067, 1379, and 1632.

✓ *Checkpoint* **What function does bark perform?**

Roots

Have you ever tried to pull a dandelion out of the soil? It's not easy, is it? That is because most roots are good anchors. **Roots anchor a plant in the ground and absorb water and nutrients from the soil.** The more root area a plant has, the more water and nutrients it can absorb. The roots of an oak tree, for example, may be twice as long as the aboveground tree. In addition, for plants such as carrots and beets, roots function as a storage area for food.

Types of Roots As you can see in Figure 9, there are two types of root systems: taproot and fibrous. A taproot system consists of a long, thick main root. Thin, branching roots grow off the main root. Turnips, radishes, dandelions, and cacti have taproots. In contrast, fibrous root systems consist of several main roots that branch

Figure 9 A plant's roots anchor the plant and absorb substances from the soil. **A.** A taproot grows deep into the soil. The plant is hard to pull out of the ground. **B.** Fibrous roots consist of several main roots that repeatedly branch. They take soil with them when you pull them out of the ground.

repeatedly to form a tangled mass of roots and soil. Lawn grass, corn, and most trees have fibrous roots.

The Structure of a Root In Figure 10 you see the structure of a typical root. Notice that the tip of the root is rounded and is covered by a structure called the **root cap.** The root cap, which contains dead cells, protects the root from injury from rocks and other material as the root grows through the soil. Behind the root cap are cells that divide to form new root cells.

Root hairs grow out of the root's surface. These hairs increase the surface area of the root that touches the soil. When more surface area is in contact with the soil, more water and nutrients can be absorbed. The root hairs also help to anchor the plant in the soil.

Locate the vascular tissue in the center of the root. The water and nutrients that are absorbed from the soil quickly move into the xylem. From there, these substances are transported upward to the plant's stems and leaves.

Phloem tissue transports food manufactured in the leaves to the root. The root tissues may then use the food for growth or store it for future use by the plant. The root also contains a layer of cambium, which produces new xylem and phloem.

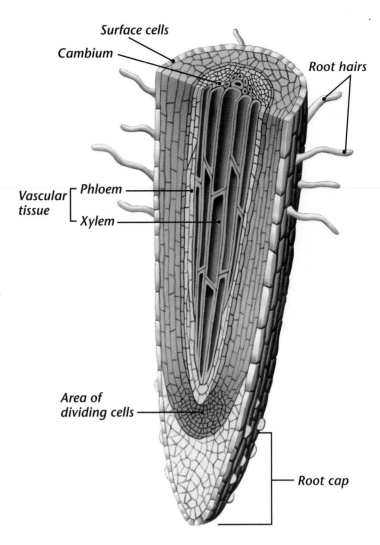

Figure 10 The root cap protects the root as it grows into the soil. Root hairs absorb water and nutrients, which are transported through the root's vascular tissue.

Section 1 Review

1. What two characteristics do all seed plants share?
2. List the three main parts of a seed. Describe the function of each part in producing a new plant.
3. What are the main functions of a plant's leaves, stems, and roots?
4. **Thinking Critically** **Predicting** Predict what would happen to a plant if you were to coat the underside of each leaf with wax. Explain your prediction.

Science at Home

Seed Germination With a family member, soak some corn seeds or lima bean seeds in water overnight. Then push them gently into some soil in a paper cup until they are just covered. Keep the soil moist. When you see the stems break through the soil, remove the seeds and examine them. Explain what you see to your family member.

DISCOVER

Are All Leaves Alike?

1. Your teacher will give you a hand lens, a ruler, and the leaves from some seed plants.

2. Using the hand lens, examine each leaf. Sketch each leaf in your notebook.

3. Measure the length and width of each leaf. Record your measurements in your notebook.

Think It Over
Classifying Divide the leaves into two groups on the basis of your observations. Explain why you grouped the leaves as you did.

GUIDE FOR READING

◆ What are the characteristics of gymnosperms?

◆ How do gymnosperms reproduce?

Reading Tip Before you read, preview *Exploring the Life Cycle of a Gymnosperm* on page 287. List any unfamiliar terms. As you read, write definitions for the terms.

Have you ever seen a tree that has grown wider than a car? Do trees this huge really exist? The answer is yes. Some giant sequoia trees, which grow almost exclusively in central California, are over ten meters wide. You can understand why giant sequoias are commonly referred to as "big trees." It takes a long time for a tree to grow so big. Scientists think that the largest giant sequoias may be about 2,000 years old. One reason they live so long is because their bark is fire-resistant.

What Are Gymnosperms?

The giant sequoia trees belong to the group of seed plants known as gymnosperms. A **gymnosperm** (JIM nuh spurm) is a seed plant that produces naked seeds. The seeds of gymnosperms are "naked" because they are not enclosed by any protective covering.

Every gymnosperm produces naked seeds. In addition, many gymnosperms also have needlelike or scalelike leaves, and deep-growing root systems. Although a few kinds of gymnosperms are shrubs or vines, most are trees.

◀ A giant sequoia in California

Types of Gymnosperms

Gymnosperms are the oldest type of seed plant. According to fossil evidence, gymnosperms first appeared on Earth about 360 million years ago. Fossils also indicate that there were many more species of gymnosperms in the past than today. Today, gymnosperms are classified into four groups—the cycads, the ginkgo, the gnetophytes, and the conifers.

Cycads About 175 million years ago, the majority of plants on Earth were cycads (SY kadz). Today, cycads grow mainly in tropical and subtropical areas. As you can see in Figure 11, cycads look like palm trees with cones. A cycad cone can grow as large as a football. In Mexico people grind seeds from the cones of one cycad to make a type of flour for tortillas.

Ginkgo Like cycads, ginkgoes (GING kohz) are also hundreds of millions of years old. Only one species of ginkgo, *Ginkgo biloba*, exists today. It probably survives only because the Chinese and Japanese cared for the species in their gardens. Ginkgoes can grow as tall as 25 meters. Today, ginkgo trees are planted along many city streets because they can tolerate the air pollution produced by city traffic.

Gnetophytes Gnetophytes (NEE tuh fyts) are the gymnosperms that you are least likely to see. These gymnosperms live only in the hot, dry deserts of southern Africa, the deserts of the western United States, and the tropical rain forests. Some gnetophytes are trees, some are shrubs, and others are vines.

Figure 11 Gymnosperms are the oldest seed plants. **A.** Cycads, similar to this sago palm, were quite common during the age of dinosaurs. **B.** Only one kind of ginkgo, *Ginkgo biloba*, lives today. **C.** Gnetophytes, such as *Welwitschia mirabilis* shown here, grow in the very dry deserts of west Africa.

Figure 12 Both the male cones (**A**) and female cones (**B**) of a Ponderosa pine are produced on a single tree. *Comparing and Contrasting How do the male and female cones differ?*

The Scoop on Cones

1. Use a hand lens to look at a female cone. Gently shake the cone over a piece of white paper. Observe what happens.

2. Break off one scale from the cone. Examine its base. If the scale contains a seed, remove the seed.

3. With a hand lens, examine the seed from Step 2, or examine a seed that fell on the paper in Step 1.

4. Wash your hands.

Inferring How does the cone protect the seeds?

Conifers Conifers (KAHN uh furz), or cone-bearing plants, are the largest and most diverse group of gymnosperms on Earth today. Most conifers, such as pines, redwoods, cedars, hemlocks, and junipers, are evergreen plants. Evergreen plants keep their leaves, or needles, year-round. Old needles drop off and are replaced by new ones throughout the life of the plant.

Reproduction

Most gymnosperms have reproductive structures called **cones.** Cones are covered with scales. Most gymnosperms produce two types of cones: male cones and female cones. Usually, a single plant produces both male and female cones. In some types of gymnosperms, however, individual trees produce either male cones or female cones. A few types of gymnosperms produce no cones at all.

Figure 12 shows the male and female cones of a Ponderosa pine. Notice that the male cones are smaller than the female cones. Male cones produce tiny grains of pollen. **Pollen** contains the microscopic cells that will later become sperm cells.

Female cones contain at least one ovule at the base of each scale. An **ovule** (OH vyool) is a structure that contains an egg cell. After fertilization occurs, the ovule develops into a seed.

You can learn how gymnosperms reproduce in *Exploring the Life Cycle of a Gymnosperm*. **First, pollen falls from a male cone onto a female cone. In time, a sperm cell and an egg cell join together in an ovule on the female cone.** After fertilization occurs, the zygote develops into the embryo part of the seed.

EXPLORING the Life Cycle of a Gymnosperm

Pine trees have a typical life cycle for a gymnosperm. Follow the steps of pollination, fertilization, and seed development in the pine tree.

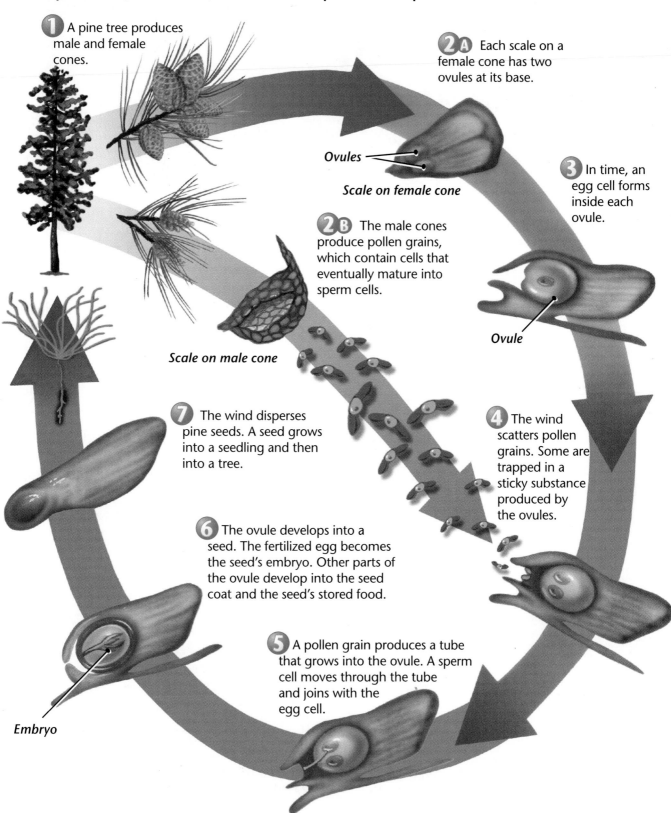

1 A pine tree produces male and female cones.

2A Each scale on a female cone has two ovules at its base.

Ovules

Scale on female cone

3 In time, an egg cell forms inside each ovule.

2B The male cones produce pollen grains, which contain cells that eventually mature into sperm cells.

Scale on male cone

Ovule

7 The wind disperses pine seeds. A seed grows into a seedling and then into a tree.

4 The wind scatters pollen grains. Some are trapped in a sticky substance produced by the ovules.

6 The ovule develops into a seed. The fertilized egg becomes the seed's embryo. Other parts of the ovule develop into the seed coat and the seed's stored food.

5 A pollen grain produces a tube that grows into the ovule. A sperm cell moves through the tube and joins with the egg cell.

Embryo

Figure 13 Conifers provided the lumber for this playground. The sap produced by some conifers is used to make turpentine and the rosin used by baseball pitchers and musicians.

Pollination and Fertilization The transfer of pollen from a male reproductive structure to a female reproductive structure is called **pollination.** In gymnosperms, wind often carries the pollen from the male cones to the female cones. The pollen collects in a sticky substance produced by each ovule. The scales of the female cone close and seal in the pollen. Inside the closed scale, fertilization occurs. The seed then develops on the scale.

Female cones stay on the tree until the seeds mature. It can take up to two years for the seeds of some gymnosperms to mature. Male cones, however, usually fall off the tree after they have shed their pollen.

Seed Dispersal As the seeds develop, the female cone increases in size. The cone's position on the branch may change as well. Cones that contain immature seeds point upward, while cones that contain mature seeds point downward. When the seeds are mature, the scales open. The wind shakes the seeds out of the cone and carries them away. Only a few seeds will land in a suitable place and grow into new plants.

Section 2 Review

1. What are three characteristics of many gymnosperms?
2. Describe how gymnosperms reproduce.
3. What are the four groups of gymnosperms?
4. **Thinking Critically Comparing and Contrasting** Compare the functions of male and female cones.

Check Your Progress

CHAPTER PROJECT

If your seeds haven't germinated yet, they soon will. For the next few days keep a close watch on your young plants to see how they grow. How do they change in height? How do the leaves appear and grow? (*Hint:* Consider using drawings or photographs as part of your record keeping.)

What Is a Fruit?

1. Your teacher will give you three different fruits that have been cut in half.

2. Use a hand lens to carefully observe the outside of each fruit. For each fruit, record its color, shape, size, and external features. Record your observations in your notebook.

3. Carefully observe the structures inside the fruit. Record your observations.

Think It Over
Forming Operational Definitions Based on your observations, how would you define the term *fruit*?

Americans who visited the Japanese pavilion at the United States Centennial Exhibition in 1876 were introduced to kudzu, an attractive Asian vine. Soon, many Americans began planting kudzu in their communities. Little did they know that this creeping vine would become a huge problem.

Kudzu is one of the world's fastest-growing plants. Although it is nicknamed the "mile-a-minute vine," kudzu really does not grow that fast. But it can grow as much as 30 centimeters a day. In the southern United States, kudzu now covers an area twice the size of Connecticut. Unfortunately, there is no effective way to control the growth of this fast-growing plant.

What Are Angiosperms?

Kudzu is a type of seed plant known as an angiosperm. An **angiosperm** (AN jee uh spurm) is a plant that produces seeds that are enclosed in a fruit. The word *angiosperm* comes from two Greek words that mean "seed in a vessel." The protective "vessel"

GUIDE FOR READING

◆ What characteristics do angiosperms share?

◆ How do angiosperms reproduce?

Reading Tip Before you read, preview the photographs in this section. Write a prediction about how angiosperms differ from gymnosperms.

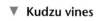

▼ Kudzu vines

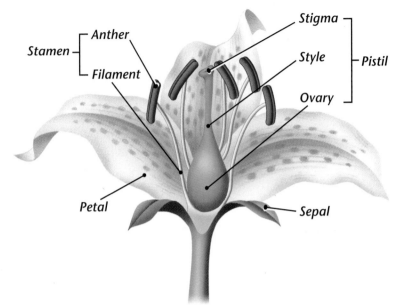

Figure 14 Like most flowers, this lily contains both male and female reproductive structures. *Interpreting Photographs What structures in the diagram can you find in the photograph?*

where seeds develop is called the **ovary.** The ovary is located within an angiosperm's **flower**—the reproductive structure of an angiosperm. **Two characteristics of angiosperms are that they produce flowers and fruits.**

Most of the familiar plants around you are angiosperms. Angiosperms live almost everywhere on Earth. They grow in frozen areas in the Arctic, tropical jungles, and barren deserts. A few angiosperms, such as mangrove trees and some sea grasses, even live in the oceans.

The Structure of Flowers

Like the plants that produce them, flowers come in all sorts of shapes, sizes, and colors. But all flowers have the same function—reproduction. Look at Figure 14 to see the parts of a typical flower. As you read about the parts, keep in mind that the description does not apply to all flowers. For example, some flowers have only male reproductive parts, and some flowers lack **petals**—the colorful structures that you see when flowers open.

When a flower is still a bud, it is enclosed by leaflike structures called **sepals** (SEE pulz). Sepals protect the developing flower. After the sepals fold back, the petals are revealed. The colors and shapes of the petals and the odors produced by the flower attract insects and other animals. These organisms ensure that pollination occurs.

Within the petals are the flower's male and female reproductive parts. Locate the thin stalks topped by small knobs inside the flower in Figure 14. These are the **stamens** (STAY munz), the male reproductive parts. The thin stalk is called the filament. Pollen is produced in the knob, or anther, at the top of the stalk.

The female parts, or **pistils** (PIS tulz), are usually found in the center of the flower. Some flowers have two or more pistils; others have only one. The sticky tip of the pistil is called the stigma. A slender tube, called a style, connects the stigma to a hollow structure at the base of the flower. This hollow structure is the ovary, which contains one or more ovules.

Reproduction

You can learn how angiosperms reproduce in *Exploring the Life Cycle of an Angiosperm* on the next page. **First, pollen falls on a stigma. In time, the sperm cell and egg cell join together in the flower's ovule. The zygote develops into the embryo part of the seed.**

Pollination and Fertilization A flower is pollinated when a grain of pollen falls on the stigma. Like gymnosperms, some angiosperms are pollinated by the wind. But most angiosperms rely on birds, bats, or insects for pollination. Nectar, a sugar-rich food, is located deep inside a flower. When an animal enters a flower to obtain the nectar, it brushes against the anthers and becomes coated with pollen. Some of the pollen can drop onto the flower's stigma as the animal leaves the flower. The pollen can also be brushed onto the sticky stigma of the next flower the animal visits. If the pollen falls on the stigma of a similar plant, fertilization can occur. The zygote then begins to develop into the seed's embryo. Other parts of the ovule develop into the rest of the seed.

Seed Dispersal As the seed develops, the ovary changes into a **fruit**—a ripened ovary and other structures that enclose one or more seeds. Apples and cherries are fruits. So are many foods you usually call vegetables, such as tomatoes and squash. For an angiosperm, a fruit is a way to disperse its seeds. Animals that eat fruits help to disperse their seeds.

✓ *Checkpoint* *What attracts pollinators to angiosperms?*

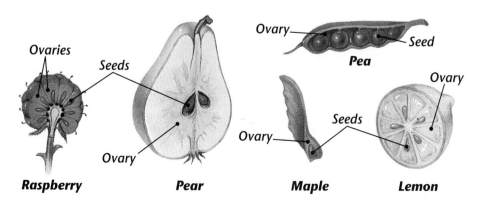

Raspberry   **Pear**   **Maple**   **Lemon**

Ovaries · Seeds · Ovary · Ovary · Seed · Pea · Seeds · Ovary

Figure 15 The seeds of angiosperms are enclosed within fruits, which protect and disperse the seed.

EXPLORING the Life Cycle of an Angiosperm

All angiosperms have a similar life cycle. Follow the steps of pollination, fertilization, and fruit development in this typical angiosperm.

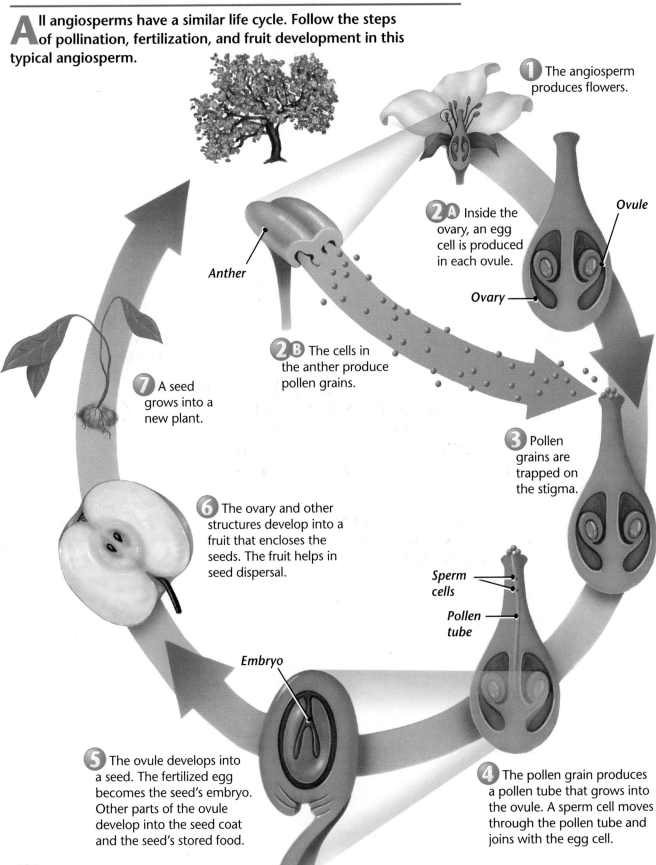

1 The angiosperm produces flowers.

2A Inside the ovary, an egg cell is produced in each ovule.

Ovule

Ovary

Anther

2B The cells in the anther produce pollen grains.

3 Pollen grains are trapped on the stigma.

7 A seed grows into a new plant.

6 The ovary and other structures develop into a fruit that encloses the seeds. The fruit helps in seed dispersal.

Sperm cells

Pollen tube

Embryo

5 The ovule develops into a seed. The fertilized egg becomes the seed's embryo. Other parts of the ovule develop into the seed coat and the seed's stored food.

4 The pollen grain produces a pollen tube that grows into the ovule. A sperm cell moves through the pollen tube and joins with the egg cell.

Monocots

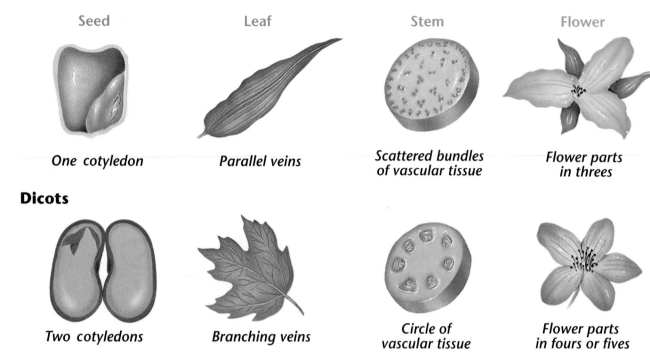

Seed	Leaf	Stem	Flower
One cotyledon	Parallel veins	Scattered bundles of vascular tissue	Flower parts in threes

Dicots

Seed	Leaf	Stem	Flower
Two cotyledons	Branching veins	Circle of vascular tissue	Flower parts in fours or fives

Types of Angiosperms

Angiosperms are divided into two major groups: monocots and dicots. "Cot" is short for *cotyledon*. Recall from Section 1 that the cotyledon, or seed leaf, provides food for the embryo. *Mono* means "one" and *di* means "two." **Monocots** are angiosperms that have only one seed leaf. **Dicots,** on the other hand, produce seeds with two seed leaves. Look at Figure 16 to compare the characteristics of monocots and dicots.

Monocots Grasses, including corn, wheat, and rice, and plants such as lilies and tulips are monocots. The flowers of a monocot usually have either three petals or a multiple of three petals. Monocots usually have long, slender leaves with veins that run parallel to one another like train rails. The bundles of vascular tissue in monocot stems are usually scattered randomly throughout the stem.

Dicots Dicots include plants such as roses and violets, as well as dandelions. Both oak and maple trees are dicots, as are food plants such as beans and apples. The flowers of dicots often have either four or five petals or multiples of these numbers. The leaves are usually wide, with veins that branch off from one another. Dicot stems usually have bundles of vascular tissue arranged in a circle.

✓ *Checkpoint* How do the petals of monocots and dicots differ in number?

Figure 16 Monocots and dicots are the two groups of angiosperms. The groups differ in the number of cotyledons, the arrangement of veins and vascular tissue, and the number of petals. *Classifying Would a plant whose flowers have 20 petals be a monocot or a dicot?*

Angiosperms and the Living World

Angiosperms are an important source of food, clothing, and medicine for other organisms. Plant-eating animals, such as cows, elephants, and beetles, eat flowering plants such as grasses as well as the leaves of trees. People eat vegetables, fruits, and cereals, all of which are angiosperms.

People also produce clothing and other products from angiosperms. For example, the seeds of cotton plants, like the ones you see in Figure 17, are covered with cotton fibers. The stems of flax plants provide linen fibers. The sap of tropical rubber trees is used to make rubber for tires and other products. Furniture is often made from the wood of maple, cherry, and oak trees.

INTEGRATING HEALTH Some angiosperms are used in the making of medicine. For example, aspirin was first made from a substance found in the leaves of willow trees. Digitalis, a heart medication, comes from the leaves of the foxglove plant. Cortisone is a medicine made from the roots of the Mexican yam. It is used to treat arthritis and other joint problems. These medicines have helped improve the health of many people.

Figure 17 Cotton seeds, which develop in structures called bolls, are covered with fibers that are manufactured into cotton fabric.

Section 3 Review

1. What two characteristics do all angiosperms share? Explain the importance of those characteristics.
2. Give a brief description of how reproduction occurs in angiosperms.
3. List the parts of a typical flower. What is the function of each part?
4. **Thinking Critically Inferring** A certain plant has small, dull-colored flowers with no scent. Do you think the plant is pollinated by animals or by the wind? Explain.

> **CHAPTER PROJECT**
> **Check Your Progress**
> Your plants should now have, or will soon have, flowers. Make a diagram of the flower's structure. When the flowers open, you'll have to pollinate them. This work is usually done by insects or birds. After pollination, watch how the flower changes. (*Hint:* Discuss with your teacher and classmates how to pollinate the flowers.)

SECTION 4 Plant Responses and Growth

DISCOVER ··· ACTIVITY ····

Can a Plant Respond to Touch?

1. Your teacher will give you two plants. Observe the first plant. Gently touch a leaf and observe what happens over the next three minutes. Record your observations.

2. Repeat Step 1 with the second plant. Record your observations.

3. Wash your hands with soap and water.

Think It Over

Inferring What advantage might a plant have if its leaves responded to touch?

The bladderwort is a freshwater plant with small yellow flowers. Attached to its floating stems are open structures called bladders. When a water flea touches a sensitive hair on a bladder, the bladder flicks open. Faster than you can blink, the water flea is sucked inside, and the bladder snaps shut. The plant then digests the trapped flea.

A bladderwort responds quickly—faster than many animals respond to a similar stimulus. You may be surprised to learn that some plants have lightning-quick responses. In fact, you might have thought that plants do not respond to stimuli at all. But plants do respond to some stimuli, although they usually do so more slowly than the bladderwort.

Tropisms

Animals usually respond to stimuli by moving. Unlike animals, plants commonly respond by growing either toward or away from a stimulus. A plant's growth response toward or away from a stimulus is called a **tropism** (TROH pihz uhm). If a plant grows toward the stimulus, it is said to show a positive tropism. If a plant grows away from a stimulus, it shows a negative tropism. **Touch, light, and gravity are three important stimuli to which plants respond.**

Touch Some plants, such as bladderworts, show a response to touch called thigmotropism. The term *thigmo* comes from a Greek word that means "touch." The stems of many vines, such as grapes and morning glories, show a positive thigmotropism. As the vines grow, they coil around any object that they touch.

GUIDE FOR READING

◆ What are three stimuli that produce plant responses?

◆ What functions do plant hormones control?

Reading Tip As you read, use the headings to make an outline about plant responses and growth.

A floating bladderwort ▶

Light All plants exhibit a response to light called phototropism. The leaves, stems, and flowers of plants grow toward light, showing a positive phototropism. For example, as the sun's position changes during the day, sunflowers move on their stalks so that they are always facing the sun.

Gravity Plants also respond to gravity. This response is called gravitropism. Roots show positive gravitropism—they grow downward, with the pull of gravity. Stems, on the other hand, show negative gravitropism—they grow upward.

Plant Hormones

Plants are able to respond to touch, light, and gravity because they produce hormones. A plant **hormone** is a chemical that affects how the plant grows and develops. **In addition to tropisms, plant hormones also control germination, the formation of flowers, stems, and leaves, the shedding of leaves, and the development and ripening of fruit.**

One important plant hormone is named **auxin** (AWX sin). Auxin speeds up the rate at which a plant's cells grow. Auxin controls a plant's response to light. When light shines on one side of a plant's stem, auxin moves to the shaded side of the stem. The cells on that side begin to grow faster. Eventually, the cells on the stem's shady side are longer than those on its sunny side. So the stem bends toward the light.

Checkpoint *What role does the hormone auxin play in a plant?*

Figure 18 The face of this sunflower turns on its stalk throughout the day so that it always faces the sun. *Making Generalizations How does a positive phototropism help a plant survive?*

Life Spans of Angiosperms

If you've ever planted a garden, you know that many flowering plants grow, flower, and die in a single year. Flowering plants that complete a life cycle within one growing season are called annuals. The word annual comes from the Latin word *annus*, which means "year." Most annuals have herbaceous stems. Annuals include many garden plants, such as marigolds, petunias, and pansies. Wheat, tomatoes, and cucumbers are also annuals.

Figure 19 A flowering plant is classified as an annual, biennial, or perennial depending on the length of its life cycle. **A.** These morning glories are annuals. **B.** Foxglove, like this *Digitalis purpurea*, is a biennial. **C.** This peony, a perennial, will bloom year after year.

Angiosperms that complete their life cycle in two years are called biennials (by EN ee ulz). The Latin prefix *bi* means "two." In the first year, biennials germinate and grow roots, very short stems, and leaves. During their second year, biennials grow new stems and leaves and then produce flowers and seeds. Once the flowers produce seeds, the plant dies. Parsley, celery, and foxglove are biennials.

Flowering plants that live for more than two years are called perennials. The Latin word *per* means "through." Perennials usually live through many years. Some perennials, such as peonies and asparagus, have herbaceous stems. The leaves and stems above the ground die each winter. New ones are produced each spring. Most perennials, however, have woody stems. Bristlecone pines, oak trees, and honeysuckle are examples of woody perennials.

Section 4 Review

1. Name three stimuli to which plants respond.
2. What is a plant hormone? List four processes that a plant's hormones control.
3. Suppose you are growing a plant on a windowsill. After a few days, you notice that the plant's leaves and flowers are facing the window. Explain why this has occurred.
4. **Thinking Critically   Applying Concepts** Is the grass that grows in most lawns an annual, a biennial, or a perennial? Explain.

Check Your Progress   CHAPTER PROJECT
Your plants should be near the end of their growth cycle. Continue to observe them. Harvest the seeds carefully, observe them, and compare them with the original seeds. If you have time, plant a few of these new seeds to begin the life cycle again.

Which Way is Up?

In this lab, you will develop and test a hypothesis about how seedlings respond to gravity.

Problem

How is the growth of a seed affected by gravity?

Materials

4 corn seeds
paper towels
water
marking pencil

plastic petri dish
scissors
masking tape
clay

Procedure

1. Read over the entire procedure. Then, with your group, develop a hypothesis about the direction in which the seedlings will grow in response to gravity.
2. Arrange four seeds that have been soaked in water for 24 hours in a petri dish. The pointed ends of the seeds should face the center of the dish, as shown in the illustration.
3. Place a circle cut from a paper towel over the seeds. Moisten one or more paper towels with water so that they are wet but not dripping. Pack them in the dish to hold the seeds firmly in place. Cover the dish, and seal it with tape.
4. Lay the dish upside-down so the seeds show. Use a marking pencil to draw a small, outward-facing arrow over one of the seeds, as shown in the illustration. Turn the dish over and write your name and the date on it.
5. Use clay to stand up the petri dish so that the arrow points upward. Put the petri dish in a dark place.

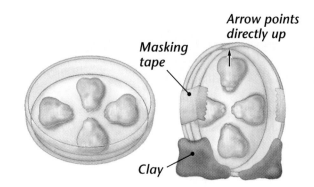

Masking tape

Arrow points directly up

Clay

6. Once a day for a week, remove the petri dish and check it. Do not open the dish. Observe and sketch the seeds. Note the seeds' direction of growth. Then return the dish, making sure that the arrow points upward.

Analyze and Conclude

1. What new structures emerged as the seeds developed? How did the direction of growth compare from seed to seed?
2. Did your results confirm your hypothesis? If not, describe any differences between your hypothesis and your results.
3. Why was it necessary to grow these seeds in the dark?
4. **Think About It** What evidence or ideas did you consider when you wrote your hypothesis? Did any of your ideas change as a result of this experiment? Explain.

Design an Experiment

How will your seedlings respond if you now allow them to grow in the light? Design an experiment to find out. Obtain your teacher's approval before carrying out your experiment.

SECTION 1 The Characteristics of Seed Plants

Key Ideas

◆ All seed plants have vascular tissue and produce seeds.

◆ A seed has three important parts: an embryo, stored food, and a seed coat.

◆ Photosynthesis occurs mainly in leaves. Stems support plants and transport materials. Roots anchor plants and absorb water and minerals.

Key Terms

phloem	cotyledon	transpiration
xylem	germination	cambium
seed	stomata	root cap
embryo		

SECTION 2 Gymnosperms

Key Ideas

◆ All gymnosperms produce naked seeds. Many gymnosperms also have needlelike or scalelike leaves, and grow deep root systems.

◆ To reproduce, pollen falls onto a female cone. A sperm cell and an egg cell join. The zygote develops into the seed's embryo.

Key Terms

gymnosperm	pollen	pollination
cone	ovule	

SECTION 3 Angiosperms

Key Ideas

◆ Angiosperms produce flowers and fruits.

◆ To reproduce, pollen falls on the stigma. In time, the sperm cell and egg cell join in the ovule. The zygote develops into the seed's embryo.

Key Terms

angiosperm	sepal	fruit
ovary	stamen	monocot
flower	pistil	dicot
petal		

SECTION 4 Plant Responses and Growth

INTEGRATING CHEMISTRY

Key Ideas

◆ A tropism is a plant's growth response toward or away from a stimulus. Plants respond to touch, light, and gravity.

◆ Plant hormones control tropisms and many other plant functions.

Key Terms

tropism
hormone
auxin

Organizing Information

Concept Map Copy the concept map about seed plants onto a separate piece of paper. Then complete the map and add a title. (For more on concept maps, see the Skills Handbook.)

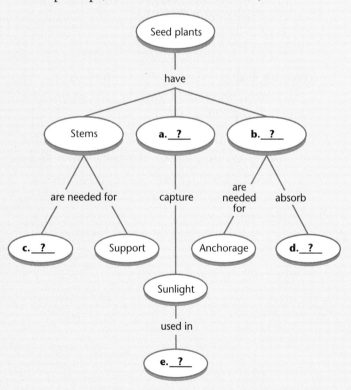

Reviewing Content

 For more review of key concepts, see the Interactive Student Tutorial CD-ROM.

Multiple Choice
Choose the letter of the best answer.

1. The process by which a seed sprouts is called
   a. pollination.
   b. fertilization.
   c. dispersal.
   d. germination.

2. Which of the following is the process by which water evaporates from leaves?
   a. pollination
   b. transpiration
   c. transportation
   d. dispersal

3. In woody stems, new xylem cells are produced by
   a. bark.
   b. cambium.
   c. phloem.
   d. pith.

4. Which of the following is the male part of the flower?
   a. pistil
   b. ovule
   c. stamen
   d. petal

5. What kind of tropism do roots display when they grow into the soil?
   a. positive gravitropism
   b. negative gravitropism
   c. positive phototropism
   d. negative thigmotropism

True or False
If the statement is true, write true. If it is false, change the underlined word or words to make the statement true.

6. <u>Stems</u> anchor plants and absorb water and minerals from the soil.

7. The needles of a pine tree are actually its <u>leaves</u>.

8. Cones are the reproductive structures of <u>angiosperms</u>.

9. The seeds of <u>gymnosperms</u> are dispersed in fruits.

10. Plants that complete their life cycle in two years are called <u>perennials</u>.

Checking Concepts

11. What is the difference between phloem and xylem? Why are these tissues important to plants?

12. Describe four different ways that seeds can be dispersed.

13. Explain the role that stomata play in a plant's leaves.

14. What are annual rings? Explain how they form.

15. Describe the structure of a female cone.

16. What is the difference between pollination and fertilization?

17. What role do plant hormones play in phototropism?

18. **Writing to Learn** Imagine that you are a seed inside a plump purple fruit that is floating in a stream. Describe your experiences on the journey you take to the place where you germinate.

Thinking Critically

19. **Relating Cause and Effect** When a strip of bark is removed all the way around the trunk of a tree, the tree dies. Explain why this happens.

20. **Classifying** Suppose you find an unusual freshly cut flower on the ground. You discover the flower has 27 petals. What does this information tell you about the plant that produced this flower? What would the plant's leaves, stems, and seeds look like?

21. **Predicting** Pesticides are designed to kill harmful insects. Sometimes, however, pesticides kill helpful insects as well. What effect could this have on angiosperms? Explain.

22. **Applying Concepts** Explain why people who grow houseplants on windowsills should turn the plants every week or so.

Applying Skills

A scientist measured the rate of transpiration in an ash tree over an 18-hour period. She also measured how much water the tree's roots took up during the same period. Use the data in the graph below to answer Questions 23–25.

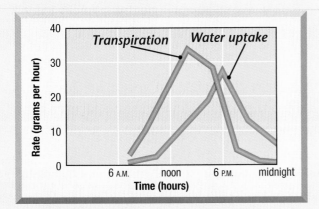

23. Interpreting Data At what time is transpiration at its highest? At what time is water uptake at its highest?

24. Inferring Why do you think the transpiration rate increases and decreases as it does during the 18-hour period?

25. Drawing Conclusions Based on the graph, what is one possible conclusion you can reach about the pattern of water loss and gain in the ash tree?

Performance ▽ **Assessment**

CHAPTER PROJECT

Present Your Project Design a poster that shows the results of your investigation. You may wish to use a cycle diagram to show the main events in the plant's life. Do you think that the later generations of plants will go through a similar life cycle? Why or why not?

Reflect and Record What new information did you learn about seed plants by doing this project? If you could do another investigation using these plants, what would you do? Why?

Test Preparation

Use these questions to prepare for standardized tests.

Use the information to answer Questions 26–29. One hundred radish seeds were planted in each of two identical trays of soil. Over the next 25 days, one tray was kept at 10°C. The other tray was kept at 20°C. The trays received equal amounts of water and sunlight. The data collected are shown below.

Day	Seeds That Germinated at:	
	10°C	20°C
0	0	0
5	0	5
10	20	35
15	45	75
20	50	85
25	50	85

26. What is the manipulated variable in this experiment?
  a. light   **b.** water
  c. seeds   **d.** temperature

27. What was the purpose of this experiment?
  a. to germinate radish seeds
  b. to determine whether radish seeds need light to germinate
  c. to determine whether radish seeds prefer a specific temperature to germinate
  d. to determine whether radish seeds need water to germinate

28. On day 15, what was the difference in the number of seeds that had germinated in the two trays?
  a. 15   **b.** 20   **c.** 30   **d.** 35

29. Which statement is a correct conclusion based on the data gathered from this experiment?
  a. The experiment failed because some seeds did not germinate.
  b. Temperature does not affect germination.
  c. More seeds germinate at a temperature of 20°C than at 10°C.
  d. Radish seeds need water and sunlight to germinate.

From Plants to CHEMICALS

Can you power a car with corn? Can you drink soda from a bottle made from plants? Can you use a farmer's corn crop to make chemicals strong enough to remove paint?

You can, thanks to scientists like Rathin Datta. Dr. Datta specializes in finding ways to get useful chemicals from plants. His discoveries will help make the environment cleaner for all of us.

Rathin is a chemical engineer at the Argonne National Laboratory in Illinois. For years, he has been finding ways to make useful products from substances found naturally in plants. He's helped find ways to turn corn into an automobile fuel called gasohol. He's researched plants that can be used to produce powerful medicines. He even worked on a way to use corn to make a stretchy fabric that athletes wear.

"I've always been interested in the plant and biological side of chemistry," says Rathin, who grew up in northern India. Even in grade school, he was interested in science. "That's because I've always been concerned about the effect of chemicals on the environment."

Rathin Datta was born in India, just north of Delhi. His interest in science was inspired in part by his father, who was a mathematician. Rathin came to the United States in 1970 to get a doctorate in chemical engineering at Princeton University. He works now at Argonne National Laboratory in Argonne, Illinois. In his free time, he enjoys tennis, hiking, and biking. He plays the sitar, an Indian lute, and has a special interest in opera.

Talking with Rathin Datta

Are Plant-Based Chemicals Safer?

Chemicals that come from crop plants are called *agrochemicals*, meaning "chemicals from agriculture," Rathin explains. Many agrochemicals are much less dangerous to the environment than chemicals made from petroleum. For one thing, although some agrochemicals can be poisonous to humans, most are not.

Because agrochemicals are made from plant materials, nature usually recycles them just as it recycles dead plants. Think of what happens to a tree after it falls to the ground. Tiny microbes work on its leaves and branches until the tree has rotted completely away. Much the same thing happens to products made from agrochemicals. A bag made from corn-based chemicals will break down and disappear after only a few weeks of being buried. In contrast, a plastic bag made from *petrochemicals*—chemicals made from petroleum—can survive hundreds of years.

Converting Carbohydrates

The starting ingredients in many agrochemicals are energy-rich substances called carbohydrates. Sugar and starch are carbohydrates. Rathin Datta converts, or changes, carbohydrates from corn into an agrochemical that can be used to make plastic. To do this, he needs help from tiny organisms—bacteria. First, he explains, he puts particular bacteria into a big vat of ground-up corn. The bacteria convert the corn's carbohydrates into acids through a

Researchers Rathin Datta (right), Mike Henry (center), and Shih-Perng Tsai (left) developed the new, low-cost solvent. The dark substance is the fermented corn mixture. The clear substance that Rathin holds is the solvent.

natural process called fermentation. Rathin then uses the acids to make agrochemical plastic.

"The bacteria do all the work of converting the carbohydrates into useful molecules," says Rathin. "The hardest part for us comes afterward. The fermentation process produces a brew that contains a whole mix of materials. We have to find ways to separate out the one kind of material that we want to use from all the others."

This sign on a gasoline pump advertises gasohol.

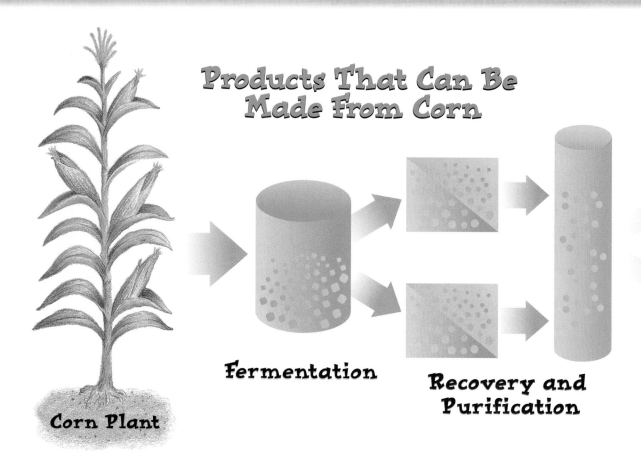

Products That Can Be Made From Corn

Corn Plant

Fermentation

Recovery and Purification

Making Paint Remover From Corn

Rathin Datta's most recent discovery is a good example of how agrochemicals can replace petrochemicals. He and his team have found a new way to use corn to make powerful solvents. Solvents are used to dissolve other substances.

"Solvents are found everywhere," says Rathin. "For example, factories use them in many processes to clean electronic parts or to remove ink from recycled newspapers. Households use them in grease-cleaning detergents and in paint removers."

Almost 4 million tons of solvents are used in the United States every year. Most are made from petro-chemicals and can be very poisonous.

"Scientists have known for a long time that much safer solvents can be made from agrochemicals," says Rathin. "But the process has been too expensive. It doesn't do any good to make something that is environmentally sound if it costs too much for people to use," says Rathin. "Our challenge as chemical engineers

Spandex was used to make the blue tops these dancers are wearing.

306

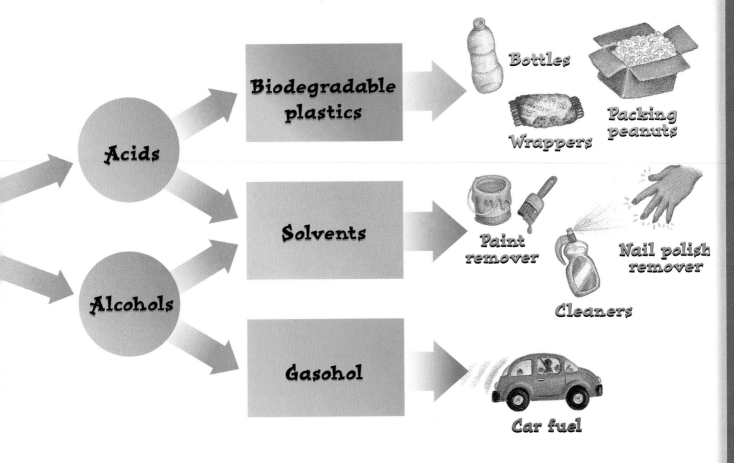

was to think about an old process in an entirely new way. We had to find a less expensive way to make these solvents."

Discovering a New Process

Rathin needed a new process to separate the solvents he wanted from a mixture. "I started working with a new kind of plastic that acts like a very fine filter. When we pass the fermented corn over this plastic, it captures the acids we want to keep and lets the other material pass through."

After two years of experimenting, Rathin perfected his process of making agrochemical solvents. His process works for less than half the cost of the old method. It also uses 90 percent less energy. Soon, most of the solvents used in the United States

could be this cleaner, safer kind made from corn. "It even makes a a great fingernail polish remover," says Datta.

"It's very satisfying to take a natural product like corn and use it to produce a chemical that will replace a less safe chemical," says Rathin. "It's rare to find a compound that can do everything that this corn solvent can do and still be nonpoisonous and easily break down in the environment."

In Your Journal

Rathin Datta and his team had discovered years ago how to make a solvent that was safer for the environment. But it was very expensive to make. Rathin could have stopped his research at that point. Instead, he chose to continue. What does this action tell you about how scientists like Datta meet challenges?

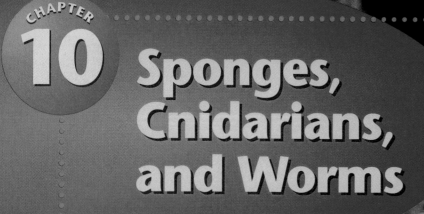

The graceful tentacles of this yellow cup coral help it to lure and catch food.

WEB ACTIVITY
www.phschool.com

SECTION
1 **What Is an Animal?**

Discover Is It an Animal?
Sharpen Your Skills Inferring

SECTION
2 *Integrating Mathematics*
Symmetry

Discover How Many Ways Can You
      Fold It?
Science at Home Front-End Advantages
Real-World Lab A Tale Told by Tracks

SECTION
3 **Sponges and Cnidarians**

Discover How Do Natural and Synthetic
      Sponges Compare?
Try This Hydra Doing?

CHAPTER 10 PROJECT

Alive and Well

When you hear the word *animal*, what picture comes to mind? You probably do not think of anything like this fingerlike yellow coral waving in the ocean current. But just like horses or sparrows, corals are animals, too.

Do animals such as corals really have anything in common with horses and sparrows? Keep this question in mind as you begin your study of animals. Instead of just reading about animals, though, you and your classmates will create a zoo in your classroom. Your zoo will feature crickets, earthworms, and other animals not usually found in zoos. In your role as zookeeper, you will select one animal to care for and study.

Your Goal To keep an animal safe and healthy for three weeks while you study its characteristics, needs, and behaviors.

To complete the project successfully, you must
- ◆ provide a healthy and safe environment for your animal
- ◆ keep the animal alive and well for the entire time of the project, and observe the animal's behavior
- ◆ prepare a report or illustrated booklet to show what you have learned about your animal
- ◆ follow the safety guidelines in Appendix A

Get Started After you have chosen an animal you want to care for, work with a partner to brainstorm questions you have about its survival needs. Then plan a way to find answers to your questions.

Check Your Progress You'll be working on this project as you study this chapter. To keep your project on track, look for Check Your Progress boxes at the following points.

Section 1 Review, page 314: Research your animal's needs and prepare its home.
Section 3 Review, page 325: Record your daily observations.
Section 4 Review, page 333: Analyze what you've learned and prepare your presentation.

Present Your Project At the end of the chapter (page 337), you will introduce your animal to your classmates and share your knowledge.

SECTION 4 Worms

Discover **What Can You See in a Worm?**
Sharpen Your Skills **Communicating**
Sharpen Your Skills **Observing**
Skills Lab **Earthworm Responses**

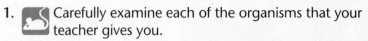

Is It an Animal?

1. Carefully examine each of the organisms that your teacher gives you.

2. Decide which ones are animals. Think about the reasons for your decision. Wash your hands after handling each of the organisms.

Think It Over

Forming Operational Definitions What characteristics did you use to decide whether each organism was an animal?

GUIDE FOR READING

◆ What characteristics do all animals have in common?

◆ What three things do animals need from their environment?

Reading Tip Before you begin to read, write your own definition of *animal*. Add to it or change it as you read.

In the waters off the north coast of Australia, a young box jellyfish floats along, looking more like a tiny transparent flower than an animal. After a time the young jellyfish will change form. As an adult, it will resemble a square bubble of clear jelly trailing bunches of long, wavy, armlike structures called tentacles.

To capture food, a box jellyfish's tentacles fire deadly venom at unlucky animals that happen to touch them. Humans are no exception. A swimmer who brushes the tentacles of a box jellyfish can die in only four minutes. In spite of their harmless appearance, adult box jellyfish have one of the strongest venoms on Earth.

Characteristics of Animals

The box jellyfish may not look like most animals you are familiar with, but it is indeed an animal. Biologists have described over 1 million different animal species, and there are certainly many more. Recall that a species is a group of organisms that can mate with each other and produce offspring, who in turn can mate and reproduce.

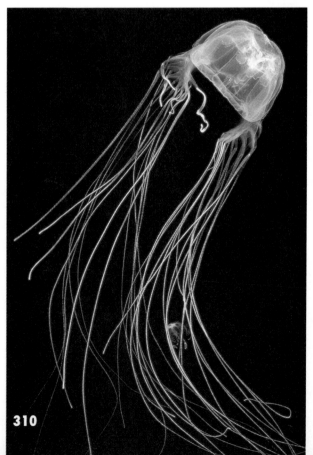

Figure 1 Don't be fooled by the delicate-looking tentacles of the Australian box jellyfish. Animals that brush against them can be killed by their venom—and become the jellyfish's next meal.

All species of animals, including the beautiful but deadly box jellyfish, are similar in some important ways. **Animals are many-celled organisms that must obtain their food by eating other organisms.** In addition, most animals reproduce sexually and can move from place to place. Biologists look for these characteristics in deciding whether an organism is an animal.

How Animal Cells Are Organized All animals are multicellular organisms. The cells of most animals are grouped together to form different kinds of tissue. A tissue is a group of similar cells that perform a specific job. For example, muscle tissue allows animals to move, while nerve tissue carries messages from one part of the body to another. Tissues may combine to form an **organ,** which is a group of different tissues that work together to perform a specific job that is more complex than the functions of each tissue by itself. Organs are made up of different types of tissue—your thigh bone, for example, is an organ that contains bone tissue, nerve tissue, and blood. In most animals, different organs combine to form an organ system, such as your skeletal system, shown in Figure 2.

How Animals Obtain Food Earlier chapters of this book described autotrophs, organisms that make their own food, and heterotrophs, organisms that cannot make their own food. Every animal is a heterotroph—it must obtain food by eating other organisms. Most animals take food into a cavity inside their bodies. Inside this cavity, the food is digested, or broken down into substances that the animal's body can absorb and use.

How Animals Reproduce Animals typically reproduce sexually. You have learned that sexual reproduction is the process by which a new organism forms from the joining of two organisms' sex cells. When a male sperm cell and a female egg cell unite, the resulting new individual has a combination of characteristics from both parents. Some animals can also reproduce asexually. Recall that asexual reproduction is the process by which a single organism produces a new organism identical to itself. A tiny animal called a hydra, for example, reproduces asexually by forming buds that eventually break off to form new hydras.

How Animals Move Many animal movements are related to obtaining food, reproducing, or escaping danger. Barnacles, for example, wave feathery arms through the water to collect tiny food particles. Some geese fly long distances each spring to the place where they mate and lay eggs. And you've probably seen a cat climb a tree to escape a snarling dog.

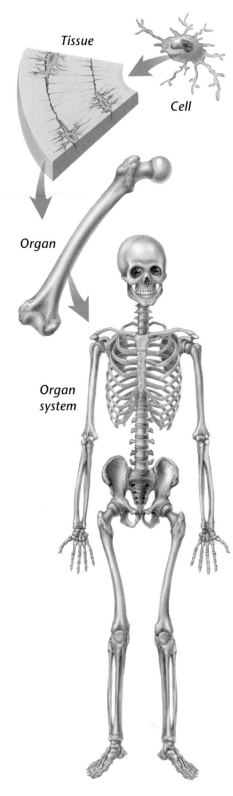

Tissue

Cell

Organ

Organ system

Figure 2 An animal's skeletal system has different levels of organization. Bone cells make up tissues, and tissues make up organs such as the thigh bone.
Classifying Is the skull best classified as an organ or as a tissue?

Some animals don't move from place to place. Adult oysters, sponges, and corals all stick firmly to underwater rocks. But most animals move freely at some point in their lives. For example, for its first few weeks of life, an oyster is a tiny swimmer. Then the young oyster swims to a solid surface. It glues itself in place and changes into an adult oyster within a shell.

How Animals Meet Their Needs

Animals need to obtain water, food, and oxygen from their environment, or surroundings. Animals need water because the chemical reactions that keep them alive, such as the breakdown of food, take place in water. Food provides animals with raw materials for growth and with energy for their bodies' activities, such as moving and breathing. To release that energy, the body's cells need oxygen. Some animals get oxygen from air; others absorb it from water.

An animal also needs to be able to respond to its environment—for example, to find food or to run away from danger. Animals' bodies and behaviors are adapted for such tasks. An **adaptation** is a characteristic that helps an organism survive in its environment or reproduce.

Adaptations for Getting Food

Unlike plants that make their own food using sunlight, animals must obtain their food. Some animals eat plants, other animals eat animals, and still others eat both plants and animals.

Herbivores Animals that eat only plants are called **herbivores.** Grasshoppers, termites, and garden snails are some common small herbivores. Larger herbivores include cows, horses, and pandas. Herbivores have adaptations such as teeth with broad, flat surfaces that are good for grinding tough plants.

Figure 3 Animals have different methods of obtaining food.
A. A macaw uses its curved beak to feed on fruits and seeds.
B. A carpet snake uses its body to strangle a lizard for a meal.
Applying Concepts
What do these animals obtain from food?

Carnivores Animals that eat only other animals are **carnivores**. Many carnivores are **predators** that hunt and kill other animals. Predators have adaptations that help them capture the animals they feed upon, their **prey.** Wolves, for example, run down their prey. A wolf's adaptations include sharp claws, speed, and excellent hearing and eyesight. The teeth of most carnivores are sharp and pointed—they are adapted for cutting and stabbing.

Unlike wolves, "sit-and-wait" predators hide and attack suddenly. Most blend in with their surroundings. Think of a frog sitting by a pond. An insect flying by doesn't see the frog. Suddenly the frog flicks out its tongue and catches the unsuspecting insect.

Omnivores An animal that eats both plants and animals is an **omnivore.** A grizzly bear eats berries and roots, as well as insects, fish, and other small animals. Humans are also omnivores, as you know if you like hamburgers with tomato.

☑ *Checkpoint* *Describe some feeding adaptations of carnivores.*

Adaptations for Escaping Predators

In addition to feeding adaptations, animals have adaptations that help them avoid being eaten by predators. Some animals, such as box turtles and hedgehogs, have hard shells or spiny skins. Opossums and pill bugs "play dead" when they are attacked, so their predators lose interest. Stingers, claws, bitter-tasting flesh, or smelly sprays protect other animals. If you see a skunk, you stay far away from it. So do most predators.

Classification of Animals

Biologists classify animals in the animal kingdom into about 35 phyla, or major groups. The branching tree on page 314 shows how biologists think some of the phyla are related. For example, from their positions on the tree, you can see that segmented worms are more closely related to arthropods than to sponges. The tree also shows the order in which biologists think animal life has evolved, or changed over time.

One important characteristic used to classify animals is the presence or absence of a backbone. An animal that does not have a backbone is called an **invertebrate.** Jellyfishes, worms, snails, crabs, spiders, and insects are all invertebrates. Most animal species—about 95 percent— are invertebrates. In contrast, a **vertebrate** is an animal that has a backbone. Fishes, amphibians, reptiles, birds, and mammals are all vertebrates.

Sharpen your Skills

Inferring ACTIVITY

The pictures show the jawbones of two animals. Look at the pictures carefully, and decide what types of food each animal probably eats. List the observations on which you base your inferences.

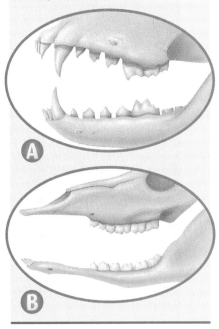

Ⓐ

Ⓑ

Figure 4 This African pygmy hedgehog can roll up into a spiny ball to protect itself from predators.

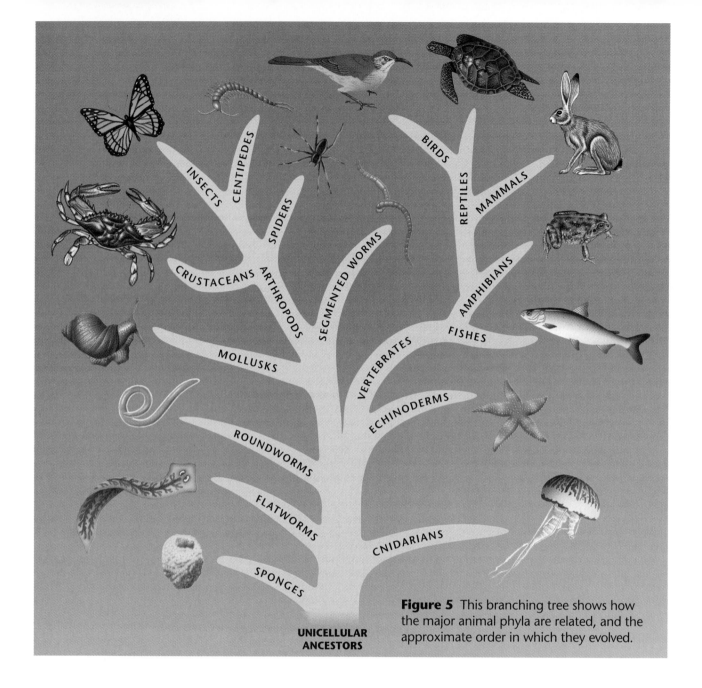

Figure 5 This branching tree shows how the major animal phyla are related, and the approximate order in which they evolved.

Section 1 Review

1. Describe two characteristics of all animals.
2. List three needs that all animals must meet in order to survive.
3. Define *invertebrate* and *vertebrate*. Give an example of each.
4. **Thinking Critically** **Comparing and Contrasting** Contrast the ways in which wolves and cows obtain their food, and identify one food-getting adaptation of each animal.

Check Your Progress

CHAPTER PROJECT

By now, you should have chosen an animal and researched how to meet its needs. Discuss with your teacher your plans for housing and caring for your animal. After preparing your animal's home and obtaining some food for it, put the animal in its new home. (*Hint:* Make a plan for your animal for holidays and weekends.)

314

SECTION 2 Symmetry

DISCOVER · ACTIVITY · · ·

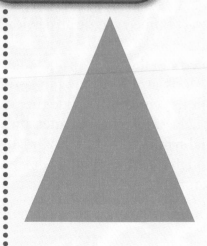

How Many Ways Can You Fold It?

1. Trace the triangle onto a sheet of paper and cut it out. Then draw a circle by tracing the rim of a glass or other round object. Cut out the circle.

2. Fold the triangle so that one half matches the other. Do the same with the circle.

3. See how many different ways you can fold each figure so that the two halves are identical.

Think It Over

Classifying Can you think of animals whose body shape could be folded in the same number of ways as the triangle? As the circle?

With its wings closed, a bright and colorful butterfly perches lightly on a flower, drinking nectar. Its delicate but strong wings are motionless as it drinks. Then, suddenly, those fragile-looking wings begin to move, and they lift the butterfly, seemingly effortlessly, into the air.

As you can see from the photo of the large copper butterfly in Figure 6, a butterfly's body has two halves, and each half looks almost like a reflection of the other. This balanced arrangement, called symmetry, is characteristic of many animals. A butterfly's symmetry contributes to its pleasing appearance. More importantly, the balanced wings help the butterfly to fly more easily.

GUIDE FOR READING

◆ What types of symmetry do complex animals exhibit?

Reading Tip Before you read, preview the illustrations in Figures 6 and 7. Write a few sentences comparing and contrasting the organisms in the illustrations.

Figure 6 If you could draw a line through this butterfly's body, it would divide the animal into two mirror-image halves. *Applying Concepts What is this balanced arrangement called?*

The Mathematics of Symmetry

In Figure 6 on page 315, you can see that a line drawn down the middle of the butterfly produces two halves that are the same—they are mirror images. This dividing line is called a line of symmetry. An object has line symmetry, or **bilateral symmetry,** if there is a line that divides it into halves that are mirror images. A large copper butterfly has bilateral symmetry, as do an oak leaf, a spoon, and a pair of eyeglasses.

Contrast the butterfly's symmetry to that of a sea anemone. A sea anemone is circular if you look at it from the top, as in Figure 7. Any line drawn through its center will divide the sea anemone into two symmetrical halves. Like the sea anemone, many circular objects exhibit **radial symmetry**—they have many lines of symmetry that all go through a central point. Pie plates and bicycle wheels have radial symmetry.

☑ *Checkpoint* *How is radial symmetry different from bilateral symmetry?*

Symmetry in Animals

There are a few animals, such as most sponges, that exhibit no symmetry. These asymmetrical animals generally have very simple body plans. Sponges, for example, have no hearts, brains, kidneys, or nerve cells. **The bodies of complex animals all have either radial or bilateral symmetry.**

Animals with Radial Symmetry The external body parts of animals with radial symmetry are equally spaced around a central point, like spokes on a bicycle wheel. Because of the circular arrangement of their parts, radially symmetrical animals, such as jellyfishes, sea anemones, and sea urchins, do not have distinct front or back ends.

Animals with radial symmetry have several characteristics in common. All of them live in water. Most of them do not move very fast—they either stay in one spot, are moved along by water currents, or creep along the bottom. Few radially symmetrical animals are able to go out in search of prey. Instead, their watery environment carries food to them.

For a water animal that does not actively chase prey, the absence of a front end creates no disadvantage. Animals with radial symmetry learn about their environment primarily through senses of touch and taste, which function on the surfaces of their bodies. Because the animals are able to sense their environment in all directions, they can be ready to grab food coming from any direction.

Figure 7 Sea anemones have radial symmetry. A radially symmetrical object has many lines of symmetry that all go through a central point. *Observing How would you describe the shape of the sea anemone?*

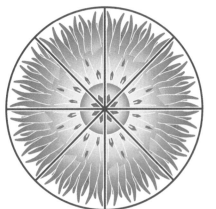

Animals with Bilateral Symmetry Most animals you are familiar with have bilateral symmetry. For example, a fish has only one line of symmetry that divides it into mirror images. Each half of a fish has one eye, one nostril, half of a mouth, and one of each of the fish's pairs of fins. Your body also has bilateral symmetry.

In general, bilaterally symmetrical animals are larger and more complex than those with radial symmetry. Animals with bilateral symmetry have a front end that goes first as the animal moves along. These animals move more quickly and efficiently than most animals with radial symmetry. This is partly because bilateral symmetry allows for a streamlined, balanced body. In addition, most bilaterally symmetrical animals have sense organs in their front ends that pick up information about what is in front of them. Swift movement and sense organs help bilaterally symmetrical animals get food and avoid enemies.

Figure 8 Radially symmetrical animals, like the sea urchin at left, have no distinct front or back ends. In contrast, bilaterally symmetrical animals, like the tiger above, have a front end with sense organs that pick up information. Because of its balanced body plan, a tiger can also move quickly.

Section 2 Review

1. What two types of symmetry do complex animals exhibit? Describe each type.
2. How can bilateral symmetry be an advantage to a predator?
3. Draw a view of a bilaterally symmetrical animal to show its symmetry. Draw the line of symmetry.
4. **Thinking Critically Applying Concepts** Which capital letters of the alphabet have bilateral symmetry? Radial symmetry?

Science at Home

Front-End Advantages With a family member, observe as many different animals as possible in your yard or at a park. Look in lots of different places, such as in the grass, under rocks, and in the air. Explain to your family member the advantage to an animal of having a distinct front end. What is this type of body arrangement called?

A TALE TOLD BY TRACKS

Suppose that, on a chilly winter day, you hike through a park. You suspect that many animals live there, but you don't actually see any of them. Instead, you see signs that the animals have left behind, such as mysterious tracks in the snow. These tracks are evidence you can use to draw inferences about the animals, such as what size they are and what they were doing. Inferences are interpretations of observations that help you to explain what may have happened in a given situation.

Problem

What can you learn about animals by studying their tracks?

Skill Focus

observing, inferring

Procedure

1. Copy the data table into your notebook.
2. The illustration at the top of the next page shows the tracks, or footprints, left in the snow by animals living in a park. The illustration has been divided into three sections. Focus on the tracks in Section 1.

3. Make two or more observations about the tracks and record them in your data table.
4. For each observation you listed, write one or more inferences that could be drawn from that observation.

DATA TABLE		
Section	Observations	Inferences
Section 1		
Section 2		
Section 3		

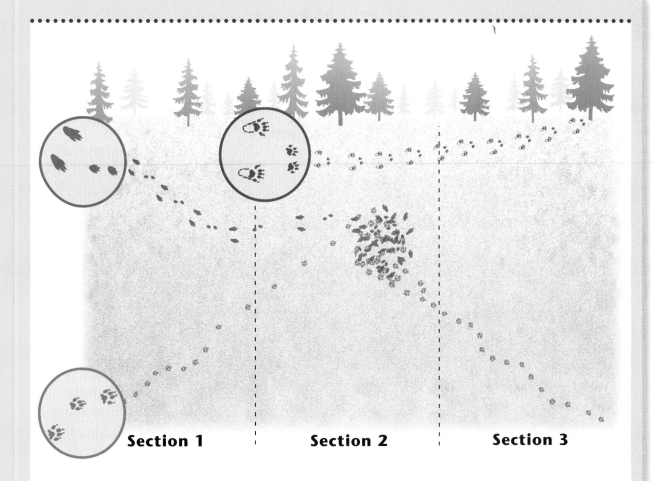

Section 1 | **Section 2** | **Section 3**

5. Now look at the tracks in Section 2. Write two or more observations in the data table. For each observation, write one or more inferences.
6. Study the tracks in Section 3. Write two or more observations in the data table. Write at least one inference for each observation.

Analyze and Conclude

1. How many types of animals made the tracks shown in the illustration? Explain.
2. What inferences, if any, can you make about the relative sizes of the animals based on their tracks? Explain.
3. What can you infer about the speed of the animals' movements? Are they walking? Running? How can you tell?

4. In a paragraph, explain what you think happened to the animals and the order in which the events happened.
5. What inference do you feel most confident about and why? Which inference do you feel least confident about and why?
6. **Apply** How might making inferences be important in the work of a real detective? Explain.

More to Explore

Take a walk around your community looking for indirect evidence of animal life such as tracks, feathers, empty nests, and holes in the ground or in dead trees. For each discovery, record its location, at least two observations, and one or more inferences to explain each observation.

SECTION
3 Sponges and Cnidarians

DISCOVER •••••••••••••••••••••••••••••••••••••••ACTIVITY•••

How Do Natural and Synthetic Sponges Compare?

1. Examine a natural sponge, and then use a hand lens or a microscope to take a closer look at its surface. Look carefully at the holes in the sponge. Draw what you see through the lens.

2. ✂ Cut out a small piece of sponge and examine it with a hand lens. Draw what you see.

3. Repeat Steps 1 and 2 with a synthetic kitchen sponge.

Think It Over
Observing What are three ways a natural and synthetic sponge are similar? What are three ways they are different?

GUIDE FOR READING

◆ How is the body of a sponge organized?

◆ What are the main characteristics of cnidarians?

Reading Tip As you read, create a compare/contrast table about sponges and cnidarians. Include information on body plans, feeding methods, defense, and reproduction.

Eagerly but carefully, you and the others in your group put on scuba gear, preparing to dive into the ocean and see firsthand what lies beneath the surface. Over the side of the boat you go; the salty ocean water feels cool on your skin. As you slowly descend, you notice that you are surrounded by animals. You see many kinds of fishes, of course, but as you get to the ocean bottom, you notice other animals, too, some as strange as creatures from a science fiction movie. Some of these strange creatures may be sponges.

Sponges live all over the world—mostly in oceans, but also in freshwater rivers and lakes. Sponges are attached to hard surfaces underwater, and they are well adapted to their watery life. Moving currents carry food and oxygen to them, and these same currents take away their waste products. Water plays a role in their reproduction and helps their young find new places to live.

Sponges

Sponges don't look or act like most animals you know. In fact, they are so different that for a long time, people thought that sponges were plants. Like plants, adult sponges stay in one place. But unlike most plants, sponges take food into their bodies, which qualifies them for membership in the animal kingdom. These strange animals have been on Earth for about 540 million years.

◀ Pink sponges on a Caribbean coral reef

The bodies of most sponges have irregular shapes, with no symmetry. While some of their cells do specialized jobs, sponges lack the tissues and organs that most other animals have.

The Structure of a Sponge You might use a brightly colored, synthetic sponge to mop up a spill. That sponge is filled with holes, and so are the animals called sponges. **The body of a sponge is something like a bag that is pierced all over with openings called pores.** In fact, the name of the phylum to which sponges belong—phylum Porifera—means "having pores." Notice the many pores in the sponge in *Exploring a Sponge*.

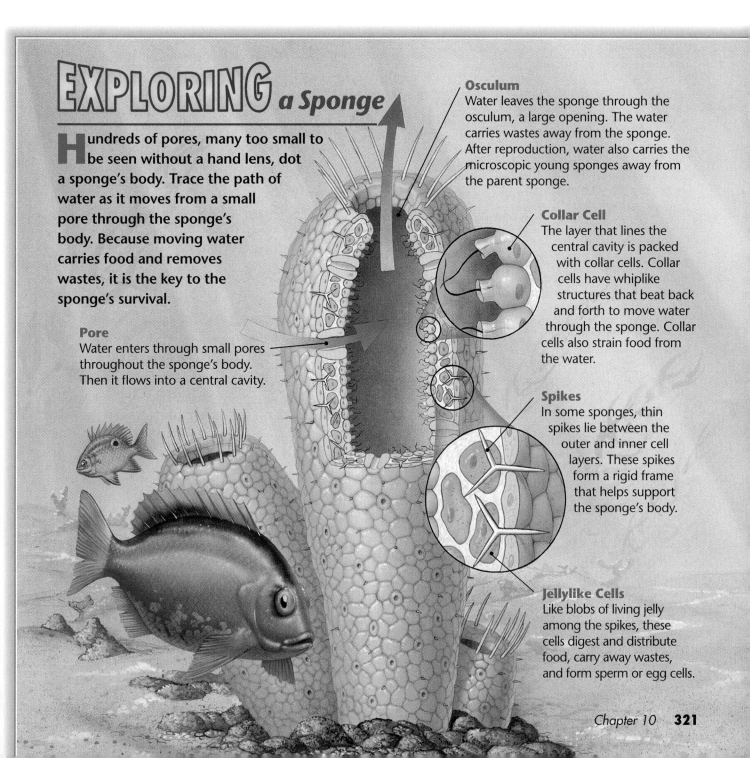

EXPLORING *a Sponge*

Hundreds of pores, many too small to be seen without a hand lens, dot a sponge's body. Trace the path of water as it moves from a small pore through the sponge's body. Because moving water carries food and removes wastes, it is the key to the sponge's survival.

Pore
Water enters through small pores throughout the sponge's body. Then it flows into a central cavity.

Osculum
Water leaves the sponge through the osculum, a large opening. The water carries wastes away from the sponge. After reproduction, water also carries the microscopic young sponges away from the parent sponge.

Collar Cell
The layer that lines the central cavity is packed with collar cells. Collar cells have whiplike structures that beat back and forth to move water through the sponge. Collar cells also strain food from the water.

Spikes
In some sponges, thin spikes lie between the outer and inner cell layers. These spikes form a rigid frame that helps support the sponge's body.

Jellylike Cells
Like blobs of living jelly among the spikes, these cells digest and distribute food, carry away wastes, and form sperm or egg cells.

In the paragraph that describes how sponges defend themselves, notice how the author says that a sponge dinner would be "like a sandwich made of thorns, sand, and cement, with a little awful-tasting goo mixed in." The author's description is a simile, which is a comparison using the word *like* or *as*. Writers use similes to paint lively word pictures and create vivid impressions.

In Your Journal

You can use similes in your own writing. For instance, you might say that a racehorse launches itself from the starting line like a rocket. Choose three different animals and write a simile describing each one. For each simile, identify the characteristic that you are trying to convey.

Getting Food and Oxygen from Water Sponges feed by straining food particles from water. As water enters a sponge, it carries tiny organisms such as bacteria and protists. Collar cells on the inside of the central cavity trap these food particles and digest them. Sponges are very efficient at removing food particles from water. A sponge the size of a teacup is able to remove food from 5,000 liters of water per day. That's enough water to fill a truckload of two-liter soft-drink bottles!

INTEGRATING CHEMISTRY A sponge gets its oxygen from water too. The water contains oxygen, which moves from the water into the sponge's cells in a process known as diffusion. In diffusion, molecules of a substance move from an area in which they are highly concentrated to an area in which they are less concentrated. Oxygen is more highly concentrated in the water than it is in the sponge's cells. So the oxygen moves from the water into the sponge. Diffusion also carries waste products from the sponge's cells into the water.

Spikes The soft bodies of most sponges are supported by a network of spikes. Those spikes can be as sharp as needles, as anyone who has touched a live sponge knows. In addition, many sponges are tougher than wood, and some produce irritating substances. Even so, some fish eat sponges. A sponge dinner is probably like a sandwich made of thorns, sand, and cement, with a little awful-tasting goo mixed in.

Sponge Reproduction Sponges reproduce both asexually and sexually. Budding is one form of asexual reproduction in sponges. In budding, small new sponges grow from the sides of an adult sponge. Eventually these tiny sponges detach and begin life on their own. Sponges reproduce sexually too. Sponges do not have separate sexes—a single sponge forms eggs at one time of the year and sperm at a different time. At any one time of the year, some sponges are producing eggs and others are producing sperm. When a sponge produces sperm, the water currents that move through the sponge carry sperm from the sponge into the open water. The sperm may then enter the pores of another sponge and fertilize egg cells in that sponge.

After fertilization, a larva develops. A **larva** (plural *larvae*) is the immature form of an animal that looks very different from the adult. A sponge larva is a hollow ball of cells that swims through the water. Eventually the larva attaches to a surface and develops into a nonmoving adult sponge.

✓ *Checkpoint* As water flows through a sponge's body, what functions does it enable the sponge to perform?

Cnidarians

Some other organisms you might notice on an underwater dive are jellyfishes, sea anemones, and corals. At first glance, those animals look like they could be creatures from another planet. Most jellyfishes look like transparent bubbles that trail curtains of streamerlike tentacles. Sea anemones look like odd, underwater flowers. Some corals have branches that make them look like trees. Jellyfishes, sea anemones, and corals are **cnidarians** (nih DAIR ee uhnz), animals that have stinging cells and take their food into a hollow central cavity. **Members of the phylum Cnidaria are carnivores that use their stinging cells to capture their prey and to defend themselves.** The stinging cells are located on the long, wavy tentacles.

Unlike sponges, cnidarians have specialized tissues. For example, because of muscle-like tissues, many cnidarians can move in interesting ways. Jellyfishes swim through the water, and hydras turn slow somersaults. Anemones stretch out, shrink down, and bend slowly from side to side. These movements are directed by nerve cells that are spread out like a spider web, or net. This nerve net helps the cnidarian respond quickly to danger or the presence of food.

Cnidarian Body Plans Cnidarians have two different body plans. Both body plans have radial symmetry. As you read about these two body plans, refer to Figure 10 on page 324. A **polyp** (PAHL ip), such as a hydra, sea anemone, or coral, is shaped something like a vase, with the mouth opening at the top. Most polyps do not move around; they are

Figure 9 All cnidarians live in watery environments. **A.** Hydras live in freshwater ponds and lakes, where they reproduce by budding. **B.** The Portuguese man-of-war is actually a colony of cnidarians living together. **C.** Sea anemones are large cnidarians that often live in groups in the ocean. *Comparing and Contrasting What characteristics do these three cnidarians share?*

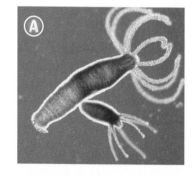

adapted for a life attached to an underwater surface. In contrast, the bowl-shaped **medusa** (muh DOO suh), such as a jellyfish, is adapted for a free-swimming life. Medusas, unlike polyps, have mouths that open downward. Some cnidarians go through both a polyp stage and a medusa stage during their lives. Others are polyps or medusas for their whole lives.

How Cnidarians Feed A cnidarian captures its prey by using its stinging cells to inject venom, a poisonous substance that paralyzes fish and other prey. Then the cnidarian's tentacles pull the prey animal to its mouth. From there the food passes into a body cavity where it is digested. Because cnidarians have a digestive system with only one opening, undigested food is expelled through the mouth.

Cnidarian Reproduction Cnidarians reproduce both asexually and sexually. For polyps, budding is the most common form of asexual reproduction. Amazingly, in some polyps the entire animal splits into pieces. Each piece then forms a new polyp. Both kinds of asexual reproduction allow the numbers of cnidarians to increase rapidly in a short time.

Sexual reproduction in cnidarians occurs in a variety of ways. Some species of cnidarians have both sexes within one individual. In others, the sexes are in separate individuals, as in humans.

☑ *Checkpoint* How does a cnidarian obtain and digest food?

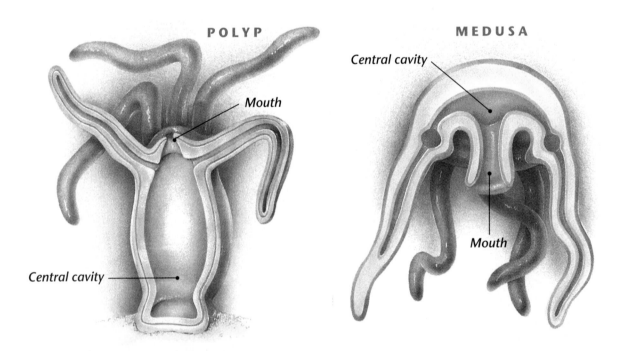

Figure 10 Cnidarians have two basic body forms, the vase-shaped polyp and the bowl-shaped medusa. *Comparing and Contrasting Contrast the location of the mouth in the polyp and the medusa.*

Life on a Coral Reef

In some warm, shallow ocean waters, just below the surface, you can find one of the most diverse ocean environments—a coral reef. Coral reefs seem to be made of stone. But in fact, coral reefs are built by cnidarians. At the beginning of its life, a free-swimming coral larva attaches to a solid surface. A broken shell, a sunken ship, or the skeleton of a once-living coral animal will do just fine. The coral polyp then produces a hard, stony skeleton around its soft body.

The coral polyp reproduces asexually, and then its offspring reproduce asexually, too. Over time, that polyp may give rise to thousands more, each with a hard skeleton. When the coral polyps die, their skeletons remain behind. Over thousands of years, as live corals add their skeletons to those that have died, rocklike masses called reefs grow up from the sea floor. Coral reefs can become enormous. The Great Barrier Reef near Australia is about 2,000 kilometers long.

Coral reefs, like the one in Figure 11, are home to more species of fishes and invertebrates than any other environment on Earth. Hundreds of sponge species live among the corals, constantly filtering water through their bodies. Worms burrow into the coral reef. Giant clams lie with their huge shells slightly open. Shrimp and crabs edge out of hiding places below the corals. At night, bright blue damsel fish settle into pockets in the coral. At dawn and dusk, sea turtles, sea snakes, and sharks all visit the reef, hunting for prey. These living things interact in complex ways, creating an environment that is rich and beautiful.

Figure 11 Coral reefs provide homes and hunting grounds for a vast variety of sea animals. The bottom photo is a close-up of a group of individual coral polyps.

Section 3 Review

1. Describe the structure of a sponge's body.
2. Explain how cnidarians capture prey and defend themselves. In your explanation, refer to specific body structures.
3. Draw a diagram to show how water travels through a sponge. Show the path with an arrow.
4. **Thinking Critically** **Classifying** Why is a sponge classified as an animal?

Check Your Progress

CHAPTER PROJECT

You should be observing your animal every day and writing your observations in your journal. Record how the animal looks, feeds, and behaves. Note any changes in the animal. Talk to your teacher before making any changes to your animal's home, feeding schedule, or other living conditions.

Coral Reefs in Danger

Coral reefs off the coasts of many nations are endangered, damaged, or threatened with destruction. Reefs house and protect many species of sea animals, including sponges, shrimp, sea turtles, and fishes. In addition, reefs protect coastlines from floods caused by ocean storms.

Although coral reefs are hard as rocks, the coral animals themselves are quite delicate. Recreational divers can damage the fragile reefs. Is it possible to protect the reefs while still allowing divers to explore them?

The Issues

What's the Harm in Diving? About 3.5 million recreational divers live in the United States. With so many divers it is hard to guarantee that no harm will occur to the coral reefs. In fact, divers can cause significant damage by standing on or even touching these fragile reefs. Carelessly dropping a boat anchor can crush part of a reef. Although most divers are careful, not all are, and accidents can always happen.

Harm to the reefs is even more likely to occur when divers collect coral for their own enjoyment or to sell for profit. You can see brightly colored coral from the sea in jewelry and in decorations.

Should Reefs Be Further Protected? The United States government has passed laws making it illegal, under most circumstances, to remove coral from the sea. Because a few divers break these laws, some people want to ban diving altogether. However, many divers say it's unfair to ban diving just because of a few lawbreakers.

Many divers consider coral reefs the most exciting and beautiful places in the ocean to explore. As recreational divers, photographers, scientists, and others visit and learn more about these delicate coral reefs, they increase their own and other's awareness of them. Public awareness may be the best way to ensure that these rich environments are protected.

More Than a Diving Issue Coral reefs in the Western Atlantic—such as those in Bermuda, the Bahamas, the Caribbean Islands, and Florida—are major tourist attractions that bring money and jobs to people in local communities. If diving were banned, local businesses would suffer significantly. Also, although divers can harm coral reefs, other human activities, such as ocean pollution, oil spills, and fishing nets, can also cause harm. In addition, natural events, such as tropical storms, changes in sea level, and changes in sea temperature, can also damage the fragile reefs.

You Decide

1. Identify the Problem

In your own words, explain the controversy surrounding diving near coral reefs.

2. Analyze the Options

List the arguments on each side of the issue. Note the pros and cons. How well would each position protect the reefs? Who might be harmed or inconvenienced?

3. Find a Solution

Write a newspaper editorial stating your position on whether diving should be allowed near coral reefs. State your position and reasons clearly.

SECTION
④ Worms

DISCOVER •••••••••••••••••••••••••••••••••••ACTIVITY••••

What Can You See in a Worm?

1. Your teacher will give you a planarian, a kind of flatworm. Pick the worm up with the tip of a paintbrush. Place it gently in a small, clear container. Use a dropper to cover the planarian with spring water.

2. Observe the planarian with a hand lens. Look for a head and tail region. Look for two spots in the head region. Draw what you see.

3. Observe and describe how the planarian moves.

4. Gently touch the planarian with a toothpick and observe how it behaves. Then return the planarian to your teacher, and wash your hands.

Think It Over

Observing How is a planarian different from a sponge?

Y ou might think that all worms are small, slimy, and wriggly. But many worms do not fit that description. Some worms are almost three meters long and are as thick as your arm. Others look like glowing, furry blobs. Worms can flutter and glide or climb around with paddle-like bristles. Still others are very small and live in white tubes cemented to rocks.

What Worms Have in Common

It's hard to say exactly what worms are, because there are many kinds of worms, all with their own characteristics. **Biologists classify worms into several phyla—the three major ones are flatworms, roundworms, and segmented worms.** Flatworms belong to the phylum Platyhelminthes (plat ee HEL minth eez); roundworms belong to the phylum Nematoda; segmented worms belong to the phylum Annelida.

GUIDE FOR READING

◆ What are the three main groups of worms?

◆ What are the characteristics of each group of worms?

Reading Tip As you read, list the characteristics of flatworms, roundworms, and segmented worms.

Figure 12 The ocean flatworm, left, and the segmented Christmas tree worm, right, show some of the wide variety of ocean worms.

Chapter 10 **327**

Figure 13 As you can tell from this spectacular spaghetti worm, not all worms are gray and tube shaped.

All worms have some characteristics in common. All worms are invertebrates, and they all have long, narrow bodies without legs. In addition, all worms have tissues, organs, and organ systems. Also, all worms have bilateral symmetry. Unlike sponges or cnidarians, worms have head and tail ends.

Response to the Environment Worms are the simplest organisms with a brain, which is a knot of nerve tissue located in the head end. Because a worm's brain and some of its sense organs are located in its head end, the worm can detect objects, food, mates, and predators quickly, and it can respond quickly, too. Sense organs, such as organs sensitive to light and touch, pick up information from the environment. The brain interprets that information and directs the animal's response. For example, if an earthworm on the surface of the ground senses a footstep, the worm will quickly return to its underground burrow.

Reproduction Both sexual and asexual reproduction are found in the worm phyla. In many species of worms, there are separate male and female animals, as in humans. In other species each individual has both male and female sex organs. A worm with both sexes does not usually fertilize its own eggs. Instead, two worms mate and exchange sperm. Many worms reproduce asexually by methods such as breaking into pieces. In fact, if you cut some kinds of worms into several pieces, a whole new worm will grow from each piece. Earthworms cannot do this, but if you cut off the tail end of an earthworm, the front end will probably grow a new tail. This ability to regrow body parts is called **regeneration.**

✓ *Checkpoint* *What type of symmetry do worms exhibit?*

Flatworms

As you'd expect from their name, flatworms are flat. The bodies of flatworms, such as planarians, flukes, and tapeworms, are soft as jelly. Although tapeworms can grow to be 10 to 12 meters long, other flatworms are almost too small to be seen.

Most flatworms are parasites that obtain their food from their hosts. As you read in Chapter 6, a parasite is an organism that lives inside or on another organism. The parasite takes its food from the organism in or on which it lives, called the host. Parasites may rob their hosts of food and make them weak. They may injure the host's tissues or organs. Sometimes a parasite will kill its host, but usually the host survives.

Tapeworms Tapeworms are one kind of parasitic flatworm. A tapeworm's body is adapted to absorbing food from the host's digestive system. Some kinds of tapeworms can live in human hosts. Many tapeworms live in more than one host during their lifetime. Notice that in *Exploring the Life Cycle of a Dog Tapeworm*, the tapeworm has two different hosts—a rabbit and a dog.

EXPLORING the Life Cycle of a Dog Tapeworm

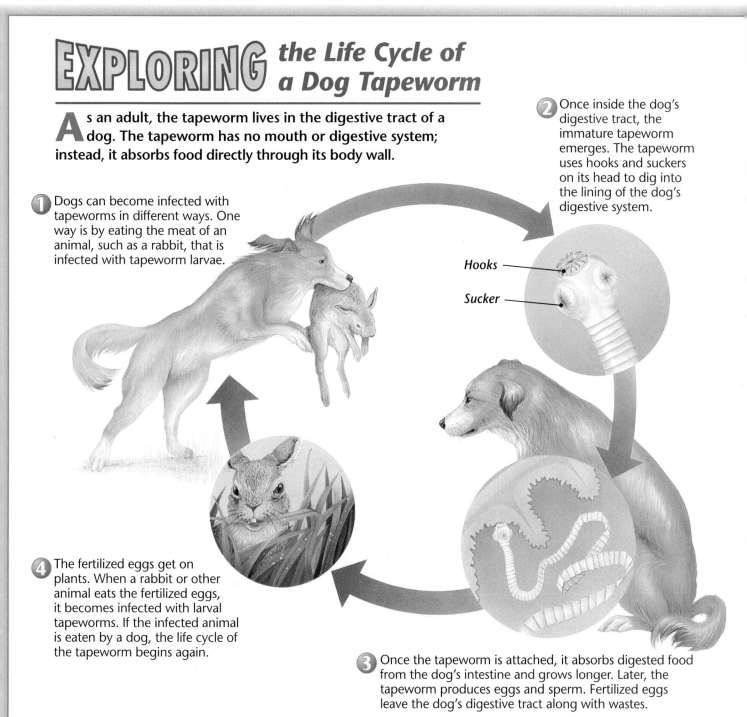

As an adult, the tapeworm lives in the digestive tract of a dog. The tapeworm has no mouth or digestive system; instead, it absorbs food directly through its body wall.

1 Dogs can become infected with tapeworms in different ways. One way is by eating the meat of an animal, such as a rabbit, that is infected with tapeworm larvae.

2 Once inside the dog's digestive tract, the immature tapeworm emerges. The tapeworm uses hooks and suckers on its head to dig into the lining of the dog's digestive system.

Hooks

Sucker

4 The fertilized eggs get on plants. When a rabbit or other animal eats the fertilized eggs, it becomes infected with larval tapeworms. If the infected animal is eaten by a dog, the life cycle of the tapeworm begins again.

3 Once the tapeworm is attached, it absorbs digested food from the dog's intestine and grows longer. Later, the tapeworm produces eggs and sperm. Fertilized eggs leave the dog's digestive tract along with wastes.

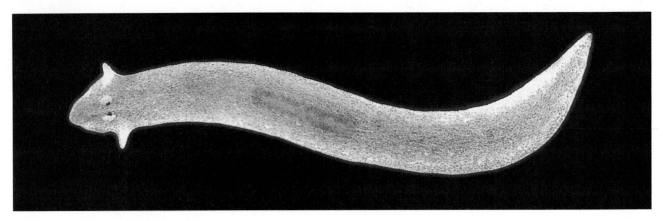

Figure 14 Planarians are flatworms that live in ponds, streams, and oceans. The eyespots on the planarian's head can distinguish between light and dark.
Inferring How is having a distinct head end an advantage to a planarian?

Planarians Some flatworms are nonparasitic, or free-living. Unlike parasites, free-living organisms do not live in or on other organisms. Small free-living flatworms glide over the rocks in ponds, slide over damp soil, or swim slowly through the oceans like ruffled, brightly patterned leaves.

Planarians, such as the one in Figure 14, are scavengers—they feed on dead or decaying material. But they are also predators and will attack any animal smaller than they are.

If you look at a planarian's head, you can see two big dots that look like eyes. These dots are called eyespots, and they function something like eyes, although they cannot see a specific image like human eyes can. A planarian's head also has cells that pick up odors. Planarians rely mainly on smell to locate food. When a planarian smells food, it moves toward the food and glides onto it.

A planarian feeds like a vacuum cleaner. The planarian inserts a feeding tube into its food. Digestive juices flow out into the food, where they begin to break down the food while it is still outside the worm's body. Then the planarian sucks up the partly digested bits of food. Digestion is then completed within a cavity inside the planarian. Food is distributed to body cells by diffusion. Like cnidarians, planarians have one opening in their digestive system. Undigested wastes exit through the feeding tube.

Roundworms

Figure 15 The transparent bodies of these roundworms have been stained for better viewing under a microscope.

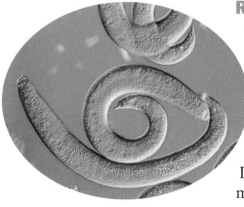

The next time you walk along a beach, consider that about a million roundworms live in each square meter of damp sand. Roundworms can live in nearly any moist environment—including forest soils, Antarctic sands, and even pools of super-hot water. Most are tiny and hard to see, but roundworms may be the most abundant animals on Earth.

Unlike flatworms, roundworms have cylindrical bodies. If you were to look at the roundworms in Figure 15 under a microscope, you'd see their bodies thrashing from side to side.

While many roundworms are carnivores or herbivores, others are parasites. Have you given worm medicine to a pet dog or cat? The medicine was probably meant to kill roundworm parasites, such as hookworms.

Unlike cnidarians or flatworms, roundworms have a digestive system that is like a tube, open at both ends. Food enters at the animal's mouth and wastes exit through an opening, called the **anus,** at the far end of the tube. Food travels in one direction through the roundworm's digestive system, as it does in most complex animals.

A one-way digestive system has certain advantages. It is something like an assembly line, with a different part of the digestive process happening at each place along the line. Digestion happens in orderly stages. First food is broken down by digestive juices. Then the digested food is absorbed into the animal's body. Finally wastes are eliminated. The advantage of this type of digestive process is that it enables the animal's body to use foods efficiently, by enabling it to absorb a large amount of the needed substances in foods.

☑ *Checkpoint You are using a microscope to look at a tiny worm. What would you look for to tell whether it is a roundworm?*

Segmented Worms

If you have ever dug in a garden in the spring, you have probably seen earthworms wriggling through the moist soil. Those familiar soil inhabitants are segmented worms. So are the exotic sea-floor worms that you see in Figure 16. Parasitic blood-sucking leeches are also segmented worms. Since their bodies are long and narrow, some segmented worms look a bit like flatworms and roundworms. But segmented worms may be more closely related to crabs and snails.

Sharpen your Skills

Communicating

🐁 Contact a veterinarian or pet-store owner to find out how to protect pets from parasitic worms. Use the information to prepare a poster that could be displayed in the veterinarian's office or a pet store.

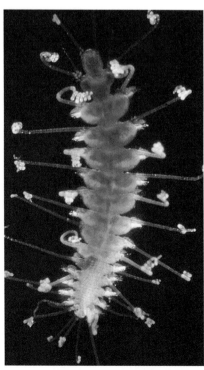

Figure 16 These segmented sea-floor worms belong to the same phylum as earthworms.

Segmented worms occupy nearly all environments, and most live in burrows or tubes. The burrow helps the worm hide both from possible predators and from possible prey. Many segmented worms that live in water are "sit-and-wait" predators. They leap out of their burrows to attack their prey.

Segmentation   When you look at an earthworm, you notice that its body seems to consist of a series of rings separated by grooves, something like a vacuum-cleaner hose. **Earthworms and other segmented worms have bodies made up of many linked sections called segments.** An earthworm usually has more than 100 segments. On the outside, the segments look nearly identical. On the inside, some organs are repeated in most segments. For example, each segment has tubes that remove wastes. Other organs, however, such as the worm's reproductive organs, are found only in some segments. Nerve cords and a digestive tube run along the length of the worm's body. Like roundworms, earthworms have a one-way digestive system with two openings.

A Closed Circulatory System   Segmented worms have a closed circulatory system. In a closed circulatory system, like your own, blood moves only within a connected network of tubes called blood vessels. In contrast, some animals, such as insects, have an open circulatory system in which blood leaves the blood vessels and sloshes around inside the body. A closed circulatory system can move blood around an animal's body much more quickly than an open circulatory system can. Blood quickly carries oxygen and food to cells. Because of this, an animal with a closed circulatory system can be larger and more active than one with an open circulatory system.

A long blood vessel runs along the top of the earthworm's body. That blood vessel pumps blood through five arches, shown in Figure 17. From the arches, the blood passes into a blood vessel that runs along the lower part of the earthworm.

Figure 17 An earthworm's body is divided into over 100 segments. Some organs are repeated in most of those segments; others exist in only a few. *Interpreting Diagrams How does blood move through an earthworm's body?*

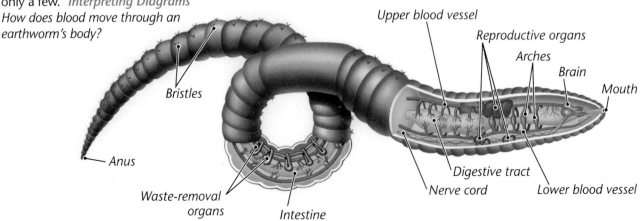

Upper blood vessel
Reproductive organs
Arches
Brain
Mouth
Bristles
Anus
Digestive tract
Nerve cord
Lower blood vessel
Waste-removal organs
Intestine

How Earthworms Live Earthworms tunnel for a living. They are scavengers that eat decayed plant and animal remains in the soil. On damp nights earthworms come up out of their burrows. They crawl on the surface of the ground, seeking leaves and soft fruits to drag underground and eat.

Night is a safe time for an earthworm to crawl on the surface, because many worm predators are asleep then. At night the air is damp, and this dampness helps keep the worm's skin moist. If a worm dries out, it will die, because it obtains oxygen through moisture on its skin.

Well-developed muscles let an earthworm move through its burrow. Stiff bristles stick out from each of the worm's segments. To crawl forward, an earthworm sticks its bristles in the ground and pulls itself along, much as a mountain climber uses an ice ax. Mountain climbers drive ice axes into a slippery slope and then pull themselves up.

Earthworms and Soil Earthworms are among the most
 INTEGRATING EARTH SCIENCE helpful inhabitants of garden and farm soil. They benefit people by improving the soil in which plants grow. Earthworm droppings make the soil more fertile. Earthworm tunnels loosen the soil and allow air, water, and plant roots to move through it. You have probably seen earthworm tunnel entrances without realizing what they were—they are extremely common in lawns. To find one, look for a small, round hole in the ground with little balls of soil next to it.

Section 4 Review

1. List the three major phyla of worms and give an example of each.
2. How does a dog tapeworm obtain its food?
3. Contrast a roundworm's digestive system to that of a planarian.
4. Describe the structure of an earthworm's body.
5. **Thinking Critically Relating Cause and Effect** How does keeping a dog on a leash reduce its risk for getting a tapeworm?

Check Your Progress CHAPTER PROJECT
Begin to analyze what you have learned about your animal from your observations. Did you see a daily pattern to the animal's behavior? Think about what each kind of behavior accomplishes—whether it helps the animal obtain food or escape from danger, for example. Choose how you are going to present what you have learned—a written report, a talk, captioned illustrations, or some other method. Prepare charts or other visual aids.

Reviewing Content

 For more review of key concepts, see the Interactive Student Tutorial CD-ROM.

Multiple Choice

Choose the letter of the best answer.

1. Organisms that eat both plants and animals are called
   a. autotrophs.
   b. omnivores.
   c. heterotrophs.
   d. carnivores.

2. An animal without a backbone is called a(n)
   a. vertebrate.
   b. invertebrate.
   c. herbivore.
   d. carnivore.

3. An animal with many lines of symmetry
   a. is bilaterally symmetrical.
   b. is radially symmetrical.
   c. has no symmetry.
   d. has line symmetry.

4. Which animal is a medusa?
   a. coral
   b. jellyfish
   c. planarian
   d. sea anemone

5. Which animal has a one-way digestive system?
   a. earthworm
   b. planarian
   c. sponge
   d. jellyfish

True or False

If the statement is true, write true. If it is false, change the underlined word or words to make the statement true.

6. <u>All</u> animals are made up of many cells.

7. An <u>organ</u> is a group of tissues that work together to perform a job.

8. Fish have <u>radial symmetry</u>.

9. The bodies of <u>cnidarians</u> contain many pores.

10. The bodies of <u>roundworms</u> are segmented.

Checking Concepts

11. Explain the relationship among cells, tissues, and organs.

12. An oxygen molecule has just passed into a sponge's cell. Describe how it probably got there.

13. Compare and contrast a medusa and a polyp.

14. Are humans parasitic or free-living animals? Explain.

15. You dig up a handful of damp soil from the floor of a forest and examine it with a microscope. What kind of animal would probably be there in the greatest numbers? Explain.

16. **Writing to Learn** You are a small fish visiting a coral reef for the first time. What interesting sights would you see? Are there any dangers you need to watch out for? In a paragraph, describe your adventures at the coral reef.

Thinking Critically

17. **Predicting** The sand in a desert is bright orange. What color would predators in that desert probably be? Explain.

18. **Classifying** Classify each of the following animals as either radially symmetrical, bilaterally symmetrical, or asymmetrical: sea stars, frogs, sponges, sharks, humans, and hydras.

19. **Comparing and Contrasting** Compare and contrast the ways in which a sponge, a planarian, and a roundworm digest their food.

20. **Relating Cause and Effect** If a pesticide killed off many of the earthworms in a garden, how might that affect the plants growing in that soil? Explain why the plants would be affected in that way.

Applying Skills

A scientist used a pesticide on one field and left a nearby field untreated. Next, she marked off five plots of equal size in each field. Then she dug up a cubic meter of soil beneath each plot, and counted the earthworms in the soil. The table below shows her data. Use the table to answer Questions 21–23.

Field with Pesticide		Untreated Field	
Plot	Worms per cubic meter	Plot	Worms per cubic meter
A	730	F	901
B	254	G	620
C	319	H	811
D	428	I	576
E	451	J	704

21. **Controlling Variables** Identify the manipulated and responding variables in this experiment.

22. **Calculating** Calculate the average number of worms per cubic meter in the treated field. Then do the same for the untreated field.

23. **Drawing Conclusions** How did this pesticide affect the population of worms?

Performance CHAPTER PROJECT **Assessment**

Present Your Project Write a summary explaining what you have learned about your animal—its physical characteristics, its habitat, the food it eats, and its behavior. Describe any surprising observations. Then introduce your animal to your classmates and share what you have discovered.

Reflect and Record Was the animal you selected a good choice? Why or why not? How might you have taken better care of your animal? What advice would you give to another student who wants to study this animal?

Test Preparation

Use these questions to prepare for standardized tests.

Read the passage. Then answer Questions 24–26.

Cnidarians use stinging cells to obtain food and to protect themselves. The stinging cells contain harpoonlike barbs at the end of coiled, hollow threads. When a cnidarian is touched by another organism, the threads of thousands of its stinging cells uncoil and shoot their barbs into its victim. Then, a paralyzing or deadly poison passes through the hollow threads and into the victim's tissues.

The stinging cells of many cnidarians are too weak to pierce human skin. However, some cnidarian species, such as the jellyfishes commonly called lion's mane and sea nettle, can harm people. A cnidarian known as the Portuguese man-of-war also has a painful and sometimes deadly sting.

It's best to avoid cnidarians. But, if you are stung, apply vinegar, meat tenderizer, or a baking soda and water paste to the stung area. Applying ice to the area can lessen the sting's pain.

24. What is the best title for this passage?
   a. The Portuguese Man-of-War
   b. The Stinging Cells of Cnidarians
   c. How to Avoid Cnidarians
   d. How Cnidarians Obtain Food

25. Which of the following objects would most closely resemble a barb?
   a. a straw   b. a string
   c. a jack-in-the-box spring   d. an arrowhead

26. What is the correct order in which a stinging cell reacts to the touch of another organism?
   a. poison passes through thread; poison enters victim; thread uncoils; barb pierces victim
   b. barb pierces victim; thread uncoils; poison passes through thread; poison enters victim
   c. thread uncoils; barb pierces victim; poison passes through thread; poison enters victim
   d. thread uncoils; poison passes through thread; barb pierces victim; poison enters victim

WEB ACTIVITY www.phschool.com

SECTION

1 Mollusks

Discover How Can You Classify Shells?
Sharpen Your Skills Classifying
Science at Home Edible Mollusks
Skills Lab A Snail's Pace

SECTION

2 Arthropods

Discover Will It Bend and Move?
Try This Pill Bugs—Wet or Dry?

SECTION

3 Insects

Discover What Kinds of Appendages Do
Insects Have?
Sharpen Your Skills Graphing
Real-World Lab What's Living in the Soil?

Going Through Changes

Look at the changes a treehopper insect goes through in its lifetime! In its white nymph stage, it doesn't look anything like an adult treehopper. Most of the animals you will read about in this chapter also change their form during their life cycles. In this project, you will view these kinds of changes firsthand as you observe mealworm development.

Your Goal To observe how different conditions affect mealworm development.

To complete this project successfully, you must
◆ compare mealworm development under two different conditions
◆ record your mealworm observations daily for several weeks
◆ draw conclusions about the effects of those conditions on development
◆ follow the safety guidelines in Appendix A

Get Started Find two containers, such as clean margarine tubs with lids, in which to keep the mealworms. Get some mealworm food, such as cornflakes, and a plastic spoon to transfer the food and count the mealworms. Choose two conditions, such as two different temperatures or food sources, and plan how to test the two conditions.

Check Your Progress You'll be working on this project as you study this chapter. To keep your project on track, look for Check Your Progress boxes at the following points.
Section 2 Review, page 353: Record your daily observations.
Section 3 Review, page 359: Sketch the stages of development.
Section 5 Review, page 368: Draw conclusions about mealworm development under each of the conditions.

Present Your Project At the end of the chapter (page 371), you will report on your results.

Treehoppers undergo dramatic changes in form during their lives. The whitish nymphs gradually turn into light green young adults. The young adults gradually change into dark green mature adults.

 Integrating Chemistry

SECTION 4 The Chemistry of Communication

Discover Can You Match the Scents?
Science at Home Chemicals and Insect Pests

SECTION 5 Echinoderms

Discover How Do Sea Stars Hold On?

DISCOVER •••**ACTIVITY**••••

How Can You Classify Shells?

1. Obtain an assortment of shells from your teacher. Examine each one carefully. Look at the shells and feel their surfaces.

2. Compare the outer surface of each shell to the inner surface.

3. Classify the shells into two or more groups based on the characteristics you observe.

Think It Over
Inferring How might it help an animal to have a shell?

GUIDE FOR READING

◆ What are the main characteristics of mollusks?

◆ What are the major groups of mollusks?

Reading Tip As you read, make a compare/contrast table to distinguish among the different mollusk groups.

From the shells of clams, Native Americans in the North-east carved purple and white beads called wampum. They wove these beads into belts with complex designs that often had special, solemn significance. A wampum belt might record a group's history. When warring groups made peace, they exchanged weavings made of wampum. Iroquois women would honor a new chief with gifts of wampum strings.

The hard shells of clams provided the material for wampum, and the soft bodies within the shells were a major source of food for Native Americans who lived along the seacoast. Today, clams and similar animals, such as scallops and oysters, are still valuable sources of food for people in many parts of the world.

What Are Mollusks?

Clams, oysters, and scallops are all mollusks (phylum Mollusca). So are snails and octopuses. **Mollusks** are invertebrates with soft, unsegmented bodies that are often protected by hard outer shells. **In addition to soft bodies often covered with shells, mollusks have a thin layer of tissue called a mantle, which covers their internal organs.** The mantle also produces the mollusk's shell. Most mollusks move with a muscular structure called a foot. The feet of different kinds of mollusks are adapted for various uses, such as crawling, digging, or catching prey.

Mollusks live nearly everywhere on Earth. Most live in water, from mountain streams to the deep ocean, but some live on land, usually in damp places.

▼ Wampum string and clamshell

Figure 1 Some mollusks, like the chambered nautilus, left, are protected by shells. Other mollusks, like the nudibranch, right, do not have shells. *Classifying What characteristics do these two organisms share?*

Like segmented worms, mollusks have bilateral symmetry. However, unlike segmented worms, the body parts of mollusks are not repeated. Instead, their internal organs, such as the stomach and reproductive organs, are all located together in one area. A mollusk's internal organs include a pair of **kidneys,** organs that remove the wastes produced by an animal's cells.

Most water-dwelling mollusks have **gills,** organs that remove oxygen from water. The gills are attached to the mantle and have a rich supply of blood vessels. Within these thin-walled blood vessels, oxygen from the surrounding water diffuses into the blood, while carbon dioxide diffuses out. The gills of most mollusks are covered by tiny, hairlike structures called cilia. The beating movement of these cilia makes water flow over the gills.

Many mollusks have an organ called a **radula** (RAJ oo luh) (plural *radulae*), which is a flexible ribbon of tiny teeth. Acting like sandpaper, the tiny teeth scrape food from a surface such as a leaf. A radula may have as many as 250,000 teeth. Biologists use the arrangement of teeth in the radula to help classify mollusks.

✓ *Checkpoint How is the body structure of a mollusk different from that of a segmented worm?*

Evidence of Early Mollusks

INTEGRATING EARTH SCIENCE Mollusks were living in Earth's oceans about 540 million years ago. Much evidence for this comes from fossil shells in limestone rocks. Some kinds of limestone are partially made from the shells of ancient, ocean-dwelling mollusks. After the mollusks died, their shells were broken into tiny pieces by waves and water currents. These shell pieces, along with the hard remains of other organisms, piled up on the ocean floor. These hard materials then underwent a chemical change in which they became cemented together to form limestone. During this process, some shells—or parts of shells—remained unbroken and eventually became fossils.

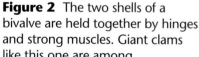
Snails and Their Relatives

Biologists classify mollusks into groups based on physical characteristics such as the presence of a shell, the type of shell, the type of foot, the arrangement of teeth in the radula, and the complexity of the nervous system. **The three major groups of mollusks are gastropods, bivalves, and cephalopods.**

The most numerous mollusks are the gastropods. **Gastropods,** which include snails and slugs, are mollusks that have a single shell or no shell at all. Most snails have a single, coiled shell, while many slugs have no shell. Gastropods usually creep along on a broad foot. Gastropods get their name, which means "stomach foot," from the fact that most of them have their foot on the same side of their body as their stomach. To learn more about the body of a gastropod, look at *Exploring a Snail* on page 343.

You can find gastropods nearly everywhere on Earth. They live in oceans, on rocky shores, in fresh water, and on dry land, too. Some snails even live in treetops.

Some gastropods are herbivores, while others are scavengers that feed on decaying material. Still others are carnivores. For example, the oyster drill is a snail that makes a hole in an oyster's shell by releasing acid and then boring a hole with its radula. The oyster drill then scrapes away the oyster's soft body.

Many snails have a tight-fitting plate or trapdoor on their foot that fits securely into the opening of their shell. When this kind of snail is threatened by a predator, it withdraws into its shell and tightly closes its trapdoor. Snails also pull back into their shells when conditions are dry and then come out when conditions are moist again. When they are sealed up in this way, gastropods can survive incredibly long times. In one museum the shells of two land snails, presumed to be dead, were glued to a piece of cardboard. Four years later, when someone put the cardboard in water, one of the snails crawled away!

Checkpoint *How did gastropods get their name?*

Figure 2 The two shells of a bivalve are held together by hinges and strong muscles. Giant clams like this one are among the largest bivalves in the world.

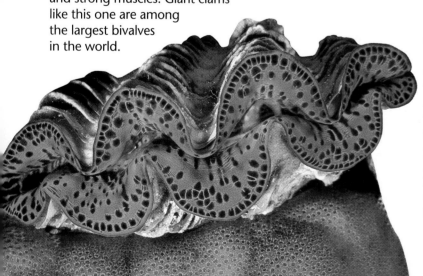

Two-Shelled Mollusks

Clams, oysters, scallops, and mussels are **bivalves,** mollusks that have two shells held together by hinges and strong muscles. Unlike other mollusks, bivalves do not have radulae. Instead, most are filter feeders; they strain their food from water. Bivalves use their gills to capture food as they breathe. Food particles stick to mucus

EXPLORING *a Snail*

Like other gastropods, a snail has a head with sense organs, and it has a wide, muscular foot. The snails shown here live in a pond.

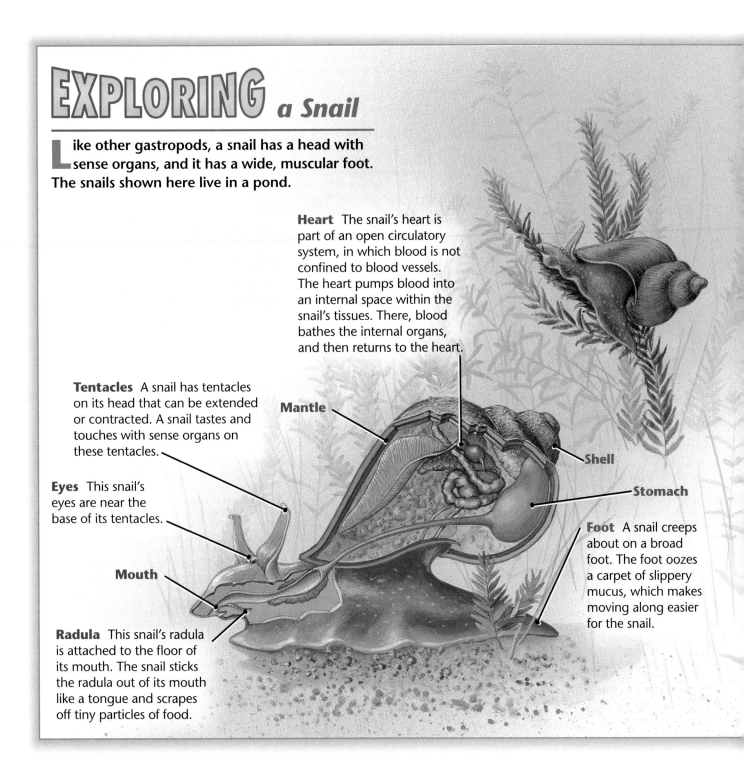

Heart The snail's heart is part of an open circulatory system, in which blood is not confined to blood vessels. The heart pumps blood into an internal space within the snail's tissues. There, blood bathes the internal organs, and then returns to the heart.

Tentacles A snail has tentacles on its head that can be extended or contracted. A snail tastes and touches with sense organs on these tentacles.

Eyes This snail's eyes are near the base of its tentacles.

Mouth

Radula This snail's radula is attached to the floor of its mouth. The snail sticks the radula out of its mouth like a tongue and scrapes off tiny particles of food.

Mantle

Shell

Stomach

Foot A snail creeps about on a broad foot. The foot oozes a carpet of slippery mucus, which makes moving along easier for the snail.

that covers the gills. The cilia on the gills then move the food particles into the bivalve's mouth.

Bivalves are found in all kinds of watery environments. As adults, most bivalves stay in one place or move slowly. After their larval stage, for example, oysters and mussels attach themselves to an underwater surface. Clams, in contrast, are active; they use a thin foot to burrow down into the sand or mud. Scallops can also move from place to place. In fact, when startled, scallops clap their shells together and leap rapidly in the water over the sand.

Sometimes sand or grit becomes lodged between a bivalve's mantle and its shell, irritating the soft mantle. Just as you might put smooth tape around rough bicycle handlebars to protect your hands, the bivalve's mantle produces a smooth, pearly coat to cover the irritating object. Eventually a pearl forms around the grit. Some oysters make pearls so beautiful that they are used in jewelry.

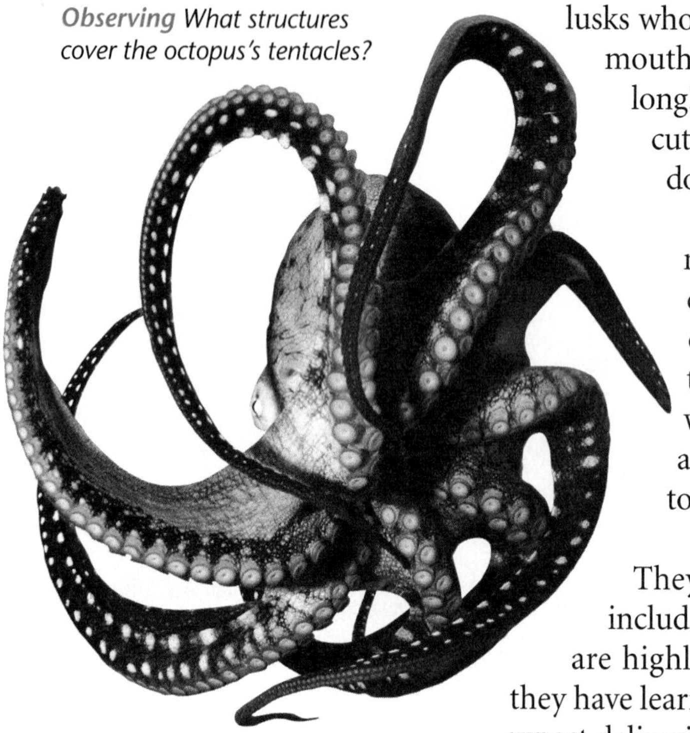

Mollusks with Tentacles

Octopuses, cuttlefish, nautiluses, and squids are **cephalopods,** mollusks whose feet are adapted to form tentacles around their mouths. Some octopuses have tentacles almost 5 meters long! While nautiluses have an external shell, squids and cuttlefish have a small shell within the body. Octopuses do not have shells.

Cephalopods capture food with their flexible, muscular tentacles. Sensitive suckers on the tentacles receive sensations of taste as well as touch. A cephalopod doesn't have to touch something to taste it; the suckers respond to chemicals in the water. For example, when an octopus feels beneath a rock, its tentacle may find a crab by taste before it touches it.

Cephalopods have large eyes and excellent vision. They also have the most complex nervous system, including a large brain, of any invertebrate. Cephalopods are highly intelligent animals that can remember things they have learned. In captivity, octopuses quickly learn when to expect deliveries of food and how to escape from their tanks.

 INTEGRATING PHYSICS All cephalopods live in the ocean, where they swim by jet propulsion. They squeeze a current of water out of the mantle cavity through a tube, and like rockets, shoot off in the opposite direction. By turning the tube around, they can steer in any direction.

Figure 3 Octopuses live in coral reefs where they hide when they are not hunting crabs and other small animals. *Observing What structures cover the octopus's tentacles?*

Section 1 Review

1. What characteristics do most mollusks have in common?
2. List the three main groups of mollusks. Describe the main characteristics of each group.
3. Explain how bivalves obtain food.
4. **Thinking Critically Predicting** Would gills function well if they had few blood vessels? Explain.

Science at Home

Edible Mollusks Visit a supermarket with a family member. Identify any mollusks that are being sold as food. Be sure to look in places other than the fish counter, such as the canned-foods section. Discuss the parts of the mollusks that are used for food and the parts that are not edible.

344

A Snail's Pace

I n this lab, you will use the skill of measuring to investigate how fast a snail moves in different water temperatures.

Problem

How do changes in environmental temperature affect the activity level of a snail?

Materials

freshwater snail   thermometer   ruler
plastic petri dish   graph paper   timer
spring water at three temperatures:
    cool (9–13°C); medium (18–22°C);
    warm (27–31°C)

Procedure

1. Create a data table for recording the water temperatures and the distance the snail travels at each temperature.
2. On one sheet of graph paper labeled *Snail,* trace a circle using the base of an empty petri dish. Divide and label the circle as shown in the illustration. On a second sheet of graph paper labeled *Data,* draw three more circles like the one in the illustration.
3. Place the petri dish over the circle on the Snail page, fill it with cool water, and record the water temperature. Then place the snail in the water just above the "S" in the circle. Be sure to handle the snail gently.
4. For five minutes, observe the snail. Record its movements by drawing a line that shows its path in the first circle on the Data page.
5. Find the distance the snail moved by measuring the line you drew. You may need to measure all the parts of the line and add them together. Record the distance in your data table.

6. Repeat Steps 3 through 5, first with medium-temperature water and then with warm water. Record the snail's paths in the second circle and third circle on the Data page.
7. Return the snail to your teacher when you are done. Wash your hands thoroughly.
8. For each temperature, compute the class average for distance traveled.

Analyze and Conclude

1. Make a bar graph showing the class average for each temperature. How does a snail's activity level change as temperature increases?
2. Do you think the pattern you found would continue at higher temperatures? Explain.
3. **Think About It** What factors in this lab were difficult to measure? How could you change the procedure to obtain more accurate measurements? Explain.

Design an Experiment

Design an experiment to measure the rate at which a snail moves in an aquarium with gravel on the bottom. Obtain your teacher's permission before trying your experiment.

SECTION 2 Arthropods

DISCOVER • ACTIVITY

Will It Bend and Move?

1. Have a partner roll a piece of cardboard around your arm to form a tube that covers your elbow. Your partner should put three pieces of tape around the tube to hold it closed—one at each end and one in the middle.

2. With the tube in place, try to write your name on a piece of paper. Then try to scratch your head.

3. Keep the tube on your arm for 10 minutes. Observe how the tube affects your ability to do things.

Think It Over

Inferring Insects and many other animals have rigid skeletons on the outside of their bodies. Why do their skeletons need joints?

GUIDE FOR READING

◆ What are the major characteristics of arthropods?

◆ What are the main groups of arthropods?

Reading Tip Before you read, rewrite the headings in this section as questions. Answer the questions as you read.

On a moonless night at the edge of a wooded area, a moth flits from flower to flower, drinking nectar. Nearby, a hungry spider waits in its web that stretches, nearly invisible, between bushes. Suddenly, the moth gets caught by the spider web. The sticky threads of the web trap one of the moth's wings. As the trapped moth struggles to free itself, the spider rushes toward it. At the last second, the moth gives a strong flap, breaks free, and flutters away—safe! Next time, the moth may not be so lucky.

The hungry spider and lucky moth are both arthropods. Insects and spiders are probably the arthropods you are most familiar with, but the phylum also includes animals such as crabs, lobsters, centipedes, and scorpions. Scientists have identified about 875,000 different species of arthropods, and there are probably many more that have not yet been discovered. Earth has more species of arthropods than of all other animals combined.

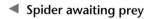

◀ Spider awaiting prey

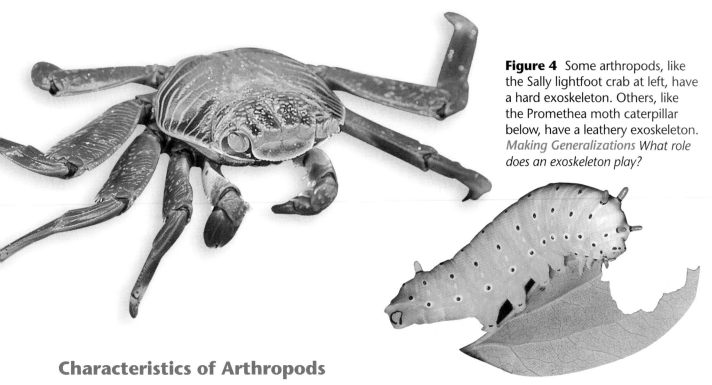

Figure 4 Some arthropods, like the Sally lightfoot crab at left, have a hard exoskeleton. Others, like the Promethea moth caterpillar below, have a leathery exoskeleton. *Making Generalizations What role does an exoskeleton play?*

Characteristics of Arthropods

Members of the **arthropod** phylum (phylum Arthropoda) share certain important characteristics. **An arthropod is an invertebrate that has an external skeleton, a segmented body, and jointed attachments called appendages.** Wings, mouthparts, and legs are all appendages. Jointed legs are such a distinctive characteristic that the arthropod phylum is named for it. *Arthros* means "joint" in Greek, and *podos* means "foot" or "leg."

Arthropods have additional characteristics in common, too. Arthropods have open circulatory systems—the blood leaves the blood vessels and bathes the internal organs. Most arthropods reproduce sexually. Unlike an earthworm, which has both male and female organs in its body, most arthropods are either male or female. Most arthropods have internal fertilization—sperm and egg unite inside the body of the female. This contrasts to external fertilization, which takes place outside an animal's body.

A Skeleton on the Outside If you were an arthropod, you would be completely covered by a waterproof shell. This waxy **exoskeleton,** or outer skeleton, protects the animal and helps prevent evaporation of water. Water animals are surrounded by water, but land animals need a way to keep from drying out. Arthropods were the first animals to move out of water and onto land, and their exoskeletons probably enabled them to do this.

INTEGRATING CHEMISTRY Arthropod exoskeletons are made of a material called **chitin** (KY tin). Chitin is made of long molecules that are built from many smaller building blocks, like links in a chain. Long-chain molecules like chitin are called polymers. Cotton fibers and rubber are polymers, too. For any

Figure 5 This rainforest cicada has just molted. You can see its old exoskeleton still hanging on the leaf below it. *Applying Concepts Why must arthropods molt?*

polymer, the kinds, numbers, and the arrangement of its small building blocks determine its characteristics. Chitin's building blocks make it tough and flexible.

As an arthropod grows larger, its exoskeleton cannot expand. The growing arthropod is trapped within its exoskeleton, like a knight in armor that is too small for him. Arthropods solve this problem by occasionally shedding their exoskeletons and growing new ones that are larger. The process of shedding an outgrown exoskeleton is called **molting.** After an arthropod has molted, its new skeleton is soft for a time. During that time, the arthropod has less protection from danger than it does after its new skeleton has hardened.

Segmented Bodies Arthropods' bodies are segmented, something like an earthworm's. The segmented body plan is easiest to see in centipedes and millipedes, which have bodies made up of many identical-looking segments. You can also see segments on the tails of shrimp and lobsters.

In some groups of arthropods, several body segments become joined into distinct sections, with each section specialized to perform specific functions. Figure 6 shows the number of body sections and other physical characteristics that are typical of the three largest groups of arthropods.

Appendages Just as your fingers are appendages attached to your palms, many arthropods have jointed appendages attached to their bodies. The joints in the appendages give the animal flexibility and enable it to move. If you did the Discover activity, you saw how important joints are for allowing movement.

Arthropod appendages tend to be highly specialized tools. For example, the appendages attached to the head of a crayfish include mouthparts that it uses for crushing its food. A crayfish also has two pairs of antennae.

Figure 6 Arthropod groups differ in the numbers of body sections, legs, and antennae, and in where they are found. *Interpreting Charts Which group of arthropods has no antennae?*

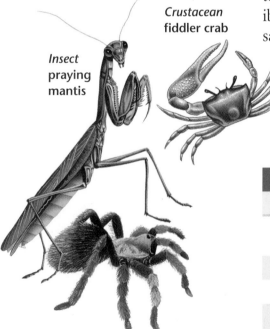

Insect **praying mantis**

Crustacean **fiddler crab**

Arachnid **tarantula**

Comparisons of the Largest Arthropod Groups			
Characteristic	**Crustaceans**	**Arachnids**	**Insects**
Number of body sections	2 or 3	2	3
Number of legs	5 or more pairs	4 pairs	3 pairs
Number of antennae	2 pairs	none	1 pair
Where found?	in water or damp places	mostly on land	mostly on land

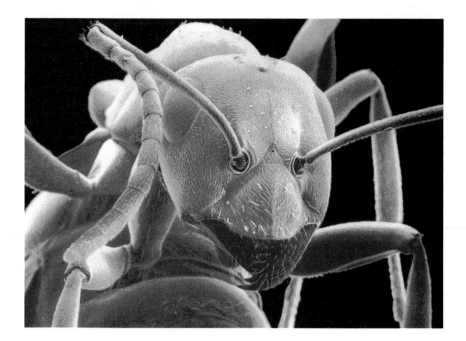

Figure 7 This wood ant's appendages include its antennae, legs, and mouthparts. It uses its mouthparts first to saw its food into small pieces and then to chew it.

An **antenna** (plural *antennae*) is an appendage on the head that contains sense organs. A crayfish's antennae have organs for smelling, tasting, touching, and keeping balance. Legs are also appendages. Most of the crayfish's legs are adapted for walking, but the crayfish uses its first pair of legs, which have claws, for catching prey and defending against predators. The wings that most insects have are also appendages.

✓ *Checkpoint* *How do exoskeletons enable many arthropods to live on land?*

Origin of Arthropods

Because both segmented worms and arthropods have segmented bodies with appendages attached to some segments, many biologists have inferred that these two groups of animals have a common ancestor. However, DNA evidence indicates that arthropods and segmented worms may not be so closely related.

Arthropods have been on Earth for about 540 million years. Like most other animal groups, arthropods first arose in the oceans. Today, however, they live almost everywhere. Some kinds of arthropods, like crayfish and crabs, are adapted to live in fresh or salt water. Very few insects, in contrast, live in salt water, but they live just about everywhere else.

Crustaceans

The major groups of arthropods are crustaceans, arachnids, centipedes, millipedes, and insects. If you've ever eaten shrimp cocktail or crab cakes, you've dined on crustaceans. A **crustacean** is an arthropod that has two or three body sections and usually has three pairs of appendages for chewing. In addition,

Pill Bugs—Wet or Dry?

Pill bugs are crustaceans

ACTIVITY

that roll up in a ball when they're disturbed. In this activity, you will find out whether they prefer a moist or dry environment.

1. Line a shoe box with aluminum foil. Tape down two paper towels side by side in the box. Tape a strip of masking tape between the two towels. Carefully moisten one of the paper towels. Keep the other towel dry.

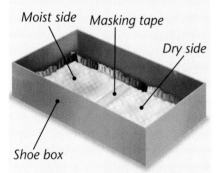

Moist side   Masking tape

Dry side

Shoe box

2. 🐾 Put ten pill bugs on the masking tape. Then put a lid on the box.

3. After 5 minutes, lift the lid and quickly count the pill bugs on the dry towel, the moist towel, and the masking tape. Record your results in a data table.

4. Repeat Steps 2 and 3 two more times. Then average the results of the three trials. Wash your hands after handling the pill bugs.

Interpreting Data Do pill bugs prefer a moist or dry environment?

crustaceans always have five or more pairs of legs; each body segment has a pair of legs or modified legs attached to it. Crustaceans are the only arthropods that have two pairs of antennae. *Exploring a Crayfish* on page 351 shows a typical crustacean.

Life Cycle Most crustaceans, such as crabs, barnacles, and shrimp, begin their lives as microscopic, swimming larvae. The bodies of these larvae do not resemble those of adults. Crustacean larvae develop into adults by **metamorphosis** (met uh MAWR fuh sis), a process in which an animal's body undergoes dramatic changes in form during its life cycle.

Environments Nearly every kind of watery environment is home to crustaceans, which usually obtain their oxygen through gills. Crustaceans thrive in freshwater lakes and rivers, and even in puddles that last a long time. You can find crustaceans in the deepest parts of oceans, floating in ocean currents, and crawling along coastlines. A few crustaceans live in damp areas on land, too. Some huge crabs even live in the tops of palm trees!

Feeding Crustaceans obtain food in many ways. Many eat dead plants and animals. Others are predators, eating animals they have killed. The pistol shrimp is a predator with an appendage that moves with such force that it stuns its prey. Krill, which are shrimplike crustaceans found in huge swarms in cold ocean waters, are herbivores that eat plantlike microorganisms. Krill, in turn, are eaten by predators such as fishes, penguins, seals, sea birds, and even by great blue whales, the world's largest animals.

☑ *Checkpoint* An animal has an exoskeleton, two body sections, and eight legs. Is it a crustacean? Why or why not?

Spiders and Their Relatives

Spiders, mites, and ticks are the arachnids that people most often encounter. To qualify as an **arachnid** (uh RAK nid), an arthropod must have only two body sections. The first section is a combined head and chest. The hind section, called the **abdomen,** contains the arachnid's reproductive organs and part of its digestive tract. Arachnids have eight legs, but no antennae. They breathe with organs called book lungs or with a network of tiny tubes that lead to openings on the exoskeleton.

Spiders Spiders are the most familiar, most feared, and most fascinating kind of arachnid. All spiders are predators, and most of them eat insects. Some spiders, such as tarantulas and wolf spiders, run down their prey, while others, such as golden garden spiders, spin webs and wait for their prey to become entangled.

EXPLORING *a Crayfish*

Crayfish are crustaceans that live in ponds, streams, or rivers, where they hide beneath rocks and burrow in the mud. Some build a tall mud "chimney" around their burrow entrance. Crayfish will eat nearly any animal or plant, dead or alive, including other crayfish.

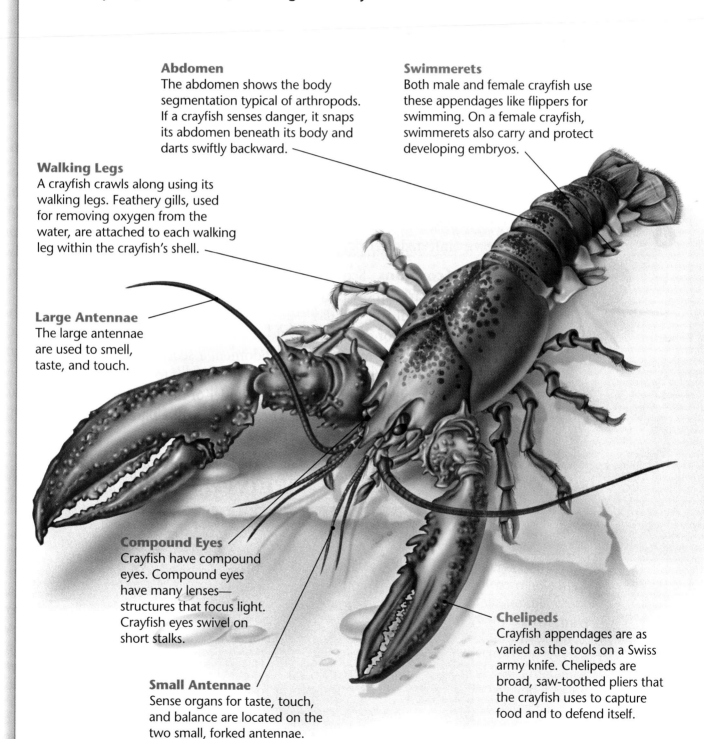

Abdomen
The abdomen shows the body segmentation typical of arthropods. If a crayfish senses danger, it snaps its abdomen beneath its body and darts swiftly backward.

Swimmerets
Both male and female crayfish use these appendages like flippers for swimming. On a female crayfish, swimmerets also carry and protect developing embryos.

Walking Legs
A crayfish crawls along using its walking legs. Feathery gills, used for removing oxygen from the water, are attached to each walking leg within the crayfish's shell.

Large Antennae
The large antennae are used to smell, taste, and touch.

Compound Eyes
Crayfish have compound eyes. Compound eyes have many lenses—structures that focus light. Crayfish eyes swivel on short stalks.

Small Antennae
Sense organs for taste, touch, and balance are located on the two small, forked antennae.

Chelipeds
Crayfish appendages are as varied as the tools on a Swiss army knife. Chelipeds are broad, saw-toothed pliers that the crayfish uses to capture food and to defend itself.

The two types of insect metamorphosis are shown in *Exploring Insect Metamorphosis* on page 357. The first type, which is called **complete metamorphosis,** has four dramatically different stages: egg, larva, pupa, and adult. As you learned in Chapter 10, a larva is an immature form of an animal that looks significantly different from the adult. Insect larvae, such as the caterpillars of butterflies and moths, usually look something like worms. Larvae are specialized for eating and growing. After a time, the larva goes into the second stage of complete metamorphosis and becomes a **pupa** (plural *pupae*). During the pupal stage, the insect is enclosed in a protective covering and gradually changes from a larva to an adult. A butterfly in a chrysalis and a moth in a cocoon are examples of insect pupae. When it has completed its development, an adult insect emerges from the protective pupa. Beetles, butterflies, houseflies, and ants all undergo complete metamorphosis.

In contrast, the second type of metamorphosis, called **gradual metamorphosis,** has no distinctly different larval stage—an egg hatches into a stage called a **nymph,** which often resembles the adult insect. A nymph may molt several times before becoming an adult. Grasshoppers, termites, cockroaches, and dragonflies go through gradual metamorphosis.

✓ *Checkpoint* **List the stages of complete metamorphosis.**

How Insects Feed

The rule seems to be this: If it is living, or if it once was living, some kind of insect will eat it. Everyone knows that insects eat plants and parts of plants, such as leaves and nectar. But insects also eat products that are made from plants, such as paper. The next time you open a very old book, watch for book lice. These very small insects live in old books, chewing tiny crooked tunnels through the pages.

Insects feed on animals, too. Some, like fleas and mosquitoes, feed on the blood of living animals. Others, like dung beetles, feed on animal droppings. Still others, like burying beetles, feed on the decaying bodies of dead animals.

Insect mouthparts are adapted for a highly specific way of getting food. For example, a bee has a bristly tongue that laps nectar from flowers, and a mosquito has sharp mouthparts for jabbing and sucking blood.

Figure 12 This caterpillar feeds almost continuously. As a larva, it must store all the energy it will need for its pupal stage.

EXPLORING *Insect Metamorphosis*

Depending on the species, an insect develops into an adult through one of the two processes shown here. Fireflies undergo complete metamorphosis, while grasshoppers undergo gradual metamorphosis.

Adult male firefly

COMPLETE METAMORPHOSIS

1 Egg Female fireflies lay their eggs in moist places. The eggs of fireflies glow in the dark.

4 Adult When its development is complete, an adult firefly crawls out of its pupal case and unfurls its crumpled wings. After its exoskeleton hardens, the adult begins a life centered around feeding, flying into new areas, and mating. Adult fireflies flash their light to attract mates.

2 Larva The eggs hatch into larvae that feed on snails and slugs. Firefly larvae are called glowworms because they give off light.

3 Pupa After a time, the firefly larva becomes a pupa. Inside the protective pupal case, wings, legs, and antennae form.

GRADUAL METAMORPHOSIS

Adult male grasshopper

2 Nymph Eggs hatch into nymphs that look much like miniature adults, except that they have no wings, or only small ones.

1 Egg A female grasshopper uses the tip of her abdomen to jab holes in the soil where she lays her eggs.

4 Adult Most insects undergoing gradual metamorphosis emerge from the final molt equipped with full-sized wings. Once its wings have hardened, the adult flies off to mate and begin the cycle again.

3 Larger Nymph A nymph feeds until its exoskeleton becomes too tight, and then it molts. The nymph molts four or five times before becoming an adult.

Chapter 11 **357**

Figure 13 The well-camouflaged thorn insect, left, and leaf insect, right, have very effective built-in defenses against predators.
Observing Why do you think the insect on the left is called a thorn insect?

Defending Themselves

Insects have many defenses against predators, including a hard exoskeleton that helps protect them. Many insects can run quickly or fly away from danger, as you know if you've ever tried to swat a fly. Some insects, such as stinkbugs, smell or taste bad to predators. Other insects, such as bees and wasps, defend themselves with painful stings.

One of the most common defenses is **camouflage,** or protective coloration, in which the insect blends with its surroundings so perfectly that it is nearly invisible to a predator. Test yourself by trying to find the camouflaged insects in Figure 13. Walking sticks, many caterpillars, and grasshoppers are just a few insects that use camouflage as a defense.

Other insects are protected by their resemblance to different animals. The spots on the wings of certain moths, for example, resemble large eyes; predators who see these spots often avoid the moths, mistaking them for much larger animals.

☑ *Checkpoint* *What are four defenses used by insects?*

Insects and Humans

For every person alive today, scientists estimate that there are at least 200 million living insects. Many of those insects have an impact on people's lives. Some species of insects do major damage to crops. In addition, insects such as flies, fleas, and mosquitoes can carry microorganisms that cause diseases in humans. For example, when they bite humans, some mosquito species can transmit the microorganism that causes malaria.

The vast majority of insects, however, are harmless or beneficial to humans. Bees make honey, and the larvae of the silkworm moth spin the fibers used to make silk cloth. Some insects prey on harmful insects, helping to reduce those insect populations. And while some insects destroy food crops, many more insects, such as butterflies and flies, enable food crops and other plants to reproduce by carrying pollen from one plant to another. If insects were to disappear from Earth, you would never get a mosquito bite. But you wouldn't have much food to eat, either.

Controlling Insect Pests

INTEGRATING ENVIRONMENTAL SCIENCE People have tried to eliminate harmful insects by applying chemicals, called pesticides, to plants. However, pesticides also kill helpful insects, such as bees, and can harm other animals, including some birds. And after a time, insect populations become resistant to the pesticides—the pesticides no longer kill the insects.

Scientists are searching for other ways to deal with harmful insects. One method is the use of biological controls. Biological controls introduce natural predators or diseases into insect populations. For example, ladybug beetles can be added to fields where crops are grown. Ladybugs prey on aphids, which are insects that destroy peaches, potatoes, and other crop plants. Soil also can be treated with bacteria that are harmless to humans but cause diseases in the larvae of pest insects such as Japanese beetles. These biological controls kill only one or a few pest species. Because biological controls kill only specific pests, they are less damaging to the environment than insecticides.

Figure 14 Bees and other pollinators are among the most beneficial of all insects. As a bee drinks nectar from a flower, pollen sticks to its body. When the insect carries that pollen to the next plant it eats from, it helps that plant to reproduce.

Section 3 Review

1. List the characteristics that insects share.
2. Identify two ways in which insects benefit humans.
3. Compare and contrast complete and gradual metamorphosis.
4. **Thinking Critically Inferring** Honeybees sting predators that try to attack them. Hover flies, which do not sting, resemble honeybees. How might this resemblance be an advantage to the hover fly?

Check Your Progress CHAPTER PROJECT

Continue observing the mealworms every day. Update the data table with your observations. As you observe the mealworms at different stages of development, make a sketch of a larva, a pupa, and an adult.

What's Living in the Soil?

The soil beneath a tree, in a garden, or under a rock is home to many organisms, including a variety of arthropods. Each of these patches of soil can be thought of as a miniature environment with its own group of living residents. In this lab, you will examine one specific soil environment.

Problem

What kinds of animals live in soil and leaf litter?

Skills Focus

observing, classifying, inferring

Materials

2-liter plastic bottle
coarse steel wool
cheesecloth
gooseneck lamp
large, wide-mouthed jar
fresh sample of soil and leaf litter
large scissors
trowel
large rubber band
hand lens
small jar

Procedure

1. Select a location where your equipment can be set up and remain undisturbed for about 24 hours. At that location, place the small jar inside the center of the large jar as shown in the photograph.

2. Use scissors to cut a large plastic bottle in half. **CAUTION:** *Cut in a direction away from yourself and others.* Turn the top half of the bottle upside down to serve as a funnel.

3. Insert a small amount of coarse steel wool into the mouth of the funnel to keep the soil from falling out. Do not pack the steel wool too tightly. Leave spaces for small organisms to crawl through. Place the funnel into the large jar as shown in the photograph.

4. Using the trowel, fill the funnel with soil and surface leaf litter. When you finish handling the leaves and soil, wash your hands thoroughly.

5. Look closely to see whether the soil and litter are dry or wet. Record your observation.

6. Make a cover for your sample by placing a piece of cheesecloth over the top of the funnel. Hold the cheesecloth in place with a large rubber band. Immediately position a lamp about 15 cm above the funnel, and turn on the light. Allow this setup to remain undisturbed for about 24 hours. **CAUTION:** *Hot light bulbs can cause burns. Do not touch the bulb.*

7. When you are ready to make your observations, turn off the lamp. Leave the funnel and jar in place while making your observations. Use a hand lens to examine each organism in the jar. **CAUTION:** *Do not touch any of the organisms.*

8. Use a data table like the one on the next page to sketch each type of organism and to record other observations. Be sure to include evidence that will help you classify the organisms. (*Hint:* Remember that some animals may be at different stages of metamorphosis.)

DATA TABLE

Sketch of Organism	Number Found	Size	Important Characteristics	Probable Phylum

9. Examine the soil and leaf litter, and record whether this material is dry or wet.

10. When you are finished, follow your teacher's directions about returning the organisms to the soil. Wash your hands with soap.

Analyze and Conclude

1. Describe the conditions of the soil environment at the beginning and end of the lab. What caused the change?

2. What types of animals did you collect in the small jar? What characteristics did you use to identify each type of animal? Which types of animals were the most common?

3. Why do you think the animals moved down the funnel away from the soil?

4. **Apply** Using what you have learned about arthropods and other animals, make an inference about the role that each animal you collected plays in the environment.

Design an Experiment

What kinds of organisms might live in other soil types—for example, soil at the edge of a pond, dry sandy soil, or commercially prepared potting soil? Design an experiment to answer this question.

INTEGRATING CHEMISTRY

SECTION 4 The Chemistry of Communication

DISCOVER ·······················ACTIVITY···

Can You Match the Scents?

1. From your teacher, obtain a container covered with aluminum foil with holes punched in it.

2. Carefully sniff the contents of the container. **CAUTION:** *Never sniff an unknown substance directly. When testing an odor, use a waving motion with your hand to direct the vapor toward your nose.*

3. One other person in your class has a container with the same substance. Use your sense of smell to find the container whose scent matches the one in your container.

Think It Over

Observing How easy was it for you and your classmates to match scents? What advantage might identifying or detecting scents have to an animal?

GUIDE FOR READING

◆ How do animals use pheromones to communicate?

Reading Tip As you read, make a list of main ideas and supporting details about pheromones and bioluminescence.

Figure 15 These ants are finding their way to the sugar by following a pheromone trail. The first ant to find the sugar began the trail, and each ant adds to its strength.

Oh no—ants have gotten into the sugar! As you watch in dismay, a stream of ants moves along the kitchen counter, heading right for the sugar bowl. Using their sense of smell, the ants follow a chemical trail that was first laid down by the ant that discovered the sugar. Each ant contributes to the trail by depositing a tiny droplet of scent onto the counter. If you watch carefully, you may see the ants doing this. The droplet quickly evaporates, making an invisible cloud of scent that hangs in the air above the path of the ants.

All the ants running to and from the sugar bowl are enveloped in an ant-sized tunnel of scent. It's like an invisible ant highway. The ants hold their antennae forward and use them to sniff their way to the sugar bowl. Then they turn around and follow the same chemical signal back to their nest.

Pheromones

The scent tunnel that leads ants to the sugar bowl is made of pheromones. A **pheromone** (FER uh mohn) is a chemical released by one animal that affects the behavior of another animal of the same

362

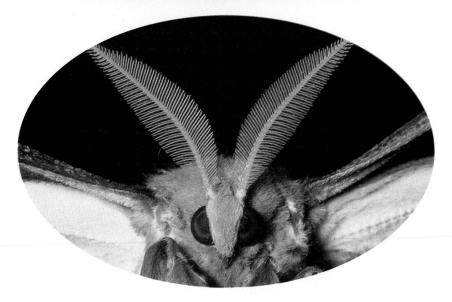

Figure 16 The antennae of this male Atlas silkworm moth allow him to find females that are ready to mate. Sense organs on the antennae pick up the female pheromone scent. The male then follows the scent to the female. *Predicting* How might injured antennae affect a male moth's ability to find a mate?

species. **Animals communicate with pheromones to locate food, attract mates, and distinguish members of their own group from members of other groups.** Animals release these very powerful chemicals only in tiny quantities.

Why Pheromones Are Specific Most pheromones are chemical compounds that are made up of long chains of atoms. Each pheromone has a unique combination of atoms in it. Because the atoms join together in specific ways, each pheromone has a different chemical shape. The different shapes of pheromones make them highly specific—when an animal releases a pheromone, it usually only causes a response in other animals of the same species. Just as the key to your front door will not work in the lock of your neighbor's door, the pheromones released by a luna moth will not trigger a response in a gypsy moth.

Pheromones and Behavior Pheromones enable many animals to recognize group members. Every ant colony, for example, has its own pheromones that identify colony members. If an ant wanders into a colony other than its own, the intruder ant's pheromones will be recognized as foreign. The intruder will be attacked and killed.

Pheromones also play an important role in mating and reproduction. A female silkworm moth, for example, releases a pheromone when she is ready to mate. When the sense organs on a male's antennae pick up the scent of the pheromone, the male flies toward the scent to mate with the female.

☑ *Checkpoint* *How do pheromones enable ants to identify members of another ant colony?*

Pheromones and Pest Control Some pheromones can be made in laboratories and then used to attract and eliminate pest insects. Manufactured pheromones lure insects into traps. In some cases, the insects are killed in the traps. In some other cases, male insects that collect in these traps can be exposed to X-rays that kill their sperm cells. Even though these altered males will mate with females after they are released, no offspring will result. The population of the insects will eventually decrease. A common pheromone trap lures Japanese beetles, which damage rosebushes. They are lured into a bag from which they can't escape. They can then be killed or relocated.

INTEGRATING
ENVIRONMENTAL SCIENCE

Figure 17 Fireflies use bioluminescence to find and attract mates.

Communicating with Light

Pheromones are only one form of chemical communication used by animals. Some animals, such as fireflies, use light to communicate. **Bioluminescence** (by oh loo muh NEHS uhns) is the production of light by a living organism. That light is generated by chemical reactions that take place in the organism's cells.

On a warm summer night, when you see a meadow lit up with fireflies, you are actually watching fireflies using bioluminescence in courtship. A male firefly sends a blinking signal to female fireflies in the grass below. Each species of firefly has a distinctive signal. When an interested female sees the signal of a male of her species, she flashes a reply. If the male sees her signal, he will land near her and they may mate.

Section 4 Review

1. List three things that animals communicate with pheromones. Using a specific animal, give an example of each type of communication.
2. How are pheromones used to control insect pests?
3. What do fireflies communicate with their bioluminescence?
4. **Thinking Critically Predicting** While a stream of ants is traveling to and from the sugar bowl, you take a sponge and wash away a six-inch section of their path. Predict how the ants will respond.

SECTION
5 Echinoderms

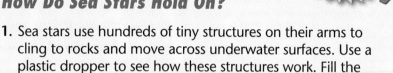

DISCOVER ••ACTIVITY••••

How Do Sea Stars Hold On?

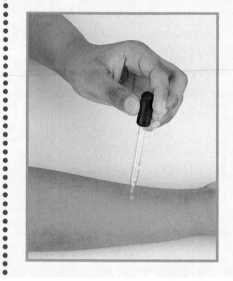

1. Sea stars use hundreds of tiny structures on their arms to cling to rocks and move across underwater surfaces. Use a plastic dropper to see how these structures work. Fill the dropper with water, and then squeeze out most of the water.

2. Squeeze one last drop of water onto the inside of your arm. Then, while squeezing the bulb, touch the tip of the dropper into the water drop. With the dropper tip against your skin, release the bulb.

3. Hold the dropper by the tube and lift it slowly, paying attention to what happens to your skin.

Think It Over
Predicting Besides moving and clinging to surfaces, what might sea stars use their suction structures for?

They look like stars, pincushions, coins, and cucumbers—are these creatures really animals? Sea stars, brittle stars, and basket stars have star-shaped bodies. Sea urchins look like living pincushions, while sand dollars are flat, round discs. Sea cucumbers, with green algae growing within their tissues, look like dill pickles—until they slowly start to crawl along the sand. All of these odd animals belong to the same phylum.

The "Spiny Skinned" Animals

Biologists classify sea stars, sea urchins, sand dollars, and sea cucumbers as echinoderms (phylum Echinodermata). An **echinoderm** (ee KY noh durm) is a radially symmetrical invertebrate that lives on the ocean floor. *Echinoderm* means "spiny skinned." This name is appropriate because the skin of most of these animals is supported by a spiny internal skeleton, or **endoskeleton,** made of plates that contain calcium.

Adult echinoderms have a unique kind of radial symmetry in which body parts, usually in multiples of five, are arranged like spokes on a wheel. If you count the legs on a sea star or the body sections of a sea urchin, you will almost always get five or a multiple of five.

GUIDE FOR READING

◆ What characteristics are typical of echinoderms?

Reading Tip Before you read, preview the photographs in this section. Write a description of the similarities you observe among these organisms.

▼ **Magnificent sea urchin**

365

In addition to five-part radial symmetry and an endoskeleton, echinoderms also have an internal fluid system called a water vascular system. The **water vascular system** consists of fluid-filled tubes within the echinoderm's body. Portions of the tubes can contract, squeezing water into structures called tube feet, which are external parts of the water vascular system. The ends of tube feet are sticky and, when filled with water, they act like small, sticky suction cups. The stickiness and suction enable the tube feet to grip the surface beneath the echinoderm. Most echinoderms also use their tube feet to move along slowly and to capture food. If you turn a sea star upside down, you will see rows of moving tube feet.

Echinoderms crawl about on the bottom of the ocean, seeking food, shelter, and mates. Like other radially symmetrical animals, echinoderms do not have a head end where sense organs and nerve tissue are found. Instead, they are adapted to respond to food, mates, or predators coming from any direction.

Most echinoderms are either male or female. Eggs are usually fertilized right in the seawater, after the female releases her eggs and the male releases his sperm. The fertilized eggs develop into tiny, swimming larvae that eventually undergo metamorphosis and become adult echinoderms.

☑ *Checkpoint* *What is the function of an echinoderm's tube feet?*

Figure 18 This red sea star is in the process of regenerating two of its arms, possibly lost in a struggle with a predator.

Sea Stars

Sea stars are predators that eat mollusks, crabs, and even other echinoderms. A sea star uses its arms and tube feet, shown in *Exploring a Sea Star* on page 367, to capture prey. The sea star grasps a clam with all five arms. Then it pulls on the tightly closed shells with its tube feet. When the shells open, the sea star forces its stomach out through its mouth and into the opening between the clam's shells. Digestive chemicals break down the clam's tissues, and the sea star sucks in the partially digested body of its prey. Sea star behavior is quite impressive for an animal that doesn't have a brain.

If a sea star loses an arm, it can grow a replacement. The process by which an animal grows a new part to replace a lost one is called regeneration. Figure 18 shows a sea star with two partially regenerated arms. A few species of sea stars can even grow a whole animal from a single arm. Some sea stars reproduce by splitting into many parts. The arms pull the sea star apart in five different directions and five new sea stars regenerate!

EXPLORING *a Sea Star*

Sea stars, which are also called starfishes, usually have five arms. However, some have as many as 50 arms.

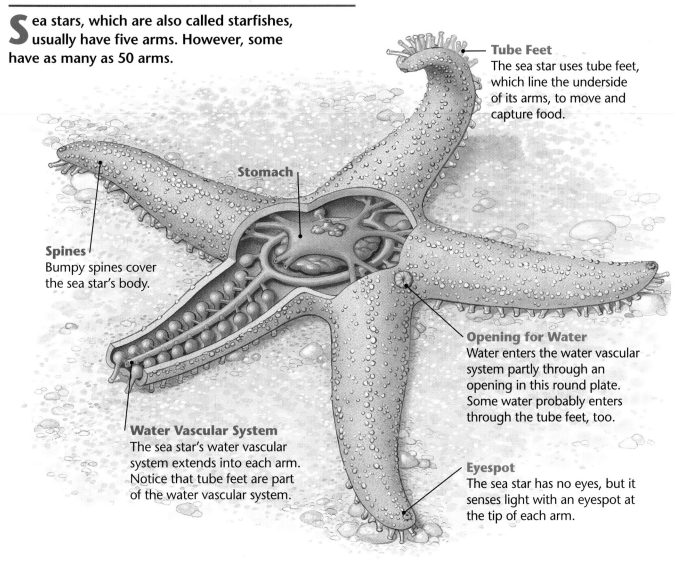

Tube Feet
The sea star uses tube feet, which line the underside of its arms, to move and capture food.

Stomach

Spines
Bumpy spines cover the sea star's body.

Water Vascular System
The sea star's water vascular system extends into each arm. Notice that tube feet are part of the water vascular system.

Opening for Water
Water enters the water vascular system partly through an opening in this round plate. Some water probably enters through the tube feet, too.

Eyespot
The sea star has no eyes, but it senses light with an eyespot at the tip of each arm.

Other Echinoderms

Brittle stars are close relatives of sea stars. Like sea stars, brittle stars have five arms, but their arms are long and slender, with flexible joints. Like sea stars, brittle stars can regenerate lost arms. Brittle stars' tube feet, which have no suction cups, are used for catching food but not for moving. Instead, brittle stars propel themselves along the ocean bottom by moving their giant arms against the ground. They are among the most mobile of all the echinoderms.

Unlike sea stars and brittle stars, sand dollars and sea urchins have no arms. Sand dollars look like large coins. Their flat bodies are covered with very short spines that help them burrow into sand.

Reviewing Content

 For more review of key concepts, see the Interactive Student Tutorial CD-ROM.

Multiple Choice

Choose the letter of the best answer.

1. Mollusks with tentacles are known as
   a. cephalopods.
   b. gastropods.
   c. bivalves.
   d. sea stars.

2. Which of these is true of the legs of arthropods?
   a. They always number six.
   b. They are always attached to the abdomen.
   c. They are rigid.
   d. They are jointed.

3. At which stage of its development is a moth enclosed in a cocoon?
   a. egg
   b. larva
   c. pupa
   d. adult

4. Chemicals released by insects that affect other insects of the same species are called
   a. camouflages.
   b. pupae.
   c. pesticides.
   d. pheromones.

5. A sea star is a(n)
   a. mollusk.
   b. arthropod.
   c. echinoderm.
   d. sponge.

True or False

If the statement is true, write true. If it is false, change the underlined word or words to make the statement true.

6. All <u>arthropods</u> have an exoskeleton.
7. All <u>sea urchins</u> have two pairs of antennae.
8. An insect's midsection is called an <u>abdomen</u>.
9. The production of light by an organism is called <u>bioluminescence</u>.
10. All echinoderms have an <u>endoskeleton</u>.

Checking Concepts

11. Explain how a snail uses its radula.
12. How is a cephalopod's way of moving different from that of most mollusks?
13. Describe five things that a crayfish can do with its appendages.
14. How is the process by which a spider digests its food similar to that of a sea star?
15. How are centipedes different from millipedes?
16. Identify some ways insects harm people.
17. How are insects different from other arthropods?
18. How does a pheromone's structure account for the fact that it usually affects the behavior of only one species?
19. How is an echinoderm's radial symmetry different from that of a jellyfish?
20. **Writing to Learn** Imagine that you are a lobster that has just molted. Using vivid, precise words, describe a dangerous situation that you might encounter before your new exoskeleton has hardened.

Thinking Critically

21. **Comparing and Contrasting** Compare and contrast bivalves and cephalopods.
22. **Applying Concepts** Explain why the development of a lion, which grows larger as it changes from a tiny cub to a 200-pound adult, is not metamorphosis.
23. **Classifying** Your friend said he found a dead insect that had two pairs of antennae and eight legs. Is this possible? Why or why not?
24. **Making Judgments** Do you think that pesticides should be used to kill harmful insects? Support your ideas with facts.
25. **Relating Cause and Effect** Sea stars sometimes get caught in fishing nets. At one time, in an attempt to protect clams from their natural predators, workers on fishing boats cut the sea stars into pieces and threw the pieces back in the water. What do you think happened to the sea star population? Explain.

Applying Skills

The following information appeared in a book on insects. Use it to answer Questions 26–29.

"A hummingbird moth beats its wings an average of 85 times per second, and it flies at a speed of about 17.8 kilometers per hour (kph). A bumblebee's wings beat about 250 times per second, and it flies about 10.3 kph. A housefly's wings beat about 190 times per second, and it flies about 7.1 kph."

26. **Creating Data Tables** Make a data table to organize the wing-beat rate and flight speed information above.
27. **Graphing** Use the data to construct two bar graphs: one showing the three insect wing-beat rates and another showing the flight speeds.
28. **Interpreting Data** Which of the three insects has the highest wing-beat rate? Which insect flies the fastest?

29. **Drawing Conclusions** On the basis of the data, do you see any relationship between the rate at which an insect beats its wings and the speed at which it flies? Explain. What factors besides wing-beat rate might affect an insect's flight speed?

Performance ▼ CHAPTER PROJECT **Assessment**

Present Your Project Prepare a display with diagrams to show how you set up your experiment and what your results were. Construct and display graphs to show the data you collected. Include pictures of the mealworms in each stage of development.

Reflect and Record In your journal, write your conclusion of how the experimental conditions affected the growth and development of the mealworms. Also suggest some possible explanations for your results.

Test Preparation

Use these questions to prepare for standardized tests.

Study the graph. Then answer Questions 30–33.

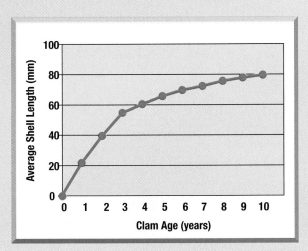

30. What is the best title for this graph?
    a. Clam Shell Growth over Time
    b. The Ages of a Clam
    c. The Maximum Size of Clams
    d. The Life Span of Clams

31. In some states, the minimum harvesting size for clams is 40 millimeters. Approximately how long does it take new clams to reach this size?
    a. 1 year   b. 2 years
    c. 3 years   d. 4 years

32. Based on the graph, which generalization about clam growth is correct?
    a. Clam growth is most rapid during years 5 through 10.
    b. Clam growth is most rapid during years 0 through 5.
    c. Clam growth is equally rapid each year.
    d. Clam growth is very slow.

33. How many millimeters larger was the average clam at age 2 compared to age 1?
    a. 8 millimeters
    b. 15 millimeters
    c. 18 millimeters
    d. 25 millimeters

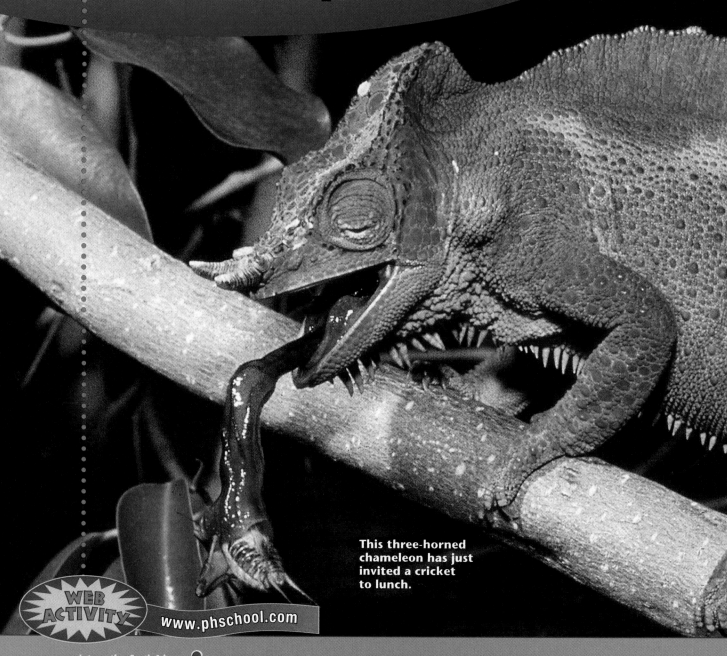

CHAPTER
12 Fishes, Amphibians, and Reptiles

This three-horned chameleon has just invited a cricket to lunch.

www.phschool.com

 SECTION
1 *Integrating Earth Science*
Evolution of Vertebrates

Discover How Is an Umbrella Like a Skeleton?
Try This Bead-y Bones
Science at Home Focus on Backbones

SECTION
2 Fishes

Discover How Does Water Flow Over a Fish's Gills?
Sharpen Your Skills Communicating
Real-World Lab Home Sweet Home

SECTION
3 Amphibians

Discover What's the Advantage of Being Green?
Try This Webbing Through Water

Animal Adaptations

The chameleon sits still on a twig, as if frozen. Only its eyes move as it sights a cricket resting nearby. Suddenly, the chameleon's long tongue shoots out and captures the unsuspecting cricket, pulling the insect into its mouth.

Watch any animal for a few minutes and you will see many ways in which it is adapted for life in its environment. How does the animal capture food, escape from predators, or obtain oxygen? To help answer these questions, you will create models of three different animals—a fish, an amphibian, and a reptile—and show how each is adapted to the environment in which it lives.

Your Goal To construct three-dimensional models of a fish, an amphibian, and a reptile that show how each is adapted to carry out an essential life function in its environment.

To complete the project successfully, you must
- ◆ select one important adaptation to show
- ◆ build a three-dimensional model of each animal, showing how it carries out the function you selected
- ◆ include a poster that explains how each animal's adaptation is suited to its environment
- ◆ follow the safety guidelines in Appendix A

Get Started Pair up with a classmate and share what you already know about fishes, amphibians, and reptiles. Discuss the following questions: Where do these organisms live? How do they move around? How do they protect themselves? Begin thinking about the characteristics that you would like to model.

Check Your Progress You'll be working on this project as you study this chapter. To keep your project on track, look for Check Your Progress boxes at the following points:

Section 2 Review, page 387: Select a fish to model, and assemble your materials.

Section 3 Review, page 394: Make a model of an amphibian.

Section 4 Review, page 404: Model a reptile. Begin your poster.

Present Your Project At the end of the chapter (page 407), you will display your models and poster.

SECTION 4 Reptiles

Discover How Do Snakes Feed?
Skills Lab Soaking Up Those Rays
Sharpen Your Skills Drawing Conclusions

① Evolution of Vertebrates

DISCOVER

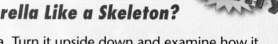

How Is an Umbrella Like a Skeleton?

1. Open an umbrella. Turn it upside down and examine how it is made.
2. Now fold the umbrella, and watch how the braces and ribs collapse against the central pole.
3. Think of what would happen if you removed the ribs from the umbrella and then tried to use it during a rainstorm.

Think It Over

Inferring What is the function of the ribs of an umbrella? How are the ribs of the umbrella similar to the bones in your skeleton? How are they different?

GUIDE FOR READING

◆ What main characteristic is shared by all vertebrates?

◆ How do vertebrates differ in the way in which they control body temperature?

Reading Tip As you read, write a definition, in your own words, of each boldfaced science term.

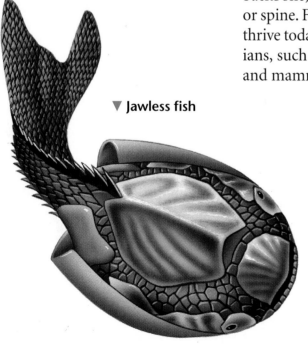

▼ Jawless fish

Look backward in time, into an ocean 530 million years ago. There you see a strange-looking creature, about as long as your middle finger. The creature is swimming with a side-to-side motion, like a flag flapping in an invisible wind. Its tail-fin is broad and flat. Tiny armorlike plates cover its small body. Its eyes are set wide apart. If you could see inside the animal, you would notice that it has a backbone. You are looking at one of the earliest vertebrates, at home in an ancient sea.

Recall from Chapter 10 that vertebrates are animals with a backbone, which is also called a vertebral column, spinal column, or spine. Fishes were the first vertebrates to appear, and they still thrive today in Earth's waters. Other vertebrates include amphibians, such as frogs, and reptiles, such as snakes, as well as birds and mammals.

The Chordate Phylum

Vertebrates are a subgroup in the phylum Chordata. Members of this phylum, called **chordates** (KAWR daytz), share these characteristics: at some point in their lives, they have a notochord, a nerve cord, and slits in their throat area. The phylum name comes from the **notochord,** a flexible rod that supports the animal's back. Some chordates, like the lancelet in Figure 1, keep the notochord all their lives. Others, such as tunicates, have a notochord as larvae, but not as adults. In vertebrates, part or all of the notochord is replaced by a backbone. A few vertebrates have backbones made of **cartilage,** a connective tissue that is softer than bone, but flexible and strong. Most vertebrates have backbones made of hard bone.

Besides a notochord, all chordates have a nerve cord that runs down their back—your spinal cord is such a nerve cord. The nerve cord is the connection between the brain and the nerves, on which messages travel back and forth. Many other groups of animals—crustaceans and worms, for example—have nerve cords, but their nerve cords do not run down their backs.

In addition, chordates have slits in their throat area called pharyngeal (fayr uhn JEE uhl) slits. Fishes keep these slits as part of their gills for their entire lives, but in many vertebrates, including humans, pharyngeal slits disappear before birth.

Figure 1 This lancelet exhibits all the typical characteristics of a chordate. It has a notochord that helps support its body, pharyngeal slits that help it to breathe, and a nerve cord.

☑ *Checkpoint* *What characteristics do all chordates share?*

The Backbone and Endoskeleton

A vertebrate's backbone runs down the center of its back. The backbone is formed by many similar bones, called **vertebrae** (singular *vertebra*), lined up in a row, like beads on a string. Joints between the vertebrae give the vertebral column flexibility. You are able to bend over and tie your sneakers partly because your backbone is flexible. Each vertebra has a hole in it that allows the spinal cord to pass through it. The spinal cord fits into the vertebrae like fingers fit into rings.

A vertebrate's backbone is part of an endoskeleton, or internal skeleton. The endoskeleton supports and protects the body, helps give it shape, and gives muscles a place to attach. In addition to the backbone, the vertebrate's endoskeleton includes

Figure 2 The bodies of all vertebrates are supported by an endoskeleton with a backbone. *Comparing and Contrasting What are two ways in which the cow and chicken skeletons are similar? What are two ways in which they are different?*

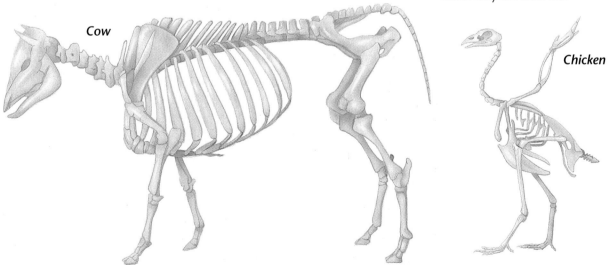

Cow

Chicken

 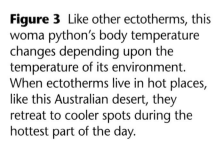
the skull and ribs. The skull protects the brain and sense organs. The ribs attach to the vertebrae and protect the heart, lungs, and other internal organs. Many vertebrates also have arm and leg bones adapted for a variety of movements.

A vertebrate's endoskeleton has several important characteristics. For one thing, unlike an arthropod's exoskeleton, it grows as the animal grows. It also forms an internal frame that supports the body against the downward pull of gravity, while allowing easy movement. Because of these endoskeleton characteristics, vertebrates can grow bigger than animals with exoskeletons or no skeletons at all.

☑ *Checkpoint* *What functions does a vertebrate's skeleton perform?*

Maintaining Body Temperature

One characteristic that distinguishes the major groups of vertebrates from one another is the way in which they control their body temperature. **Most fishes, amphibians, and reptiles have a body temperature that is close to the temperature of their environment. In contrast, birds and mammals have a stable body temperature that is typically much warmer than their environment.** Fishes, amphibians, and reptiles are ectotherms. An **ectotherm** is an animal whose body does not produce much internal heat—its body temperature changes depending upon the temperature of its environment. For example, when a turtle is lying in the sun on a riverbank, it has a higher body temperature than when it is swimming in a cool river. Ectotherms are sometimes called "coldblooded," but this term is misleading because the blood of ectotherms is often quite warm.

Figure 3 Like other ectotherms, this woma python's body temperature changes depending upon the temperature of its environment. When ectotherms live in hot places, like this Australian desert, they retreat to cooler spots during the hottest part of the day.

Figure 4 Though Antarctic winter temperatures can fall to −50°C, a dense coat keeps adult penguins warm. A thick, fluffy baby coat keeps a penguin chick warm until it gets its adult coat.
Inferring Do you think the emperor penguin is an ectotherm or an endotherm?

In contrast to a turtle, a beaver would have the same body temperature whether it was in cool water or on warm land. The beaver is a mammal, and mammals and birds are endotherms. An **endotherm** is an animal whose body controls and regulates its temperature by controlling the internal heat it produces. An endotherm's body temperature usually does not change much, even when the temperature of its environment changes.

Endotherms also have other adaptations, such as fur or feathers and sweat glands, for maintaining their body temperature. Fur and feathers keep endotherms warm on cool days. On hot days, on the other hand, some endotherms sweat. As the sweat evaporates, the animal is cooled. Because endotherms can keep their body temperatures stable, they can live in a greater variety of environments than ectotherms can.

Vertebrate History in Rocks

The information scientists have about early vertebrates comes from fossils. A **fossil** is the hardened remains or other evidence of a living thing that existed a long time in the past. Sometimes a fossil is an imprint in rock, such as an animal's footprint or the outline of a leaf. Other fossils are the remains of bones or other parts of living things—a chemical process has taken place in which the organism's tissues have become replaced by hard minerals. Because most living tissues decay rapidly, only a very few organisms become preserved as fossils.

Figure 5 The diagram shows fossils in sedimentary rock layers.
Interpreting Diagrams Which rock layer probably contains the oldest fossils? Explain.

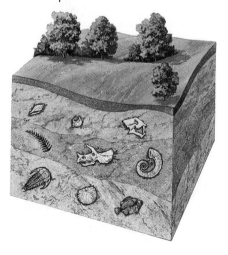

Fossils occur most frequently in the type of rock known as sedimentary rock. **Sedimentary rock** is made of hardened layers of sediments—particles of clay, sand, mud, or silt. Sediments build up in many ways. For example, wind can blow a thick layer of sand onto dunes. Sediments can also form when muddy water stands in an area for a long time. Muddy sediment in the water will eventually settle to the bottom and build up.

Over a very long time, layers of sediments can be pressed and cemented together to form rock. As sedimentary rock forms, traces of living things that have been trapped in the sediments are sometimes preserved as fossils.

Discovering Vertebrate Fossils

People have been discovering fossils since ancient times. However, it is only within the last few centuries that people have understood that fossils are the remains of organisms. Here are some especially important fossil discoveries.

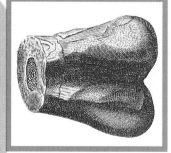

1822
Dinosaur Tooth

In a quarry near Lewes, England, Mary Ann Mantell discovered a strange-looking tooth embedded in stone. Her husband Gideon drew the picture of the tooth shown here. The tooth belonged to the dinosaur *Iguanodon.*

| 1675 | 1725 | 1775 | 1825 |

1677
Dinosaur-Bone Illustration

Robert Plot, the head of a museum in England, published a book that had an illustration of a huge fossilized thighbone. Plot thought that the bone belonged to a giant human, but it probably was the thighbone of a dinosaur.

1811
Sea Reptile

Along the cliffs near Lyme Regis, England, 12-year-old Mary Anning discovered the fossilized remains of the giant sea reptile now called *Ichthyosaurus.* Mary became one of England's first professional fossil collectors.

Applying Skills

A scientist performed an experiment on five goldfish to test the effect of water temperature on "breathing rate"—the rate at which the fish open and close their gill covers. The graph shows the data that the scientist obtained at four different temperatures. Use the graph to answer Questions 24–26.

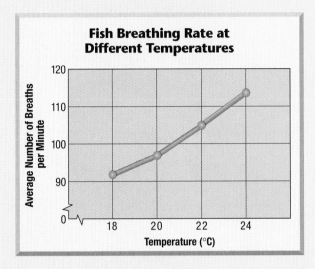

Fish Breathing Rate at Different Temperatures

Average Number of Breaths per Minute vs *Temperature (°C)*

24. Controlling Variables Identify the manipulated variable and the responding variable in this experiment.

25. Interpreting Data How does the breathing rate at 18°C compare to the breathing rate at 22°C?

26. Drawing Conclusions Based on the data, what is the relationship between water temperature and fish breathing rate?

Performance ▼ Assessment
CHAPTER PROJECT

Present Your Project Display your models in a creative and interesting way—for example, show the models in action and show details of the animals' habitats. Also display your poster.

Reflect and Record In your journal, list all the adaptations you learned about from your classmates' presentations. How did constructing a three-dimensional model help you understand the characteristics of these groups?

Test Preparation
Use these questions to prepare for standardized tests.

Read the passage. Then answer Questions 27–29.

When the snake, *Bothrops jararaca*, attacks, deadly venom enters its victim through its razor-sharp fangs. The bitten animal's blood pressure drops, its lungs burst, and it soon dies.

Why does the snake venom cause the animal's blood pressure to drop? Could the same substance be used to reduce blood pressure in humans? Because hypertension, or high blood pressure, is a leading cause of death in humans, scientists wanted to find answers to these questions.

Scientists collected the venom from many *Bothrops jararaca* snakes and injected it into laboratory animals. The animals' blood vessels widened, causing a large drop in blood pressure. The scientists then set to work to develop an artificial version of the snake venom. The result was captopril, a blood pressure medication that has saved many lives.

27. What is the best title for this passage?
   a. How Poisonous Snakes Kill Their Prey
   b. Hypertension—A Leading Cause of Death
   c. Turning Poison into a Promising New Medication
   d. Is *Bothrops jararaca* a Serious Threat to Humans?

28. Which of the following words is a synonym for *venom?*
   a. medication
   b. poison
   c. chemical
   d. vein

29. What observation led scientists to carry out further investigations of the snake venom?
   a. The bitten animal died.
   b. The venom entered the animal from the snake's razor-sharp fangs.
   c. The bitten animal's lungs burst.
   d. The bitten animal's blood pressure dropped.

WEB ACTIVITY
www.phschool.com

SECTION
1 Birds

Discover **What Are Feathers Like?**
Skills Lab **Looking at an Owl's Leftovers**
Try This **Eggs-amination**

Integrating Physics
SECTION
2 **The Physics of Bird Flight**

Discover **What Lifts Airplanes and Birds Into the Air?**
Try This **It's Plane to See**

SECTION
3 **What Is a Mammal?**

Discover **What Are Mammals' Teeth Like?**
Try This **Insulated Mammals**
Sharpen Your Skills **Classifying**
Science at Home **Mammals' Milk**
Real-World Lab **Keeping Warm**

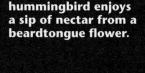

Bird Watch

One of the best ways to learn about animals is to watch them in action. In this project, you'll watch birds and other animals that visit a bird feeder. You may be surprised at how much you will discover. How do birds eat? Which ones eat first? How do different birds interact? What happens if a squirrel arrives on the scene? Careful observation and record keeping will reveal answers to these questions. They may also raise new questions for you to answer.

Your Goal To make detailed observations of the birds that appear at a bird feeder.

To complete this project successfully, you must
◆ observe the feeder regularly for at least two weeks, and identify the kinds of birds that visit the feeder
◆ make detailed observations of how the birds at your feeder eat
◆ describe the most common kinds of bird behavior
◆ follow the safety guidelines in Appendix A

Get Started Begin by meeting with some classmates to share your knowledge about the birds in your area. What kinds of birds can you expect to see? What types of foods do birds eat? Brainstorm how you could find out more about the birds that live in your area.

Check Your Progress You'll be working on this project as you study this chapter. To keep your project on track, look for Check Your Progress boxes at the following points.
Section 1 Review, page 419: Identify birds (and mammals) that come to the feeder. Observe how the animals interact.
Section 2 Review, page 422: Observe how birds feed.
Section 4 Review, page 436: Interpret your bird-feeding data, and prepare your graphs.

Present Your Project At the end of this chapter (page 439), you will share what you have learned about birds and their behavior.

This broad-tailed hummingbird enjoys a sip of nectar from a beardtongue flower.

SECTION
4 **Diversity of Mammals**

Discover How Is a Thumb Useful?

1 Birds

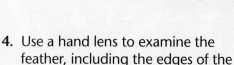

DISCOVER

What Are Feathers Like?

1. Examine a feather. Observe its overall shape and structure. Use a hand lens to examine the many hairlike barbs that project out from the feather's central shaft.

2. With your fingertip, gently stroke the feather from bottom to top. Observe whether the barbs stick together or separate.

3. Gently separate two barbs in the middle of the feather. Rub the separated edges with your fingertip.

4. Use a hand lens to examine the feather, including the edges of the two separated barbs. Draw a diagram of what you observe.

5. Now rejoin the two separated barbs by gently pulling outward from the shaft. Then wash your hands.

Think It Over

Observing Once barbs have been separated, is it easy to rejoin them? How might this be an advantage to the bird?

GUIDE FOR READING

◆ What characteristics do birds have in common?

◆ How are birds adapted to their environments?

Reading Tip Before you read, look at *Exploring a Bird* on page 413 and make a list of unfamiliar terms. As you read, write definitions for the terms.

One day in 1861, in a limestone quarry in what is now Germany, Hermann von Meyer was inspecting rocks. Meyer, who was a fossil hunter, spotted something dark in one of the rocks. It was the blackened fossil imprint of a feather! Excited, Meyer began searching for a fossil of an entire bird. Though it took a month, he eventually found what he was looking for—a skeleton surrounded by the clear imprint of many feathers. The fossil was given the scientific name *Archaeopteryx* (ahr kee AHP tur iks), meaning "ancient, winged thing."

Paleontologists estimate that *Archaeopteryx* lived about 145 million years ago. *Archaeopteryx* didn't look much like the birds you know. It looked more like a reptile with wings. While no modern bird has any teeth, *Archaeopteryx* had a mouthful of them. No modern bird has a long, bony tail, either, but *Archaeopteryx* did. However, unlike any reptile, extinct or modern, *Archaeopteryx* had feathers— its wings and tail were covered with them. Paleontologists think that *Archaeopteryx* and today's birds descended from some kind of reptile, possibly from a dinosaur.

Figure 1 The extinct bird *Archaeopteryx* may have looked like this.

Figure 2 John James Audubon painted this little blue heron in 1832.
(© Collection of the New York Historical Society)

What Is a Bird?

Modern **birds** all share certain characteristics. **A bird is an endothermic vertebrate that has feathers and a four-chambered heart, and lays eggs.** Birds have scales on their feet and legs, evidence of their descent from reptiles. In addition, most birds can fly.

The flight of birds is an amazing feat that people watch with delight and envy. All modern birds—including ostriches, penguins, and other flightless birds—evolved from ancestors that could fly.

The bodies of birds are adapted for flight. For example, the bones of a bird's forelimbs form wings. In addition, many of a bird's bones are nearly hollow, making the bird's body extremely lightweight. Flying birds have large chest muscles that move the wings. Finally, feathers are a major adaptation that help birds fly.

☑ *Checkpoint* *List four ways in which birds are adapted for flight.*

Feathers

The rule is this: If it has feathers, it's a bird. Feathers probably evolved from reptiles' scales. Both feathers and reptile scales are made of the same tough material as your fingernails.

Birds have different types of feathers. If you've ever picked up a feather from the ground, chances are good that it was a contour feather. A **contour feather** is one of the large feathers that give shape to a bird's body. The long contour feathers that extend beyond the body on the wings and tail are called flight feathers. When a bird flies, these feathers help it balance and steer.

Visual Arts
CONNECTION

John James Audubon (1785–1851) was an American artist who painted pictures of birds and other kinds of animals. Audubon grew up in France. Even as a child he loved to sketch the birds that he observed while roaming through the forest. Later, as an adult in America, he began to study and draw birds seriously, traveling to various parts of the country in search of different varieties of birds.

Audubon's four-volume work, *The Birds of America*, published between 1827 and 1838, contains 435 pictures showing 489 different bird species. Audubon's paintings, such as that of the little blue heron in Figure 2, are known for their accuracy and remarkable detail as well as their beauty.

In Your Journal

List five observations that you can make about the little blue heron in Audubon's painting, such as the shape of its bill and the pattern of color on its body. Then describe the heron's environment.

In Figure 3, you can see that a contour feather consists of a central shaft and many hairlike projections, called barbs, that are arranged parallel to each other. If you examined a contour feather in the Discover activity, you know that you can "unzip" its flat surface by pulling apart the barbs. When birds fly, their feathers sometimes become "unzipped." To keep their flight feathers in good condition, birds often pull the feathers through their bills in an action called preening. Preening "zips" the barbs back together again, smoothing the ruffled feathers.

INTEGRATING PHYSICS In addition to contour feathers, birds have short, fluffy **down feathers** that are specialized to trap heat and keep the bird warm. Down feathers are found right next to a bird's skin, at the base of contour feathers. Down feathers are soft and flexible, unlike contour feathers. Down feathers mingle and overlap, trapping air. Air is a good **insulator**—a material that does not conduct heat well and therefore helps prevent it from escaping. By trapping a blanket of warm air next to the bird's skin, down feathers slow the rate at which the skin loses heat. In effect, down feathers cover a bird in lightweight long underwear.

✓ *Checkpoint* *Why do you think quilts and jackets are often stuffed with down feathers?*

Food and Body Temperature

Birds have no teeth. To capture, grip, and handle food, birds primarily use their bills. Each species of bird has a bill shaped to help it feed quickly and efficiently. For example, the pointy, curved bill of a hawk acts like a meathook. A hawk holds its prey with its claws and uses its sharp bill to pull off bits of flesh. In contrast, the straight, sharp bill of a woodpecker is a tool for chipping into wood. When a woodpecker chisels a hole in a tree and finds a tasty insect, the woodpecker spears the insect with its long, barbed tongue.

After a bird eats its food, digestion begins. Each organ in a bird's digestive system is adapted to process food. Many birds have an internal storage tank, or **crop,** that allows them to store food inside the body after swallowing it. Find the crop in *Exploring a Bird.* The crop is connected to the stomach.

Figure 3 Birds are the only animals that have feathers. **A.** Down feathers act as insulation to trap warmth next to a bird's body. **B.** Contour feathers, like this one from a Steller's jay, give a bird its shape and help it to fly.
Observing Where do you see down feathers and contour feathers on the family of Emperor geese above?

The first part of the stomach is long and has thin walls. Here food is bathed in chemicals that begin to break it down. Then the partially digested food moves to a thick-walled, muscular part of the stomach called the **gizzard,** which squeezes and grinds the partially digested food. Remember that birds do not have teeth—their gizzard performs the grinding function of teeth. The gizzard may contain small stones that the bird has swallowed. These stones help with the grinding by rubbing against the food and crushing it.

EXPLORING *a Bird*

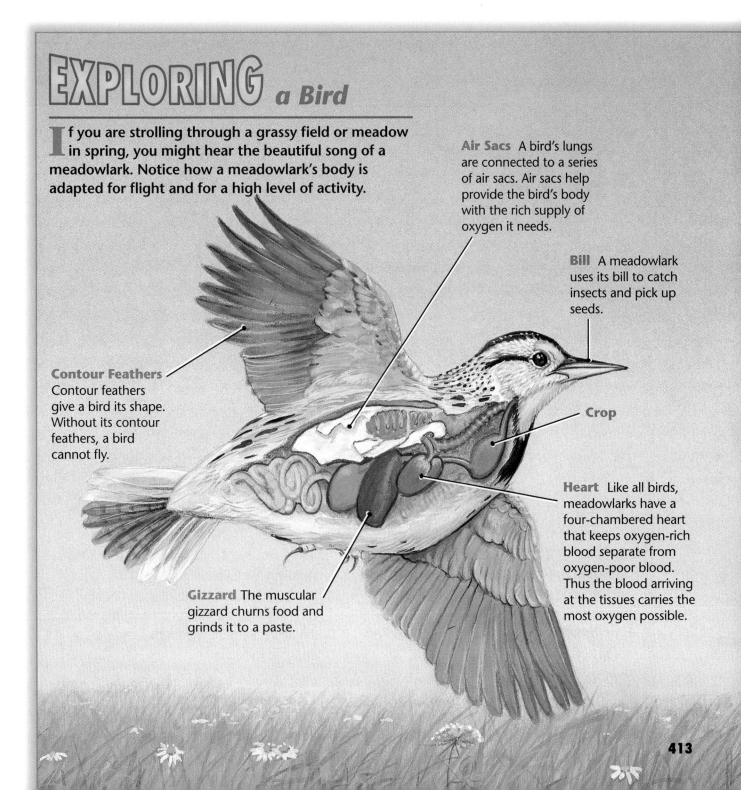

If you are strolling through a grassy field or meadow in spring, you might hear the beautiful song of a meadowlark. Notice how a meadowlark's body is adapted for flight and for a high level of activity.

Air Sacs A bird's lungs are connected to a series of air sacs. Air sacs help provide the bird's body with the rich supply of oxygen it needs.

Bill A meadowlark uses its bill to catch insects and pick up seeds.

Contour Feathers Contour feathers give a bird its shape. Without its contour feathers, a bird cannot fly.

Crop

Heart Like all birds, meadowlarks have a four-chambered heart that keeps oxygen-rich blood separate from oxygen-poor blood. Thus the blood arriving at the tissues carries the most oxygen possible.

Gizzard The muscular gizzard churns food and grinds it to a paste.

413

Like all animals, birds use the food they eat for energy. Because birds are endotherms, they need a lot of energy to maintain their body temperature. It also takes an enormous amount of energy to power the muscles used in flight. Each day an average bird eats food equal to about a quarter of its body weight. When people say, "You're eating like a bird," they usually mean that you're eating very little. But if you were actually eating as a bird does, you would be eating huge meals. You might eat 100 hamburger patties in one day!

Drawing Conclusions

LOOKING AT AN OWL'S LEFTOVERS

In this lab, you will gather evidence and draw conclusions about an owl's diet.

Problem

What can you learn about owls' diets from studying the pellets that they cough up?

Materials

owl pellet   hand lens   dissecting needle
metric ruler   forceps

Procedure

1. An owl pellet is a collection of undigested materials that an owl coughs up after a meal. Write a hypothesis describing what items you expect an owl pellet to contain. List the reasons for your hypothesis.
2. Use a hand lens to observe the outside of an owl pellet. Record your observations.

3. Use one hand to grasp the owl pellet with forceps. Hold a dissecting needle in your other hand, and use it to gently separate the pellet into pieces. **CAUTION:** *Dissecting needles are sharp. Never cut material toward you; always cut away from your body.*
4. Using the forceps and dissecting needle, carefully separate the bones from the rest of the pellet. Remove any fur that might be attached to bones.

Delivering Oxygen to Cells

Cells must receive plenty of oxygen to release the energy contained in food. Flying requires much energy. Therefore, birds need a highly efficient way to get oxygen into their body and to their cells. Birds have a system of air sacs in their body that connects to the lungs. The air sacs enable birds to extract much more oxygen from each breath of air than other animals can.

The circulatory system of a bird is also efficient at getting oxygen to the cells. Unlike amphibians and most reptiles,

Shrew	House mouse	Meadow vole	Mole	Rat

Upper jaw has at least 18 teeth; teeth are brown. Skull length is 23 mm or less.	Upper jaw has 2 biting teeth and extends past lower jaw. Skull length is 22 mm or less.	Upper jaw has 2 biting teeth that are smooth, not grooved. Skull length is more than 23 mm.	Upper jaw has at least 18 teeth. Skull length is 23 mm or more.	Upper jaw has 2 biting teeth. Upper jaw extends past lower jaw. Skull length is 22 mm or more.

5. Group similar bones together in separate piles. Observe the skulls, and draw them. Record the number of skulls, their length, and the number, shape, and color of the teeth.

6. Use the chart on this page to determine what kinds of skulls you found. If any skulls do not match the chart exactly, record which animal the skulls resemble most.

7. Try to fit together any of the remaining bones to form complete or partial skeletons. Sketch your results.

8. Wash your hands thoroughly with soap when you are finished.

Analyze and Conclude

1. How many animals' remains were in the pellet? What data led you to that conclusion?

2. Combine your results with those of your classmates. Which three animals were eaten most frequently? How do these results compare to your hypothesis?

3. Owls cough up about two pellets a day. Based on your class's data, what can you conclude about the number of animals an owl might eat in one month?

4. **Think About It** In this lab, you were able to examine only the part of the owl's diet that it did not digest. How might this fact affect your confidence in the conclusions you reached?

Design an Experiment

Design a study that might tell you how an owl's diet varies at different times of the year. Give an example of a conclusion you might expect to draw from such a study.

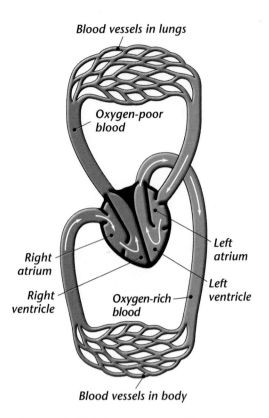

Blood vessels in lungs

Oxygen-poor blood

Right atrium

Right ventricle

Oxygen-rich blood

Left atrium

Left ventricle

Blood vessels in body

Figure 4 Birds have hearts with four chambers. Notice how the left side of the heart is completely separate from the right side. This separation prevents oxygen-rich blood from mixing with oxygen-poor blood.
Comparing and Contrasting
Contrast a bird's circulatory system with that of an amphibian, as shown on page 390, Figure 14. How do the circulatory systems differ?

whose hearts have three chambers, birds have hearts with four chambers—two atria and two ventricles. Trace the path of blood through a bird's two-loop circulatory system in Figure 4. The right side of a bird's heart pumps blood to the lungs, where the blood picks up oxygen. Oxygen-rich blood then returns to the left side of the heart, which pumps it to the rest of the body. The advantage of a four-chambered heart is that there is no mixing of oxygen-rich and oxygen-poor blood. Therefore, blood that arrives in the body's tissues has plenty of oxygen.

Nervous System and Senses

In order to fly, birds must have very quick reactions. To appreciate why, imagine how quickly you would have to react if you were a sparrow trying to land safely on a tree branch. You approach the tree headfirst, diving into a maze of tree branches. As you approach, you only have an instant to find a place where you can land safely and avoid crashing into those branches. If birds had slow reactions, they would not live very long.

A bird can react so quickly because of its well-developed brain and finely tuned senses of sight and hearing. The brain of a bird controls such complex activities as flying, singing, and finding food. Most birds have keener eyesight than humans. A flying vulture, for example, can spot food on the ground from a height of more than one and a half kilometers. Some birds have excellent hearing, too. How could keen hearing help an owl search for prey in a dark forest?

Reproducing and Caring for Young

Like reptiles, birds have internal fertilization and lay eggs. Bird eggs are similar to reptile eggs, except that their shells are harder. In most bird species, the female lays the eggs in a nest that has been prepared by one or both parents.

Bird eggs will only develop at a temperature close to the body temperature of the parent bird. A parent bird usually incubates the eggs by sitting on them to keep them warm. In some species, incubating the eggs is the job of one parent. Female robins, for example, incubate their delicate blue eggs. In other species, such as pigeons, the parents take turns incubating the eggs.

Birds differ in the length of time that it takes for their chicks to develop until hatching. Sparrow eggs take only about 12 days. Chicken eggs take about 21 days, and albatross eggs take about 80 days. In general, the larger the bird species, the longer its incubation time.

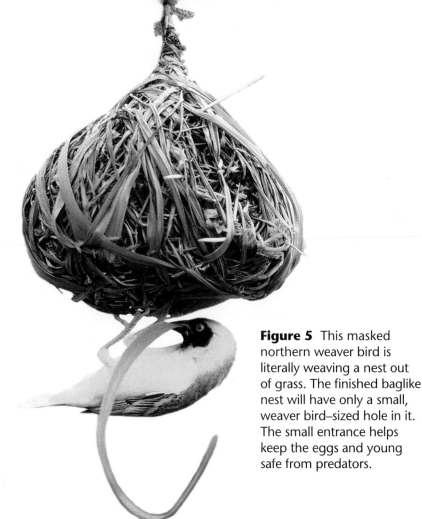

Figure 5 This masked northern weaver bird is literally weaving a nest out of grass. The finished baglike nest will have only a small, weaver bird–sized hole in it. The small entrance helps keep the eggs and young safe from predators.

When it is ready to hatch, a chick pecks its way out of the eggshell. Some newly hatched chicks, such as bluebirds and robins, are featherless, blind, and so weak they can barely lift their heads to beg for food. Other chicks, such as ducks, chickens, and pheasants, are covered with down and can run about soon after they have hatched. Most parent birds feed and protect their young at least until they are able to fly.

☑ *Checkpoint* *How do bird eggs differ from reptile eggs?*

Diversity of Birds

With almost 10,000 species, birds are the most diverse land-dwelling vertebrates. **In addition to adaptations for flight, birds have adaptations—such as the shapes of their legs, claws, and bills—for living in widely diverse environments.** For example, the long legs and toes of wading birds, such as herons and cranes, make wading easy, while the toes of perching birds, such as goldfinches and mockingbirds, can automatically lock onto a branch or other perch. The bills of ducks enable them to filter tiny plants and animals from water. Birds also have adaptations for flying, finding mates, and caring for their young. You can see a variety of bird adaptations in *Exploring Birds* on the next page.

EXPLORING Birds

Every bird has adaptations that help it live in its environment. Note how the bill and feet of each of these birds are adapted to help the bird survive.

▲ Bee-eaters
This rainbow bee-eater feeds on bees and other insects, which it catches as it flies. Bee-eaters, which are found in Africa, Europe, Australia, and Asia, help control insect pests such as locusts.

▲ Long-Legged Waders
The roseate spoonbill is found in the southern United States and throughout much of South America. The spoonbill catches small animals by sweeping its long, flattened bill back and forth underwater.

▲ Woodpeckers
The pileated woodpecker is the largest woodpecker in North America—adults average about 44 centimeters in length. This woodpecker feeds on insects it finds in holes it has chiseled into trees.

Ostriches
The ostrich, found in Africa, is the largest living bird. It cannot fly, but it can run at speeds greater than 60 kilometers per hour. Its speed helps it escape from predators. ▼

Birds of Prey
The American kestrel, a small falcon, catches its food by hovering in the air and scanning the ground. When it sees prey, such as an insect, the kestrel swoops down and grabs it. Kestrels are found worldwide.
▼

Owls are predators that hunt mostly at night. Sharp vision and keen hearing help owls find prey in the darkness. Razor-sharp claws and great strength allow larger owls, like this eagle owl, to prey on animals as large as deer.

Why Birds Are Important

A walk through the woods or a park would be dull without birds. You wouldn't hear their musical songs, and you wouldn't see them flitting gracefully from tree to tree. But people benefit from birds in practical ways, too. Birds and their eggs provide food, while feathers are used to stuff pillows and clothing.

 INTEGRATING ENVIRONMENTAL SCIENCE Birds also play an important role in the environment. Nectar-eating birds, like hummingbirds, carry pollen from one flower to another, thus enabling some flowers to reproduce. Seed-eating birds, like painted buntings, carry the seeds of plants to new places. This happens when the birds eat the fruits or seeds of a plant, fly to a new location, and then eliminate some of the seeds in digestive wastes. In addition, birds are some of the chief predators of pest animals. Hawks and owls eat many rats and mice, while many perching birds feed on insect pests.

▲ **Perching Birds**
There are over 5,000 species of perching birds. They represent more than half of all the bird species in the world. The painted bunting, a seed-eating bird, lives in the southern United States and northern Mexico.

Section 1 Review

1. What characteristics do modern birds share with reptiles? How are birds different from reptiles?
2. Choose two different bird species and describe how they are adapted to obtain food in their environment.
3. Predict how the size of crop harvests might be affected if all birds disappeared from Earth.
4. **Thinking Critically Comparing and Contrasting** Compare contour feathers with down feathers, noting both similarities and differences.

Check Your Progress

CHAPTER PROJECT

By now you should have set up your bird feeder. As you begin making observations, use a field guide to identify the species of birds. Count and record the number of each species that appears. Also observe the birds' behaviors. How long do birds stay at the feeder? How do birds respond to other birds and mammals? Look for signs that some birds are trying to dominate others.

Teeth

Endotherms need a lot of energy to maintain their body temperature, and that energy comes from food. Mammals' teeth are adapted to chew their food, breaking it into small bits that make digestion easier. Unlike reptiles and fishes, whose teeth usually all have the same shape, most mammals have teeth with four different shapes. **Incisors** are flat-edged teeth used to bite off and cut parts of food. **Canines** are sharply pointed teeth that stab food and tear into it. **Premolars** and **molars** grind and shred food into tiny bits.

The size, shape, and hardness of a mammal's teeth reflect its diet. For example, the canines of carnivores are especially large and sharp. Large carnivores, such as lions and tigers, use their canines as meat hooks that securely hold the prey while the carnivore kills it. The molars of herbivores, such as deer and woodchucks, have upper surfaces that are broad and flat—ideal for grinding and mashing plants.

Getting Oxygen to Cells

To release energy, food molecules must combine with oxygen inside cells. Therefore, a mammal needs an efficient way to get oxygen into the body and to the cells that need it.

Like reptiles and birds, all mammals breathe with lungs—even mammals such as whales that live in the ocean. Mammals breathe in and out because of the combined action of rib muscles and a large muscle called the **diaphragm** located at the bottom of the chest. The lungs have a huge, moist surface area where oxygen can dissolve and then move into the bloodstream.

Like birds, mammals have a four-chambered heart and a two-loop circulation. One loop pumps oxygen-poor blood from the heart to the lungs and then back to the heart. The second loop pumps oxygen-rich blood from the heart to the tissues of the mammal's body, and then back to the heart.

Figure 9 Lions have sharp, pointed teeth. Note the especially long canine teeth.
Inferring What kind of diet do lions eat?

☑ *Checkpoint* *How do mammals take air into their bodies?*

Nervous System and Senses

The nervous system and senses of an animal receive information about its environment and coordinate the animal's movements. The brains of mammals enable them to learn, remember, and behave in complex ways. Squirrels, for example, feed on

nuts. In order to do this, they must crack the nutshell to get to the meat inside. Squirrels learn to use different methods to crack different kinds of nuts, depending on where the weak points in each kind of shell are located.

The senses of mammals are highly developed and adapted for the ways that individual species live. Tarsiers, which are active at night, have huge eyes that enable them to see in the dark. Humans, monkeys, gorillas, and chimpanzees are able to see objects in color. This ability is extremely useful because these mammals are most active during the day when colors are visible.

Most mammals hear well. Bats even use their sense of hearing to navigate. Bats make high-pitched squeaks that bounce off objects. The echoes give bats information about the shapes of objects around them and about how far away the objects are. Bats use their hearing to fly at night and to capture flying insects.

Most mammals have highly developed senses of smell. Many mammals, including dogs and cats, use smell to track their prey. By detecting the scent of an approaching predator, antelopes use their sense of smell to protect themselves.

Movement

One function of a mammal's nervous system is to direct and coordinate complex movement. No other group of vertebrates can move in as many different ways as mammals can. Like most mammals, camels and leopards have four limbs and can walk and run. Other four-limbed mammals have specialized ways of moving. For example, kangaroos hop, gibbons swing by their arms from branch to branch, and flying squirrels glide down from high perches. Moles use their powerful front limbs to burrow through the soil. Bats, in contrast, are adapted to fly through the air—their front limbs are wings. Whales, dolphins, and other sea mammals have no hind limbs—their front limbs are flippers adapted for swimming in water.

Classifying

Unlike humans, birds and bats both fly. Does this mean that bats are more closely related to birds than to humans? Use the diagrams below to find out. The diagrams show the front-limb bones of a bird, a bat, and a human. Examine them carefully, noting similarities and differences. Then decide which two animals are more closely related. Give evidence to support your classification.

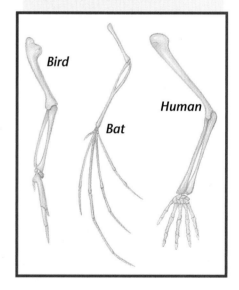

Bird

Bat

Human

Figure 10 Mammals, like these springboks, have large brains. A springbok's brain processes complex information about its environment and then quickly decides on an appropriate action.

Figure 11 This young giraffe is feeding on milk produced by its mother, as do all young mammals.

Reproducing and Caring for Young

Like reptiles and birds, mammals have internal fertilization. Although a few kinds of mammals lay shelled eggs, the young of most mammals develop within their mothers' bodies and are never enclosed in an eggshell. All mammals, even those that lay eggs, feed their young with milk produced in **mammary glands.** In fact, the word *mammal* comes from the term *mammary.*

Young mammals are usually quite helpless for a long time after being born. Many are born without a coat of insulating fur. Their eyes are often sealed and may not open for weeks. For example, black bear cubs are surprisingly tiny when they are born. The blind, nearly hairless cubs have a mass of only 240 to 330 grams—about as small as a grapefruit. The mass of an adult black bear, in contrast, ranges from about 120 to 150 kilograms—about 500 times as large as a newborn cub!

Young mammals usually stay with their mother or both parents for an extended time. After black bear cubs learn to walk, they follow their mother about for the next year, learning how to be a bear. They learn things that are important to their survival, such as which mushrooms and berries are good to eat and how to rip apart a rotten log and find good-tasting grubs within it. During the winter, when black bears go through a period of inactivity, the young bears stay with their mother. The following spring, she will usually force them to live independently.

Section 3 Review

1. List five characteristics that all mammals share.
2. Name three ways in which mammals are similar to birds. Then list three ways in which they are different.
3. Relate the shape of any mammal's teeth to its diet.
4. Explain how a keen sense of hearing is an advantage to a bat.
5. **Thinking Critically Making Generalizations** What characteristics enable mammals to live in colder environments than reptiles can?

Science at Home

Mammals' Milk With a family member, examine the nutrition facts listed on a container of whole milk. What types of nutrients does whole milk contain? Discuss why milk is an ideal source of food for young, growing mammals.

KEEPING WARM

Any time you wear a sweater or socks made of wool, you are using a mammalian adaptation to keep yourself warm. Suppose a manufacturer claims that its wool socks keep your feet as warm when the socks are wet as when they are dry. In this investigation, you will test that claim.

Problem

Do wool products provide insulation from the cold? How well does wool insulate when it is wet?

Skills Focus

controlling variables, interpreting data

Materials

tap water, hot
beaker, 1 L
clock or watch
a pair of wool socks
tap water, room temperature
3 containers, 250 mL, with lids
scissors
3 thermometers
graph paper

Procedure

1. Put one container into a dry woolen sock. Soak a second sock with water at room temperature, wring it out so it's not dripping, and then slide the second container into the wet sock. Both containers should stand upright. Leave the third container uncovered.
2. Create a data table in your notebook, listing the containers in the first column. Provide four more columns in which to record the water temperatures during the experiment.

3. Use scissors to carefully cut a small "X" in the center of each lid. Make the X just large enough for a thermometer to pass through.
4. Fill a beaker with about 800 mL of hot tap water. Then pour hot water nearly to the top of each of the three containers. **CAUTION:** *Avoid spilling hot water on yourself or others.*
5. Place a lid on each of the containers, and insert a thermometer into the water through the hole in each lid. Gather the socks around the thermometers above the first two containers so that the containers are completely covered.
6. Immediately measure the temperature of the water in each container, and record it in your data table. Take temperature readings every 5 minutes for at least 15 minutes.

Analyze and Conclude

1. Graph your results using a different color to represent each container. Graph time in minutes on the horizontal axis and temperature on the vertical axis.
2. Compare the temperature changes in the three containers. Relate your findings to the insulation characteristics of mammal skin coverings.
3. **Apply** Suppose an ad for wool gloves claims that the gloves keep you warm even if they get wet. Do your findings support this claim? Why or why not?

Design an Experiment

Design an experiment to compare how wool's insulating properties compare with those of other natural materials (such as cotton) or manufactured materials (such as acrylic). Obtain your teacher's approval before conducting your experiment.

Animals and Medical Research

In laboratories around the world, scientists search for cures for cancer, AIDS, and other diseases. Scientists use millions of animals each year in research—mostly to test drugs and surgical procedures. Finding treatments could save millions of human lives. However, these experiments can hurt and even kill animals.

The Issues

Why Is Animal Testing Done? If you have ever used an antibiotic or other medicine, animal testing has helped you. The United States Food and Drug Administration requires that new medicines be tested on research animals before they can be used by humans. Through testing, researchers can learn whether a drug works and what doses are safe. Because of animal research, many serious diseases can now be treated or prevented. New treatments for AIDS, cancer, and Alzheimer's disease are also likely to depend on animal testing.

Which Animals Are Used for Testing? Most often mice, rats, and other small mammals are used. These animals reproduce rapidly, so scientists can study many generations in a year. Since apes and monkeys are similar to humans in many ways, they are often used to test new treatments for serious diseases. In other cases, researchers use animals that naturally get diseases common to humans. Cocker spaniels, for example, often develop glaucoma, an eye disease that can cause blindness. Surgeons may test new surgical treatments for the disease on cocker spaniels.

What Happens to Research Animals? In a typical laboratory experiment, a group of animals will first be infected with a disease. Then they will be given a drug to see if it can fight off the disease. In many cases, the animals suffer, and some die. Some people are concerned that laboratory animals do not receive proper care.

What Are the Alternatives? Other testing methods do exist. For example, in some cases, scientists can use computer models to test drugs or surgical treatments. Another testing method is to mix drugs with animal cells grown in petri dishes. Unfortunately, neither computer models nor cell experiments are as useful as tests on living animals.

You Decide

1. Identify the Problem

In a sentence, describe the controversy over using animals in medical research.

2. Analyze the Options

Review the different positions. Is animal testing acceptable? Is it acceptable for some animals but not for others? Is animal research never acceptable? List the benefits and drawbacks of each option.

3. Find a Solution

Suppose you are a scientist who has found a possible cure for a type of cancer. The drug needs to be tested on research animals first, but you know that testing could harm the animals. What would you do? Support your opinion with sound reasons.

SECTION
4 Diversity of Mammals

DISCOVER ··· ACTIVITY

How Is a Thumb Useful?

1. Tape the thumb of your writing hand to your palm so that you cannot move your thumb. The tape should keep your thumb from moving but allow your other fingers to move freely.

2. Pick up a pencil with the taped hand and try to write your name.

3. Keep the tape on for 5 minutes. During that time, try to use your taped hand to do such everyday activities as lifting a book, turning the pages, and untying and retying your shoes.

4. Remove the tape and repeat all the activities you tried to do when your thumb was taped. Observe the position and action of your thumb and other fingers as you perform each activity.

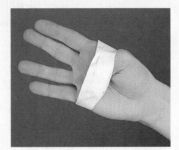

Think It Over

Inferring Humans, chimpanzees, and gorillas all have thumbs that can touch the other four fingers. What advantage does that kind of thumb give to the animal?

How is a koala similar to a panda? Both are furry, cuddly-looking mammals that eat leaves. How is a koala different from a panda? Surprisingly, koalas and pandas belong to very different groups of mammals—koalas are marsupials, and pandas are placental mammals. **Members of the three groups of mammals—monotremes, marsupials, and placental mammals—are classified on the basis of how their young develop.**

GUIDE FOR READING

◆ What characteristic is used to classify mammals into three groups?

Reading Tip As you read this section, write a definition in your own words for each new science term.

Giant panda (left) and koala (right)

Figure 12 The spiny anteater, left, and the duck-billed platypus, right, could share the "Weirdest Mammal" award. Both are monotremes, the only mammals whose young hatch from eggs.

Monotremes

If you held a "Weirdest Mammal in the World" contest, two main contenders would be spiny anteaters and duck-billed platypuses. There are two species of spiny anteaters and only one species of duck-billed platypus, all living in Australia and New Guinea. These are the only species of monotremes that are alive today. **Monotremes** are mammals that lay eggs.

Spiny Anteaters These monotremes look like pincushions with long noses. They have sharp spines scattered throughout their brown hair. As their name implies, spiny anteaters eat ants, which they dig up with their powerful claws.

A female spiny anteater lays one to three leathery-shelled eggs directly into the pouch on her belly. After the young hatch, still in the pouch, they drink milk that seeps out of pores on the mother's skin. They stay in the pouch until they are six to eight weeks old, when their spines start to irritate the mother anteater, and she scratches them out of her pouch.

Duck-billed Platypuses The duck-billed platypus has webbed feet and a bill, but it also has fur and feeds its young with milk. Platypuses, which live in the water, construct a maze of tunnels in muddy banks. The female lays her eggs in an underground nest. The eggs hatch about two weeks later. After they hatch, the tiny offspring feed by lapping at the milk that oozes onto the fur of their mother's belly.

Marsupials

Koalas, kangaroos, wallabies, and opossums are some of the better-known marsupials. **Marsupials** are mammals whose young are born alive, but at an early stage of development, and they usually continue to develop in a pouch on their mother's body.

Marsupials were once widespread, but today they are found mostly in South America, Australia, and New Guinea. Opossums are the only marsupials found in North America.

Marsupials have a very short **gestation period,** the length of time between fertilization and birth. Opossums, for example, have a gestation period of only about 13 days. Newborn marsupials are tiny—the newborns of one opossum species are only about 10 millimeters long! When they are born, marsupials are blind, hairless, and pink. They crawl along the wet fur of their mother's belly until they reach her pouch. Once inside, they find one of her nipples and attach to it. They remain in the pouch at least until they have grown enough to peer out of the pouch opening.

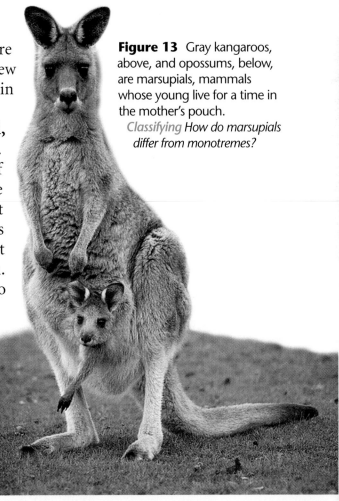

Figure 13 Gray kangaroos, above, and opossums, below, are marsupials, mammals whose young live for a time in the mother's pouch.
Classifying How do marsupials differ from monotremes?

Kangaroos The largest marsupials are kangaroos, which are found in Australia and nearby islands. Some male kangaroos are over 2 meters tall—taller than most humans. Kangaroos have powerful hind legs for jumping and long tails that help them keep their balance. A female kangaroo gives birth to only one baby, called a joey, at a time. Kangaroos are herbivores, so they eat foods such as leaves and grasses.

Opossums The common opossum is an omnivore that comes out of its nest at dusk to search for fruits, plants, insects, or other small animals to eat. Opossums are good climbers. They can grasp branches with their long tails. If a predator attacks it, an opossum will often "play dead"—its body becomes limp, its mouth gapes open, and its tongue lolls out of its mouth. Female opossums may give birth to 21 young at a time, but most female opossums have only 13 nipples. The first 13 young opossums that get into the pouch and attach to nipples are the only ones that survive.

☑ *Checkpoint* *What do the young of marsupials do immediately after they are born?*

Placental Mammals

Unlike a monotreme or a marsupial, a **placental mammal** develops inside its mother's body until its body systems can function independently. In *Exploring Placental Mammals* on the next page, you can see some members of this group.

EXPLORING *Placental Mammals*

From tiny moles to huge elephants, placental mammals exhibit a great variety of size and body form. Note how each group is adapted for obtaining food or for living in a particular environment.

▲ Rabbits and Hares
Leaping mammals like this black-tailed jack rabbit have long hind legs specialized for spectacular jumps. Rabbits and hares have long, curved incisors for gnawing.

▲ Insect-eaters
Star-nosed moles and their relatives have sharp cutting surfaces on all of their teeth. Star-nosed moles spend much of their time in water searching for prey with their sensitive, tentacled snouts.

Flying Mammals ▲
Bats fly, but they are mammals, not birds. The wings of bats are made of a thin skin that stretches from their wrists to the tips of their long finger bones.

Rodents ▲
Rodents are gnawing mammals such as rats, beavers, squirrels, mice, and the North American porcupine shown here. Their teeth are adapted to grind down their food. The four incisors of most rodents keep growing throughout their lives but are constantly worn down by gnawing.

▲ Primates
This group of mammals with large brains includes humans, monkeys, and apes such as this chimpanzee. Many primates have opposable thumbs—thumbs that can touch the other four fingers. An opposable thumb makes the hand capable of complex movements, such as grasping and throwing.

▲ Hoofed Mammals
Mammals with hooves are divided into two groups—those with an even number of toes and those with an odd number of toes. Cows, deer, and pigs all have an even number of toes, while horses and zebras belong to the odd-numbered group.

▲ Toothless Mammals
Sloths, such as the one shown here, are toothless mammals, as are armadillos. Although a few members of this group have small teeth, most have none.

Carnivores ▶
This river otter belongs to the group known as carnivores, or meat eaters. Other mammals in this group include dogs, cats, raccoons, bears, weasels, and seals. Large canine teeth and toes with claws help carnivores catch and eat their prey.

Marine Mammals
Whales, manatees, and these Atlantic spotted dolphins are ocean-dwelling mammals that evolved from cowlike, land-dwelling ancestors. The bodies of marine mammals show no external trace of hind limbs, although hind limbs have been found in their fossilized ancestors. ▼

Mammals With Trunks ▲
Elephants' noses are long trunks that they use for collecting food and water.

Figure 14 Young mammals usually require much parental care. On a rocky slope in Alaska, this Dall's sheep, a placental mammal, keeps a close watch on her lamb.

The name of this group comes from the **placenta,** an organ in pregnant female mammals that passes materials between the mother and the developing embryo. Food and oxygen pass from the mother to her young through the placenta. Wastes pass from the young through the placenta to the mother, where they are eliminated by her body. The umbilical cord connects the young to the placenta. Most mammals, including humans, are placental mammals.

Placental mammals are classified into groups on the basis of characteristics such as how they eat and how their bodies are adapted for moving. For example, whales, dolphins, and porpoises all form one group of mammals that have adaptations for swimming. The mammals in the carnivore group, which includes cats, dogs, otters, and seals, are all predators that have enlarged canine teeth. Primates, which include monkeys, apes, and humans, all have large brains and eyes that face forward. In addition, the forelimbs of many primates have adaptations for grasping. For example, the human thumb can touch all four other fingers. As you learned if you did the Discover activity, it is difficult to grasp objects if you cannot use your thumb.

Placental mammals vary in the length of their gestation periods. Generally, the larger the placental mammal, the longer its gestation period. For example, African elephants are the largest land-dwelling placental mammals. The gestation period for an elephant averages about 21 months. A house mouse, on the other hand, gives birth after a gestation period of only about 20 days.

Section 4 Review

1. Explain the difference in the development of the young of monotremes, marsupials, and placental mammals.
2. What is the function of the placenta?
3. Describe the feeding adaptations of three groups of placental mammals.
4. **Thinking Critically** Inferring Many hoofed mammals feed in large groups, or herds. What advantage could this behavior have?

Check Your Progress

CHAPTER PROJECT

Continue to observe bird behavior at your bird feeder and record your observations in your notebook. Now is the time to plan your presentation. You may want to include the following information in your presentation: drawings of the different birds you observed, detailed descriptions of bird behaviors, and other interesting observations you made. (Hint: Prepare bar graphs to present numerical data, such as the number of times that different species visited the feeder.)

SECTION 1 Birds

Key Ideas

◆ Birds are endothermic vertebrates that have feathers and a four-chambered heart and lay eggs. Most birds can fly.

◆ Birds care for their young by keeping the eggs warm until hatching and by protecting the young at least until they can fly.

◆ Birds have adaptations, such as the shapes of their toes and bills, for living and obtaining food in different environments.

Key Terms

bird	down feather	crop
contour feather	insulator	gizzard

SECTION 2 The Physics of Bird Flight

INTEGRATING PHYSICS

Key Ideas

◆ Air flowing over the curved upper surface of a moving wing exerts less downward pressure than the upward pressure from the air flowing beneath the wing. The difference in pressure produces lift that causes the wing to rise.

◆ Birds fly by flapping, soaring, and gliding.

Key Term

lift

SECTION 3 What Is a Mammal?

Key Ideas

◆ Mammals are vertebrates that are endothermic, have skin covered with hair or fur, feed their young with milk from the mother's mammary glands, and have teeth of different shapes adapted to their diets.

◆ Mammals use a large muscle called the diaphragm to breathe. Mammals have a four-chambered heart and a two-loop circulation.

Key Terms

mammal	premolars	diaphragm
incisors	molars	mammary gland
canines		

SECTION 4 Diversity of Mammals

Key Ideas

◆ Mammals are classified into three groups on the basis of how their young develop. Monotremes lay eggs. Marsupials give birth to live young who continue to develop in the mother's pouch. The young of placental mammals develop more fully before birth than do the young of marsupials.

◆ Placental mammals are divided into groups on the basis of adaptations, such as those for feeding and moving.

Key Terms

monotreme
marsupial
gestation period
placental mammal
placenta

Organizing Information

Compare/Contrast Table Copy the table comparing mammal groups onto a separate sheet of paper. Complete it and add a title. (For more on compare/contrast tables, see the Skills Handbook.)

Characteristic	Monotremes	Marsupials	Placental Mammals
How Young Begin Life	a. ?	b. ?	c. ?
How Young Are Fed	milk from pores or slits on mother's skin	d. ?	e. ?
Example	f. ?	g. ?	h. ?

Reviewing Content

 For more review of key concepts, see the Interactive Student Tutorial CD-ROM.

Multiple Choice

Choose the letter of the best answer.

1. Which of these characteristics is found only in birds?
   a. scales
   b. wings
   c. feathers
   d. four-chambered heart

2. A four-chambered heart is an advantage because
   a. it keeps oxygen-rich and oxygen-poor blood separate.
   b. it allows oxygen-rich and oxygen-poor blood to mix.
   c. blood can move through it quickly.
   d. it slows the flow of blood.

3. What causes the lift that allows a bird's wing to rise?
   a. reduced air pressure beneath the wing
   b. reduced air pressure above the wing
   c. air that is not moving
   d. jet propulsion

4. Which muscle helps mammals move air into and out of their lungs?
   a. air muscle
   b. diaphragm
   c. placenta
   d. gestation

5. Kangaroos, koalas, and opossums are all
   a. monotremes.
   b. primates.
   c. marsupials.
   d. placental mammals.

True or False

If the statement is true, write true. If it is false, change the underlined word or words to make the statement true.

6. *Archaeopteryx* shows the link between birds and reptiles.

7. A bird's gizzard grinds food.

8. The slower air moves, the less pressure it exerts.

9. Fur and down feathers have a similar function.

10. Marsupials are mammals that lay eggs.

Checking Concepts

11. Explain how the skeleton of a bird is adapted for flight.

12. How is a bird's ability to fly related to the shape of its wings?

13. Explain how soaring and gliding birds such as vultures and eagles use air currents in their flight.

14. Contrast the structure and function of incisors and molars.

15. Identify and explain two ways in which mammals are adapted to live in cold climates.

16. How is a mammal's ability to move related to the function of its nervous system?

17. What is one way in which the bodies of dolphins are different from those of land mammals?

18. **Writing to Learn** You are a documentary filmmaker preparing to make a short film about spiny anteaters. First, think of a title for the film. Then plan two scenes that you would include in the film and write the narrator's script. Your scenes should show what the animals look like and what they do.

Thinking Critically

19. **Making Generalizations** What is the general relationship between whether an animal is an endotherm and whether it has a four-chambered heart? Relate this to the animal's need for energy.

20. **Comparing and Contrasting** Why do you think some scientists might consider monotremes to be a link between reptiles and mammals?

21. **Predicting** If a rodent were fed a diet consisting only of soft food that it did not need to gnaw, what might its front teeth look like after several months? Explain your prediction.

Applying Skills

The data table below shows the approximate gestation period of several mammals and the approximate length of time that those mammals care for their young after birth. Use the information in the table to answer Questions 22–24.

Mammal	Gestation Period	Time Spent Caring for Young After Birth
Deer mouse	0.75 month	1 month
Chimpanzee	8 months	24 months
Harp seal	11 months	0.75 month
Elephant	21 months	24 months
Bobcat	2 months	8 months

22. **Graphing** Decide which kind of graph would be best for showing the data in the table. Then construct two graphs—one for gestation period and the other for time spent caring for young.

23. **Interpreting Data** Which mammals in the table care for their young for the longest time? The shortest time?

24. **Drawing Conclusions** What seems to be the general relationship between the size of the mammal and the length of time for which it cares for its young? Which animal is the exception to this pattern?

Performance ▽CHAPTER PROJECT Assessment

Present Your Project When you present your project, display the graphs, charts, and pictures you constructed. Be sure to describe the ways in which birds eat and interesting examples of bird behavior you observed.

Reflect and Record In your journal, analyze how successful the project was. Was the bird feeder located in a good place for attracting and observing birds? Did many birds come to the feeder—if not, why might this have happened? What are the advantages and limitations of using field guides for identifying birds?

Test Preparation

Use these questions to prepare for standardized tests.

Use the information to answer Questions 25–27.
Sankong wanted to find out which type of birdseed the birds in his neighborhood preferred—sunflower seeds or thistle. He set up two identical bird feeders on a tree in his backyard. He filled one feeder with sunflower seeds and the other with thistle. He spent one hour each day counting how many birds visited each feeder. The chart below shows the data he collected.

Type of Birdseed	Number of Birds			
	Day 1	Day 2	Day 3	Day 4
Sunflower Seeds	23	6	14	7
Thistle	19	9	16	5

25. What was the manipulated variable in Sankong's experiment?
   a. the day
   b. the number of birds
   c. the type of seed
   d. the type of feeder

26. What was the responding variable?
   a. the day   b. the number of birds
   c. the type of seed   d. the type of feeder

27. Based on the data, what conclusion could Sankong reach?
   a. The birds in the neighborhood preferred thistle to sunflower seeds.
   b. The birds in the neighborhood preferred sunflower seeds to thistle.
   c. The birds in the neighborhood showed no clear preference.
   d. Sankong's experiment was flawed.

CHAPTER 14 Animal Behavior

WEB ACTIVITY www.phschool.com

SECTION 1
Integrating Psychology
Why Do Animals Behave as They Do?

Discover **What Can You Observe About a Vertebrate's Behavior?**
Sharpen Your Skills **Predicting**
Try This **Line Them Up**
Skills Lab **Become a Learning Detective**

SECTION 2
Patterns of Behavior

Discover **What Can You Express Without Words?**
Try This **Worker Bees**
Real-World Lab **One for All**

Horn-butting is a common way for male antelopes, like these gemsboks in Africa, to compete for food, water, and mates.

Learning New Tricks

These male gemsboks are butting horns in a contest to see which one is stronger. The victorious gemsbok will become the leader of a herd consisting of himself and several females. Have you ever watched dogs or other animals interacting like the gemsboks on this page? If so, did you wonder whether the animals were playing or fighting? Were they born knowing how to act this way, or did they have to learn this behavior? These and other kinds of questions are part of the study of animal behavior.

As you learn in this chapter about animal behavior, you will have a chance to study an animal on your own. Your challenge will be to teach the animal a new behavior.

Your Goal To monitor an animal's learning process as you teach it a new skill.

To complete the project successfully, you must
◆ observe an animal to learn about its general behavior patterns
◆ choose one new skill for the animal to learn, and develop a plan to teach it the new skill
◆ monitor the animal's learning over a specific period of time
◆ follow the safety guidelines in Appendix A

Get Started Select an animal to train from those to which you have access. The animal could be a family pet, a neighbor's pet, or another animal approved by your teacher. Begin by observing the animal carefully to learn about its natural behaviors. Then think about an appropriate new skill to teach to the animal.

Check Your Progress You'll be working on this project as you study this chapter. To keep your project on track, look for Check Your Progress boxes at the following points.
Section 1 Review, page 448: Develop a day-by-day plan.
Section 2 Review, page 457: Make and record observations.

Present Your Project At the end of the chapter (page 461), your animal will be a star! As your animal demonstrates its new accomplishment, you will describe your training technique.

SECTION 1 Why Do Animals Behave as They Do?

DISCOVER • ACTIVITY

What Can You Observe About a Vertebrate's Behavior?

1. For a few minutes, carefully observe the behavior of a small vertebrate, such as a gerbil or a goldfish. Write down your observations.

2. Place some food near the animal and watch what the animal does.

3. If there are other animals in the cage or aquarium, observe how the animals interact—for example, do they fight, groom one another, or ignore one another?

4. Tap gently on the cage or aquarium and see how the animal reacts. Note any other events that seem to make the animal change its behavior (from resting to moving, for example).

Think It Over

Predicting What are some circumstances under which you might expect an animal's behavior to change suddenly?

GUIDE FOR READING

◆ What are the functions of most of an animal's behaviors?

◆ How does instinctive behavior compare with learned behavior?

Reading Tip Before you read, rewrite the headings in the section as *how, why,* or *what* questions. As you read, write answers to those questions.

A male anole—a kind of lizard—stands in a patch of sun. As another male approaches, the first anole begins to lower and raise its head and chest in a series of quick push-ups. From beneath its neck a dewlap, a bright red flap of skin, flares out and then collapses, over and over. The anoles stare at each other, looking like miniature dinosaurs about to do battle. The first anole seems to be saying, "This area belongs to me. You'll have to leave or fight!"

The push-ups, piercing stares, and dewlap displays are all behaviors that warn another male to go away.

Figure 1 These two anoles are displaying their dewlaps in a dispute over space.

442

coordina
to develc
    Anin
conditio

Conditi

leash, the
learned t
to conne
called **co**
stimulus
walk. An
Think of
The skun
smells aw
because t
rible spra
    Durir
performe
Figure 3,
stimulus

❶ Whe
or sme
saliva.
and th
salivati
usually
to othe
sound

An animal's **behavior** consists of all the actions it performs—for example, the things that it does to obtain food, avoid predators, and find a mate. To understand animals, it is important to know not only what their body structures are like, but also how and why they behave as they do. Like their body structures, the behaviors of animals are adaptations that have evolved over long periods of time.

Most behavior is a complicated process in which different parts of an animal's body work together. The first anole saw the second anole with his eyes and interpreted the sight with his brain. His brain and nervous system then directed his muscles to perform the push-up movement and to display his bright red dewlap.

Why Behavior Is Important

When an animal looks for food or hides to avoid a predator, it is obviously doing something that helps it stay alive. When animals search for mates and build nests for young, they are behaving in ways that help them reproduce. **Most behaviors help an animal survive or reproduce.**

As an example of a survival behavior, consider what happens when a water current carries a small crustacean to a hydra's tentacles. After stinging cells on the tentacles paralyze the prey, the tentacles bend, pulling the captured crustacean toward the hydra's mouth. At the same time, the hydra's mouth opens to receive the food. If the tentacles didn't pull the food toward the hydra's mouth, or if the mouth didn't open, then the hydra couldn't take the food into its body. If the hydra couldn't feed, it would die.

The small crustacean acted as a stimulus to the hydra. A **stimulus** (plural *stimuli*) is a signal that causes an organism to react in some way. The organism's reaction to the stimulus is called a **response**. The hydra responded to the crustacean by stinging it and then eating it. All animal behavior is caused by stimuli. Some stimuli come from an animal's external environment, while other stimuli, such as hunger, come from inside the animal's body. An animal's response may include external actions, internal changes (such as a faster heartbeat), or both.

☑ *Checkpoint* **Give an example of a stimulus to which a hydra would respond.**

Figure 2 When a hungry sea star finds a clam, the clam acts as a stimulus. The sea star's response is to approach the clam, grab the clam's shell with its tube feet, and open it. The sea star can then force its stomach inside the shell to consume the clam.
Applying Concepts How is this behavior important to the sea star's survival?

Sha...
Sk...

Predicti...

Hawks, wh
have short
necks, pre
Geese, wh
do not pre
When new
chicks see
they instin
down. As t
older, they
when they
a hawk, bu
crouch wh
goose's sha
older gull
when they
shaped like
type of lea
behavior sl

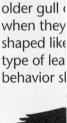

A

B

C

Real-World Lab

ONE FOR ALL

H ave you ever stopped to watch a group of busy ants? In this lab, you will find out what goes on in an ant colony.

Problem

How does an ant society operate?

Skills Focus

observing, inferring, posing questions

Materials

large glass jar	sandy soil	shallow pan
water	wire screen	sponge
20–30 ants	sugar	bread crumbs
wax pencil	black paper	tape
large, thick rubber band		forceps

Procedure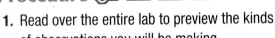

1. Read over the entire lab to preview the kinds of observations you will be making.
2. Mark the outside of a large jar with four evenly spaced vertical lines. Label the sections A, B, C, and D.
3. Fill the jar about three-fourths full with soil. Place the jar in a shallow pan of water to prevent any ants from escaping. Place a wet sponge in the jar as a water source.
4. Observe the condition of the soil, both on the surface and along the sides of the jar. Record your observations for each section.
5. Add the ants to the jar. Immediately cover the jar with the wire screen, using the rubber band to hold the screen firmly in place.
6. Observe the ants for 10 minutes. Look for differences among the adult ants. Look for eggs, larvae, and pupae. Examine both individual behavior and interactions.
7. Remove the screen, and add some bread crumbs and sugar to the jar. Close the cover. Observe for 10 more minutes.
8. Wrap black paper around the jar above the water line. Remove the paper only when making your observations.
9. Observe the ants every day for two weeks. Look at the soil as well, and always examine the food. If any food is moldy, use forceps to remove it. Place the moldy food in a plastic bag, seal the bag, and throw it away. Add more food as necessary, and keep the sponge moist. When you finish your observations, replace the paper.

Analyze and Conclude

1. Describe the various types of ants you saw. What evidence, if any, did you observe that different kinds of ants perform different tasks?
2. How do the different behaviors you observed contribute to the survival of the colony?
3. How did the soil change over the period of your observations? What caused those changes? How do you know?
4. **Apply** Based on this lab, what kinds of environmental conditions do you think ant colonies need to thrive outdoors?

Design an Experiment

Design an experiment to investigate how an ant colony responds to change. Obtain your teacher's approval before carrying out your experiment.

SECTION 1 — Why Do Animals Behave as They Do?

INTEGRATING PSYCHOLOGY

Key Ideas

◆ Most behaviors help an animal survive and reproduce. Examples include behaviors involved in obtaining food, avoiding predators, and finding a mate.

◆ An instinct is an inborn behavior pattern that the animal performs correctly the first time. Most behaviors of invertebrates are instinctive.

◆ Learning changes an animal's behavior as a result of experience. Some ways in which animals learn include conditioning, trial-and-error learning, and insight learning.

◆ Imprinting, in which very young animals learn to follow the first moving object they see, involves both instinct and learning.

Key Terms

behavior	conditioning
stimulus	trial-and-error learning
response	insight learning
instinct	artificial intelligence
learning	imprinting

SECTION 2 — Patterns of Behavior

Key Ideas

◆ Animals use aggression to compete for limited resources, such as food or shelter.

◆ Many animals establish territories from which they exclude other members of their species.

◆ Courtship behavior ensures that males and females of the same species recognize one another so that they can reproduce.

◆ There is usually some survival advantage to living in a group, such as cooperation in getting food and protection from danger.

◆ Animals use chemicals, sounds, body positions, and movements to communicate.

◆ Some animal behaviors occur in regular patterns. Circadian rhythms are one-day behavior cycles. Hibernation is a period of inactivity during winter.

◆ Some animals migrate to places where they can more easily find food, reproduce, or both.

Key Terms

aggression	circadian rhythm
territory	hibernation
courtship behavior	migration
society	

Organizing Information

Concept Map Copy the concept map below onto a separate sheet of paper. Then complete the map. (For more on concept maps, see the Skills Handbook.)

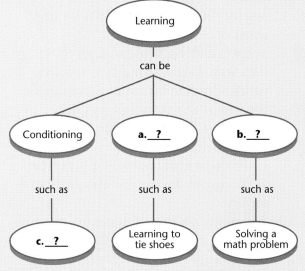

Reviewing Content

 For more review of key concepts, see the Interactive Student Tutorial CD-ROM.

Multiple Choice

Choose the letter of the best answer.

1. The scent of a female moth causes a male to fly toward her. The scent is an example of
   a. a response. b. a stimulus.
   c. aggression. d. insight learning.

2. If you could play the saxophone by instinct, you would
   a. play well the first time you tried.
   b. need someone to teach you.
   c. have to practice frequently.
   d. know how to play other instruments.

3. When a male and female falcon share an acrobatic flight display, they exhibit
   a. learning. b. imprinting.
   c. migration. d. courtship behavior.

4. Some squirrels sleep all day and are active all night. This is an example of
   a. migration. b. hibernation.
   c. circadian rhythm. d. aggression.

5. When a bird travels from its winter home in South America to New York, this is called
   a. learning. b. conditioning.
   c. migration. d. hibernation.

True or False

If the statement is true, write true. If it is false, change the underlined word or words to make the statement true.

6. A spider building a web exhibits <u>learned</u> behavior.

7. Every day after school, you take your dog for a walk. Lately, he greets your arrival with his leash in his mouth. Your dog's behavior is an example of <u>instinct</u>.

8. A <u>territory</u> is an area that an animal will fight to defend.

9. Closely related animals of the same species work together for the group's benefit in a <u>society</u>.

10. Salmon return to fresh water to reproduce. This is an example of <u>circadian rhythm</u>.

Checking Concepts

11. Explain how both instinct and learning are involved in imprinting.

12. Your German shepherd puppy has just shredded your favorite pair of sneakers. When you loudly scold him, he rolls over on his back. What kind of behavior are you exhibiting to the dog? What is the meaning of his response?

13. Explain how courtship and territorial behavior are related.

14. Because a highway has been constructed through a forest, many of the animals that once lived there have had to move to a different wooded area. Is their move an example of migration? Explain.

15. **Writing to Learn** After landing on a distant planet, you discover creatures who look something like humans but whose society is organized like that of honeybees. Write an interview with one creature, who explains the structure of the society and the roles of different members.

Thinking Critically

16. **Applying Concepts** Explain how a racehorse's ability to win races is a combination of inherited and learned characteristics.

17. **Problem Solving** A dog keeps jumping onto a sofa. Describe a procedure that the owner might use to train the dog not to do this. The procedure must not involve any pain or harm to the dog.

18. **Applying Concepts** Give an example of something that you have learned by insight learning. Explain how you made use of your past knowledge and experience in learning it.

19. **Predicting** Suppose that a disease caused a population of crickets to become deaf. How might the reproduction rate of the cricket population be affected? Explain.

Applying Skills

The toad in the pictures below caught a bee and then spit it out. Use the pictures to answer Questions 20–22.

20. **Inferring** Explain why the toad probably behaved as it did in picture B.
21. **Predicting** If another bee flies by, how will the toad probably behave? Why?
22. **Classifying** What type of learning will probably result from the toad's experience? Explain.

Present Your Project Now is your chance to explain—or demonstrate—what your trained animal can do and to describe your training plan. Obtain your teacher's permission before bringing an animal to class. If you cannot bring in the animal, you can show photographs or illustrations of the animal's training. Be sure to discuss any surprises or setbacks you experienced.

Reflect and Record In your journal, describe your success in training your animal. What did you discover about the animal's learning process? How could you have improved your training plan? What questions do you still have about your animal's behavior?

Test Preparation

Use these questions to prepare for standardized tests.

Use the information to answer Questions 23–25.
A scientist conducted an experiment to learn whether mice would learn to run a maze more quickly if they were given rewards. She set up two identical mazes. In one maze, cheese was placed at the end of the correct route through the maze. No cheese was placed in the second maze. The graph below shows the results.

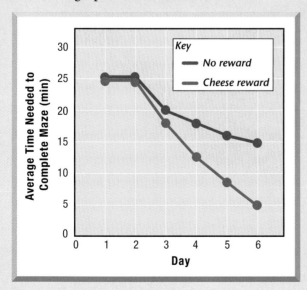

23. Based on the graph, which statement is true?
   a. Learning occurred more quickly when the mice received a reward.
   b. Learning occurred more slowly when the mice received a reward.
   c. The reward had no effect on how quickly the mice learned to run the maze.
   d. None of the mice learned to run the maze.

24. What was the manipulated variable in the experiment?
   a. the length of the maze
   b. the amount of time it took to run the maze
   c. the day
   d. whether or not a reward of cheese was given

25. What type of learning did the mice exhibit in the maze with the cheese reward?
   a. insight learning
   b. conditioning
   c. imprinting
   d. instinctive behavior

The Secret of Silk

What animal—

was a secret for thousands of years?

was smuggled across mountains in a hollow cane?

is good to eat, especially stir-fried with garlic and ginger?

is not really what its name says it is?

If you guessed that this amazing animal is the silkworm, you are right. The silk thread that this caterpillar spins is woven into silk cloth. For at least 4,000 years people have treasured silk.

Chinese legends say that in 2640 B.C., a Chinese empress accidentally dropped a silkworm cocoon in warm water and watched the thread unravel. She had discovered silk. But for thousands of years, the Chinese people kept the work of silkworms a secret. Death was the penalty for telling the secret.

Then, it is said, in about A.D. 550, two travelers from Persia visited China and returned to the West carrying silkworm eggs hidden in their hollow canes. Ever since then, the world has enjoyed the beauty of silk—its warmth, strength, softness, and shimmer.

Metamorphosis of the Silkworm

The silkworm is not really a worm; it's the larva of an insect—a moth named *Bombyx mori*. In its entire feeding period, this larva consumes about 20 times its own weight in mulberry leaves. The silkworm undergoes complete metamorphosis during its life.

1 The adult female moth lays 300 to 500 eggs, each the size of a pinhead. After about ten days at 27°C, the larvae—which people call silkworms—hatch from the eggs and begin to eat. Mulberry leaves are the insects' source of food.

2 For the next 40 to 45 days, the larvae consume great quantities of mulberry leaves. The silkworms molt each time their exoskeletons become too tight. After the last molting and feeding stage, the silkworms begin to build their cocoons.

3 To spin its cocoon, each silkworm produces two single strands from its two silk glands. Another pair of glands produces a sticky substance that binds the two strands together. The silkworm pushes this single strand out through a small tube in its head. Once in the air, the strand hardens and the silkworm winds the strand around itself in many layers to make a thick cocoon. The single silk strand may be as long as 900 meters—more than two laps around an Olympic track.

Science Activity

Examine a silkworm cocoon. After softening the cocoon in water, find the end of the strand of silk. Pull this strand, wind it onto an index card, and measure its length.

With a partner, design an experiment to compare the strength of the silk thread you just collected to that of cotton and/or nylon thread of the same weight or thickness.

◆ Develop a hypothesis about the strength of the threads.

◆ Decide on the setup you will use to test the threads.

◆ Check your safety plan with your teacher.

4 After 14 to 18 days, the adult moths emerge from the cocoons. The new moth does not eat or fly. It mates, the female lays eggs, and 2 to 3 days later both the male and female die.

The Silk Road

Long before the rest of the world learned how silk was made, the Chinese were trading this treasured fabric with people west of China. Merchants who bought and sold silk traveled along a system of hazardous routes that came to be known as the Silk Road. The Silk Road stretched 6,400 kilometers from Ch'ang-an in China to the Mediterranean Sea. Silk, furs, and spices traveled west toward Rome along the road. Gold, wool, glass, grapes, garlic, and walnuts moved east toward China.

Travel along the Silk Road was treacherous and difficult. For safety, traders traveled in caravans of many people and animals. Some kinds of pack animals were better equipped to handle certain parts of the journey than others. Camels, for instance, were well suited to the desert; they could go without drinking for several days and withstand most sandstorms. Yaks were often used in the high mountains.

The entire journey along the Silk Road could take years. Many people and animals died along the way. Very few individuals or caravans traveled the whole length of the Silk Road.

Silk fabric became highly prized in Rome. In fact, it was said that the first silk products to reach Rome after 50 B.C. were worth their weight in gold. The Chinese, of course, kept the secret of the silkworm and controlled silk production. They were pleased that the Romans thought that silk grew on trees. It was not until about A.D. 550 that the Romans learned the secret of silk.

In time, silk production spread around the world. The Silk Road, though, opened forever the exchange of goods and ideas between China and the West.

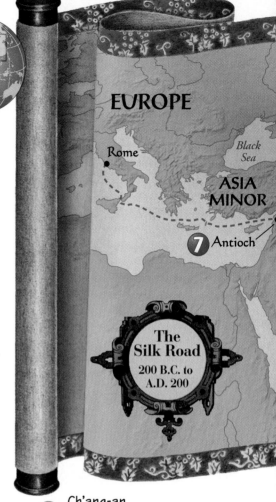

① Ch'ang-an
From Ch'ang-an in northern China, the Silk Road headed west along a corridor between the Nan Shan Mountains and the Gobi Desert.

② Dunhuang
At Dunhuang, in an oasis, or fertile green area, of the Gobi Desert, caravans took on rested pack animals. Beyond Dunhuang, the silk route split.

③ Takla Makan Desert
The desert is well named— Takla Makan means "Go in and you won't come out!" Most travelers avoided the scorching heat of the desert and journeyed along the edges of this great wasteland of sand.

Social Studies Activity

Suppose you are a merchant traveling from Dunhuang to Kashgar. You will be carrying silk, furs, and cinnamon to Kashgar where you'll trade for gold, garlic, and glass, which you will carry back to Dunhuang. Plan your route and hire a guide.

◆ Look at the map to find the distances and the physical features you will see on your journey.

◆ Explain why you chose the route you did.

◆ List the animals and supplies that you will take.

◆ Write a help-wanted ad for a guide to lead your caravan.

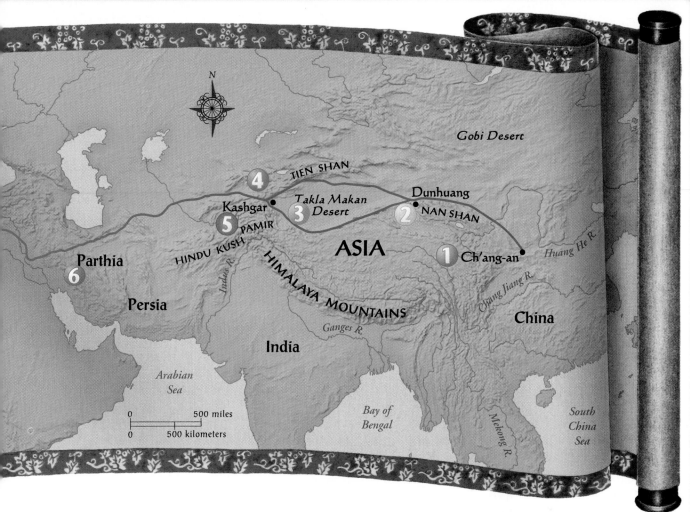

Gobi Desert

N

TIEN SHAN
④
Kashgar
⑤ PAMIR
③ Takla Makan
Desert
Dunhuang
② NAN SHAN

HINDU KUSH
Indus R.
HIMALAYA MOUNTAINS

ASIA
① Ch'ang-an
Huang He R.

Chang Jiang R.

China

Parthia
⑥

Persia

Ganges R.

India

Arabian
Sea

Bay of
Bengal

Mekong R.

South
China
Sea

0   500 miles
0   500 kilometers

④ **Kashgar**

The silk routes along the northern and southern edges of the Takla Makan Desert came together at Kashgar. The perilous part of the Silk Road was still ahead.

⑤ **Pamir Mountains**

Traveling west from Kashgar, caravans faced some of the highest mountains in the world. The towering Pamir Mountains are more than 6,000 meters high. Once traders crossed the mountains, though, travel on the Silk Road was less difficult. Traders journeyed west through Persia to cities located on the Mediterranean Sea.

⑥ **Parthia**

For a while, Parthian traders controlled part of the Silk Road. In 53 B.C., Rome was a mighty power around the Mediterranean Sea. That year when the Roman and Parthian armies were at battle, the Parthians suddenly turned to face their enemy and attacked with deadly arrows. Then, in the bright light of noon, the Parthians unrolled huge banners of gold-embroidered silk. The Romans were so dazzled by the brilliance that they surrendered.

⑦ **Antioch**

Trade flourished in Antioch, where silk was traded for gold. Ships carried silk and spices on the Mediterranean Sea from Antioch to Rome, Egypt, and Greece.

The Gift of Silk

A myth is a story handed down from past cultures—often to explain an event or natural phenomenon. Myths may be about gods and goddesses or about heroes.

The Yellow Emperor, Huang Di, who is mentioned in this Chinese myth, was a real person. Some stories say that he was the founder of the Chinese nation. He was thought to be a god who came to rule on Earth. Here the silkworm goddess appears to him at a victory celebration.

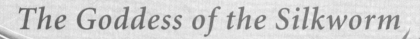

The Goddess of the Silkworm

A *GODDESS* descended from the heavens with a gift for the Yellow Emperor. Her body was covered with a horse's hide, and she presented two shining rolls of silk to the god. She was the "goddess of the silkworm," sometimes called the "lady with a horse's head." Long, long ago she had been a beautiful girl, but now a horse's skin grew over her body. If she pulled the two sides of the skin close to her body she became a silkworm with a horse's head, spinning a long, glittering thread of silk from her mouth. It is said she lived in a mulberry tree, producing silk day and night in the wild northern plain. This is her story.

Once in ancient times there lived a man, his daughter and their horse. Often the man had to travel, leaving his daughter alone at home to take care of the beast. And often the girl was lonely. One day, because she missed her father she teased the horse: "Dear long-nosed one, if you could bring my father home right how, I'd marry you and be your wife." At that the horse broke out of his harness. He galloped away and came quickly to the place where the master was doing business. The master, surprised to see his beast, grasped his mane and jumped up on his back. The horse stood mournfully staring in the direction he had come from, so the man decided there must be something amiss at home and hurried back.

When they arrived home, the daughter explained that she had only remarked that she missed her father and the horse had dashed off wildly. The man said nothing but was secretly pleased to own such a remarkable animal and fed him special sweet hay. But the horse would not touch it and whinnied and reared each time he saw the girl.

The man began to worry about the horse's strange behavior, and one day he said to the girl,

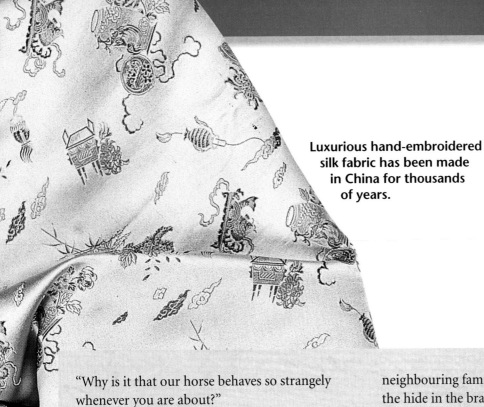

Luxurious hand-embroidered silk fabric has been made in China for thousands of years.

"Why is it that our horse behaves so strangely whenever you are about?"

So the young girl confessed the teasing remark she had made.

When he heard this the father was enraged, "For shame to say such a thing to an animal! No one must know of this! You will stay locked in the house!"

Now the man had always liked this horse, but he would not hear of its becoming his son-in-law. That night, to prevent any more trouble, he crept quietly into the stable with his bow and arrow and shot the horse through the heart. Then he skinned it and hung up the hide in the courtyard.

Next day, when the father was away, the girl ran out of the house to join some other children playing in the courtyard near the horse hide. When she saw it she kicked it angrily and said, "Dirty horse hide! What made you think such an ugly long-snouted creature as you could become my . . . ."

But before she could finish, the hide suddenly flew up and wrapped itself around her, swift as the wind, and carried her away out of sight. The other children watched dumbfounded; there was nothing they could do but wait to tell the old man when he arrived home.

Her father set out immediately in search of his daughter, but in vain. Some days later a neighbouring family found the girl wrapped up in the hide in the branches of a mulberry tree. She had turned into a wormlike creature spinning a long thread of shining silk from her horse-shaped head, spinning it round and round her in a soft cocoon.

Such is the story of the goddess of the silkworm. The Yellow Emperor was delighted to receive her exquisite gift of silk. . . . He ordered his official tailor, Bo Yu, to create new ceremonial robes and hats. And Lei Zu, the revered queen mother of gods and people, wife of the Emperor, began then to collect silkworms and grow them. And so it was that the Chinese people learned of silk.

—Yuan Ke, *Dragons and Dynasties*, translated by Kim Echlin and Nie Zhixiong

Language Arts Activity

What two details in the myth tell you that silkworms were important to the Chinese people?

The girl in the myth gets into trouble because she breaks her promise. Write a story of your own using the idea of a broken promise.

◆ Decide on the place, time, and main characters.
◆ Think about the events that will happen and how your story will conclude.

Mathematics

Counting on Caterpillars

Lai opened the door to the silkworm room. She was greeted by the loud sound of thousands of silkworms crunching on fresh leaves from mulberry trees. Lai enjoyed raising silkworms, but it was hard work. Over its lifetime, each silkworm eats about twenty times its own weight.

Lai had a chance to care for more silkworms. But first she had to figure out how many more she could raise. She now had 6,000 silkworms that ate the leaves from 125 mulberry trees. Should she have her parents buy another piece of land with another 100 mulberry trees? If she had 100 more trees, how many more silkworms could she feed?

Analyze. 125 trees can feed 6,000 silkworms. You want to know the number of silkworms 100 trees will feed. Write a proportion, using n to represent the number of silkworms.

Write the proportion.

$$\frac{\text{trees} \rightarrow}{\text{silkworms} \rightarrow} \quad \frac{125}{6{,}000} = \frac{100}{n} \quad \frac{\leftarrow \text{trees}}{\leftarrow \text{silkworms}}$$

Cross multiply. $\qquad 125 \times n = 6{,}000 \times 100$

Simplify. $\qquad\qquad 125n = 600{,}000$

Solve. $\qquad n = \dfrac{600{,}000}{125} \qquad n = 4{,}800$

Think about it. "Yes," she decided. She could raise 4,800 more silkworms!

▲ Silkworms are fed fresh mulberry leaves every four hours, around the clock.

Math Activity

Solve the following problems.

1. Lai's friend Cheng also raises silkworms. He buys mulberry leaves. If 20 sacks of leaves feed 12,000 silkworms a day, how many sacks of leaves will 9,600 silkworms eat per day?

2. When Lai's silkworms are ready to spin, she places them in trays. If 3 trays can hold 150 silkworms, how many trays does Lai use for her 6,000 silkworms?

3. A silkworm spins silk at a rate of about 30.4 centimeters per minute. (a) How many centimeters can it spin in an hour? (b) It takes a silkworm 60 hours to spin the entire cocoon. How many centimeters is that?

4. Lai's silk thread contributes to the creation of beautiful silk clothes. It takes the thread of 630 cocoons to make a blouse and the thread of 110 cocoons to make a tie. (a) If each of Lai's 6,000 silkworms produces a cocoon, how many blouses can be made from the thread? (b) How many ties can be made?

Tie It Together

Plan a Silk Festival

People use silk in many ways other than just to make fine clothing. Did you know that silk was used for parachutes during World War II? Or that some bicycle racers choose tires containing silk because they provide good traction? Today, silk is used for a variety of purposes, including:

◆ recreation: fishing lines and nets, bicycle tires;

◆ business: electrical insulations, typewriter and computer ribbons, surgical sutures;

◆ decoration: some silkscreen printing, artificial flowers

Work in small groups to learn about one of the ways that people have used silk in the past or are using it today. Devise an interesting way to share your project with the class, such as

◆ a booth to display or advertise a silk product;

◆ a skit in which you wear silk;

◆ a historical presentation on the uses of silk in other countries;

◆ a presentation about a process, such as silkscreen painting or silk flowers.

Ask volunteers to bring pictures or silk products to class. After rehearsing or reviewing your presentation, work with other groups to decide how to organize your Silk Festival.

▼ **Racers at the Tour de France often use tires containing silk on their bicycles.**

469

CHAPTER
15 Bones, Muscles, and Skin

WEB ACTIVITY
www.phschool.com

SECTION
1 _Integrating Health_ 🌐
Body Organization and Homeostasis

SECTION
2 **The Skeletal System**

SECTION
3 **The Muscular System**

Discover How Do You Lift Books?
Try This How Is a Book Organized?

Discover Hard as a Rock?
Try This Soft Bones?
Sharpen Your Skills Classifying
Science at Home Exercising Safely

Discover How Do Muscles Work?
Try This Get a Grip
Skills Lab A Look Beneath the Skin

On the Move

People are able to perform an amazing variety of movements. For example, a baseball player can swing a bat, a chef can twirl pizza dough, and an artist can mold clay into a sculpture. Behind every human movement, there's a complex interaction of bones, muscles, and other parts of the body.

In this chapter, you'll find out how bones and muscles work. And in this project, you'll take a close look at a simple movement, such as stretching a leg, bending an arm at the elbow, or another movement you choose.

Your Goal To make a working model that shows how bones and muscles interact to move the body in a specific way.

To complete this project you will
◆ select a specific movement, and identify all of the major bones, joints, and muscles that are involved
◆ design an accurate physical model of the movement
◆ explain how the bones and muscles make the movement possible
◆ follow the safety guidelines in Appendix A

Get Started Let all group members name a motion from a sport or other familiar activity that they'd like to investigate. If the motion is long or complicated, discuss how to simplify it for the project. Also consider what kind of model you'll make, such as a wood or cardboard cutout, clay structure, or computer animation. Then write up a plan for your teacher's approval.

Check Your Progress You'll be working on this project as you study this chapter. To keep your project on track, look for Check Your Progress boxes at the following points.
Section 1 Review, page 479: Choose a simple motion to analyze and sketch.
Section 3 Review, page 492: Create your working model.

Present Your Project At the end of the chapter (page 503), you'll demonstrate your working model.

For this baseball player to hit the ball, his bones and muscles must work together in a coordinated manner.

SECTION
4 **The Skin**

Discover **What Can You Observe About Skin?**
Try This **Sweaty Skin**
Real-World Lab **Sun Safety**
Science at Home **Protection From the Sun**

1 Body Organization and Homeostasis

DISCOVER • ACTIVITY

How Do You Lift Books?

1. Stack one book on top of another one.

2. Lift the two stacked books in front of you so the lowest book is about level with your shoulders. Hold the books in this position for 30 seconds. While you are performing this activity, note how your body responds. For example, how do your arms feel at the beginning and toward the end of the 30 seconds?

3. Balance one book on the top of your head. Walk a few steps with the book on your head.

Think It Over
Inferring List all the parts of your body that worked together as you performed the activities in Steps 1 through 3.

GUIDE FOR READING

◆ What are the levels of organization in the body?

◆ What are the four basic types of tissue in the human body?

◆ What is homeostasis?

Reading Tip Before you read, preview *Exploring Levels of Organization in the Body.* Write down any unfamiliar words. Then, as you read, write their definitions.

The bell rings—lunchtime at last! You hurry down the noisy halls toward the cafeteria. The unmistakable aroma of hot pizza makes your mouth water. At last, after waiting in line, you pick up a plate with a slice of pizza and some salad. When you get to the cashier, you dig in your pocket for lunch money. Then, carefully balancing your tray, you scan the crowded cafeteria for your friends. You spot them, walk to their table, sit down, and begin to eat.

Think for a minute about how many parts of your body were involved in the simple act of getting and eating your lunch. You heard the bell with your ears and smelled the pizza with your nose. Bones and muscles worked together as you walked to the cafeteria, picked up your food, and sat down at the table. Without your brain, you couldn't have remembered where you put your lunch money. Once you began to eat, your teeth chewed the food and your throat muscles swallowed it. Then other parts of your digestive system, such as your stomach, began to process the food for your body to use.

Levels of Organization

Every minute of the day, whether you are eating, studying, playing basketball, or even sleeping, your body is busily at work. Each part of the body has a specific job to do, and all the different parts work together. This smooth functioning is due partly to the way in which the human body is organized. **The levels of organization in the human body consist of cells, tissues, organs, and organ systems.** The smallest unit is the cell, and the largest is the organ system.

Cells

A **cell** is the basic unit of structure and function in a living thing. Complex organisms are composed of many cells in the same way a building is composed of many bricks. The human body contains about 100 trillion cells. Cells are quite tiny, and most cannot be seen without a microscope.

Most animal cells, including those in the human body, have a structure similar to the cell in Figure 1. The **cell membrane** forms the outside boundary of the cell. Inside the cell membrane is a large structure called the **nucleus.** The nucleus is the control center that directs the cell's activities and contains information that determines the cell's characteristics. When the cell divides, or reproduces, this information is passed on to the newly formed cells. The area between the cell membrane and the nucleus is called the **cytoplasm.** The cytoplasm contains a clear, jellylike substance in which many important cell structures, called organelles, are found.

Cells carry on the processes that keep organisms alive. Inside cells, for example, molecules from digested food undergo chemical reactions that provide energy for the body's activities. Cells also get rid of waste products, grow, and reproduce. For more information on cells, look back at Chapters 1 and 2.

Checkpoint **What is the function of the nucleus?**

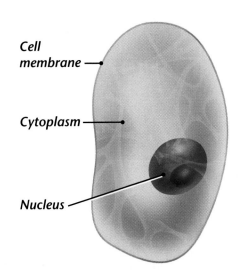

Figure 1 The cells in your body are surrounded by a cell membrane, and most have a nucleus. The cytoplasm is the area between the cell membrane and the nucleus.

Cell membrane

Cytoplasm

Nucleus

Tissues

Tissue is the next largest unit of organization in your body. A **tissue** is a group of similar cells that perform the same function. **The human body contains four basic types of tissue: muscle tissue, nerve tissue, connective tissue, and epithelial tissue.** To see examples of each of these tissues, look at Figure 2.

Like the muscle cells that form it, **muscle tissue** can contract, or shorten. By doing this, muscle tissue makes parts of your body move.

While muscle tissue carries out movement, nerve tissue directs and controls it. **Nerve tissue** carries messages back and forth between the brain and every other part of the body. Your brain is made up mostly of nerve tissue.

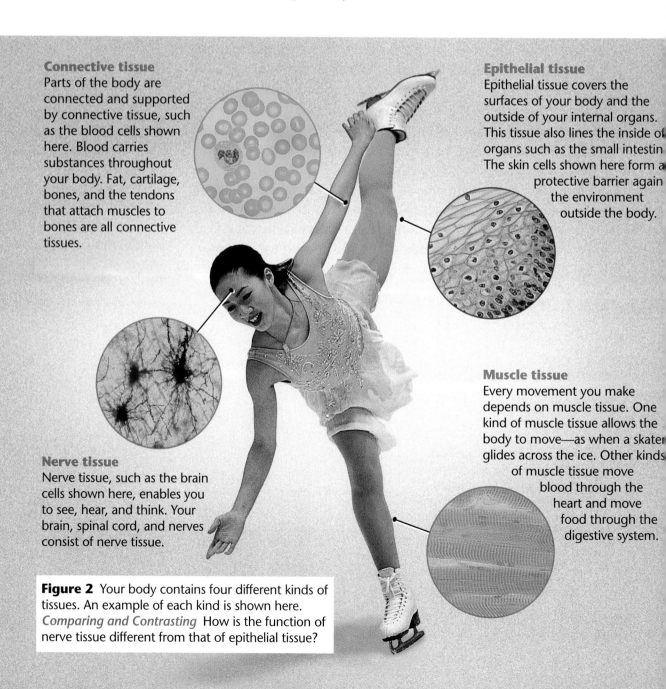

Connective tissue
Parts of the body are connected and supported by connective tissue, such as the blood cells shown here. Blood carries substances throughout your body. Fat, cartilage, bones, and the tendons that attach muscles to bones are all connective tissues.

Epithelial tissue
Epithelial tissue covers the surfaces of your body and the outside of your internal organs. This tissue also lines the inside of organs such as the small intestin. The skin cells shown here form a protective barrier again the environment outside the body.

Nerve tissue
Nerve tissue, such as the brain cells shown here, enables you to see, hear, and think. Your brain, spinal cord, and nerves consist of nerve tissue.

Muscle tissue
Every movement you make depends on muscle tissue. One kind of muscle tissue allows the body to move—as when a skater glides across the ice. Other kinds of muscle tissue move blood through the heart and move food through the digestive system.

Figure 2 Your body contains four different kinds of tissues. An example of each kind is shown here. *Comparing and Contrasting* How is the function of nerve tissue different from that of epithelial tissue?

Connective tissue provides support for your body and connects all its parts. Bone is one kind of connective tissue; its strength and hardness support your body and protect its internal structures. Fat is also a connective tissue. It pads parts of your body, provides insulation from cold, and stores energy.

Epithelial tissue (ep uh THEE lee ul) covers the surfaces of your body, inside and out. Some epithelial tissue, such as the outermost layer of your skin, protects the delicate structures that lie beneath it. Other kinds of epithelial tissue absorb or release substances. The lining of your digestive system consists of epithelial tissue that releases chemicals used in digestion.

Organs and Organ Systems

Your stomach, heart, brain, and lungs are all organs. An **organ** is a structure that is composed of different kinds of tissue. Like a tissue, an organ performs a specific job. The job of an organ, however, is generally more complex than that of a tissue. The heart, for example, pumps blood throughout your body, over and over again. The heart contains all four kinds of tissue— muscle, nerve, connective, and epithelial. Each tissue type contributes to the overall job of pumping blood.

Each organ in your body is part of an **organ system,** a group of organs that work together to perform a major function. Your heart is part of your circulatory system, which carries oxygen and other materials throughout the body. Besides the heart, blood vessels are organs in the circulatory system. Figure 3 describes the major organ systems in the human body.

Figure 3 The human body is made up of eleven organ systems. *Interpreting Charts* Which two systems work together to get oxygen to your cells?

Organ Systems in the Human Body

◀ **Circulatory** Carries needed materials to the body cells; carries wastes away from body cells; helps fight disease.

Digestive Takes food into the body, breaks food down, and absorbs the digested materials.

Endocrine Controls many body processes—such as intake of sugar by cells—by means of chemicals.

Excretory Removes wastes.

Immune Fights disease.

Muscular Enables the body to move; moves food through the digestive system; keeps the heart beating.

Nervous Detects and interprets information from the environment outside the body and from within the body; controls most body functions.

Reproductive Produces sex cells that can unite with other sex cells to create offspring; controls male and female characteristics.

Respiratory Takes oxygen into the body and eliminates carbon dioxide.

Skeletal Supports the body, protects it, and works with muscles to allow movement; makes blood cells and stores some materials.

Skin Protects the body, keeps water inside the body, and helps regulate body temperature.

In Edgar Allan Poe's story, "The Pit and the Pendulum," the author's detailed descriptions paint a vivid picture of a person's physical reactions to a stressor. The character was frightened by a razor-sharp pendulum swinging overhead. "I at once started to my feet, trembling compulsively in every fibre....Perspiration burst from every pore, and stood in cold, big beads upon my forehead."

In Your Journal

Create a situation in which a character faces an extremely stressful situation. Describe the character's physical reactions and feelings. Make sure to use vivid and precise descriptive words that clearly convey the character's reactions.

The effects of adrenaline, which take only a few seconds, are dramatic. Your breathing quickens, sending more oxygen to your body cells to provide energy for your muscles. That extra oxygen gets to your cells rapidly because your heart begins to beat faster. The faster heartbeat increases the flow of blood to your muscles and some other organs. In contrast, less blood flows to your skin and digestive system, so that more is available for your arms and legs. The pupils of your eyes become wider, allowing you to see better.

Fight or Flight The reactions caused by adrenaline are sometimes called the "fight-or-flight" response, because they prepare you either to fight the stressor or to take flight and escape. Scientists think that the fight-or-flight response was important for primitive people who faced wild-animal attacks and similar dangers. Today, the same reactions still occur with any stressor, whether it is a snarling dog or a social studies test.

During the fight-or-flight response, your body systems work together to respond to the stressor. For example, your respiratory system provides you with extra oxygen, which your circulatory system delivers to the parts of your body that need it. Your muscular system, in turn, works with your skeletal system to help you move—fast.

☑ *Checkpoint* *During the alarm stage, how do your eyes and ears respond?*

Figure 6 Oops! One sure way to cause stress is to do too many things at once. *Relating Cause and Effect How does stress affect a person's heartbeat and breathing rates?*

Long-Term Stress

The alarm stage of stress only lasts for a short time. If the stress is over quickly, your body soon returns to its normal state. Some kinds of stressors, however, continue for a long time. Suppose, for example, you are stressed because you are moving to a new community. You cannot fight the stressor, and you cannot run away from it either. When a stressful situation does not go away quickly, your body cannot restore homeostasis. If you do not deal with the stress, you may become tired, irritable, and have trouble getting along with others. In addition, you may be more likely to become ill.

Dealing With Stress

Stress is a normal part of life. No one can avoid stress entirely. When you are in a stressful situation, it is important that you recognize it and take action to deal with it, rather than pretending that the stressor doesn't exist. For example, suppose you aren't doing well in math class. If you accept the problem and deal with it—perhaps by asking your teacher for help—your stress will probably decrease.

In addition, when you are experiencing long-term stress, physical activity can help you feel better. Riding a bike, skating, or even raking leaves can take your mind off the stress. It is also important to talk about the situation and your feelings with friends and family members.

Figure 7 When you are under stress, it is important to find ways to relax.

Section 1 Review

1. List the four levels of organization in the human body. Give an example of each level.
2. Name the four types of tissue in the human body. Give an example of where each is located.
3. What is homeostasis?
4. Describe what happens during the alarm stage of stress.
5. **Thinking Critically** **Applying Concepts** What systems of the body are involved when you prepare a sandwich and then eat it?

Check Your Progress CHAPTER PROJECT

By now, you should have your teacher's approval for modeling the movement you chose. Ask a classmate or friend to perform the movement. Make drawings to study the motion. Find out what bones are involved, and determine their sizes and shapes. (*Hint:* Notice the direction of bone movement and the kinds of joints that are involved.)

SECTION 2 The Skeletal System

ACTIVITY

Hard as a Rock?

1. Your teacher will give you a leg bone from a cooked turkey or chicken and a rock.
2. Use a hand lens to examine both the rock and the bone.
3. Gently tap both the rock and the bone on a hard surface.
4. Pick up each object to feel how heavy it is.
5. Wash your hands. Then make notes of your observations.

Think It Over

Observing Based on your observations, why do you think bones are sometimes compared to rocks? List some ways in which bones and rocks are similar and different.

GUIDE FOR READING

◆ What are the functions of the skeleton?

◆ What role do movable joints play in the body?

◆ How can you keep your bones strong and healthy?

Reading Tip Before you read, rewrite the headings in the section as *how, why,* or *what* questions. As you read, write answers to the questions.

A construction site is a busy place. After workers have prepared the building's foundation, they begin to assemble thousands of steel pieces into a frame for the building. People watch as the steel pieces are joined to create a rigid frame that climbs toward the sky. By the time the building is finished, however, the building's framework will no longer be visible.

Like a building, you also have an inner framework, but it is made up of bones instead of steel. Your framework, or skeleton, is shown in Figure 9. The number of bones in your skeleton depends on your age. A newborn baby has about 275 bones. An adult, however, has about 206 bones. As a baby grows, some of the bones fuse together. For example, as a baby, you had many more individual bones in your skull than you do now. As you grew, some of your bones grew together to form the larger bones of your skull.

What the Skeletal System Does

Just as a building could not stand without its frame, you would collapse without your skeleton. **Your skeleton has five major functions. It provides shape and support, enables you to move, protects your internal organs, produces blood cells, and stores certain materials until your body needs them.**

Figure 8 Like the steel beams that support a building, your skeleton supports your body.

Your skeleton determines the shape of your body, much as a steel frame determines the shape of a building. The backbone, or vertebral column, is the center of the skeleton. Locate the backbone in Figure 9. Notice that all the bones of the body are in some way connected to this column. If you move your fingers down the center of your back, you can feel the 26 small bones, or **vertebrae** (VUR tuh bray)(singular **vertebra**), that make up your backbone. Bend forward at the waist and feel the bones adjust as you move. You can think of each individual vertebra as a bead on a string. Just as a beaded necklace is flexible and able to bend, so too is your vertebral column. If your backbone were just one bone, you would not be able to bend or twist.

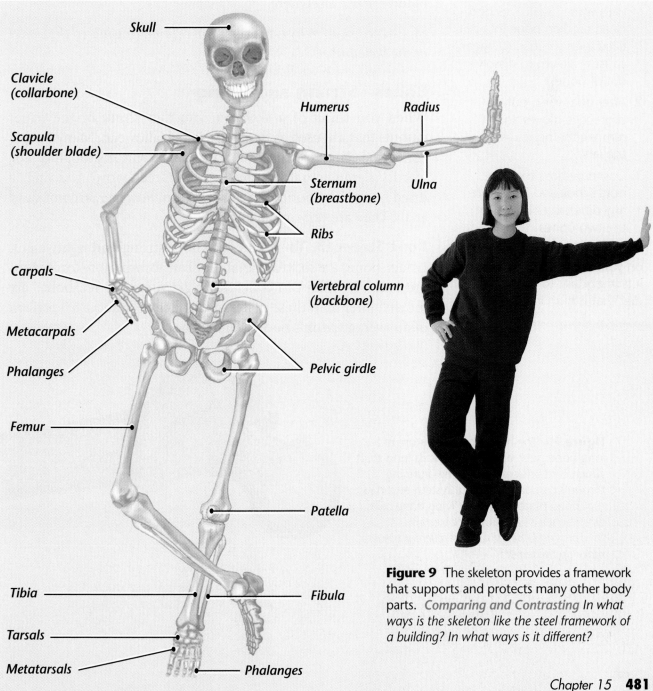

Skull
Clavicle (collarbone)
Scapula (shoulder blade)
Humerus
Radius
Sternum (breastbone)
Ulna
Ribs
Carpals
Vertebral column (backbone)
Metacarpals
Phalanges
Pelvic girdle
Femur
Patella
Tibia
Fibula
Tarsals
Metatarsals
Phalanges

Figure 9 The skeleton provides a framework that supports and protects many other body parts. *Comparing and Contrasting In what ways is the skeleton like the steel framework of a building? In what ways is it different?*

Your skeleton also allows you to move. Most of the body's bones are associated with muscles. The muscles pull on the bones to make the body move. Bones also protect many of the organs in your body. For example, your skull protects your brain, and your breastbone and ribs form a protective cage around your heart and lungs.

Some of the bones in your body produce substances that your body needs. You can think of the long bones of your arms and legs as factories that make blood cells. Bones also store minerals such as calcium and phosphorus. Calcium and phosphorus make bones strong and hard. When the body needs these minerals, the bones release small amounts of them into the blood for use elsewhere.

☑ *Checkpoint* *Why is the vertebral column considered the center of the skeleton?*

Bones—Strong and Living

When you think of a skeleton, you may think of the paper cutouts that are used as decorations at Halloween. Many people connect skeletons with death. The ancient Greeks did, too. The word *skeleton* actually comes from a Greek word meaning "a dried body." The bones of your skeleton, however, are not dead at all. They are very much alive.

Bone Strength Your bones are both strong and lightweight. In fact, bones are so strong that they can absorb more force without breaking than can concrete or granite rock. Yet, bones are much lighter than these materials. In fact, only about 20 percent of an average adult's body weight is bone.

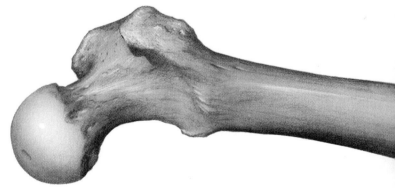

Figure 10 The most obvious feature of a long bone, such as the femur, is its long shaft, which contains compact bone. Running through compact bone is a system of canals that bring materials to the living bone cells. One canal is seen in the photograph.
Interpreting Diagrams *What different tissues make up the femur?*

Have you ever heard the phrase "as hard as a rock"? Most rock is hard because it is made up of minerals that are packed tightly together. In a similar way, bones are hard because they are made up of two minerals—phosphorus and calcium.

Bone Growth Bones also contain cells and tissues, such as blood and nerves. And, because your bone cells are alive, they form new bone tissue as you grow. But even after you are grown, bone tissue continues to form within your bones. For example, every time you play soccer or basketball, your bones absorb the force of your weight. They respond by making new bone tissue.

Sometimes, new bone tissue forms after an accident. If you break a bone, for example, new bone tissue forms to fill the gap between the broken ends of the bone. The healed region of new bone may be stronger than the original bone.

The Structure of Bones

Figure 10 shows the structure of the femur, or thighbone. The femur, which is the body's longest bone, connects the pelvic bones to the lower leg bones. Notice that a thin, tough membrane covers all of the bone except the ends. Blood vessels and nerves enter and leave the bone through the membrane. Beneath the membrane is a layer of compact bone, which is hard and dense, but not solid. As you can see in Figure 10, small canals run through the compact bone. These canals carry blood vessels and nerves from the bone's surface to the living cells within the bone.

Just inside the compact bone is a layer of spongy bone. Spongy bone is also found at the ends of the bone. Like a sponge, spongy bone has many small spaces within it. This structure makes spongy bone lightweight but strong.

CANAL

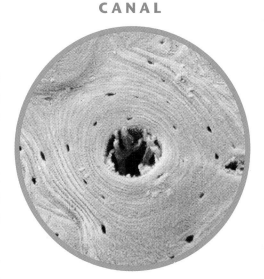

COMPACT BONE

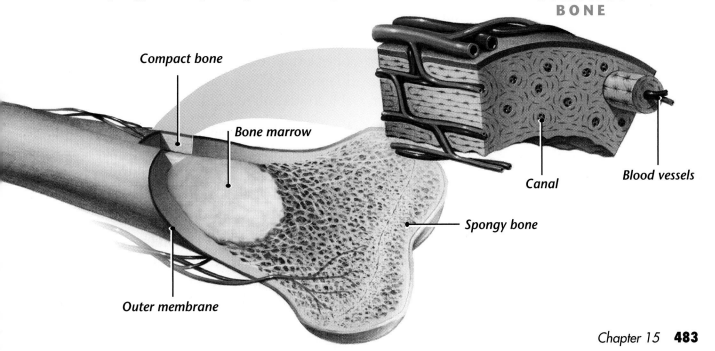

Compact bone

Bone marrow

Outer membrane

Canal

Blood vessels

Spongy bone

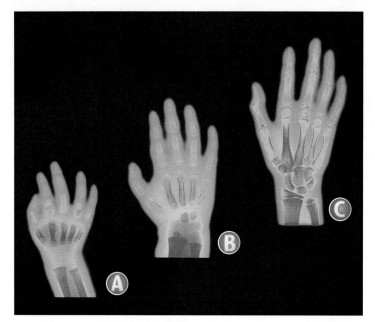

Figure 11 X-rays of the hands of a 1-year-old **(A)** and a 3-year-old **(B)** show that the cartilage in the wrist has not yet been replaced by bone. In the X-ray of the 13-year-old's hand **(C)**, the replacement of cartilage by bone is almost complete.

The spaces in bone contain a soft connective tissue called **marrow.** There are two types of marrow—red and yellow. Red bone marrow produces the body's blood cells. As a child, most of your bones contained red bone marrow. As a teenager, only the ends of your femurs, skull, hip bones, and sternum (breastbone) contain red marrow. Your other bones contain yellow marrow. This marrow stores fat, which serves as an energy reserve.

How Bones Form

Try this activity: Move the tip of your nose from side to side between your fingers. Notice that the tip of your nose is not stiff. That is because it contains cartilage. **Cartilage** (KAHR tuh lij) is a connective tissue that is more flexible than bone. As an infant, much of your skeleton was cartilage. Over time, most of the cartilage has been replaced with hard bone tissue.

The replacement of cartilage by bone tissue usually is complete by the time you stop growing. But not all of your body's cartilage is replaced by bone. Even in adulthood, cartilage covers the ends of many bones. For example, in the knee, cartilage acts like a cushion that keeps your femur from rubbing against the bones of your lower leg.

✓ *Checkpoint* *What happens to cartilage as you grow?*

Joints of the Skeleton

Imagine what life would be like if your femur ran the length of your leg. How would you get out of bed in the morning? How would you run for the school bus? Luckily, your body contains many small bones rather than fewer large ones. A place in the body where two bones come together is a **joint.** Joints allow bones to move in different ways. There are two kinds of joints in the body—immovable joints and movable joints.

Immovable Joints Some joints in the body connect bones in a way that allows little or no movement. These joints are called immovable joints. The bones of the skull are held together by immovable joints. The joints that attach the ribs to the sternum are also immovable.

Movable Joints Most of the joints in the body are movable joints. **Movable joints allow the body to make a wide range of movements.** Look at *Exploring Movable Joints* to see the variety of movements that these joints make possible.

EXPLORING *Movable Joints*

Without movable joints, your body would be as stiff as a board. The four types of movable joints shown here allow your body to move in a variety of ways.

Ball-and-socket joint Ball-and-socket joints allow the greatest range of motion. In your shoulder, the top of the arm bone fits into the deep, bowl-like socket of the scapula (shoulder blade). The joint allows you to swing your arm freely in a circle. Your hips also have ball-and-socket joints.

Pivot joint A pivot joint allows one bone to rotate around another. The pivot joint in the top of your neck gives you limited ability to turn your head from side to side.

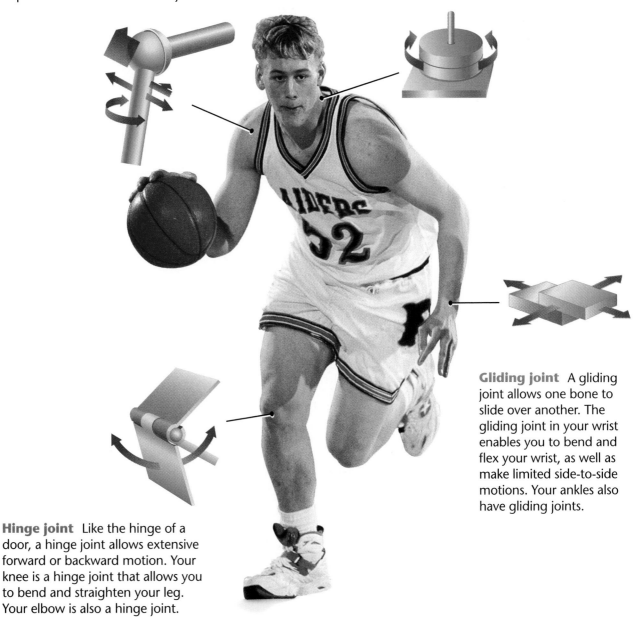

Gliding joint A gliding joint allows one bone to slide over another. The gliding joint in your wrist enables you to bend and flex your wrist, as well as make limited side-to-side motions. Your ankles also have gliding joints.

Hinge joint Like the hinge of a door, a hinge joint allows extensive forward or backward motion. Your knee is a hinge joint that allows you to bend and straighten your leg. Your elbow is also a hinge joint.

The bones in movable joints are held together by strong connective tissues called **ligaments.** Cartilage that covers the ends of the bones keeps them from rubbing against each other. In addition, a fluid lubricates the ends of the bones, allowing them to move smoothly over each other.

Taking Care of Your Bones

INTEGRATING HEALTH Because your skeleton performs so many necessary functions, it is important to keep it healthy. This is especially true while you are still growing. **A combination of a balanced diet and regular exercise can start you on the way to a lifetime of healthy bones.**

One way to ensure healthy bones is to eat a well-balanced diet. A well-balanced diet includes enough calcium and phosphorus to keep your bones strong while they are growing. Meats, whole grains, and leafy green vegetables are all excellent sources of both calcium and phosphorus. Dairy products, including milk, are excellent sources of calcium.

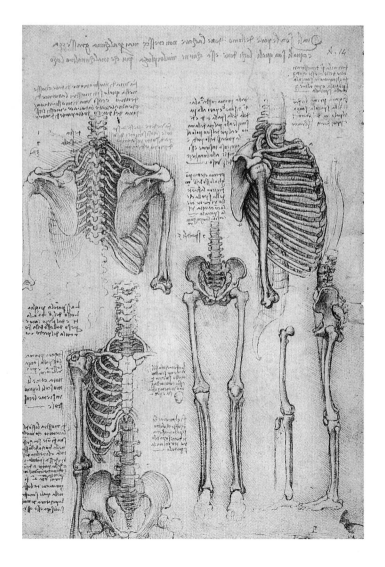

Visual Arts
CONNECTION

Leonardo da Vinci (1452–1519), was an Italian artist, inventor, and scientist. Although he is well known for his paintings, including the Mona Lisa, Leonardo also made accurate sketches of the human body. As a scientist, Leonardo used dissections and took precise measurements to create accurate drawings of bones, ligaments, tendons, and other body parts. His sketches are considered to be the first accurate drawings of the human body.

In Your Journal

Leonardo da Vinci relied on measurements and visual observations to make his drawings. Use a metric ruler to measure the lengths of the bones in your arm or leg. Then try to make an accurate drawing of your arm or leg.

Figure 12 Leonardo da Vinci drew these sketches of the human chest, hip, and leg bones in 1510.

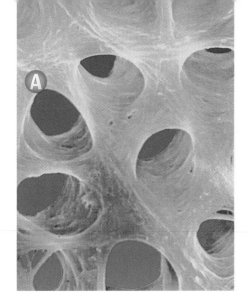

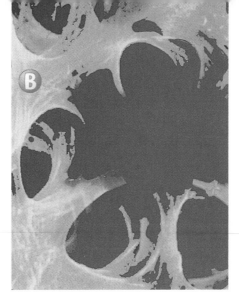

Figure 13 Without enough calcium in the diet, a person's bones weaken. **A.** This magnified view of healthy bone shows a continuous framework. **B.** Notice the large empty space in this bone from a person with osteoporosis. *Relating Cause and Effect What can you do to prevent osteoporosis?*

Another way to build and maintain strong bones is to get plenty of exercise. During activities such as walking, soccer, or basketball, your bones support the weight of your entire body. This helps your bones grow stronger and denser. Running, skating, and aerobics are other activities that help keep your bones healthy and strong. To prevent injuries while exercising, be sure to wear appropriate safety equipment, such as a helmet, knee pads, or shoulder pads.

As people become older, their bones begin to lose some of the minerals they contain. Mineral loss can lead to **osteoporosis** (ahs tee oh puh ROH sis), a condition in which the body's bones become weak and break easily. You can see the effect of osteoporosis in Figure 13B. Osteoporosis is more common in women than in men. Evidence indicates that regular exercise throughout life can help prevent osteoporosis. A diet with enough calcium can also help prevent osteoporosis. If you eat enough calcium-rich foods now, during your teenage years, you may help prevent osteoporosis later in life.

Section 2 Review

1. List five important functions that the skeleton performs in the body.
2. What is the role of movable joints in the body?
3. What behaviors are important for keeping your bones healthy?
4. Compare the motion of a hinge joint to that of a pivot joint.
5. **Thinking Critically** Predicting How would your life be different if your backbone consisted of just one bone?

Science at Home

Exercising Safely List the types of exercise you and your family members do. With your family, brainstorm a list of safety gear and precautions to use for each activity. (For example, for bicycling, you might list wearing a helmet, stretching before riding, and avoiding busy streets and nighttime riding.) How can you put these safety measures into practice?

3 The Muscular System

DISCOVER

How Do Muscles Work?

1. Grip a spring-type clothespin with the thumb and index finger of your writing hand. Squeeze the clothespin open and shut as quickly as possible for two minutes. Count how many times you can squeeze the clothespin before your muscles tire.

2. Rest for one minute. Then repeat Step 1.

Think It Over
Predicting What do you think would happen if you repeated Steps 1 and 2 with your other hand? Give a reason for your prediction. Then test your prediction.

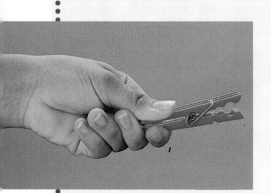

GUIDE FOR READING

◆ **What three types of muscles are found in the body?**

◆ **Why do skeletal muscles work in pairs?**

Reading Tip **Before you read, preview Figure 14. Predict the functions of skeletal, smooth, and cardiac muscle. After you read the section, look back at your predictions to see whether they were correct.**

A rabbit becomes still when it senses danger. The rabbit sits so still that it doesn't seem to move a muscle. Could you sit without moving any muscles? If you tried to, you'd find that it is impossible to sit still for very long. Saliva builds up in your mouth. You swallow. You need to breathe. Your chest expands to let air in. All of these actions involve muscles.

There are about 600 muscles in your body. Muscles have many functions. For example, they keep your heart beating, pull your mouth into a smile, and move the bones of your skeleton.

Muscle Action

Some of your body's movements, such as smiling, are easy to control. Other movements, such as the beating of your heart, are impossible to control completely. That is because some muscles are not under your conscious control. Those muscles are called **involuntary muscles.** Involuntary muscles are responsible for activities such as breathing and digesting food.

The muscles that are under your control are called **voluntary muscles.** Smiling, turning a page in a book, and getting out of your chair when the bell rings are all actions controlled by voluntary muscles.

◀ **A rabbit "frozen" in place**

Types of Muscles

Your body has three types of muscle tissue—skeletal muscle, smooth muscle, and cardiac muscle. In Figure 14, you see a magnified view of each type of muscle in the body. Both skeletal and smooth muscles are found in many places in the body. Cardiac muscle is found only in the heart. Each muscle type performs specific functions in the body.

Skeletal Muscle Every time you type on a computer keyboard, shoot a basketball, or walk across a room, you are using skeletal muscles. As their name suggests, **skeletal muscles** are attached

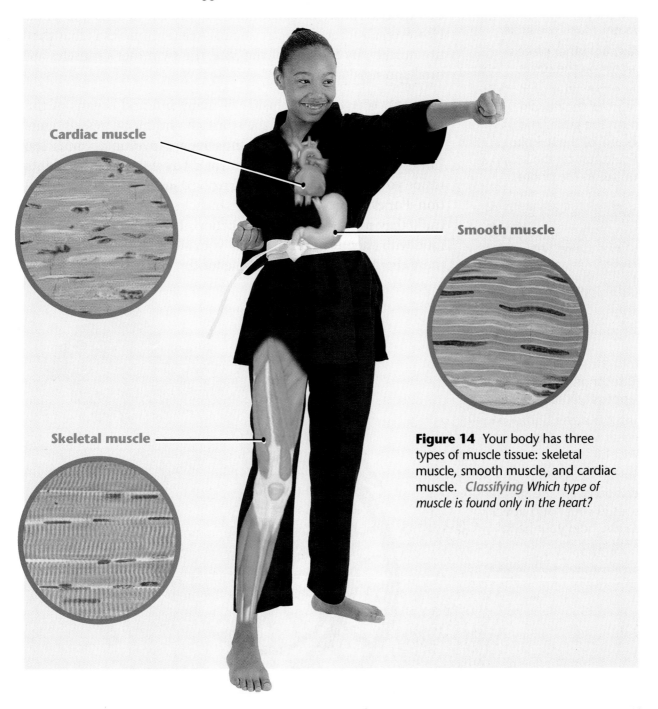

Cardiac muscle

Smooth muscle

Skeletal muscle

Figure 14 Your body has three types of muscle tissue: skeletal muscle, smooth muscle, and cardiac muscle. *Classifying Which type of muscle is found only in the heart?*

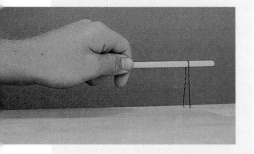
to the bones of your skeleton. These muscles provide the force that moves your bones. At each end of a skeletal muscle is a tendon. A **tendon** is a strong connective tissue that attaches muscle to bone. As you can see in Figure 14, skeletal muscle cells appear banded, or striated (STRY ay tid). For this reason, skeletal muscle is sometimes called striated muscle.

Because you have conscious control of skeletal muscles, they are classified as voluntary muscles. One characteristic of skeletal muscles is that they react very quickly. You can see an example of just how quickly skeletal muscle reacts by watching a swim meet. Immediately after the starting gun sounds, a swimmer's leg muscles quickly push the swimmer off the block into the pool. However, another characteristic of skeletal muscles is that they tire quickly. By the end of the race, the swimmer's muscles are tired and need a rest.

Smooth Muscle The inside of many internal organs of the body, such as the walls of the stomach and blood vessels, contain smooth muscles. **Smooth muscles** are involuntary muscles. They work automatically to control many types of movements inside your body, such as those involved in the process of digestion. For example, as the smooth muscles of your stomach contract, they produce a churning action. The churning mixes the food with chemicals produced by your stomach. This action and these chemicals help to digest the food.

Unlike skeletal muscles, smooth muscle cells are not striated. Smooth muscles behave differently than skeletal muscles, too. Smooth muscles react more slowly and tire more slowly.

Cardiac Muscle The tissue called **cardiac muscle** has characteristics in common with both smooth and skeletal muscles. Like smooth muscle, cardiac muscle is involuntary. Like skeletal muscle, cardiac muscle cells are striated. However, unlike skeletal muscle, cardiac muscle does not get tired. It can contract repeatedly. You call those repeated contractions heartbeats.

✓ *Checkpoint* *Which type of muscle reacts and tires quickly?*

Muscles at Work

Has anyone ever asked you to "make a muscle"? If so, you probably tightened your fist, bent your arm at the elbow, and made the muscles in your upper arm bulge. Like other skeletal muscles, the muscles in your arm do their work by contracting, or becoming shorter and thicker. Muscle cells contract when they receive messages from the nervous system. **Because muscle cells can only contract, not extend, skeletal muscles must work in pairs. While one muscle contracts, the other muscle in the pair returns to its original length.**

Figure 15 shows the muscle action involved in bending the arm at the elbow. First, the biceps muscle on the front of the upper arm contracts to bend the elbow, lifting the forearm and hand. As the biceps contracts, the triceps on the back of the upper arm returns to its original length. Then to straighten the elbow, the triceps muscle contracts. As the triceps contracts to extend the arm, the biceps returns to its original length. Another example of muscles that work in pairs are those in your thigh that bend and straighten the knee joint.

Figure 15 Because muscles can only contract, or shorten, they must work in pairs. To bend the arm at the elbow, the biceps contracts while the triceps returns to its original length.
Interpreting Diagrams What happens to each muscle to straighten the arm?

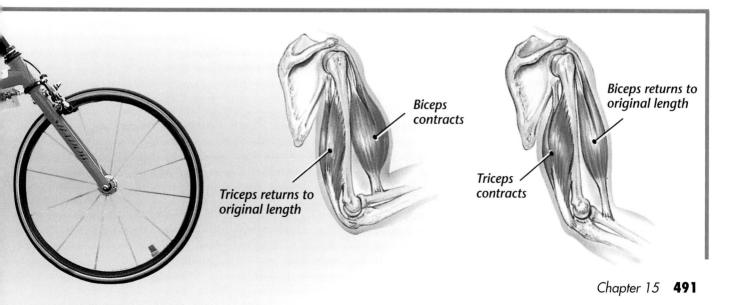

Biceps contracts

Biceps returns to original length

Triceps returns to original length

Triceps contracts

Figure 16 When you warm up before exercising, you increase the flexibility of your muscles.

Taking Care of Your Skeletal Muscles

INTEGRATING HEALTH Exercise is important for maintaining both muscular strength and flexibility. Exercise makes individual muscle cells grow wider. This, in turn, causes the whole muscle to become thicker. The thicker a muscle is, the stronger the muscle is. When you stretch and warm up thoroughly, your muscles become more flexible. This helps prepare your muscles for the work involved in exercising or playing.

Like your bones and joints, your skeletal muscles are subject to injuries. Some of the same precautions that help prevent bone and joint injuries can also help prevent muscle injuries. For example, warming up increases the flexibility of joints as well as muscles. In addition, using proper safety equipment can protect all of your tissues, including muscles and tendons.

Sometimes, despite taking proper precautions, muscles can become injured. A muscle strain, or a pulled muscle, can occur when muscles are overworked or overstretched. Tendons can also be overstretched or partially torn. After a long period of exercise, a skeletal muscle can cramp. When a muscle cramps, the entire muscle contracts strongly and stays contracted. If you injure a muscle or tendon, it is important to follow medical instructions and to rest the injured area until it heals.

Section 3 Review

1. Name the three types of muscle tissue. Where is each type found?
2. Describe how the muscles in your upper arm work together to bend and straighten your arm.
3. How do voluntary and involuntary muscles differ? Give an example of each type of muscle.
4. **Thinking Critically Predicting** The muscles that move your fingers are attached to the bones in your fingers by long tendons. Suppose one of the tendons in a person's index finger were cut all the way through. How would this injury affect the person's ability to move his or her index finger? Explain.

CHAPTER PROJECT

Check Your Progress
You should now be assembling your working model. Be sure that you include the muscles involved in the movement you are modeling. Also, remember that your model must show how muscle contractions produce the chosen movement. (*Hint:* After you have assembled your model, do a final check to be sure it functions the way it should.)

A Look Beneath the Skin

In this lab, you will learn about your own skeletal muscles by observing the "arm" muscles of a chicken.

Problem

What are some characteristics of skeletal muscles? How do skeletal muscles work?

Materials

protective gloves
paper towels
scissors

water
dissection tray
uncooked chicken wing, treated with bleach

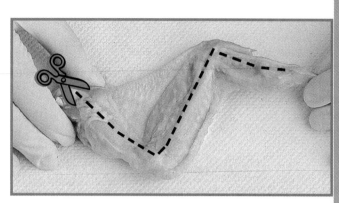

Procedure

1. Put on protective gloves. **CAUTION:** *Wear gloves whenever you handle the chicken.*

2. Your teacher will give you a chicken wing. Rinse it well with water, dry it with paper towels, and place it in a dissecting tray.

3. Carefully extend the wing to find out how many major parts it has. Draw a diagram of the external structure. Label the upper arm, elbow, lower arm, and hand (wing tip).

4. Use scissors to remove the skin. Cut along the cut line as shown in the photo. Only cut through the skin. **CAUTION:** *Cut away from your body and your classmates.*

5. Examine the muscles, the bundles of pink tissue around the bones. Find the two groups of muscles in the upper arm. Hold the arm down at the shoulder, and alternately pull on each muscle group. Observe what happens.

6. Find the two groups of muscles in the lower arm. Hold down the arm at the elbow, and alternately pull on each muscle group. Then make a diagram of the wing's muscles.

7. Find the tendons—shiny white tissue at the ends of the muscles. Notice what parts the tendons connect. Add the tendons to your diagram.

8. Remove the muscles and tendons. Find the ligaments, the whitish ribbonlike structures between bones. Add them to your diagram.

9. Dispose of the chicken parts according to your teacher's instructions. Wash your hands.

Analyze and Conclude

1. How does a chicken wing move at the elbow? How does the motion compare to how your elbow moves? What type of joint is involved?

2. What happened when you pulled on one of the arm muscles? What muscle action does the pulling represent?

3. Classify the muscles you observed as smooth, cardiac, or skeletal.

4. **Think About It** Why is it valuable to record your observations with accurate diagrams?

More to Explore

Use the procedures from this lab to examine an uncooked chicken thigh and leg. Compare how the chicken leg and a human leg move.

SECTION 4 The Skin

DISCOVER •••••••••••••••••••••••••••••••••••••• ACTIVITY ••••

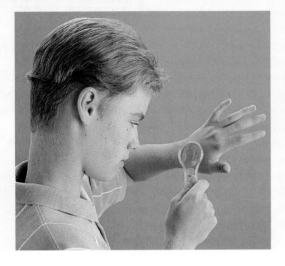

What Can You Observe About Skin?

1. Using a hand lens, examine the skin on your hand. Look for pores and hairs on both the palm and back of your hand.

2. Place a plastic glove on your hand. After five minutes, remove the glove. Then examine the skin on your hand with the hand lens.

Think It Over

Inferring Compare your hand before and after wearing the glove. What happened to the skin when you wore the glove? Why did this happen?

GUIDE FOR READING

◆ What are the functions of skin?

◆ What habits can help keep your skin healthy?

Reading Tip As you read, create a table that shows the two major layers of skin. Include columns to record the location, structures, and functions of each layer.

Figure 17 The skin forms a barrier that protects the inside of the body from substances such as the chlorine in pool water.

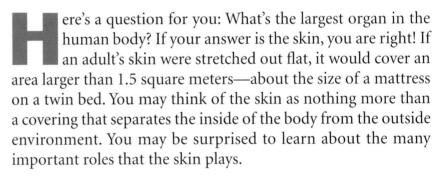

Here's a question for you: What's the largest organ in the human body? If your answer is the skin, you are right! If an adult's skin were stretched out flat, it would cover an area larger than 1.5 square meters—about the size of a mattress on a twin bed. You may think of the skin as nothing more than a covering that separates the inside of the body from the outside environment. You may be surprised to learn about the many important roles that the skin plays.

The Body's Tough Covering

The skin performs several major functions in the body. **The skin covers the body and prevents the loss of water. It protects the body from injury and infection. The skin also helps to regulate body temperature, eliminate wastes, gather information about the environment, and produce vitamin D.**

The skin protects the body by forming a barrier that keeps disease-causing microorganisms and harmful substances outside the body. In addition, the skin helps keep important substances inside the body. Like plastic wrap that keeps food from drying out, the skin prevents the loss of important fluids such as water.

Figure 18 When you exercise, your body becomes warmer. Sweat glands in the skin produce perspiration, which leaves the body through pores like the one you see here. *Relating Cause and Effect How does perspiration help cool your body?*

Another function of the skin is to help the body maintain a steady temperature. Many blood vessels run through skin. When you become too warm, these blood vessels enlarge to increase the amount of blood that flows through them. This allows heat to move from your body into the outside environment. In addition, sweat glands in the skin respond to excess heat by producing perspiration. As perspiration evaporates from your skin, heat moves into the air. Because perspiration contains some dissolved waste materials, your skin also helps to eliminate wastes.

The skin also gathers information about the environment. To understand how the skin does this, place your fingertips on the skin of your arm and press down firmly. Then lightly pinch yourself. You have just tested some of the nerves in your skin. The nerves in skin provide information about such things as pressure, pain, and temperature. Pain messages are important because they warn you that something in your surroundings may have injured you.

Lastly, some skin cells produce vitamin D in the presence of sunlight. Vitamin D is important for healthy bones. This is because Vitamin D helps the cells in your digestive system to absorb the calcium in your food. Your skin cells need only a few minutes of sunlight to produce all the vitamin D you need in a day.

☑ *Checkpoint How does your skin help eliminate waste materials from your body?*

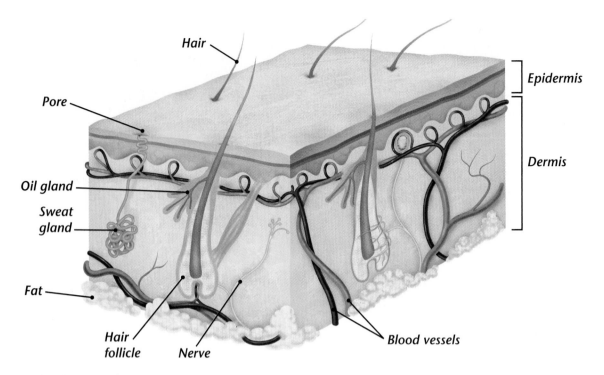

Figure 19 labels: Hair, Pore, Oil gland, Sweat gland, Fat, Hair follicle, Nerve, Blood vessels, Epidermis, Dermis

Figure 19 The skin is made of two main layers. The top layer is called the epidermis. The bottom layer is called the dermis.
Interpreting Diagrams In which layer of the skin do you find blood vessels?

The Epidermis

The skin is organized into two main layers, the epidermis and the dermis. You can see these layers in Figure 19. The **epidermis** is the outermost layer of the skin. In most places, the epidermis is thinner than the dermis. The epidermis does not have nerves or blood vessels. This is why you usually don't feel pain from very shallow scratches and why shallow scratches do not bleed.

Dead or Alive? The cells in the epidermis have a definite life cycle. Each epidermal cell begins life deep in the epidermis, where cells divide to form new cells. The new cells gradually mature and move upward in the epidermis as new cells form beneath them. After about two weeks, the cells die and become part of the surface layer of the epidermis. Under a microscope, this surface layer of dead cells resembles flat bags laid on top of each other. Cells remain in this layer for about two weeks. Then they are shed and replaced by the dead cells below.

Protecting the Body In some ways, the cells of the epidermis are more valuable to the body dead than alive. Most of the protection provided by the skin is due to the layer of dead cells on the surface. The thick layer of dead cells on your fingertips, for example, protects and cushions your fingertips. The shedding of dead cells also helps to protect the body. As the cells fall away, they carry with them bacteria and other substances that settle on the skin. Every time you rub your hands together, you lose hundreds, even thousands, of dead skin cells.

Some cells in the inner layer of the epidermis help to protect the body, too. On your fingers, for example, some cells produce hard fingernails, which protect the fingertips from injury and help you scratch and pick up objects.

Other cells deep in the epidermis produce **melanin,** a pigment, or colored substance, that gives skin its color. The more melanin in your skin, the darker it is. Exposure to sunlight stimulates the skin to make more melanin. Melanin production helps to protect the skin from burning.

☑ *Checkpoint How do dead skin cells help to protect the body?*

The Dermis

The **dermis** is the lower layer of the skin. Find the dermis in Figure 19. Notice that it is located below the epidermis and above a layer of fat. This fat layer pads the internal organs and helps keep heat in the body.

The dermis contains nerves and blood vessels. The dermis also contains other structures as well—sweat glands, hairs, and oil glands. Sweat glands produce perspiration, which reaches the surface through openings called **pores.** Strands of hair grow within the dermis in structures called **follicles** (FAHL ih kulz). The hair that you see above the skin's surface is made up of dead cells. Oil produced in glands around the hair follicles waterproofs the hair. In addition, oil that reaches the surface helps to keep the skin moist.

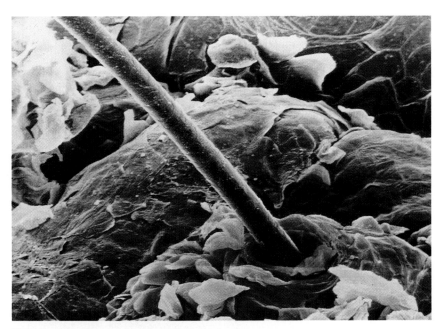

Figure 20 Hairs grow from follicles in the dermis of the skin. Hair is made of dead cells.

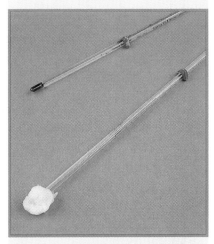

Caring for Your Skin

Because your skin has so many important functions, it is important to take care of it. **Four simple habits can help you keep your skin healthy. Eat properly. Drink enough water. Limit your exposure to the sun. Keep your skin clean and dry.**

Eating Properly Your skin is always active. The cells in the epidermis are replaced, hair strands and nails grow, and oil is produced. These activities require energy—and a well-balanced diet provides the energy needed for these processes. You will learn more about healthy diets in Chapter 16.

Real-World Lab

You and Your Environment

Sun Safety

In this lab, you'll investigate how sunscreen products and various fabrics protect your skin from the sun.

Problem

How well do different materials protect the skin from the sun?

Skills Focus

predicting, observing, drawing conclusions

Materials

scissors
3 different fabrics
photosensitive paper
white construction paper
resealable plastic bag
2 sunscreens with SPF ratings of 4 and 30

pencil
plastic knife
metric ruler
stapler
staple remover

Procedure

1. Read over the procedure. Then write a prediction about how well each of the sunscreens and fabrics will protect against the sun.

2. Use scissors to cut five strips of photosensitive paper that measure 5 cm by 15 cm.

3. Divide each strip into thirds by drawing lines across the strips as shown in the photo.

4. Cover one third of each strip with a square of white construction paper. Staple each square down.

Part 1 Investigating Sunscreens

5. Use a pencil to write the lower SPF (sun protection factor) rating on the back of the first strip. Write the other SPF rating on the back of a second strip.

6. Place the two strips side by side in a plastic bag. Seal the bag, then staple through the white squares to hold the strips in place.

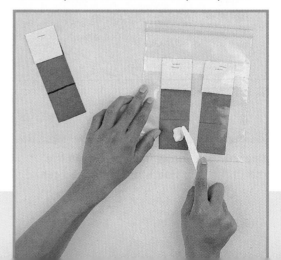

Drinking Water To keep your skin healthy, it is also important to drink plenty of water. When you participate in strenuous activities, such as playing soccer, you can perspire up to 10 liters of liquid a day. You need to replace the water lost in perspiration by drinking water or other beverages and by eating foods, such as fruits, that contain water.

Limiting Sun Exposure You can also take actions to protect your skin from cancer and early aging. **Cancer** is a disease in which some body cells divide uncontrollably. Repeated exposure to sunlight can damage skin cells and cause them to become

7. With a plastic knife, spread a thin layer of each sunscreen on the bag over the last square of each strip. Make certain each layer has the same depth. Be sure not to spread sunscreen over the middle squares.
8. Place the bag in direct sunlight with the sunscreen side up. Leave it there until the middle squares turn white.
9. Remove the strips from the bag, and take off the construction paper. Rinse the strips for one minute in cold water. Then dry them flat.
10. Observe all the squares. Record your observations.

Part 2 Investigating Fabrics
11. Obtain three fabrics of different thicknesses. Staple a square of each fabric over the last square of a photosensitive strip. Write a description of the fabric on the back of the strip.
12. Expose the strips to the sun, fabric-side up, until the middle square turns white. Then follow Steps 9 and 10.

3. Did the fabrics protect against sun exposure? How do you know?
4. Which fabric provided the most protection? The least protection? How did your results compare with your predictions?
5. **Apply** What advice would you give people about protecting their skin from the sun?

Analyze and Conclude

1. Did the sunscreens protect against sun exposure? How do you know?
2. Which sunscreen provided more protection? Was your prediction correct?

Design an Experiment

Design an experiment to find out whether ordinary window glass protects skin against sun exposure. Obtain your teacher's approval before carrying out this experiment.

Figure 21 This person is taking precautions to protect her skin from the sun. *Applying Concepts What other behaviors can provide protection from the sun?*

cancerous. In addition, exposure to the sun can cause the skin to become leathery and wrinkled.

There are many things you can do to protect your skin from damage by the sun. When you are outdoors, wear a hat and sunglasses and use a sunscreen on exposed skin. The clothing you wear can also protect you. Choose clothing made of tightly woven fabrics for the greatest protection. In addition, avoid exposure to the sun between the hours of 10 A.M. and 2 P.M. That is the time when sunlight is the strongest.

Keeping Skin Clean When you wash your skin with mild soap, you get rid of dirt and harmful bacteria. Good washing habits are particularly important during the teenage years when oil glands are more active. When oil glands become clogged with oil, bacterial infections can occur.

One bacterial infection of the skin that can be difficult to control is known as **acne.** If you develop acne, your doctor may prescribe an antibiotic to help control the infection. When you wash, you help to control oiliness and keep your skin from becoming infected with more bacteria.

Other organisms, called fungi, can also live on and infect the skin. Fungi grow best in warm, moist surroundings. Athlete's foot is a very common fungal infection that occurs on the feet, especially between the toes. You can prevent athlete's foot by keeping your feet, especially the spaces between your toes, clean and dry.

Section 4 Review

1. Describe the functions of the skin.
2. List three things you can do to keep your skin healthy.
3. Describe the structure of the two layers of skin.
4. **Thinking Critically Making Judgments** Do you think it is possible to wash your skin too much and damage it as a result? Why or why not?

Science at Home

Protection From the Sun With a family member, look for products in your home that provide protection from the sun. You may also want to visit a store that sells these products. Make a list of the products and place them in categories such as sunblocks, clothing, eye protectors, and other products. Explain to your family member why it is important to use such products.

SECTION 1 Body Organization and Homeostasis

Key Ideas
◆ The levels of organization in the body consist of cells, tissues, organs, and organ systems.
◆ Homeostasis is the process by which an organism's internal environment is kept stable in spite of changes in the external environment.

Key Terms
cell	muscle tissue	organ
cell membrane	nerve tissue	organ system
nucleus	connective tissue	homeostasis
cytoplasm	epithelial tissue	stress
tissue		

SECTION 2 The Skeletal System

Key Ideas
◆ The skeleton provides shape and support, enables movement, protects internal organs, produces blood cells, and stores materials.
◆ Movable joints allow the body to make a wide range of motions.
◆ A combination of a balanced diet and regular exercise helps keep bones healthy.

Key Terms
vertebra	cartilage	ligament
marrow	joint	osteoporosis

SECTION 3 The Muscular System

Key Ideas
◆ Skeletal muscles are voluntary muscles that are attached to the bones of the skeleton.
◆ Smooth muscles, which are involuntary muscles, line the walls of many internal organs and blood vessels. Cardiac muscles are involuntary muscles found only in the heart.

Key Terms
involuntary muscle	tendon
voluntary muscle	smooth muscle
skeletal muscle	cardiac muscle

SECTION 4 The Skin

Key Ideas
◆ Skin covers and protects the body from injury and infection. It also helps to regulate body temperature, get rid of wastes, gather information about the environment, and produce vitamin D.
◆ The epidermis is the top layer of the skin. The dermis is the lower layer of the skin.
◆ For healthy skin, eat a well-balanced diet and drink enough water. Also limit your exposure to the sun and keep your skin clean.

Key Terms
epidermis	follicle
melanin	cancer
dermis	acne
pore	

Organizing Information

Concept Map Copy the concept map about muscles onto a separate sheet of paper. Then complete it and add a title. (For more information on concept maps, see the Skills Handbook.)

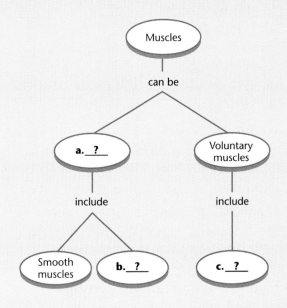

Reviewing Content

For more review of key concepts, see the Interactive Student Tutorial CD-ROM.

Multiple Choice

Choose the letter of the best answer.

1. A group of similar cells that perform a similar function is called a(n)
   a. cell.
   b. organ.
   c. tissue.
   d. organ system.

2. The term most closely associated with homeostasis is
   a. growth.
   b. stability.
   c. temperature.
   d. energy.

3. Blood cells are produced in
   a. compact bone.
   b. marrow.
   c. cartilage.
   d. ligaments.

4. Muscles that help the skeleton move are
   a. cardiac muscles.
   b. smooth muscles.
   c. skeletal muscles.
   d. involuntary muscles.

5. Which structures help to maintain body temperature?
   a. oil glands   b. follicles
   c. sweat glands   d. ligaments

True or False

If the statement is true, write true. If it is false, change the underlined word or words to make the statement true.

6. <u>Epithelial</u> tissue makes parts of your body move.

7. The <u>circulatory</u> system carries needed materials to the body cells.

8. Spongy bone is filled with <u>cartilage</u>.

9. <u>Skeletal</u> muscle is sometimes called striated muscle.

10. The <u>epidermis</u> contains nerve endings and blood vessels.

Checking Concepts

11. Explain the relationship among cells, tissues, organs, and organ systems.

12. How does hunger help your body maintain homeostasis?

13. Think of a situation that might cause long-term stress. Identify some ways in which a person might deal with that stress.

14. Describe the structure of a bone.

15. List the four kinds of movable joints. Describe how each kind of joint functions.

16. How does the appearance of smooth muscle differ from that of skeletal muscle when viewed with a microscope?

17. Explain how skeletal muscles work in pairs to move a body part.

18. Why is it important to limit your exposure to the sun?

19. **Writing to Learn** Write an article for your school newspaper about preventing skeletal and muscular injuries. The article should focus on ways in which athletes can strengthen their muscles and bones and decrease the risk of injuries during sports.

Thinking Critically

20. **Inferring** Why do you think scientists classify blood as a connective tissue?

21. **Making Generalizations** How is homeostasis important to survival?

22. **Applying Concepts** At birth, the joints in an infant's skull are flexible and not yet fixed. As the child develops, the bones become more rigid and grow together. Why is it important that the bones of an infant's skull not grow together too rapidly?

23. **Predicting** If smooth muscle had to be consciously controlled, what problems could you foresee in day-to-day living?

24. **Relating Cause and Effect** A person who is exposed to excessive heat may suffer from a condition known as heat stroke. The first sign of heat stroke is that the person stops sweating. Why is this condition a life-threatening emergency?

Applying Skills

The graph below shows the effects of the temperature of the environment on a girl's skin temperature and on the temperature inside her body. Use the graph to answer Questions 25–27.

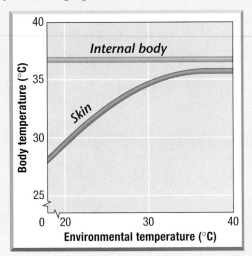

25. Interpreting Data As the temperature of the environment rises, what happens to the girl's internal temperature? How does this demonstrate homeostasis?

26. Inferring What happens to the temperature of the girl's skin? Why is this pattern different from the pattern shown by the girl's internal temperature?

27. Developing Hypotheses Suppose the girl went outdoors on a chilly fall morning. Write a hypothesis that predicts what would happen to her internal body temperature and skin temperature.

Performance ▼ CHAPTER PROJECT Assessment

Present Your Project Demonstrate your model for the class. Explain how your model shows your chosen motion. Describe how the contraction of muscle is involved.

Reflect and Record Why did you select the motion that you modeled? What new information did you discover about the human body? If you could do the project again, what would you change? Write your thoughts in your journal.

Test Preparation
Use these questions to prepare for standardized tests.

Read the passage. Then answer Questions 28–30.

Magnetic resonance imaging, or MRI, is a method used to take clear images of both the bones and soft tissues of the body. An MRI scanner is a large cylinder that contains electromagnets. The person is placed on a platform that slides into the center of the cylinder. The person is then exposed to short bursts of magnetic energy. This magnetic energy causes atoms within the body to vibrate, or resonate. A computer then analyzes the vibration patterns and produces an image of the area.

   MRI can produce images of body tissues at any angle. The images clearly show muscles and other soft tissues that an X-ray image cannot show. Another advantage of MRI is that it does not damage cells. Because MRI machines are very expensive to buy and use, this technique is not used to examine broken bones.

28. Which of the following is the best title for this passage?
   a. Using X-Rays to Diagnose Bone Injuries
   b. Using MRI to Diagnose Injuries
   c. The Dangers of MRI
   d. Two Methods for Diagnosing Injuries

29. Why is MRI often used to diagnose muscle and other soft tissue injuries?
   a. MRI creates clear images of soft tissues.
   b. MRI can produce images from many angles.
   c. MRI does not damage body cells.
   d. all of the above

30. According to the passage, why are X-rays used instead of MRI to examine broken bones?
   a. X-ray images are less expensive to produce.
   b. MRI involves placing a person inside a cylinder.
   c. Vibration of atoms is uncomfortable.
   d. MRI causes damage to cells.

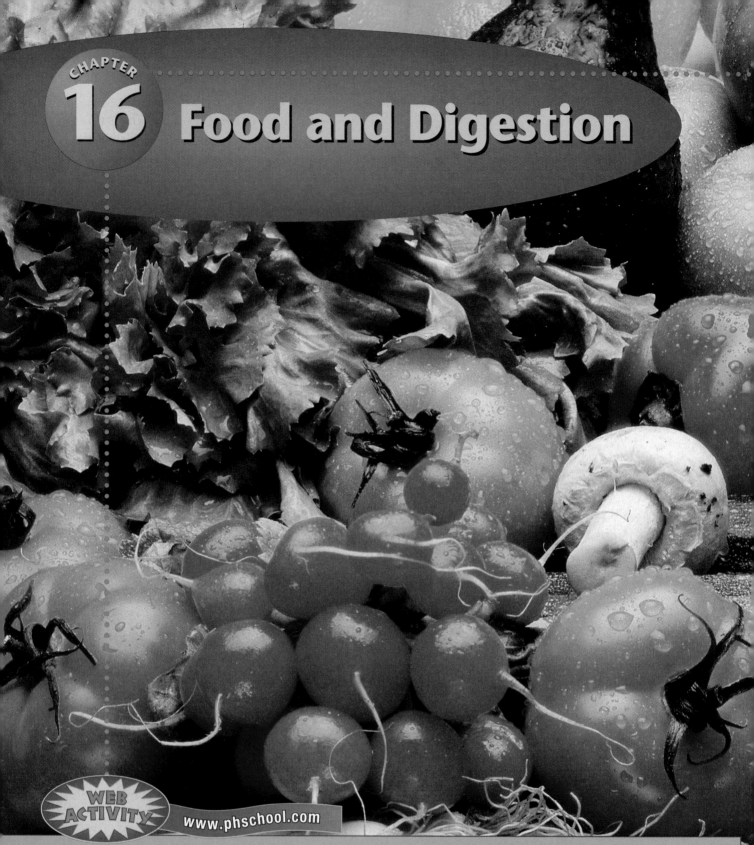

SECTION 1 Integrating Chemistry
Food and Energy

Discover **Food Claims—Fact or Fiction?**
Sharpen Your Skills **Predicting**
Real-World Lab **Iron for Breakfast**

SECTION 2 **The Digestive Process Begins**

Discover **How Can You Speed up Digestion?**
Try This **Modeling Peristalsis**
Skills Lab **As the Stomach Churns**

SECTION 3 **Final Digestion and Absorption**

Discover **Which Surface Is Larger?**
Try This **Break Up!**

504

CHAPTER 16 PROJECT

What's on Your Menu?

When you see fresh vegetables in a market, which kinds appeal to you? In the school cafeteria at lunch time, which foods do you select? When you're hungry and grab a snack, what do you choose? This chapter looks at foods and the process of digestion that goes on in your body. It also explains how your food choices affect your health. In this project, you'll take a close look at the foods you select each day.

Your Goal To compare your eating pattern to the recommendations in the Food Guide Pyramid.

To complete this project successfully, you must

◆ keep an accurate record of everything you eat and drink for three days

◆ create graphs to compare your eating pattern with the recommendations in the Food Guide Pyramid

◆ make changes, if needed, during another three-day period to bring your diet closer to the recommendations in the Food Guide Pyramid

Get Started Begin by deciding how to best keep an accurate, complete food log. How will you make sure you record everything you eat, including snacks and drinks? How will you decide which category each food falls into? How will you determine serving sizes? Prepare a plan for keeping a food log, and give it to your teacher for approval.

Check Your Progress You'll be working on this project as you study this chapter. To keep your project on track, look for Check Your Progress boxes at the following points.

Section 1 Review, page 516: Keep a food log for three days.
Section 2 Review, page 523: Create graphs to compare your food choices to the recommended number of servings.
Section 3 Review, page 529: Make changes to improve your diet.

Present Your Project At the end of the chapter (page 533), you'll prepare a written summary of what you've learned.

Take your pick! Local markets offer a wide choice of tasty fruits and vegetables.

SECTION 1 Food and Energy

DISCOVER • ACTIVITY

Food Claims—Fact or Fiction?

1. Examine the list of statements at the right. Copy the list onto a separate sheet of paper.

2. Next to each statement, write *agree* or *disagree*. Give a reason for your response.

3. Discuss your responses with a small group of classmates. Compare the reasons you gave for agreeing or disagreeing with each statement.

Think It Over

Posing Questions List some other statements about nutrition that you have heard. How could you find out whether the statements are true?

Fact or Fiction?

a. Athletes need more protein in their diets than other people do.

b. The only salt that a food contains is the salt that you have added to it.

c. As part of a healthy diet, everyone should take vitamin supplements.

d. You can go without water for longer than you can go without food.

GUIDE FOR READING

◆ What are the six nutrients needed by the body?

◆ How can the Food Guide Pyramid and food labels help you plan a healthy diet?

Reading Tip As you read, create a table that includes the function and sources of each nutrient group.

Imagine a Thanksgiving dinner—roast turkey on a platter, delicious stuffing, and lots of vegetables—an abundance of colors and aromas. Food is an important part of many happy occasions, of times shared with friends and family. Food is also essential. Every living thing needs food to stay alive.

Why You Need Food

Food provides your body with materials for growing and for repairing tissues. Food also provides energy for everything you do—running, playing a musical instrument, reading, and even sleeping. By filling those needs, food enables your body to maintain homeostasis. Recall that homeostasis is the body's ability to keep a steady internal state in spite of changing external conditions. Suppose, for example, that you cut your finger. Food provides both the raw materials necessary to grow new skin and the energy that powers this growth.

Your body converts the foods you eat into nutrients. **Nutrients** (NOO tre unts) are the substances in food that provide the raw materials and energy the body needs to carry out all the essential processes. **There are six kinds of nutrients necessary for human health— carbohydrates, fats, proteins, vitamins, minerals, and water.**

INTEGRATING PHYSICS Carbohydrates, fats, and proteins all provide the body with energy. When nutrients are used by the body for energy, the amount of energy they release can be measured in units called calories. One **calorie** is the amount of energy needed to raise the temperature of one gram of water by one Celsius degree. Most foods contain many thousands of calories of energy. Scientists usually use the term *Calorie*, with a capital *C*, to measure the energy in foods. One Calorie is the same as 1,000 calories. For example, one serving of popcorn may contain 60 Calories, or 60,000 calories, of energy. The more Calories a food has, the more energy it contains.

You need to eat a certain number of Calories each day to meet your body's energy needs. This daily energy requirement depends on a person's level of physical activity. It also changes as a person grows and ages. Infants and small children grow very rapidly, so they generally have the highest energy needs. Your current growth and level of physical activity affect the number of Calories you need. The more active you are, the higher your energy needs are.

Carbohydrates

The nutrients called **carbohydrates** (kar boh HY drayts), which are composed of carbon, oxygen, and hydrogen, are a major source of energy. One gram of carbohydrate provides your body with four Calories of energy. Carbohydrates also provide the raw materials to make parts of cells. Based on their chemical structure, carbohydrates are divided into two groups, simple carbohydrates and complex carbohydrates.

Figure 1 Your body obtains energy from carbohydrates. The sugars in fruits are simple carbohydrates. Starch is a complex carbohydrate found in grains and other plant products.

Figure 2 Fiber is found in fruits, whole-grain foods, and the other foods shown here. *Applying Concepts Why is fiber important in the diet?*

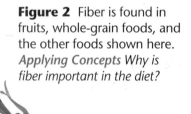

Simple Carbohydrates Simple carbohydrates are also known as sugars. There are many types of sugars. They are found naturally in fruits, milk, and some vegetables. Sugars are also added to foods such as cookies, candies, and soft drinks. One sugar, **glucose** (GLOO kohs), is the major source of energy for your body's cells. However, most foods do not contain large amounts of glucose. The body converts other types of sugars into glucose, the form of sugar the body can use.

Complex Carbohydrates Complex carbohydrates are made up of many sugar molecules linked together in a chain. Starch is a complex carbohydrate found in plant foods such as potatoes, rice, corn, and grain products, such as pasta, cereals, and bread. To use starch as an energy source, your body first breaks it down into smaller, individual sugar molecules. These sugar molecules are then involved in chemical reactions where energy is produced.

Like starch, **fiber** is a complex carbohydrate found in plant foods. However, unlike starch, fiber cannot be broken down into sugar molecules by your body. Instead, the fiber passes through the body and is eliminated. Because your body cannot digest it, fiber is not considered a nutrient. Fiber is an important part of the diet, however, because it helps keep the digestive system functioning properly. Fruits, vegetables, and nuts contain fiber. So do products made with whole grains, such as some breads and cereals.

Nutritionists recommend that 50 to 60 percent of the Calories in a diet come from carbohydrates. When choosing foods containing carbohydrates, it is better to eat more complex carbohydrates than simple carbohydrates. Sugars can give a quick burst of energy, but starches provide a more even, long-term energy source. In addition, foods that are high in starch usually contain a variety of other nutrients. Foods made with a lot of sugar, such as candy, cookies, and soft drinks, usually have few valuable nutrients.

Checkpoint *What are the two types of carbohydrates? Give an example of each.*

Figure 3 You obtain fats from foods such as steak, ice cream, and cooking oils.
Classifying Which of these foods contain saturated fats?

Fats

Like carbohydrates, **fats** are high-energy nutrients that are composed of carbon, oxygen, and hydrogen. However, fats contain more than twice as much energy as an equal amount of carbohydrates. In addition, fats perform other important functions. For example, they form part of the structure of cells. Fatty tissue also protects and supports your internal organs and acts as insulation to keep heat inside your body.

Fats are classified as either unsaturated fats or saturated fats, based on their chemical structure. **Unsaturated fats** are usually liquid at room temperature. Most oils, such as olive oil and canola oil, are unsaturated fats. Unsaturated fat is also found in some types of seafood, such as salmon. **Saturated fats** are usually solid at room temperature. Animal products, such as meat, dairy products, and egg yolks, contain relatively large amounts of saturated fat. Some oils, such as palm oil and coconut oil, are also high in saturated fat.

Foods that contain saturated fat often contain cholesterol as well. **Cholesterol** (kuh LES tur awl) is a waxy, fatlike substance found only in animal products. Like fats, cholesterol is an important part of your body's cells. But your liver makes all of the cholesterol your body needs. Therefore, cholesterol is not a necessary part of the diet.

Although people need some fats in their diet, they only need a small amount. Nutritionists recommend that no more than 30 percent of the Calories eaten each day come from fats. In particular, people should limit their intake of saturated fats and cholesterol. Extra fats and cholesterol in the diet can lead to a buildup of a fatty material in the blood vessels. This fatty buildup can cause heart disease. You will learn about the connections among fats, cholesterol, and heart disease in Chapter 17.

Math TOOLBOX

Calculating Percent

A percent (%) is a number compared to 100. For example, 30% means 30 out of 100.

Here is how to calculate the percent of Calories from fat in a person's diet. Suppose that a person eats a total of 2,000 Calories in one day. Of those Calories, 500 come from fats.

1. Write the comparison as a fraction:

$$\frac{500}{2,000}$$

2. Multiply the fraction by 100% to express it as a percent:

$$\frac{500}{2,000} \times \frac{100\%}{1} = 25\%$$

Calories from fat made up 25% of the person's diet that day.

Figure 4 Meats and these other foods are sources of protein.

Social Studies
CONNECTION

Industry grew rapidly in the 1800s. During that time, many children of factory workers developed rickets, a condition in which the bones become soft. Rickets is caused by a lack of vitamin D. The main source of vitamin D is sunlight, which acts on skin cells to produce the vitamin.

Factory workers in the 1800s often lived in cities with dark, narrow streets. Air pollution from factories also blocked some sunlight. One researcher, Theobald A. Palm, wrote this statement in 1890: "It is in the narrow alleys, the haunts and playgrounds of the children of the poor, that this exclusion of sunlight is at its worst, and it is there that the victims of rickets are to be found in abundance."

In Your Journal

Write several questions that a newspaper reporter might have asked Dr. Palm about rickets among poor city residents. Then write the answers he might have given.

Proteins

Proteins are nutrients that contain nitrogen as well as carbon, hydrogen, and oxygen. Proteins are needed for tissue growth and repair. They also play a part in chemical reactions within cells. Proteins can serve as a source of energy, but they are a less important source of energy than carbohydrates or fats. Foods that contain high amounts of protein include meat, poultry, fish, dairy products, nuts, beans, and lentils. About 12 percent of your daily Calorie intake should come from proteins.

Amino Acids Proteins are made up of small units called **INTEGRATING CHEMISTRY** **amino acids** (uh MEE noh), which are linked together chemically to form large protein molecules. Thousands of different proteins are built from only about 20 different amino acids. Your body can make about half of the amino acids it needs. The others, called essential amino acids, must come from the foods you eat.

Complete and Incomplete Proteins Proteins from animal sources, such as meat and eggs, are called complete proteins because they contain all the essential amino acids. Proteins from plant sources, such as beans, grains, and nuts, are called incomplete proteins because they are missing one or more essential amino acids. Different plant foods lack different amino acids. Therefore, to obtain all the essential amino acids from plant sources alone, people need to eat a variety of plant foods.

☑ *Checkpoint* *What is meant by the term* incomplete protein?

Vitamins

The life of a sailor in the 1700s could be difficult indeed. For one thing, sailors on long voyages ate hard, dry biscuits, salted meat, and not much else. In addition, many sailors developed a serious disease called scurvy. People with scurvy suffer from bleeding gums, stiff joints, and sores that do not heal.

A Scottish doctor, James Lind, hypothesized that scurvy was the result of the sailors' poor diet. Lind divided sailors with scurvy into groups and fed different foods to each group. The sailors who were fed citrus fruits—oranges and lemons—quickly recovered from the disease. In 1754, Lind recommended that all sailors eat citrus fruits. When Lind's recommendations were finally carried out by the British Navy in 1795, scurvy disappeared from the navy.

Scurvy is caused by the lack of a nutrient called vitamin C. **Vitamins** act as helper molecules in a variety of chemical reactions within the body. The body needs only small amounts of vitamins. Figure 5 lists the vitamins necessary for health. The body can make a few of these vitamins. For example, bacteria that live in your intestines make small amounts of vitamin K.

Figure 5 Both fat-soluble vitamins and water-soluble vitamins are necessary to maintain health. *Interpreting Charts What foods provide a supply of both vitamins A and B_6?*

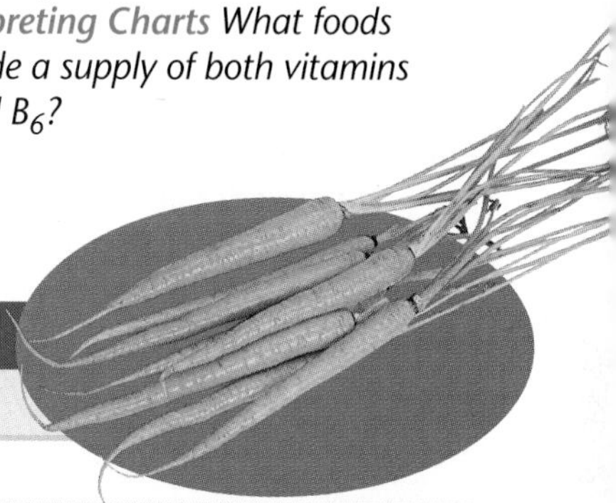

Essential Vitamins

Vitamin	Sources	Function
Fat-soluble		
A	Dairy products; eggs; liver; yellow, orange, and dark green vegetables; fruits	Maintains healthy skin, bones, teeth, and hair; aids vision in dim light
D	Fortified dairy products; fish; eggs; liver; made by skin cells in presence of sunlight	Maintains bones and teeth; helps in the use of calcium and phosphorus
E	Vegetable oils; margarine; green, leafy vegetables; whole-grain foods; seeds; nuts	Aids in maintenance of red blood cells
K	Green, leafy vegetables; milk; liver; made by bacteria in the intestines	Aids in blood clotting
Water-soluble		
B_1 (thiamin)	Pork; liver; whole-grain foods; legumes; nuts	Needed for breakdown of carbohydrates
B_2 (riboflavin)	Dairy products; eggs; leafy, green vegetables; whole-grain breads and cereals	Needed for normal growth
B_3 (niacin)	Many protein-rich foods; milk; eggs; meat; fish; whole-grain foods; nuts; peanut butter	Needed for release of energy
B_6 (pyridoxine)	Green and leafy vegetables; meats; fish; legumes; fruits; whole-grain foods	Helps in the breakdown of proteins, fats, and carbohydrates
B_{12}	Meats; fish; poultry; dairy products; eggs	Maintains healthy nervous system; needed for red blood cell formation
Biotin	Liver; meat; fish; eggs; legumes; bananas; melons	Aids in the release of energy
Folic acid	Leafy, green vegetables; legumes; seeds; liver	Needed for red blood cell formation
Pantothenic acid	Liver; meats; fish; eggs; whole-grain foods	Needed for the release of energy
C	Citrus fruits; tomatoes; potatoes; dark green vegetables; mangoes	Needed to form connective tissue and fight infection

However, people must obtain most vitamins from foods. If people eat a wide variety of foods, they will probably get enough of each vitamin. Most people do not need to take vitamin supplements.

Vitamins are classified as either fat-soluble or water-soluble. Fat-soluble vitamins dissolve in fat, and they are stored in fatty tissues in the body. Vitamins A, D, E, and K are all fat-soluble vitamins. Water-soluble vitamins dissolve in water and are not stored in the body. This fact makes it especially important to include sources of water-soluble vitamins—vitamin C and all the B vitamins—in your diet every day.

Minerals

Like vitamins, minerals are needed by your body in small amounts. **Minerals** are nutrients that are not made by living things. They are present in soil and are absorbed by plants through their roots. You obtain minerals by eating plant foods or animals that have eaten plants. Figure 6 lists some minerals you need. As you know from Chapter 15, calcium is needed for strong bones and teeth. Iron is needed for the proper function of red blood cells.

Figure 6 Eating a variety of foods each day provides your body with the minerals it needs.
Interpreting Charts Which minerals play a role in regulating water levels in the body?

◀ **Source of calcium**

▼ **Source of potassium**

Essential Minerals		
Mineral	**Sources**	**Function**
Calcium	Milk; cheese; dark green, leafy vegetables; tofu; legumes	Helps build bones and teeth; important for blood-clotting, nerve and muscle function
Chlorine	Table salt; soy sauce; processed foods	Helps maintain water balance; aids in digestion
Fluorine	Fluoridated drinking water; fish	Helps form bones and teeth
Iodine	Seafood; iodized salt	Makes up part of hormones that regulate the release of energy
Iron	Red meats; seafood; green, leafy vegetables; legumes; dried fruits	Forms an important part of red blood cells
Magnesium	Green, leafy vegetables; legumes; nuts; whole-grain foods	Needed for normal muscle and nerve function; helps in the release of energy
Phosphorus	Meat; poultry; eggs; fish; dairy products	Needed for healthy bones and teeth; helps in the release of energy
Potassium	Grains; fruits; vegetables; meat; fish	Helps maintain water balance; needed for normal muscle and nerve function
Sodium	Table salt; soy sauce; processed foods	Helps maintain water balance; needed for normal nerve function

Source of sodium ▶

512

Water

Imagine that a boat is sinking. The people are getting into a lifeboat. They have room for one of the following: a bag of fruit, a can of meat, a loaf of bread, or a jug of water. Which item should they choose?

You might be surprised to learn that the lifeboat passengers should choose the water. Although people can probably survive for weeks without food, they will die within days without fresh water. Water is the most abundant substance in the body. It accounts for about 65 percent of the average person's body weight.

Water is the most important nutrient because the body's vital processes—including chemical reactions such as the breakdown of nutrients—take place in water. Water makes up most of the body's fluids, including blood. Nutrients and other important substances are carried throughout the body dissolved in the watery part of the blood. Your body also needs water to produce perspiration.

Under normal conditions, you need to take in about 2 liters of water every day. You can do this by drinking water and other beverages, and by eating foods with lots of water, such as fruits and vegetables. If the weather is hot or you are exercising, you need to drink even more to replace the water that you lose in sweat.

Figure 7 Like all living things, you need water. Without regular water intake, your body cannot carry out the processes that keep you alive.

The Food Guide Pyramid

The **Food Guide Pyramid** was developed by nutritionists to help people plan a healthy diet. **The Food Guide Pyramid classifies foods into six groups. It also indicates how many servings from each group should be eaten every day to maintain a healthy diet.** You can combine the advice within the pyramid with knowledge of your own food preferences. By doing this, you can have a healthy diet containing foods you like.

You can see the six food groups in *Exploring the Food Guide Pyramid* on page 514. Notice that the food group at the base of the pyramid includes foods made from grains, such as bread, cereal, rice, and pasta. This bottom level is the widest part of the pyramid. The large size indicates that these foods should make up the largest part of the diet.

The second level in the pyramid is made of two food groups, the Fruit group and the Vegetable group. Notice that this level is not as wide as the bottom level. This size difference indicates that people need fewer servings of these foods than of foods from the bottom level.

EXPLORING *the Food Guide Pyramid*

The Food Guide Pyramid recommends the number of servings that a person should eat each day from six food groups. Note that each number of servings is listed as a range. Active, growing teenagers may need to eat the larger number of servings for each group.

Fats, Oils, and Sweets (Use sparingly.)
Soft drinks, candy, ice cream, mayonnaise, and other foods in this group have few valuable nutrients. In addition, these foods are high in Calories. They should be eaten only in small quantities.

Milk, Yogurt, and Cheese Group (2–3 servings) Milk and other dairy products are rich in proteins, carbohydrates, vitamins, and minerals. Try to select low-fat dairy foods, such as low-fat milk.

Meat, Poultry, Fish, Dry Beans, Eggs, and Nuts Group (2–3 servings)
These foods are high in protein. They also supply vitamins and minerals. Since eggs, nuts, and some meats are high in fat, they should be eaten sparingly.

Vegetable Group (3–5 servings)
Vegetables are low-fat sources of carbohydrates, fiber, vitamins, and minerals.

Fruit Group (2–4 servings)
Fruits are good sources of carbohydrates, fiber, vitamins, and water.

Bread, Cereal, Rice, and Pasta Group (6–11 servings)
The foods at the base of the pyramid are rich in complex carbohydrates and also provide proteins, fiber, vitamins, and some minerals.

● *Fat (naturally occurring and added)*
▲ *Sugars (naturally occurring and added)*

The third level of the pyramid contains the Milk, Yogurt, and Cheese group; and the Meat, Poultry, Fish, Dry Beans, Eggs, and Nuts group. People need still smaller amounts of food from this level.

At the top of the pyramid are foods containing large amounts of fat, sugar, or both. Notice that this is the smallest part of the pyramid. The small size indicates that intake of these foods should be limited. There is a good reason for this advice. Foods in the other groups already contain fats and sugars. Limiting intake of *additional* fats and sugars can help you prevent heart disease and other problems.

☑ *Checkpoint* *What types of foods should make up the largest portion of a person's diet?*

Food Labels

After a long day, you and your friends stop into a store on your way home from school. What snack should you buy? How can you make a wise choice? One thing you can do is to read the information provided on food labels. The United States Food and Drug Administration (FDA) requires that all food items except meat, poultry, fresh vegetables, and fresh fruit must be labeled with specific nutritional information. **Food labels allow you to evaluate a single food as well as to compare the nutritional values of two foods.**

Figure 8 shows a food label that might appear on a box of cereal. Refer to that label as you read about some of the important nutritional information it contains.

Serving Size Notice that the serving size and the number of servings in the container are listed at the top of the label. The FDA has established standard serving sizes for all types of foods. This means that all containers of ice cream, for example, use the same serving size on their labels. The information on the rest of the label, including Calorie counts and nutrient content, is based on the serving size. Therefore, if you eat a portion that's twice as large as the serving size, you'll consume twice the number of Calories and nutrients listed on the label.

Calories from Fat The next item on the food label is the number of Calories in a serving and the number of Calories that come from fat. Notice that a single serving of this cereal supplies the body with 110 Calories of energy.

Figure 8 By law, specific nutritional information must be listed on food labels. *Calculating How many servings of this product would you have to eat to get 90 percent of the Daily Value for iron?*

Nutrition Facts

Serving Size	1 cup (30g)
Servings Per Container	About 10

Amount Per Serving

Calories 110	Calories from Fat 15

	% Daily Value*
Total Fat 2g	**3%**
Saturated Fat 0g	**0%**
Cholesterol 0mg	**0%**
Sodium 280mg	**12%**
Total Carbohydrate 22g	**7%**
Dietary Fiber 3g	**12%**
Sugars 1g	
Protein 3g	

Vitamin A	10%	•	Vitamin C	20%
Calcium	4%	•	Iron	45%

* Percent Daily Values are based on a 2,000 Calorie diet. Your daily values may be higher or lower depending on your caloric needs:

	Calories	2,000	2,500
Total Fat	Less than	65g	80g
Sat. Fat	Less than	20g	25g
Cholesterol	Less than	300mg	300mg
Sodium	Less than	2,400mg	2,400mg
Total Carbohydrate		300g	375g
Fiber		25g	30g

Calories per gram:
Fat 9   •   Carbohydrate 4   •   Protein 4

Ingredients: Whole grain oats, sugar, salt, milled corn, oat fiber, dried whey, hone~ almonds, d~

Figure 9 If you are very active, you need to eat more servings to provide your body with the Calories and nutrients you need.

Recall that no more than 30 percent of the Calories you consume should come from fats. To calculate whether a specific food falls within this guideline, divide the number of Calories from fat by the total number of Calories, then multiply by 100%. For this cereal,

$$\frac{15}{110} \times \frac{100\%}{1} = 13.6\%.$$

That number shows you that a serving of this cereal is well within the recommended limits for fat intake.

Daily Values Locate the % Daily Value column in Figure 8. The **Percent Daily Value** indicates how the nutritional content of one serving fits into the diet of a person who consumes a total of 2,000 Calories a day. One serving of this cereal contains 280 milligrams of sodium. That's 12 percent of the total amount of sodium a person should consume in one day.

Ingredients Packaged foods, such as crackers and soup mixes, usually contain a mixture of ingredients. The food label lists those ingredients in order by weight, starting with the main ingredient. In a breakfast cereal, for example, that may be corn, oats, rice, or wheat. Often, sugar and salt are added for flavor. The list can alert you to substances that have been added to a food to improve its flavor or color, or to keep it from spoiling. In addition, some people can become sick or break out in a rash if they eat certain substances. By reading ingredient lists, people can find foods that contain nutrients they need and avoid foods that contain substances to which they are allergic.

Section 1 Review

1. List the six nutrients that are needed by the body.
2. What information does the Food Guide Pyramid provide? Into how many groups are foods classified?
3. Explain how food labels can help a person make healthy food choices.
4. Why should you eat more complex carbohydrates than simple carbohydrates?
5. **Thinking Critically Applying Concepts** Why is it especially important that vegetarians eat a varied diet?

CHAPTER PROJECT

Check Your Progress

By now, you should have given your teacher your plan for keeping your food log. Adjust the plan as your teacher suggests. Then start your three days of record-keeping. If possible, your record-keeping should span two weekdays and one weekend day. Be sure to keep an accurate record of all the foods and beverages you consume. (*Hint:* Either make your log portable, or plan a method for recording your food intake when you're away from home.)

Iron for Breakfast

Have you ever looked at the nutrition facts on a cereal box? Some of the listed nutrients occur naturally in the cereal. Others are added as it is processed. In this lab, you will look for evidence that extra iron has been added to some cereals.

Problem

How can you test whether iron has been added to cereals?

Skills Focus

observing, predicting, interpreting data

Materials

long bar magnet   balance
white paper towels   plastic spoon
instant oatmeal   warm water
watch or clock
wooden dowel
2 dry breakfast cereals
3 sealable plastic freezer bags
plastic jar with sealable cover

Procedure

1. Read the nutrition facts listed on the packages of the cereals that you'll be testing. Record the percent of iron listed for each of the cereals.
2. Put a paper towel on the pan of a balance. Use a spoon to measure out 50 grams of instant oatmeal. **CAUTION:** *Do not eat any of the cereals in this lab.*
3. Place the oatmeal in a plastic bag. Push down gently on the bag to remove most of the air, then seal the bag. Roll a dowel over the cereal repeatedly to crush it into a fine powder.

4. Pour the powdered cereal into a plastic jar. Cover the cereal with warm water. Cover the jar tightly and shake it for about 15 minutes.
5. Move a bar magnet along the outside of the jar. Observe the results.
6. Repeat Steps 2 through 5 with your other cereal samples.

Analyze and Conclude

1. Describe the material you saw inside the jar near the magnet. What evidence do you have that this material is iron?
2. Which sample appeared to have the most added iron? The least? Were those results consistent with the listed amounts?
3. Why is it likely that any iron metal present in the cereal was added during the processing?
4. What roles does iron play in the body?
5. **Apply** Why might adding iron to breakfast cereal be a good way to ensure that children receive an adequate amount of that mineral?

More to Explore

Read the labels on five snack foods. Make a bar graph showing their iron content.

SECTION 2 The Digestive Process Begins

DISCOVER ········· ACTIVITY····

How Can You Speed up Digestion?

1. Obtain two plastic jars with lids. Fill the jars with equal amounts of water.

2. At the same time, place a whole sugar cube into one jar. Place a crushed sugar cube into the other jar.

3. Fasten the lids on the jars. Holding one jar in each hand, shake the two jars gently and equally.

4. Place the jars on a flat surface. Observe whether the whole cube or the crushed cube dissolves faster.

Think It Over

Predicting Use the results of this activity to predict which would take longer to digest: a large piece of food or one that has been cut up into many small pieces. Explain your answer.

GUIDE FOR READING

◆ What general functions are carried out in the digestive system?

Reading Tip Before you read, preview the headings in this section. Predict the functions of the mouth, the esophagus, and the stomach.

Dr. William Beaumont ▼

In June of 1822, nineteen-year-old Alexis St. Martin was wounded in the stomach while hunting. William Beaumont, a doctor with the United States Army, saved St. Martin's life. However, the wound left an opening in St. Martin's stomach that never closed completely. Beaumont realized that by looking through the opening, he could observe what was happening inside St. Martin's stomach.

Beaumont observed that milk changed chemically inside the stomach. He hypothesized that chemical reactions inside the stomach broke down foods into smaller particles. To test his hypothesis, Beaumont removed liquid from St. Martin's stomach. He had the liquid analyzed to determine what materials it contained. The stomach liquid contained an acid that could break down foods into simpler substances.

Functions of the Digestive System

Beaumont's observations helped scientists understand the role of the stomach in the digestive system. The digestive system has three main functions. **First, it breaks down food into molecules the body can use. Then, the molecules are absorbed into the blood and carried throughout the body. Finally, wastes are eliminated from the body.**

The process by which your body breaks down food into small nutrient molecules is called **digestion.** There are two kinds of digestion—mechanical and chemical. In mechanical digestion, foods are physically broken down into smaller pieces. Mechanical digestion occurs when you bite into

518

a sandwich and chew it into small pieces. In chemical digestion, chemicals produced by the body break foods into their smaller chemical building blocks. For example, the starch in bread is broken down into individual sugar molecules.

After your food is digested, the molecules are ready to be transported throughout your body. **Absorption** (ab SAWRP shun) is the process by which nutrient molecules pass through the wall of your digestive system into your blood. Materials that are not absorbed, such as fiber, are eliminated from the body as wastes.

Figure 10 shows the organs of the digestive system, which is about nine meters long from beginning to end. As food moves through the digestive system, the processes of digestion, absorption, and elimination occur one after the other in an efficient, continuous process.

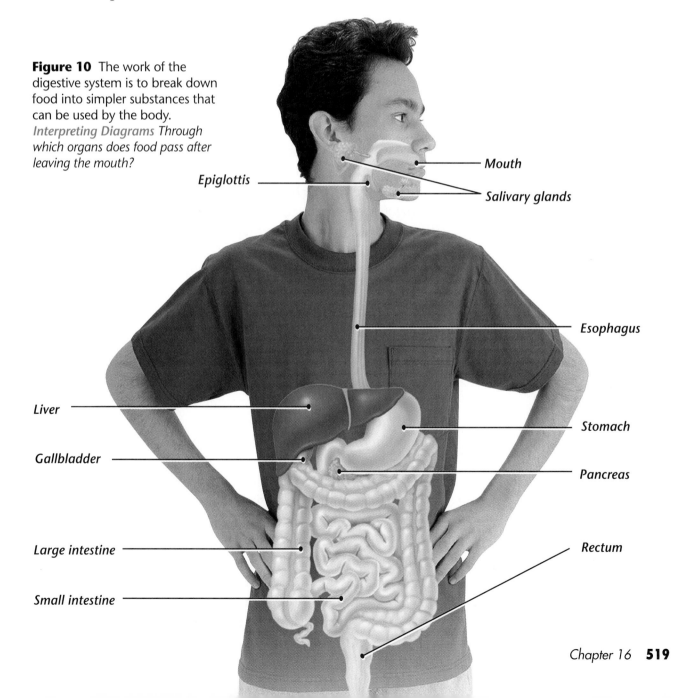

Figure 10 The work of the digestive system is to break down food into simpler substances that can be used by the body. *Interpreting Diagrams Through which organs does food pass after leaving the mouth?*

Mouth

Epiglottis

Salivary glands

Esophagus

Liver

Gallbladder

Large intestine

Small intestine

Stomach

Pancreas

Rectum

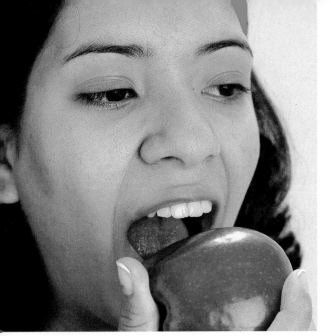

Figure 11 Mechanical digestion begins in the mouth, where the teeth cut and tear food into smaller pieces. *Observing Which teeth are specialized for biting into a juicy apple?*

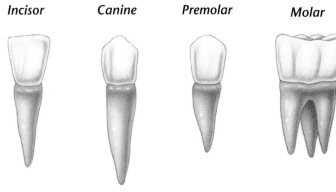

Incisor   *Canine*   *Premolar*   *Molar*

The Mouth

Have you ever walked past a bakery or restaurant and noticed your mouth watering? Smelling or even just thinking about food when you're hungry is enough to start your mouth watering. This response isn't accidental. Your body is responding to hunger and thoughts of food by preparing for the delicious meal it expects. The fluid released when your mouth waters is called **saliva** (suh LY vuh). Saliva plays an important role in both the mechanical and chemical digestive processes that take place in the mouth.

Mechanical Digestion   The process of mechanical digestion begins as you take your first bite of food. Your teeth carry out the first stage of mechanical digestion. Your center teeth, or incisors (in SY zurz), cut the food into bite-sized pieces. On either side of the incisors are sharp, pointy teeth called canines (KAY nynz). These teeth tear and slash the food in your mouth into smaller pieces. Behind the canines are the premolars and molars, which crush and grind the food. As the teeth do their work, saliva mixes with the pieces of food, moistening them into one slippery mass.

Chemical Digestion   Like mechanical digestion, chemical

INTEGRATING CHEMISTRY

digestion begins in the mouth. If you take a bite of a cracker and roll it around your mouth, the cracker begins to taste sweet. It tastes sweet because a chemical in the saliva has broken down the starch in the cracker into sugar molecules. Chemical digestion—the breakdown of complex molecules into simpler ones—has taken place. Chemical digestion is accomplished by enzymes. An **enzyme** is a protein that speeds up chemical reactions in the body. The chemical in saliva that digests starch is an enzyme. Your body produces many different enzymes. Each enzyme has a specific chemical shape. Its shape enables it to take part in only one kind of chemical reaction. For example, the enzyme that breaks down starch into sugars cannot break down proteins into amino acids.

The Esophagus

If you've ever choked on food, someone may have said that your food "went down the wrong way." That's because there are two openings at the back of your mouth. One opening leads to your windpipe, which carries air into your lungs. Usually, your body keeps food out of your windpipe. As you swallow, muscles in your throat move the food downward. While this happens, a flap of tissue called the **epiglottis** (ep uh GLAHT is) seals off your windpipe, preventing the food from entering. As you swallow, food goes into the **esophagus** (ih SAHF uh gus), a muscular tube that connects the mouth to the stomach. The esophagus is lined with mucus. **Mucus** is a thick, slippery substance produced by the body. In the digestive system, mucus makes food easier to swallow and to be moved along.

Food remains in the esophagus for only about 10 seconds. After food enters the esophagus, contractions of smooth muscles push the food toward the stomach. These involuntary waves of muscle contraction are called **peristalsis** (pehr ih STAWL sis). The action of peristalsis is shown in Figure 12. Peristalsis also occurs in the stomach and farther down the digestive system. These muscular waves keep food moving in one direction.

✓ *Checkpoint* How is food prevented from entering the windpipe?

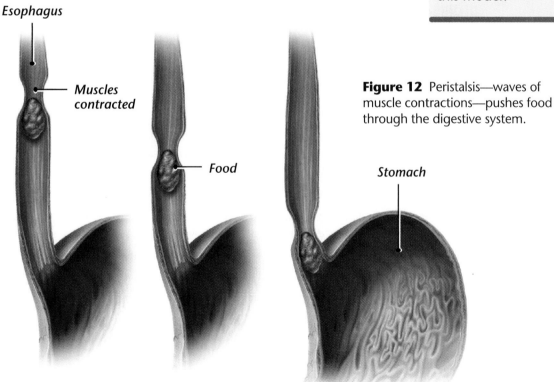

Esophagus

Muscles contracted

Food

Stomach

Figure 12 Peristalsis—waves of muscle contractions—pushes food through the digestive system.

The Stomach

When food leaves the esophagus, it enters the **stomach,** a J-shaped, muscular pouch located in the abdomen. As you eat, your stomach expands to hold all of the food that you swallow. An average adult's stomach holds about 2 liters of food.

Most mechanical digestion occurs in the stomach. Three strong layers of muscle contract to produce a churning motion. This action squeezes the food, mixing it with fluids in somewhat the same way that clothes and soapy water are mixed in a washing machine.

INTEGRATING CHEMISTRY While mechanical digestion is taking place, so too is chemical digestion. The churning of the stomach mixes food with digestive juice, a fluid produced by cells in the lining of the stomach.

Digestive juice contains the enzyme pepsin. Pepsin chemically digests the proteins in your food, breaking them down into amino acids. Digestive juice also contains hydrochloric acid, a very strong acid. This acid would burn a hole in clothes if it were spilled on them. Without this strong acid, however, your stomach could not function properly. First, pepsin works best in an acidic environment. Second, the acid kills many bacteria that you swallow along with your food.

Since the acid is so strong, you may wonder why it doesn't burn a hole in your stomach. The reason is that digestive juice

Figure 13 As food passes through the digestive system, the digestive juices gradually break down large food molecules into smaller ones. *Interpreting Charts Which enzymes aid in protein digestion?*

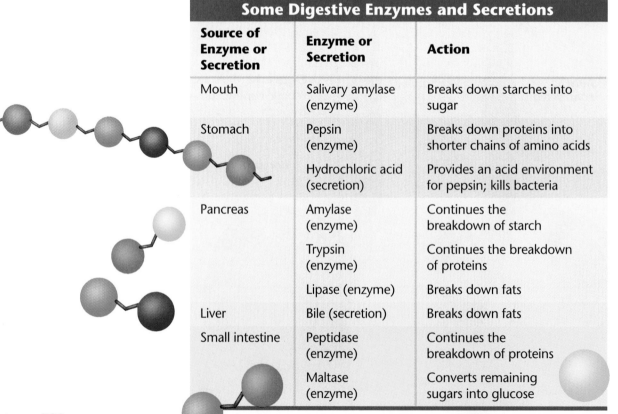

Some Digestive Enzymes and Secretions		
Source of Enzyme or Secretion	**Enzyme or Secretion**	**Action**
Mouth	Salivary amylase (enzyme)	Breaks down starches into sugar
Stomach	Pepsin (enzyme)	Breaks down proteins into shorter chains of amino acids
	Hydrochloric acid (secretion)	Provides an acid environment for pepsin; kills bacteria
Pancreas	Amylase (enzyme)	Continues the breakdown of starch
	Trypsin (enzyme)	Continues the breakdown of proteins
	Lipase (enzyme)	Breaks down fats
Liver	Bile (secretion)	Breaks down fats
Small intestine	Peptidase (enzyme)	Continues the breakdown of proteins
	Maltase (enzyme)	Converts remaining sugars into glucose

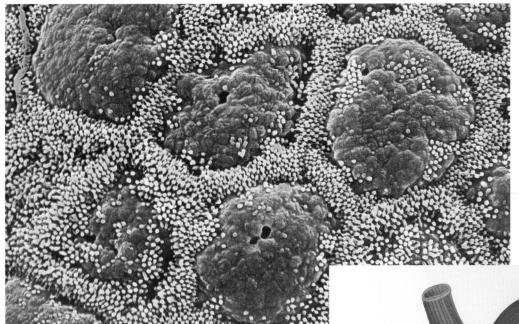

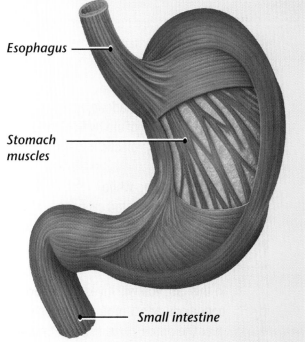

Figure 14 The stomach walls (left) produce mucus, shown here in yellow. Mucus protects the stomach from its own acid and enzymes. The stomach has powerful muscles (below) that help grind up food.

Esophagus

Stomach muscles

Small intestine

also contains mucus, which coats and protects the lining of your stomach. In addition, the cells that line the stomach are quickly replaced when they are damaged or worn out.

Food remains in the stomach until all of the solid material has been broken down into liquid form. A few hours after you finish eating, the stomach completes mechanical digestion of the food. By that time, most of the proteins have been chemically digested into shorter chains of amino acids. The food, now a thick liquid, is released into the next part of the digestive system. That is where final chemical digestion and absorption will take place.

Section 2 Review

1. List the functions of the digestive system.
2. What role does saliva play in digestion?
3. Describe peristalsis and explain its function in the digestive system.
4. What is the function of pepsin?
5. **Thinking Critically** Predicting If your stomach could no longer produce acid, how do you think that would affect digestion?

Check Your Progress CHAPTER PROJECT

By this point, you should have completed three full days of record keeping. Now create bar graphs to compare your food intake to the recommended numbers of servings in the Food Guide Pyramid. Analyze your graphs to identify changes you could make in your diet.

AS THE STOMACH CHURNS

The proteins you eat are constructed of large, complex molecules. Your body begins to break down those complex molecules in the stomach. In this lab, you will draw conclusions about the process by which proteins are digested.

Problem

What conditions are needed for the digestion of proteins in the stomach?

Materials

test tube rack   marking pencil
pepsin   dilute hydrochloric acid
water   plastic stirrers
litmus paper
cubes of boiled egg white
10-mL plastic graduated cylinder
4 test tubes with stoppers

Procedure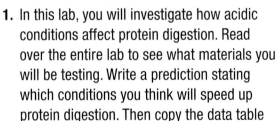

1. In this lab, you will investigate how acidic conditions affect protein digestion. Read over the entire lab to see what materials you will be testing. Write a prediction stating which conditions you think will speed up protein digestion. Then copy the data table into your notebook.

2. Label four test tubes *A, B, C,* and *D* and place them in a test tube rack.

3. In this lab, the protein you will test is boiled egg white, which has been cut into cubes about 1 cm on each side. Add 3 cubes to each test tube. Note and record the size and overall appearance of the cubes in each test tube. **CAUTION:** *Do not put any egg white into your mouth.*

4. Use a graduated cylinder to add 10 mL of the enzyme pepsin to test tube A. Observe the egg white cubes to determine whether an immediate reaction takes place. Record your observations under *Day 1* in your data table. If no changes occur, write "no immediate reaction."

5. Use a clean graduated cylinder to add 5 mL of pepsin to test tube B. Then rinse the graduated cylinder and add 5 mL of water to test tube B. Observe whether or not an immediate reaction takes place.

6. Use a clean graduated cylinder to add 10 mL of hydrochloric acid to test tube C. Observe whether or not an immediate reaction takes place. **CAUTION:** *Hydrochloric acid can burn skin and clothing. Avoid direct contact with it. Wash any splashes or spills with plenty of water, and notify your teacher.*

	DATA TABLE			
Test Tube	Egg White Appearance		Litmus Color	
	Day 1	Day 2	Day 1	Day 2
A				
B				
C				
D				

7. Use a clean graduated cylinder to add 5 mL of pepsin to test tube D. Then rinse the graduated cylinder and add 5 mL of hydrochloric acid to test tube D. Observe whether or not an immediate reaction takes place. Record your observations.

8. Obtain four strips of blue litmus paper. (Blue litmus paper turns pink in the presence of an acid.) Dip a clean plastic stirrer into the solution in each test tube, and then touch the stirrer to a piece of litmus paper. Observe what happens to the litmus paper. Record your observations.

9. Insert stoppers in the four test tubes and store the test tube rack as directed by your teacher.

10. The next day, examine the contents of each test tube. Note any changes in the size and overall appearance of the egg white cubes. Then test each solution with litmus paper. Record your observations in your data table.

Analyze and Conclude

1. Which material(s) were the best at digesting the egg white? What observations enabled you to determine this?

2. Do you think that the chemical digestion of protein in food is a fast reaction or a slow one? Explain.

3. What did this lab demonstrate about the ability of pepsin to digest protein?

4. Why was it important that the cubes of egg white all be about the same size?

5. **Think About It** How did test tubes A and C help you draw conclusions about protein digestion in this investigation?

Design an Experiment

Design a way to test whether protein digestion is affected by the size of the food pieces. Write down the hypothesis that you will test. Then create a data table for recording your observations. Obtain your teacher's permission before carrying out your plan.

SECTION 3 Final Digestion and Absorption

DISCOVER

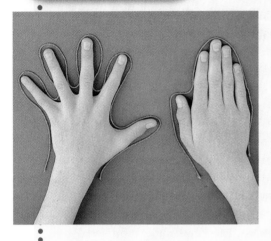

Which Surface Is Larger?

1. Work with a partner to carry out this investigation.

2. Begin by placing your hand palm-side down on a table. Keep your thumb and fingers tightly together. Lay string along the outline of your hand. Have your partner help you determine how long a string you need to outline your hand.

3. Use a metric ruler to measure the length of that string.

Think It Over

Predicting How long would you expect your hand outline to be if you spread out your thumb and fingers? Use string to test your prediction. Compare the two string lengths.

GUIDE FOR READING

◆ What role does the small intestine play in digestion?

◆ What role does the large intestine play in digestion?

Reading Tip As you read, create a table with the headings *Small Intestine, Liver, Pancreas,* and *Large Intestine.* Under each heading, list that organ's digestive function.

Have you ever been part of a huge crowd attending a concert or sports event? Barriers and passageways often guide people in the right direction. Ticket takers make sure that only those with tickets get in, and that they enter in an orderly fashion.

In some ways, the stomach can be thought of as the "ticket taker" of the digestive system. Once the food has been changed into a thick liquid, the stomach releases a little liquid at a time into the next part of the digestive system. This slow, smooth passage of food through the digestive system ensures that digestion and absorption take place smoothly.

The Small Intestine

After the thick liquid leaves the stomach, it enters the small intestine. The **small intestine** is the part of the digestive system where most of the chemical digestion takes place. If you look back at Figure 10, you may wonder how the small intestine got its name. After all, at about 6 meters—longer than many full-sized cars— it makes up two thirds of the digestive system. The small intestine was named for its small diameter. It is about two to three centimeters wide, about half the diameter of the large intestine.

When food reaches the small intestine, it has already been mechanically digested into a thick liquid. But chemical digestion has just begun. Although starches and proteins have been partially broken down, fats haven't been digested at all. **Almost all chemical digestion and absorption of nutrients takes place in the small intestine.**

The small intestine is bustling with chemical activity. As the liquid moves into the small intestine, it mixes with enzymes and secretions. The enzymes and secretions are produced in three different organs—the small intestine, the liver, and the pancreas. The liver and the pancreas deliver their substances to the small intestine through small tubes.

The Role of the Liver The **liver** is located in the upper portion of the abdomen. It is the largest and heaviest organ inside the body. You can think of the liver as an extremely busy chemical factory that plays a role in many body processes. For example, the liver breaks down medicines and other substances, and it helps eliminate nitrogen from the body. As part of the digestive system, the liver produces **bile,** a substance that breaks up fat particles. Bile flows from the liver into the **gallbladder,** the organ that stores bile. After you eat, bile passes through a tube from the gallbladder into the small intestine.

Bile is not an enzyme. It does not chemically digest foods. It does, however, break up large fat particles into smaller fat droplets. You can compare the action of bile on fats with the action of soap on a greasy frying pan. Soap physically breaks up the grease into small droplets that can mix with the soapy water and be washed away. Bile mixes with the fats in food to form small fat droplets. The droplets can then be chemically broken down by enzymes produced in the pancreas.

Break Up!

In this activity, you will model **ACTIVITY** the breakup of fat particles in the small intestine.

1. Fill two plastic jars half full of water. Add a few drops of oil to each jar.

2. Add $\frac{1}{4}$ teaspoon baking soda to one of the jars.

3. Stir the contents of both jars. Record your observations.

Observing In which jar did the oil begin to break up? What substance does the baking soda represent?

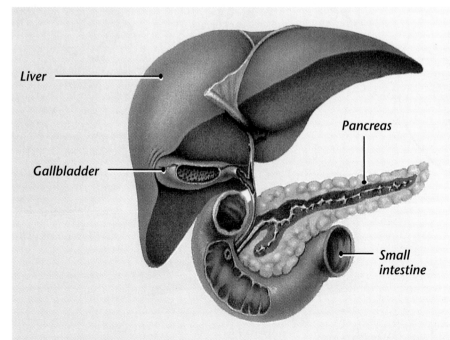

Liver

Gallbladder

Pancreas

Small intestine

Figure 15 Substances produced by the liver and pancreas aid in the digestion of food. *Applying Concepts Where is bile produced? Where is it stored before it is released into the small intestine?*

Help From the Pancreas The **pancreas** is a triangular organ that lies between the stomach and the first part of the small intestine. Like the liver, the pancreas plays a role in many body processes. As part of the digestive system, the pancreas produces enzymes that flow into the small intestine. These enzymes help break down starches, proteins, and fats.

The digestive enzymes produced by the pancreas and other organs do not break down all food substances, however. Recall that the fiber in food isn't broken down. Instead, fiber thickens the liquid material in the intestine. This makes it easier for peristalsis to push the material forward.

✓ *Checkpoint* *How does the pancreas aid in digestion?*

Absorption in the Small Intestine After chemical digestion takes place, the small nutrient molecules are ready to be absorbed by the body. The structure of the small intestine makes it well suited for absorption. The inner surface, or lining, of the small intestine looks bumpy. Millions of tiny finger-shaped structures called **villi** (VIL eye) (singular *villus*) cover the surface. The villi absorb nutrient molecules. Notice that tiny blood vessels run through the center of each villus. Nutrient molecules pass from cells on the surface of a villus into blood vessels. The blood carries the nutrients throughout the body for use by body cells.

The presence of villi increases the surface area of the small intestine. If all of the villi were laid out flat, the total surface area of the small intestine would be about as large as a tennis court.

Figure 16 Tiny finger-shaped projections called villi line the inside of the small intestine. In the diagram, you can see that the blood vessels in the villi are covered by a single layer of cells. The photograph shows a closeup view of villi. *Interpreting Diagrams How does the structure of the villi help them carry out their function?*

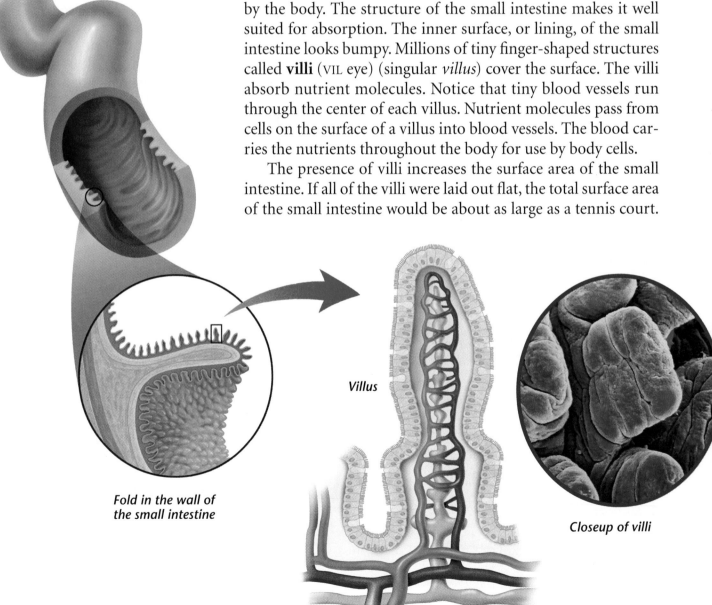

Small intestine

Fold in the wall of the small intestine

Villus

Closeup of villi

This greatly increased surface enables digested food to be absorbed faster than if the walls of the small intestine were smooth.

The Large Intestine

By the time material reaches the end of the small intestine, most nutrients have been absorbed. The remaining material moves from the small intestine into the large intestine. The **large intestine** is the last section of the digestive system. It is about one and a half meters long—about as long as the average bathtub. As you can see in Figure 17, the large intestine is shaped somewhat like a horseshoe. It runs up the right-hand side of the abdomen, across the upper abdomen, and then down the left-hand side. The large intestine contains bacteria that feed on the material passing through. These bacteria normally do not cause disease. In fact, they are helpful because they make certain vitamins, including vitamin K.

The material entering the large intestine contains water and undigested food such as fiber. **As the material moves through the large intestine, water is absorbed into the bloodstream. The remaining material is readied for elimination from the body.**

The large intestine ends in a short tube called the **rectum.** Here waste material is compressed into a solid form. This waste material is eliminated from the body through the **anus,** a muscular opening at the end of the rectum.

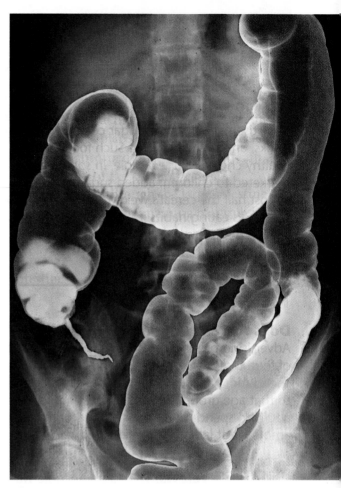

Figure 17 Notice the shape of the large intestine. As material passes through this structure, most of the water is absorbed by the body.

Section 3 Review

1. What two digestive processes occur in the small intestine? Briefly describe each process.
2. Which nutrient is absorbed in the large intestine?
3. How do the liver and pancreas function in the digestive process?
4. **Thinking Critically** **Relating Cause and Effect** Some people are allergic to a protein in wheat. When these people eat foods made with wheat, a reaction destroys the villi in the small intestine. What problems would you expect these people to experience?

CHAPTER PROJECT
Check Your Progress
You should now be trying to eat a more healthful diet. Be sure you keep an accurate log of your food intake during this three-day period. Then graph the results. (*Hint:* You might find it helpful to focus on one food category when trying to improve your eating habits.)

Reviewing Content

 For more review of key concepts, see the Interactive Student Tutorial CD-ROM.

Multiple Choice

Choose the letter of the best answer.

1. Which nutrient makes up about 65 percent of the body's weight?
   a. carbohydrate
   b. protein
   c. water
   d. fat

2. According to the Food Guide Pyramid, from which group should you eat the most servings?
   a. Milk, Yogurt, and Cheese
   b. Meat, Poultry, Fish, Beans, Eggs, and Nuts
   c. Vegetables
   d. Bread, Cereal, Rice, and Pasta

3. Most mechanical digestion takes place in the
   a. mouth.   b. esophagus.
   c. stomach.   d. small intestine.

4. The enzyme in saliva chemically breaks down
   a. fats.   b. proteins.
   c. sugars.   d. starches.

5. Bile is produced by the
   a. liver.   b. pancreas.
   c. small intestine. d. large intestine.

True or False

If the statement is true, write true. If it is false, change the underlined word or words to make the statement true.

6. Proteins that come from animal sources are <u>incomplete</u> proteins.

7. Vitamins that are stored in the fatty tissue of the body are <u>water-soluble</u>.

8. To determine which of two cereals supplies more iron, you can check the <u>Percent Daily Value</u> on the food label.

9. The physical breakdown of food is called <u>mechanical</u> digestion.

10. Most materials are absorbed into the bloodstream in the <u>large</u> intestine.

Checking Concepts

11. How does a person's level of physical activity affect his or her daily energy needs?

12. Why is fiber necessary in a person's diet even though it is not considered a nutrient?

13. Why does the Food Guide Pyramid give the recommended daily servings as a range instead of a single number?

14. Describe the location and function of the epiglottis.

15. Explain the role of peristalsis in the digestive system.

16. What is the function of villi? Where are villi located?

17. **Writing to Learn** Imagine that you are a bacon, lettuce, and tomato sandwich. Describe your journey through a person's digestive system, starting in the mouth and ending with absorption.

Thinking Critically

18. **Applying Concepts** Before winter arrives, animals that hibernate often prepare by eating foods that contain a lot of fat. How is this behavior helpful?

19. **Comparing and Contrasting** The digestive system is sometimes said to be "an assembly line in reverse." Identify some similarities and some differences between your digestive system and an assembly line.

20. **Relating Cause and Effect** "Heartburn" occurs when stomach acid enters the esophagus. Use your knowledge of the digestive system to explain how this condition affects the esophagus and how "heartburn" got its name.

21. **Inferring** Why is it important for people to chew their food thoroughly before swallowing?

22. **Relating Cause and Effect** Suppose a medicine killed all the bacteria in your body. How might this affect vitamin production in your body? Explain.

Applying Skills

Use the chart below to answer Questions 23–25.

Food (1 cup)	Calcium (% Daily Value)	Calories	Calories from Fat
Chocolate Milk	30	230	80
Low-fat Milk	35	110	20
Plain Yogurt	35	110	35

23. Classifying To which group in the Food Guide Pyramid do the foods in the chart belong? What is the recommended range of daily servings for that group?

24. Interpreting Data How many cups of low-fat milk provide the daily recommended amount of calcium?

25. Calculating Which of the foods meet the recommendation that no more than 30 percent of a food's Calories come from fat? Explain.

Performance CHAPTER PROJECT **Assessment**

Present Your Project Write a summary of what you've learned from keeping a food log. Address these questions in your summary: How close were your eating patterns to those recommended in the Food Guide Pyramid? How did you attempt to change your diet during the second three days? How successful were you at making those changes in your diet?

Reflect and Record Did your eating patterns surprise you? What additional changes could help you improve your diet? How might others help you make those changes? If your eating patterns match those that are recommended in the Food Guide Pyramid, how can you be sure to continue those patterns?

Test Preparation

Use these questions to prepare for standardized tests.

Use the information to answer Questions 26–29.

A scientist performed an experiment to determine the amount of time needed to digest protein. She placed small pieces of hardboiled egg white (a protein) in a test tube containing hydrochloric acid, water, and the enzyme pepsin. She measured the rate at which the egg white was digested over a 24-hour period. Her data is recorded in the table below.

Time (hours)	Percent of Egg White Digested
0	0%
4	15%
8	25%
12	40%
16	70%
20	85%
24	90%

26. During which 4-hour period did the most digestion take place?
  a. 0–4 hours **b.** 4–8 hours
  c. 8–12 hours **d.** 12–16 hours

27. After about how many hours would you estimate that half of the protein was digested?
  a. 8 hours **b.** 12 hours
  c. 14 hours **d.** 16 hours

28. How much digestion occurred in 16 hours?
  a. 25% **b.** 40%
  c. 70% **d.** 90%

29. What would have happened if no hydrochloric acid were added to the test tube?
  a. The protein would have been digested faster.
  b. The protein would have been digested slower.
  c. There would have been no change in the rate of protein digestion.
  d. Pepsin alone would have digested the protein.

CHAPTER 17 Circulation

WEB ACTIVITY
www.phschool.com

 SECTION 1 The Body's Transportation System

Discover How Hard Does Your Heart Work?

SECTION 2 A Closer Look at Blood Vessels

Discover How Does Pressure Affect the Flow of Blood?
Sharpen Your Skills Creating Data Tables
Skills Lab Heart Beat, Health Beat

 SECTION 3 Blood and Lymph

Discover What Kinds of Cells Are in Blood?
Try This Caught in the Web
Real-World Lab Do You Know Your A-B-O's?

534

Travels of a Red Blood Cell

Every day, you travel from home to school and then back home again. Your path makes a loop, or circuit, ending where it began. In this chapter, you'll learn how your blood also travels in circuits. You'll find out how your heart pumps your blood throughout your body, bringing that essential fluid to all your living cells. As you learn more about the heart and circulatory system, you'll create a display to show how blood circulates throughout the body.

Your Goal To design and construct a display showing a complete journey of a red blood cell through the human body.

To complete the project successfully, your display must
◆ show a red blood cell that leaves from the heart and returns to the same place
◆ show where the red blood cell picks up and delivers oxygen and carbon dioxide
◆ provide written descriptions of the circuits made by the red blood cell, either with captions or in a continuous story
◆ be designed following the safety guidelines in Appendix A

Get Started Look ahead at the diagrams in the chapter. Then discuss the kinds of displays you could use, including a three-dimensional model, posters, a series of drawings, a flip-book, or a video animation. Write down any content questions you'll need to answer.

Check Your Progress You'll be working on this project as you study this chapter. To keep your project on track, look for Check Your Progress boxes at the following points.
Section 1 Review, page 542: Make a sketch of your display.
Section 2 Review, page 547: Begin to construct your display.
Section 3 Review, page 554: Add a written description to your display.

Present Your Project At the end of the chapter (page 563), you will use your display to show how blood travels through the body.

Blood cells travel in blood vessels to all parts of the body.

Integrating Health

SECTION 4 Cardiovascular Health

Discover **Which Foods Are "Heart Healthy"?**
Try This **Blocking the Flow**
Science at Home **Healthy Hearts**

WEB ACTIVITY www.phschool.com

SECTION **1** **The Respiratory System**

Discover How Big Can You Blow Up a Balloon?
Try This Do You Exhale Carbon Dioxide?
Science at Home Modeling Alveoli
Skills Lab A Breath of Fresh Air

Integrating Health

SECTION **2** **Smoking and Your Health**

Discover What Are the Dangers of Smoking?
Sharpen Your Skills Calculating

SECTION **3** **The Excretory System**

Discover How Does Filtering a Liquid Change What Is in It?
Real-World Lab Clues About Health

Get the Message Out

Lively music fills the air as the band marches along the parade route. To play many musical instruments, you need powerful, healthy lungs, which are part of the respiratory system. In this chapter, you will learn about the respiratory and excretory systems.

One way that people can keep their respiratory systems healthy is by choosing not to smoke. You've probably seen antismoking advertisements on television and in magazines. Imagine that you're part of a team of writers and designers who create advertisements. You've just been given the job of creating antismoking ads for different age groups. As you learn about the respiratory system, you can use your knowledge in your ad campaign.

Your Goal To create three different antismoking ads: one telling young children about the dangers of smoking; the second one discouraging teenagers from trying cigarettes; and the third encouraging adult smokers to quit.

To complete the project successfully, each ad must
- accurately communicate at least three health risks associated with smoking
- address at least two pressures that influence people to start or continue smoking
- use images and words in convincing, creative ways that gear your message to each audience

Get Started Brainstorm a list of reasons why people smoke. Consider the possible influence of family and friends as well as that of ads, movies, videos, and television. Also decide which types of ads you will produce, such as magazine ads or billboards. Begin to plan your ads.

Check Your Progress You'll be working on this project as you study this chapter. To keep your project on track, look for Check Your Progress boxes at the following points.
> **Section 2 Review**, page 580: Plan your ads.
> **Section 3 Review**, page 586: Design and produce your ads.

Present Your Project At the end of the chapter (page 589), you will display your completed ads. Be prepared to discuss your reasons for choosing the images and persuasive messages that you used.

Trombone players in a marching band need strong, healthy lungs.

Figure 11 Your skin and lungs also function as excretory organs. Water and some chemical wastes are excreted in perspiration. And when you exhale on a cold morning, you can see the water in your breath. *Applying Concepts* What other waste product does your exhaled breath contain?

however, the day is cool and you've drunk a lot of water, less water will be reabsorbed. Your body will produce a larger volume of urine.

Every day, you need to take at least 2 liters of water into your body. You can do this either by drinking or by eating foods such as apples that contain a lot of water. This helps your kidneys maintain the proper water balance in your body.

Other Organs of Excretion

Most of the wastes produced by the body are removed through the kidneys, but not all. **The other organs of excretion are the lungs, skin, and liver.** You've already learned how the lungs and skin remove wastes. When you breathe out, carbon dioxide and some water are removed from the body. Sweat glands also function in excretion, because water and some chemical wastes are excreted in perspiration.

Have you ever torn apart a large pizza box so that it could fit in a wastebasket? If so, then you can understand that some wastes need to be broken down before they can be excreted. The liver performs this function. For example, urea, which comes from the breakdown of proteins, is produced by the liver. The liver also converts part of the hemoglobin molecule from old red blood cells into substances such as bile. Recall from Chapter 16 that bile helps break down fats during digestion. Because the liver produces a usable material from old red blood cells, you can think of the liver as a recycling factory.

Section 3 Review

1. What is the function of the excretory system?
2. Describe the two stages of urine formation.
3. What roles do the lungs, skin, and liver play in excretion?
4. How do the kidneys help regulate the amount of water in the body?
5. **Thinking Critically** **Predicting** On a long bus trip, Laura does not drink any water for several hours. How will the volume of urine she produces that day compare to the volume on a day when she drinks several glasses of water? Explain.

Check Your Progress CHAPTER PROJECT

By now you should be creating your ads. If you are producing ads for a newspaper or magazine, you need to create original drawings or use images from other sources. If you are preparing television or radio ads, you need to arrange for actors and any necessary props. Write and edit the text or script of your ads. Arrange for a place to display your ads or for a time to present the ads.

SECTION 1 The Respiratory System

Key Ideas

◆ The respiratory system moves oxygen into the body and removes carbon dioxide from the body.

◆ In the process of respiration in cells, glucose is broken down using oxygen to produce energy.

◆ As air travels from the outside environment to the lungs, it passes through the nose, pharynx, trachea, and bronchi.

◆ In the alveoli, oxygen moves from the air into the blood, while carbon dioxide and water pass from the blood into the air.

◆ During inhalation, the diaphragm and rib muscles make the chest cavity expand. The air pressure inside the lungs decreases, and air rushes into the lungs. During exhalation, the chest cavity becomes smaller, pushing air out of the body.

◆ When air passes over the vocal cords, which are folds of tissue in the larynx, they vibrate to produce sound.

Key Terms

respiration   bronchi   diaphragm
cilia   lungs   larynx
pharynx   alveoli   vocal cords
trachea

SECTION 2 Smoking and Your Health

INTEGRATING HEALTH

Key Ideas

◆ The most harmful substances in tobacco smoke are tar, carbon monoxide, and nicotine.

◆ When people inhale tobacco smoke, they increase their chances of developing respiratory diseases such as bronchitis, emphysema, and lung cancer.

◆ Smokers are more likely to have heart attacks than are nonsmokers.

Key Terms

tar   bronchitis
carbon monoxide   emphysema
nicotine   passive smoking
addiction

SECTION 3 The Excretory System

Key Ideas

◆ The excretory system removes carbon dioxide, urea, water, and other wastes from the body.

◆ The kidneys are the major organs of excretion. By filtering the blood, the kidneys produce urine.

◆ Urine travels from the kidneys through the ureters to the urinary bladder.

◆ In the kidney's nephrons, wastes and other materials are filtered from the blood. Some useful substances, such as glucose and water, are then reabsorbed into the blood.

◆ The lungs, skin, and liver are also organs of excretion.

Key Terms

excretion   urine   urethra
urea   ureters   nephron
kidney   urinary bladder

Organizing Information

Flowchart The kidneys eliminate wastes from the body in a series of steps. Copy the flowchart below and complete it by filling in the missing steps.

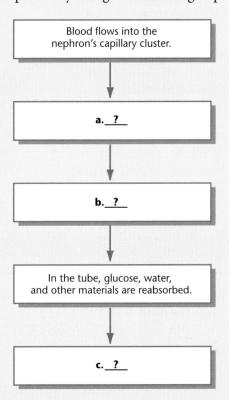

Blood flows into the nephron's capillary cluster.

a. ?

b. ?

In the tube, glucose, water, and other materials are reabsorbed.

c. ?

Reviewing Content

 For more review of key concepts, see the Interactive Student Tutorial CD-ROM.

Multiple Choice

1. The process in which glucose and oxygen react in cells to release energy is called
   a. digestion.
   b. respiration.
   c. breathing.
   d. gas exchange.
2. The trachea divides into two tubes called
   a. bronchi.
   b. alveoli.
   c. windpipes.
   d. diaphragms.
3. Your voice is produced by the
   a. pharynx.
   b. larynx.
   c. trachea.
   d. alveoli.
4. The disease in which the respiratory passages become narrower than normal is called
   a. bronchitis.
   b. lung cancer.
   c. diabetes.
   d. emphysema.
5. Normal urine contains both
   a. water and carbon monoxide.
   b. water and large amounts of glucose.
   c. urea and proteins.
   d. urea and water.

True or False

If the statement is true, write true. If it is false, change the underlined word or words to make the statement true.

6. Dust particles trapped in mucus are swept away by tiny, hairlike <u>blood vessels</u>.
7. The clusters of air sacs in the lungs are called <u>alveoli</u>.
8. <u>Tar</u> is a chemical in tobacco smoke that makes the heart beat faster.
9. The <u>ureter</u> is the tube through which urine leaves the body.
10. The <u>lungs</u> are excretory organs.

Checking Concepts

11. Explain the difference between breathing and respiration.
12. Explain how the alveoli provide a large surface area for gas exchange in the lungs.
13. Describe how the diaphragm and rib muscles work together to control inhaling and exhaling.
14. Why do men have deeper voices than women?
15. Describe what happens when carbon monoxide enters the body. How does this affect the body?
16. Explain two ways in which the kidneys help to maintain homeostasis in the body.
17. **Writing to Learn** Imagine that you are a molecule of oxygen. Write an adventure story that describes what happens to you between the time you are inhaled through someone's nose and the time you are used in respiration in a body cell.

Thinking Critically

18. **Comparing and Contrasting** How is respiration similar to the burning of fuel? How is it different?
19. **Inferring** If you exhale onto a mirror, the mirror will become clouded with a thin film of moisture. Explain why this happens.
20. **Applying Concepts** Explain how babies can develop smoking-related respiratory problems.
21. **Making Judgments** Do you think that drugstores, which sell medicines, should also sell cigarettes and other tobacco products? Why or why not?
22. **Predicting** If the walls of the capillary cluster in a nephron were damaged or broken, what substance might you expect to find in urine that is not normally present? Explain.

Applying Skills

Use your knowledge of the respiratory system and the information in the graphs to answer Questions 23–25.

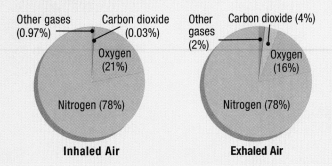

Other gases (0.97%) Carbon dioxide (0.03%) Oxygen (21%) Nitrogen (78%)
Inhaled Air

Other gases (2%) Carbon dioxide (4%) Oxygen (16%) Nitrogen (78%)
Exhaled Air

23. **Interpreting Data** Compare the percentage of carbon dioxide in inhaled air and in exhaled air. How can you account for the difference?

24. **Drawing Conclusions** Based on the data, which gas is used by the body? How is this gas used?

25. **Inferring** Explain why the percentage of nitrogen is the same in both inhaled air and exhaled air.

Performance ▽ CHAPTER PROJECT Assessment

Present Your Project Your three ads should be ready for display. Be prepared to explain why you chose the message you did for each group of viewers. Why do you think your ads would be effective?

Reflect and Record Of all the ads produced by your classmates, which seemed the most effective? Why? Did any ads change your own ideas about smoking? How can you protect yourself from pressures that might tempt you to smoke? Record your ideas in your journal.

Test Preparation

Use these questions to prepare for standardized tests.

Study the table. Then answer Questions 26–29.

Average Daily Loss of Water in Humans (mL)			
Source	**Normal Weather**	**Hot Weather**	**Extended Heavy Exercise**
Lungs	350	250	650
Urine	1,400	1,200	500
Sweat	450	1,750	5,350
Digestive Waste	200	200	200

26. During normal weather, what is the major source of water loss?
    a. lungs
    b. urine
    c. sweat
    d. digestive waste

27. During hot weather, what is the major source of water loss?
    a. lungs
    b. urine
    c. sweat
    d. digestive waste

28. What is the total amount of water lost on a hot weather day?
    a. 2,400 mL
    b. 3,200 mL
    c. 3,400 mL
    d. 6,700 mL

29. What is the benefit of sweat during heavy exercise?
    a. Sweat helps blood flow to the exercising muscles.
    b. Sweat helps lubricate muscles during heavy exercise.
    c. Sweat evaporates from the skin and helps cool the body.
    d. Sweat helps energy get to the exercising muscles.

CHAPTER
19 Fighting Disease

A white blood cell
(shown in purple) attacks
a cancer cell (yellow).

WEB ACTIVITY
www.phschool.com

SECTION
1 Infectious Disease

Discover How Does a Disease Spread?
Sharpen Your Skills Posing Questions

SECTION
2 The Body's Defenses

Discover Which Pieces Fit Together?
Real-World Lab The Skin as a Barrier
Try This Stuck Together

SECTION
Integrating Health
3 Preventing Infectious
Disease

Discover What Substances Can Kill
Pathogens?
Science at Home Vaccination History
Skills Lab Causes of Death, Then and Now

Stop the Invasion!

When you catch a cold, your body is being attacked. The attackers are cold viruses. If they're not stopped, they'll multiply in great numbers and cause infection. Many other diseases are also caused in this way—by viruses or bacteria that invade your body. In this chapter, you'll learn how your body defends itself against such invasions. And you'll put that knowledge to use as you develop a series of informative news reports in this chapter project.

Your Goal To create a series of imaginary news broadcasts from "battlefield sites" where the body is fighting an infectious disease.

To complete the project successfully you must
◆ choose a specific disease and represent the sequence of events that occur when that disease strikes the body
◆ describe the stages of the disease as if they were battles between two armies
◆ present your story creatively in at least three reports using newspaper, radio, or television news-reporting techniques

Get Started With some classmates, list your ideas about delivering a good newspaper, radio, or television news report. Think about what techniques reporters use to make stories interesting or to explain complicated information. Also, recall the times you've had a cold, flu, or other infectious disease. Write down how your body responded, how long you were sick, and any other useful information you can remember.

Check Your Progress You'll be working on this project as you study this chapter. To keep your project on track, look for Check Your Progress boxes at the following points.
Section 1 Review, page 595: Select a specific disease to research. Learn how it affects the body and how the body responds.
Section 2 Review, page 604: Write scripts for your news reports.
Section 4 Review, page 616: Make any necessary revisions, and practice your presentation.

Present Your Project At the end of the chapter (page 619), you will "broadcast" your news reports for the rest of the class.

SECTION 4 Noninfectious Disease

Discover **What Happens When Airflow Is Restricted?**
Sharpen Your Skills **Drawing Conclusions**

SECTION
1 Infectious Disease

DISCOVER • ACTIVITY • • • •

How Does a Disease Spread?

1. On a sheet of paper, write three headings: *Round 1, Round 2,* and *Round 3.*

2. Everyone in the class should shake hands with two people. Under *Round 1,* record the names of the people whose hand you shook.

3. Now shake hands with two different people. Record the name of each person whose hand you shook under *Round 2.*

4. Once again, shake hands with two additional people. Under *Round 3,* record the names of the people whose hand you shook.

Think It Over
Calculating Suppose you had a disease that was spread by shaking hands. Everyone whose hand you shook has caught the disease. So has anyone who later shook those people's hands. Calculate how many people you "infected."

GUIDE FOR READING

◆ What kinds of organisms cause disease?

◆ Where do pathogens come from?

Reading Tip As you read, use the headings in the section to make an outline. Write the important concepts under each heading.

Before the twentieth century, surgery was a very risky business. Even if people lived through an operation, they were not out of danger. After the operation, many patients' wounds became infected, and the patients often died. No one knew what caused these infections.

In the 1860s, a British surgeon named Joseph Lister hypothesized that microorganisms caused the infections. To protect his patients, Lister used carbolic acid, a chemical that kills microorganisms. Before performing an operation, Lister washed his hands and surgical instruments with carbolic acid. After the surgery, he covered the patient's wounds with bandages dipped in carbolic acid.

Figure 1 Doctors at Massachusetts General Hospital perform surgery on a patient in 1846. In the 1800s, surgery was performed under conditions that were very different from those used today.

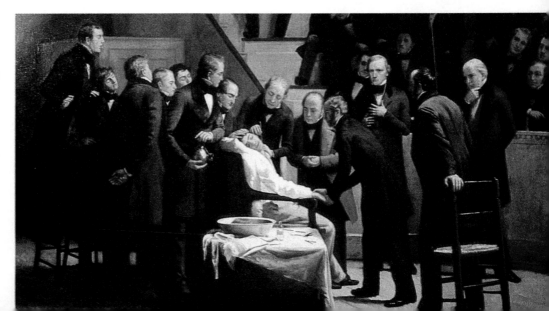

Lister's results were dramatic. Before he used his new method, about 45 percent of his surgical patients died from infection. With Lister's new techniques, only 15 percent died.

Disease and Pathogens

Like the infections that Lister observed after surgery, many illnesses, such as strep throat and food poisoning, are caused by organisms that are too small to see without microscopes. Until Lister's time, few people thought these tiny organisms could cause disease. Most people believed that things like evil spirits and swamp air made people sick.

Organisms that cause disease are called **pathogens.** Diseases caused by pathogens are infectious. An **infectious disease** is a disease that can pass from one organism to another. When you have an infectious disease, pathogens have gotten inside your body and harmed it. Even though you may feel pain in a whole organ or throughout your body, pathogens make you sick by damaging individual cells. For example, when you have an ear infection, pathogens have damaged cells in your ear.

Each infectious disease is caused by a specific pathogen. **The four major groups of human pathogens are bacteria, viruses, fungi, and protists.** Strep throat is caused by a bacterium, a unicellular organism. Colds and influenza are caused by viruses, nonliving things that can reproduce only inside living cells. Athlete's foot is an infectious disease caused by a fungus. Malaria is an example of a tropical disease caused by a protist.

Lister's work with pathogens was influenced by Louis Pasteur, a French scientist. In the 1860s, Pasteur showed that microorganisms cause certain diseases. In addition, Pasteur showed that killing the microorganisms could prevent the spread of those diseases. Pasteur's work led to **pasteurization,** a heating process that is widely used today to kill microorganisms in food products such as milk.

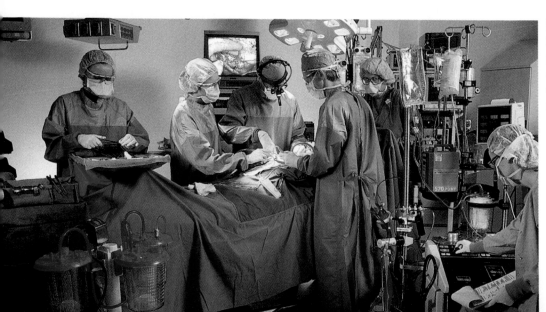

Figure 2 Surgery today is performed in operating rooms that have been cleaned thoroughly to eliminate disease-causing organisms.
Comparing and Contrasting Contrast Figures 1 and 2. How does surgery today differ from surgery in 1846?

How Diseases Are Spread

Pathogens are something like ants at a picnic. They aren't trying to harm you. However, just like the ants, pathogens need food. They also need a place to live and reproduce. Unfortunately, your body may be just the right place for a pathogen to meet those needs.

You can become infected by a pathogen in one of several ways. **Some sources of pathogens include another person, a contaminated object, an animal bite, and the environment.**

Person-to-Person Transfer Many pathogens are transferred from one person to another person. Pathogens often pass from one person to another through direct physical contact, such as kissing, hugging, and shaking hands. For example, if you kiss someone who has a cold sore, cold-sore viruses can then get into your body.

Diseases are also spread through indirect contact with an infected person. For example, if a person with pneumonia sneezes, pathogens shoot into the air. Pathogens from a sneeze can travel most of the way across a small room! Other people may catch pneumonia if they inhale these pathogens. Colds, flu, and tuberculosis can be spread through coughing and sneezing.

☑ *Checkpoint* *In what ways can pathogens pass from one person to another?*

Figure 3 The map shows the location of cholera cases in the 1854 epidemic in London, England.

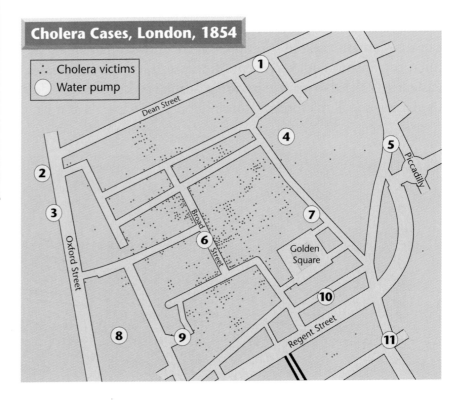

Cholera Cases, London, 1854

∴ Cholera victims
◯ Water pump

Contaminated Objects Some pathogens can survive for a time outside a person's body. Water and food can become contaminated. If people then eat the food or drink the water, they may become sick. Some pathogens that cause severe diarrhea are spread through contaminated food and water. People can also pick up pathogens by using objects, such as towels or silverware, that have been handled by an infected person. Colds and flu can be spread in this way. Tetanus bacteria can enter the body if a person steps on a contaminated nail.

Animal Bites If an animal is infected with certain pathogens and then bites a person, it can pass the pathogens to the person. People can get rabies, a serious disease that affects the nervous system, from the bite of an infected animal, such as a dog or a raccoon. Lyme disease and Rocky Mountain spotted fever are both spread by tick bites. The protist that causes malaria is transferred by the bites of mosquitoes that live in tropical regions.

Pathogens from the Environment Some pathogens occur naturally in the environment. The bacterium that causes tetanus lives in soil or water. The bacterium that causes botulism, an especially severe form of food poisoning, also lives in soil. Botulism bacteria can produce a toxin in foods that have been improperly canned. The toxin is extremely powerful.

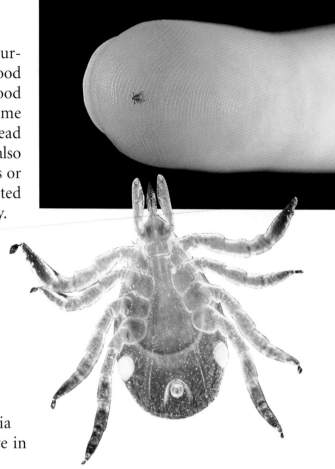

Figure 4 The tiny deer tick may carry the bacterium that causes Lyme disease, a serious condition that can damage the joints. If a deer tick that is carrying Lyme disease bacteria bites a person, the person may get Lyme disease. *Problem Solving How might people reduce their risk of catching Lyme disease?*

Section 1 Review

1. Name four kinds of pathogens that cause disease in humans.
2. Describe four ways that pathogens can infect humans.
3. Explain how Pasteur contributed to the understanding of infectious disease.
4. **Thinking Critically Applying Concepts** If you have a cold, what steps can you take to keep from spreading it to other people? Explain.

CHAPTER PROJECT

Check Your Progress
At this stage, you should have chosen a specific infectious disease to research. You should also decide whether to do newspaper articles, radio programs, or a television series. Begin to plan how you will explain the way in which the body is invaded by pathogens. Also begin thinking about how you will make your show appropriate for your audience. (*Hint:* To get ideas on how to present news stories, read newspapers or watch or listen to news programs about international conflicts.)

DISCOVER •

Which Pieces Fit Together?

1. Your teacher will give you a piece of paper with one jagged edge.

2. One student in the class has a piece of paper whose edges match your paper edge, like two pieces of a jigsaw puzzle.

3. Find the student whose paper matches yours and fit the two edges together.

Think It Over

Inferring Imagine that one of each pair of matching pieces is a pathogen. The other is a cell in your body that defends your body against the invading pathogen. How many kinds of invaders can each defender cell recognize?

GUIDE FOR READING

◆ What is the body's first line of defense against pathogens?

◆ What happens during the inflammatory response?

◆ How does the immune system respond to pathogens?

Reading Tip Before you read, preview *Exploring the Immune Response* on page 602. List any unfamiliar terms. As you read, write definitions of those terms in your own words.

Your eyes are glued to the screen. The situation in the video game is desperate. Enemy troops have gotten through an opening in the wall. Your soldiers have managed to hold back most of the invaders. However, some enemy soldiers are breaking through the defense lines. You need your backup defenders. They can zap the invaders with their powerful weapons. If your soldiers can fight off the enemy until the backup team arrives, you can save your fortress.

Video games create fantasy wars, but in your body, real battles happen all the time. In your body, the "enemies" are invading pathogens. You are hardly ever aware of these battles. The body's disease-fighting system is so effective that most people get sick only occasionally. By eliminating pathogens that can destroy your cells, your body maintains homeostasis.

Figure 5 The pathogens that invade your body are something like the enemy soldiers in a video game. Your body has to defend itself against the pathogens.

596

Barriers That Keep Pathogens Out

Your body has three lines of defense against pathogens. The first line consists of barriers that keep pathogens from getting into the body. You do not wear a sign that says "Pathogens Keep Out," but that doesn't matter. **Barriers such as the skin, breathing passages, mouth, and stomach trap and kill most pathogens with which you come into contact.**

The Skin When pathogens land on the skin, they are exposed to destructive chemicals in oil and sweat. Even if these chemicals don't kill them, the pathogens may fall off with dead skin cells. Washing your skin regularly with soap and warm water can help decrease the number of pathogens on your skin.

If the pathogens manage to stay on the skin, they must get through the tightly packed dead cells that form a barrier on top of living skin cells. Most pathogens get through the skin only when it is cut. Scabs form over cuts so rapidly that the period in which pathogens can enter the body in this way is very short.

The Breathing Passages As you know, you can inhale pathogens when you breathe in. The nose, pharynx, trachea, and bronchi, however, contain mucus and cilia. Together, the mucus and cilia trap and remove most of the pathogens that enter the respiratory system. In addition, irritation by pathogens may make you sneeze or cough. Both actions force the pathogens out of your body.

The Mouth and Stomach Some pathogens are found in foods, even if the foods are washed, cooked, and stored properly. Like the skin on the outside of your body, your mouth and digestive system is an intact passageway that keeps its contents separate from the rest of the body. Unless you have cuts in your mouth or a stomach ulcer, for example, the pathogens you take into your mouth do not mix with blood or other parts of your body. The saliva in your mouth contains destructive chemicals and your stomach produces acid that combats these pathogens. Most pathogens that you swallow are destroyed by saliva or stomach acid.

☑ *Checkpoint* How do the breathing passages prevent pathogens from entering the body?

Figure 6 Skin is covered with bacteria. The dots in the photo are colonies of bacteria living on a person's hand.
Relating Cause and Effect How can a cut in the skin lead to an infection?

THE SKIN AS A BARRIER

Bacteria are all around you. Many of those bacteria can cause disease, yet you usually remain free of disease. In this lab, you will investigate how the skin protects you from infectious disease.

Problem

How does skin act as a barrier to pathogens?

Skills Focus

making models, controlling variables, drawing conclusions

Materials

sealable plastic bags, 4   marking pen
fresh apples, 4   paper towels
rotting apple   toothpick
cotton swabs   rubbing alcohol

Procedure

1. Read over the entire procedure to see how you will treat each of four fresh apples. Write a prediction in your notebook about the change(s) you expect to see in each apple. Then copy the data table into your notebook.
2. Label four plastic bags *1, 2, 3,* and *4.*
3. Gently wash four fresh apples with water, then dry them carefully with paper towels. Place one apple in plastic bag 1, and seal the bag.
4. Insert a toothpick tip into a rotting apple and withdraw it. Lightly draw the tip of the toothpick down the side of the second apple without breaking the skin. Repeat these actions three more times, touching the toothpick to different parts of the apple without breaking the skin. Insert the apple in plastic bag 2, and seal the bag.

5. Insert the toothpick tip into the rotting apple and withdraw it. Use the tip to make a long, thin scratch down the side of the third apple. Be sure to pierce the apple's skin. Repeat these actions three more times, making additional scratches on different parts of the apple. Insert the apple into plastic bag 3, and seal the bag.
6. Repeat Step 5 to make four scratches in the fourth apple. However, before you place the apple in the bag, dip a cotton swab in rubbing alcohol, and swab the scratches. Then place the apple in plastic bag 4, and seal the bag. **CAUTION:** *Alcohol and its vapors are flammable. Work where there are no sparks, exposed flames, or other heat sources.*
7. Store the four bags in a warm, dark place. Wash your hands thoroughly with soap and water.
8. Every day for one week, remove the apples from their storage place, and observe them without opening the bags. Record your observations, then return the bags to their storage location. At the end of the activity, dispose of the unopened bags as directed by your teacher.

Analyze and Conclude

1. How did the appearance of the four apples compare? Explain your results.
2. In this activity, what condition in the human body is each of the four fresh apples supposed to model?
3. What is the control in this experiment?
4. What is the role of the rotting apple in this activity?
5. **Apply** How does this investigation show why routine cuts and scrapes should be cleaned and bandaged?

Design an Experiment

Using apples as you did in this activity, design an experiment to model how washing hands can prevent the spread of disease. Obtain your teacher's permission before carrying out your investigation.

DATA TABLE

Date	Apple 1 (no contact with decay)	Apple 2 (contact with decay, unbroken skin)	Apple 3 (contact with decay, scratched, untreated)	Apple 4 (contact with decay, scratched, treated with alcohol)

Today the Panama Canal is an important shipping route that links the Atlantic and Pacific oceans. But because of two diseases that cause high fever—malaria and yellow fever—the Panama Canal almost didn't get built. Much of the canal passes through the mosquito-filled rain forests of Panama. Mosquitoes carry the pathogens that cause malaria and yellow fever.

In 1889 an attempt at digging a canal was abandoned, partly because so many workers became sick. In 1904, an American physician, Colonel William C. Gorgas, began a project in which swamps in the work area were drained. In addition, brush and grass were cut down. Gorgas's project destroyed the places where mosquitoes lived and reproduced. This action greatly reduced the mosquito population. The Panama Canal was completed in 1914

Panama Canal

In Your Journal

Write a newspaper article about the construction of the Panama Canal. The article should focus on the problem of disease and the contribution of Colonel Gorgas.

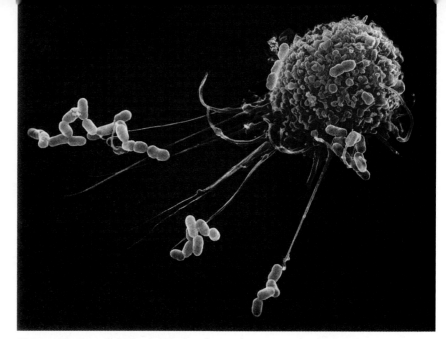

Figure 7 Caught! The bacteria, shown in green, don't stand a chance against the phagocyte, shown in red. Phagocytes are white blood cells that engulf and destroy bacteria.

General Defenses

In spite of barriers, pathogens sometimes get into your body and begin to damage cells. When body cells are damaged, they release chemicals that trigger the **inflammatory response,** which is the second line of defense. **In the inflammatory response, fluid and certain types of white blood cells leak from blood vessels into nearby tissues. The white blood cells then fight the pathogens.** Because the inflammatory response is the same no matter what the pathogen, it is sometimes called the body's general defense.

All white blood cells are disease fighters, but there are different types, each with its own particular function. The kinds involved in the inflammatory response are called phagocytes. A **phagocyte** (FAG uh syt) is a white blood cell that engulfs pathogens and destroys them by breaking them down.

During the inflammatory response, blood vessels widen in the area affected by the pathogens. This enlargement increases blood flow to the area. The enlarged blood vessels—and the fluid that leaks out of them—make the affected area red and swollen. If you touch the swollen area, it will feel slightly warmer than normal. In fact, the term *inflammation* comes from a Latin word meaning "to set on fire."

In some cases, chemicals produced during the inflammatory response cause a fever, raising your body temperature above its normal temperature of 37° Celsius. Although fever makes you feel bad, it actually may help your body fight the infection. Some pathogens may not grow and reproduce well at higher temperatures.

Tumor Formation As cancerous cells divide over and over, they often form abnormal tissue masses called **tumors.** Cancerous tumors invade the healthy tissue around them and destroy the tissue. Cancer cells can break away from a tumor and invade blood or lymph vessels. The blood or lymph then carries the cancer cells to other parts of the body, where they may begin to divide and form new tumors. Unless stopped by treatment, cancer progresses through the body.

Causes of Cancer Different factors may work together to determine what makes cells become cancerous. One such factor is the characteristics that people inherit from their parents. Because of their inherited characteristics, some people are more likely than others to develop certain kinds of cancer. For example, women whose mothers had breast cancer have a higher risk of developing breast cancer than do women with no family history of the disease.

Some substances or factors in the environment, called **carcinogens** (kahr SIN uh junz), can cause cancer. The tar in cigarette smoke is a carcinogen. Ultraviolet light, which is part of sunlight, can also be a carcinogen.

Cancer Treatment Surgery, drugs, and radiation are all used to treat cancer. If cancer is detected before it has spread, doctors remove the cancerous tumors through surgery. Sometimes, however, a surgeon can't remove all of the cancer. In some cases, drugs or radiation may be used to kill the cancer cells or slow their spread.

INTEGRATING PHYSICS Radiation treatment uses high-energy waves to kill cancer cells. X-rays and gamma rays are two types of radiation used in cancer treatment. These waves are similar to sunlight and the

Figure 16 The large orange mass in the X-ray is a cancerous tumor in the lung. The graph shows leading types of cancer that affect men and women in the United States. *Interpreting Graphs Do more women or men develop lung cancer each year?*

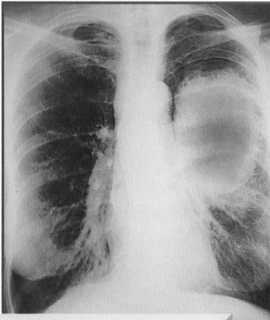

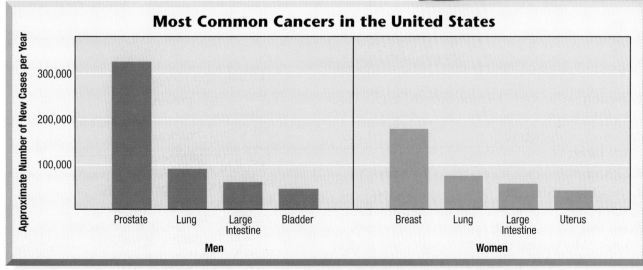

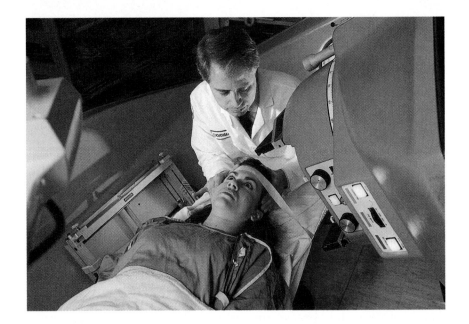

Figure 17 Radiation is one method that is used to treat cancer. The machine beams high-energy radiation at the tumor. This radiation kills cancer cells.

waves that make radios and microwave ovens work. However, X-rays and gamma rays have far more energy than sunlight, radio waves, or microwaves. When X-rays and gamma rays are aimed at tumors, they blast the cancer cells and kill them.

Cancer Prevention People can take steps to reduce their risk of developing cancer. For instance, they can avoid any form of tobacco, since tobacco and tobacco smoke contain carcinogens. Chewing tobacco and snuff contain carcinogens as well—they can cause cancers in the mouth. To prevent skin cancer, people can protect their skin from exposure to too much sunlight. A diet that is low in fat and includes plenty of fruits and vegetables can help people avoid some kinds of cancer, such as certain cancers of the digestive system.

Regular medical checkups are also important. Physicians or nurses may notice signs of cancer during a checkup. The earlier cancer is detected, the more likely it can be treated successfully.

 Section 4 Review

1. What is an allergy? Describe how the body reacts to the presence of an allergen.
2. How does diabetes affect the level of glucose in the blood?
3. Describe how cancer cells harm the body.
4. **Thinking Critically** **Inferring** Doctors sometimes recommend that people with diabetes eat several small meals rather than three large ones. Why do you think doctors give this advice?

Check Your Progress

CHAPTER PROJECT

Before your presentation, make your final revisions. If you are doing broadcasts, practice reading your scripts aloud. Experiment with different ways of bringing your series to a dramatic ending. Try to include answers to questions that might occur to your audience. For instance, are people around the patient at risk of invasion? If so, how can they defend themselves?

SECTION 1 Infectious Disease

Key Ideas

◆ Infectious diseases are caused by pathogens: bacteria, viruses, fungi, and protists.

◆ Pathogens that infect humans can come from another person, a contaminated object, an animal bite, or the environment.

Key Terms

pathogen   infectious disease   pasteurization

 ## SECTION 2 The Body's Defenses

Key Ideas

◆ The body has three lines of defense against pathogens.

◆ The immune system targets specific pathogens. T cells identify pathogens and distinguish one kind from another. B cells produce antibodies that destroy pathogens.

◆ HIV, the virus that causes AIDS, infects and destroys T cells.

Key Terms

inflammatory response   antigen
phagocyte   B cell
immune response   antibody
lymphocyte   AIDS
T cell

 ## SECTION 3 Preventing Infectious Disease

INTEGRATING HEALTH

Key Ideas

◆ In active immunity, a person's own immune system produces antibodies. A person can acquire active immunity by having the disease or by being vaccinated.

◆ In passive immunity, the antibodies come from a source other than the person's body.

Key Terms

immunity   vaccination   passive immunity
active immunity   vaccine   antibiotic

SECTION 4 Noninfectious Disease

Key Ideas

◆ Noninfectious diseases are diseases that are not spread from person to person.

◆ An allergy is a disorder in which the immune system is overly sensitive to a foreign substance, called an allergen.

◆ In diabetes, the body does not produce enough insulin or can't use it properly.

◆ In cancer, cells multiply uncontrollably, destroying healthy tissues.

Key Terms

noninfectious disease   insulin
allergy   diabetes
allergen   tumor
histamine   carcinogen
asthma

Organizing Information

Flowchart Complete the flowchart, which shows what happens after tuberculosis bacteria begin to multiply in the lungs. (For more information on flowcharts, see the Skills Handbook.)

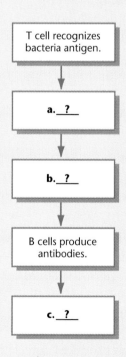

T cell recognizes bacteria antigen.

↓

a. ?

↓

b. ?

↓

B cells produce antibodies.

↓

c. ?

Reviewing Content

 For more review of key concepts, see the Interactive Student Tutorial CD-ROM.

Multiple Choice
Choose the letter of the best answer.

1. Some pathogenic bacteria produce poisons called
   a. histamines.
   b. toxins.
   c. phagocytes.
   d. pathogens.
2. Antibodies are produced by
   a. phagocytes.
   b. B cells.
   c. T cells.
   d. pathogens.
3. Which disease is caused by HIV?
   a. diabetes
   b. flu
   c. AIDS
   d. tetanus
4. A chemical that kills bacteria or slows their growth without harming body cells is called a(n)
   a. pathogen
   b. antibiotic
   c. allergen
   d. histamine
5. A carcinogen causes
   a. cancer.
   b. colds.
   c. allergies.
   d. food poisoning.

True or False
If a statement is true, write true. If it is false, change the underlined word or words to make the statement true.

6. Bacteria, viruses, fungi, and protists are the major human phagocytes.
7. People can get Lyme disease and rabies from animal bites.
8. A T cell engulfs pathogens and destroys them.
9. Vaccination produces active immunity.
10. A tumor is a mass of cancer cells.

Checking Concepts

11. Explain why pasteurization is important in food processing today.
12. Explain why it is difficult for pathogens to get to a part of the body in which they can cause disease.
13. What is the relationship between antigens and antibodies?
14. Explain the differences between active immunity and passive immunity. Then describe one way in which a person can acquire each type of immunity.
15. How does diabetes harm the body?
16. Identify two factors that can make a person likely to develop cancer.
17. **Writing to Learn** A patient of Joseph Lister is angry because Lister has covered her surgery wound with a bandage dipped in carbolic acid. The acid stings and the bandage is uncomfortable. Write a conversation between Lister and the patient in which Lister explains why she shouldn't take the bandage off.

Thinking Critically

18. **Inferring** Given all the sources of pathogens detailed in this chapter, name as many things as you can that must be sterilized in a hospital operating room.
19. **Applying Concepts** Can you catch a cold by sitting in a chilly draft? Explain.
20. **Comparing and Contrasting** Compare the functions of T cells and B cells.
21. **Relating Cause and Effect** Why can the immune system successfully fight most pathogens, but not HIV?
22. **Making Generalizations** If diabetes is not treated, the body cells of the diabetic person do not get enough glucose to function properly. List four symptoms of diabetes. Then explain how the lack of glucose can lead to each of the symptoms you listed.

Applying Skills

A person had an illness caused by bacteria. The table shows how the person's temperature and antibody level changed over the course of the disease. Use the table to answer Questions 23–25.

Week	Body Temperature (°C)	Antibody Level
0	37	low
1	39.8	low
2	39	medium
3	37	high
4	37	medium
5	37	low

23. **Graphing** Make a line graph of the temperature data. Label the horizontal axis "Week Number" and the vertical axis "Body Temperature."

24. **Interpreting Data** During what week did the person's temperature return to normal?

25. **Drawing Conclusions** When do antibody levels start to rise? What effect do antibodies have on the illness? Explain.

Performance ▼ CHAPTER PROJECT Assessment

Present Your Project Now you can share your news series with your classmates. Before your presentation, make sure any sound effects and props support the story.

Reflect and Record In your notebook, reflect on what you learned by using your imagination to explore a science topic. Did it help you to better understand how the body fights disease? What new information did you learn from presentations made by other groups? If you had your project to do over, what would you do differently?

Test Preparation

Use these questions to prepare for standardized tests.

Use the information to answer Questions 26–28.
A Glucose Tolerance Test is used to determine whether a person may have diabetes. A doctor gives a patient a sugar drink (at time 0) and measures the blood glucose level every 30 minutes for two hours. The graph below reveals that Person A is normal, while Person B has diabetes.

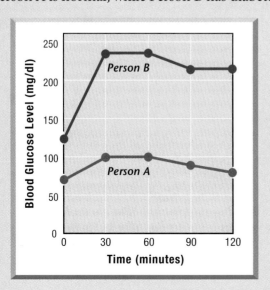

26. What would be the best title for this graph?
    a. How Blood Glucose Levels Rise Over Time
    b. Blood Glucose Levels in a Diabetic and a Non-Diabetic
    c. Normal Blood Glucose Levels
    d. How to Measure Blood Glucose Levels

27. According to the graph, which of the following statements is true?
    a. Person A's starting glucose level is higher than Person B's.
    b. Person A's glucose level rose quickly and then fell to near the starting level.
    c. Person B's glucose level rose quickly and then fell to near the starting level.
    d. Person A's blood glucose level was highest after 90 minutes.

28. What is the name of the hormone that normally controls blood glucose levels?
    a. estrogen   c. insulin
    b. testosterone   d. collagen

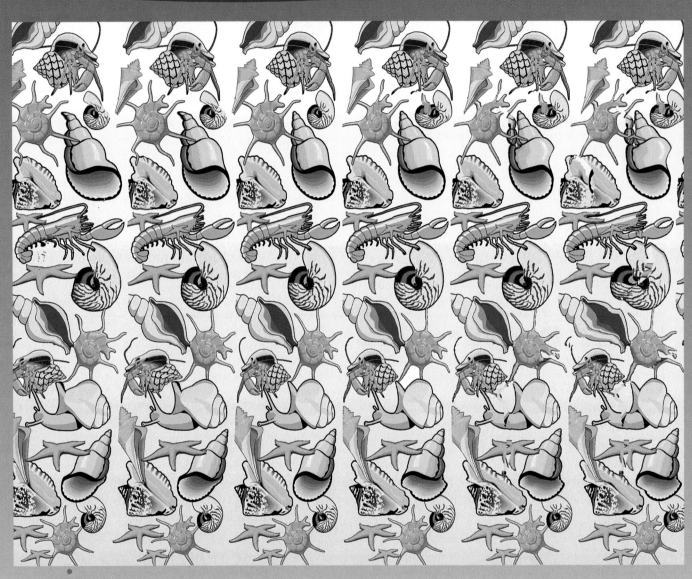

www.phschool.com

 How the Nervous System Works

Discover **How Simple Is a Simple Task?**
Science at Home **Stimulus and Response**
Skills Lab **Ready or Not**

 Divisions of the Nervous System

Discover **How Does Your Knee React?**
Sharpen Your Skills **Controlling Variables**

 The Senses

Discover **What's in the Bag?**
Try This **Why Do You Need Two Eyes?**
Try This **Tick, Tick, Tick**
Sharpen Your Skills **Designing Experiments**

Tricks and Illusions

Can you be sure of what you see, hear, smell, taste, or touch? In this chapter, you'll learn how you experience your environment through your senses. You'll see how the senses send information to your nervous system and how your brain interprets the messages.

But things aren't always what they seem. For example, an optical illusion is a picture or other visual effect that tricks you into seeing something incorrectly. In this project, you'll investigate how your senses can sometimes be fooled by illusions.

Your Goal To set up a science fair booth to demonstrate how different people respond to one or more illusions.

To complete this project, you must
- try out a variety of illusions, including some that involve the senses of hearing or touch as well as sight
- select one or more illusions, and set up an experiment to monitor people's responses to the illusions
- learn why the illusions fool the senses
- follow the safety guidelines in Appendix A

Get Started In a small group, discuss optical illusions or other illusions that you know about. Look in books to learn about others. Try them out. Which illusions would make an interesting experiment? How could you set up such an experiment at a science fair?

Check Your Progress You'll be working on this project as you study this chapter. To keep your project on track, look for Check Your Progress boxes at the following points.

Section 2 Review, page 634: Plan the experiment you will perform.
Section 3 Review, page 643: Carry out your experiment.
Section 4 Review, page 652: Explain why the illusions trick the senses.

Present Your Project At the end of the chapter (page 655), be prepared to share your findings with your classmates. Then explain how your illusions work.

Now you see it. Now you don't. Sometimes your eyes can play tricks on you. The picture shows rows of seashells and sea animals. Or does it?

Stare at the picture for several seconds, as if it were far away. The picture should look slightly out of focus. After a while, does anything seem to pop out from the picture?

SECTION

4

Integrating Health

Alcohol and Other Drugs

Discover How Can You Best Say No?
Sharpen Your Skills Communicating
Real-World Lab With Caffeine or Without?

1 How the Nervous System Works

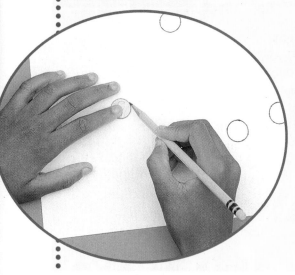

How Simple Is a Simple Task?

1. Trace the outline of a penny in twelve different places on a piece of paper.

2. Number the circles from 1 through 12. Write the numbers randomly, in no particular order.

3. Now pick up the penny again. Put it in each circle, one after another, in numerical order, beginning with 1 and ending with 12.

Think it Over

Inferring Make a list of all the sense organs, muscle movements, and thought processes in this activity. Compare your list with your classmates' lists. What organ system coordinated all the different processes involved in this task?

GUIDE FOR READING

◆ What are the functions of the nervous system?

◆ What are the three types of neurons and how do they interact?

Reading Tip Before you read, preview *Exploring the Path of a Nerve Impulse* on page 625. List any unfamiliar terms. Then, as you read, write a definition for each term.

The drums roll, and the crowd suddenly becomes silent. The people in the audience hold their breaths as the tightrope walker begins his long and dangerous journey across the wire. High above the circus floor, he inches along, slowly but steadily. One wrong movement could mean disaster.

To keep from slipping, tightrope performers need excellent coordination and a keen sense of balance. In addition, they must remember what they have learned from years of practice.

Even though you aren't a tightrope walker, you also need coordination, a sense of balance, memory, and the ability to learn. Your nervous system carries out all those functions. The nervous system consists of the brain, spinal cord, and nerves that run throughout the body. It also includes sense organs such as the eyes and ears.

Jobs of the Nervous System

The Internet lets people gather information from anywhere in the world with the click of a button. Like the Internet, your nervous system is a communications network. Your nervous system is much more efficient, however.

The nervous system receives information about what is happening both inside and outside your body. It also directs the way in which your body responds to this information. In addition, your nervous system helps maintain homeostasis. Without your nervous system, you could not move, think, feel pain, or taste a spicy taco.

Receiving Information Because of your nervous system, you are aware of what is happening in the environment around you. For example, you know that a soccer ball is zooming toward you, that the wind is blowing, or that a friend is telling a funny joke. Your nervous system also checks conditions inside your body, such as the level of glucose in your blood.

Responding to Information Any change or signal in the environment that can make an organism react is a **stimulus** (STIM yoo lus)(plural *stimuli*). A zooming soccer ball is a stimulus. After your nervous system analyzes the stimulus, it causes a response. A **response** is what your body does in reaction to a stimulus—you kick the ball toward the goal.

Some nervous system responses, such as kicking a ball, are voluntary, or under your control. However, many processes necessary for life, such as heartbeat rate, are controlled by involuntary actions of the nervous system.

Maintaining Homeostasis The nervous system helps maintain homeostasis by directing the body to respond appropriately to the information it receives. For example, when you are hungry, your nervous system directs you to eat. This action maintains homeostasis by supplying your body with nutrients and energy it needs.

☑ *Checkpoint* What is a stimulus?

The Neuron—A Message-Carrying Cell

The cells that carry information through your nervous system are called **neurons** (NOO rahnz), or nerve cells. The message that a neuron carries is called a **nerve impulse.** The structure of a neuron enables it to carry nerve impulses.

Figure 1 The sparkling water is a stimulus. This toddler responds by thrusting her hands into the water and splashing.

The Structure of a Neuron A neuron has a large cell body that contains the nucleus. The cell body has threadlike extensions. One kind of extension, a **dendrite,** carries impulses toward the cell body. An **axon** carries impulses away from the cell body. Nerve impulses begin in a dendrite, move toward the cell body, and then move down the axon. A neuron can have many dendrites, but it has only one axon. An axon, however, can have more than one tip, so the impulse can go to more than one other cell.

Axons and dendrites are sometimes called nerve fibers. Nerve fibers are often arranged in parallel bundles covered with connective tissue, something like a package of uncooked spaghetti wrapped in cellophane. A bundle of nerve fibers is called a **nerve.**

Kinds of Neurons Different kinds of neurons perform different functions. **Three kinds of neurons are found in the body—sensory neurons, interneurons, and motor neurons. Together they make up a chain of nerve cells that carry an impulse through the nervous system.** *Exploring the Path of a Nerve Impulse* shows how these three kinds of neurons work together.

A **sensory neuron** picks up stimuli from the internal or external environment and converts each stimulus into a nerve impulse. The impulse travels along the sensory neuron until it reaches an interneuron, usually in the brain or spinal cord. An **interneuron** is a neuron that carries nerve impulses from one neuron to another. Some interneurons pass impulses from sensory neurons to motor neurons. A **motor neuron** sends an impulse to a muscle, and the muscle contracts in response.

☑ *Checkpoint* *What is the function of an axon?*

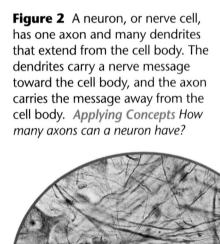

Figure 2 A neuron, or nerve cell, has one axon and many dendrites that extend from the cell body. The dendrites carry a nerve message toward the cell body, and the axon carries the message away from the cell body. *Applying Concepts How many axons can a neuron have?*

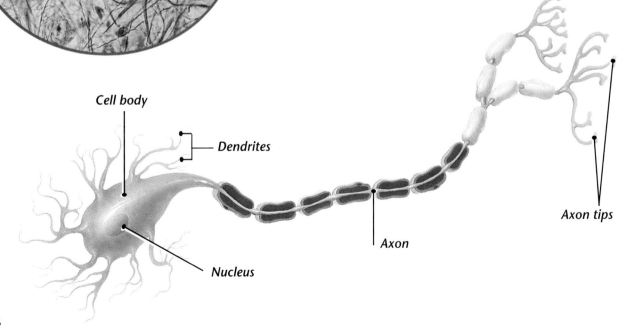

Cell body

Dendrites

Nucleus

Axon

Axon tips

EXPLORING the Path of a Nerve Impulse

When you hear the phone ring, you pick it up to answer it. Many sensory neurons, interneurons, and motor neurons are involved in this action.

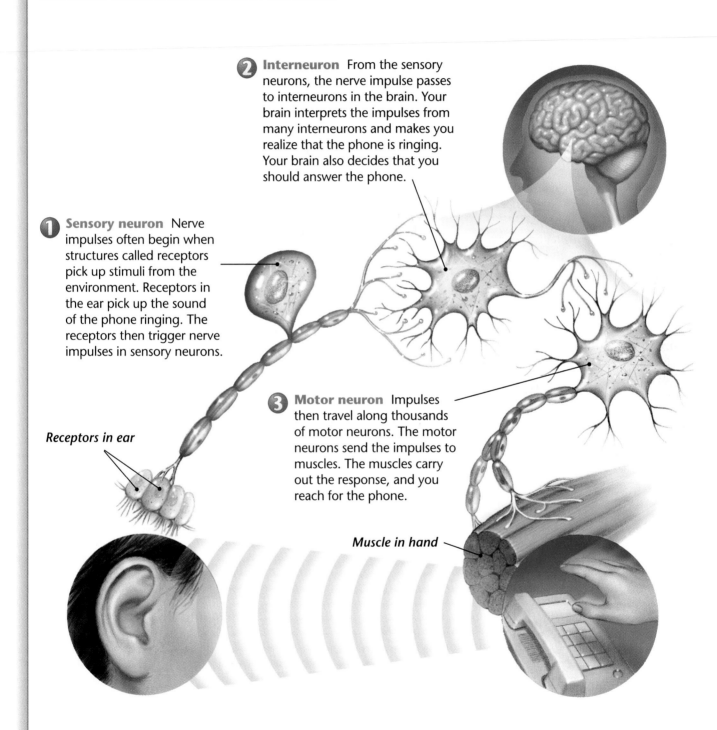

2 Interneuron From the sensory neurons, the nerve impulse passes to interneurons in the brain. Your brain interprets the impulses from many interneurons and makes you realize that the phone is ringing. Your brain also decides that you should answer the phone.

1 Sensory neuron Nerve impulses often begin when structures called receptors pick up stimuli from the environment. Receptors in the ear pick up the sound of the phone ringing. The receptors then trigger nerve impulses in sensory neurons.

3 Motor neuron Impulses then travel along thousands of motor neurons. The motor neurons send the impulses to muscles. The muscles carry out the response, and you reach for the phone.

Receptors in ear

Muscle in hand

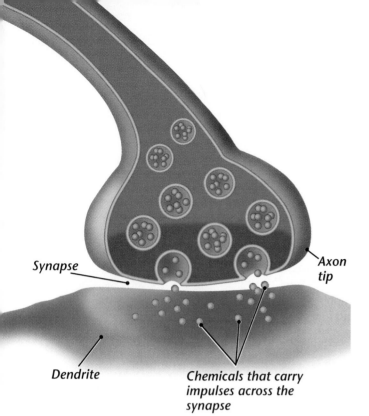

Synapse

Axon tip

Dendrite

Chemicals that carry impulses across the synapse

Figure 3 A synapse is the tiny space between the axon of one neuron and the dendrite of another neuron. When a nerve impulse reaches the end of an axon, chemicals are released into the synapse. These chemicals enable the nerve impulse to cross the synapse.

How a Nerve Impulse Travels

Every day of your life, millions of nerve impulses travel through your nervous system. Each of those nerve impulses begins in the dendrites of a neuron. The impulse moves rapidly toward the neuron's cell body and then down the axon until it reaches the axon tip. A nerve impulse travels along the neuron in the form of electrical and chemical signals. Nerve impulses can travel as fast as 120 meters per second!

There is a tiny space called a **synapse** (SIN aps) between each axon tip and the next structure. Sometimes this next structure is a dendrite of another neuron. Other times the next structure can be a muscle or a cell in another organ, such as a sweat gland. Figure 3 illustrates a synapse between the axon of one neuron and a dendrite of another neuron.

In order for a nerve impulse to be carried along, it must cross the gap between the axon and the next structure. The axon tips release chemicals that enable the impulse to cross the synapse. If that didn't happen, the impulse would stop at the end of the axon. The impulse would not be passed from sensory neuron, to interneuron, to motor neuron. Nerve impulses would never reach your brain or make your muscles contract.

You can think of a synapse as a river, and an axon as a road that leads up to the riverbank. The nerve impulse is like a car traveling on the road. To get to the other side, the car has to cross the river. The car gets on a ferry boat, which carries it across the river. The chemicals that the axon tips release are like a ferry that carries the nerve impulse across the synapse.

Section 1 Review

1. Describe three functions of the nervous system.
2. Identify the three kinds of neurons that are found in the nervous system. Describe how they interact to carry nerve impulses.
3. How does a nerve impulse cross a synapse?
4. **Thinking Critically** **Predicting** What would happen to a nerve impulse carried by an interneuron if the tips of the interneuron's axon were damaged? Explain.

Science at Home

Stimulus and Response During dinner, ask a family member to pass the salt and pepper to you. Observe what your family member then does. Explain that the words you spoke were a stimulus and that the family member's reaction was a response. Discuss other examples of stimuli and responses with your family.

Ready or Not

Do people carry out tasks better at certain times of day? In this lab, you will design an experiment to answer this question.

Problem

Do people's reaction times vary at different times of day?

Materials

meter stick

Design a Plan

Part 1 Observing a Response to a Stimulus

1. Have your partner hold a meter stick with the zero end about 50 cm above a table.
2. Get ready to catch the meter stick by positioning the top of your thumb and forefinger just at the zero position as shown in the photograph.
3. Your partner should drop the meter stick without any warning. Using your thumb and forefinger only (no other part of your hand), catch the meter stick as soon as you can. Record the distance in centimeters that the meter stick fell. This distance is a measure of your reaction time.

Part 2 Design Your Experiment

4. With your partner, discuss how you can use the activity from Part 1 to find out whether people's reaction times vary at different times of day. Be sure to consider the questions below. Then write up your experimental plan.
   - What hypothesis will you test?
   - What variables do you need to control?
   - How many people will you test? How many times will you test each person?

5. Submit your plan for your teacher's review. Make any changes your teacher recommends. Create a data table to record your results. Then perform your experiment.

Analyze and Conclude

1. In this lab, what is the stimulus? What is the response? Is this response voluntary or involuntary? Explain.
2. Why can you use the distance on the meter stick as a measure of reaction time?
3. Based on your results, do people's reaction times vary at different times of day? Explain.
4. **Think About It** In Part 2, why is it important to control all variables except the time of day?

More to Explore

Do you think people can do arithmetic problems more quickly and accurately at certain times of the day? Design an experiment to investigate this question. Obtain your teacher's permission before trying your experiment.

Divisions of the Nervous System

・・・ACTIVITY・・・・

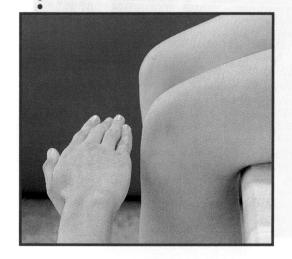

How Does Your Knee React?

1. Sit on a table or counter so that your legs dangle freely. Your feet should not touch the floor.

2. Have your partner use the side of his or her hand to *gently* tap one of your knees just below the kneecap. Observe what happens to your leg. Note whether you have any control over your reaction.

3. Change places with your partner. Repeat Steps 1 and 2.

Think It Over

Inferring When might it be an advantage for your body to react very quickly and without your conscious control?

GUIDE FOR READING

◆ What is the function of the central nervous system?

◆ What functions does the peripheral nervous system perform?

◆ What is a reflex?

Reading Tip As you read, write four multiple choice questions about the content in this section. Exchange questions with a partner and answer each other's questions.

A concert is about to begin. The conductor gives the signal, and the musicians begin to play. The sound of music, beautiful and stirring, fills the air.

To play music in harmony, an orchestra needs both musicians and a conductor. The musicians play the music, and the conductor directs the musicians and coordinates their playing.

Similarly, your nervous system has two divisions that work together—the central nervous system and the peripheral nervous system. The **central nervous system** consists of the brain and spinal cord. The **peripheral nervous system** consists of all the nerves located outside of the central nervous system. The central nervous system is like a conductor. The nerves of the peripheral nervous system are like the musicians.

Figure 4 In an orchestra, the conductor and musicians work together to make music. Similarly, the central and peripheral nervous systems work together to control body functions.

In addition, steroid abuse can cause serious health problems, such as heart damage, liver damage, and increased blood pressure. Steroid use is especially dangerous for teenagers, whose growing bodies can be permanently damaged.

Alcohol

Alcohol is a drug found in many beverages, including beer, wine, cocktails, and hard liquor. Alcohol is a powerful depressant. In the United States, it is illegal for people under the age of 21 to buy or possess alcohol. In spite of this fact, alcohol is the most commonly abused drug in people aged 12 to 17.

6. Remove the slide from the microscope. Use a plastic dropper to add 1 drop of adrenaline solution to the water flea chamber. (Adrenaline is a substance that is produced by the human body that acts in a manner similar to a stimulant.)
7. Place the slide on the microscope. Using low power, locate a water flea. Count and record the number of heartbeats in a minute.

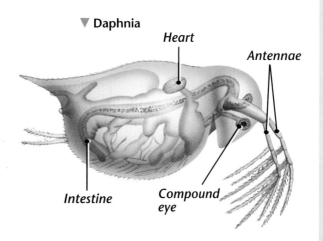

▼ **Daphnia**

Heart

Antennae

Intestine

Compound eye

Part 2 Testing the Effects of Caffeine

8. Using the procedures you followed in Part 1, design an experiment that tests the effect of caffeine on *Daphnia's* heartbeat. You can use beverages with and without caffeine in your investigation. Be sure to write a hypothesis and control all necessary variables.
9. Submit your experimental plan to your teacher for review. After making any necessary changes, carry out your experiment.

Analyze and Conclude

1. What effect does a stimulant have on the body?

2. In Part 1, how did you know that adrenaline acted as a stimulant?
3. In Part 2, did caffeine act as a stimulant?
4. **Apply** Based on your work in Part 2, how do you think your body would react to drinks with caffeine? To drinks without caffeine?

Design an Experiment

Do you think that "decaffeinated" products will act as a stimulant in *Daphnia?* Design a controlled experiment to find out. Obtain your teacher's approval before performing this experiment.

How Alcohol Affects the Body Alcohol is absorbed by the digestive system quickly. If a person drinks alcohol on an empty stomach, the alcohol enters the blood and gets to the brain and other organs almost immediately. If alcohol is drunk with a meal, it takes longer to get into the blood.

To understand what alcohol does to the body, look at *Exploring the Effects of Alcohol.* The more alcohol in the blood, the more serious the effects. The amount of alcohol in the blood is usually expressed as blood alcohol concentration, or BAC. A BAC value of 0.1 percent means that one tenth of one percent of the fluid in the blood is alcohol. In some states, if car drivers have a BAC of 0.08 percent or more, they are legally drunk. In other states, drivers with a BAC of 0.1 are considered drunk.

Alcohol produces serious effects, including loss of normal judgment, at a BAC of less than 0.08 percent. This loss of judgment can have serious consequences. For example, people who have been drinking may not realize that they cannot drive a car safely. In the United States, alcohol is involved in about 40 percent of traffic-related deaths. About every two minutes, a person in the United States is injured in a car crash related to alcohol.

Long-Term Alcohol Abuse Many adults drink occasionally, and in moderation, without serious safety or health problems. However, heavy drinking, especially over a long period, can result in significant health problems. **The abuse of alcohol can cause the destruction of cells in the brain and liver, and it can also lead to addiction and emotional dependence.** Damage to the brain can cause mental disturbances, such as hallucinations and

Figure 23 Alcohol is involved in many car crashes. Alcohol decreases a driver's ability to react quickly to traffic and road conditions.

loss of consciousness. The liver, which breaks down alcohol for elimination from the body, can become so scarred that it does not function properly. In addition, long-term alcohol abuse can increase the risk of getting certain kinds of cancer.

Abuse of alcohol can result in **alcoholism,** a disease in which a person is both physically addicted to and emotionally dependent on alcohol. To give up alcohol, alcoholics must go through withdrawal, as with any addictive drug. To give up drinking,

EXPLORING *the Effects of Alcohol*

Alcohol is a drug that affects every system of the body. It also impacts a person's thought processes and judgment.

Nervous system Vision becomes blurred. Speech becomes unclear. Control of behavior is reduced. Judgment becomes poor.

Cardiovascular system At first, heartbeat rate and blood pressure increase. Later, with large amounts of alcohol, the heartbeat rate and blood pressure may decrease.

Excretory system Alcohol causes the kidneys to produce more urine. As a result, the drinker loses more water than usual.

Skin Blood flow to the skin increases, causing rapid loss of body heat.

Liver The liver breaks down alcohol. Over many years, liver damage can result.

Digestive system Alcohol is absorbed directly from the stomach and small intestine. The alcohol passes into the bloodstream quickly.

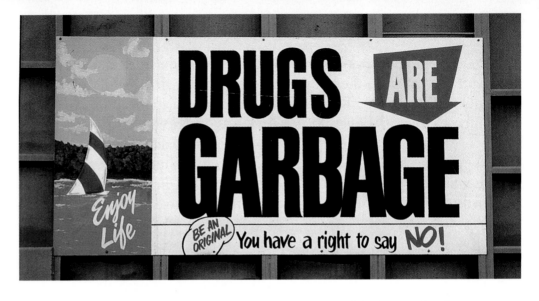

Figure 24 The message is clear: drugs are dangerous, and you have the right to refuse to take them.

alcoholics need both medical and emotional help. Medical professionals and organizations such as Alcoholics Anonymous can help a person stop drinking.

Avoiding Drugs and Alcohol

The best way to avoid depending on drugs and alcohol is not to start using them. Many teenagers who start do so because of peer pressure from people who are abusing drugs. Try to avoid situations in which there is a possibility that drugs may be used.

If you are faced with pressure to use drugs, give a simple but honest reason for your refusal. For example, you might say that you don't want to risk getting into trouble with the law. You do not need to apologize for your decision. And remember that people who don't respect your feelings aren't very good friends.

To stay away from drugs, it is important to find healthy things to do with friends. Become involved in sports and other school or community activities in which you and your friends can have fun together. Such activities help you feel good about yourself. By deciding not to use drugs, you are protecting your health.

Section 4 Review

1. How do abused drugs affect the nervous system? Why can these effects be dangerous?
2. What are the effects of long-term alcohol abuse?
3. What is alcoholism?
4. **Thinking Critically Comparing and Contrasting** Contrast the effects that stimulants and depressants have on the body.

Check Your Progress

CHAPTER PROJECT

By now you should have finished collecting your data and recording your observations. Now begin preparing a report about your findings. Think about the best way to communicate the procedures you followed and the results you obtained. Your report should explain how you think the illusions you chose trick the senses. Decide how to use graphs and other visuals in your report.

How the Nervous System Works

Key Ideas
◆ The nervous system receives information about the external and internal environment and helps maintain homeostasis.

Key Terms
stimulus	dendrite	interneuron
response	axon	motor neuron
neuron	nerve	synapse
nerve impulse	sensory neuron	

Divisions of the Nervous System

Key Ideas
◆ The central nervous system consists of the brain and spinal cord.
◆ The peripheral nervous system links the central nervous system to the rest of the body.

Key Terms
central nervous system	cerebellum
peripheral nervous system	brainstem
	somatic nervous system
brain	autonomic nervous system
spinal cord	reflex
cerebrum	concussion

The Senses

Key Ideas
◆ The senses change information about the environment to nerve impulses.
◆ After light enters the eye, it passes through the lens, which focuses it on the retina. Impulses then travel to the brain.
◆ Sound waves start vibrations in structures in the ear. When the vibrations reach the cochlea, impulses are sent to the brain.

Key Terms
cornea	retina	eardrum
pupil	nearsightedness	cochlea
iris	farsightedness	semicircular canal
lens		

Alcohol and Other Drugs

INTEGRATING HEALTH

Key Ideas
◆ Abused drugs act on the nervous system. Depressants slow down the central nervous system. Stimulants speed up body processes. Marijuana, alcohol, amphetamines, and anabolic steroids are commonly abused drugs.
◆ The long-term abuse of alcohol can damage the liver and brain and lead to alcoholism.

Key Terms
drug	withdrawal	anabolic steroid
drug abuse	depressant	alcoholism
tolerance	stimulant	

Organizing Information

Concept Map Complete the following concept map about nerve cells and their functions. (For more on concept maps, see the Skills Handbook.)

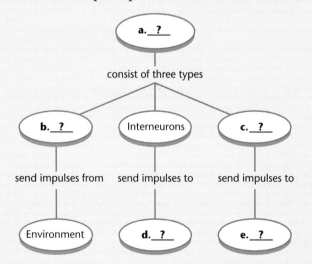

Reviewing Content

 For more review of key concepts, see the Interactive Student Tutorial CD-ROM.

Multiple Choice
Choose the letter of the best answer.

1. A change or signal in the environment that makes the nervous system react is called a
   a. stimulus.   **b.** response.
   c. receptor.   **d.** synapse.
2. The structures that carry messages toward a neuron's cell body are
   a. axons.
   b. dendrites.
   c. nerves.
   d. impulses.
3. Which structure links the brain and the peripheral nervous system?
   a. the cerebrum
   b. the cerebellum
   c. the cochlea
   d. the spinal cord
4. Which structure adjusts the size of the pupil?
   a. the cornea
   b. the retina
   c. the lens
   d. the iris
5. Physical dependence on a drug is called
   a. withdrawal.
   b. response.
   c. addiction.
   d. tolerance.

True or False
If the statement is true, write true. If it is false, change the underlined word or words to make the statement true.

6. A nerve message is also called a <u>nerve impulse</u>.
7. The <u>brainstem</u> is the part of the brain that controls involuntary actions.
8. In <u>nearsightedness</u>, a person cannot see nearby objects clearly.
9. The hammer, anvil, and <u>wrench</u> are the three bones in the middle ear.
10. Alcohol is a <u>depressant</u>.

Checking Concepts

11. Compare the functions of axons and dendrites.
12. What is the function of the autonomic nervous system?
13. How do the cerebrum and cerebellum work together when you ride a bicycle?
14. What are some steps you can take to protect your central nervous system from injury?
15. Describe how lenses in eyeglasses correct nearsightedness and farsightedness.
16. List all the structures in your ear that must vibrate before you hear a sound. List them in the order in which they vibrate.
17. What are the effects of anabolic steroids on the body?
18. **Writing to Learn** Imagine that Earth has been invaded by space aliens who are exactly like humans except for the fact that they have no sense of touch. These aliens plan to take over Earth. Write a plan for fighting the aliens that makes use of the fact that they lack a sense of touch.

Thinking Critically

19. **Relating Cause and Effect** When a person has a stroke, blood flow to part of the brain is reduced, and severe brain damage can result. Suppose that after a stroke, a woman is unable to move her right arm and right leg. In which side of her brain did the stroke occur? Explain.
20. **Applying Concepts** As a man walks barefoot along a beach, he steps on a sharp shell. His foot automatically jerks upward, even before he feels pain. What process is this an example of? How does it help protect the man?
21. **Making Judgments** If someone tried to persuade you to take drugs, what arguments would you use as a way of refusing? Why do you think these arguments would be effective?

Applying Skills

A person with normal vision stood at different distances from an eye chart and tried to identify the letters on the chart. The table gives the results. Use the table to answer Questions 22–24.

Distance from Eye Chart	Percent of Letters Identified Correctly
2 meters	100
4 meters	92
6 meters	80
8 meters	71
10 meters	60

22. Graphing Make a line graph of the data. Plot the distance from the chart on the horizontal axis. On the vertical axis, plot the percent of letters identified correctly.

23. Controlling Variables What was the manipulated variable in this experiment? What was the responding variable?

24. Predicting How would you expect the results to differ for a farsighted person? Explain.

Performance ▽ CHAPTER PROJECT Assessment

Present Your Project Your report should include an explanation of how you did your research, what you were trying to find out, and how your actual results compared with your expected results. Also include information on how the nervous system was involved in your illusions. If you can, try to explain why the illusions work.

Reflect and Record In your journal, summarize what you learned from doing this project. Did the project go as you expected, or were you surprised by some results? If you had a chance to continue your investigations, what would you do next? Why?

Test Preparation

Use these questions to prepare for standardized tests.

Study the diagram. Then answer Questions 25–28.

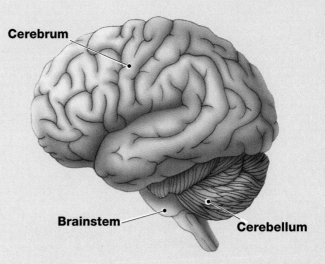

25. Which part of the brain controls muscle coordination and balance?
   a. right half of cerebrum
   b. left half of cerebrum
   c. cerebellum
   d. brainstem

26. Which part of the brain controls involuntary actions such as breathing and the heartbeat?
   a. right half of cerebrum
   b. left half of cerebrum
   c. cerebellum
   d. brainstem

27. Which part of the brain controls your ability to raise your right hand high over your head?
   a. right half of cerebrum
   b. left half of cerebrum
   c. spinal cord
   d. brainstem

28. Which body system consists of the brain and spinal cord?
   a. central nervous system
   b. peripheral nervous system
   c. somatic nervous system
   d. autonomic nervous system

CHAPTER
21
The Endocrine System and Reproduction

www.phschool.com

"Breakfast now!"
A baby may need
care at any moment
of the day or night.

Integrating Health

SECTION 1 The Endocrine System

Discover What's the Signal?

SECTION 2 The Male and Female Reproductive Systems

Discover What's the Big Difference?
Sharpen Your Skills Graphing

SECTION 3 The Human Life Cycle

Discover How Many Ways Does a Child Grow?
Try This Way to Grow!
Skills Lab Growing Up

656

A Precious Bundle

With the arrival of their first baby, most new parents discover that their lives are totally changed. Their usual schedules are disrupted, and they suddenly need a new set of skills. Parents must begin to learn how to keep the infant comfortable and happy.

As you learn about reproduction and development, you'll experience what it's like to care for a "baby." Although your baby will be only a physical model, you'll have a chance to learn about the responsibilities of parenthood.

Your Goal To develop and follow a plan to care for a "baby" for three days and nights.

To complete this project, you must
- ◆ list all the essential tasks involved in caring for a young infant, and prepare a 24-hour schedule of those tasks
- ◆ make a model "baby" from a bag of flour, and care for the baby according to your schedule
- ◆ keep a journal of your thoughts and feelings as you care for your "baby," making entries at least twice a day

Get Started With classmates write down all the things that parents must do when caring for infants. Prepare a plan describing how to carry out those activities with your "baby." List the materials you'll need. If you require more information, write down your questions, then consult adult caregivers, day care facilities, or other resources.

Check Your Progress You'll be working on this project as you study this chapter. To keep your project on track, look for Check Your Progress boxes at the following points.

Section 1 Review, page 662: Present your child-care plan to your teacher for review.

Section 2 Review, page 668: Care for your "baby," and record your experiences in your journal.

Section 4 Review, page 677: Summarize your experiences.

Present Your Project At the end of the chapter (page 681), you'll share what you learned about parenthood.

The Endocrine System

DISCOVER

What's the Signal?

1. Stand up and move around the room until your teacher says "Freeze!" Then stop moving immediately. Stay perfectly still until your teacher says "Start!" Then begin moving again.

2. Anyone who moves between the "Freeze!" command and the "Start!" command has to leave the game.

3. Play until only one person is left in the game. That person is the winner.

Think It Over

Inferring Why is it important for players in this game to respond to signals? What types of signals does the human body use?

GUIDE FOR READING

◆ What is the function of the endocrine system?

◆ How does negative feedback control hormone levels?

Reading Tip Before you read, preview *Exploring the Endocrine System* on pages 660–661. List the terms in the diagram that are new to you. Look for their meanings as you read.

You're playing softball on a hot afternoon. Without warning, thick, dark clouds form. Suddenly, there's a flash of lightning. Thunder cracks overhead. Someone screams, you jump, and everyone runs for cover. Your heart is pounding, your palms are sweaty, and your muscles are tight.

Your body's reaction to the sudden storm was caused mainly by your body's endocrine system. In this section, you will learn about the role of the endocrine system in many body processes—from the quick response to a thunder clap, to the slower body changes that turn a child into an adult.

The Role of the Endocrine System

The human body has two systems that regulate its activities. You learned about one, the nervous system, in Chapter 20. The endocrine system is the other regulating system. **The endocrine system controls many of the body's daily activities as well as long-term changes such as development.**

The endocrine system is made up of glands. Glands are organs that produce chemicals. You already know about some glands, such as those that produce saliva and sweat. Those glands release their chemicals into tiny tubes. The tubes deliver the chemicals to a specific location within the body or to the skin's surface.

The endocrine system does not have delivery tubes. **Endocrine glands** (EN duh krin) produce and release their chemical products directly into the bloodstream. The blood then carries those chemicals throughout the body.

Applying Skills

The data table below shows how the length of a developing baby changes during pregnancy. Use the table to answer Questions 23–25.

Week of Pregnancy	Average Length (mm)	Week of Pregnancy	Average Length (mm)
4	7	24	300
8	30	28	350
12	75	32	410
16	180	36	450
20	250	38	500

23. Measuring Use a metric ruler to mark each length on a piece of paper. During which four-week period did the greatest increase in length occur?

24. Graphing Graph the data by plotting time on the horizontal axis and length on the vertical axis.

25. Interpreting Data At the twelfth week, a developing baby measures about 75 mm. By which week has the fetus grown to four times that length? Six times that length?

CHAPTER PROJECT

Performance Assessment

Present Your Project You now have the chance to discuss what you learned as you cared for your "baby." What do you now know about parenting that you didn't know before? Consider reading passages from your journal to the class, including the summary you wrote.

Reflect and Record In your journal, describe how well you carried out this project. Did you care for the baby for three complete days? Did you do each task as carefully as you would have for a real infant? How do you think this project was similar to caring for a real baby? How was it different?

Test Preparation

Use these questions to prepare for standardized tests.

Study the graph. Then answer Questions 26–29.

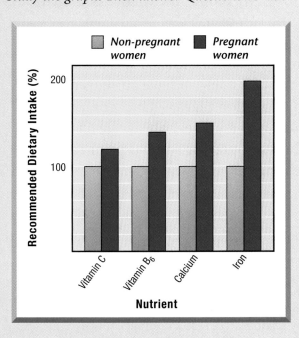

26. What would be the best title for this graph?
   a. Nutrient Needs of Pregnant Women
   b. Recommended Dietary Intake
   c. Vitamin Needs of Pregnant Women
   d. Mineral Needs of Non-pregnant Women

27. How much more iron does a pregnant woman need than a non-pregnant woman?
   a. 20%   **b.** 100%
   c. 120%   **d.** 150%

28. If non-pregnant adult women normally need 800 mg of calcium a day, how much calcium do pregnant women need?
   a. 800 mg   **b.** 1,000 mg
   c. 1,200 mg   **d.** 1,600 mg

29. Which nutrient do pregnant women need in the greatest amount?
   a. vitamin C
   b. vitamin B_6
   c. iron
   d. can't tell from the information in this graph

PROTECTING DESERT WILDLIFE

Elroy Masters likes working outdoors. One day he hikes a mountain trail, looking for desert tortoises. The next morning he may be in a boat on the Colorado River, counting birds along the riverbank. Another day he may be in the Arizona hills, building a water container for thirsty bighorn sheep. Elroy is a biologist working for the federal government's Bureau of Land Management (BLM). His job is to protect wildlife habitat in the desert along the Colorado River between California and Arizona.

"People may come in wanting to run a pipeline across public land or needing to build a road," he explains. "Part of my job is to check out the biological effect of that action on different species of animals and plants. If people are going to build a road where there are a lot of tortoises, we might try to have them work from November to March. Since tortoises hibernate during those months, we reduce the chance of a tortoise getting run over."

Growing up in Arizona, Elroy lived in a farming community. "I was always out-doors. I was able to have animals that a lot of people don't have—chickens, pigeons, ducks, and a horse. I always loved animals. I always hoped for some type of career with them."

Elroy Masters studied biology at Phoenix College and Northern Arizona University. He started working for the Bureau of Land Management when he was still a college student. He now works as a Wildlife Management Biologist. In this photograph, Elroy is about to release a razorback sucker, an endangered species of fish, into the Colorado River.

Today, Elroy and his co-workers make surveys of desert animals. They count the animals in different areas and make maps of their habitats. They locate where the animals live, what they eat, and where they build their nests and raise their young. Elroy uses that information to protect the animals when natural events or human activities threaten them.

Elroy Masters works in the area around Lake Havasu in western Arizona.

TALKING WITH ELROY MASTERS

Q *What wildlife do you protect?*

A One of the neatest animals we deal with is the desert bighorn sheep. In an average summer, it can get as hot as 120 degrees here. Sometimes the heat lasts for weeks. But with the number of people living around the river, the animals are no longer able to travel to water. So we go up into the mountains to construct catchments (containers) to collect water and store it. That way the sheep can stay in the mountains without trying to cross freeways to get to water.

We fly in big storage tanks that hold about 10,000 gallons of water. We bury them in the ground or put them on a platform. We use paint to mask them into the color of the scenery. We sometimes build a dam or put out a metal sheet to catch drizzle rain.

A catchment can hold 10,000 gallons of water (right). It is buried in the ground. The drinking container provides water for desert bighorn sheep (below), mule deer, and other wildlife.

Q *What else are you doing to protect the bighorn sheep?*

A We're going to work with the Fish and Wildlife Department to capture and transplant bighorn sheep to a mountain range in my area. There are already sheep and some mountain lions here. But the sheep aren't doing as well as we expected. We want to bring in some bighorn sheep that are used to lions. We hope these lion-savvy sheep will teach the sheep in our area how to avoid lions. To catch the sheep, we'll use a helicopter. We'll shoot a net over the sheep and a couple of guys will jump out to secure the animals and then bring them to our herd.

The Colorado River valley is home to the Southwestern willow flycatcher and the desert tortoise.

Q *What other animals are you responsible for protecting?*

A I work a lot with desert tortoises. I'm responsible for two different populations, one on either side of the river. The tortoises live in the drier, hilly areas away from the river. Any time we go out into the field, we try to collect data. We keep track of where they've been and where they feed.

Q *How do you find the tortoises?*

A We have maps that indicate their habitat. Based on the habitat, we'll go out, walk around, and look under rocks and boulders to see if we can find a burrow. The tortoises are good diggers. They find a good boulder and go underground 10 or 12 feet. That's where they'll spend the winter.

Southwestern willow flycatcher

Desert tortoise

Q *Do you also work with birds?*

A Right now we're working with the Southwestern willow flycatcher. It's a small bird that depends on thick riparian (riverbank) vegetation to build nests and breed. The flycatcher is a migratory bird. Each spring, the birds fly to Arizona from Central America and Mexico. In the early summer months, we go out to find how many are breeding. We're trying to learn what's needed to prevent flycatchers from becoming extinct. We need to survey and protect the remaining stands of habitat. The flycatchers like to nest in thick stands of willow. But they will also build nests in another tree, salt cedar. The birds don't prefer it, but sometimes salt cedar is the only vegetation remaining, so they use it.

Q *What's threatening the riverbank plants?*

A The low water level in the river—due to human use—is a big threat. So is fire. During summer months, there are large numbers of recreational boats. Careless boaters can cause fires. Some fires get pretty big along the river and destroy a lot of the habitat where the birds nest and raise their young.

Q *Can you see the benefits of your work?*

A Yes, I see it especially in riverbank zones where areas are protected so that vegetation and trees can grow back. This year we did a new bird count in one area. Species that hadn't been seen in a while, like tanagers, showed up. Some of the migratory birds are already stopping in young cottonwood trees. That's the best gauge I've had—seeing birds returning to these new trees.

There are also quick results with the water catchments in the hills. We put the water in a year ago. They're aimed at bighorn sheep and mule deer. But now we've also got a lot of different birds—doves and quails—that come into the area.

Elroy Masters also works with populations of the California leaf-nosed bat. This bat has large ears and a leaf-shaped, turned-up nose. The bats are threatened by the loss of their habitat.

In Your Journal

Elroy Masters and his co-workers "survey" the wildlife in their area in order to learn how to protect them. Think of a wild animal that lives in a park or open area near you—squirrels, frogs, birds, even insects. Work out a step-by-step plan to draw a simple map marking the places where the animal is found.

685

 WEB ACTIVITY www.phschool.com

SECTION
1 Living Things and the Environment

Discover **What's in the Scene?**
Try This **With or Without Salt?**
Skills Lab **A World in a Bottle**

Integrating Mathematics
SECTION
2 Studying Populations

Discover **What's the Bean Population?**
Sharpen Your Skills **Calculating**
Try This **Elbow Room**
Science at Home **Word Estimates**
Real-World Lab **Counting Turtles**

SECTION
3 Interactions Among Living Things

Discover **How Well Can You Hide a Butterfly?**
Sharpen Your Skills **Classifying**

What's a Crowd?

How many sunflowers are there in this photograph? Certainly too many to count! But there is a limit to how many more sunflowers can grow in this fertile field. The limit is determined by what the sunflowers need to survive.

In this chapter, you will explore how living things obtain the things they need from their surroundings. You will also learn how organisms interact with the living and nonliving things around them. As you study this chapter, you will observe plants as sample organisms.

Your Goal To design and conduct an experiment to determine the effect of crowding on plant growth.

To complete your project successfully, you must

◆ develop a plan for planting different numbers of seeds in identical containers
◆ observe and collect data on the growing plants
◆ present your results in a written report and a graph
◆ follow the safety guidelines in Appendix A

Get Started With your group, brainstorm ideas for your plan. What conditions do plants need to grow? How will you arrange your seeds in their containers? What types of measurements will you make when the plants begin to grow? Submit your draft plan to your teacher for review.

Check Your Progress You'll be working on this project as you study this chapter. To keep your project on track, look for Check Your Progress boxes at the following points.

Section 1 Review, page 693: Plant the seeds. Measure the plants' growth and record your observations.
Section 3 Review, page 710: Analyze your data and prepare your report.

Present Your Project At the end of the chapter (page 713), your group will present your results and conclusions to the class.

Row after row of bright sunflowers blanket a field in Provence, France.

Living Things and the Environment

What's in the Scene?

1. Choose a magazine picture of a nature scene. Paste the picture onto a sheet of paper, leaving space all around the picture.

2. Identify all the things in the picture that are alive. Use a colored pencil to draw a line from each living thing, or organism. Label the organism if you know its name.

3. Use a different colored pencil to draw a line from each nonliving thing and label it.

Think It Over

Inferring How do the organisms in the picture depend on the nonliving things? Using a third color, draw lines connecting organisms to the nonliving things they need.

GUIDE FOR READING

◆ What needs are met by an organism's surroundings?

◆ What are the levels of organization within an ecosystem?

Reading Tip Write the section headings in your notebook. As you read, make a list of main ideas and supporting details under each heading.

Black-tailed prairie dogs ▼

As the sun rises on a warm summer morning, the Nebraska town is already bustling with activity. Some residents are hard at work building homes for their families. They are building underground, where it is dark and cool. Other inhabitants are collecting seeds for breakfast. Some of the town's younger residents are at play, chasing each other through the grass.

Suddenly, an adult spots a threatening shadow approaching—an enemy has appeared in the sky! The adult cries out several times, warning the others. Within moments, the town's residents disappear into their underground homes. The town is silent and still, except for a single hawk circling overhead.

Have you guessed what kind of town this is? It is a prairie dog town on the Nebraska plains. As these prairie dogs dug their burrows, searched for food, and hid from the hawk, they interacted with their environment, or surroundings. The prairie dogs interacted with living things, such as the grass and the hawk, and with nonliving things, such as the soil. All the living and nonliving things that interact in a particular area make up an **ecosystem.**

A prairie is just one of the many different ecosystems found on Earth. Other ecosystems in which living things make their homes include mountain streams, deep oceans, and dense forests.

Habitats

A prairie dog is one type of organism, or living thing. Organisms live in a specific place within an ecosystem. **An organism obtains food, water, shelter, and other things it needs to live, grow, and reproduce from its surroundings.** The place where an organism lives and that provides the things the organism needs is called its **habitat.**

A single ecosystem may contain many habitats. For example, in a forest ecosystem, mushrooms grow in the damp soil, bears live on the forest floor, termites live in fallen tree trunks, and flickers build nests in the trunks.

Organisms live in different habitats because they have different requirements for survival. A prairie dog obtains the food and shelter it needs from its habitat. It could not survive in a tropical rain forest or on the rocky ocean shore. Likewise, the prairie would not meet the needs of a gorilla, a penguin, or a hermit crab.

Figure 1 A stream tumbles over mossy rocks in a lush Tennessee forest. This ecosystem contains many different habitats. *Comparing and Contrasting How is the mushrooms' habitat in the forest different from the flicker's habitat?*

Biotic Factors

An organism interacts with both the living and nonliving things in its environment. The living parts of an ecosystem are called **biotic factors** (by AHT ik factors). Biotic factors in the prairie dogs' ecosystem include the grass and plants that provide seeds and berries. The hawks, ferrets, badgers, and eagles that hunt the prairie dogs are also biotic factors. In addition, worms, fungi, and bacteria are biotic factors that live in the soil underneath the prairie grass. These organisms keep the soil rich in nutrients as they break down the remains of other living things.

☑ *Checkpoint Name a biotic factor in your environment.*

Figure 2 This eastern banjo frog is burrowing in the sand to stay cool in the hot Australian desert. *Interpreting Photographs With which abiotic factors is the frog interacting in this scene?*

With or Without Salt?

In this activity you will explore salt as an abiotic factor.

ACTIVITY

1. Label four 600-mL beakers A, B, C, and D. Fill each with 500 mL of room-temperature spring water.

2. Set beaker A aside. It will contain fresh water. To beaker B, add 2.5 grams of noniodized salt. Add 7.5 grams of salt to beaker C and 15 grams of salt to beaker D. Stir beakers B, C, and D.

3. Add about $\frac{1}{4}$ of a spoonful of brine shrimp eggs to each beaker.

4. Cover each beaker with a square of paper. Keep them away from direct light or heat. Wash your hands.

5. Observe the beakers daily for three days.

Drawing Conclusions In which beakers did the eggs hatch? What can you conclude about the amount of salt in the shrimps' natural habitat?

Abiotic Factors

The nonliving parts of an ecosystem are called **abiotic factors** (ay by AHT ik factors). Abiotic factors that affect living things in the prairie are similar to those found in most ecosystems. They include water, sunlight, oxygen, temperature, and soil.

Water All living things require water to carry out their life processes. Water also makes up a large part of the bodies of most organisms. Your body, for example, is about 65 percent water. A watermelon consists of more than 95 percent water! Water is particularly important to plants and algae. As you have learned, these organisms use water, along with sunlight and carbon dioxide, to make food in a process called photosynthesis. Other living things eat the plants and algae to obtain energy.

Sunlight Because sunlight is necessary for photosynthesis, it is an important abiotic factor for plants, algae, and other living things. In places that do not receive sunlight, such as dark caves, plants cannot grow. Without plants or algae to provide a source of food, few other organisms can live.

Oxygen Most living things require oxygen to carry out their life processes. Oxygen is so important to the functioning of the human body that you can live only a few minutes without it. Organisms that live on land obtain oxygen from the air, which is about 20 percent oxygen. Fish and other water organisms obtain dissolved oxygen from the water around them.

Temperature The temperatures that are typical of an area determine the types of organisms that can live there. For example, if you took a trip to a warm tropical island, you would see palm trees, bright hibiscus flowers, and tiny lizards. These organisms could not survive on the frozen plains of Siberia. But the thick, warm fur of wolves and short, strong branches of dwarf willows are suited to the blustery winters there.

Some animals alter their environments to overcome very hot or very cold temperatures. For example, prairie dogs dig underground dens to find shelter from the blazing summer sun. They line the dens with grass. The grass keeps the prairie dogs warm during the cold and windy winters.

Soil Soil is a mixture of rock fragments, nutrients, air, water, and the decaying remains of living things. Soil in different areas consists of varying amounts of these materials. The type of soil in an area influences the kinds of plants that can grow there. Many animals, such as the prairie dogs, use the soil itself as a home. Billions of microscopic organisms such as bacteria also live in the soil. These tiny organisms play an important role in the ecosystem by breaking down the remains of other living things.

☑ *Checkpoint* *How do biotic factors differ from abiotic factors?*

Populations

In 1900, travelers saw a prairie dog town in Texas covering an area twice the size of the city of Dallas. The sprawling town contained more than 400 million prairie dogs! These prairie dogs were all members of one species. Recall from Chapter 6 that a species is a group of organisms that are physically similar and can reproduce with one another to produce fertile offspring.

All the members of one species in a particular area are referred to as a **population.** The 400 million prairie dogs in the Texas town are one example of a population. All the pigeons in New York City make up a population, as do all the daisies in a field. In contrast, all the trees in a forest do not make up a population, because they do not all belong to the same species. There may be pines, maples, birches, and many other tree species in the forest.

The area in which a population lives can be as small as a single blade of grass or as large as the whole planet. Scientists studying a type of organism usually limit their study to a population in a defined area. For example, they might study the population of bluegill fish in a pond, or the population of alligators in the Florida Everglades.

Some populations, however, do not stay in a contained area. For example, to study the population of finback whales, a scientist might need to use the entire ocean.

Figure 3 This milkweed plant is home to a small population of ladybug beetles.

Organism	Population

Language Arts
CONNECTION

The word *ecology* comes from two Greek root words: *oikos*, which means house or place to live, and *logos*, which means *study*. Put together, these root words create a term for studying organisms in the place where they live. Many science terms are derived from Greek and Latin root words.

In Your Journal

Use a dictionary to find root words for the following terms from this section: *habitat, biotic, community,* and *population.* For each root word, list its meaning, original language, and other English words containing the root.

Communities

Of course, most ecosystems contain more than one type of organism. The prairie, for instance, includes prairie dogs, hawks, grasses, badgers, and snakes, along with many other organisms. All the different populations that live together in an area make up a **community.**

Figure 4 shows the levels of organization in the prairie ecosystem. **The smallest unit of organization is a single organism, which belongs to a population of other members of its species. The population belongs to a community of different species. The community and abiotic factors together form an ecosystem.**

To be considered a community, the different populations must live close enough together to interact. One way the populations in a community may interact is by using the same resources, such as food and shelter. For example, the tunnels dug by the prairie dogs also serve as homes for burrowing owls and black-footed ferrets. The prairie dogs share the grass with other animals. Meanwhile, prairie dogs themselves serve as food for many species.

What Is Ecology?

Because the populations in the prairie ecosystem interact with one another, any changes in a community affect all the different populations that live there. The study of how living things interact with one another and with their environment is called **ecology.** Ecologists, scientists who study ecology, look at how all the biotic and abiotic factors in an ecosystem are related.

Community

Ecosystem

Figure 4 The smallest level of ecological organization is an individual organism. The largest is the entire ecosystem.

As part of their work, ecologists study how organisms react to changes in their environment. Living things constantly interact with their surroundings, responding to changes in the conditions around them. Some responses are very quick. When a prairie dog sees a hawk overhead, it gives a warning bark. The other prairie dogs hear the bark and respond by returning to their burrows to hide. Other responses to change in the environment occur more slowly. For example, after a fire on the prairie, it takes some time for the grass to reach its former height and for all the animals to return to the area.

Section 1 Review

1. What basic needs are provided by an organism's habitat?
2. List these terms in order from the smallest unit to the largest: population, organism, ecosystem, community.
3. Explain how water and sunlight are two abiotic factors that are important to all organisms.
4. Why do ecologists study both biotic and abiotic factors in an ecosystem?
5. **Thinking Critically** **Applying Concepts** Would all the insects in a forest be considered a population? Why or why not?

CHAPTER PROJECT

Check Your Progress

After your teacher has reviewed your plan, prepare the containers and plant the seeds. Design a data table to record the information you will use to compare the growth in the different containers. When the plants begin to grow, examine them daily and record your observations. Be sure to continue caring for your plants according to your plan. *(Hint:* Use a metric ruler to measure your growing plants. Besides size, look for differences in leaf color and the number of buds among the plants.)

Making Models

A World in a Bottle

In this lab, you will study the interactions between biotic and abiotic factors in a model ecosystem.

Problem

How do organisms survive in a closed ecosystem?

Materials

pre-cut, clear plastic bottle
gravel
soil
moss plants
plastic spoon
charcoal
spray bottle

2 vascular plants
plastic wrap

Procedure

1. In this lab, you will place plants in moist soil in a bottle that is then sealed. This setup is called a terrarium. Predict whether the plants can survive in this habitat.
2. Spread about 2.5 cm of gravel on the bottom of a pre-cut bottle. Then sprinkle a spoonful or two of charcoal over the gravel.
3. Use the spoon to layer about 8 cm of soil over the gravel and charcoal. As you add the soil, tap it down to pack it.
4. Scoop out two holes in the soil. Remove the vascular plants from their pots. Gently place their roots in the holes. Then pack the loose soil firmly around the plants' stems.

5. Fill the spray bottle with water. Spray the soil until you see water collecting in the gravel.
6. Cover the soil with the moss plants, including the areas around the stems of the vascular plants. Lightly spray the mosses with water.
7. Tightly cover your terrarium with plastic wrap. Secure the cover with a rubber band. Place the terrarium in bright, indirect light.
8. Observe the terrarium daily for two weeks. Record your observations in your notebook. If its sides fog, move the terrarium to an area with a different amount of light. You may have to move it a few times before the fog disappears. Write down any changes you make in your terrarium's location.

Analyze and Conclude

1. What biotic and abiotic factors are part of the ecosystem in the bottle?
2. Were any biotic or abiotic factors able to enter the terrarium? If so, which ones?
3. Draw a diagram of the interactions between the terrarium's biotic and abiotic factors.
4. Suppose a plant-eating insect were added to the terrarium. Predict whether it would be able to survive. Explain your prediction.
5. **Think About It** Explain how your terrarium models an ecosystem. How does your model differ from an ecosystem on Earth?

More to Explore

Make a plan to model a freshwater ecosystem. How would this model be different from the land ecosystem? Obtain your teacher's approval before carrying out your plan.

SECTION
2 Studying Populations

DISCOVER ·· ACTIVITY····

What's the Bean Population?

1. Fill a plastic jar with dried beans. This is your model population.

2. Your goal is to determine the number of beans in the jar, but you will not have time to count every bean. You may use any of the following to help you determine the size of the bean population: a ruler, a small beaker, another large jar. Set a timer for two minutes when you are ready to begin.

3. After two minutes, record your answer. Then count the actual number of beans. How close was your answer?

Think It Over
Forming Operational Definitions
In this activity, you came up with an estimate of the size of the bean population. Write a definition of the term *estimate* based on what you did.

How would you like to change jobs for the day? Instead of being a student, today you are an ecologist. You are working on a project to study the bald eagle population in your area. One question you might ask is how the population has changed over time. Is the number of bald eagles more, less, or the same as it was 50 years ago? To answer these questions, you must first determine the present size of the bald eagle population.

Population Density

One way to state the size of a population is in terms of **population density**—the number of individuals in a specific area. Population density can be written as an equation:

$$Population\ density = \frac{Number\ of\ individuals}{Unit\ area}$$

For instance, suppose you counted 50 monarch butterflies in a garden measuring 10 square meters. The population density would be 50 butterflies per 10 square meters, or 5 butterflies per square meter.

GUIDE FOR READING

◆ How do ecologists determine the size of a population?

◆ What causes populations to change in size?

◆ What factors limit population growth?

Reading Tip Before you read, predict some factors that might cause a population to increase or decrease.

Bald eagles in Alaska ▶

695

Figure 5 These cone-shaped structures are nests built by cliff swallows in Dinosaur National Monument, Utah. Counting the nests is one way to estimate the cliff swallow population.

Calculating

A bed of oysters measures 100 meters long and 50 meters wide. In a one-square-meter area you count 20 oysters. Estimate the population of oysters in the bed. *(Hint:* Drawing a diagram may help you set up your calculation.)

Determining Population Size

In your work as an ecologist, how can you determine the size of the population you are studying? **Some methods of determining the size of a population are direct and indirect observations, sampling, and mark-and-recapture studies.**

Direct Observation The most obvious way to determine the size of a population is to count, one by one, all of its members. You could count all the bald eagles that live along a river, all the red maple trees in a forest, or all the elephants in a valley in Kenya.

Indirect Observation The members of a population may be small or hard to find. It may then be easier to observe their tracks or other signs rather than the organisms themselves. Look at the mud nests built by cliff swallows in Figure 5. Each nest has one entrance hole. By counting the entrance holes, you can determine the number of swallow families nesting in this area. Suppose that the average number of swallows per nest is four: two parents and two offspring. If there are 120 nests in an area, you can find the number of swallows by multiplying 120 by 4, or 480 swallows.

Sampling In most cases, it is not possible to count every member of a population. The population may be very large, or it may be spread over a wide area. It may be hard to find every individual or to remember which ones have already been counted. Instead, ecologists usually make an estimate. An **estimate** is an approximation of a number, based on reasonable assumptions.

One type of estimating involves counting the number of organisms in a small area (a sample), and then multiplying to find the number in a larger area. To get an accurate estimate, the sample should have the same population density as the larger area. For example, suppose you count 8 red maples in a 10 meter-by-10 meter area of the forest. If the entire forest were 100 times that size, you would multiply your count by 100 to estimate the total population, or 800 red maples.

Mark-and-Recapture Studies Another estimating method is a technique called "mark and recapture." This technique gets its name because some animals are first captured, marked, and released into the environment. Then another group of animals is captured. The number of marked animals in this second group indicates the population size. For example, if half the animals in the second group are marked, it means that the first sample represented about half the total population.

Here's an example showing how mark and recapture works. First, deer mice in a field are caught in a trap that does not harm the mice. Ecologists count the mice and mark each mouse's belly with a dot of hair dye before releasing it again. Two weeks later, the researchers return and capture mice again. They count how many mice have marks, showing that they were captured the first time, and how many are unmarked. Using a mathematical formula, the scientists can estimate the total population of mice in the field. You can try this technique for yourself in the Real-World Lab at the end of this section.

Figure 6 This young hawk is part of a mark-and-recapture study in a Virginia marsh. *Inferring What is the purpose of the silver band on the hawk's leg?*

✓ *Checkpoint* *When is sampling used to estimate a population?*

Changes in Population Size

By returning to a location often and using one of the methods described here, ecologists can monitor the size of a population over time. **Populations can change in size when new members enter the population or when members leave the population.**

Births and Deaths The major way in which new individuals are added to a population is through the birth of offspring. The **birth rate** of a population is the number of births in a population in a certain amount of time. For example, suppose a population of 1,000 snow geese produces 1,400 goslings in a year. The birth rate in this population would be 1,400 goslings per year.

Similarly, the major way that individuals leave a population is by dying. The **death rate** is the number of deaths in a population in a certain amount of time. Suppose that in the same population, 100 geese die in a year. The death rate would be 100 geese per year.

Figure 7 The birth of new individuals can increase the size of a population. This cheetah mother added five offspring to the population in her area.

Math TOOLBOX

Inequalities

The population statement is an example of an inequality. An inequality is a mathematical statement that compares two expressions. Two signs that represent inequalities are:

< (is less than)
> (is greater than)

For example, an inequality comparing the fraction $\frac{1}{2}$ to the decimal 0.75 would be written:

$$\frac{1}{2} < 0.75$$

Write an inequality comparing each pair of expressions below.

1. 5 **?** −6
2. 0.4 **?** $\frac{3}{5}$
3. −2 − (−8) **?** 7 − 1.5

The Population Statement

When the birth rate in a population is greater than the death rate, the population will generally increase in size. This statement can be written as a mathematical statement using the "is greater than" sign:

If birth rate > death rate, population size increases.

For example, in the snow goose population, the birth rate of 1,400 goslings per year was greater than the death rate of 100 geese per year, and the population would increase in size.

However, if the death rate in a population is greater than the birth rate, the population size will generally decrease. This can also be written as a mathematical statement:

If death rate > birth rate, population size decreases.

Immigration and Emigration The size of a population also can change when individuals move into or out of the population, just as the population of your town changes when families move into town or move away. **Immigration** (im ih GRAY shun) means moving into a population. **Emigration** (em ih GRAY shun) means leaving a population. Emigration can occur when part of a population gets cut off from the rest of the population. For instance, if food is scarce, some members of an antelope herd may wander off in search of better grassland. If they become permanently separated from the original herd, they will no longer be part of that population.

Graphing Changes in Population You can see an example of changes in a population of rabbits in Figure 8. The vertical axis shows the numbers of rabbits in the population, while the horizontal axis shows time. The graph shows the size of the population over a 10-year period.

☑ *Checkpoint* *Name two ways individuals can join a population.*

Figure 8 From Year 0 to Year 4, more rabbits joined the population than left it, so the population increased. From Year 4 to Year 8, more rabbits left the population than joined it, so the population decreased. From Year 8 to Year 10, the rates of rabbits leaving and joining the population were about equal, so the population remained steady. *Interpreting Graphs In what year did the rabbit population reach its highest point? What was the size of the population in that year?*

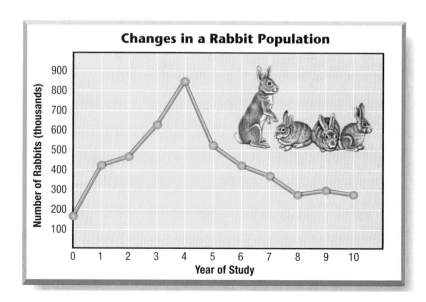

Figure 9 These gannets seem to have heard the saying "Birds of a feather flock together." When there are more birds than the space can support, the population will have exceeded the carrying capacity of the shore.

Limiting Factors

When conditions are good, a population will generally increase. But a population does not keep growing forever. Eventually, some factor in its environment causes the population to stop growing. A **limiting factor** is an environmental factor that prevents a population from increasing. **Some limiting factors for populations are food, space, and weather conditions.**

Food Organisms require food to survive. In an area where food is scarce, this becomes a limiting factor. Suppose a giraffe needs to eat 10 kilograms of leaves each day to survive. The trees in an area can provide 100 kilograms of leaves a day while remaining healthy. Five giraffes could live easily in this area, since they would only require a total of 50 kilograms of food. But 15 giraffes could not all survive—there would not be enough food for all of them. No matter how much shelter, water, and other resources there might be, the population will not grow much higher than 10 giraffes. The largest population that an environment can support is called its **carrying capacity.** The carrying capacity of this environment is 10 giraffes.

Space The birds in Figure 9 are rarely seen on land. These birds, called gannets, spend most of their lives flying over the ocean. They only land on this rocky shore to nest. But as you can see, the shore is very crowded. If a pair of gannets does not have room to build a nest, that pair will not be able to produce any offspring.

Elbow Room

Using masking tape, mark off several one-meter squares on the floor of your classroom. Your teacher will form groups of 2, 4, and 6 students. Each group's task is to put together a small jigsaw puzzle in one of the squares. All the group members must keep their feet within the square. Time how long it takes your group to finish the puzzle.

Making Models How long did it take each group to complete the task? How does this activity show that space can be a limiting factor? What is the carrying capacity of puzzle-solvers in a square meter?

Figure 10 A snowstorm can limit the size of the orange crop.

Those gannets will not contribute to an increase in the gannet population. This means that space for nesting is a limiting factor for these gannets. If the shore were bigger, more gannets would be able to nest there, and the population would increase.

Space is often a limiting factor for plants. The amount of space in which a plant grows can determine how much sunlight, water, and other necessities the plant can obtain. For example, many pine seedlings sprout each year in a forest. But as the trees get bigger, those that are too close together do not have room to spread their roots underground. Other tree branches block out the sunlight they need to live. Some of the seedlings die, limiting the size of the pine population.

Weather Weather conditions such as temperature and amount of rainfall can also limit population growth. Many insect species breed in the warm spring weather. As winter begins, the first frost kills many of the insects. This sudden rise in the death rate causes the insect population to decrease.

A single severe weather event can dramatically change the size of a population by killing many organisms. For instance, a flood or hurricane can wash away nests and burrows just as it damages the homes of humans. If you live in a northern state, you may have seen an early frost limit the population of tomatoes in a vegetable garden.

Section 2 Review

1. List four ways of determining population size.
2. How is birth rate related to population size?
3. List three limiting factors for populations. Choose one and explain how this factor can limit population growth.
4. Explain why it is often necessary for ecologists to estimate the size of a population.
5. **Thinking Critically** Problem Solving A field measures 50 meters by 90 meters. In one square meter, you count 3 mice. Estimate the total population of mice in the field. What method did you use to make your estimate?

Science at Home

Word Estimates Choose a page of a dictionary or other book that has a lot of type on it. Challenge your family members to estimate the number of words on the page. After everyone has come up with an estimate, have each person explain the method he or she used. Now count the actual number of words on the page. Whose estimate was closest?

Counting Turtles

For three years, ecologists have been using the mark-and-recapture method to monitor the population of turtles in a pond. In this lab, you will model recapturing the turtles to complete the study. Then you will analyze the results.

Problem

How can the mark-and-recapture method help ecologists monitor the size of a population?

Skills Focus

calculating, graphing, predicting

Materials

model paper turtle population
calculator   graph paper

Procedure

1. The data table shows the results from the first three years of the study. Copy it into your notebook, leaving spaces for your data as shown.
2. Your teacher will give you a box representing the pond. Fifteen of the turtles have been marked, as shown in the data table for Year 4.
3. Capture a member of the population by randomly selecting one turtle. Set it aside.
4. Repeat Step 3 nine times. Record the total number of turtles you captured.
5. Examine each turtle to see whether it has a mark. Count the number of recaptured (marked) turtles. Record this number in your data table.

Analyze and Conclude

1. Use the equation below to estimate the turtle population for each year. The first year is done for you as a sample. If your answer is a decimal, round it to the nearest whole number so that your estimate is in "whole turtles." Record the population for each year in the last column of the data table.

$$\text{Total population} = \frac{\text{Number marked} \times \text{Total number captured}}{\text{Number recaptured (with marks)}}$$

Sample (Year 1):

$$\frac{32 \times 28}{15} = 59.7 \text{ or } 60 \text{ turtles}$$

2. Graph the estimated total populations for the four years. Mark years on the horizontal axis. Mark population size on the vertical axis.
3. Describe how the turtle population has changed over the four years of the study. Suggest three possible causes for the changes.
4. **Apply** Use your graph to predict the turtle population in Year 5. Explain your prediction.

Getting Involved

Find out whether any wildlife populations in your area are being monitored by national, state, or local agencies. Make a poster or write an article for the school paper about the population and the method being used to study it.

DATA TABLE

Year	Number Marked	Total Number Captured	Number Recaptured (with Marks)	Estimated Total Population
1	32	28	15	
2	25	21	11	
3	23	19	11	
4	15			

SCIENCE AND SOCIETY

Animal Overpopulation: How Can People Help?

Populations of white-tailed deer are growing rapidly in many parts of the United States. As populations soar, food becomes a limiting factor. Many deer die of starvation. Others grow up small and unhealthy. In search of food, hungry deer move closer to where humans live. There they eat farm crops, garden vegetables, shrubs, and even trees. This affects birds and small animals that depend on the plants for shelter or food. In addition, increased numbers of deer near roads can cause more automobile accidents.

People admire the grace, beauty, and swiftness of deer. Most people don't want these animals to suffer from starvation or illness. Should people take action to limit growing deer populations?

The Issues

Should People Take Direct Action?
Many people argue that hunting is the simplest way to reduce animal populations. Wildlife managers look at the supply of resources in an area and determine its carrying capacity. Then hunters are issued licenses to help reduce the number of deer to the level that can be supported.

Other people favor nonhunting approaches to control deer populations. One plan is to trap the deer and relocate them. But this method is expensive and requires finding another location that can accept the deer without unbalancing its own system. Few such locations are available.

Scientists are also working to develop chemicals to reduce the birth rate in deer populations. This plan will help control overpopulation, but it is effective for only one year at a time.

Should People Take Indirect Action?
Some suggest bringing in natural enemies of deer, such as wolves, mountain lions, and bears, to areas with too many deer. But these animals could also attack cattle, dogs, cats, and even humans. Other communities have built tall fences around areas they don't want deer to invade. Although this solution can work for people with small yards, it is impractical for farmers or ranchers.

Should People Do Nothing?
Some people oppose any kind of action. They support leaving the deer alone and allowing nature to take its course. Animal populations in an area naturally cycle up and down over time. Doing nothing means that some deer will die of starvation or disease. But eventually, the population will be reduced to a size within the carrying capacity of the environment.

You Decide

1. Identify the Problem
In your own words, explain the problem created by the over-population of white-tailed deer.

2. Analyze the Options
List the ways that people can deal with overpopulation of white-tailed deer. State the negative and positive points of each method.

3. Find a Solution
Suppose you are an ecologist in an area that has twice as many deer as it can support. Propose a way for the community to deal with the problem.

SECTION
3 Interactions Among Living Things

How Well Can You Hide a Butterfly?

1. Using the outline at the right, trace a butterfly onto a piece of paper.

2. Look around the classroom and pick a spot where you will place your butterfly. The butterfly must be placed completely in the open. Color your butterfly so it will blend in with the spot you choose.

3. Tape your butterfly to its spot. Someone will now enter the room to look for the butterflies. This person will have one minute to find all the butterflies he or she can. Will your butterfly be found?

Think It Over

Predicting Over time, how do you think the population size would change for butterflies that blend in with their surroundings?

Imagine giving a big hug to the plant in the photo. Ouch! The sharp spines on its trunk would make you think twice before hugging—or even touching—the saguaro (suh GWAHR oh) cactus. But if you could spend a day hidden inside a saguaro, you would see that many species do interact with this spiky plant.

As the day breaks, you hear a twittering noise coming from a nest tucked in one of the sagauro's arms. Two young red-tailed hawks are preparing to fly for the first time. Farther down the trunk, a tiny elf owl peeks out of its nest in a small hole. The elf owl is so small it could fit in your palm! A rattlesnake slithers around the base of the saguaro, looking for lunch. Spying a nearby shrew, the snake moves in for the kill. With a sudden movement, it strikes the shrew with its sharp fangs.

The activity around the saguaro doesn't stop after the sun goes down. At night, long-nosed bats feed on the nectar from the saguaro's blossoms. They stick their faces into the flowers to feed, covering their long snouts with a dusting of white pollen in the process. As the bats move from plant to plant, they carry the pollen along. This enables the cactuses to reproduce.

GUIDE FOR READING

◆ How do an organism's adaptations help it to survive?

◆ What are the major types of interactions among organisms?

◆ What are the three forms of symbiotic relationships?

Reading Tip As you read, use the section headings to make an outline. Fill in details under each heading.

◀ Saguaro cactus in the Arizona desert

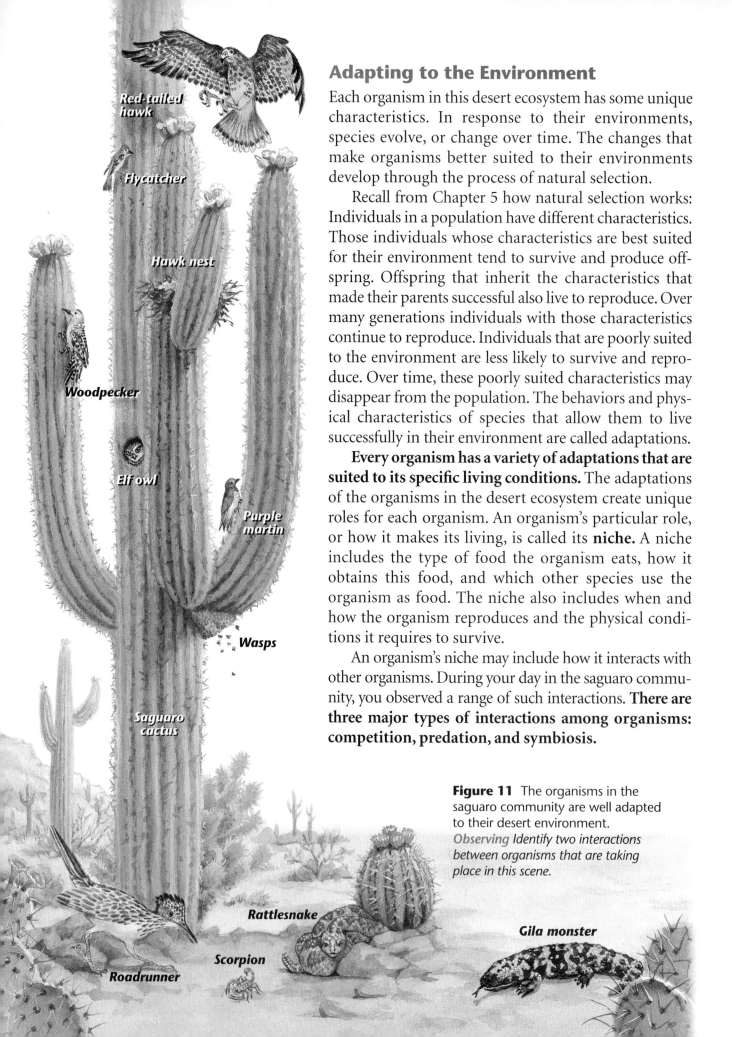

Adapting to the Environment

Each organism in this desert ecosystem has some unique characteristics. In response to their environments, species evolve, or change over time. The changes that make organisms better suited to their environments develop through the process of natural selection.

Recall from Chapter 5 how natural selection works: Individuals in a population have different characteristics. Those individuals whose characteristics are best suited for their environment tend to survive and produce off-spring. Offspring that inherit the characteristics that made their parents successful also live to reproduce. Over many generations individuals with those characteristics continue to reproduce. Individuals that are poorly suited to the environment are less likely to survive and repro-duce. Over time, these poorly suited characteristics may disappear from the population. The behaviors and phys-ical characteristics of species that allow them to live successfully in their environment are called adaptations.

Every organism has a variety of adaptations that are suited to its specific living conditions. The adaptations of the organisms in the desert ecosystem create unique roles for each organism. An organism's particular role, or how it makes its living, is called its **niche.** A niche includes the type of food the organism eats, how it obtains this food, and which other species use the organism as food. The niche also includes when and how the organism reproduces and the physical condi-tions it requires to survive.

An organism's niche may include how it interacts with other organisms. During your day in the saguaro commu-nity, you observed a range of such interactions. **There are three major types of interactions among organisms: competition, predation, and symbiosis.**

Figure 11 The organisms in the saguaro community are well adapted to their desert environment.
Observing Identify two interactions between organisms that are taking place in this scene.

The bay-breasted warbler *feeds in the middle part of the tree.*

The Cape May warbler *feeds at the tips of branches near the top of the tree.*

The yellow-rumped warbler *feeds in the lower part of the tree and at the bases of the middle branches.*

Figure 12 Each of these warblers occupies a different niche in its spruce tree habitat. By feeding in different areas of the tree, the birds avoid competing with one another for food.

Competition

Different species can share the same habitat, such as the many animals that live in and around the saguaro. Different species can also share similar food requirements. For example, the red-tailed hawk and the elf owl both live on the saguaro and eat similar food. However, these two species do not occupy exactly the same niche. The hawk is active during the day, while the owl is active mostly at night. If two species occupy the same niche, one of the species will eventually die off. The reason for this is **competition,** the struggle between organisms to survive in a habitat with limited resources.

An ecosystem cannot satisfy the needs of all the living things in a particular habitat. There is a limited amount of food, water, and shelter. Organisms that survive have adaptations that enable them to reduce competition. For example, the three species of warblers in Figure 12 live in the same spruce forest habitat. They all eat insects that live in the spruce trees. How do these birds avoid competing for the limited insect supply? Each warbler "specializes" in feeding in a certain part of a spruce tree. By finding their own places to feed, the three species can coexist.

INTEGRATING CHEMISTRY Many plants use chemicals to ward off their competition. Plants often compete with one another for growing space and water. Some shrubs release toxic, or poisonous, chemicals into the ground around them. These chemicals keep grass and weeds from growing around the shrubs, sometimes forming a ring of bare ground a meter or two wide.

✓ *Checkpoint* *Why can't two species occupy the same niche?*

Predation

A tiger shark lurks beneath the surface of the clear blue water, looking for shadows of young albatross floating above it. The shark sees a chick and silently swims closer. Suddenly, the shark bursts through the water and seizes the albatross with one snap of its powerful jaw. This interaction between two organisms has an unfortunate ending for the albatross.

An interaction in which one organism hunts and kills another for food is called **predation.** Recall from Chapter 10 that the organism that does the killing, in this case the tiger shark, is the **predator.** The organism that is caught, the albatross, is the **prey.**

Predator Adaptations Predators have adaptations that help them catch and kill their prey. For example, a cheetah can run very fast for a short time, enabling it to catch its prey. A jellyfish's tentacles contain a poisonous substance that paralyzes tiny water

EXPLORING *Defense Strategies*

Organisms display a wide array of adaptations that help them avoid becoming prey.

Camouflage ▲
These delicate spiny bugs are a perfect match for their branch habitat. The more an organism resembles its surroundings, the less likely it is that a predator will notice it. Some animals, such as flounder, can even change their colors to match a variety of settings.

Protective Coverings
This sea urchin sends a clear message to predators: "Don't touch!" Porcupines, hedgehogs, and cactuses all use the same spiny strategy. After a few painful encounters, a predator will look for less prickly prey. ▼

animals. You can probably think of many predators that have claws, sharp teeth, or stingers. Some plants, too, have adaptations for catching prey. The sundew is covered with sticky bulbs on stalks—when a fly lands on the plant, it remains snared in the sticky goo while the plant digests it.

Some predators have adaptations that enable them to hunt at night. For example, the big eyes of an owl let in as much light as possible to help it see in the dark. Bats can hunt without seeing at all. Instead, they locate their prey by producing pulses of sound and listening for the echoes. This precise method enables a bat to catch a flying moth in complete darkness.

Prey Adaptations How do prey organisms manage to avoid being caught by such effective predators? In *Exploring Defense Strategies*, below, you can see some examples of how an organism's physical characteristics can help protect it.

Warning Coloring ▲
A frog this bright certainly can't hide. How could such a color be an advantage? The bright red and blue of this poison arrow frog warn predators not to eat it— glands on the frog's back that release toxic chemicals make it a bad choice for a meal.

Mimicry
If you've ever been stung by a bee, you'd probably keep your distance from this insect. But actually this "bee" is a harmless fly. The fly's resemblance to a stinging bee protects it from birds and other predators, who are fooled into staying away. ▼

◄ False Coloring
Which way is this butterfly fish swimming? The black dot on its tail is a false eye. A predator may bite this end of the fish, allowing it to escape with only part of its tail missing.

Figure 13 The populations of wolves and moose on Isle Royale are related. The predator wolf population depends on the size of the prey moose population, and vice versa.
Predicting How might a disease in the wolf population one year affect the moose population the next year?

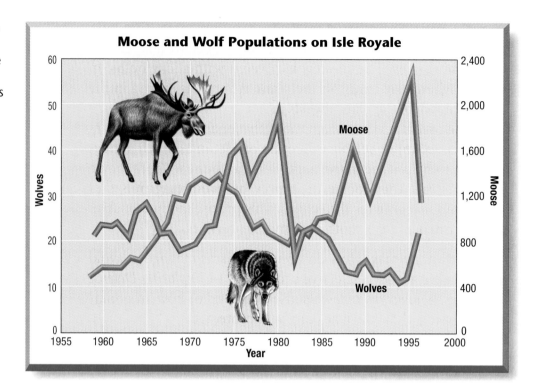

The Effect of Predation on Population Size Predation can have a major effect on the size of a population. As you learned in Section 2, when the death rate exceeds the birth rate in a population, the size of the population usually decreases. If predators are very effective at hunting their prey, the result is often a decrease in the size of the prey population. But a decrease in the prey population in turn affects the predator population.

To see how predator and prey populations can affect each other, look at the graph above. The graph shows the number of moose and wolves living on Isle Royale, an island in Lake Superior. From 1965 to 1975, the number of prey moose increased. The wolves now had enough to eat, so more of them survived. Within a few years, the wolf population began to increase. The growing number of wolves killed more and more moose. The moose population decreased. By 1980, the lack of moose had greatly affected the wolves. Some wolves starved, and others could not raise as many young. Soon the moose population began to climb again. This cycle for the two species has continued.

Of course, other factors also affect the populations on Isle Royale. For instance, cold winters and disease can also reduce the size of one or both of the populations.

☑ *Checkpoint* *If predation removes more members of a population than are born, how will the population change?*

Symbiosis

Many of the interactions in the saguaro community you read about earlier are examples of symbiosis. **Symbiosis** (sim bee OH sis) is a close relationship between two species that benefits at least one of the species. **The three types of symbiotic relationships are mutualism, commensalism, and parasitism.**

Mutualism   A relationship in which both species benefit is called **mutualism** (MYOO choo uh liz um). The relationship between the saguaro and the long-eared bats is an example of mutualism. The bat benefits because the cactus flowers provide it with food. The saguaro benefits as its pollen is carried on the bat's nose to another plant.

INTEGRATING HEALTH   At this very moment, you are participating in a mutualistic relationship with a population of bacteria in your large intestine. These bacteria, called *Escherichia coli,* live in the intestines of most mammals. These bacteria break down some foods that the mammal cannot digest. The bacteria benefit by receiving food and a place to live. You also benefit from the relationship because the bacteria provide you with vitamin K, a nutrient that is needed to make your blood clot.

Commensalism   A relationship in which one species benefits and the other species is neither helped nor harmed is called **commensalism** (kuh MEN suh liz um). The red-tailed hawks' interaction with the saguaro is an example of commensalism. The hawks are helped by having a place to build their nest, while the cactus is not affected by the birds.

Commensalism is not very common in nature because two species are usually either helped or harmed a little by any interaction. For example, by creating a small hole for its nest in the cactus trunk, the elf owl slightly damages the cactus.

Figure 14 Three yellow-billed oxpeckers get a cruise and a snack aboard an obliging hippopotamus. The oxpeckers eat ticks living on the hippo's skin. Since both the birds and the hippo benefit from this interaction, it is an example of mutualism.

Figure 15 The white objects on this sphinx moth larva are wasp cocoons. When the wasps emerge, they will feed on the larva.
Applying Concepts Which organism in this interaction is the parasite? Which organism is the host?

Parasitism The third type of symbiosis is called parasitism. **Parasitism** (PA ruh sit iz um) involves one organism living on or inside another organism and harming it. Recall from Chapter 6 that the organism that benefits is called a **parasite.** The organism the parasite lives on or in is called a **host.** The parasite is usually smaller than the host. In a parasitic relationship, the parasite benefits from the interaction while the host is harmed.

Some common parasites you may be familiar with are fleas, ticks, and leeches. These parasites have adaptations that enable them to attach to their host and feed on its blood. Other parasites live inside the host's body, such as tapeworms that live inside the digestive systems of many mammals, such as dogs and wolves.

Unlike a predator, a parasite does not usually kill the organism it feeds on. If the host dies, the parasite loses its source of food. An interesting example of this rule is shown by a species of mite that lives in the ears of moths. The mites almost always live in just one of the moth's ears. If they live in both ears, the moth's hearing is so badly affected that it is likely to be quickly caught and eaten by its predator, a bat.

Section 3 Review

1. How do an organism's adaptations help it to survive?
2. Name and define the three major types of interactions among organisms.
3. List the three types of symbiosis. For each one, explain how the two organisms are affected.
4. A walking stick is an insect that resembles a small twig. How do you think this insect avoids predators?
5. **Thinking Critically** **Comparing and Contrasting** How are parasitism and predation similar? How are they different?

Check Your Progress CHAPTER PROJECT
By now you should be making your final observations of your plants and planning your report. How can you present your data in a graph? Think about what you should put on each axis of your graph. (*Hint:* Draft the written portion of your report early enough to look it over and make any necessary changes.)

SECTION 1 Living Things and the Environment

Key Ideas

◆ An organism's habitat provides food, water, shelter, and other things the organism needs to live, grow, and reproduce.

◆ An ecosystem includes both biotic and abiotic factors. Abiotic factors found in many environments include water, sunlight, oxygen, temperature, and soil.

◆ A population consists of a single species. The different populations living together in one area make up a community. The community plus abiotic factors form an ecosystem.

◆ Ecologists study how the biotic and abiotic factors interact within an ecosystem.

Key Terms

ecosystem	population
habitat	community
biotic factor	ecology
abiotic factor	

 SECTION 2 Studying Populations

INTEGRATING **MATHEMATICS**

Key Ideas

◆ Ecologists can estimate population size by direct and indirect observations, sampling, and mark-and-recapture studies.

◆ A population changes in size as a result of changes in the birth rate or death rate, or when organisms move into or out of the population.

◆ Population size is controlled by limiting factors such as food, space, and weather conditions.

Key Terms

population density	immigration
estimate	emigration
birth rate	limiting factor
death rate	carrying capacity

 SECTION 3 Interactions Among Living Things

Key Ideas

◆ Over time, species of organisms develop specialized adaptations and behaviors that help them succeed in their environments.

◆ The major types of interactions among organisms are competition, predation, and symbiosis.

◆ Symbiosis is a close relationship between two species. The three types of symbiotic relationships are mutualism, commensalism, and parasitism.

Key Terms

niche	prey	parasitism
competition	symbiosis	parasite
predation	mutualism	host
predator	commensalism	

Organizing Information

Concept Map Copy the concept map about interactions among organisms onto a sheet of paper. Complete it and add a title. (For more on concept maps, see the Skills Handbook.)

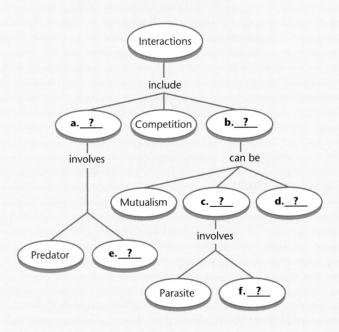

Reviewing Content

 For more review of key concepts, see the Interactive Student Tutorial CD-ROM.

Multiple Choice

Choose the letter of the best answer.

1. Which of the following is *not* an example of a population?
   a. the pets in your neighborhood
   b. the people in a city
   c. the rainbow trout in a stream
   d. the ants in an anthill

2. A prairie dog, a hawk, and a badger all are members of the same
   a. habitat.   b. community.
   c. species.   d. population.

3. All of the following are examples of limiting factors for populations *except*
   a. space   b. food
   c. time   d. weather

4. In which type of interaction do both species benefit?
   a. predation   b. mutualism
   c. commensalism   d. parasitism

5. Which of these relationships is an example of parasitism?
   a. a bird building a nest on a tree branch
   b. a bat pollinating a saguaro cactus
   c. a flea living on a cat's blood
   d. *Escherichia coli* bacteria making vitamin K in your intestine

True or False

If the statement is true, write true. If it is false, change the underlined word or words to make the statement true.

6. Grass is an example of a(n) <u>abiotic</u> factor in a habitat.

7. A rise in birth rate while the death rate remains steady will cause a population to <u>increase</u> in size.

8. An organism's specific role in its habitat is called its <u>niche</u>.

9. The struggle between organisms for limited resources is called <u>mutualism</u>.

10. A parasite lives on or inside its <u>predator</u>.

Checking Concepts

11. Name two biotic and two abiotic factors you might find in a forest ecosystem.

12. Explain how sunlight is used by plants and algae. How is this process important to other living things in an ecosystem?

13. Describe how ecologists use the technique of sampling to estimate population size.

14. Give an example showing how space can be a limiting factor for a population.

15. What are two adaptations that prey organisms have developed to protect themselves? Describe how each adaptation protects the organism.

16. **Writing to Learn** Write a description of your niche in the environment. Include details about your habitat, including both biotic and abiotic factors around you. Be sure to describe your feeding habits as well as any interactions you have with members of other species.

Thinking Critically

17. **Making Generalizations** Explain why ecologists usually study a specific population of organisms rather than studying the entire species.

18. **Problem Solving** In a summer job working for an ecologist, you have been assigned to estimate the population of grasshoppers in a field. Propose a method to get an estimate and explain how you would carry it out.

19. **Relating Cause and Effect** Competition for resources in an area is usually more intense within a single species than between two different species. Can you suggest an explanation for this observation? (*Hint:* Consider how niches help organisms avoid competition.)

20. **Comparing and Contrasting** Explain how parasitism and mutualism are similar and how they are different.

Applying Skills

Ecologists monitoring a deer population collected data during a 30-year study. Use the data to answer Questions 21–24.

Year	0	5	10	15	20	25	30
Population (thousands)	15	30	65	100	40	25	10

21. **Graphing** Make a line graph using the data in the table. Plot years on the horizontal axis and population on the vertical axis.

22. **Interpreting Data** In which year did the deer population reach its highest point? Its lowest point?

23. **Communicating** Write a few sentences describing how the deer population changed during the study.

24. **Developing Hypotheses** In Year 16 of the study, this region experienced a very severe winter. How might this have affected the deer population?

Performance ▽ CHAPTER PROJECT Assessment

Present Your Project Review your report and graph to be sure that they clearly state your conclusion about the effects of crowding on plant growth. With your group, decide how you will present your results. Do a practice run-through to make sure all group members feel comfortable with their part.

Reflect and Record Compare your group's results with those of your classmates. Suggest possible explanations for any differences. How could you have improved your plan for your experiment?

Test Preparation

Use these questions to prepare for standardized tests.

Study the graph. Then answer Questions 25–28.

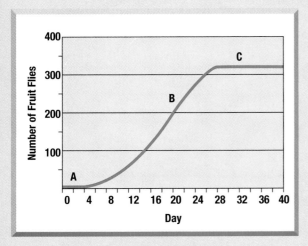

25. What is the best title for this graph?
    a. Fruit Fly Population Density
    b. Abiotic Factors and Fruit Flies
    c. Fruit Fly Population Growth
    d. Fruit Fly Death Rate

26. At what point on the graph is the population of fruit flies increasing?
    a. Point A   b. Point B
    c. Point C   d. none of the above

27. Which of the following statements may be true of the fruit fly population at Point C?
    a. The death rate is approximately equal to the birth rate.
    b. A limiting factor in the environment is preventing the population from increasing.
    c. There may not be enough food or space to support a larger population.
    d. All of the above statements may be true.

28. Based on the graph, what is the carrying capacity of the environment in which the fruit flies live?
    a. approximately 320 fruit flies
    b. approximately 220 fruit flies
    c. approximately 410 fruit flies
    d. approximately 160 fruit flies

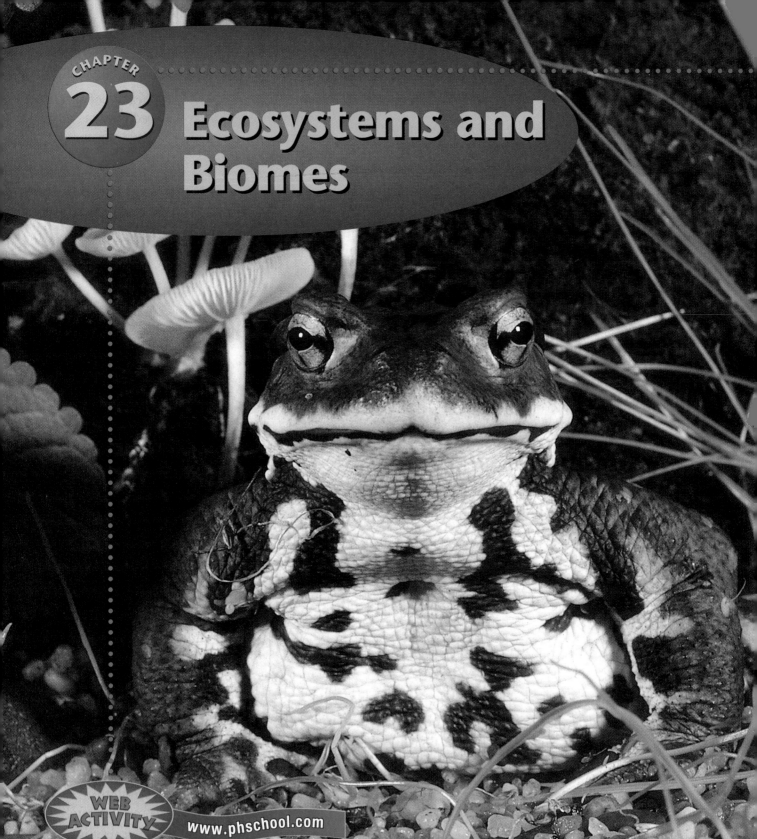

CHAPTER

23 Ecosystems and Biomes

WEB ACTIVITY www.phschool.com

Integrating Chemistry

SECTION 1 Energy Flow in Ecosystems

Discover Where Did Your Dinner Come From?
Sharpen Your Skills Observing
Try This Weaving a Food Web

SECTION 2 Cycles of Matter

Discover Are You Part of a Cycle?
Sharpen Your Skills Developing Hypotheses

SECTION 3 Biogeography

Discover How Can You Move a Seed?
Science at Home Sock Walk

Breaking It Down

Nothing in this toad's ecosystem is wasted. Even when the living things die, they will be recycled by other organisms like the mushrooms. This natural breakdown process is called decomposition. In this chapter, you will study decomposition and other processes in ecosystems.

When fallen leaves and other waste products decompose, a fluffy, brown mixture called compost is formed. You can observe decomposition firsthand by building a compost chamber.

Your Goal To design an experiment to learn more about the process of decomposition.

To complete your project successfully, you must

◆ build two compost chambers
◆ investigate the effect of one of the following variables on decomposition: moisture, oxygen, temperature, or activity of soil organisms
◆ analyze your data and present your results
◆ follow the safety guidelines in Appendix A

Get Started Your teacher will provide you with a sample of compost material. Observe the wastes in the mixture with a hand lens. Write a hypothesis about which kinds of waste will decay and which will not. Begin thinking about which variable you will test.

Check Your Progress You'll be working on this project as you study this chapter. To keep your project on track, look for Check Your Progress boxes at the following points.

Section 1 Review, page 722: Build your compost chambers and design your experimental plan.
Section 2 Review, page 727: Observe your compost chambers and collect data.
Section 4 Review, page 745: Analyze your data.

Present Your Project At the end of the chapter (page 753), you will compare the compost produced in each of your compost chambers. Will your results support your hypothesis?

This toad is right at home in its habitat. It is surrounded by living leaves, grass, and mushrooms, as well as nonliving rocks, soil, and air.

 Earth's Biomes

Real-World Lab **Biomes in Miniature**
Discover **How Much Rain Is That?**
Try This **Desert Survival**
Sharpen Your Skills **Inferring**
Sharpen Your Skills **Interpreting Data**

 Succession

Skills Lab **Change in a Tiny Community**
Discover **What Happened Here?**
Science at Home **Succession Interview**

Energy Flow in Ecosystems

DISCOVER ·ACTIVITY· · · ·

Where Did Your Dinner Come From?

1. Across the top of a page, list the different types of foods you ate for dinner last night.

2. Under each item, write the name of the plant, animal, or other organism that is the source of that food. Some foods have more than one source. For example, bread is made from flour (which is made from a plant such as wheat) and yeast (which is a fungus).

Think It Over

Classifying Count all the different organisms that contributed to your dinner. How many of your food sources were plants? How many were animals?

GUIDE FOR READING

◆ What energy roles do organisms play in an ecosystem?

◆ How much energy is available at each level of an energy pyramid?

Reading Tip As you read, create a flowchart showing one possible path of energy through an ecosystem.

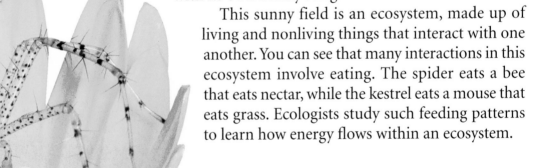
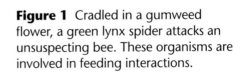

Pushing off from its perch on an oak tree limb, the kestrel glides over a field dotted with yellow flowers. In the middle of the field, the bird pauses. It hovers above the ground like a giant hummingbird. Despite strong gusts of wind, the bird's head remains steady as it looks for prey. It takes a lot of energy for the kestrel to hover in this way, but from this position it can search the field below for food.

Soon the kestrel spots a mouse munching the ripening seed-head of a blade of grass. Seconds later the kestrel swoops down and grasps the mouse in its talons. The bird carries the mouse back to the tree to feed.

Meanwhile, a lynx spider hides among the petals of a nearby flower. An unsuspecting bee lands on the flower for a sip of nectar. The spider grabs the bee and injects its venom into the bee's body. The venom kills the bee before it can respond with its own deadly sting.

This sunny field is an ecosystem, made up of living and nonliving things that interact with one another. You can see that many interactions in this ecosystem involve eating. The spider eats a bee that eats nectar, while the kestrel eats a mouse that eats grass. Ecologists study such feeding patterns to learn how energy flows within an ecosystem.

Figure 1 Cradled in a gumweed flower, a green lynx spider attacks an unsuspecting bee. These organisms are involved in feeding interactions.

Energy Roles

Do you play an instrument in your school band? If so, you know that each instrument has a role in a piece of music. For instance, the flute may provide the melody, while the drum provides the beat. Although the two instruments are quite different, they both play important roles in creating the band's music. In the same way, each organism has a role in the movement of energy through its ecosystem. This role is part of the organism's niche in the ecosystem. The kestrel's role is different from that of the giant oak tree where it was perched. But all parts of the ecosystem, like all parts of the band, are necessary for the ecosystem to work.

An organism's energy role is determined by how it obtains energy and how it interacts with the other living things in its ecosystem. **An organism's energy role in an ecosystem may be that of a producer, consumer, or decomposer.**

Producers Energy first enters most ecosystems as sunlight. Some organisms, such as plants, algae, and certain microorganisms, are able to capture the energy of sunlight and store it as food energy. These organisms use the sun's energy to turn water and carbon dioxide into molecules such as sugars and starches through photosynthesis.

As you have learned, organisms that carry out photosynthesis are called autotrophs. Another word for an organism that can make its own food is a **producer.** Producers are the source of all the food in an ecosystem. For example, the grass and oak tree are the producers for the field ecosystem.

In a few ecosystems the producers obtain energy from a source other than sunlight. One such ecosystem is found in rocks deep beneath the ground. Since the rocks are never exposed to sunlight, how is energy brought into this ecosystem? Certain bacteria in this ecosystem produce their own food using the energy in a gas, hydrogen sulfide, which is found in their environment.

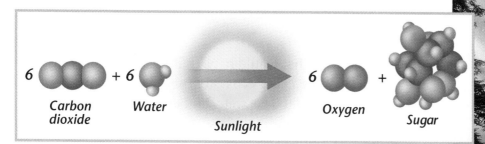

Figure 2 The sunlight streaming through this redwood forest is the source of energy for the ecosystem. Plants convert the sun's energy to stored food energy through the process of photosynthesis.
Interpreting Diagrams What substances are needed for photosynthesis? What substances are produced?

Figure 3 Consumers are classified by what they eat. **A.** An agile gerenuk stands on its hind legs to reach these leaves. Consumers that eat plants are called herbivores. **B.** Carnivores like this collared lizard eat only animals. **C.** A black vulture is a scavenger, a carnivore that feeds on the remains of dead organisms.

Consumers Recall that other members of an ecosystem, called heterotrophs, cannot make their own food. These organisms depend on the producers for food and energy. Another word for an organism that obtains energy by feeding on other organisms is a **consumer.**

Consumers are classified by what they eat. Consumers that eat only plants are called **herbivores.** This term comes from the Latin words *herba,* which means grass or herb, and *vorare,* which means to eat. Some familiar herbivores are caterpillars, cattle, and deer. Consumers that eat only animals are called **carnivores.** This term comes from the same root word *vorare,* plus the Latin word for flesh, *carnis.* Lions, spiders, and snakes are some examples of carnivores. A consumer that eats both plants and animals is called an **omnivore.** The Latin word *omni* means all. Crows, goats, and most humans are examples of omnivores.

Some carnivores are scavengers. A **scavenger** is a carnivore that feeds on the bodies of dead organisms. Scavengers include catfish and vultures.

Decomposers What would happen if there were only producers and consumers in an ecosystem? As the organisms in the ecosystem continued to take water, minerals, and other raw materials from their surroundings, these materials would begin to run low. If these materials were not replaced, new organisms would not be able to grow.

All the organisms in an ecosystem produce waste and eventually die. If these wastes and dead organisms were not somehow removed from the ecosystem, they would pile up until they overwhelmed the living things. Organisms that break down wastes and dead organisms and return the raw materials to the environment are called **decomposers.** Two major groups of decomposers are bacteria and fungi, such as molds and mushrooms. While obtaining energy for their own needs, decomposers return simple molecules to the environment. These molecules can be used again by other organisms.

☑ *Checkpoint* *How are herbivores and carnivores similar?*

Food Chains and Food Webs

As you have read, energy enters most ecosystems as sunlight, and is converted into sugar and starch molecules by producers. This energy is transferred to each organism that eats a producer, and then to other organisms that feed on these consumers. The movement of energy through an ecosystem can be shown in diagrams called food chains and food webs.

A **food chain** is a series of events in which one organism eats another and obtains energy. You can follow one food chain from the field ecosystem below. The first organism in a food chain is always a producer, such as the grass in the field. The second organism is a consumer that eats the producer, and is called a first-level consumer. The mouse is a first-level consumer. Next, a second-level consumer eats the first-level consumer. The second-level consumer in this example is the kestrel.

A food chain shows one possible path along which energy can move through an ecosystem. But just as you do not eat the same thing every day, neither do most other organisms. Most producers and consumers are part of many food chains. A more realistic way to show the flow of energy through an ecosystem is a food web. A **food web** consists of the many overlapping food chains in an ecosystem.

Figure 4 A cluster of honey mushrooms grows among dead leaves. Mushrooms are familiar decomposers.

Kestrel
(Second-level consumer)

Figure 5 These organisms make up one food chain in a field ecosystem.
Classifying Which organism shown is acting as an herbivore? Which is a carnivore?

Grass
(Producer)

Mouse
(First-level consumer)

EXPLORING a Food Web

A food web consists of many inter-connected food chains. Trace the path of energy through the producers, consumers, and decomposers.

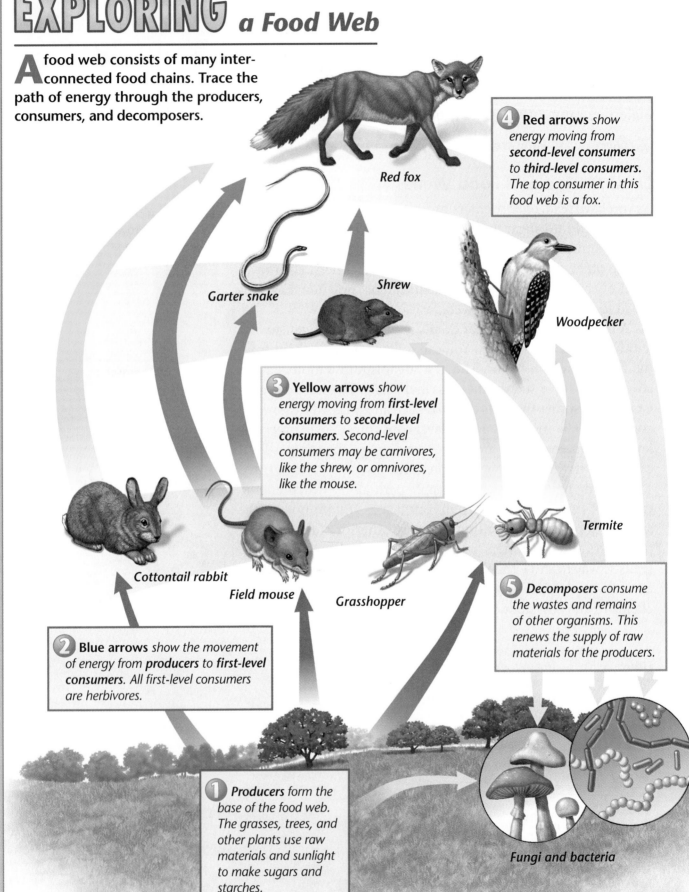

4 **Red arrows** *show energy moving from **second-level consumers** to **third-level consumers**. The top consumer in this food web is a fox.*

Red fox

Garter snake

Shrew

Woodpecker

3 **Yellow arrows** *show energy moving from **first-level consumers** to **second-level consumers**. Second-level consumers may be carnivores, like the shrew, or omnivores, like the mouse.*

Cottontail rabbit

Field mouse

Grasshopper

Termite

5 **Decomposers** *consume the wastes and remains of other organisms. This renews the supply of raw materials for the producers.*

2 **Blue arrows** *show the movement of energy from **producers** to **first-level consumers**. All first-level consumers are herbivores.*

1 **Producers** *form the base of the food web. The grasses, trees, and other plants use raw materials and sunlight to make sugars and starches.*

Fungi and bacteria

720

In *Exploring a Food Web* on the facing page, you can trace the many food chains in a woodland ecosystem. Note that an organism may play more than one role in an ecosystem. For example, an omnivore such as the mouse is a first-level consumer when it eats grass. But when the mouse eats a grasshopper, it is a second-level consumer.

☑ *Checkpoint* *What are the organisms in one food chain shown in the food web on the facing page?*

Energy Pyramids

When an organism in an ecosystem eats, it obtains energy. The organism uses some of this energy to move, grow, reproduce, and carry out other life activities. This means that only some of the energy will be available to the next organism in the food web.

A diagram called an **energy pyramid** shows the amount of energy that moves from one feeding level to another in a food web. The organisms at each level use some of the energy to carry out their life processes. **The most energy is available at the producer level. At each level in the pyramid, there is less available energy than at the level below.** An energy pyramid gets its name from the shape of the diagram—wider at the base and narrower at the top, resembling a pyramid.

In general, only about 10 percent of the energy at one level of a food web is transferred to the next, higher, level. The other

Weaving a Food Web

This activity shows how the organisms in a food web are interconnected.

ACTIVITY

1. Your teacher will assign you a role in the food web.

2. Hold one end of each of several pieces of yarn in your hand. Give the other ends of your yarn to the other organisms to which your organism is linked.

3. Your teacher will now eliminate one of the organisms. Everyone who is connected to that organism should drop the yarn connecting them to it.

Making Models How many organisms were affected by the removal of one organism? What does this activity show about the importance of each organism in a food web?

Figure 6 Organisms use energy to carry out their life activities. A lioness uses energy to chase her zebra prey. The zebras use energy to flee.

Figure 7 This energy pyramid diagram shows the energy available at each level of a food web. Energy is measured in kilocalories, or kcal.
Calculating How many times more energy is available at the producer level than at the second-level consumer level?

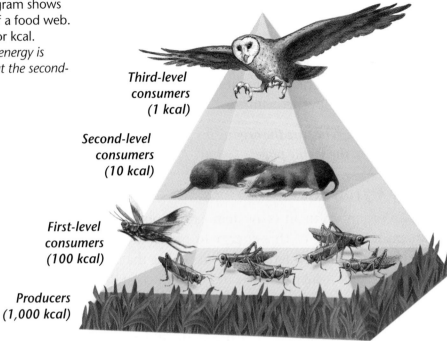

Third-level consumers (1 kcal)

Second-level consumers (10 kcal)

First-level consumers (100 kcal)

Producers (1,000 kcal)

90 percent of the energy is used for the organism's life processes or is lost as heat to the environment. Because of this, most food webs only have three or four feeding levels. Since 90 percent of the energy is lost at each step, there is not enough energy to support many feeding levels.

But the organisms at higher feeding levels of an energy pyramid do not necessarily require less energy to live than organisms at lower levels. Since so much energy is lost at each level, the amount of energy in the producer level limits the number of consumers the ecosystem can support. As a result, there usually are few organisms at the highest level in a food web.

Section 1 Review

1. Name the three energy roles of organisms in an ecosystem. How does each type of organism obtain energy?
2. How does the amount of available energy change from one level of an energy pyramid to the next level up?
3. Name and define the four types of consumers.
4. What is the source of energy for most ecosystems?
5. **Thinking Critically Making Generalizations** Why are food webs a more realistic way of portraying ecosystems than food chains?

Check Your Progress CHAPTER PROJECT
By now you should have constructed your compost chambers and chosen a variable to investigate. Design your plan for observing the effect of this variable on the decomposition process. Submit your plan to your teacher for approval. (*Hint:* As part of your plan, include how you will collect data to measure decomposition in your compost chambers.)

SECTION 2 Cycles of Matter

DISCOVER ● ACTIVITY ● ● ● ●

Are You Part of a Cycle?

1. Hold a small mirror a few centimeters from your mouth.
2. Exhale onto the mirror.
3. Observe the surface of the mirror.

Think It Over

Inferring What is the substance that forms on the mirror? Where did this substance come from?

A pile of crumpled cars is ready for loading into a giant compactor. Junkyard workers have already removed many of the cars' parts. The aluminum and copper pieces were removed so that they could be recycled, or used again. Now a recycling plant will reclaim the steel in the bodies of the cars. Earth has a limited supply of aluminum, copper, and the iron needed to make steel. Recycling old cars is one way to provide a new supply of these materials.

Recycling Matter

The way matter is recycled in ecosystems is similar to the way the metal in old cars is recycled. Like the supply of metal for building cars, the supply of matter in an ecosystem is limited. If matter could not be recycled, ecosystems would quickly run out of the raw materials necessary for life.

Energy, on the other hand, is not recycled. You must constantly supply a car with energy in the form of gasoline. Ecosystems must also be constantly supplied with energy, usually in the form of sunlight. Gasoline and the sun's energy cannot be recycled—they must be constantly supplied.

As you read in Section 1, energy enters an ecosystem and moves from the producers to the consumers to the decomposers. In contrast, matter cycles through an ecosystem over and over. Matter in an ecosystem includes water, oxygen, carbon, nitrogen, and many other substances. To understand how these substances cycle through an ecosystem, you need to know a few basic terms that describe the structure of matter. Matter is made

GUIDE FOR READING

◆ What three major processes make up the water cycle?

◆ How is carbon dioxide used by producers?

Reading Tip As you read, use the section headings to make an outline of the section.

Cars awaiting recycling at a Utah plant ▼

723

Figure 8 In the water cycle, water moves continuously from Earth's surface to the atmosphere and back. *Interpreting Diagrams In which step of the water cycle does water return to Earth's surface?*

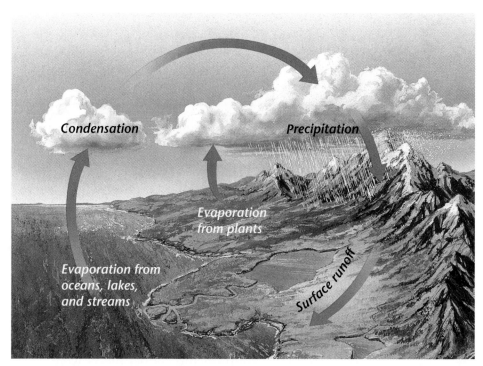

Condensation

Precipitation

Evaporation from plants

Evaporation from oceans, lakes, and streams

Surface runoff

up of tiny particles called atoms. Combinations of two or more atoms chemically bonded together are called molecules. For example, a molecule of water consists of two hydrogen atoms bonded to one oxygen atom. In this section, you will learn about some of the most important cycles of matter: the water cycle, the carbon and oxygen cycles, and the nitrogen cycle.

The Water Cycle

How could you determine whether life has ever existed on another planet in the solar system? One piece of evidence scientists look for is the presence of water. This is because water is the most common compound in all living cells on Earth. Water is necessary for life as we know it.

Water is recycled through the water cycle. The **water cycle** is the continuous process by which water moves from Earth's surface to the atmosphere and back. **The processes of evaporation, condensation, and precipitation make up the water cycle.** As you read about these processes, follow the cycle in Figure 8.

Evaporation The process by which molecules of liquid water absorb energy and change to the gas state is called **evaporation.** In the water cycle liquid water evaporates from Earth's surface and forms water vapor, a gas, in the atmosphere. Most water evaporates from the surfaces of oceans and lakes. The energy for evaporation comes from the sun.

Sharpen your Skills

Developing Hypotheses

ACTIVITY

You're having cocoa at a friend's house on a cold, rainy day. As your friend boils some water, you notice that a window next to the stove is covered with water droplets. Your friend thinks the window is leaking. Using what you know about the water cycle, can you propose another explanation for the water droplets on the window?

Some water is also given off by living things. For example, plants take in water through their roots and release water vapor from their leaves. You take in water when you drink and eat. You release liquid water in your wastes and water vapor when you exhale.

Condensation What happens next to the water vapor in the atmosphere? As the water vapor rises higher in the atmosphere, it cools down. When it cools to a certain temperature the vapor turns back into tiny drops of liquid water. The process by which a gas changes to a liquid is called **condensation.** The water droplets collect around particles of dust in the air, eventually forming clouds like those in Figure 8.

Precipitation As more water vapor condenses, the drops of water in the cloud grow larger and heavier. Eventually the heavy drops fall back to Earth as a form of **precipitation**—rain, snow, sleet, or hail. Most precipitation falls back into oceans or lakes. The precipitation that falls on land may soak into the soil and become groundwater. Or the precipitation may run off the land, ultimately flowing into a river or ocean once again.

☑ *Checkpoint* *What change of state occurs when water from the surface of the ocean enters the atmosphere as water vapor?*

The Carbon and Oxygen Cycles

Two other chemicals necessary for life are carbon and oxygen. The processes by which they are recycled are linked together, as shown in Figure 9. Carbon is the building block for the matter that makes up the bodies of living things. It is present in the atmosphere in the gas carbon dioxide. Producers take in carbon

Figure 9 This scene shows how the carbon and oxygen cycles are linked together. Producers use carbon dioxide to carry out photosynthesis. In this process, carbon is used to create sugar molecules such as those found in apples. The producers release oxygen, which is then used by other organisms. These organisms take in carbon in food and release it in the form of carbon dioxide again.

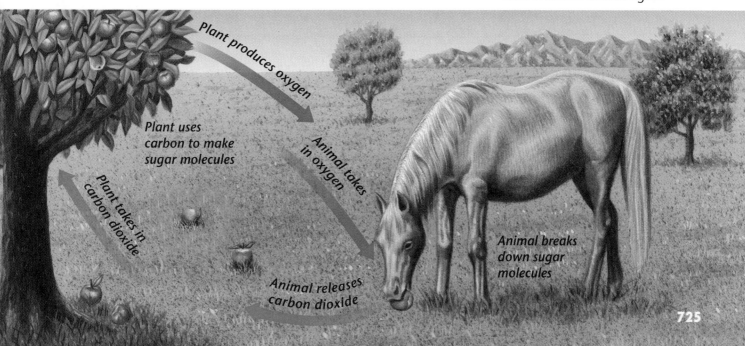

Plant produces oxygen

Plant uses carbon to make sugar molecules

Animal takes in oxygen

Plant takes in carbon dioxide

Animal breaks down sugar molecules

Animal releases carbon dioxide

725

dioxide from the atmosphere during photosynthesis. **In this process, the producers use carbon from the carbon dioxide to produce other carbon-containing molecules.** These molecules include sugars and starches. To obtain energy from these molecules, consumers break them down into simpler molecules. Consumers release water and carbon dioxide as waste products.

At the same time, oxygen is also cycling through the ecosystem. Producers release oxygen as a result of photosynthesis. Other organisms take in oxygen from the atmosphere and use it in their life processes.

☑ *Checkpoint* *How is oxygen returned to the environment?*

The Nitrogen Cycle

Like carbon, nitrogen is a necessary building block in the matter that makes up living things. Since the air around you is about 78 percent nitrogen gas, you might think that it would be easy for living things to obtain nitrogen. However, most organisms cannot use the nitrogen gas in the air. Nitrogen gas is called "free" nitrogen, meaning it is not combined with other kinds of atoms. Most organisms can use nitrogen only once it has been "fixed," or combined with other elements to form nitrogen-containing compounds. You can follow this process in Figure 10 below.

Figure 10 In the nitrogen cycle, nitrogen moves from the air to the soil, into living things, and back into the air.
Interpreting Diagrams How do consumers obtain nitrogen?

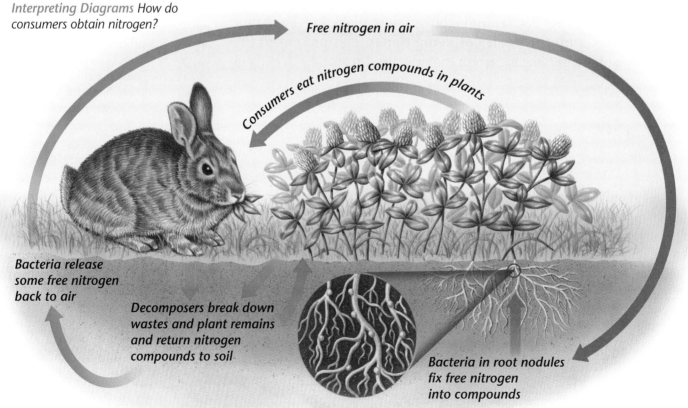

Free nitrogen in air

Consumers eat nitrogen compounds in plants

Bacteria release some free nitrogen back to air

Decomposers break down wastes and plant remains and return nitrogen compounds to soil

Bacteria in root nodules fix free nitrogen into compounds

Nitrogen Fixation The process of changing free nitrogen gas into a usable form of nitrogen is called **nitrogen fixation.** Most nitrogen fixation is performed by certain kinds of bacteria. Some of these bacteria live in bumps called **nodules** (NAHJ oolz) on the roots of certain plants. These plants, known as legumes, include clover, beans, peas, alfalfa, and peanuts.

The relationship between the bacteria and the legumes is an example of mutualism. As you recall from Chapter 22, a symbiotic relationship in which both species benefit is called mutualism. Both the bacteria and the plant benefit from this relationship: The bacteria feed on the plant's sugars, and the plant is supplied with nitrogen in a usable form.

 INTEGRATING TECHNOLOGY Many farmers make use of the nitrogen-fixing bacteria in legumes to enrich their fields. Every few years, a farmer may plant a legume such as alfalfa in a field. The bacteria in the alfalfa roots build up a new supply of nitrogen compounds in the soil. The following year, the new crops planted in the field benefit from the improved soil.

Return of Nitrogen to the Environment Once the nitrogen has been fixed into chemical compounds, it can be used by organisms to build proteins and other complex substances. Decomposers break down these complex compounds in animal wastes and in the bodies of dead organisms. This returns simple nitrogen compounds to the soil. Nitrogen can cycle from the soil to producers and consumers many times. At some point, however, bacteria break down the nitrogen compounds completely. These bacteria release free nitrogen back into the air. Then the cycle starts again.

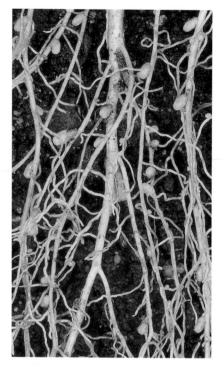

Figure 11 Lumpy nodules are clearly visible on the roots of this clover plant. Bacteria inside the nodules carry out nitrogen fixation.

Section 2 Review

1. Name and define the three major processes that occur during the water cycle.
2. Explain the role of plants in the carbon cycle.
3. How is nitrogen fixation a necessary part of the nitrogen cycle?
4. Where do nitrogen-fixing bacteria live?
5. **Thinking Critically Comparing and Contrasting** Explain how the movement of matter through an ecosystem is different from the movement of energy through an ecosystem.

Check Your Progress

CHAPTER PROJECT

Once your teacher has approved your plan, place the waste into your compost chambers. Record your hypothesis about the effect of the variable you are investigating. Observe the two containers daily. (*Hint:* If there are no signs of decomposition after several days, you may wish to stir the contents of each chamber. Stirring allows more oxygen to enter the mixture.)

DISCOVER ·· ACTIVITY····

How Can You Move a Seed?

1. Place a few corn kernels at one end of a shallow pan.

2. Make a list of ways you could move the kernels to the other side of the pan. You may use any of the simple materials your teacher has provided.

3. Now try each method. Record whether or not each was successful in moving the kernels across the pan.

Think It Over

Predicting How might seeds be moved from place to place on Earth?

GUIDE FOR READING

◆ How does dispersal of organisms occur?

◆ What factors can limit the distribution of a species?

Reading Tip As you read, look for reasons why organisms live in certain places in the world. Make a list of these reasons.

◀ Australian wallaby

Imagine how European explorers must have felt when they saw the continent of Australia for the first time. Instead of familiar grazing animals such as horses and deer, they saw what looked like giant rabbits with long tails. Peering into the branches of eucalyptus trees, these explorers saw bearlike koalas. And who could have dreamed up an egg-laying animal with a beaver's tail, a duck's bill, and a thick coat of fur? You can see why people who heard the first descriptions of the platypus accused the explorers of lying!

Ecologists had many questions about the plants and animals of Australia. Why had no one ever seen a kangaroo, a eucalyptus tree, or a koala in Europe? Why were there no reindeer, camels, or gorillas in Australia?

Different species live in different parts of the world. The study of where organisms live is called **biogeography.** The word *biogeography* is made up of three Greek word roots: *bio,* meaning "life"; *geo,* meaning "Earth"; and *graph,* meaning "description." Together, these root words tell what biogeographers do—they describe where living things are found on Earth.

Continental Drift

INTEGRATING EARTH SCIENCE In addition to studying where species live today, biogeographers also study how these species spread into different parts of the world. One factor that has affected how species are distributed is the motion of Earth's continents. The continents are huge blocks of solid rock floating on a layer of hot, dense liquid. The very slow motion of the continents is called **continental drift.**

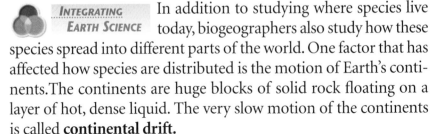

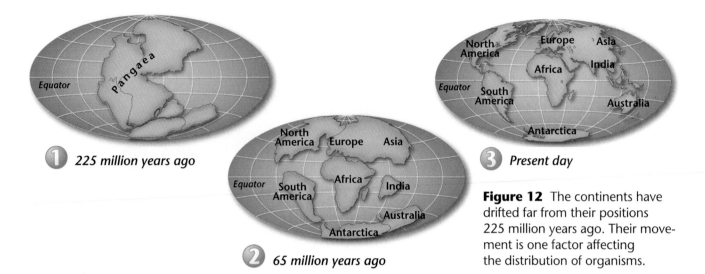

① **225 million years ago**

② **65 million years ago**

③ *Present day*

Figure 12 The continents have drifted far from their positions 225 million years ago. Their movement is one factor affecting the distribution of organisms.

Figure 12 shows how much the continents have moved. About 225 million years ago, all the continents were touching one another. But after millions of years of slow drifting, they have moved apart. Looking at the globe today, it is hard to believe that at one time India was next to Antarctica, or that Europe and North America were once connected.

The movement of the continents has had a great impact on the distribution of species. Consider Australia, for example. Millions of years ago Australia drifted apart from the other land masses. Organisms from other parts of the world could not reach the isolated continent. Kangaroos, koalas, and other unique species developed in this isolation.

Means of Dispersal

The movement of organisms from one place to another is called **dispersal.** Organisms may be dispersed in several different ways. **Dispersal can be caused by wind, water, or living things, including humans.**

Wind and Water Many animals move into new areas by simply walking, swimming, or flying. But plants and small organisms need assistance to move from place to place. Wind provides a means of dispersal for seeds, the spores of fungi, tiny spiders, and many other small, light organisms. Similarly, water transports objects that float, such as coconuts and leaves. Insects and small animals may get a free ride to a new home on top of these floating rafts.

Other Living Things Organisms may also be dispersed by other living things. For example, a goldfinch may eat seeds in one area and deposit them elsewhere in its wastes. A duck may carry algae or fish eggs on its feet from pond to pond. And if your dog or cat has ever come home covered with sticky plant burs, you know another way seeds can get around.

Figure 13 The stiff brown pods of the milkweed plant contain seeds fringed with silky threads.
Inferring By what means of dispersal are milkweed seeds spread?

Figure 14 Clumps of purple loosestrife line the banks of a Massachusetts river. Loosestrife is an exotic species that has thrived in its new home, often crowding out native species.

Humans are important to the dispersal of other species. As people move around the globe, they take plants, animals, and other organisms with them. Sometimes this is intentional, such as when people bring horses to a new settlement. Sometimes it is unintentional, such as when someone carries a parasite into a country.

Species that have naturally evolved in an area are referred to as **native species.** When an organism is carried into a new location by people, it is referred to as an **exotic species.** Some exotic species are so common in their new environment that people think of them as native. For example, you probably know the dandelion, one of the most common flowering plants in North America. But the dandelion is not a native species. It was brought by colonists who valued its leaves for eating and for tea for the sick.

☑ *Checkpoint* *How can humans disperse a species?*

Limits to Dispersal

With all these means of dispersal, you might expect to find the same organisms everywhere in the world. Of course, that's not so. Why not? What determines the limits of a species' distribution? **Three factors that limit dispersal of a species are physical barriers, competition, and climate.**

Physical Barriers Barriers such as water, mountains, and deserts are hard to cross. These features can limit the movement of organisms. For example, once Australia became separated from the other continents, the ocean acted as a barrier to dispersal. Organisms could not easily move to or from Australia.

Competition When an organism enters a new area, it must compete for resources with the species already there. To survive, the organism must find a unique niche. If the existing species are thriving, they may outcompete the new species. In this case competition is a barrier to dispersal. Sometimes, however, the new species is more successful than the existing species. The native species may be displaced.

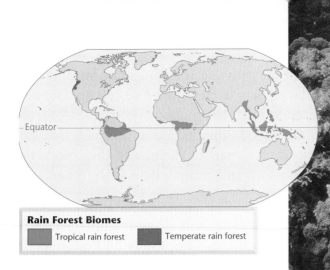

Rain Forest Biomes

Tropical rain forest ■ Temperate rain forest ■

Rain Forest Biomes

The first stop on your expedition is a tropical rain forest close to the equator. The rain forest is warm and humid—in fact, it's pouring rain! Fortunately, you remembered to pack a poncho. After just a short rain shower, the sun reappears. But even though the sun is shining, very little light penetrates the thick vegetation.

Plants are everywhere in the rain forest. Some, such as the ferns, orchids, and vines you observe hanging from tree limbs, even grow on other plants. Among the plants are many species of birds as bright as the numerous flowers all around you.

Tropical Rain Forests Tropical rain forests are found in warm regions close to the equator. Tropical rain forests typically receive a lot of rain. The warm temperatures do not vary much throughout the year, and the sunlight is fairly constant all year.

Tropical rain forests contain an astounding variety of species. For example, scientists studying a 100-square-meter area of one rain forest identified 300 different kinds of trees! These trees form several distinct layers. The tall trees form a leafy roof called the **canopy.** A few giant trees poke out above the canopy. Below the canopy, a second layer of shorter trees and vines form an **understory.** Understory plants grow well in the shade formed by the canopy. Finally, some plants thrive in the near-darkness of the forest floor.

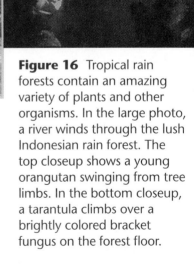

Figure 16 Tropical rain forests contain an amazing variety of plants and other organisms. In the large photo, a river winds through the lush Indonesian rain forest. The top closeup shows a young orangutan swinging from tree limbs. In the bottom closeup, a tarantula climbs over a brightly colored bracket fungus on the forest floor.

The abundant plant life provides many habitats for animals. The number of insect species in tropical rain forests is not known, but has been estimated to be in the millions. These in turn feed many bird species, which feed other animals. Although tropical rain forests cover only a small part of the planet, they probably contain more species of plants and animals than all the other land biomes combined.

Temperate Rain Forests The land along the northwestern coast of the United States resembles a tropical rain forest in some ways. This region receives more than 300 centimeters of rain a year. Huge trees grow there, including cedars, redwoods, and Douglas firs. However, it is difficult to classify this region. It is too far north and too cool to be a tropical rain forest. Instead many ecologists refer to this ecosystem as a temperate rain forest. The term *temperate* means having moderate temperatures.

Desert Biomes

The next stop on your expedition is a desert. It couldn't be more different from the tropical rain forest you just left. You step off the bus into the searing summer heat. At midday, you cannot even walk into the desert—the sand feels as hot as the hot water that comes from your bathroom faucet at home.

A **desert** is an area that receives less than 25 centimeters of rain per year. The amount of evaporation in a desert is greater than the amount of precipitation. Some of the driest deserts may not receive any rain at all in a year! Deserts often also undergo large shifts in temperature during the course of a day. A scorching hot desert like the

Figure 17 Desert organisms have adaptations that enable them to live in the harsh conditions of their biome. For example, this shovel-snouted lizard "dances" to avoid burning its feet on the hot sand dunes of the Namib Desert in Africa. *Making Generalizations Describe the climate conditions of a typical desert.*

Equator

Desert and Grassland Biomes
☐ Desert   ☐ Grassland

Namib Desert cools rapidly each night when the sun goes down. Other deserts, such as the Gobi in central Asia, are cooler, even experiencing freezing temperatures in the winter.

The organisms that live in the desert are adapted to the lack of rain and to the extreme temperatures. For example, the trunk of a saguaro cactus has folds that work like the pleats in an accordion. The trunk of the cactus expands to hold more water when it is raining. Many desert animals are most active at night when the temperatures are cooler. A gila monster, for instance, spends much of its time in a cool underground burrow. It may go for weeks without coming up to the surface of the desert.

☑ *Checkpoint* *What are some adaptations that help an organism to live in the desert?*

Grassland Biomes

The next stop on the expedition is a grassland called a prairie. The temperature here is much more comfortable than that in the desert. The breeze carries the scent of soil warmed by the sun. This rich soil supports grass as tall as you and your classmates. Sparrows flit among the grass stems, looking for their next meal. Startled by your approach, a rabbit quickly bounds away.

Like other grasslands located in the middle latitudes, this prairie receives more rain than deserts, but not enough for many trees to grow. A **grassland** receives between 25 and 75 centimeters of rain each year, and is typically populated by grasses and other non-woody plants. Grasslands that are located closer to the equator than prairies, called **savannas,** receive as much as 120 centimeters of

Desert Survival

✂ Use a hand lens **ACTIVITY** to carefully observe a small potted cactus. Be careful of the spines! With a pair of scissors, carefully snip a small piece from the tip of the cactus. Observe the inside of the plant. Note any characteristics that seem different from those of other plants.

Observing How is the inside of the cactus different from the outside? Suggest how the features you observe might be related to its desert habitat.

Figure 18 Migrating wildebeest make their way across a vast Kenyan savanna.

Forest Biomes

Deciduous forest | Boreal forest

Figure 19 This Michigan forest in autumn is a beautiful example of a deciduous forest. The closeup shows a red fox, a common resident of North American deciduous forests. *Comparing and Contrasting How do deciduous forests differ from rain forests?*

rain each year. Scattered shrubs and small trees grow on savannas along with the grass.

Grasslands are home to many of the largest animals on Earth—herbivores such as bison, antelopes, zebras, rhinoceros, giraffes, and kangaroos. Grazing by these large herbivores helps to maintain the grasslands. They keep young trees and bushes from sprouting and competing with the grass for water and sunlight.

Deciduous Forest Biomes

Your trip to the next biome takes you to another forest. It is now late summer. Cool mornings here give way to warm days. Several members of the expedition are busy recording the numerous plant species. Others are looking through their binoculars, trying to identify the songbirds in the trees. You step carefully to avoid a small salamander on the forest floor. Chipmunks chatter at all the disturbance.

You are now visiting the deciduous forest biome. The trees found in this forest, called **deciduous trees** (dee SIJ oo us), shed their leaves and grow new ones each year. Oaks and maples are examples of deciduous trees. Deciduous forests receive enough rain to support the growth of trees and other plants, at least 50 centimeters per year. Temperatures vary during the year. The growing season usually lasts five to six months. As in the rain forest, different plants grow to different heights, ranging from a canopy of tall trees to small ferns and mosses on the forest floor.

The variety of plants in the forest creates many different habitats. You and your classmates note that different species of birds live at each level, eating the insects and fruits that live and grow there. You observe opossums, mice, and a skunk looking for food in the thick layer of damp leaves on the ground. Other common North American deciduous forest species include wood thrushes, white-tailed deer, and black bears.

If you were to return to this biome in the winter, you would not see much of the wildlife you are now observing. One reason is that many of the bird species migrate to warmer areas. Some of the mammals enter a low-energy state similar to sleep called hibernation. During hibernation an animal relies on fat it has stored in its body.

☑ *Checkpoint* *What are deciduous trees?*

Boreal Forest Biomes

Now the expedition heads north into a colder climate. The expedition leaders claim they can identify the next biome, a boreal forest, by its smell. When you arrive, you catch a whiff of the spruce and fir trees that blanket the hillsides. Feeling the chilly early fall air, you pull a jacket and hat out of your bag.

This forest contains **coniferous trees** (koh NIF ur us), that produce their seeds in cones and have leaves shaped like needles. The boreal forest is sometimes referred to by its Russian name, the *taiga* (TY guh). Winters in these forests are very cold. The yearly

Sharpen your Skills

Inferring ACTIVITY

Observe the map on the facing page showing the locations of deciduous and boreal forests. How do they compare? Can you suggest a reason why no boreal forests are shown in the Southern Hemisphere?

Figure 20 Common organisms of the boreal forest include moose like this one in Alaska's Denali National Park, and porcupines.

snowfall can reach heights well over your head—or even two or three times your height! Even so, the summers are rainy and warm enough to melt all the snow.

A limited number of trees have adapted to the cold climate of boreal forests. Fir, spruce, and hemlock are the most common species because their thick, waxy needles keep water from evaporating. Since water is frozen for much of the year in these areas, prevention of water loss is a necessary adaptation for trees in the boreal forest.

Many of the animals of the boreal forest eat the seeds produced by the conifers. These animals include red squirrels, insects, and birds such as finches and chickadees. Some of the larger herbivores, such as porcupines, deer, elk, moose, and beavers, eat tree bark and new shoots. This variety of herbivores in the boreal forest supports a variety of large predators, including wolves, bears, wolverines, and lynxes.

Tundra Biomes

The driving wind brings tears to the eyes of the members of the expedition as you arrive at your next stop. It is now fall. The slicing wind gives everyone an immediate feel for this biome, the tundra. The **tundra** is an extremely cold, dry, land biome. Expecting deep snow, many are surprised that the tundra may receive no more precipitation than a desert. Most of the soil in the tundra is frozen all year. This frozen soil is called **permafrost.**

Figure 21 Far from being a barren terrain, the tundra explodes with color in summer. Mosses, wildflowers, and shrubs flourish despite the short growing season. *Relating Cause and Effect Why are there no tall trees on the tundra?*

Tundra Biomes, Mountains, and Ice

Tundra   Mountains   Ice

Equator

During the short summer the top layer of soil on the tundra thaws, but the underlying soil remains frozen.

Plants on the tundra include mosses, grasses, shrubs, and dwarf forms of a few trees, such as willows. Looking across the tundra, you observe that the landscape is already brown and gold. The short growing season is over. Most of the plant growth takes place during the long summer days when many hours of sunshine combine with the warmest temperatures of the year. North of the Arctic Circle the sun does not set during midsummer.

If you had visited the tundra during the summer, the animals you might remember most are insects. Swarms of black flies and mosquitos provide food for many birds. The birds take advantage of the plentiful food and long days by eating as much as they can. Then, when winter approaches again, many birds migrate south to warmer climates.

Mammals of the tundra include caribou, foxes, wolves, and hares. The animals that remain in the tundra during the winter grow thick fur coats. What can these animals find to eat on the tundra in winter? The caribou scrape snow away to find lichens, which are fungi and algae that grow together on rocks. Wolves follow the caribou and look for weak members of the herd to prey upon.

☑ *Checkpoint* *What is the climate of the tundra?*

Mountains and Ice

Some areas of land on Earth do not fall into one of the major land biomes. These areas include mountain ranges and land that is covered with thick sheets of ice.

You read in Section 3 that the climate conditions of a mountain change from its base to its summit. As a result, different species of plants and other organisms inhabit different parts of the mountain. If you hiked to the top of a tall mountain, you would pass through a series of biomes. At the base of the mountain, you might find a grassland. As you climbed, you might pass through a deciduous forest, and then a boreal forest. Finally, as you neared the top, the trees would disappear. Your surroundings would resemble the rugged tundra.

Some land on Earth is covered year-round with thick ice sheets. Most of the island of Greenland and the continent of Antarctica fall into this category. Some organisms are adapted to life on the ice, including penguins, polar bears, and seals.

Figure 22 Many waterfowl spend summers on the tundra. This black brant is tending her nest.

Interpreting Data

An ecologist has collected climate data from two locations. The total yearly precipitation is 250 cm in Location A and 14 cm in Location B. The graph below shows the average monthly temperature in the two locations. Based on this information, of which biome is each location a part? Explain.

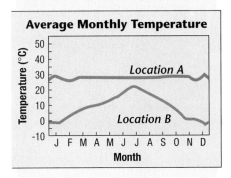

Figure 23 Ponds and rivers are two types of freshwater habitats. **A.** At the edge of a pond, two western pond turtles sun themselves on a log. **B.** A brown bear fishes for salmon in the rushing waters of a river. *Comparing and Contrasting How are these habitats similar? How are they different?*

Freshwater Biomes

The next stops for the expedition are located in water biomes. Since almost three quarters of Earth's surface is covered with water, it is not surprising that many living things make their homes in the water. Water biomes include both freshwater and saltwater (also called marine) biomes. All of these are affected by the same abiotic factors: temperature, sunlight, oxygen, and salt content.

An especially important factor in water biomes is sunlight. Sunlight is necessary for photosynthesis in the water just as it is on land. **However, because water absorbs sunlight, there is only enough light for photosynthesis near the surface or in shallow water.** The most common producers in most water biomes are algae rather than plants.

Ponds and Lakes First stop among the freshwater biomes is a calm pond. Ponds and lakes are bodies of standing, or still, fresh water. Lakes are generally larger and deeper than ponds. Ponds are often shallow enough that sunlight can reach the bottom even in the center of the pond, allowing plants to grow there. Plants that grow along the shore have their roots in the soil, while their leaves stretch to the sunlit water at the surface. In the center of a lake, algae floating at the surface are the major producers.

Many animals are adapted for life in the still water. Along the shore of the pond you observe insects, snails, frogs, and salamanders. Sunfish live in the open water, feeding on insects and algae from the surface. Scavengers such as catfish live near the pond bottom. Bacteria and other decomposers also feed on the remains of other organisms.

Streams and Rivers When you arrive at a mountain stream, you immediately notice how different it is from the still waters of a lake. Where the stream begins, called the headwaters, the cold, clear water flows rapidly. Animals that live in this part must be adapted to the strong current. Trout, for instance, have streamlined bodies that allow them to swim despite the pull of the rushing water. Insects and other small animals may have hooks or suckers to help them cling to rocks. Few plants or algae can grow in this fast-moving water. Instead, first-level consumers rely on leaves and seeds that fall into the stream.

As the river flows along, it is joined by other streams. The current slows. The water becomes cloudy with soil. With fewer rapids, the slower-moving, warmer water contains less oxygen. Different organisms are adapted to live in this lower part of the river. More plants take root among the pebbles on the river bottom, providing homes for insects and frogs. As is true in every biome, organisms are adapted to live in this specific habitat.

☑ *Checkpoint* *What are two abiotic factors that affect organisms in a river?*

Marine Biomes

Next the members of the expedition head down the coast to explore some marine biomes. The oceans contain many different habitats. These habitats differ in sunlight amount, water temperature, wave action, and water pressure. Different organisms are adapted to life in each type of habitat. The first habitat, called an **estuary** (ES choo ehr ee), is found where the fresh water of a river meets the salt water of the ocean.

Estuaries The shallow, sunlit water, plus a large supply of nutrients carried in by the river, makes an estuary a very rich habitat for living things. The major producers in estuaries are plants, such as marsh grasses, as well as algae.

Figure 24 Fresh river water and salty ocean water meet in an estuary. Estuaries such as this Georgia salt marsh provide a rich habitat for many organisms, including a wading tricolored heron.

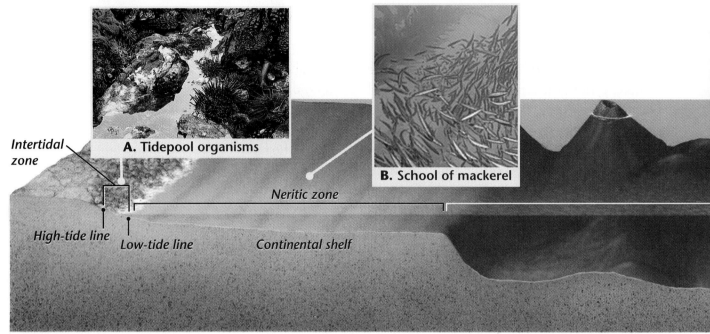

Intertidal zone

A. Tidepool organisms

B. School of mackerel

Neritic zone

High-tide line

Low-tide line

Continental shelf

Figure 25 The marine biome is divided into several zones. **A.** Tidepools are common in the intertidal zone. This zone lies between the highest high-tide line and lowest low-tide line. **B.** Many fish, such as these silvery mackerel, inhabit the shallow waters over the continental shelf, called the neritic zone. **C.** A humpback whale feeds on algae at the surface of the open-ocean zone. **D.** This eerie deep-sea gulper is a predator in the deepest part of the ocean.

These organisms provide food and shelter for a variety of animals, including crabs, worms, clams, oysters, and fish. Many of these organisms use the calm waters of estuaries for breeding grounds.

Intertidal Zone Next, you take a walk along the rocky shore-line. The part of the shore between the highest high-tide line and the lowest low-tide line is called the **intertidal zone.** Organisms here must be able to withstand the pounding action of waves, sudden changes in temperature, and being both covered with water and then exposed to the air. It is a difficult place to live! You observe many animals, such as barnacles and sea stars, clinging to the rocks. Others, such as clams and crabs, burrow in the sand.

Neritic Zone Now it's time to set out to sea to explore the waters near shore. From your research vessel, your group will explore the next type of marine habitat. The edge of a continent extends into the ocean for a short distance, like a shelf. Below the low-tide line is a region of shallow water, called the **neritic zone** (nuh RIT ik), that extends over the continental shelf. Just as in freshwater biomes, the shallow water in this zone allows photo-synthesis to occur. As a result, this zone is particularly rich in living things. Many large schools of fish such as sardines and anchovies feed on the algae in the neritic zone. In the warm ocean waters of the tropics, coral reefs may form in the neritic zone. Though a coral reef may look like stone, it is actually a living home to a wide variety of other organisms.

Surface Zone Out in the open ocean, light penetrates through the water only to a depth of a few hundred meters. Algae float-ing in these surface waters carry out photosynthesis. These algae

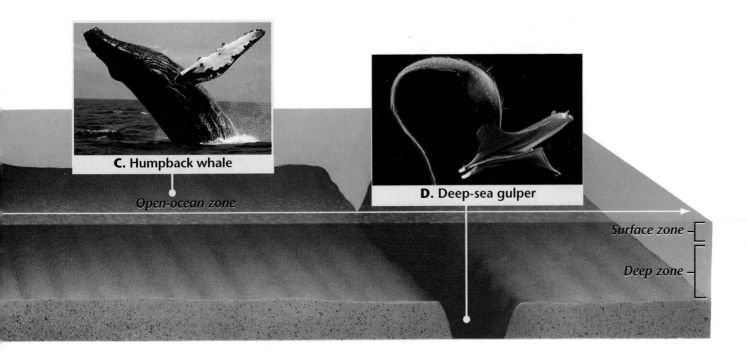

C. Humpback whale

Open-ocean zone

D. Deep-sea gulper

Surface zone

Deep zone

are the producers that form the base of almost all open-ocean food webs. Other marine animals, such as tuna, swordfish, and whales, depend directly or indirectly on the algae for food.

Deep Zone The deep zone is located in the open ocean below the surface zone. Throughout most of the deep ocean, the water is completely dark. Your expedition will need to use a submarine with bright headlights to explore this region. How can anything live in a place with no sunlight? Most animals in this zone feed on remains of organisms that sink down from the surface zone. The deepest parts of the deep zone are home to bizarre-looking animals, such as giant squid that glow in the dark and fish with rows and rows of sharp teeth.

After you have recorded your deep-zone observations, your long expedition is over at last. You can finally return home.

Section 4 Review

1. How does climate determine a biome's characteristics?
2. Where in water biomes can photosynthesis occur?
3. Which land biome receives the most precipitation? Which two receive the least?
4. In which biome would you find large herbivores such as antelope and elephants? Explain your answer.
5. **Thinking Critically Comparing and Contrasting** How are the three forest biomes (rain forests, deciduous forests, and boreal forests) alike? How are they different?

Check Your Progress CHAPTER PROJECT

By now you should be ready to start analyzing the data you have collected about your compost chambers. Do your observations of the two chambers support your hypothesis? Begin to prepare your report.

CHANGE IN A TINY COMMUNITY

The types of organisms in an ecosystem may change gradually over time. You will learn more about this process, called succession, in the next section. In this lab you will observe succession in a pond community.

Problem

How does a pond community change over time?

Materials

hay solution
small baby-food jar
plastic dropper
coverslip

pond water
wax pencil
microscope slide
microscope

Procedure

1. Use a wax pencil to label a small jar with your name.

2. Fill the jar about three-fourths full with hay solution. Add pond water until the jar is nearly full. Examine the mixture, and record your observations in your notebook.

3. Place the jar in a safe location out of direct sunlight where it will remain undisturbed. Always wash your hands thoroughly with soap after handling the jar or its contents.

4. After two days, examine the contents of the jar, and record your observations.

5. Use a plastic dropper to collect a few drops from the surface of the solution in the jar. Make a slide following the procedures in the box at the right. **CAUTION:** *Slides and coverslips are fragile, and their edges are sharp. Handle them carefully.*

6. Examine the slide under a microscope using both low and high power following the procedures in the box at the right. Draw each type of organism you observe. Estimate the number of each type in your sample. The illustration below shows some of the organisms you might see.

7. Repeat Steps 5 and 6 with a drop of solution taken from the side of the jar beneath the surface.

8. Repeat Steps 5 and 6 with a drop of solution taken from the bottom of the jar. When you are finished, follow your teacher's directions about cleaning up.

9. After 3 days, repeat Steps 5 through 8.

10. After 3 more days, repeat Steps 5 through 8 again. Then follow your teacher's directions for returning the solution.

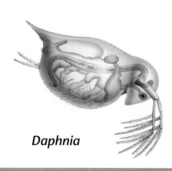

Daphnia

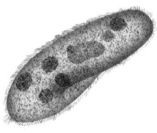

Paramecium

Spirogyra

Making and Viewing a Slide

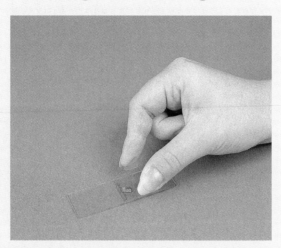

A. Place one drop of the solution to be examined in the middle of a microscope slide. Place one edge of a coverslip at the edge of the drop, as shown above. Gently lower the coverslip over the drop. Try not to trap any air bubbles.

B. Place the slide on the stage of a microscope so the drop is over the opening in the stage. Adjust the stage clips to hold the slide.

C. Look from the side of the microscope, and use the coarse adjustment knob to move the low-power objective close to, but not touching, the coverslip.

D. Look through the eyepiece, and use the coarse adjustment knob to raise the body tube and bring the slide into view. Use the fine adjustment knob to bring the slide into focus.

E. To view the slide under high power, look from the side of the microscope, and revolve the nosepiece until the high-power objective clicks into place just over, but not touching, the slide.

F. While you are looking through the eyepiece, use the fine adjustment knob to bring the slide into focus.

Analyze and Conclude

1. Identify as many of the organisms you observed as possible. Use the diagrams on the facing page and any other resources your teacher provides.
2. How did the community change over the time that you made your observations?
3. What factors may have influenced the changes in this community?
4. Where did the organisms you observed in the jar come from?

5. **Think About It** Do you think your observations gave you a complete picture of the changes in this community? Explain your answer.

Design an Experiment

Write a hypothesis about what would happen if you changed one biotic or abiotic factor in this activity. Design a plan to test your hypothesis. Obtain your teacher's permission before carrying out your experiment.

What Happened Here?

1. The two photographs at the right show the same area in Yellowstone National Park in Wyoming. Photograph A was taken soon after a major fire. Photograph B was taken a few years later. Observe the photographs carefully.

2. Make a list of all the differences you notice between the two scenes.

Think It Over

Posing Questions How would you describe what happened during the time between the two photographs? What questions do you have about this process?

◆ How are primary and secondary succession different?

Reading Tip Before you read, write a definition of what you think the term *succession* might mean. As you read, revise your definition.

In 1988, a huge fire raged through Yellowstone National Park. The fire was so hot that it jumped from tree to tree without burning along the ground between them. In an instant, huge trees burst into flame from the intense heat. It took weeks for the fires to burn themselves out. All that remained of that part of the forest were thousands of blackened tree trunks sticking out of the ground like charred toothpicks.

You might think it unlikely that Yellowstone could recover from such a disastrous fire. But within just a few months, signs of life had returned. First tiny green shoots of new grass appeared in the black ground. Then small tree seedlings began to grow again. The forest was coming back!

Fires, floods, volcanoes, hurricanes, and other natural disasters can change communities in a very short period of time. But even without a disaster, communities change. The series of predictable changes that occur in a community over time is called **succession.** This section describes two types of succession: primary succession and secondary succession.

Applying Skills

Use the diagram of a food web below to answer Questions 23–25.

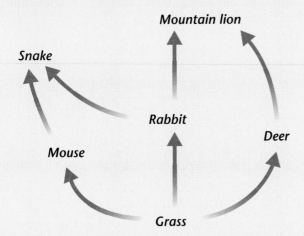

23. Classifying Identify the energy role of each organism in this food web. For consumers, specify whether they are first-level, second-level, or third-level.

24. Inferring Which level of the food web contains the greatest amount of available energy?

25. Predicting If a disease were to kill most of the rabbits in this area, predict how the snakes, deer, and mountain lions would be affected.

Performance ▽ Assessment
CHAPTER PROJECT

Present Your Project Check over your report, poster, or other product. It should clearly present your data and conclusions about the effect of your variable on the decomposition process.

Reflect and Record In your notebook, compare your results to your predictions about the different waste materials in the compost mixture. Were you surprised by any of your results? Based on what you have learned from your project and those of your classmates, make a list of the ideal conditions for decomposition.

Test Preparation
Use these questions to prepare for standardized tests.

Study the diagram. Then answer Questions 26–29.

26. Which of the following is a producer in the jar ecosystem?
a. fresh water
b. fish
c. snails
d. water plants

27. Which of the following is a consumer in the jar ecosystem?
a. gravel
b. snails
c. water plants
d. fresh water

28. Which gas do the snails and fish release into the water?
a. hydrogen
b. oxygen
c. carbon dioxide
d. nitrogen

29. A gas released by the water plants as a result of photosynthesis is
a. hydrogen   b. oxygen
c. carbon dioxide   d. nitrogen

WEB ACTIVITY www.phschool.com

SECTION Integrating Environmental Science
1 **Environmental Issues**

Discover **How Do You Decide?**
Real-World Lab **Is Paper a Renewable
Resource?**

SECTION
2 **Forests and Fisheries**

Discover **What Happened to the Tuna?**
Sharpen Your Skills **Calculating**
Science at Home **Renewable Survey**
Skills Lab **Tree Cookie Tales**

SECTION
3 **Biodiversity**

Discover **How Much Variety Is There?**
Sharpen Your Skills **Communicating**

Variety Show

The colors in this meadow show that many different types of organisms live here. In other places, life's variety is less obvious. In this chapter's project, you will become an ecologist as you study the diversity of life in a small plot of land. Keep in mind that the area you will study has just a small sample of the huge variety of organisms that live on Earth.

Your Goal To observe the diversity of organisms in a plot of land.

To complete this project you must
◆ stake out a 1.5 meter-by-1.5 meter plot of ground
◆ keep a record of your observations of the abiotic conditions
◆ identify the species of organisms you observe
◆ follow the safety guidelines in Appendix A

Get Started Read over the project and prepare a notebook in which to record your observations. Include places to record the date, time, air temperature, and other weather conditions during each observation. Leave space for drawings or photographs of the organisms in your plot.

Check Your Progress You'll be working on this project as you study this chapter. To keep your project on track, look for Check Your Progress boxes at the following points.
  Section 1 Review, page 760: Stake out your plot, and begin to observe it.
  Section 3 Review, page 776: Identify the organisms in your plot. Begin to prepare your presentation.

Present Your Project At the end of the chapter (page 779), you will present your findings to the class. You will describe your observations and share the diversity of life in your plot.

A woodchuck feasts on wildflowers in a meadow exploding with color. Black-eyed Susans, Queen Anne's lace, and butterflyweed are part of the meadow's diversity.

SECTION 1 Environmental Issues

DISCOVER • ACTIVITY

How Do You Decide?

1. On a sheet of paper, list the three environmental issues you think are most important.

2. Form a group with three other classmates. Share your lists. As a group decide which one of the issues is the most important.

Think It Over
Forming Operational Definitions
Based on your group's discussion, how would you define the term *environmental issue*?

GUIDE FOR READING

◆ What are the main types of environmental issues?

◆ What is environmental science?

Reading Tip Before you read, make a list of ways that humans depend on the environment. As you read, add examples from the text.

Here's a puzzle for you: What is bigger than the United States and Mexico combined; is covered with two kilometers of ice; is a source of oil, coal, and iron; and is a unique habitat for many animals? The answer is Antarctica. People once thought of Antarctica as a useless, icy wasteland. But when explorers told of its huge populations of seals and whales, hunters began going to Antarctica. Then scientists set up research stations to study the unique conditions there. They soon discovered valuable minerals beneath the thick ice.

Now the puzzle is what to do with Antarctica. Many people want its rich deposits of minerals and oil. Others worry that mining will harm the delicate ecosystems there. Some people propose building hotels, parks, and ski resorts. But others feel that Antarctica should remain undisturbed. It is not even obvious who should decide Antarctica's fate.

In 1998, 26 nations agreed to ban mining and oil exploration in Antarctica for at least 50 years. As resources become more scarce elsewhere in the world, the debate will surely continue. What is the best use of Antarctica?

Figure 1 This leopard seal's habitat could be affected if oil drilling is allowed in Antarctica. This tradeoff is an example of an environmental issue.

Types of Environmental Issues

People have always used Earth's resources. But as the human population has grown, so has its effect on the environment. People compete with each other and with other living things for Earth's limited resources. Disposing of wastes created by people can change ecosystems. And while people are continuing to take resources from the environment, many of them cannot be replaced. These resources could eventually run out.

Figure 2 Cherries are a renewable resource. After they are harvested, new cherries will grow in their place. In contrast, the aluminum and iron used to make these kitchen tools are nonrenewable resources.

The three main types of environmental issues are resource use, population growth, and pollution. These issues are all connected, making them very difficult to solve.

Resource Use Any living or nonliving thing in the environment that is used by people is a natural resource. Some natural resources, called **renewable resources,** are naturally replaced in a relatively short time. Renewable resources include sunlight, wind, and trees. But it is possible to use up some renewable resources. For example, if people cut down trees faster than they can grow back, the supply of this resource will decrease.

Natural resources that are not replaced as they are used are called **nonrenewable resources.** Most nonrenewable resources, such as coal and oil, exist in a limited supply. As nonrenewable resources are used, the supply may eventually be depleted.

Population Growth Figure 3 shows how the human population has changed in the last 3,000 years. You can see that the population grew very slowly until about A.D. 1650. Around that time, improvements in medicine, agriculture, and sanitation enabled people to live longer. The death rate decreased. But as the population has continued to grow, the demand for resources has also grown.

Pollution Any change to the environment that has a negative effect on living things is called **pollution.** Pollution is an issue because it is often the result of an activity that benefits humans. For example, generating electricity by burning coal can result in air pollution. Some pesticides used to kill insects that eat crops are harmful to other animals.

☑ *Checkpoint* *What is a natural resource?*

Figure 3 If two's company, six billion is certainly a crowd! The human population has grown rapidly in the last few centuries. *Calculating How much has the population grown since 1650?*

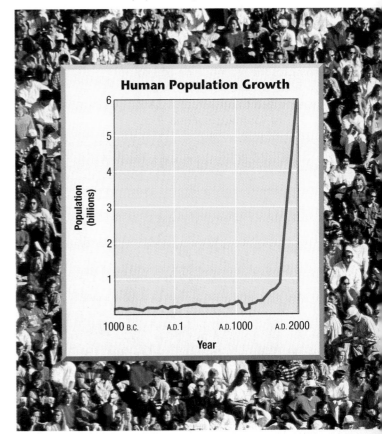

Human Population Growth

Approaches to Environmental Issues

Dealing with environmental issues means making choices. These choices can be made at personal, local, national, or global levels. Whether to ride in a car, take a bus, or ride your bicycle to the mall is an example of a personal choice. Whether to build a landfill or an incinerator for disposing of a town's wastes is a local choice. Whether the United States should allow oil drilling in a wildlife refuge is a national choice. How to protect Earth's atmosphere is a global choice.

Choices that seem personal are often part of much larger issues. Choices of what you eat, what you wear, and how you travel all affect the environment in a small way. When the choices made by millions of people are added together, each person's actions can make a difference.

SCIENCE & History

Making a Difference

Can one individual change the way people think? The leaders featured in this time line have influenced the way that many people think about environmental issues.

1892

California writer John Muir founds the Sierra Club. The group promotes the setting aside of wild areas as national parks. Muir's actions lead to the establishment of Yosemite National Park.

1905

Forestry scientist Gifford Pinchot is appointed the first director of the United States Forest Service. His goal is to manage forests scientifically to meet current and future lumber needs.

1875   **1900**   **1925**

1903

President Theodore Roosevelt establishes the first National Wildlife Refuge on Pelican Island, Florida, to protect the brown pelican.

Theodore Roosevelt (left) and John Muir (right)

The first step in making environmental decisions is to understand how humans interact with the environment. **Environmental science is the study of the natural processes that occur in the environment and how humans can affect them.**

When people make decisions about environmental issues, the information provided by environmental scientists is a starting point. The next step is to decide what to do with the information. But environmental decisions also involve discussions of values, not just facts and figures. The lawmakers and government agencies that make environmental decisions must consider the needs and concerns of people with many different viewpoints.

☑ *Checkpoint* *What is an example of a local choice about an environmental issue?*

In Your Journal

Find out more about one of the people featured in this time line. Write a short biography of the person's life explaining how he or she became involved in environmental issues. What obstacles did the person overcome to accomplish his or her goal?

1949

Naturalist Aldo Leopold publishes *A Sand County Almanac.* This classic book links wildlife management to the science of ecology.

1969

At the age of 79, journalist Marjory Stoneman Douglas founds Friends of the Everglades. This grassroots organization is dedicated to preserving the unique Florida ecosystem. She continues to work for the Everglades until her death in 1998.

| 1950 | 1975 | 2000 |

1962

Biologist Rachel Carson writes *Silent Spring*, which describes the harmful effects of pesticides on the environment. The book raises awareness of how human activities can affect the environment.

1977

Biologist Wangari Maathai founds the Green Belt Movement. This organization encourages restoring forests in Kenya and other African nations.

Figure 4 The environment is valued for many different reasons.
Applying Concepts In what other ways might this area be valuable?

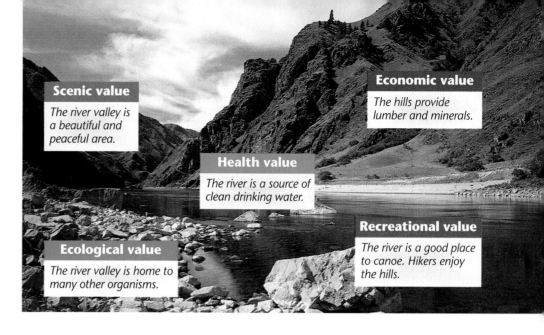

Scenic value
The river valley is a beautiful and peaceful area.

Economic value
The hills provide lumber and minerals.

Health value
The river is a source of clean drinking water.

Recreational value
The river is a good place to canoe. Hikers enjoy the hills.

Ecological value
The river valley is home to many other organisms.

Weighing Costs and Benefits

To help balance different opinions, decision makers weigh the costs and benefits of a proposal. Costs and benefits are often economic. Will a proposal provide jobs? Will it cost too much money? But costs and benefits are not only measured in terms of money. For example, building an incinerator might reduce the beauty of a natural landscape (a scenic cost). But the incinerator might be safer than an existing open dump (a health benefit). It is also important to consider short-term and long-term effects. A proposal's short-term costs might be outweighed by its long-term benefits.

Consider the costs of drilling for oil in Antarctica. It would be very expensive to set up a drilling operation in such a cold and distant place. Transporting the oil would be difficult and costly. An oil spill in the seas around Antarctica could harm the fish, penguins, and seals there.

On the other hand, there would be many benefits to the drilling. A new supply of oil would provide fuel for heat, electricity, and transportation. The plan would create many new jobs. There would be more opportunity to study Antarctica. Do the benefits of drilling outweigh the costs? This is the kind of question people ask when they make environmental decisions.

Section 1 Review

1. List the three main types of environmental issues.
2. Define environmental science.
3. List three costs and three benefits of drilling for oil in Antarctica.
4. **Thinking Critically Comparing and Contrasting** Compare renewable and non-renewable resources. Give an example of each.

Check Your Progress

CHAPTER PROJECT

Stake out a square plot measuring 1.5 meters on each side. Record the date, time, temperature, and weather. Observe and record the organisms in your plot. (*Hint:* Also note evidence such as feathers or footprints that shows that other organisms have visited the plot.)

Is Paper a Renewable Resource?

Recycling is a common local environmental issue. In this lab, you will explore how well paper can be recycled.

Problem

What happens when paper is recycled?

Skills Focus

observing, designing experiments

Materials

newspaper	microscope	water
eggbeater	square pan	screen
plastic wrap	mixing bowl	heavy book
microscope slide		

Procedure

1. Tear off a small piece of newspaper. Place the paper on a microscope slide and examine it under a microscope. Record your observations.
2. Tear a sheet of newspaper into pieces about the size of postage stamps. Place the pieces in the mixing bowl. Add enough water to cover the newspaper. Cover the bowl and let the mixture stand overnight.
3. The next day, add more water to cover the paper if necessary. Use the eggbeater to mix the wet paper until it is smooth. This thick liquid is called paper pulp.
4. Place the screen in the bottom of the pan. Pour the pulp onto the screen, spreading it out evenly. Then lift the screen above the pan, allowing most of the water to drip into the pan.

5. Place the screen and pulp on several layers of newspaper to absorb the rest of the water. Lay a sheet of plastic wrap over the pulp. Place a heavy book on top of the plastic wrap to press more water out of the pulp.
6. After 30 minutes, remove the book. Carefully turn over the screen, plastic wrap, and pulp. Remove the screen and plastic wrap. Let the pulp sit on the newspaper for one or two more days to dry. Replace the newspaper layers if necessary.
7. When the pulp is dry, observe it closely. Record your observations.

Analyze and Conclude

1. What kind of structures did you observe when you examined torn newspaper under a microscope? What are these structures made of? Where do they come from?
2. What do you think happens to the structures you observed when paper is recycled?
3. Based on your results, predict how many times a sheet of newspaper can be recycled.
4. **Apply** Should paper be classified as a renewable or nonrenewable resource? Explain.

Using procedures like those in this lab, design an experiment to recycle three different types of paper, such as shiny magazine paper, paper towels, and cardboard. Find out how the resulting papers differ. Obtain your teacher's approval for your plans before you try your experiment.

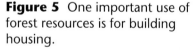

DISCOVER •• ACTIVITY

What Happened to the Tuna?

1. Use the data in the table to make a line graph. Label the axes of the graph and add a title. (To review graphing, see the Skills Handbook.)
2. Mark the high and low points on the graph.

Think It Over

Inferring How did the tuna population change during this period? Can you suggest a possible reason for this change?

Year	Western Atlantic Bluefin Tuna Population
1970	240,000
1975	190,000
1980	90,000
1985	60,000
1990	45,000
1994	60,000

GUIDE FOR READING

◆ How can forests and fisheries be managed?

Reading Tip As you read, make a list of ways to conserve forests and fisheries.

Figure 5 One important use of forest resources is for building housing.

At first glance, a bluefin tuna and a pine tree may not seem to have much in common. One is an animal and the other is a plant. One lives in the ocean and the other lives on land. However, tuna and pine trees are both living resources. Tuna are a source of food for people. People don't eat pine trees, but they do use them to make lumber, paper, and turpentine. People also use pine needles as mulch in gardens.

Every day you use many different products that are made from living organisms. In this section, you will read about two major types of living resources: forests and fisheries. As you read, think about how they are similar and how they are different.

Forest Resources

Forests are a resource because they contain valuable materials. Many products are made from the flowers, fruits, seeds, and other parts of forest plants. Some of these products, such as maple syrup, rubber, and nuts, come from living trees. Other products, such as lumber and pulp for paper, require cutting trees down. Conifers, including pine and spruce, are used for construction and for making paper. Hardwoods, such as oak, cherry, and maple, are used for furniture because of their strength and beauty.

Trees and other plants produce oxygen that other organisms need to survive. They also absorb carbon dioxide and many pollutants from the air. Trees also help prevent flooding and control soil erosion. Their roots absorb rainwater and hold the soil together.

Figure 6 Clear-cutting has left large portions of these hillsides bare. *Interpreting Photographs What problems might clear-cutting cause?*

Managing Forests

There are about 300 million hectares of forests in the United States. That's nearly a third of the nation's area! Many forests are located on publicly owned land. Others are owned by private timber and paper companies or by individuals. Forest industries provide jobs for 1.5 million people.

Because new trees can be planted to replace trees that are cut down, forests can be renewable resources. The United States Forest Service and environmental organizations work with forestry companies to conserve forest resources. They try to develop logging methods that maintain forests as renewable resources.

Logging Methods There are two major methods of logging: clear-cutting and selective cutting. **Clear-cutting** is the process of cutting down all the trees in an area at once. Cutting down only some trees in a forest and leaving a mix of tree sizes and species behind is called **selective cutting.**

Each logging method has advantages and disadvantages. Clear-cutting is usually quicker and cheaper than selective cutting. It may also be safer for the loggers. In selective cutting, the loggers must move the heavy equipment and logs around the remaining trees in the forest. But selective cutting is usually less damaging to the forest environment than clear-cutting. When an area of forest is clear-cut, the habitat changes. Clear-cutting exposes the soil to wind and rain. Without the protection of the tree roots, the soil is more easily blown or washed away. Soil washed into streams may harm the fish and other organisms that live there.

Sustainable Forestry Forests can be managed to provide a sustained yield. A **sustainable yield** is a regular amount of a renewable resource such as trees that can be harvested without reducing the future supply. This works sort of like a book swap: as long as you donate a book each time you borrow one, the total supply of books will not be affected. Planting a tree to replace one being cut down is like donating a book to replace a borrowed one.

Part of forest management is planning how frequently the trees must be replanted to keep a constant supply. Different species grow at different rates. Trees with softer woods, such as pines, usually mature faster than trees with harder woods, such as hickory, oak, and cherry. Forests containing faster-growing trees can be harvested and replanted more often. For example, pine forests may be harvested every 20 to 30 years. On the other hand, some hardwood forests may be harvested only every 40 to 100 years. One sustainable approach is to log small patches of forest. This way, different sections of forest can be harvested every year.

Certified Wood Forests that are managed in a sustainable way can be certified by the Forest Stewardship Council. Once a forest is certified, all wood logged from that forest may carry a "well-managed" label. This label allows businesses and individuals to select wood from forests that are managed for sustainable yields.

☑ *Checkpoint* *What is a sustainable yield?*

Figure 7 Two logging methods are clear-cutting and selective cutting. **A.** After clear-cutting, the new trees are usually all the same age and species. **B.** Selective cutting results in a more diverse forest.

Original forest *Clear-cutting* *Replanted growth*

Original forest *Selective cutting* *Diverse regrowth*

Figure 8 A fishing boat returns to harbor at the end of a long day. Overfishing has forced the crews of many boats to find other work until the fisheries recover.

Fisheries

Until recently, the oceans seemed like an unlimited resource. The waters held huge schools of fish, and fish reproduce in incredible numbers. A single codfish can lay as many as nine million eggs in a single year! It seemed impossible that fish populations could ever disappear. But people have discovered that this resource has limits. After many years of big catches, the number of sardines off the California coast suddenly declined. The same thing happened to the huge schools of cod off the New England coast. What caused these changes?

An area with a large population of valuable ocean organisms is called a **fishery.** Some major fisheries include the Grand Banks off Newfoundland, Georges Bank off New England, and Monterey Canyon off California. Fisheries like these are valuable renewable resources. But if fish are caught at a faster rate than they can breed, the population decreases. This situation is known as overfishing.

Scientists estimate that 70 percent of the world's major fisheries have been overfished. But if those fish populations are allowed to recover, a sustainable yield of fish can once again be harvested. **Managing fisheries for a sustainable yield includes setting fishing limits, changing fishing methods, developing aquaculture techniques, and finding new resources.**

Fishing Limits Laws can help protect individual fish species. Laws may also limit the amount that can be caught or require that fish be at least a certain size. This ensures that young fish

Sharpen your Skills

Calculating

In a recent year, the total **ACTIVITY** catch of fish in the world was 112.9 million metric tons. Based on the data below, calculate the percent of this total each country caught.

Country	Catch (millions of metric tons)
China	24.4
Japan	6.8
United States	5.6
Peru	8.9

survive long enough to reproduce. Also, setting an upper limit on the size of fish caught ensures that breeding fish remain in the population. But if a fishery has been severely overfished, the government may need to completely ban fishing until the populations can recover.

Fishing Methods Today fishing practices are regulated by laws. Some fishing crews now use nets with a larger mesh size to allow small, young fish to escape. Some methods have been outlawed. These methods include poisoning fish with cyanide and stunning them by exploding dynamite underwater. These techniques kill all the fish in an area rather than selecting certain fish.

Aquaculture The practice of raising fish and other water-dwelling organisms for food is called **aquaculture.** The fish may be raised in artificial ponds or bays. Salmon, catfish, and shrimp are farmed in this way in the United States.

However, aquaculture is not a perfect solution. The artificial ponds and bays often replace natural habitats such as salt marshes. Maintaining the farms can cause pollution and spread diseases into wild fish populations.

New Resources Today about 9,000 different fish species are harvested for food. More than half the animal protein eaten by people throughout the world comes from fish. One way to help feed a growing human population is to fish for new species. Scientists and chefs are working together to introduce people to deep-water species such as monkfish and tile fish, as well as easy-to-farm freshwater fish such as tilapia.

Figure 9 As fishing limits become stricter, aquaculture is playing a larger role in meeting the worldwide demand for fish. This fish farm in Hawaii raises tilapia.

Section 2 Review

1. Describe one example of a sustainable forestry practice.
2. What are three ways fisheries can be managed so that they will continue to provide fish for the future?
3. Why are forests considered renewable resources?
4. **Thinking Critically Comparing and Contrasting** Describe the advantages and disadvantages of clear-cutting and selective cutting.

Science at Home

Renewable Survey With a family member, conduct a "Forest and Fishery" survey of your home. Make a list of all the things that are made from either forest or fishery products. Then ask other family members to predict how many items are on the list. Are they surprised by the answer?

Tree Cookie Tales

Tree cookies aren't snacks! They're slices of a tree trunk that contain clues about the tree's age, past weather conditions, and fires that occurred during its life. In this lab, you'll interpret the data hidden in a tree cookie.

Problem

What can tree cookies reveal about the past?

Materials

tree cookie   metric ruler   hand lens
colored pencils   calculator (optional)

Procedure

1. Use a hand lens to examine your tree cookie. Draw a simple diagram of your tree cookie. Label the bark, tree rings, and center, or pith.
2. Notice the light-colored and dark-colored rings. The light ring results from fast springtime growth. The dark ring, where the cells are smaller, results from slower summertime growth. Each pair of rings represents one year's growth, so the pair is called an annual ring. Observe and count the annual rings.

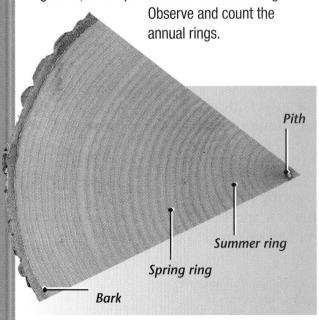

Pith

Summer ring

Spring ring

Bark

3. Compare the spring and summer portions of the annual rings. Identify the thinnest and thickest rings.
4. Measure the distance from the center to the outermost edge of the last summer growth ring. This is the radius of your tree cookie. Record your measurement.
5. Measure the distance from the center to the outermost edge of the 10th summer growth ring. Record your measurement.
6. Examine your tree cookie for any other evidence of its history, such as damaged bark or burn marks. Record your observations.

Analyze and Conclude

1. How old was your tree? How do you know?
2. What percent of the tree's growth took place during the first 10 years of its life? (*Hint:* Divide the distance from the center to the 10th growth ring by the radius. Then multiply by 100. This gives you the percent of growth that occurred during the tree's first 10 years.)
3. How did the spring rings compare to the summer rings for the same year? Suggest a reason.
4. Why might the annual rings be narrower for some years than for others?
5. Using evidence from your tree cookie, summarize the history of the tree.
6. **Think About It** Suppose you had cookies from two other trees of the same species that grew near your tree. How could you verify the interpretations you made in this lab?

More to Explore

Examine and compare several tree cookies. Do you think any of the tree cookies came from trees growing in the same area? Support your answer with specific evidence.

SECTION
3 Biodiversity

DISCOVER • **ACTIVITY**

How Much Variety Is There?

1. You will be given two cups of seeds and a paper plate. The seeds in Cup A represent the trees in a section of tropical rain forest. The seeds in Cup B represent the trees in a section of deciduous forest.

2. Pour the seeds from Cup A onto the plate. Sort the seeds by type. Count the different types of seeds. This number represents the number of different kinds of trees in that type of forest.

3. Pour the seeds back into Cup A.

4. Repeat Steps 2 and 3 with the seeds in Cup B.

5. Share your results with your class. Use the class results to calculate the average number of different kinds of seeds in each type of forest.

Think It Over

Inferring How does the variety of trees in the tropical rain forest compare with the variety of trees in a deciduous forest? Can you suggest any advantages of having a wide variety of species?

GUIDE FOR READING

◆ What factors affect an area's biodiversity?

◆ Which human activities threaten biodiversity?

◆ How can biodiversity be protected?

Reading Tip Before you read, use the headings to make an outline on biodiversity.

No one knows exactly how many species live on Earth. So far, more than 1.7 million species have been identified. The number of different species in an area is called its **biodiversity.** It is difficult to estimate the total biodiversity on Earth because many areas of the planet have not been thoroughly studied. Some experts think that the deep oceans alone could contain 10 million new species! Protecting this diversity is a major environmental issue today.

Factors Affecting Biodiversity

Biodiversity varies from place to place on Earth. **Factors that affect biodiversity in an ecosystem include area, climate, and diversity of niches.**

Area Within an ecosystem, a large area will contain more species than a small area. For example, suppose you were counting tree species in a forest. You would find far more tree species in a 10-square-meter area than in a 1-square-meter area.

Diversity of Species

Insects
751,000

Protists —
57,700

Other animals
281,000

Plants
248,400

Fungi
69,000

Bacteria
4,800

Figure 10 Organisms of many kinds are part of Earth's biodiversity.
Interpreting Graphs Which group of organisms has the greatest number of species?

In Costa Rica, which is half the size of Tennessee, there are 850 species of birds—200 more than in all the rest of North America.

A 10-hectare area of forest in Borneo contains 700 species of trees, as many as all of North America.

A single river in Brazil contains more species than all of the rivers in the United States combined.

Figure 11 Tropical ecosystems tend to be more diverse than those farther from the equator.

Climate In general, the number of species increases from the poles toward the equator. The tropical rain forests of Latin America, southeast Asia, and central Africa are the most diverse ecosystems in the world. These forests cover about 6 percent of Earth's land surface and contain over half of the world's species.

The reason for the great biodiversity in the tropics is not fully understood. Many scientists hypothesize that it has to do with climate. For example, tropical rain forests have fairly constant temperatures and large amounts of rainfall throughout the year. Many plants in these regions have year-round growing seasons. This means that food is available for other organisms year-round.

Figure 12 Coral reefs are the second most diverse ecosystems. *Applying Concepts What is one reason why coral reefs are so diverse?*

Niche Diversity Coral reefs make up less than 1 percent of the oceans' area. But reefs are home to 20 percent of the world's saltwater fish species. Coral reefs are the second most diverse ecosystems in the world. Found only in shallow, warm waters, coral reefs are often called the rain forests of the sea. A reef provides many different niches for organisms that live under, on, and among the coral. This enables more species to live in the reef than in a more uniform habitat such as a flat sandbar.

☑ *Checkpoint What is one possible reason that tropical regions have the greatest biodiversity?*

The Value of Biodiversity

Perhaps you are wondering how biodiversity is important. Does it matter whether there are 50 or 5,000 species of ferns in some faraway rain forest? Is it necessary to protect every one of these species?

Figure 13 Ecosystem tours such as safaris can provide income for local people. These tourists are observing giraffes in Botswana.

There are many reasons why preserving biodiversity is important. The simplest reason is that wild organisms and ecosystems are a source of beauty and recreation.

Economic Value Many plants, animals, and other organisms are essential for human survival. In addition to providing food and oxygen, these organisms supply raw materials for clothing, medicine, and other products. No one knows how many other useful species have not yet been identified.

Ecosystems are economically valuable, too. For example, many companies now run wildlife tours in rain forests, savannas, mountain ranges, and other locations. This ecosystem tourism, or "ecotourism," is an important source of jobs and money for nations such as Brazil, Costa Rica, and Kenya.

Value to the Ecosystem All the species in an ecosystem are connected to one another. Species may depend on one another for food and shelter. A change that affects one species will surely affect all the others.

Some species play a particularly important role. A species that influences the survival of many other species in an ecosystem is called a **keystone species.** If a keystone species disappears, the entire ecosystem may change. For example, the sea stars in Figure 14 are a keystone species in their ecosystem. The sea stars prey mostly on the mussels that live in tide pools. When researchers removed the sea stars from an area, the mussels began to outcompete many of the other species in the tide pool. The sea star predators had kept the population of mussels in check, allowing other species to live. When the keystone species disappeared, the balance in the ecosystem was destroyed.

Figure 14 These sea stars on the Washington coast are an example of a keystone species. By preying on mussels, the sea stars keep the mussels from taking over the ecosystem.

Gene Pool Diversity

The organisms in a healthy population have a diversity of traits. As you learned in Chapter 3, these traits are determined by genes. Every organism receives a combination of genes from its parents. Genes determine the organism's characteristics, from its size and appearance to its ability to fight disease. The organisms in one species share many genes. But each organism also has some genes that differ from those of other individuals. These individual differences make up the total gene "pool" of that species.

Species that lack a diverse gene pool are less able to adapt to disease or parasites. For example, most crops, such as wheat and corn, have very little diversity. These species are bred to be very uniform. If a disease or parasite attacks, the whole population could be affected. A fungus once wiped out much of the corn crop in the United States in this way. Fortunately, there are many wild varieties of corn that have slightly different genes. At least some of these plants contain genes that make them more resistant to the fungus. Scientists were able to breed corn that was not affected by the fungus. Keeping a diverse gene pool helps ensure that crops can survive such problems.

Figure 15 Just as diversity of species is important to an ecosystem, diversity of genes is important within a species. Diverse genes give these potatoes their rainbow of colors.

☑ *Checkpoint* *What do an organism's genes determine?*

Extinction of Species

The disappearance of all members of a species from Earth is called **extinction.** Extinction is a natural process. Many species that once lived on Earth, from dinosaurs to dodos, are now extinct. But in the last few centuries, the number of species becoming extinct has increased dramatically.

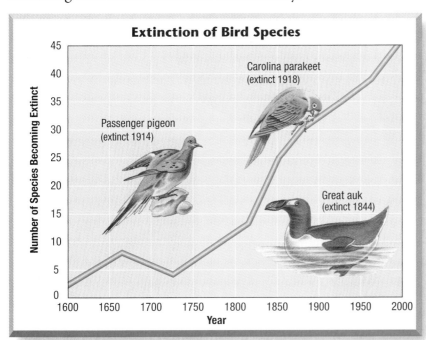

Extinction of Bird Species

Carolina parakeet (extinct 1918)

Passenger pigeon (extinct 1914)

Great auk (extinct 1844)

Figure 16 This graph shows the rate of extinction of bird species in the last 400 years.
Interpreting Graphs How many bird species became extinct in 1750? In 1850? In 1950?

Once a population drops below a certain level, the species may not be able to recover. For example, millions of passenger pigeons once darkened the skies in the United States. People hunted the birds for sport and food, killing many hundreds of thousands. This was only part of the total population of passenger pigeons. But at some point, there were not enough birds to reproduce and increase the population. Only after the birds disappeared did people realize that the species could not survive without its enormous numbers.

Species in danger of becoming extinct in the near future are considered **endangered species.** Species that could become endangered in the near future are considered **threatened species.**

EXPLORING *Endangered Species*

A broad range of species and habitats are represented on the endangered list in the United States.

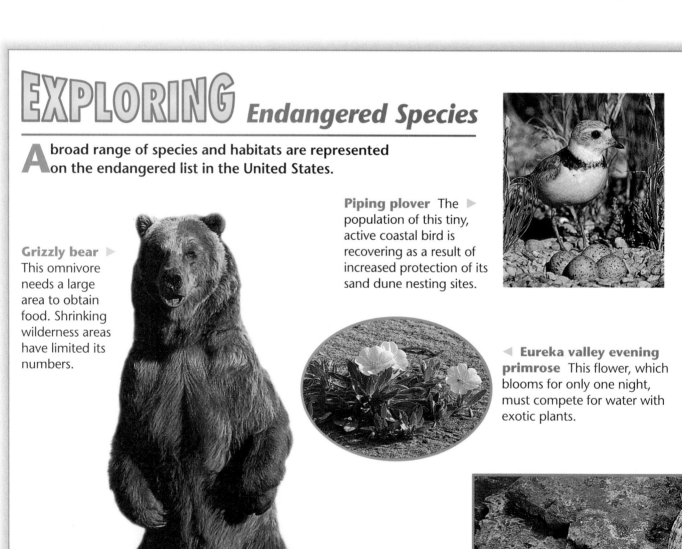

Grizzly bear ▶ This omnivore needs a large area to obtain food. Shrinking wilderness areas have limited its numbers.

Piping plover The ▶ population of this tiny, active coastal bird is recovering as a result of increased protection of its sand dune nesting sites.

◀ **Eureka valley evening primrose** This flower, which blooms for only one night, must compete for water with exotic plants.

Exploring Endangered Species shows some organisms that are endangered in the United States. Threatened and endangered species are found on every continent and in every ocean. Ensuring that these species survive is one way to protect Earth's biodiversity.

Causes of Extinction

A natural event, such as an earthquake or volcano, can damage an ecosystem, wiping out populations or even some species. **Human activities can also threaten biodiversity. These activities include habitat destruction, poaching, pollution, and the introduction of exotic species.**

◄ **Steller's sea lion** This mammal competes with fishermen for its prey along the Pacific coast.

Schaus swallowtail ▶ butterfly Threatened by habitat loss and pesticide pollution in the Florida Keys, this butterfly was nearly wiped out by Hurricane Andrew.

◄ **New Mexico ridgenose rattlesnake** Illegal collectors have reduced the population of this rare snake, the largest known group of which lives in a single canyon.

▲ **Whooping crane** Threatened by habitat destruction and disease, half of the remaining population of this wading bird is in captivity. The species seems to be recovering well since its lowest point in the 1940s.

Figure 17 Building this subdivision caused the habitats in the area to change. Open land was replaced by houses, streets, and yards.
Inferring How would these changes affect species in this area?

Communicating

ACTIVITY

Use references from enviromental organizations or your library to discover what threatened and endangered species live in your state. With your classmates, develop a brochure featuring pictures and facts about these species. With your teacher's permission, distribute your brochure at stores or libraries in your area.

Habitat Destruction   The major cause of extinction is **habitat destruction,** the loss of a natural habitat. This can occur when forests are cleared to build towns or create grazing land. Plowing grasslands or filling in wetlands greatly changes those ecosystems. Some species may not be able to survive such changes to their habitats.

Breaking larger habitats into smaller, isolated pieces, or fragments, is called **habitat fragmentation.** For example, building a road through a forest disrupts habitats. This makes trees more vulnerable to wind damage. Plants may be less likely to successfully disperse their seeds. Habitat fragmentation is also very harmful to large mammals. These animals usually need large areas of land to find enough food to survive. They may not be able to obtain enough resources in a small area. They may also be injured trying to cross to another area.

Poaching   The illegal killing or removal of wildlife species is called **poaching.** Many endangered animals are hunted for their skin, fur, teeth, horns, or claws. These things are used for making medicines, jewelry, coats, belts, and shoes.

People illegally remove organisms from their habitats to sell them as exotic pets. Tropical fish, tortoises, and parrots are very popular pets, making them valuable to poachers. Endangered plants may be illegally dug up and sold as houseplants. Others are poached to be used as medicines.

Pollution   Some species are endangered because of pollution. Substances that cause pollution, called pollutants, may reach animals through the water they drink or air they breathe. Pollutants may also settle in the soil. From there they are absorbed by plants, and build up in other organisms through the food chain. Pollutants may kill or weaken organisms or cause birth defects.

Exotic Species   Introducing exotic species into an ecosystem can threaten biodiversity. When European sailors began visiting Hawaii a couple of hundred years ago, rats from their ships escaped onto the islands. Without any predators in Hawaii, the rats multiplied quickly. They ate the eggs of the nene goose. To protect the geese, people brought the rat-eating mongoose from India to help control the rat population. Unfortunately, the mongooses preferred eating eggs to eating rats. With both the rats and the mongoose eating its eggs, the nene goose is now endangered.

Protecting Biodiversity

Many people are working to preserve the world's biodiversity. Some focus on protecting individual endangered species, such as the giant panda or the Florida panther. Others try to protect entire ecosystems, such as the Great Barrier Reef in Australia. **Many programs to protect biodiversity combine scientific and legal approaches.**

Captive Breeding One scientific approach to protecting severely endangered species is captive breeding. **Captive breeding** is the mating of animals in zoos or wildlife preserves. Scientists care for the young to increase their chance of survival. These offspring are then released back into the wild.

A captive breeding program was the only hope for the California condor. California condors are the largest birds in North America. They became endangered as a result of habitat destruction, poaching, and pollution. By the mid-1980s there were fewer than ten California condors in the wild. Fewer than 30 were in zoos. Scientists captured all the wild condors and brought them to the zoos. Soon afterward, the first California condor chick was successfully bred in captivity. Today, there are more than 100 California condors in zoos. Some condors have even been returned to the wild. Though successful, this program has cost more than $20 million. It is not possible to save many species in this costly way.

Laws and Treaties Laws can help protect individual species. Some nations have made it illegal to sell endangered species or products made from them. In the United States, the Endangered Species Act of 1973 prohibits importing or trading products made from threatened or endangered species. This law also requires the development of plans to save endangered species.

Figure 18 Captive breeding programs use a scientific approach to protect endangered species.
A. California condor chicks raised in captivity need to learn what adult condors look like. Here, a scientist uses a condor puppet to feed and groom a chick.
B. These young green turtles were hatched in the laboratory. Now a researcher is releasing the turtles into their natural ocean habitat.

Figure 19 Preserving whole habitats is probably the most effective way to protect biodiversity.

American alligators, Pacific gray whales, and green sea turtles are just a few of the species that have begun to recover as a result of legal protection.

The most important international treaty protecting wildlife is the Convention on International Trade in Endangered Species. Eighty nations signed this treaty in 1973. This treaty lists nearly 700 threatened and endangered species that cannot be traded for profit. Laws like these are difficult to enforce. Even so, they have helped to reduce the poaching of many endangered species, including African elephants, snow leopards, sperm whales, and mountain gorillas.

Habitat Preservation The most effective way to preserve biodiversity is to protect whole ecosystems. Preserving whole habitats saves not only endangered species, but also other species that depend on them.

Beginning in 1872 with Yellowstone National Park, the world's first national park, many countries have set aside wildlife habitats as parks and refuges. In addition, private organizations have purchased millions of hectares of endangered habitats throughout the world. Today, there are about 7,000 nature parks, preserves, and refuges in the world.

To be most effective, reserves must have the characteristics of diverse ecosystems. For example, they must be large enough to support the populations that live there. The reserves must contain a variety of niches. And of course, it is still necessary to keep the air, land, and water clean, remove exotic species, and control poaching.

Section 3 Review

1. What are three factors that affect biodiversity?
2. List four possible causes of extinction.
3. Give an example of a legal approach and a scientific approach to preventing extinction.
4. Which are the most diverse ecosystems on Earth?
5. Identify three ways in which biodiversity is important.
6. **Thinking Critically Making Generalizations** Explain how the statement "In the web of life, all things are connected" relates to keystone species.

CHAPTER PROJECT

Check Your Progress

Visit your plot regularly. Use field guides to identify the organisms you observe. Record their locations within your plot along with their common and scientific names. You should also be planning how to present your findings. Consider using a series of drawings, a flip chart, a computer presentation, or a video of your plot with closeups of the species you have identified. (*Hint:* Be sure to include the data you collected on abiotic factors.)

SECTION 1 Environmental Issues

INTEGRATING ENVIRONMENTAL SCIENCE

Key Ideas

◆ Three types of environmental issues are resource use, population growth, and pollution.

◆ Environmental science is the study of the natural processes that occur in the environment and how humans can affect them.

◆ Making environmental decisions requires balancing different viewpoints and weighing the costs and benefits of proposals.

Key Terms

renewable resources
nonrenewable resources
pollution

SECTION 2 Forests and Fisheries

Key Ideas

◆ Because new trees can be planted to replace those that are cut down, forests can be renewable resources.

◆ Managing fisheries involves setting fishing limits, changing fishing methods, developing aquaculture techniques, and finding new resources.

Key Terms

clear-cutting
selective cutting
sustainable yield
fishery
aquaculture

SECTION 3 Biodiversity

Key Ideas

◆ Factors that affect biodiversity include area, climate, and diversity of niches.

◆ Tropical rain forests and coral reefs are the two most diverse ecosystems.

◆ Human activities that threaten biodiversity include habitat destruction, poaching, pollution, and the introduction of exotic species.

◆ Three techniques for protecting biodiversity are regulating capture and trade, captive breeding, and habitat preservation.

Key Terms

biodiversity   habitat destruction
keystone species   habitat fragmentation
extinction   poaching
endangered species   captive breeding
threatened species

Organizing Information

Concept Map Copy the biodiversity concept map below onto a sheet of paper. Complete it and add a title. (For more on concept maps, see the Skills Handbook.)

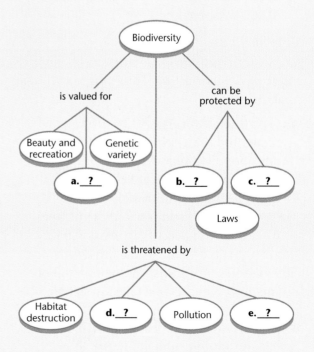

Reviewing Content

 For more review of key concepts, see the Interactive Student Tutorial CD-ROM.

Multiple Choice

Choose the letter of the best answer.

1. Which of the following is a benefit of drilling for oil in Antarctica?
   a. It would be expensive to drill there.
   b. It would create new jobs.
   c. It could harm the area wildlife.
   d. It would be difficult to transport the oil.

2. The practice of raising fish for food is called
   a. aquaculture.   b. overfishing.
   c. poaching.   d. captive breeding.

3. The most diverse ecosystems in the world are
   a. coral reefs.   b. deserts.
   c. grasslands.   d. tropical rain forests.

4. If all members of a species disappear from Earth, that species is
   a. extinct.   b. endangered.
   c. nonrenewable.   d. threatened.

5. The illegal removal from the wild or killing of an endangered species is called
   a. habitat destruction.
   b. poaching.
   c. pollution.
   d. captive breeding.

True or False

If the statement is true, write true. If it is false, change the underlined word or words to make the statement true.

6. The three main types of environmental issues today are resource use, pollution, and population growth.

7. Forests and fisheries are examples of nonrenewable resources.

8. A sustainable yield is a number of trees that can be regularly harvested without affecting the health of the forest.

9. A species that influences the survival of many other species in an ecosystem is called a(n) endangered species.

10. The most effective way to protect biodiversity is through habitat fragmentation.

Checking Concepts

11. Give an example of a personal or local environmental issue and an example of a national or global environmental issue.

12. Explain how environmental decisions are made.

13. Compare the effects of clear-cutting and selective cutting on forest ecosystems.

14. Describe one way that people can prevent overfishing.

15. Explain how habitat destruction affects species.

16. **Writing to Learn** You are a member of the county land use commission. Hundreds of people are moving to your county every day. You must make a decision regarding how to manage a 5,000-hectare woodland area in your county. The proposals include using the land for housing, for a new factory, for community gardens, or for a wildlife refuge. List the costs and benefits of each option. Then choose one and write an editorial for a newspaper explaining your position.

Thinking Critically

17. **Relating Cause and Effect** Explain how human population growth affects other species on Earth.

18. **Making Generalizations** Describe how an exotic species can threaten other species in an ecosystem.

19. **Predicting** How could the extinction of a species today affect your life 20 years from now?

20. **Making Judgments** Suppose you were given $1 million toward saving an endangered turtle species. You could use the money to start a captive breeding program for the turtles. Or you could use the money to purchase and protect part of the turtle's habitat. How would you spend the money? Explain your answer.

Applying Skills

One study identifies the reasons that mammal and bird species are endangered or threatened. Use the table to answer Questions 21–23.

Reason	Mammals	Birds
Poaching	31%	20%
Habitat loss	32%	60%
Exotic species	17%	12%
Other causes	20%	8%

21. **Graphing** Make a bar graph comparing the reasons that mammals and birds are endangered and threatened. Show percents for each animal group on the vertical axis and reasons on the horizontal axis.

22. **Interpreting Data** What is the major reason that mammals become endangered or threatened? What mainly endangers or threatens birds?

23. **Developing Hypotheses** Suggest explanations for the differences between the data for mammals and birds.

Performance ▽ CHAPTER PROJECT Assessment

Present Your Project In your presentation, describe the biodiversity in your plot. Suggest an explanation for any patterns you observed. Make sure each person in your group has a role in the presentation. Before the presentation day, brainstorm questions your classmates might ask. Then prepare answers for them.

Reflect and Record In your journal, write what you learned from observing a single location. Which of your findings were surprising? What was the hardest part of this project? What would you do differently if you did this project again?

Test Preparation

Use these questions to prepare for standardized tests.

Read the passage. Then answer Questions 24–26.

The Pacific yew tree is very resistant to disease and insects. Scientists began studying the bark of the Pacific yew to find out why it was so hardy. They discovered a chemical in the tree's bark, named taxol, that protects the tree from damage.

When scientists experimented with taxol in the laboratory, they found that the chemical affects cancer cells in an unusual way. Typically, cancer cells grow and divide rapidly, forming a mass of cells called a tumor. Taxol prevents cancer cells from dividing and shrinks certain types of tumors. Today, taxol is used to treat thousands of cancer patients each year.

Many scientists are concerned that the supply of Pacific yew trees has dwindled. Unfortunately, much of the yew tree's natural habitat has been lost. Only recently have people realized the importance of protecting the remaining Pacific yew trees for future generations.

24. What is the main idea of this passage?
    a. Taxol is used to treat cancer patients.
    b. Pacific yew trees produce a cancer-fighting substance.
    c. The Pacific yew tree is resistant to diseases.
    d. Cancer cells grow and divide rapidly.

25. According to this passage, what effect does taxol have on cancer cells?
    a. Taxol causes cancerous tumors to form.
    b. Taxol causes cancer cells to divide rapidly.
    c. Taxol prevents cancer cells from dividing.
    d. Taxol has no effect on cancer cells.

26. Why did scientists first become interested in studying the Pacific yew tree?
    a. The tree's habitat was being destroyed.
    b. They wanted to understand how taxol shrunk tumors.
    c. They wanted to learn about taxol's chemical structure.
    d. They wanted to find out why the Pacific yew tree was so hardy.

African Rain Forests
Preserving Diversity

What forest—

is home to a beetle with wings larger than a sparrow's?

contains a frog that's 30 cm long?

is home to gorillas, chimpanzees, and pygmy hippos?

▲ Ball python

▲ Comet moth

I t's an African rain forest. Thousands of plants and animals live here, from colorful orchids to fruit bats, tree frogs, and elephants.

The rain forests of Africa grow in a band near the equator. About 80 percent of the rain-forested area is in central Africa, in the vast basin of the great Congo River. Some parts of the central African rain forest are so dense and hard to reach that explorers have never visited them. East Africa, which is drier and more heavily populated, has only scattered areas of rain forest.

The rain forest regions of the world have similar life forms and niches. But the rain forests of different continents have very different species.

African Rain Forests

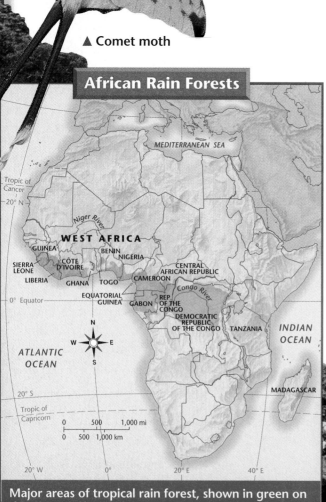

MEDITERRANEAN SEA

Tropic of Cancer
20° N

Niger River

WEST AFRICA

GUINEA
BENIN
NIGERIA
SIERRA LEONE
CÔTE D'IVOIRE
LIBERIA
GHANA
TOGO
CAMEROON
CENTRAL AFRICAN REPUBLIC

0° Equator

EQUATORIAL GUINEA
GABON
REP. OF THE CONGO
Congo River
DEMOCRATIC REPUBLIC OF THE CONGO
TANZANIA
INDIAN OCEAN

ATLANTIC OCEAN

20° S

MADAGASCAR

Tropic of Capricorn

0   500   1,000 mi
0 500 1,000 km

20° W   0°   20° E   40° E

Major areas of tropical rain forest, shown in green on the map, are located near the equator.

Bonobo chimpanzee ▶

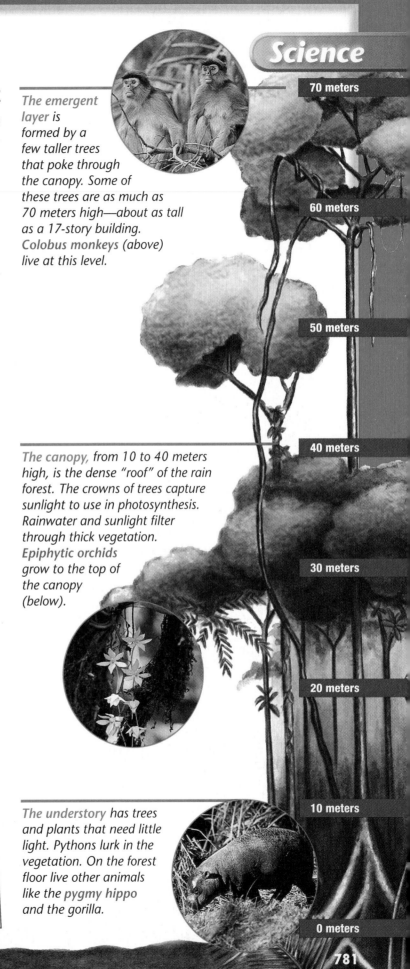

Layers of the Rain Forest

From above, the rain forest may look like a mass of broccoli. But it's really many forests in one—like different levels in an apartment building.

Each layer from the forest floor to the emergent, or top, layer varies in climate and is home to different plants and animals. The emergent layer captures the most rain, sunlight, heat, and wind. Colobus monkeys swing from vines and branches. Vast numbers of birds live in the trees.

Over time, African rain forest plants and animals have developed unusual adaptations to life at different layers of the forest. Some monkeys living in the canopy have long, muscular legs. They can run and leap through the branches. Guenons and baboons have strong teeth and jaws that allow them to crunch fruits, nuts, and seeds. Other monkeys have shorter tails but longer front legs. They live mainly on the forest floor.

In the understory, small animals such as frogs and squirrels "fly." They have tough membranes that stretch between their front and hind legs and allow them to glide from branch to branch.

The forest floor is dark, humid, and still. Termites feed on dead leaves and brush. Many plants have large leaves that allow them to catch the dim light. Some animals, such as frogs and insects, grow to gigantic sizes. Others are little, like the pygmy hippo that runs through the forest.

Science Activity

Design a rain forest animal that is adapted to life at a certain level of the rain forest. Consider how your animal lives, how it travels, and what food it eats. Outline its characteristics and explain how each adaptation helps the animal survive. Draw a sketch.

The emergent layer is formed by a few taller trees that poke through the canopy. Some of these trees are as much as 70 meters high—about as tall as a 17-story building. Colobus monkeys (above) live at this level.

The canopy, from 10 to 40 meters high, is the dense "roof" of the rain forest. The crowns of trees capture sunlight to use in photosynthesis. Rainwater and sunlight filter through thick vegetation. Epiphytic orchids grow to the top of the canopy (below).

The understory has trees and plants that need little light. Pythons lurk in the vegetation. On the forest floor live other animals like the pygmy hippo and the gorilla.

70 meters

60 meters

50 meters

40 meters

30 meters

20 meters

10 meters

0 meters

781

Mathematics

Reaching for Sunlight

Most rain forest trees are evergreens with broad leathery leaves. Some, like the African yellowwood, are conifers. Because the forest is so dense, trees must grow tall and straight to reach sunlight at the top of the canopy.

Along rivers, the floor and understory of the rain forest are a tangle of plants. Early explorers traveling the rivers assumed that the entire rain forest had similar thick vegetation, or jungle. In fact, the rain forest floor is surprisingly bare.

The canopy trees block the sunlight from plants below. Shaded by the dense canopy, the understory and forest floor are humid and dark. Water drips from the leaves of the canopy high overhead. Young trees have the best chance to grow when trees fall, opening up sunny clearings.

West Africa's tropical forests contain many valuable trees. African mahogany and teak are used to make furniture, tools, and boats. Oil from the oil palm is used in soaps, candles, and some foods. Trees such as ebony that can tolerate shade, grow slowly and develop dark, hard, long-lasting wood.

Trees of the Rain Forest	
Tree	Maximum Height
African oil palm	18 m
African yellowwood	20 m
Cape fig	7 m
Ebony	30 m
Kapok	70 m
Raffia palm	12 m
Teak	46 m

Math Activity

The table on this page gives the height of some of the trees in the rain forest. Use the information in the table to make a bar graph. On the horizontal axis, label the trees. Use the vertical axis to show the height of the trees.

◆ Which tree has the greatest maximum height? The least maximum height?

◆ What is the height difference between the tallest and the shortest trees?

◆ What is the average height of all the trees shown in the graph?

African oil palms ▲ grow in Nigeria.

◀ This African sculpture is made of wood from the African rain forest.

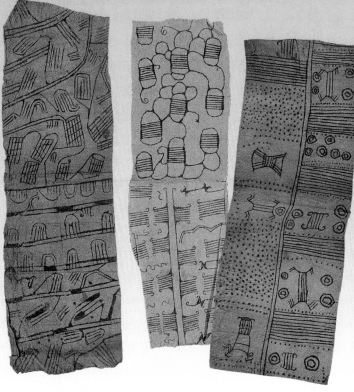

The Mbuti (above) hunt and fish along the Congo River. Their clothing is made of bark cloth (left).

Ituri Forest People

The native peoples of the African rain forest live as they have for thousands of years—by hunting and gathering. The forest supplies them with everything they need—food, water, firewood, building materials, and medicines.

One group of rain forest dwellers is the Mbuti people. The Mbuti live in the Ituri forest of the Democratic Republic of the Congo. Many of the Mbuti are quite small. The men hunt game, such as gazelle and antelope. The women gather wild fruits, nuts, and greens. Their traditional Mbuti clothing is made of tree bark and is wrapped around the waist. The bark is beaten to make it soft. It is then decorated with geometric designs.

Most Mbuti live as nomads, with no single settled home. Every few months they set up new hunting grounds. They build temporary dome-shaped huts of branches and leaves. Hunting groups of about 10 to 25 families live together. They divide the hunting area among the family groups. On occasion, larger groups gather for ceremonies with dances and ritual music.

Modern Africa has brought changes to the forest people, especially for those who live near the edges of the rain forest. For a few months of the year, some Mbuti work as laborers for farmers who live in villages at the edge of the forest. When their work is finished, the Mbuti return to the Ituri forest. Most forest people prefer not to cultivate their own land. Since the farmers don't hunt, they trade their goods for meat. In exchange for meat, the Mbuti receive goods such as iron tools, cooking pots, clothes, bananas, and other farm produce.

Social Studies Activity

List the goods that forest people and farmers might have to trade. Assume that no modern conveniences, such as tractors and stoves, are available. Write a paragraph or two explaining how goods might be exchanged. Assign a value to the farmers' goods and the Mbuti goods, depending upon each group's needs. For example, decide how much meat a farmer should pay for medicines from the rain forest. How would the trading process change if money were exchanged?

783

Climbing the Canopy

Much of the rain forest is still a mystery because it's so difficult for scientists to study the canopy. Native forest people sometimes climb these tall trees using strong, thick vines called lianas as support. But rain forest scientists have had to find different methods. Naturalist Gerald Durrell, working in the African rain forest, was lucky enough to find another way to observe the canopy. He describes it here:

While the canopy is one of the most richly inhabited regions of the forest it is also the one that causes the naturalist the greatest frustration. There he is, down in the gloom among the giant tree trunks, hearing the noises of animal life high above him and having half-eaten fruit, flowers, or seeds rained on him by legions of animals high in their sunlit domain—all of which he cannot see. Under these circumstances the naturalist develops a very bad temper and a permanent crick in the neck.

However, there was one occasion when I managed to transport myself into the forest canopy, and it was a magical experience. It happened in West Africa when I was camped on the thickly forested lower slopes of a mountain called N'da Ali. Walking through the forest one day I found I was walking along the edge of a great step cut out of the mountain. The cliff face, covered with creepers, dropped away for about 50 yards, so that although I was walking through forest, just next to me and slightly below was the canopy of the forest growing up from the base of the cliff. This cliff was over half a mile in length and provided me with a natural balcony from which I could observe the treetop life simply by lying on the cliff edge, concealed in the low undergrowth.

Over a period of about a week I spent hours up there and a whole pageant of wildlife passed by. The numbers of birds were incredible, ranging from minute glittering sunbirds in rainbow coloring, zooming like helicopters from blossom to blossom as they fed on the nectar, to the flocks of huge black hornbills with their monstrous yellow beaks who flew in such an ungainly manner and made such a noise over their choice of forest fruits.

From early morning to evening when it grew too dark to see, I watched this parade of creatures. Troops of monkeys swept past, followed by attendant flocks of birds who fed eagerly on the insects that the monkeys disturbed during their noisy crashing through the trees. Squirrels chased each other, or hotly pursued lizards, or simply lay spread-eagled on branches high up in the trees, enjoying the sun.

Language Arts Activity

◆ Besides being an experienced naturalist and writer, Gerald Durrell is also a careful observer. In this selection, he describes in detail the "magical experience" of being in the canopy. Reread Durrell's description. Now work with a partner to write and design a pamphlet that will persuade visitors to come to an African rain forest. For your pamphlet, write strong, lively descriptions of what you might see, hear, and experience. Be persuasive.

Tie It Together

Celebrate Diversity

Rain forests have the greatest biodiversity—variety of plant and animal life—of any ecosystem on Earth. Many species have yet to be discovered! Plan a display for your school to celebrate biodiversity in the rain forests. Include drawings, photos, and detailed captions.

◆ On a large map, locate and label Earth's tropical rain forests. Divide into groups to choose one rain forest region to research, such as Africa, Brazil, Costa Rica, Hawaii, Indonesia, or Borneo.

◆ Have your group study several animal and plant species in its chosen rain forest. You might choose monkeys, butterflies, birds, orchids, or medicinal plants.

◆ For each species, describe its appearance, where it occurs in the rain forest, its role in the ecosystem, and how it is useful to humans.

British conservationist Gerald Durrell wrote about his adventures with wildlife around the world. He established a zoo on the British island of Jersey and worked to preserve threatened species. In the photo, Durrell holds an anteater.

Think Like a Scientist

Although you may not know it, you think like a scientist every day. Whenever you ask a question and explore possible answers, you use many of the same skills that scientists do. Some of these skills are described on this page.

Observing

When you use one or more of your five senses to gather information about the world, you are **observing.** Hearing a dog bark, counting twelve green seeds, and smelling smoke are all observations. To increase the power of their senses, scientists sometimes use microscopes, telescopes, or other instruments that help them make more detailed observations.

An observation must be an accurate report of what your senses detect. It is important to keep careful records of your observations in science class by writing or drawing in a notebook. The information collected through observations is called evidence, or data.

Inferring

When you interpret an observation, you are **inferring,** or making an inference. For example, if you hear your dog barking, you may infer that someone is at your front door. To make this inference, you combine the evidence—the barking dog—and your experience or knowledge—you know that your dog barks when strangers approach—to reach a logical conclusion.

Notice that an inference is not a fact; it is only one of many possible interpretations for an observation. For example, your dog may be barking because it wants to go for a walk. An inference may turn out to be incorrect even if it is based on accurate observations and logical reasoning. The only way to find out if an inference is correct is to investigate further.

Predicting

When you listen to the weather forecast, you hear many predictions about the next day's weather—what the temperature will be, whether it will rain, and how windy it will be. Weather forecasters use observations and knowledge of weather patterns to predict the weather. The skill of **predicting** involves making an inference about a future event based on current evidence or past experience.

Because a prediction is an inference, it may prove to be false. In science class, you can test some of your predictions by doing experiments. For example, suppose you predict that larger paper airplanes can fly farther than smaller airplanes. How could you test your prediction?

 Use the photograph to answer the questions below.

Observing Look closely at the photograph. List at least three observations.

Inferring Use your observations to make an inference about what is happening. What experience or knowledge did you use to make the inference?

Predicting Predict what will happen next. On what evidence or experience do you base your prediction?

Classifying

Could you imagine searching for a book in the library if the books were shelved in no particular order? Your trip to the library would be an all-day event! Luckily, librarians group books on similar topics or by the same author. Grouping items that are alike in some way is called **classifying.** You can classify items in many ways: by size, by shape, by use, and by other important characteristics.

Like librarians, scientists use the skill of classifying to organize information and objects. When things are sorted into groups, the relationships among them become easier to understand.

Classify the objects in the photograph into two groups based on any characteristic you choose. Then use another characteristic to classify the objects into three groups.

ACTIVITY

Making Models

Have you ever drawn a picture to help someone understand what you were saying? Such a drawing is one type of model. A model is a picture, diagram, computer image, or other representation of a complex object or process. **Making models** helps people understand things that they cannot observe directly.

Scientists often use models to represent things that are either very large or very small, such as the planets in the solar system, or the parts of a cell. Such models are physical models—drawings or three-dimensional structures that look

like the real thing. Other models are mental models—mathematical equations or words that describe how something works.

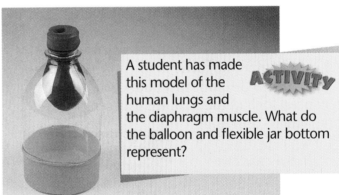

A student has made this model of the human lungs and the diaphragm muscle. What do the balloon and flexible jar bottom represent?

ACTIVITY

Communicating

Whenever you talk on the phone, write a letter, or listen to your teacher at school, you are communicating. **Communicating** is the process of sharing ideas and information with others. Communicating effectively requires many skills, including writing, reading, speaking, listening, and making models.

Scientists communicate to share results, information, and opinions. Scientists often communicate about their work in journals, over the telephone, in letters, and on the Internet. They also attend scientific meetings where they share their ideas with one another in person.

On a sheet of paper, write out clear, detailed directions for making a peanut butter and jelly sandwich. Then exchange directions with a partner. Take your partner's directions home and follow the directions exactly. How successful were you at making the sandwich? How could your partner have communicated more clearly?

ACTIVITY

Making Measurements

When scientists make observations, it is not sufficient to say that something is "big" or "heavy." Instead, scientists use instruments to measure just how big or heavy an object is. By measuring, scientists can express their observations more precisely and communicate more information about what they observe.

Measuring in SI

The standard system of measurement used by scientists around the world is known as the International System of Units, which is abbreviated as SI (in French, *Système International d'Unités*). SI units are easy to use because they are based on multiples of 10. Each unit is ten times larger than the next smallest unit and one tenth the size of the next largest unit. The table lists the prefixes used to name the most common SI units.

Common SI Prefixes

Prefix	Symbol	Meaning
kilo-	k	1,000
hecto-	h	100
deka-	da	10
deci-	d	0.1 (one tenth)
centi-	c	0.01 (one hundredth)
milli-	m	0.001 (one thousandth)

Length To measure length, or the distance between two points, the unit of measure is the **meter (m)**. One meter is the approximate distance from the floor to a doorknob. Long distances, such as the distance between two cities, are measured in kilometers (km). Small lengths are measured in centimeters (cm) or millimeters (mm). Scientists use metric rulers and meter sticks to measure length.

Common Conversions

1 km = 1,000 m
1 m = 100 cm
1 m = 1,000 mm
1 cm = 10 mm

The larger lines on the metric ruler in the picture show centimeter divisions, while the smaller, unnumbered lines show millimeter divisions. How many centimeters long is the leaf? How many millimeters long is it? **ACTIVITY**

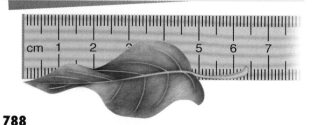

Liquid Volume To measure the volume of a liquid, or the amount of space it takes up, you will use a unit of measure known as the **liter (L)**. One liter is the approximate volume of a medium-sized carton of milk. Smaller volumes are measured in milliliters (mL). Scientists use graduated cylinders to measure liquid volume.

Common Conversion

1 L = 1,000 mL

The graduated cylinder in the picture is marked in milliliter divisions. Notice that the water in the cylinder has a curved surface. This curved surface is called the *meniscus*. To measure the volume, you must read the level at the lowest point of the meniscus. What is the volume of water in this graduated cylinder? **ACTIVITY**

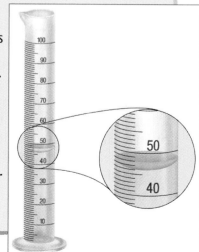

Mass To measure mass, or the amount of matter in an object, you will use a unit of measure known as the **gram (g).** One gram is approximately the mass of a paper clip. Larger masses are measured in kilograms (kg). Scientists use a balance to find the mass of an object.

Common Conversion

1 kg = 1,000 g

The electronic balance displays the mass of an egg in kilograms. What is the mass of the egg? Suppose a recipe for egg salad called for one kilogram of eggs. About how many eggs would you need?

ACTIVITY

Temperature
To measure the temperature of a substance, you will use the **Celsius scale.** Temperature is measured in degrees Celsius (°C) using a Celsius thermometer. Water freezes at 0°C and boils at 100°C.

ACTIVITY

What is the temperature of the liquid in degrees Celsius?

Converting SI Units

To use the SI system, you must know how to convert between units. Converting from one unit to another involves the skill of **calculating,** or using mathematical operations. Converting between SI units is similar to converting between dollars and dimes because both systems are based on multiples of ten.

Suppose you want to convert a length of 80 centimeters to meters. Follow these steps to convert between units.

1. Begin by writing down the measurement you want to convert—in this example, 80 centimeters.
2. Write a conversion factor that represents the relationship between the two units you are converting. In this example, the relationship is *1 meter = 100 centimeters.* Write this conversion factor as a fraction, making sure to place the units you are converting from (centimeters, in this example) in the denominator.

3. Multiply the measurement you want to convert by the fraction. When you do this, the units in the first measurement will cancel out with the units in the denominator. Your answer will be in the units you are converting to (meters, in this example).

Example

80 centimeters = ____?____ meters

$$80 \text{ centimeters} \times \frac{1 \text{ meter}}{100 \text{ centimeters}} = \frac{80 \text{ meters}}{100}$$

$$= 0.8 \text{ meters}$$

Convert between the following units.

ACTIVITY

1. 400 millimeters = __?__ meters
2. 0.25 liters = __?__ milliliters
3. 1,350 grams = __?__ kilograms

Conducting a Scientific Investigation

In some ways, scientists are like detectives, piecing together clues to learn about a process or event. One way that scientists gather clues is by carrying out experiments. An experiment tests an idea in a careful, orderly manner. Although not all experiments follow the same steps in the same order, many follow a pattern similar to the one described here.

Posing Questions

Experiments begin by asking a scientific question. A scientific question is one that can be answered by gathering evidence. For example, the question "Which freezes faster—fresh water or salt water?" is a scientific question because you can carry out an investigation and gather information to answer the question.

Developing a Hypothesis

The next step is to form a hypothesis. A **hypothesis** is a possible explanation for a set of observations or answer to a scientific question. In science, a hypothesis must be something that can be tested. A hypothesis can be worded as an *If…then…* statement. For example, a hypothesis might be *"If I add salt to fresh water, then the water will take longer to freeze."* A hypothesis worded this way serves as a rough outline of the experiment you should perform.

Designing an Experiment

Next you need to plan a way to test your hypothesis. Your plan should be written out as a step-by-step procedure and should describe the observations or measurements you will make.

Two important steps involved in designing an experiment are controlling variables and forming operational definitions.

Controlling Variables In a well-designed experiment, you need to keep all variables the same except for one. A **variable** is any factor that can change in an experiment. The factor that you change is called the **manipulated variable.** In this experiment, the manipulated variable is the amount of salt added to the water. Other factors, such as the amount of water or the starting temperature, are kept constant.

The factor that changes as a result of the manipulated variable is called the responding variable. The **responding variable** is what you measure or observe to obtain your results. In this experiment, the responding variable is how long the water takes to freeze.

An experiment in which all factors except one are kept constant is a **controlled experiment.** Most controlled experiments include a test called the control. In this experiment, Container 3 is the control. Because no salt is added to Container 3, you can compare the results from the other containers to it. Any difference in results must be due to the addition of salt alone.

Forming Operational Definitions

Another important aspect of a well-designed experiment is having clear operational definitions. An **operational definition** is a statement that describes how a particular variable is to be measured or how a term is to be defined. For example, in this experiment, how will you determine if the water has frozen? You might decide to insert a stick in each container at the start of the experiment. Your operational definition of "frozen" would be the time at which the stick can no longer move.

EXPERIMENTAL PROCEDURE

1. Fill 3 containers with 300 milliliters of cold tap water.

2. Add 10 grams of salt to Container 1; stir. Add 20 grams of salt to Container 2; stir. Add no salt to Container 3.

3. Place the 3 containers in a freezer.

4. Check the containers every 15 minutes. Record your observations.

Interpreting Data

The observations and measurements you make in an experiment are called data. At the end of an experiment, you need to analyze the data to look for any patterns or trends. Patterns often become clear if you organize your data in a data table or graph. Then think through what the data reveal. Do they support your hypothesis? Do they point out a flaw in your experiment? Do you need to collect more data?

Drawing Conclusions

A conclusion is a statement that sums up what you have learned from an experiment. When you draw a conclusion, you need to decide whether the data you collected support your hypothesis or not. You may need to repeat an experiment several times before you can draw any conclusions from it. Conclusions often lead you to pose new questions and plan new experiments to answer them.

Do birds in your neighborhood prefer to eat sunflower seeds or worms? Using the steps just described, plan a controlled experiment to investigate this problem.

ACTIVITY

Organizing Information

As you read this textbook, how can you make sense of all the information it contains? Some useful tools to help you organize information are shown on this page. These tools are called **graphic organizers** because they give you a visual picture of a topic, showing at a glance how key concepts are related.

Concept Maps

Concept maps are useful tools for organizing information on broad topics. A concept map begins with a general concept and shows how it can be broken down into more specific concepts. In that way, relationships between concepts become easier to understand.

A concept map is constructed by placing concept words (usually nouns) in ovals and connecting them with linking words. Often, the most general concept word is placed at the top, and the words become more specific as you move downward. Often the linking words, which are written on a line extending between two ovals, describe the relationship between the two concepts they connect. If you follow any string of concepts and linking words down the map, it should read like a sentence.

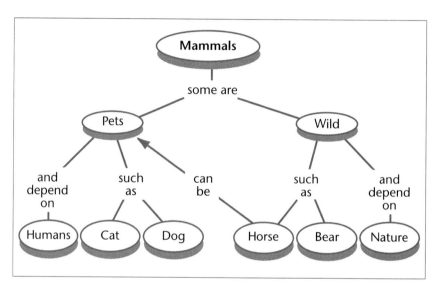

Some concept maps include linking words that connect a concept on one branch of the map to a concept on another branch. These linking words, called cross-linkages, show more complex interrelationships among concepts.

Compare/Contrast Tables

Compare/contrast tables are useful tools for sorting out the similarities and differences between two or more items. A table provides an organized framework in which to compare items based on specific characteristics that you identify.

To create a compare/contrast table, list the items to be compared across the top of a table. Then list the characteristics that will form the basis of your comparison in the left-hand

Characteristic	Baseball	Basketball
Number of Players	9	5
Playing Field	Baseball diamond	Basketball court
Equipment	Bat, baseball, mitts	Basket, basketball

column. Complete the table by filling in information about each characteristic, first for one item and then for the other.

Venn Diagrams

Another way to show similarities and differences between items is with a Venn diagram. A Venn diagram consists of two or more circles that partially overlap. Each circle represents a particular concept or idea. Common characteristics, or similarities, are written within the area of overlap between the two circles. Unique characteristics, or differences, are written in the parts of the circles outside the area of overlap.

To create a Venn diagram, draw two overlapping circles. Label the circles with the names of the items being compared. Write the

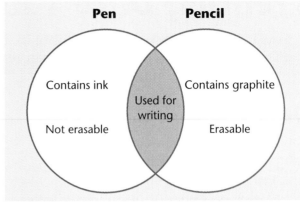

unique characteristics in each circle outside the area of overlap. Then write the shared characteristics within the area of overlap.

Flowcharts

A flowchart can help you understand the order in which certain events have occurred or should occur. Flowcharts are useful for outlining the stages in a process or the steps in a procedure.

To make a flowchart, write a brief description of each event in a box. Place the first event at the top of the page, followed by the second event, the third event, and so on. Then draw an arrow to connect each event to the one that occurs next.

Preparing Pasta

Boil water

↓

Cook pasta

↓

Drain water

↓

Add sauce

Cycle Diagrams

A cycle diagram can be used to show a sequence of events that is continuous, or cyclical. A continuous sequence does not have an end because, when the final event is over, the first event begins again. Like a flowchart, a cycle diagram can help you understand the order of events.

To create a cycle diagram, write a brief description of each event in a box. Place one event at the top of the page in the center. Then, moving in a clockwise direction around an imaginary circle, write each event in its proper sequence. Draw arrows that connect each event to the one that occurs next, forming a continuous circle.

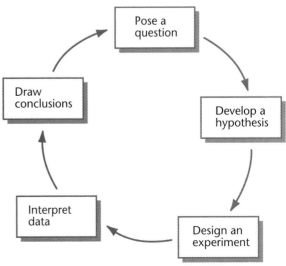

Steps in a Science Experiment

Creating Data Tables and Graphs

How can you make sense of the data in a science experiment? The first step is to organize the data to help you understand them. Data tables and graphs are helpful tools for organizing data.

Data Tables

You have gathered your materials and set up your experiment. But before you start, you need to plan a way to record what happens during the experiment. By creating a data table, you can record your observations and measurements in an orderly way.

Suppose, for example, that a scientist conducted an experiment to find out how many Calories people of different body masses burn while doing various activities. The data table shows the results.

Notice in this data table that the manipulated variable (body mass) is the heading of one column. The responding variable (for Experiment 1, the number of Calories burned while bicycling) is the heading of the next column. Additional columns were added for related experiments.

CALORIES BURNED IN 30 MINUTES OF ACTIVITY			
Body Mass	Experiment 1 Bicycling	Experiment 2 Playing Basketball	Experiment 3 Watching Television
30 kg	60 Calories	120 Calories	21 Calories
40 kg	77 Calories	164 Calories	27 Calories
50 kg	95 Calories	206 Calories	33 Calories
60 kg	114 Calories	248 Calories	38 Calories

Bar Graphs

To compare how many Calories a person burns doing various activities, you could create a bar graph. A bar graph is used to display data in a number of separate, or distinct, categories. In this example, bicycling, playing basketball, and watching television are three separate categories.

To create a bar graph, follow these steps.
1. On graph paper, draw a horizontal, or *x*-, axis and a vertical, or *y*-, axis.
2. Write the names of the categories to be graphed along the horizontal axis. Include an overall label for the axis as well.
3. Label the vertical axis with the name of the responding variable. Include units of measurement. Then create a scale along the axis by marking off equally spaced numbers that cover the range of the data collected.
4. For each category, draw a solid bar using the scale on the vertical axis to determine the

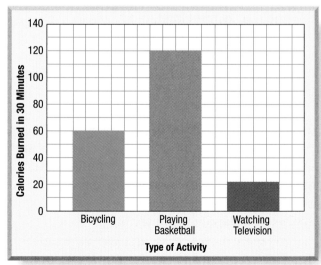

Calories Burned by a 30-kilogram Person in Various Activities

appropriate height. For example, for bicycling, draw the bar as high as the 60 mark on the vertical axis. Make all the bars the same width and leave equal spaces between them.
5. Add a title that describes the graph.

Line Graphs

To see whether a relationship exists between body mass and the number of Calories burned while bicycling, you could create a line graph. A line graph is used to display data that show how one variable (the responding variable) changes in response to another variable (the manipulated variable). You can use a line graph when your manipulated variable is *continuous*, that is, when there are other points between the ones that you tested. In this example, body mass is a continuous variable because there are other body masses between 30 and 40 kilograms (for example, 31 kilograms). Time is another example of a continuous variable.

Line graphs are powerful tools because they allow you to estimate values for conditions that you did not test in the experiment. For example, you can use the line graph to estimate that a 35-kilogram person would burn 68 Calories while bicycling.

To create a line graph, follow these steps.

1. On graph paper, draw a horizontal, or *x*-, axis and a vertical, or *y*-, axis.
2. Label the horizontal axis with the name of the manipulated variable. Label the vertical axis with the name of the responding variable. Include units of measurement.
3. Create a scale on each axis by marking off equally spaced numbers that cover the range of the data collected.
4. Plot a point on the graph for each piece of data. In the line graph above, the dotted lines show how to plot the first data point (30 kilograms and 60 Calories). Draw an imaginary vertical line extending up from the horizontal axis at the 30-kilogram mark. Then draw an imaginary horizontal line extending across from the vertical axis at the 60-Calorie mark. Plot the point where the two lines intersect.

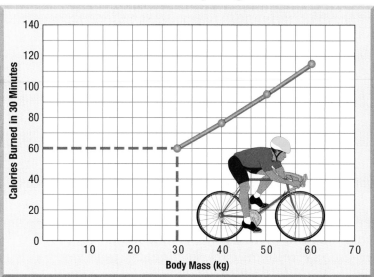

Effect of Body Mass on Calories Burned While Bicycling

5. Connect the plotted points with a solid line. (In some cases, it may be more appropriate to draw a line that shows the general trend of the plotted points. In those cases, some of the points may fall above or below the line. Also, not all graphs are linear and it may be more appropriate to draw a curve to connect the points.)
6. Add a title that identifies the variables or relationship in the graph.

> **ACTIVITY**
> Create line graphs to display the data from Experiment 2 and Experiment 3 in the data table.

> **ACTIVITY**
> In one middle school there are 190 sixth graders, 245 seventh graders, and 175 eighth graders. What type of graph would you use to display these data? Use graph paper to create the graph.

Circle Graphs

Like bar graphs, circle graphs can be used to display data in a number of separate categories. Unlike bar graphs, however, circle graphs can only be used when you have data for *all* the categories that make up a given topic. A circle graph is sometimes called a pie chart because it resembles a pie cut into slices. The pie represents the entire topic, while the slices represent the individual categories. The size of a slice indicates what percentage of the whole a particular category makes up.

The data table below shows the results of a survey in which 24 teenagers were asked to identify their favorite sport. The data were then used to create the circle graph at the right.

Sports That Teens Prefer

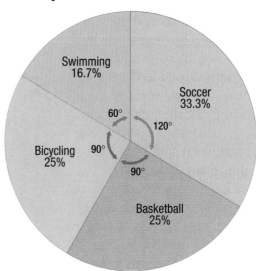

FAVORITE SPORTS

Sport	Number of Students
Soccer	8
Basketball	6
Bicycling	6
Swimming	4

To create a circle graph, follow these steps.

1. Use a compass to draw a circle. Mark the center of the circle with a point. Then draw a line from the center point to the top of the circle.

2. Determine the size of each "slice" by setting up a proportion where x equals the number of degrees in a slice. (NOTE: A circle contains 360 degrees.) For example, to find the number of degrees in the "soccer" slice, set up the following proportion:

$$\frac{\text{students who prefer soccer}}{\text{total number of students}} = \frac{x}{\text{total number of degrees in a circle}}$$

$$\frac{8}{24} = \frac{x}{360}$$

Cross-multiply and solve for x.

$$24x = 8 \times 360$$
$$x = 120$$

The "soccer" slice should contain 120 degrees.

3. Use a protractor to measure the angle of the first slice, using the line you drew to the top of the circle as the 0° line. Draw a line from the center of the circle to the edge for the angle you measured.

4. Continue around the circle by measuring the size of each slice with the protractor. Start measuring from the edge of the previous slice so the wedges do not overlap. When you are done, the entire circle should be filled in.

5. Determine the percentage of the whole circle that each slice represents. To do this, divide the number of degrees in a slice by the total number of degrees in a circle (360), and multiply by 100%. For the "soccer" slice, you can find the percentage as follows:

$$\frac{120}{360} \times 100\% = 33.3\%$$

6. Use a different color to shade in each slice. Label each slice with the name of the category and with the percentage of the whole it represents.

7. Add a title to the circle graph.

> **ACTIVITY**
>
> An ice cream shop sold 80 ice cream cones today—24 vanilla cones, 36 chocolate cones, and 20 pistachio cones. Create a circle graph to display these data.

Laboratory Safety

Safety Symbols

These symbols alert you to possible dangers in the laboratory and remind you to work carefully.

Safety Goggles Always wear safety goggles to protect your eyes in any activity involving chemicals, flames or heating, or the possibility of broken glassware.

Lab Apron Wear a laboratory apron to protect your skin and clothing from damage.

Breakage You are working with materials that may be breakable, such as glass containers, glass tubing, thermometers, or funnels. Handle breakable materials with care. Do not touch broken glassware.

Heat-resistant Gloves Use an oven mitt or other hand protection when handling hot materials. Hot plates, hot glassware, or hot water can cause burns. Do not touch hot objects with your bare hands.

Heating Use a clamp or tongs to pick up hot glassware. Do not touch hot objects with your bare hands.

Sharp Object Pointed-tip scissors, scalpels, knives, needles, pins, or tacks are sharp. They can cut or puncture your skin. Always direct a sharp edge or point away from yourself and others. Use sharp instruments only as instructed.

Electric Shock Avoid the possibility of electric shock. Never use electrical equipment around water, or when the equipment is wet or your hands are wet. Be sure cords are untangled and cannot trip anyone. Disconnect the equipment when it is not in use.

Corrosive Chemical You are working with an acid or another corrosive chemical. Avoid getting it on your skin or clothing, or in your eyes. Do not inhale the vapors. Wash your hands when you are finished with the activity.

Poison Do not let any poisonous chemical come in contact with your skin, and do not inhale its vapors. Wash your hands when you are finished with the activity.

Physical Safety When an experiment involves physical activity, take precautions to avoid injuring yourself or others. Follow instructions from your teacher. Alert your teacher if there is any reason you should not participate in the activity.

Animal Safety Treat live animals with care to avoid harming the animals or yourself. Working with animal parts or preserved animals also requires caution. Wash your hands when you are finished with the activity.

Plant Safety Handle plants in the laboratory or during field work only as directed by your teacher. If you are allergic to certain plants, tell your teacher before doing an activity in which those plants are used. Avoid touching harmful plants such as poison ivy, poison oak, or poison sumac, or plants with thorns. Wash your hands when you are finished with the activity.

Flames You may be working with flames from a lab burner, candle, or matches. Tie back loose hair and clothing. Follow instructions from your teacher about lighting and extinguishing flames.

No Flames Flammable materials may be present. Make sure there are no flames, sparks, or other exposed heat sources present.

Fumes When poisonous or unpleasant vapors may be involved, work in a ventilated area. Avoid inhaling vapors directly. Only test an odor when directed to do so by your teacher, and use a wafting motion to direct the vapor toward your nose.

Disposal Chemicals and other laboratory materials used in the activity must be disposed of safely. Follow the instructions from your teacher.

Hand Washing Wash your hands thoroughly when finished with the activity. Use antibacterial soap and warm water. Lather both sides of your hands and between your fingers. Rinse well.

General Safety Awareness You may see this symbol when none of the symbols described earlier appears. In this case, follow the specific instructions provided. You may also see this symbol when you are asked to develop your own procedure in a lab. Have your teacher approve your plan before you go further.

Using the Microscope

T he microscope is an essential tool in the study of life science. It allows you to see things that are too small to be seen with the unaided eye.

You will probably use a compound microscope like the one you see here. The compound microscope has more than one lens that magnifies the object you view.

Typically, a compound microscope has one lens in the eyepiece, the part you look through. The eyepiece lens usually magnifies 10 ×. Any object you view through this lens would appear 10 times larger than it is.

The compound microscope may contain one or two other lenses called objective lenses. If there are two objective lenses, they are called the low-power and high-power objective lenses. The low-power objective lens usually magnifies 10 ×. The high-power objective lens usually magnifies 40 ×.

To calculate the total magnification with which you are viewing an object, multiply the magnification of the eyepiece lens by the magnification of the objective lens you are using. For example, the eyepiece's magnification of 10 × multiplied by the low-power objective's magnification of 10 × equals a total magnification of 100 ×.

Use the photo of the compound microscope to become familiar with the parts of the microscope and their functions.

The Parts of the Compound Microscope

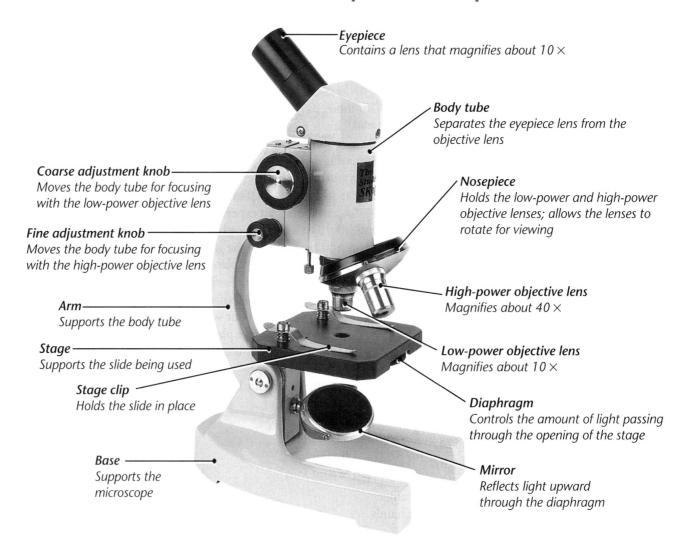

Eyepiece
Contains a lens that magnifies about 10 ×

Body tube
Separates the eyepiece lens from the objective lens

Coarse adjustment knob
Moves the body tube for focusing with the low-power objective lens

Nosepiece
Holds the low-power and high-power objective lenses; allows the lenses to rotate for viewing

Fine adjustment knob
Moves the body tube for focusing with the high-power objective lens

High-power objective lens
Magnifies about 40 ×

Arm
Supports the body tube

Stage
Supports the slide being used

Low-power objective lens
Magnifies about 10 ×

Stage clip
Holds the slide in place

Diaphragm
Controls the amount of light passing through the opening of the stage

Base
Supports the microscope

Mirror
Reflects light upward through the diaphragm

To prep
laborat
Then r
unders
teacher
unders

Dress (
1. To p
   safet
   burn
   into
   your
2. Wea
   corr
3. Tie l
   cher
4. Rem
   jewe
   flam
   slee
5. Nev

Gener
6. Rea
   bef
   wri
   abc
   for
7. Ne
   aut
   bef
   any
8. Ne
   sup
9. Ne
10. Ke
    on
    pr
    as
    de
11. Do

Using the Microscope

Use the following procedures when you are working with a microscope.

1. To carry the microscope grasp the microscope's arm with one hand. Place your other hand under the base.

2. Place the microscope on a table with the arm toward you.

3. Turn the coarse adjustment knob to raise the body tube.

4. Revolve the nosepiece until the low-power objective lens clicks into place.

5. Adjust the diaphragm. While looking through the eyepiece, also adjust the mirror until you see a bright white circle of light. **CAUTION:** *Never use direct sunlight as a light source.*

6. Place a slide on the stage. Center the specimen over the opening on the stage. Use the stage clips to hold the slide in place. **CAUTION:** *Glass slides are fragile.*

7. Look at the stage from the side. Carefully turn the coarse adjustment knob to lower the body tube until the low-power objective almost touches the slide.

8. Looking through the eyepiece, very slowly turn the coarse adjustment knob until the specimen comes into focus.

9. To switch to the high-power objective lens, look at the microscope from the side. Carefully revolve the nosepiece until the high-power objective lens clicks into place. Make sure the lens does not hit the slide.

10. Looking through the eyepiece, turn the fine adjustment knob until the specimen comes into focus.

Making a Wet-Mount Slide

Use the following procedures to make a wet-mount slide of a specimen.

1. Obtain a clean microscope slide and a coverslip. **CAUTION:** *Glass slides and coverslips are fragile.*

2. Place the specimen on the slide. The specimen must be thin enough for light to pass through it.

3. Using a plastic dropper, place a drop of water on the specimen.

4. Gently place one edge of the coverslip against the slide so that it touches the edge of the water drop at a 45° angle. Slowly lower the coverslip over the specimen. If air bubbles are trapped beneath the coverslip, tap the coverslip gently with the eraser end of a pencil.

5. Remove any excess water at the edge of the coverslip with a paper towel.

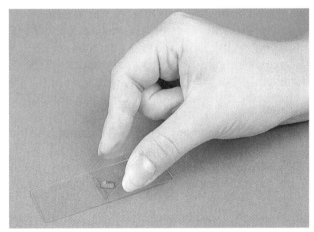

Glossary

······ **A** ······

abdomen The hind section of an arachnid's body that contains its reproductive organs and part of its digestive tract; the hind section of an insect's body. (p. 350)

abiotic factor A nonliving part of an ecosystem. (p. 690)

absolute dating A technique used to determine the actual age of a fossil. (p. 160)

absorption The process by which nutrient molecules pass through the wall of the digestive system into the blood. (p. 519)

acne A bacterial infection of the skin in which the oil glands become blocked and swollen. (p. 500)

active immunity Immunity that occurs when a person's own immune system produces antibodies in response to the presence of a pathogen. (p. 605)

active transport The movement of materials through a cell membrane using energy. (p. 59)

adaptation A characteristic that helps an organism survive in its environment or reproduce. (pp. 149, 312)

addiction A physical dependence on a substance; an intense need by the body for a substance. (p. 577)

adolescence The stage of development between childhood and adulthood when children become adults physically and mentally. (p. 675)

aggression A threatening behavior that one animal uses to gain control over another. (p. 451)

AIDS (acquired immunodeficiency syndrome) A disease caused by a virus that attacks the immune system. (p. 603)

alcoholism A disease in which a person is both physically addicted to and emotionally dependent on alcohol. (p. 651)

alga A plantlike protist. (p. 224)

algal bloom The rapid growth of a population of algae. (p. 228)

alleles The different forms of a gene. (p. 89)

allergen A substance that causes an allergy. (p. 613)

allergy A disorder in which the immune system is overly sensitive to a foreign substance. (p. 612)

alveoli Tiny sacs of lung tissue specialized for the movement of gases between the air and the blood. (p. 570)

amino acids Small units that are linked together chemically to form large protein molecules. (pp. 53, 510)

amniocentesis A technique by which a small amount of the fluid that surrounds a developing baby is removed; the fluid is analyzed to determine whether the baby will have a genetic disorder. (p. 128)

amniotic sac A fluid-filled sac that cushions and protects a developing fetus in the uterus. (p. 670)

amphibian An ectothermic vertebrate that spends its early life in water and its adulthood on land, returning to water to reproduce. (p. 390)

anabolic steroids Synthetic chemicals that are similar to hormones produced in the body and that may increase muscle size and cause mood swings. (p. 648)

angiosperm A plant that produces seeds that are enclosed in a protective structure. (p. 289)

antenna An appendage on the head of some animals that contains sense organs. (p. 349)

antibiotic A chemical that kills bacteria or slows their growth without harming the body cells of humans. (pp. 201, 609)

antibody A chemical produced by a B cell of the immune system that destroys a specific kind of pathogen. (p. 602)

antigen A molecule on a cell that the immune system can recognize either as part of the body or as coming from outside the body. (p. 601)

anus The opening at the end of an organism's digestive system through which wastes exit. (pp. 331, 529)

aorta The largest artery in the body. (p. 542)

aquaculture The practice of raising fish and other water organisms for food. (p. 766)

arachnid An arthropod with only two body sections. (p. 350)

artery A blood vessel that carries blood away from the heart. (p. 540)

arthropod An invertebrate that has an external skeleton, a segmented body, and jointed attachments called appendages. (p. 347)

artificial intelligence The capacity of a computer to perform complex tasks such as learning from experience and solving problems. (p. 446)

asexual reproduction The reproductive process that involves only one parent and produces offspring that are identical to the parent. (p. 195)

asthma A disorder in which the respiratory passages narrow significantly. (p. 613)

atherosclerosis A condition in which an artery wall thickens as a result of the buildup of fatty materials. (p. 557)

atom The smallest unit of an element. (p. 52)

atrium Each of the two upper chambers of the heart that receives blood that comes into the heart. (pp. 390, 538)

autonomic nervous system The group of nerves that controls involuntary actions. (p. 632)

autotroph An organism that makes its own food. (p. 23)

auxin The plant hormone that speeds up the rate of growth of plant cells. (p. 298)

axon A threadlike extension of a neuron that carries nerve impulses away from the cell body. (p. 624)

··········· **B** ···········

B cell A lymphocyte that produces chemicals that help destroy a specific kind of pathogen. (p. 602)

bacteriophage A virus that infects bacteria. (p. 206)

bacterium A single-celled organism that is a prokaryote; belongs to one of two kingdoms—Archaebacteria or Eubacteria. (p. 193)

behavior All the actions an animal performs. (p. 443)

bilateral symmetry Line symmetry; the quality of being divisible into two halves that are mirror images. (p. 316)

bile A substance produced by the liver that breaks up fat particles. (p. 527)

binary fission A form of asexual reproduction in which one cell divides to form two identical cells. (p. 195)

binomial nomenclature The naming system for organisms in which each organism is given a two-part name—a genus name and a species name. (p. 183)

biodiversity The number of different species in an area. (p. 768)

biogeography The study of where organisms live. (p. 728)

bioluminescence The production of light by a living organism. (p. 364)

biome A group of ecosystems with similar climates and organisms. (p. 734)

biotic factor A living part of an ecosystem. (p. 689)

bird An endothermic vertebrate that has feathers and a four-chambered heart, and lays eggs. (p. 411)

birth rate The number of births in a population in a certain amount of time. (p. 697)

bivalve A mollusk that has two shells held together by hinges and strong muscles. (p. 342)

blood pressure The pressure that is exerted by the blood against the walls of blood vessels. (p. 547)

blood transfusion The transference of blood from one person to another. (p. 552)

bog A wetland where sphagnum moss grows on top of acidic water. (p. 258)

brain The part of the central nervous system that is located in the skull and controls most functions in the body. (p. 629)

brainstem The part of the brain that controls many body functions that occur automatically. (p. 631)

branching tree A diagram that shows how scientists think different groups of organisms are related. (p. 168)

bronchi The passages that branch from the trachea and direct air into the lungs. (p. 570)

bronchitis An irritation of the breathing passages in which the small passages become narrower than normal and often clogged with mucus. (p. 578)

budding A form of asexual reproduction in which a new organism grows out of the body of a parent. (p. 236)

buoyant force The force that water exerts upward on any underwater object. (p. 386)

···········  ···········

calorie The amount of energy needed to raise the temperature of one gram of water by one Celsius degree. (p. 507)

cambium The layer of cells in a plant that produces new phloem and xylem cells. (p. 281)

camouflage Protective coloration; a common animal defense. (p. 358)

cancer A disease in which some body cells grow and divide uncontrollably, damaging the parts of the body around them. (p. 499)

canines Sharply pointed teeth that stab food and tear into it. (p. 426)

canopy A leafy roof formed by tall trees. (p. 735)

capillary A tiny blood vessel where substances are exchanged between the blood and the body cells. (p. 540)

captive breeding The mating of endangered animals in zoos or preserves. (p. 775)

carbohydrates Energy-rich organic compounds, such as sugars and starches, that are made of the elements carbon, hydrogen, and oxygen. They provide the raw materials to make parts of cells. (pp. 54, 507)

carbon monoxide A colorless, odorless gas produced when substances—including tobacco—are burned. (p. 577)

carcinogen A substance or a factor in the environment that can cause cancer. (p. 615)

cardiac muscle Muscle tissue found only in the heart. (p. 489)

cardiovascular system The body system that consists of the heart, blood vessels, and blood, and that carries needed substances to cells and carries waste products away from cells. (p. 536)

carnivore An animal that eats only other animals. (pp. 313, 718)

carrier A person who has one recessive allele for a trait and one dominant allele, but does not have the trait. (p. 122)

carrying capacity The largest population that an area can support. (p. 699)

cartilage A connective tissue that is more flexible than bone and that gives support to some parts of the body. (pp. 375, 484)

cast A fossil that is a copy of an organism's shape, formed when minerals seep into a mold. (p. 158)

cell The basic unit of structure and function in living things. (pp. 19, 473)

cell cycle The regular sequence of growth and division that cells undergo. (p. 73)

cell membrane The outside boundary of a cell; controls which substances can enter or leave the cell. (pp. 35, 473)

cell theory A widely accepted explanation of the relationship between cells and living things. (p. 30)

cell wall A rigid layer of nonliving material that surrounds the cells of plants and some other organisms. (p. 35)

central nervous system The brain and spinal cord; the control center of the body. (p. 628)

cephalopod A mollusk with feet adapted to form tentacles around its mouth. (p. 344)

cerebellum The part of the brain that coordinates the actions of the muscles and helps maintain balance. (p. 631)

cerebrum The part of the brain that interprets input from the senses, controls the movement of skeletal muscles, and carries out complex mental processes. (p. 630)

chitin The tough, flexible material from which arthropod exoskeletons are made. (p. 347)

chlorophyll A green pigment found in the chloroplasts of plants, algae, and some bacteria. (p. 63)

chloroplast A structure in the cells of plants and some other organisms that captures energy from sunlight and uses it to produce food. (p. 40)

cholesterol A waxy, fatlike substance, found only in animal products, that is an important part of the body's cells; can build up on artery walls. (p. 509)

chordate The phylum whose members have a notochord, a nerve cord, and slits in their throat area at some point in their lives. (p. 374)

chromatid One of the identical rods of a chromosome. (p. 74)

chromatin Material in cells that contains DNA and carries genetic information. (p. 37)

chromosome A rod-shaped cellular structure made of condensed chromatin; contains DNA, which carries the genetic information that controls inherited characteristics such as eye color and blood type. (pp. 74, 664)

cilia The hairlike projections on the outside of cells that move in a wavelike manner. (pp. 221, 568)

circadian rhythm Behavior cycles that occur over a period of approximately one day. (p. 455)

classification The process of grouping things based on their similarities. (p. 182)

clear-cutting The process of cutting down all the trees in an area at once. (p. 763)

climate The typical weather pattern in an area over a long period of time. (p. 731)

clone An organism that is genetically identical to the organism from which it was produced. (p. 134)

cnidarians Animals whose stinging cells are used to capture their prey and defend themselves, and who take their food into a hollow central cavity. (p. 323)

cochlea A snail-shaped tube in the inner ear lined with sound receptors; nerve impulses are sent from the cochlea to the brain. (p. 641)

codominance A condition in which neither of two alleles of a gene is dominant or recessive. (p. 98)

commensalism A relationship between two species in which one species benefits and the other is neither helped nor harmed. (p. 709)

community All the different populations that live together in an area. (p. 692)

competition The struggle between organisms for the limited resources in a habitat. (p. 705)

complete metamorphosis A type of metamorphosis characterized by four dramatically different stages: egg, larva, pupa, and adult. (p. 356)

compound Two or more elements that are chemically combined. (p. 52)

compound microscope A light microscope that has more than one lens. (p. 28)

concussion A bruiselike injury of the brain that occurs when the soft tissue of the cerebrum bumps against the skull. (p. 634)

conditioning The process of learning to connect a stimulus with a good or bad event. (p.445)

cone The reproductive structure of a gymnosperm. (p. 286)

condensation The process by which a gas changes to a liquid (p. 725)

coniferous trees Trees that produce their seeds in cones and have needle-shaped leaves. (p. 739)

conjugation The process in which a unicellular organism transfers some of its genetic material to another unicellular organism. (p. 196)

connective tissue A body tissue that provides support for the body and connects all of its parts. (p. 474)

consumer An organism that obtains energy by feeding on other organisms. (p. 718)

continental drift The very slow motion of the continents. (p. 728)

contour feather A large feather that helps give shape to a bird's body. (p. 411)

contractile vacuole The cell structure that collects extra water from the cytoplasm and then expels it from the cell. (p. 220)

controlled experiment An experiment in which all of the variables except for one remain the same. (pp. 7, 21)

convex lens A curved lens in which the center is thicker than the edges. (p. 32)

cornea The clear tissue that covers the front of the eye. (p. 637)

coronary artery An artery that supplies blood to the heart itself. (p. 543)

cotyledon A seed leaf that stores food. (p. 276)

courtship behavior The behavior that animals of the same species engage in to prepare for mating. (p. 452)

crop A bird's internal storage tank that allows it to store food inside its body after swallowing it. (p. 412)

crustacean An arthropod that has two or three body sections, five or more pairs of legs, two pairs of antennae, and usually three pairs of appendages for chewing. (p. 349)

cuticle The waxy, waterproof layer that covers the leaves and stems of some plants. (p. 249)

cytokinesis The final stage of the cell cycle, in which the cell's cytoplasm divides, distributing the organelles into each of the two new cells. (p. 75)

cytoplasm The region of a cell located inside the cell membrane (in prokaryotes) or between the cell membrane and nucleus (in eukaryotes); contains a gel-like material and cell organelles. (pp. 37, 473)

data The facts, figures, and other evidence gathered through observation. (p. 5)

death rate The number of deaths in a certain amount of time. (p. 697)

deciduous trees Trees that shed their leaves and grow new ones each year. (p. 738)

decomposer An organism that breaks down large chemicals from dead organisms into small chemicals and returns important materials to the soil and water. (pp. 199, 719)

dendrite A threadlike extension of a neuron that carries nerve impulses toward the cell body. (p. 624)

depressant A drug that slows down the activity of the central nervous system. (p. 646)

dermis The lower layer of the skin. (p. 497)

desert An area in which the yearly amount of evaporation is greater than the amount of precipitation. (p. 736)

development The process of change that occurs during an organism's life to produce a more complex organism. (p. 20)

diabetes A condition in which either the pancreas fails to produce enough insulin, or the body's cells can't use it properly. (p. 614)

diaphragm A large, dome-shaped muscle that plays an important role in breathing. (pp. 426, 572)

dicot An angiosperm that has two seed leaves. (p. 293)

diffusion The process by which molecules move from an area in which they are highly concentrated to an area in which they are less concentrated. (pp. 57, 545)

digestion The process by which the body breaks down food into small nutrient molecules. (p. 578)

dispersal The movement of organisms from one place to another. (p. 729)

DNA Deoxyribonucleic acid; the genetic material that carries information about an organism and is passed from parent to offspring. (p. 55)

dominant allele An allele whose trait always shows up in the organism when the allele is present. (p. 89)

down feathers Short, fluffy feathers that trap heat and keep a bird warm. (p. 412)

drug Any chemical that causes changes in a person's body or behavior. (p. 644)

drug abuse The deliberate misuse of drugs for purposes other than appropriate medical ones. (p. 645)

eardrum The membrane that separates the outer ear from the middle ear, and that vibrates when sound waves strike it. (p. 641)

echinoderm A radially symmetrical invertebrate that lives on the ocean floor and has a spiny internal skeleton. (p. 365)

ecology The study of how living things interact with each other and their environment. (p. 692)

ecosystem All the living and nonliving things that interact in an area. (p. 688)

ectotherm An animal whose body does not produce much internal heat. (p. 376)

egg A female sex cell. (pp. 102, 663)

element A type of matter in which all the atoms are the same; cannot be broken down into simpler substances. (p. 52)

embryo The young plant that develops from a zygote. (p. 276) Also, a developing human during the first eight weeks after fertilization has occurred. (p. 669)

emigration Leaving a population. (p. 698)

emphysema A serious disease that destroys lung tissue and causes difficulty in breathing. (p. 578)

endangered species A species in danger of becoming extinct in the near future. (p. 772)

endocrine gland An organ of the endocrine system that produces and releases its chemical products directly into the bloodstream. (p. 658)

endoplasmic reticulum A cell structure that forms a maze of passageways in which proteins and other materials are carried from one part of the cell to another. (p. 40)

endoskeleton An internal skeleton. (p. 365)

endospore A small, rounded, thick-walled, resting cell that forms inside a bacterial cell. (p. 197)

endotherm An animal whose body controls and regulates its temperature by controlling the internal heat it produces. (p. 377)

energy pyramid A diagram that shows the amount of energy that moves from one feeding level to another in a food web. (p. 721)

enzyme A protein that speeds up chemical reactions in the bodies of living things. (pp. 54, 520)

epidermis The outermost layer of the skin. (p. 496)

epiglottis A flap of tissue that seals off the windpipe and prevents food from entering. (p. 521)

epithelial tissue A body tissue that covers the surfaces of the body, inside and out. (p. 474)

esophagus A muscular tube that connects the mouth to the stomach. (p. 521)

estimate An approximation of a number based on reasonable assumptions. (p. 696)

estrogen A hormone produced by the ovaries that controls the development of adult female characteristics. (p. 666)

estuary A habitat in which the fresh water of a river meets the salt water of the ocean. (p. 743)

eukaryote An organism with cells that contain nuclei and other cell structures. (p. 41)

eutrophication The buildup over time of nutrients in freshwater lakes and ponds that leads to an increase in the growth of algae. (p. 230)

evaporation The process by which molecules of a liquid absorb energy and change to the gas state. (p. 724)

evolution The gradual change in a species over time. (p. 149)

excretion The process by which wastes are removed from the body. (p. 581)

exoskeleton An outer skeleton. (p. 347)

exotic species Species that are carried to a new location by people. (p. 730)

extinct A species that does not have any living members. (p. 160)

extinction The disappearance of all members of a species from Earth. (p. 771)

farsightedness The condition in which distant objects can be seen clearly but nearby objects look blurry. (p. 639)

fats High-energy nutrients that are composed of carbon, oxygen, and hydrogen and contain more than twice as much energy as an equal amount of carbohydrates. (p. 509)

fermentation The process by which cells break down molecules to release energy without using oxygen. (p. 69)

fertilization The joining of a sperm cell and an egg cell. (pp. 252, 663)

fetus A developing human from the ninth week of development until birth. (p. 671)

fiber A complex carbohydrate, found in plant foods, that cannot be broken down into sugar molecules by the body. (p. 508)

fibrin A chemical that is important in blood clotting because it forms a net of tiny fibers that traps red blood cells. (p. 552)

fish A vertebrate that lives in the water and has fins. (p. 381)

fishery An area with a large population of valuable ocean organisms. (p. 765)

flagellum A long, whiplike structure that helps a unicellular organism move. (p. 194)

flower The reproductive structure of an angiosperm. (p. 290)

follicle A structure in the dermis of the skin from which a strand of hair grows. (p. 497)

food chain A series of events in which one organism eats another. (p. 719)

food web The pattern of overlapping food chains in an ecosystem. (p. 719)

Food Guide Pyramid A chart that classifies foods into six groups to help people plan a healthy diet. (p. 513)

force A push or a pull exerted on an object. (p. 542)

fossil The preserved remains or traces of an organism that lived in the past. (pp. 46, 157, 377)

fossil record The millions of fossils that scientists have collected. (p. 160)

frond The leaf of a fern plant. (p. 264)

fruit The ripened ovary and other structures that enclose one or more seeds of an angiosperm. (p. 291)

fruiting body The reproductive hypha of a fungus. (p. 236)

gallbladder The organ that stores bile after it is produced by the liver. (p. 527)

gamete A sperm cell or an egg cell. (p. 253)

gametophyte The stage in the life cycle of a plant in which the plant produces gametes, or sex cells. (p. 253)

gastropod A mollusk with a single shell or no shell. (p. 342)

gene A segment of DNA on a chromosome that codes for a specific trait. (p. 89)

gene therapy The insertion of working copies of a gene into the cells of a person with a genetic disorder in an attempt to correct the disorder. (p. 136)

genetic disorder An abnormal condition that a person inherits through genes or chromosomes. (p. 125)

genetic engineering The transfer of a gene from the DNA of one organism into another organism, in order to produce an organism with desired traits. (p. 134)

genetics The scientific study of heredity. (p. 86)

genome All of the DNA in one cell of an organism. (p. 138)

genotype An organism's genetic makeup, or allele combinations. (p. 98)

genus A classification grouping that consists of a number of similar, closely related species. (p. 184)

germination The early growth stage of the embryo plant in a seed. (p. 278)

gestation period The length of time between fertilization and the birth of a mammal. (p. 433)

gill An organism's breathing organ that removes oxygen from water. (p. 341)

gizzard A thick-walled, muscular part of a bird's stomach that squeezes and grinds partially digested food. (p. 413)

glucose A sugar that is the major source of energy for the body's cells. (p. 508)

Golgi body A structure in a cell that receives proteins and other newly formed materials from the endoplasmic reticulum, packages them, and distributes them to other parts of the cell. (p. 40)

gradual metamorphosis A type of metamorphosis in which an egg hatches into a nymph that resembles an adult, and which has no distinctly different larval stage. (p. 356)

gradualism The theory that evolution occurs slowly but steadily. (p. 164)

grassland An area populated by grasses that gets 25 to 75 centimeters of rain each year. (p. 737)

gymnosperm A plant that produces seeds that are not enclosed by a protective covering. (p. 284)

habitat The place where an organism lives and that provides the things the organism needs. (p. 394, 689)

habitat destruction The loss of a natural habitat. (p. 774)

habitat fragmentation The breaking of a habitat into smaller, isolated pieces. (p. 774)

half-life The time it takes for half of the atoms of a radioactive element to decay. (p. 160)

heart A hollow, muscular organ that pumps blood throughout the body. (p. 538)

heart attack A condition in which blood flow to a part of the heart muscle is blocked, which causes heart cells to die. (p. 557)

hemoglobin An iron-containing protein that binds chemically to oxygen molecules and makes up most of a red blood cell. (p. 550)

herbivore An animal that eats only plants. (pp. 312, 718)

heredity The passing of traits from parents to offspring. (p. 86)

heterotroph An organism that cannot make its own food. (p. 24)

heterozygous Having two different alleles for a trait. (p. 98)

hibernation A state of greatly reduced body activity that occurs during the winter. (p. 456)

histamine A chemical that is responsible for the symptoms of an allergy. (p. 613)

homeostasis The process by which an organism's internal environment is kept stable in spite of changes in the external environment. (pp. 25, 476)

homologous structures Body parts that are structurally similar in related species; provide evidence that the structures were inherited from a common ancestor. (p. 166)

homozygous Having two identical alleles for a trait. (p. 98)

hormone A chemical that affects a plant's growth and development. (p. 298) Also, the chemical product of an endocrine gland that speeds up or slows down the activities of an organ or tissue. (p. 659)

host An organism that provides a source of energy or a suitable environment for a virus or for another organism to live. (pp. 205, 710)

hybrid An organism that has two different alleles for a trait; an organism that is heterozygous for a particular trait. (p. 90)

hybridization A selective breeding method in which two genetically different individuals are crossed. (p. 133)

hydroponics The method of growing plants in a solution of nutrients instead of in soil. (p. 268)

hypertension A disorder in which a person's blood pressure is consistently higher than normal. (p. 557)

hypha One of many branching, threadlike tubes that make up the body of a fungus. (p. 234)

hypothalamus A tiny part of the brain that links the nervous system and the endocrine system. (p. 660)

hypothesis A possible explanation for a set of observations or answer to a scientific question; must be testable. (p. 6)

immigration Moving into a population. (p. 698)

immune response Part of the body's defense against pathogens in which cells of the immune system react to each kind of pathogen with a defense targeted specifically at that pathogen. (p. 601)

immunity The ability of the immune system to destroy pathogens before they can cause disease. (p. 605)

imprinting A process in which newly hatched birds or newborn mammals learn to follow the first object they see. (p. 447)

inbreeding A selective breeding method in which two individuals with identical or similar sets of alleles are crossed. (p. 133)

incisors Flat-edged teeth used to bite off and cut parts of food. (p. 426)

infectious disease A disease that can pass from one organism to another. (pp. 200, 593)

inference An interpretation of an observation that is based on evidence or prior knowledge. (p. 5)

inflammatory response Part of the body's defense against pathogens, in which fluid and white blood cells leak from blood vessels into tissues; the white blood cells destroy pathogens by breaking them down. (p. 600)

inorganic compound A compound that does not contain carbon. (p. 53)

insect An arthropod with three body sections, six legs, one pair of antennae, and usually one or two pairs of wings. (p. 355)

insight learning The process of learning how to solve a problem or do something new by applying what is already known. (p. 446)

instinct An inborn behavior pattern that an animal performs correctly the first time. (p. 444)

insulator A material that does not conduct heat well and thus helps to prevent heat from escaping. (p. 412)

insulin A chemical produced in the pancreas that enables the body's cells to take in glucose from the blood and use it for energy. (p. 614)

interneuron A neuron that carries nerve impulses from one neuron to another. (p. 624)

interphase The stage of the cell cycle that takes place before cell division occurs; during this stage, the cell grows, copies its DNA, and prepares to divide. (p. 73)

intertidal zone The area between the highest high-tide line and the lowest low-tide line. (p. 744)

invertebrate An animal that does not have a backbone. (p. 313)

involuntary muscle A muscle that is not under conscious control. (p. 488)

iris The circular structure that surrounds the pupil and regulates the amount of light entering the eye. (p. 637)

joint A place where two bones come together. (p. 484)

karyotype A picture of all the chromosomes in a cell arranged in pairs. (p. 129)

keystone species A species that influences the survival of many other species in an ecosystem. (p. 770)

kidney A major organ of the excretory system; eliminates urea, excess water, and other waste materials from the body. (pp. 341, 581)

large intestine The last section of the digestive system, where water is absorbed from food and the remaining material is eliminated from the body. (p. 529)

larva The immature form of an animal that looks very different from the adult. (p. 322)

larynx The voice box, located in the top part of the trachea, underneath the epiglottis. (p. 573)

learning The process that leads to change in behavior based on practice or experience. (p. 444)

lens The flexible structure that focuses light that has entered the eye. (p. 637)

lichen The combination of a fungus and either an alga or an autotrophic bacterium that live together in a mutualistic relationship. (p. 242)

lift An upward force on an object that results from the difference in pressure between the upper and lower surfaces of the object. (p. 421)

ligament Strong connective tissue that holds together the bones in a movable joint. (p. 486)

limiting factor An environmental factor that prevents a population from increasing. (p. 699)

lipids Energy-rich organic compounds, such as fats, oils, and waxes, that are made of carbon, hydrogen, and oxygen. (p. 54)

liver The largest and heaviest organ inside the body; it breaks down substances and eliminates nitrogen from the body. (p. 527)

lungs The main organs of the respiratory system, where gas exchange takes place. (p. 570)

lymph The fluid that the lymphatic system collects and returns to the bloodstream. (p. 554)

lymph node A small knob of tissue in the lymphatic system that filters lymph. (p. 554)

lymphatic system A network of veinlike vessels that returns the fluid that leaks out of blood vessels to the bloodstream. (p. 554)

lymphocyte White blood cell that reacts to each kind of pathogen with a defense targeted specifically at that pathogen. (p. 601)

lysosome A small round cell structure that contains chemicals that break down large food particles into smaller ones. (p. 41)

magnification The ability to make things look larger than they are. (p. 32)

mammal An endothermic vertebrate with a four-chambered heart, skin covered with fur or hair, and has young fed with milk from the mother's body. (p. 423)

mammary glands The organs that produce the milk with which mammals feed their young. (p. 428)

manipulated variable The one factor that a scientist changes to test a hypothesis during an experiment; also called the independent variable. (p. 7)

marrow The soft tissue that fills the internal spaces in bone. (p. 484)

marsupial A mammal whose young are born alive at an early stage of development, and which usually continue to develop in a pouch on their mother's body. (p. 432)

medusa The cnidarian body plan characterized by a bowl shape and which is adapted for a free-swimming life. (p. 324)

meiosis The process that occurs in sex cells (sperm and egg) by which the number of chromosomes is reduced by half. (p. 104)

melanin A pigment that gives the skin its color. (p. 497)

menstrual cycle The monthly cycle of changes that occurs in the female reproductive system, during which an egg develops and the uterus prepares for the arrival of a fertilized egg. (p. 667)

menstruation The process that occurs if fertilization does not take place, in which the thickened lining of the uterus breaks down and blood and tissue then pass out of the female body through the vagina. (p. 668)

messenger RNA RNA that copies the coded message from DNA in the nucleus and carries the message into the cytoplasm. (p. 109)

metamorphosis A process in which an animal's body undergoes dramatic changes in form during its life cycle. (p. 350)

microscope An instrument that makes small objects look larger. (p. 28)

migration The regular, periodic journey of an animal from one place to another and back again for the purpose of feeding or reproducing. (p. 456)

minerals Nutrients that are needed by the body in small amounts and are not made by living things. (p. 512)

mitochondria Rod-shaped cell structures that produce most of the energy needed to carry out the cell's functions. (p. 37)

mitosis The stage of the cell cycle during which the cell's nucleus divides into two new nuclei and one copy of the DNA is distributed into each daughter cell. (p. 74)

molars Teeth that, along with premolars, grind and shred food into tiny bits. (p. 426)

mold A fossil formed when an organism buried in sediment dissolves, leaving a hollow area. (p. 158)

molecule The smallest unit of most compounds. (p. 52)

mollusk An invertebrate with a soft, unsegmented body; most are protected by hard outer shells. (p. 340)

molting The process of shedding an outgrown exoskeleton. (p. 348)

monocot An angiosperm that has only one seed leaf. (p. 293)

monotreme A mammal that lays eggs. (p. 432)

motor neuron A neuron that sends an impulse to a muscle, causing the muscle to contract. (p. 624)

mucus A thick, slippery substance produced by the body. (p. 521)

multicellular A type of organism that is made up of many cells. (p. 19)

multiple alleles Three or more forms of a gene that code for a single trait. (p. 119)

muscle tissue A body tissue that contracts or shortens, making body parts move. (p. 474)

mutation A change in a gene or chromosome. (p. 110)

mutualism A type of symbiosis in which both partners benefit from living together. (pp. 222, 709)

native species Species that have naturally evolved in an area. (p. 730)

natural selection The process by which individuals that are better adapted to their environment are more likely to survive and reproduce than other members of the same species. (p. 150)

nearsightedness The condition in which nearby objects can be seen clearly but distant objects look blurry. (p. 639)

negative feedback A process in which a system is turned off by the condition it produces; examples of negative feedback systems include regulation of temperature by a thermostat and the regulation of the levels of many hormones in the blood. (p. 662)

nephron One of a million tiny, filtering structures found in the kidneys that removes wastes from blood and produces urine. (p. 582)

neritic zone The region of shallow ocean water over the continental shelf. (p. 744)

nerve A bundle of nerve fibers. (p. 624)

nerve impulse The message carried by a neuron. (p. 623)

nerve tissue A body tissue that carries messages back and forth between the brain and every other part of the body. (p. 474)

neuron A cell that carries messages through the nervous system. (p. 623)

niche An organism's particular role in an ecosystem, or how it makes its living. (p. 704)

nicotine A drug in tobacco that speeds up the activities of the nervous system, heart, and other organs of the body. (p. 577)

nitrogen fixation The process of changing free nitrogen gas into a usable form. (p. 727)

nodules Bumps on the roots of certain plants that house nitrogen-fixing bacteria. (p. 727)

noninfectious disease A disease that is not spread from person to person. (p. 612)

nonrenewable resource A natural resource that is not replaced as it is used. (p. 85)

nonvascular plant A low-growing plant that lacks vascular tissue. (p. 256)

notochord A flexible rod that supports a chordate's back. (p. 374)

nucleic acid A very large organic molecule made of carbon, oxygen, hydrogen, nitrogen, and phosphorus, that contains instructions that cells need to carry out all the functions of life. (p. 55)

nucleus The control center of a cell that directs the cell's activities; contains the chemical instructions that direct all the cell's activities and determine the cell's characteristics. (pp. 36, 473)

nutrients Substances in food that provide the raw materials and energy the body needs to carry out all the essential life processes. (p. 506)

nymph A stage of gradual metamorphosis that usually resembles the adult insect. (p. 356)

observation A skill that involves the use of one or more of the senses—sight, hearing, touch, smell, and sometimes taste—to gather information and collect data. (p. 5)

omnivore An animal that eats both plants and animals. (pp. 313, 718)

operational definition A statement that describes how a particular variable is to be measured or how a term is to be defined. (p. 791)

organ A structure in the body that is composed of different kinds of tissue. (pp. 311, 475)

organ system A group of organs that work together to perform a major function in the body. (p. 475)

organelle A tiny cell structure that carries out a specific function within the cell. (p. 35)

organic compound A compound that contains carbon. (p. 53)

organism A living thing. (p. 18)

osmosis The diffusion of water molecules through a selectively permeable membrane. (p. 58)

osteoporosis A condition in which the body's bones become weak and break easily. (p. 487)

ovary A protective structure in plants that encloses the developing seeds. (p. 290) Also, an organ of the female reproductive system in which eggs and estrogen are produced. (p. 666)

oviduct A passageway for eggs from an ovary to the uterus; the place where fertilization usually occurs. (p. 666)

ovulation The process in which a mature egg is released from the ovary into an oviduct; occurs about halfway through a typical menstrual cycle. (p. 667)

ovule A plant structure in seed plants that contains an egg cell. (p. 286)

pacemaker A group of cells located in the right atrium that sends out signals that make the heart muscle contract and that regulates heartbeat rate. (p. 540)

pancreas A triangular organ that produces enzymes that flow into the small intestine. (p. 528)

parasite An organism that lives on or in a host and causes harm to the host. (pp. 205, 710)

parasitism A relationship in which one organism lives on or inside another and harms it. (p. 710)

passive immunity Immunity in which the antibodies that fight a pathogen come from another organism rather than from the person's own body. (p. 608)

passive smoking The involuntary inhalation of smoke from other people's cigarettes, cigars, or pipes. (p. 579)

passive transport The movement of materials through a cell membrane without using energy. (p. 59)

pasteurization A heating process that is widely used to kill microorganisms in food products such as milk. (p. 593)

pathogen An organism that causes disease. (p. 593)

peat The blackish-brown material consisting of compressed layers of dead sphagnum mosses that grow in bogs. (p. 258)

pedigree A chart or "family tree" that tracks which members of a family have a particular trait. (p. 123)

peer pressure The pressure from friends and classmates to behave in certain ways. (p. 676)

penis The organ through which both semen and urine leave the male body. (p. 665)

Percent Daily Value An indication on a food label of how the nutritional content of a food fits into the diet of a person who consumes a total of 2,000 Calories a day. (p. 516)

peripheral nervous system All the nerves located outside the central nervous system; connects the central nervous system to all parts of the body. (p. 628)

peristalsis Involuntary waves of muscle contraction that keep food moving along in one direction through the digestive system. (p. 521)

permafrost Soil that is frozen all year. (p. 740)

petal One of the colorful, leaflike structures of a flower. (p. 290)

petrified fossil A fossil in which minerals replace all or part of an organism. (p. 158)

phagocyte A white blood cell that destroys pathogens by engulfing them and breaking them down. (p. 600)

pharynx The throat; part of both the respiratory and digestive systems. (p. 568)

phenotype An organism's physical appearance, or visible traits. (p. 98)

pheromone A chemical released by one animal that affects the behavior of another animal of the same species. (p. 362)

phloem The vascular tissue through which food moves in some plants. (p. 275)

photosynthesis The process by which plants and some other organisms capture light energy and use it to make food from carbon dioxide and water. (p. 62)

pigment A colored chemical compound that absorbs light, producing color. (pp. 63, 225)

pioneer species The first species to populate an area. (p. 749)

pistil The female reproductive parts of a flower. (p. 291)

pituitary gland An endocrine gland just below the hypothalamus that communicates with the hypothalamus to control many body activities. (p. 661)

placenta A membrane that becomes the link between the developing embryo or fetus and the mother. (pp. 436, 670)

placental mammal A mammal that develops inside its mother's body until its body systems can function independently. (p. 433)

plasma The liquid part of blood. (p. 549)

platelet A cell fragment that plays an important part in forming blood clots. (p. 552)

poaching The illegal killing or removal of wildlife species. (p. 774)

pollen Tiny particles produced by plants that contain the microscopic cells that later become sperm cells. (p. 286)

pollination The transfer of pollen from male reproductive structures to female reproductive structures in plants. (p. 288)

pollution A change to the environment that has a negative effect on living things. (p. 757)

polyp The cnidarian body plan characterized by a vaselike shape and which is usually adapted for life attached to an underwater surface. (p. 323)

population All the members of one species in a particular area. (p. 691)

population density The number of individuals in a specific area. (p. 695)

pore An opening through which sweat reaches the surface of the skin. (p. 497)

precipitation Rain, snow, sleet, or hail. (p. 725)

predation An interaction in which one organism hunts and kills another animal for food. (p. 706)

predator A carnivore that hunts and kills other animals for food and has adaptations that help it capture the animals it preys upon. (pp. 313, 706)

premolars Teeth that, along with molars, grind and shred food into tiny bits. (p. 426)

pressure The force that something exerts over a given area. (p. 546)

prey An animal that a predator feeds upon. (pp. 313, 706)

primary succession The changes that occur in an area where no ecosystem had existed. (p. 749)

probability The likelihood that a particular event will occur. (p. 94)

producer An organism that can make its own food. (p. 717)

prokaryote An organism whose cells lack a nucleus and some other cell structures. (p. 41)

proteins Large organic molecules made of carbon, hydrogen, oxygen, nitrogen, and sometimes sulfur; they are needed for tissue growth and repair and play a part in chemical reactions within cells. (pp. 53, 510)

protozoan An animal-like protist. (p. 219)

pseudopod A "false foot" or temporary bulge of the cell membrane used for feeding and movement in some protozoans. (p. 219)

puberty The period of sexual development during the teenage years in which the body becomes able to reproduce. (p. 675)

punctuated equilibria The theory that species evolve during short periods of rapid change. (p. 164)

Punnett square A chart that shows all the possible combinations of alleles that can result from a genetic cross. (p. 96)

pupa The second stage of complete metamorphosis, in which an insect is enclosed in a protective covering and gradually changes from a larva to an adult. (p. 356)

pupil The opening through which light enters the eye. (p. 637)

purebred An organism that always produces offspring with the same form of a trait as the parent. (p. 87)

radial symmetry The quality of having many lines of symmetry that all pass through a central point. (p. 316)

radioactive element An unstable particle that breaks down into a different element. (p. 160)

radula A flexible ribbon of tiny teeth in mollusks. (p. 341)

recessive allele An allele that is masked when a dominant allele is present. (p. 89)

rectum A short tube at the end of the large intestine where waste material is compressed into a solid form before being eliminated. (p. 529)

red blood cell A cell in the blood that takes up oxygen in the lungs and delivers it to cells elsewhere in the body. (p. 550)

red tide An algal bloom that occurs in salt water. (p. 229)

reflex An automatic response that occurs very rapidly and without conscious control. (p. 633)

regeneration The ability of an organism to regrow body parts. (p. 328)

relative dating A technique used to determine which of two fossils is older. (p. 159)

renewable resource A resource that is naturally replaced in a relatively short time. (p. 757)

replication The process by which a cell makes a copy of the DNA in its nucleus. (p. 73)

reproduce The production of offspring that are similar to the parents. (p. 21)

reproduction The process by which living things produce new individuals of the same type. (p. 663)

reptile An ectothermic vertebrate with lungs and scaly skin; lays eggs with tough, leathery shells. (p. 395)

resolution The ability to clearly distinguish the individual parts of an object. (p. 33)

respiration The process by which cells break down simple food molecules to release the energy they contain. (pp. 67, 567)

responding variable The factor that changes as a result of changes to the manipulated variable in an experiment; also called the dependent variable. (p. 7)

response An action or change in behavior that occurs as a result of a stimulus. (pp. 21, 443, 623)

retina The layer of receptor cells at the back of the eye on which an image is focused; nerve impulses are sent from the retina to the brain. (p. 638)

rhizoid The thin, rootlike structure that anchors a moss and absorbs water and nutrients for the plant. (p. 257)

ribosome A tiny structure in the cytoplasm of a cell where proteins are made. (p. 40)

RNA Ribonucleic acid; a nucleic acid that plays an important role in the production of proteins. (p. 55)

root cap A structure that covers the tip of a root, protecting the root from injury. (p. 283)

saliva The fluid released when the mouth waters that plays an important role in both mechanical and chemical digestion. (p. 520)

saturated fats Fats, such as butter, that are usually solid at room temperature. (p. 509)

savanna A grassland close to the equator. (p. 737)

scavenger A carnivore that feeds on the bodies of dead organisms. (p. 718)

science A way of learning about the natural world and the knowledge gained through that process. (p. 4)

scientific inquiry The diverse ways in which scientists study the natural world. (p. 4)

scientific theory A well-tested concept that explains a wide range of observations. (pp. 9, 149)

scrotum An external pouch of skin in which the testes are located. (p. 664)

secondary succession The changes that occur after a disturbance in an ecosystem. (p. 750)

sedimentary rock A type of rock that forms when particles from other rocks or the remains of plants and animals are pressed and cemented together. (pp. 158, 378)

seed The plant structure that contains a young plant inside a protective covering. (p. 276)

selective breeding The process of selecting a few organisms with desired traits to serve as parents of the next generation. (p. 132)

selective cutting The process of cutting down only some trees in an area. (p. 763)

selectively permeable A property of cell membranes that allows some substances to pass through, while others cannot. (p. 56)

semen A mixture of sperm cells and fluids. (p. 665)

semicircular canals Structures in the inner ear that are responsible for the sense of balance. (p. 641)

sensory neuron A neuron that picks up stimuli from the internal or external environment and converts each stimulus into a nerve impulse. (p. 624)

sepal A leaflike structure that encloses the bud of a flower. (p. 290)

sex-linked gene A gene that is carried on the X or Y chromosome. (p. 122)

sexual reproduction The reproductive process that involves two parents who combine their genetic material to produce a new organism, which differs from both parents. (p. 196)

skeletal muscle A muscle that is attached to the bones of the skeleton. (p. 489)

small intestine The part of the digestive system in which most chemical digestion takes place. (p. 526)

smooth muscle Involuntary muscle found inside many internal organs of the body. (p. 489)

society A group of closely related animals that work together for the benefit of the whole group. (p. 454)

somatic nervous system The group of nerves that controls voluntary actions. (p. 632)

species A group of similar organisms whose members can mate with one another and produce fertile offspring. (pp. 147, 184)

sperm A male sex cell. (pp. 102, 663)

sphygmomanometer An instrument that measures blood pressure. (p. 547)

spinal cord The thick column of nerve tissue that is enclosed by the vertebrae and that links the brain to most of the nerves in the peripheral nervous system. (p. 629)

spontaneous generation The mistaken idea that living things arise from nonliving sources. (p. 21)

spore A tiny cell that is able to grow into a new organism. (p. 223)

sporophyte The stage in the life cycle of a plant in which the plant produces spores for reproduction. (p. 253)

stamen The male reproductive parts of a flower. (p. 290)

stimulant A drug that speeds up body processes. (p. 646)

stimulus A change in an organism's surroundings that causes the organism to react. (pp. 20, 443, 623)

stomach A J-shaped, muscular pouch located in the abdomen that expands to hold all of the food that is swallowed. (p. 522)

stomata The small openings on the undersides of most leaves through which oxygen and carbon dioxide can move. (pp. 63, 278)

stress The reaction of a person's body and mind to threatening, challenging, or disturbing events. (p. 477)

succession The series of predictable changes that occur in a community over time. (p. 748)

sustainable yield A regular amount of a renewable resource that can be harvested without reducing the future supply. (p. 763)

swim bladder An internal gas-filled organ that helps a bony fish stabilize its body at different water depths. (p. 386)

symbiosis A close relationship between two organisms in which at least one of the organisms benefits. (pp. 222, 709)

synapse The tiny space between the tip of an axon and the next structure. (p. 626)

T

T cell A lymphocyte that identifies pathogens and distinguishes one pathogen from another. (p. 601)

tar A dark, sticky substance produced when tobacco burns. (p. 576)

target cell A cell in the body that recognizes a hormone's chemical structure; a cell to which a hormone binds chemically. (p. 659)

taxonomic key A series of paired statements that describe the physical characteristics of different organisms. (p. 186)

taxonomy The scientific study of how living things are classified. (p. 183)

tendon Strong connective tissue that attaches a muscle to a bone. (p. 490)

territory An area that is occupied and defended by an animal or group of animals. (p. 451)

testis Organ of the male reproductive system in which sperm and testosterone are produced. (p. 664)

testosterone A hormone produced by the testes that controls the development of physical characteristics in men. (p. 664)

thorax An insect's mid-section, to which its wings and legs are attached. (p. 355)

threatened species A species that could become endangered in the near future. (p. 772)

tissue A group of similar cells that perform a specific function in an organism. (pp. 252, 474)

tolerance A state in which a drug user, after repeatedly taking a drug, needs larger and larger doses of the drug to produce the same effect. (p. 645)

toxin A poison that can harm an organism. (p. 200)

trachea The windpipe; a passage through which air moves in the respiratory system. (p. 569)

trait A characteristic that an organism can pass on to its offspring through its genes. (p. 86)

transfer RNA RNA in the cytoplasm that carries an amino acid to the ribosome and adds it to the growing protein chain. (p. 109)

transpiration The process by which water is lost through a plant's leaves. (p. 280)

trial-and-error-learning The learning that occurs when an animal learns to perform a behavior more and more skillfully through repeated practice. (p. 446)

tropism The growth response of a plant toward or away from a stimulus. (p. 297)

tumor A mass of abnormal cells that develops when cancerous cells divide and grow uncontrollably. (p. 615)

tundra An extremely cold, dry biome. (p. 740)

U

umbilical cord A ropelike structure that forms in the uterus between the embryo and the placenta. (p. 670)

understory A layer of shorter plants that grow in the shade of a forest canopy. (p. 735)

unicellular A type of organism that is made up of a single cell. (p. 19)

unsaturated fats Fats, such as olive oil and canola oil, that are usually liquid at room temperature. (p. 509)

urea A chemical that comes from the breakdown of proteins and is removed from the body by the kidneys. (p. 581)

ureter A narrow tube that carries urine from one of the kidneys to the urinary bladder. (p. 581)

urethra A small tube through which urine flows from the body. (p. 582)

urinary bladder A sacklike muscular organ that stores urine until it is eliminated from the body. (p. 582)

urine A watery fluid produced by the kidneys that contains urea and other waste materials. (pp. 397, 581)

uterus The hollow muscular organ of the female reproductive system in which a baby develops. (p. 666)

V

vaccination The process by which harmless antigens are deliberately introduced into a person's body to produce active immunity. (p. 607)

vaccine A substance used in a vaccination that consists of pathogens that have been weakened or killed but can still trigger the immune system into action. (pp. 211, 607)

vacuole A water-filled sac inside a cell that acts as a storage area. (p. 41)

vagina A muscular passageway through which a baby leaves the mother's body. (p. 667)

valve A flap of tissue in the heart or a vein that prevents blood from flowing backward. (p. 538)

variable Any factor that can change in an experiment. (pp. 6, 21)

variation Any difference between individuals of the same species. (p. 151)

vascular plant A plant that has vascular tissue. (p. 262)

vascular tissue The internal transporting tissue in some plants that is made up of tubelike structures. (p. 252)

vein A blood vessel that carries blood back to the heart. (p. 540)

ventricle A lower chamber of the heart that pumps blood out to the lungs and body. (pp. 390, 538)

vertebrae The bones that make up the backbone of an animal. (pp. 375, 481)

vertebrate An animal with a backbone. (p. 313)

villi Tiny finger-shaped structures that cover the inner surface of the small intestine and provide a large surface area through which digested food is absorbed. (p. 528)

virus A small, nonliving particle that invades and then reproduces inside a living cell. (p. 204)

vitamins Molecules that act as helpers in a variety of chemical reactions within the body. (p. 511)

vocal cords Folds of connective tissue that stretch across the opening of the larynx and produce a person's voice. (p. 573)

voluntary muscle A muscle that is under conscious control. (p. 488)

water cycle The continuous process by which water moves from Earth's surface to the atmosphere and back. (p. 724)

water vascular system A system of fluid-filled tubes in an echinoderm's body. (p. 366)

white blood cell A blood cell that fights disease. (p. 551)

withdrawal A period of adjustment that occurs when a drug-dependent person stops taking the drug. (p. 646)

xylem The vascular tissue through which water and nutrients move in some plants. (p. 275)

zygote A fertilized egg, produced by the joining of a sperm and an egg. (pp. 252, 663)

Abbé, Ernst 31
abdomen
  of arachnid 350
  of crayfish 351
  of insect 355
Abert squirrel 155
abiotic factors 690
absolute dating 160
absorption 519, 528–529
acne 500
acquired immunodeficiency syndrome
  (AIDS) 210, 603–604
active immunity 605–608
active transport 59–60
active viruses 207–208
adaptations 149, 312, 373
  of animals 312–313
  of birds 417–418
  to environment 704, 706
  of plants 250–251
  predator 313, 706–707
  prey 313, 706–707
  of primates for grasping 436
  in reptiles to conserve water 395–396
addiction, drug 646
  alcoholism 651
  nicotine 577
adenine 78, 108
adolescence 675–676
adrenal glands 660, 661
adrenaline 477–478, 659
adulthood 677
advertising, nutrition and 530
African rain forests 780–785
afterbirth 672
aggression 451, 454
aging 677
agrochemicals 305, 306
AIDS 210, 603–604
air pressure, bird wings and 420–421
air sacs in bird lungs 412, 413, 415
Akita 177
alcohol 645, 647, 649–652
  effects of 650–652
alcoholic fermentation 70
alcoholism 651
algae 224–230, 249
  brown 227
  colors of 225
  diatoms 218, 226, 229
  dinoflagellates 226, 229
  euglenoids 225
  green 226
  red 227
algal blooms 228–230
alleles 89–90
  dominant 122
  multiple 119–120
  recessive 122
  sickle-cell 127
allergens 613
allergies 612–613
alligators 403
alveoli 570, 571
ameba 220

amino acids 53, 510, 522–523
amniocentesis 128
amniotic sac 670
amphetamines 646, 647
amphibians 389–394
  circulation in 390
  frogs 391, 392, 393
  mobility of 392
  reproduction in 390–391
  respiration in 390
  salamanders 389, 391, 392–393
  threats to 394
  toads 392
anabolic steroids 647, 648
anal pore 221
anaphase 74, 77
Andes Mountains 572
anemone fish 387
angiosperms 289–296
  flowers 290–95
  life cycle of 292
  reproduction in 291
  types of 293
  uses of 296
animal(s) 191, 309, 310–439. See also
  invertebrates; vertebrates
  adaptations of 312–313
  amphibians 389–394
  arthropods 346–353
  of boreal forest 740
  characteristics of 310–312
  classification of 313–314
  cloning of 134
  cnidarians 323–325
  of deciduous forests 739
  of desert 737
  echinoderms 365–368
  fishes 381–387
  in freshwater biomes 742, 743
  of grassland 738
  insects 346, 348, 354–364
  in marine biomes 744, 745
  mollusks 340–344
  of mountains and ice biome 741
  movement by 311–312
  needs of 312
  of rain forest 736
  reptiles 395–404
  sponges 320–322
  symmetry in 316–317, 341, 365
  of tundra 741
  worms 327–334
animal behavior 441–458
  aggression 451, 454
  behavior cycles 455–456
  communication 450, 454
  competition 451
  conditioning 445–446
  group living 453–454, 455, 458
  imprinting 447–448
  instinctive 444
  learning 444–447, 449
  mating 452–453
  migration 456–457
  parenting 453

  pheromones and 363
  territory, establishing 451–452
animal bites, disease spread by 595
animal cells 19, 39, 43, 75, 311
animalcules 29
animal-like protists 219–223
Annelida (phylum) 327
Anning, Mary 378
annual plants 298
annual rings 281–282
anole 442
Antarctica 756, 760
antennae of crayfish 348–349, 351
anther 290, 292
antibiotics 201, 609
antibodies 602, 605
antigens 601
ants 362
anus 331, 529
anvil 641
aorta 539, 542
appendages, arthropod 347, 348–349
appendix 165
aquaculture 766
arachnids 348, 350–352
Archaebacteria 189–190, 194
Archaeopteryx 379, 410
Aristotle 183
arteries 540, 543–545
Arthropoda (phylum) 347
arthropods 346–353. See also insects
  arachnids 348, 350–352
  centipedes 353
  characteristics of 347–349, 360–361
  crustaceans 348, 349–350, 351
  millipedes 353
  origin of 349
artificial heart 559
artificial intelligence 446–447
asexual reproduction 195, 236, 311
  in bacteria 195
  budding 236
  in cnidarians 324
  in corals 325
  in fungi 236
  in paramecium 221
  in sponges 322
  in worms 328
asthma 613
atherosclerosis 557, 579
atmosphere 567
  of early Earth 44–45
atom 52, 724
atrium, atria of heart 390, 538, 539
Audubon, John James 411
Australia 156
autonomic nervous system 632
autotrophs 23, 65, 249, 717
auxin 298
axons 624, 626, 632

baby
  birth of 671–672
  in infancy 673–674
  sex of 121

backbone 374, 375–376, 481. *See also* **vertebrates**
bacteria 29, 181, 192–203, 593, 719
  cell of 41, 192–194
  environmental recycling by 199–200
  fermentation and 305
  in food 198–199
  fuel produced by 197
  genetic engineering in 135–136
  health-promoting 201
  infectious diseases caused by 200–201
  kingdoms of 189–190, 194–195
  nitrogen-fixing 727
  reproduction in 192, 195–196
  survival needs of 196–197
bacteriophage 205, 206
ball-and-socket joint 485
balloonfish 387
barbiturates 647
bases, nitrogen 78, 108, 109
basset hound 176
bats 434
B cells 601, 602, 606
Beaumont, William 518
bee-eaters 418
behavior 443. *See also* **animal behavior**
biceps 491
biennials 299
bighorn sheep, desert 683, 684
bilateral symmetry 316, 317, 341
bile 527, 586
bill of bird 412, 413
binary fission 195
binomial nomenclature 183
biodiversity 768–776, 780–785
  factors affecting 768–769
  of gene pool 771
  protection of 775–776
  species extinction and 771–774
  value of 769–770
biogeography 728–731
  continental drift 156, 728–729
  dispersal, means and limits of 729–731
biological controls 359
bioluminescence 364
biomes 732–751
  boreal forest 739–740
  deciduous forest 738–739
  desert 736–737
  freshwater 742–743
  grassland 737–738
  marine 743–745
  mountains and ice 741
  rain forest 735–736, 780–785
  succession 746–750
  tundra 740–741
biotic factors 689
birds 409, 410–422
  body temperature of 414
  diversity of 417–419
  feathers of 411–412
  flight of 411, 420–422
  food of 412–415
  getting oxygen 415–416
  importance of 419

  nervous system of 416
  of prey 418
  reproduction and caring for young in 416–417
birth 671–673
birth canal 667
birth rate 697
bivalves 342–344
bladderwort 297
Blalock, Alfred 558
blood
  blood types and 552–553, 555
  components of 549–553
  plasma 549
  platelets 549, 551, 552
  red blood cells 42, 58, 126, 531, 549, 550–551
  water content of 24
  white blood cells 531, 549, 551, 600
blood alcohol concentration (BAC) 650
blood banks 558
blood cells 42, 58, 126, 531, 535, 549, 550–552, 600
blood flow, regulating 544–545, 546
blood pressure 546–547
blood transfusion 552–553, 555
blood types 119, 552–553, 555, 558
blood vessels 540–546
  arteries 540, 543–545
  capillaries 540, 544, 545, 570, 582–583
  veins 540, 545, 546
body defenses against infectious disease 596–600
body organization 472–479
  cells 473
  homeostasis in 25, 476–479
  levels of 472–475
  organs 311, 475
  tissues 474–475
body temperature 477
  of birds 414
  skin and maintenance of 495
  in vertebrates 376–377
bog 258
bones 480–487. *See also* **skeletal system**
  growth 483
  strength 482–483
bony fish 383, 385–386
Border collie 176
Border terrier 178
boreal forest biome 739–740
Borrelia burgdorferi 193
botanists 12
botulism 595
box jellyfish 310
Brachiosaurus 404
brain
  of bird 416
  concussion of 634
  of human 629–630
  of worm 328
brainstem 630, 631
branching tree diagram 168–169, 314, 380
breathing 567, 572–573, 575
  path of air in 568–570

  processing of 572–573
breeding 132–133, 150
bristlecone pine 250
brittle stars 367
bronchi 568, 569, 570
bronchitis 578
Brown, Barnum 379
brown algae 227
bubonic plague (Black Death) 358
budding 236, 322, 324
buoyancy 386
  swim bladders in fish and 385–386
butterflies 315, 354, 773

caffeine 648–649
calcium 482, 483, 486, 512
California condors, captive breeding of 775
California leaf-nosed bat 685
calipers 7
calorie 507
Calorie (1000 calories) 507
  from fat 515–516
cambium 281, 283
Cambrian period 162
camouflage 358, 706
cancer 112, 499–500, 578, 579, 614–616
  causes of 615
  prevention of 616
  treatment of 615–616
canines 426, 520
canopy 735, 781, 782, 784–785
capillaries 540, 544, 545, 570, 582–583
captive breeding 775
carbohydrates 19, 46, 53, 54, 506, 507–508
  converting to agrochemicals 305
carbolic acid 592
carbon 53
carbon cycle 725–726
carbon dioxide 44, 53
  in alcoholic fermentation 70
  in gas exchange 571
  photosynthesis and 63, 64
  in red blood cells 550
Carboniferous period 162
carbon monoxide 577
carcinogens 615, 616
cardiac muscle 489, 491, 538
cardiovascular diseases 557–559, 612
  atherosclerosis 557,558,559
  heart attack 557,559
  hypertension 557–559
cardiovascular health 556–560
  advances in 558–559
  maintaining 560
cardiovascular system 536–537. *See also* **circulation**
  alcohol's effect on 651
carnivores 313, 718
  mammal 435, 436
carrageenan 227
carrier 122, 123
  of hemophelia 127
carrying capacity 699
Carson, Rachel 759
cartilage 375, 484

cartilaginous fish 383, 384
casts 158
cell(s) 16–49, 473
    active transport in 59–60
    animal 19, 39, 43, 75, 311
    bacterial 41, 192–194
    chemical composition of 19, 52–55
    diffusion in 57, 58–59
    energy use by 20, 67
    first (early) 46
    first sightings of 28–29
    fungal 234
    nucleus of 36–37, 38, 39
    osmosis in 58–59
    plant 19, 35, 38, 43, 54, 75
    sex 102–106, 663–664
    specialized 19, 42
cell cycle 73–77
    cytokinesis 75, 76
    interphase 73–74, 76
    length of 75, 80
    mitosis 74, 76–77
cell division
    cytokinesis 75, 76
    DNA replication 78–79
    mitosis 74, 76–77
    preparation for 74
cell membrane 35–36, 38, 39, 53, 54, 220, 473
    engulfment by 60
    selective permeability of 56
cell theory 30–31
cellular organization 19
cellular respiration 67
cellulose 35, 54
cell wall 35, 38
Celsius scale 789
Cenozoic era 163
centipedes 353
central nervous system 628, 629–631
    brain 629–630
    spinal cord 629, 631
centromere 74, 77
cephalopods 342, 344
cerebellum 630, 631
cerebrum 630
certified wood 764
cervix 666, 667
chameleon 373, 397, 398
chelipeds 351
chemical digestion 519, 520, 522, 523, 526–528
chemicals
    compund cells in 53–55
    plant-based 304–307
    in tobacco smoke 576–577
chicken pox 210
chitin 347–348
Chlamydomonas 190
chlorine 512
chlorophyll 63, 64, 278
chloroplast 38, 40, 62–63, 278, 279
cholera 594
cholesterol 509
Chordata (phylum) 374
chordates 374–375

Chow chow 177
chromatids 74, 77
chromatin 36, 37, 74
chromosomes 74, 106, 664
    DNA and 108
    inheritance and 102–103
    sex 121, 122
chrysalis 357
cilia 221, 341, 568, 569, 597
ciliates 221
circadian rhythms 455
circle graphs 798
circulation 535–560
    blood, components of 549–553
    blood pressure 546–547
    blood vessels and 540–546
    cardiovascular health and 556–560
    functions of 536–537
    heart and 538–540
    lymphatic system and 554
circulatory system 475, 536–537, 567
    closed 332, 382
    of amphibians 390
    of arthropods 347
    of bird 415–416
    of fish 382
    of mammals 426
    of segmented worms 332
    open 332, 347
    smoking and 579
clams 343
classification 182–188, 787
    early systems of 183
    of fungi 237
    levels of 185–186, 187
    Linnean system of 183–185
    reasons for 182–183
    using 186
clear-cutting 763
climate
    biodiversity and 769
    biome and 734
    as limit to dispersal 731
cloning 134
Closterium 226
Clostridium tetani 200–201
club fungi 237
club mosses 265
cnidarians 323–325
    body plans of 323–324
    characteristics of 323
    in coral reef 325–326
    feeding by 324
    reproduction in 324
coal, formation of 262
cocaine 645, 647
cochlea 641
cocoon 357
codominance 98–99
cold sores 209
Colorado River valley 684
colorblindness, red-green 122–123
commensalism 709
commons 763
communication

animal 450, 454
    insect 362–364
    in science 9, 787
communities
    in ecosystem 692
    succession in 746–750
compact bone 483
compare/contrast tables 794
competition 151, 451, 704, 705, 730
complete metamorphosis 356, 357
complete proteins 510
complex carbohydrates 508
compound eyes 351, 355
compound microscope 28, 30, 31, 802
compounds 52
    in cells 53–55
    inorganic 53
    organic 53
concave lenses 639
concept maps 794
conclusions, drawing 8, 791
concussion 634
condensation 725
conditioning 445–446
cones 286, 287, 288, 638
coniferous trees (conifers) 286, 288, 739–740
conjugation 196
connective tissue 474, 475, 484, 490
consumers 718, 719, 720
contaminated objects, spread of disease by 595
continental drift 156, 728–729
contour feathers 411, 413
contractile vacuole 220, 221
controlled experiment 7, 21, 22, 791
Convention on International Trade in Endangered Species (1973) 776
convex lens 32, 639
coral reef 323, 325–326, 769
corn, products made from 306
cornea 637
coronary arteries 543, 557
cortisone 296
cotton plants 296
cotyledons 276
cough 570
courtship behavior 452–453, 454
crayfish 348–349, 351
Cretaceous period 163
Crick, Francis 78
critical thinking skills 792–793
crocodiles 403
crop 412, 413
cross matching of blood types 553
crustaceans 348, 349–350, 351
Culex nigripalpus 211
cuticle 249, 264, 279
cuttlefish 344
cycads 285
cycle diagrams 795
cycles of matter 723–727
    carbon and oxygen cycle 725–726
    nitrogen cycle 726–727
    recycling matter 723–724
    water cycle 724–725

cystic fibrosis 126
cytokinesis 75, 76
cytoplasm 37–41, 75, 220, 473
    respiration in 68
cytosine 78, 108

dachshund 176
Dall's sheep 436
dandelions 274
Darwin, Charles 146–151
data 5
    collecting 7
    interpreting 8, 791
data tables 8, 796
date palm 251
dating techniques 159–160
Datta, Rathin 304–307
death, leading causes of 610–611
death rate 697
deciduous forest biome 738–739
decomposers 199–200, 718–719, 720, 727
deep zone 745
defenses against infectious disease 596–600
defense strategies 706–707
defensive communication 454
Deinonychus 379
dendrite 624, 626
deoxyribonucleic acid. See DNA
deoxyribose 78
dependent (responding) variable 7, 791
depressants 646
    alcohol 649–652
dermis 496, 497, 643
desert biome 736–737
desert wildlife, protecting 682–685
development. See also human life cycle
    evolutionary similarities in early 166–167
    of living things 20
Devonian period 162
DeVries, William 559
dewlap 398
diabetes 584, 614
diaphragm 426, 572, 573
diarrhea 595
diatomaceous earth 226
diatoms 218, 226, 229
dicots 293
diffusion 57, 59, 322, 545
    of water molecules 58–59
digestion 518–530
    chemical 519, 520, 522, 523, 526–528
    esophagus and 519, 521
    large intestine 519, 529
    liver function in 519, 527
    mechanical 518–519, 520, 522, 523
    mouth and 519, 520
    pancreas function in 519, 528
    small intestine and 519, 526–528
    stomach and 519, 522–525
digestive system 475, 567
    alcohol's effect on 651
    of birds 412–413
    functions of 518–519
    organs of 519, 520–529
    of planarian 330

of roundworms 331
digitalis 296
dinoflagellates 226, 229
dinosaur eggs 379
dinosaurs 378–379, 404
direct observation 696
disease(s). See also infectious disease;
        noninfectious disease
    analyzing urine for signs of 584
    cardiovascular 557, 612
    cardiovascular system and fight against
        537
    fungal 240–241
    insects carrying 358
dispersal 729
    limits of 730–731
    means of 729–730
DNA 55, 107–112
    chromosomes and 108
    evolutionary similarities in 167–168
    extracted from fossils 168
    genetic code 107–108
    mutations and 110–112
    replication of 73, 78–79
    structure of 78–79
DNA fingerprinting 137
dogs 174–179
dog tapeworms 329
Dolly (cloned sheep) 116, 134
dolphins 435
dominant alleles 89–90, 122
double helix 78
Douglas, Marjory Stoneman 759
down feathers 412
Down syndrome 128
downy mildews 223
Drew, Charles 558
drinking and driving 650
drone (bee) 455
drugs 644–652
    alcohol 645, 647, 649–652
    drug abuse 645–646, 647
    kinds of 646–649
    medicines 644
duck-billed platypuses 432
Durrell, Gerald 784–785

ear, hearing and 640–641
eardrum 641
Earth, early atmosphere of 44–45
earthworms 331, 332–333, 334, 444
Ebola virus 205
Echinodermata (phylum) 365
echinoderms 365–368
    brittle stars 367
    characteristics of 365–366
    sand dollars 367
    sea cucumbers 368
    sea stars 366–367
    sea urchins 365, 368
ecological interactions 703–710
    competition 151, 451, 704, 705, 730
    environmental adaptations 704, 706
    predation 704, 706–708
    symbiosis 222, 704, 709–710

ecology 692–693
economic value of biodiversity 770
ecosystems 688–694, 715–731. See also
        biomes
    abiotic factors in 690
    biogeography 728–731
    biotic factors in 689
    communities in 692
    cycles of matter in 723–727
    ecology and 692–693
    energy flow in 716–722
    habitats 394, 689
    populations in 691
ecotourism 770
ectotherm 376. See also amphibians; fishes;
        reptiles
egg cells 102
    human 663, 666–667
eggs
    bird 416-417
    dinosaur 379
    insect 356, 357
    reptile 396
Eldridge, Niles 164
electron microscopes 33
elements 52, 160
elephants 435
elephant shrew 167–168
elimination of wastes 529
embryo 669
    development of 669–670
    of seed 276
emergency medical technician (EMT) 13
emergent layer of rain forest 781
emigration 698
emphysema 578, 579
endangered species 772–773
Endangered Species Act of 1973 775
endocrine glands 658
endocrine system 475, 658–662
    in adolescence 675
    hormones 659, 666, 668, 675
    hypothalamus 660, 661
    menstrual cycle and 668
    negative feedback and 662
    pituitary gland 660, 661
    role of 658, 660–661
endoplasmic reticulum 38, 39, 40
endoskeleton 365
    backbone 375–376
endospores 197
endotherm 377, 379. See also birds;
        mammals
energy
    as product of respiration 68
    in carbohydrates 54
    cellular use of 20, 67
    in lipids 54
    mitochondrial production of 37
    organisms' need for 23–24
    photosynthesis and 62–63, 64
energy flow in ecosystems 716–722
    energy pyramids 721–722
    energy roles 717–719
    food chains and food webs 719–721

energy pyramids 721–722
English peppered moth 154
engulfment by cell membrane 60
environment. *See also* **ecosystems**
    adaptations to 704, 706
    of crustaceans 350
    genetics and 120
    pathogens from 595
environmental issues 755–776
    approaches to 758–760
    biodiversity 768–776, 780–785
    fisheries 765–766
    forest resources 762–764, 767
    history of 758–759
    types of 756–757
environmental recycling
    by bacteria 199–200
    by fungi 240
environmental science 759
enzymes 54, 520, 522
epidermis 496–497
epiglottis 519, 521, 569, 570
epithelial tissue 474, 475
Epstein-Barr virus 205
Escher, M.C. 631
Escherichia coli 193, 195, 709
esophagus 519, 521
estrogen 666
estuary 743–744
Eubacteria 190, 194–195, 200
euglena 225
euglenoids 225
eukaryotes 41, 249.
Eureka valley evening primrose 772
eutrophication 230, 231–232
evaporation 724–725
evolution 146–173
    in action 154
    adaptations and 149
    body structure similarities and 165–166
    combining evidence of 168–169
    continental drift and 156
    Darwin's work and 146–151
    defined 149
    DNA similarities and 167–168
    early development similarities and 166–167
    fossil record of 157–164
    genes and 154
    natural selection 146, 150–153, 154, 704
    protein structure and 170
    rate of 164
    species formation 155–156
    of vertebrates 374–380
excretion 581
excretory system 475, 581–586
    kidneys 581–586
    other organs of 586
    water balance and 585–586
exercise
    cardiovascular health and 560
    healthy bones and 487
    healthy muscles and 492
exoskeleton 347–348
exotic species 730, 774

experiment 790–791
    controlled 21, 22
    designing 6–7, 10, 26, 791
    laboratory safety 11, 799–801
extinction 771–774
    causes of 773–774
    of dinosaurs 404
extinct species 160
eye
    amphibian 392
    vision and 637–639
eye dominance 120
eyespots 330, 367

"fairy rings" 241
farms, efficiency of 267–268
farsightedness 639
fats 54, 506, 509
    Calories from 515–516
fat-soluble vitamins 511, 512
feathers 411–412
Felis genus 184
female reproductive system 666–668
    egg cells 663, 666–667
    menstrual cycle 667–668
    ovaries 660, 666
fermentation 69–70, 305
ferns 261, 263–264
fertilization. *See also* **reproduction**
    in amphibians 390
    in angiosperms 291, 292
    in arthropods 347
    in birds 416
    in fishes 383
    in gymnosperms 287, 288
    in humans 663
    in mammals 428
    in plants 252, 253
fertilizer 5, 268
fetus, development of 671
fiber 508, 528
fibrin 552
fibrous roots 282–283
fiddleheads 264
fight-or-flight response 478
filament 290
filter feeders 342
finches 149, 154
fins 381, 382, 385
fireflies 357, 364
fisheries 765–766
fishes 381–387
    bony 383, 385–386
    cartilaginous 383, 384
    classification of 383–386
    feeding by 382
    as food 387
    getting oxygen 382, 388
    jawless 374, 383
    mobility of 382
    reproduction in 383
fishing limits 765–766
flagellum, flagella 194, 222
flapping flight 422
flatworms 328–329

Fleming, Alexander 241, 607
flight of birds 411, 420–422
flowcharts 795
flowers 292
    of monocots vs. dicots 293
    structure of 290–291, 294–295
fluorine 512
flying gurnards 386
follicles 497
food 196, 504–516. *See also* **digestion**
    animal adaptations for getting 312–313
    bacteria in 198–199
    carbohydrates 19, 46, 53, 54, 305, 506, 507–508
    contaminated, disease spread by 595
    efficiency of farms 267–268
    fats 54, 506, 509, 515–516
    Food Guide Pyramid 513–515
    functions of 506–507
    fungi and 240
    hydroponics 268
    as limiting factor 699
    minerals 506, 512, 517
    photosynthesis and 63
    plants as 266–268
    proteins 19, 53–54, 506, 510
    vitamins 506, 510–512
food, methods of obtaining 311
    in alligators and crocodiles 403
    in birds 412–415
    of cnidarians 324
    in crustaceans 350
    by fishes 382
    in fungi 235
    in insects 356
    in lizards 398
    in snakes 399
    of sponges 322
    in turtles 402
food chains 719–721
food groups 513, 514
Food Guide Pyramid 513–515
food labels 515–516
food vacuole 220, 221
food web 719–721
foot
    mollusk 342
    of snail 343
force, ventricular 542
forest(s)
    boreal 739–740
    deciduous 738–739
    rain 248, 735–736, 780–785
forest resources 762–764, 767
Forest Stewardship Council 764
fossil record 160
fossils 46, 157–164, 377, 410
    determining age of 159–160
    DNA extracted from 168
    formation of 157–159
    Geologic Time Scale and 161–164
    information yielded by 160–161
    of mollusks 341
    petrified 158
    vertebrate history in 377–379

fraternal twins 673
free nitrogen 726
freshwater biome 742–743
freshwater blooms 230
Friedman, Cindy xxii, 1–3
Friends of the Everglades 759
frogs 391, 392, 393
fronds 264
fruiting bodies 236
fruits 291, 292
fuel
    bacteria and production of 197
    coal deposits 262
    peat 258
fungi 191, 233–245, 593, 719
    cell structure of 234
    classification of 237
    food acquisition by 235
    living world and 240–242
    reproduction in 235–236
    skin infection with 500
funguslike protists 223–224
fur 424–425, 429

Galapagos Islands 147–148
gallbladder 519, 527
gametes 253
gametophytes 253, 257, 264, 275
gannets 699–700
gas exchange 571
gasohol 304
gastropods 342
gemsboks 441
gene(s) 89, 102, 106
    on chromosomes 106
    evolution and 154
    main function of 107
    sex-linked 122–123
    traits controlled by many 120
    traits controlled by single 118–119
gene pool diversity 771
generalizations, making 793
gene therapy 136–137
genetic code 107–108
genetic counseling 129
genetic crosses 100–101
genetic disorders 125–131
    cystic fibrosis 126
    diagnosing 128–129
    Down syndrome 128
    genetic counseling and 129
    hemophilia 127
    from inbreeding 175
    sickle-cell disease 126–127
genetic engineering 134–137, 267
genetics 84–143. See also DNA; traits
    alleles 89–90, 119–120, 122, 127
    cloning 134
    codominance 98–99
    environment and 120
    genetic engineering 134–137, 267
    Human Genome Project 138–139
    Mendel's work on 86–91
    mutations 110–112, 125
    pedigrees in 117, 123–124

phenotypes and genotypes 98, 112
    probability and 94–101
    Punnett squares and 96–97, 104
    selective breeding 132–133, 150
    sex of baby and 121
    symbols in 90–91
genetic testing 139
genotypes 98
genus 184, 186
geographic isolation 155–156
Geologic Time Scale 161–164
germination 278
gestation period 433, 436
giant clams 342
giant kelps 227
giant sequoia trees 284
Giardia lamblia 222
gills 341, 381, 382, 385
ginkgo 285
gizzard 413
glands 658. See also endocrine system
gliding flight 422
gliding joint 485
glucose 67, 508
    diabetes and blood level of 614
    from photosynthesis 63, 64
gnetophytes 285
Golden retriever 176
Golgi body 38, 39, 40
Gonyaulax 226
Gorgas, William C. 600
Gould, Stephen Jay 164
gradualism 164
gradual metamorphosis 356, 357
gram (g) 789
graphic organizers 794–795
grasshopper 357
grassland biome 737–738
gravitropism 298, 300
gray wolf 174
great horned owl 186, 187
green algae 226
Green Belt Movement 759
87–88, 90, 96–97, 98–99
Greyhound 176
grizzly bear 772
group living 453–454, 455, 458
growth of living things 20
growth spurt 675
guanine 78, 108
gymnosperms 284–288
    life cycle of 287
    reproduction in 286–288
    types of 285–286

habitat 394, 689
habitat destruction 774
habitat fragmentation 774
habitat preservation 776
hagfishes 383
hair 424–425, 429
hair follicles 497
half-life 160
hallucinogens 647, 648
hammer 641

hares 434
hearing 636, 640–641
heart 538–540
    action of 538–539, 548
    amphibian 390
    artificial 559
    of bird 416
    mammal 426
    regulation of beat of 540
    of snail 343
    structure of human 538
heart attack 557, 579
heartbeat 538
heart transplants 559
heartwood 281
helmets, wearing 634, 635
hemoglobin 550, 577
hemophilia 127
Henry, Mike 305
herbaceous stems 280–281
herbivores 312, 718
heredity 86. See also genetics
Herriot, James 178
heterotrophs 24, 65, 311, 718
heterozygous trait 98
hibernation 456, 739
hidden viruses 208–209
hinge joint 485
histamine 613
HIV 603, 646
Hoh rain forest (Washington State) 248
homeostasis 25, 476–479
    hypothalamus and 660
    negative feedback and 662
    nervous system and maintaining 623
    stress and 477–479
    water balance in body 585–586
homologous structures 166
homozygous trait 98
honeybees 454–455
hoofed mammals 435
Hooke, Robert 28, 30
hormones 659–662
    in adolescence 675
    estrogen 666
    menstruation triggered by 668
    plant 298
    testosterone 664
hornworts 259
horsetails 265
host 205, 710
Human Genome Project 138–139
human immunodeficiency virus (HIV) 603, 646
human life cycle 669–678
    adolescence 675–676
    adulthood 677
    birth 671–673
    childhood 674
    embryo, development of 669–670
    fetus, development of 671
    infancy 657, 673–674
humans, as means of dispersal 730
hybridization 133
hybrids 90

hydra 29
hydrochloric acid 522
hydroponics 268
hypertension 557–559
hyphae 234, 235, 241
hypothalamus 660, 661
hypothesis 6, 8, 790

ice sheets 741
Ichthyosaurus 378
identical twins 673
iguanas, green 398
Iguanodon 378
immigration 698
immovable joints 484
immune response 601, 602, 606
immune system 475, 601–602
   AIDS and 603–604
imperfect fungi 237
imprinting 447–448
inbreeding 133, 175
incisors 426, 520
incomplete proteins 510
independent (manipulated) variable 7
indirect observation 696
Industrial Revolution 154
infancy 657, 673–674
infectious disease 592–611
   active immunity to 605–608
   AIDS 210, 603–604
   from bacteria 200–201
   body defenses against 596–600
   immune system and 601–602
   medications and 609
   passive immunity to 608
   pathogens and 593
   prevention of 605–608, 609
   spread of 594–595
   from viruses 200, 210–211
inference 5, 786
inflammatory response 600
influenza 210
inhalants 647
inheritance, chromosomes and 102–103.
      See also genetics
inherited traits 89, 444–445
inner ear 640, 641
inorganic compounds 53
insect-eating mammals 434
insects 346, 348, 354–364
   body of 355
   communication by 362–364
   control of 359
   defenses of 358
   development of 355–356, 357
   humans and 358–359
insight learning 446
instinctive behavior 444
insulator 412
   fat as 425
   fur and hair as 424–425
insulin 135, 614
interneurons 624, 625, 629
interphase 73–74, 76
intertidal zone 744

invertebrates 313. *See also* **arthropods**
involuntary muscles 488
iodine 512
iris 637
iron 512, 517
isolation, geographic 155–156
Ituri forest 783

Janssen, Hans and Zacharias 30
Jarvik, Robert 559
jawless fish 374, 383
jellyfish 310, 323
Jenner, Edward 606
jet propulsion, swimming by 344
Jurassic period 163

Kaibab squirrel 155
kangaroos 433
karyotype 129
kelps 227
kestrels 418, 716
keystone species 770
kidneys 581–586
   as filters 582–583
   of mollusks 341
   reptile 397
   water balance in body and 585–586
king cobra 395
kingdoms 186, 189–191
   bacterial 189–190, 194–195
   Plant Kingdom 248–255
Koch, Robert 607
krill 350, 450
kudzu 289

laboratory safety 11, 799–801
labor during birth 671
Labrador retrievers 175
lactic-acid fermentation 69, 70
lakes 742
lampreys 383
Landsteiner, Karl 552, 558
large intestine 519, 529
large nucleus 221
larva 322
   amphibian 390, 391
   insect 357
larynx 573, 574
laser surgery 559
lateral line 385
laws to protect biodiversity 775–776
leafy sea dragon 386
learning 444–447, 449
   conditioning 445–446
   insight 446
   trial and error 446
leaves
   controlling water loss in 280
   of monocots vs. dicots 293
   photosynthesis and 278–279
   of seed plants 278–280
   structure of 278, 279
Leeuwenhoek, Anton van 29, 30, 192
legumes 727
length, measuring 788

lens 637, 638–639
   in microscopes 32
Leonardo da Vinci 486
Leopold, Aldo 759
Lessing, Doris 566
Lhasa apso 177
lice 33
lichens 242
life. *See* living things
life cycle
   of angiosperms 292
   of crustaceans 350
   of gymnosperms 287
   human 669–678
   of plants 253
life science
   branches of 11–13
   careers in 12–13
life span of seed plants 298–299
lift 421
ligaments 486
light
   insect communication with 364
   plant responses to 298
light microscope 31, 32–33
limestone 341
limiting factors 699–700
Lind, James 511
line graphs 797
Linnaeus, Carolus 183–185
lipids 19, 53, 54
liquid volume 788
Lister, Joseph 592–593, 606
liter (L) 788
liver
   alcohol's effect on 651
   digestion and 519, 527
   excretion and 586
liverworts 259
living space, organisms' need for 25
living things 18–49
   cell theory and 30–31
   characteristics of 18–21
   chemical composition of 19, 45–46
   as means of dispersal 729–730
   needs of 22–28
   origin of 44–46
   photosynthesis and 65
   water and 55
lizards 397–398, 400–401
lodgepole pines 275
logging methods 763
Lorenz, Konrad 448
Lovejoy, Asa L. 94
lung cancer 578, 579
lungs
   circulation to and from 541
   excretion and 586
   mammal 426
   breathing and 569, 570, 571
Lyme disease 352, 595
lymph 554
lymphatic system 554
lymph nodes 554
lymphocytes 601, 602

lynx spider 716
lysosomes 39, 41

Maathai, Wangari 759
magnesium 512
magnification of microscope 32
malaria 223, 595, 600
male reproductive system 664–665
mammals 423–436
   diversity of 431–436
   early 424
   fur and hair of 424–425, 429
   getting oxygen 426
   marsupials 156, 431, 432–433
   monotremes 431, 432
   movement of 428
   nervous system and senses of 426–427
   placental 431, 433–436
   reproduction and parenting in 428
   teeth of 426
   of tundra 741
mammary glands 428
mangrove trees 251
manipulated variable 7, 791
Mantell, Mary Ann and Gideon 378
mantle of mollusk 340, 343
marijuana 645, 647
marine biologists 12
marine biome 743–745
marine mammals 435
mark-and-recapture studies 696–697, 701
marker molecules 552–553
marrow 485
marsupials 156, 431, 432–433
mass, measuring 789
Masters, Elroy 682–685
mating 452–453. See also reproduction
matter 723–724
   cycles of 723–727
   recycling 723–724
Mbuti people 783
measles 210
measurements, making 7, 788–789
mechanical digestion 518–519, 520, 522, 523
medications, infectious disease and 609
medicine 296, 644
medusa 324
meiosis 104–106
melanin 497
Mendel, Gregor 86–91, 96
meniscus 788
menstrual cycle 667–668
menstruation 668
mental changes
   in adolescence 676
   in childhood 674
Mesozoic era 163
messenger RNA 109, 110–111
metamorphosis 350, 463
   amphibian 390, 391
   insect 355–356
metaphase 74, 77
meter (m) 788
methane 44, 197
Meyer, Hermann von 410

microscope 29, 192–193
   improvements over time 3–31
   invention of 28
   magnification of 32
   resolution of 33
   types of 28, 30, 31, 32–33, 802
   use of 802–803
middle ear 640, 641
migration 456–457
Miller, Stanley 45
millipedes 353
mimicry as defense strategy 707
minerals 506, 512, 517
mites 352
mitochondria 37, 38, 39, 68
mitosis 74, 76–77
models, making 787
molars 426, 520
molds 18, 223–224
molds (fossil) 158
molecules 52, 724
   diffusion of 57
Mollusca (phylum) 340
mollusks 340–344
   evidence of early 341
   snails 342, 343, 345
   with tentacles 343, 344
   two-shelled 342–344
molting 348
monarch butterflies 354
monocots 293
monotremes 431, 432
mood-altering drugs 645
moray eel 381
mosses 257–258, 260
motor neuron 624, 625, 632
mountains and ice biome 741
mouth
   as barrier against pathogens 597
   digestion and 519, 520
movable joints 484, 485
movement of animals 311–312
   of fish 382
   of mammals 428
   mobility of amphibians 392
   mobility of fishes 382
   skeleton and 482
mucus 521, 523, 568, 569, 597
Muir, John 758
multicellular organisms 19
multiple alleles 119–120
multiple births 673
muscles and muscular system 488–493
   action of 488
   for breathing 572
   care of 492
   types of muscles 489–491, 492, 493
   at work 491, 493
muscle tissue 474
muscular system 475
mushrooms 217
musk oxen 453
mussels 343
mutations 110–112, 125
mutualism 222, 709, 727

nanometers (nm) 206
narcotics 647
native species 730
natural selection 146, 150–153, 154, 704
nautiluses 344
nearsightedness 639
negative feedback 662
Nematoda (phylum) 327
nephrons 582, 583
neritic zone 744
nerve cells 19, 42
nerve cord 375
nerve impulse 623, 624, 625–626
   how it travels 626
   path of 625
nerve tissue 474
nervous system 475, 621–652
   alcohol's effect on 651
   of birds 416
   divisions of 628–632
   drugs and 644–652
   functions of 523, 527
   of mammals 426–427
   nerve impulse 623, 624, 625–626
   nerves in skin 495
   neurons in 623–624, 625, 629, 632
   reflexes and 633–634
   safety and 634, 635
   senses 636–642
neurons 623–624, 625, 632
   in brains 629
New Mexico ridgenose rattlesnake 773
niche diversity 769
niches 704, 731
nicotine 577, 647
Nightingale, Florence 606
nitrogen 44
nitrogen bases 78, 108, 109
nitrogen cycle 726–727
nitrogen fixation 726, 727
nodules 727
noninfectious disease 612
   allergies 612–613
   cancer 112, 499–500, 578, 579, 614–616
   diabetes 584, 614
nonrenewable resources 756
nonvascular plants 256–260
   characteristics of 256–257
   hornworts 259
   liverworts 259
   mosses 257–258, 260
nose 568, 569
notochord 374
nuclear membrane 36
nucleic acids 19, 46, 53, 55
nucleolus 36, 37
nucleus 220, 221, 473
   cell 36–37, 38, 39
nutrients 506. See also food
nutrition 506–507
nymph 356, 357

observation 5, 6, 696, 786
octopuses 344
oil glands 497

O'Keeffe, Georgia 291
omnivore 313, 718
open-ocean zone 745
operational definition 791
opossums 433
optical illusions 620–621
optic nerve 638
oral groove 221
Orchrobactrum anthropi 200
orders 186
Ordovician period 162
organelles 35, 37–41, 53
organic compounds 53
organisms 18. *See also* living things
    classifying 182–188
    multicellular 19
    unicellular (single-celled) 19
organizing information 794–795
organpipe cacti 275
organs 311, 475
organ systems 475. *See also* circulatory
    system; digestive system; endocrine
    system; excretory system; muscles
    and muscular system; nervous
    system; skeletal system; skin
Origin of Species, The (Darwin) 150
osculum 321
osmosis 58–59
osteoporosis 487
ostriches 418
Ostrom, John 379
outer ear 640, 641
ovaries 660, 666
    of angiosperm 290, 291, 292
overfishing 387
overpopulation 702
overproduction 150
oviduct 666
ovulation 667
ovules 286, 287, 291, 292
owls 186, 187, 419
oxygen 67
    as abiotic factor 690
    body's need for 566–567
    in gas exchange 571
    methods of obtaining. *See* breathing
    from photosynthesis 63, 64
    in red blood cells 550
oxygen cycle 725–726
oyster drill 342
oysters 343, 344

pacemaker 539, 540
Paleozoic era 162–163
Palm, Theobald A. 510
Panama Canal, disease and construction of
    600
pancreas 527, 660, 661
    digestion and 519, 528
pandas 168–169
Pangaea 156
papilloma viruses 205
paralysis 634
paramecium 221
parasites 205, 710

flatworms 328–329
    roundworms 331
    tapeworms 329
parasitism 710
parathyroid glands 660, 661
parenting, animal 428, 453
park rangers 13
pasque flower 250
passive immunity 608
passive smoking 579
passive transport 59
Pasteur, Louis 22, 23, 45, 593, 607
pasteurization 593
pathogens 593
    barriers keeping out 597
    transfer of 594–595
Pavlov, Ivan 445
peas, Mendel's experiments on 86–91
peat 258
peat moss 256, 258
pedigree (family tree) 117, 123–124
peer pressure 676
Pekingese 177
penicillin 201, 241, 607
Penicillium 235, 237, 241
Penicillium roqueforti 240
penis 665
pepsin 522
Percent Daily Value 516
perching birds 419
peregrine falcon 422
perennials 299
peripheral nervous system 632
peristalsis 521, 528
permafrost 740
permeability, selective 56
Permian period 163
person-to-person transfer of pathogens 594
perspiration 495
pest control, pheromones and 364
pesticides 359
petals 87, 290
petrified fossils 158
petrochemicals 305, 306
Pettygrove, Francis W. 94
phagocytes 600
pharyngeal slits 375
pharynx 568, 569
phenotypes 98, 112
pheromones 362–364
phloem 275, 279, 281, 283
phosphate 78
phosphorus 482, 483, 486, 512
photosynthesis 61–65, 249, 254–255
    in chloroplast 62–63
    energy capture process 62–63, 64
    equation for 64
    food production process 63
    leaves and 278–279
    living things and 65
    by producers 717
    respiration and 69
    in water biomes 742, 744
phototropism 298
physical changes

in adolescence 675
    in adulthood 677
    in childhood 675
    in infancy 673
physical therapists 13
physicians 12
pie charts 798
pigments 63, 225
pill bugs 350
Pinchot, Gifford 758
pioneer plants 258
pioneer species 749
piping plover 772
pistil 87, 290, 291
pith 281
pituitary gland 660, 661
pivot joint 485
placenta 436, 670
placental mammals 431, 433–436
planarians 330
plant(s) 191, 247–268. *See also* forest(s);
    seed plants
    adaptations of 250–251
    chemicals from 304–307
    cloning of 134
    competition among 705
    desert 737
    as food 266–268
    fungi and 241
    life cycles of 253
    limiting factors for 700
    living on land 249–252
    nonvascular plants 256–260
    obtaining and retaining water in 249
    photosynthesis. *See* photosynthesis
    reproduction in 252, 253
    seedless vascular plants 261–265
    support in 252
    transporting materials in 252
    vascular plants 252, 272–299
plant cells 19, 35, 38, 43, 54, 75
plantlike protists 224–230
plasma 549
Plasmodium 222–223
platelets 549, 551, 552
Platyhelminthes (phylum) 327
Plot, Robert 378
poliomyelitis 210
pollen 286
pollination 287, 288
    of angiosperms 291, 292
pollution 757, 774
polymers 347–348
polyp 323–324
ponds 742, 746–747
population growth 757
populations 695–702
    in ecosystem 691
    limiting factors in 699–700
    overpopulation in 702
    population density 695
    size of 696–698, 701, 708
population statement 698
pores 36, 497
    in sponge 321

Porifera (phylum) 321
potassium 512
prairie 737
prairie dogs 688, 689, 692–693
Precambrian 161, 162
precipitation 725
precision farming 267–268
predation 704, 706–708
predator 313, 706–707
preening 412
pregnancy 669
premolars 426, 520
preserved remains 158–159
pressure 546
prey 313, 706–707
primary succession 749
primates 434, 436
probability 94–101
   calculating 95
problem solving 793
producers 717, 719, 720
prokaryotes 41, 190
prophase 74, 77
protective coverings 706
protein(s) 19, 53–54, 506, 510
   blood clotting 136
   digestion of 524–525
   evolutionary similarities in 170
   genes and 107
   plasma, groups of 549
   ribosomal production of 40
   RNA's role in 109, 110
   structure of 53
   transport 59
   in viral coat 207
protein synthesis 108–111
protists 190, 218–232, 593
   animal-like 219–223
   funguslike 223–224
   plantlike 224–230
protozoans 219–223
   with cilia 221
   with flagella 222
   with pseudopods 219–220
   sporozoans 222–223
pseudopods 219–220
puberty 675
punctuated equilibria 164
Punnett squares 96–97, 104
pupa 357
pupil (eye) 637
purebred 87

Quaternary period 163
queen bee 455

rabbits 434
rabies 205, 210, 595, 608
radial symmetry 316, 365
radiation treatment 615–616
radioactive elements 160
radula 341, 343
rafflesia 251
rain forest biome 248, 735–736
   African 780–785

trees of 782
rays 384
recessive alleles 89–90, 122
rectum 529
recycling 199–200, 240, 723–724, 761
red algae 227
red blood cell 42, 58, 126, 531, 549, 550–551
Redi, Francesco 21, 22, 45
red tides (saltwater blooms) 229
reefs, coral 323, 325–326, 769
reflexes 633–634
regeneration 328, 366
relative dating 159
renewable resources 757, 761
   forests as 763
replication, DNA 73, 78–79
reproduction 21
   in amphibians 390–391
   in angiosperms 291
   asexual 195, 236, 311, 322, 324, 325, 328
   in bacteria 192, 195–196
   in birds 416–417
   in cnidarians 324
   in ferns 264
   in fishes 383
   in fungi 235–236
   in gymnosperms 286–288
   in humans 663
   in mammals 428
   in plants 252, 253
   sexual 196, 236, 311, 324, 328, 347
   in sponges 322
   spores for 263
   in worms 328
reproductive systems 475, 663–668
   in females 666–668
   in males 664–665
   sex cells 102–106, 663–664
reptiles 395–404
   adaptations to conserve water in 395–396
   alligators 403
   crocodiles 403
   dinosaurs 378–379, 404
   eggs with shells in 396
   lizards 397–398, 400–401
   obtaining oxygen from air 397
   skin and kidneys in 397, 398
   snakes 395, 399
   turtles 402
resolution of microscope 33
resource use 756
   forest resources 762–764
respiration 66–71, 567
   bacterial 196
   equation for 68
   fermentation 69–70
   photosynthesis and 69
respiratory system 475, 566–580
   barriers keeping pathogens out of 597
   breathing 567, 572–573, 575
   gas exchange 571
   lungs 569, 570, 571
   need for oxygen and 566–567
   path of air through 568–570
   smoking and 577–578

speaking 573–574
responding variable 7, 791
response 443, 444, 623
   to surroundings 20–21
retina 638
rhizoids 257
ribonucleic acid (RNA) 55, 109, 110–111
ribosomes 37, 38, 39, 40, 110
ribs 376
rickets 510
ringworm 240–241
RNA 55
   protein synthesis and 109, 110
   types of 109–111
rocks, vertebrate history in 377–379
rockweed 227
Rocky Mountain spotted fever 595
rodents 434
rods 638
Roosevelt, Theodore 758
root cap 283
roots 282–283
roseate spoonbill 418
roundworms 330–331
Ruska, Ernst 31

sac fungi 237
safety
   in groups 453
   laboratory 11, 799–801
   nervous system and 634, 635
saguaro cactus 703
salamanders 389, 391, 392–393
saliva 520, 597
salivary glands 519
salmonella xxii
saltwater blooms (red tides) 229
sampling 696
sand dollars 367
sarcodines 219–220
saturated fats 509
savannas 737–738
scales on fish 381, 385
scallops 343
scanning electron microscope (SEM) 31
scanning tunneling microscope (STM) 31
scavenger 330, 333, 718
Schaus swallowtail butterfly 773
science 4
   communicating in 9, 787
scientific inquiry 4
scientific investigation, conducting 4–9, 790–791
scientific theory 9, 149
scorpions 352
scrotum 664
scuba divers, coral reefs and 326
scurvy 510–511
sea anemones 323
sea cucumbers 368
sea stars 366–367
sea urchins 365, 368
seaweeds 227
secondary succession 750

sedimentary rock 158, 378
seed(s) 276–278
    germination of 278
    of monocot vs. dicots 293
seed coat 276
seed dispersal 277
    of angiosperms 291, 292
    for gymnosperms 288
seedless vascular plants 261–265
    characteristics of 262–263
    club mosses 265
    ferns 261, 263–264
    horsetails 265
seed plants 272–300
    angiosperms 289–296
    characteristics of 274–283
    growth of 298–299, 300
    gymnosperms 284–288
    responses of 297–299
segmented bodies of arthropods 348
segmented worms 331–333, 334
selective breeding 132–133, 150
selective cutting 763
selective permeability 56
self-pollination 87
semen 665
semicircular canals 641–642
senses 636–642
    balance 636, 641–642
    hearing 636, 640–641
    of mammals 427
    smell 636, 642–643
    taste 636, 642–643
    touch 636, 643
    vision 636, 637–639
sensory neuron 624, 625, 632
sepals 290
septum 539
serving size 515
sex cell 102–106, 663–664
sex chromosomes 121, 122
sex-linked genes 122–123
sexual reproduction 196, 236, 311
    of arthropods 347
    in cnidarians 324
    in worms 328
sharks 384
Siberian husky 177
sickle-cell disease 126–127
Sierra Club 758
SI Système International d'Unités 7,
    788–789
silk 462–469
    feeding silkworms 468
    goddess of 466–467
    metamorphosis of silkworm and 463
    Silk Road and 464–465
Silk Road 464–465
silkworm moth 363
Silurian period 162
simple carbohydrates 508
skates 384
skeletal muscles 489–490, 492, 493
skeletal system 311, 475, 480–487
    bone growth 483

bone strength 482–483
    formation of 484
    functions of 480–482
    joints 484–486
    structure of 483–484
skeleton. See endoskeleton; exoskeleton
skin 475, 494–500
    as barrier against pathogens 597, 598–599
    care of 498–500
    dermis 496, 497, 643
    epidermis 496–497
    excretion and 586
    functions of 494–495
    as sense organ 643
skin cancer 112
skull 376
slime molds 18, 224
sloths 435
slugs 342
small intestine 519, 526–528
smallpox 606
smoking 576–580
    cardiovascular health and 560
    chemicals in tobacco smoke 576–577
    choosing not to smoke 580
    circulatory system problems from 579
    passive 579
    respiratory system problems from
        577–578
smooth muscle 489, 490–491
snails 342, 343, 345
snakes 395, 399
Snow, John 594
soaring flight 422
society, animal 454, 455
sodium 512
    hypertension and intake of 559
soil
    as abiotic factor 691
    arthropods living in 360–361
    earthworms and 333
solvents, agrochemical 306–307
somatic nervous system 632
sound vibrations 640–641
southwestern willow flycatcher 685
speaking 573–574
species 147, 184
    extinct 160, 771–774
    formation of new 155–156
sperm 102, 663, 665
sphagnum moss 258
sphygmomanometer 547
spiders 346, 350–352
spikes in sponges 321, 322
spinal cord 629, 631
spinal cord injuries 634
spinal nerves 632
spindle fibers 77
spiny anteaters 432
sponges 320–322
    characteristics of 320–321
    food and oxygen, obtaining 322, 323
    reproduction in 322
    spikes in 321, 322
    structure of 321

spongy bone 483
spontaneous generation 21–22
spore cases 264
spores 223, 235, 236
    for reproduction 263
sporophyte 253, 257, 264, 275
sporozoans 222–223
squids 344
squirrels 155
staghorn fern 250
stamens 87, 290
Staphylococcus aureus 193
starch 54, 508. See also carbohydrates
starfishes. See sea stars
star-nosed moles 434
Steller's sea lion 773
stems 280–282
    of monocots vs. dicots 293
    structure of 280–281
stigma 290, 291
stimulants 646
stimulus/stimuli 20–21, 443, 444, 623
stirrup 641
stomach
    as barrier against pathogens 597
    digestion and 519, 522–525
stomach acid 597
stomata 63, 278, 279
Streptococci 190
stress 477–479
    dealing with 479
    fight-or-flight response 478
    long-term 479
    physical responses to 477–478
striated muscle 489–490. See also skeletal
    muscle
succession 746–750
    primary 749
    secondary 750
sugars 54, 508. See also carbohydrates
sunlight 690
    limiting exposure to 499–500
sunscreens 498–499
surface zone 744–745
survival behavior 443
sustainable yield 763–764
Sutton, Walter 102–103
sweat glands 497
swim bladders 385–386
swimmerets 351
symbiosis 222, 704, 709–710
symmetry 315–317
    in animals 316–317, 341, 365
synapse 626

tadpoles 390, 391
tail fin 385
tail of iguana 398
taproot system 282
tar 576
target cells 659–660
taste buds 642–643
Taussig, Helen 558
taxonomic key 186–188
taxonomy 183, 186. See also classification

T cells 601, 602, 603, 606
teeth 426, 520
telophase 74, 76
temperate rain forest 736
temperature. *See also* **body temperature**
    as abiotic factor 690–691
    measuring 789
temperature regulation 25
tendons 490
tentacles, mollusks with 343, 344
territory, establishing 451–452
Tertiary period 163
testes 661, 664
testosterone 664
tetanus 595
theory, scientific 9, 149
thigmotropism 297
thorax 355
threadlike fungi 237
threatened species 772
thumb 436
thymine 78, 108
thymus 660, 661
thyroid gland 660, 661, 662
thyroid-stimulating hormone (TSH) 662
thyroxine 662
ticks 352, 595
tissues 474–475
    animal 311
    plant 252
toads 392
tobacco mosaic viruses 205
tolerance, drug 645
toothless mammals 435
tortoises, desert 684
toxin 200–201
trachea 568, 569–570
traits 98, 175. *See also* **genetics**
    controlled by many genes 120
    controlled by single gene 118–119
    inheritance of 89, 444–445
tranquilizers 647
transfer RNA 109, 110–111
transmission electron microscope (TEM) 31
transpiration 280
transport proteins 59
tree cookies, data hidden in 767
trees, annual rings of 281–282. *See also* **forest(s)**
trial and error learning 446
Triassic period 163
triceps 491
tropical ecosystems, diversity in 769
tropical rain forests 735–736
tropisms 297–298
Tsai, Shih-Perng 305
tumors, formation of 615
tundra biome 740–741
tunicates 374
turtles 402
twins 673
Tyrannosaurus rex 379, 404

ulva 226
umbilical cord 670
understory 735, 781, 782
unicellular organisms 19
United States Food and Drug
    Administration (FDA) 430, 515
unsaturated fats 509
uracil 109
urea 581
ureters 581
urethra 582, 665
Urey, Harold 45
urinary bladder 582
urine 397, 581, 583–584, 665
Ursus horribilis 184
uterus 666

vaccination 607–608
vaccine 211, 607
vacuoles 38, 39, 41
vagina 666, 667
valve 538
variables 6–7, 21, 791
vascular plants 252
    seedless 261–265
vascular tissue 252, 257, 262–263, 275, 283
veins 540, 545, 546
Venette, Jean de 358
Venn diagrams 795
ventricle of heart 538, 539
    amphibian 390
    blood pressure and contraction of 547
    force of 542
Venus fly trap 251
vertebra, vertebrae 375, 481
vertebrates 313
    backbone and endoskeleton of 374,
        375–376, 481
    body temperature in 376–377
    chordates 374–375
    evolution of 374–380
    history of 377–380
veterinarians 13
vibrations, sound 640–641
villi 528, 571
Virchow, Rudolf 29
viruses 181, 204–212, 593
    active 207–208
    hidden 208–209
    infectious diseases caused by 200, 210–211
    multiplication of 205, 207–209
    shapes and sizes of 206, 212
    structure of 206–207
vision 636, 637–639
vision problems, correcting 638–639
vitamin(s) 506, 510–512
    C 511
    D 495, 510
    K 511
vocal cords 573–574
voluntary muscles 488

walking legs of crayfish 351
Wallace, Alfred Russel 150
wampum 340
waste products. *See also* **excretory system**
    cellular 36
    movement by cardiovascular system 537
water
    as abiotic factor 690
    in cells 19
    diffusion of water molecules 58–59
    importance to plants of 249
    living things and 55
    molecular structure of 52
    as nutrient 506, 513
    organisms' need for 24
water balance, excretory system and
    585–586
water biomes 742–745
water cycle 724–725
water lily 250
water molds 223
water-soluble vitamins 511, 512
water vapor 44
water vascular system 366, 367
Watson, James 78
waxes 54
weather as limiting factor 700
Weiss Lake 232
wet-mount slide 803
whales, communication among 450
wheat 275
white blood cells 531, 549, 551, 600
whooping crane 773
windpipe. *See* **trachea**
wing of bird 420–421
withdrawal 646
woodpeckers 418
woody stems 281
worker bee 455
worms 327–334
    classification of 327
    flatworms 328–329
    reproduction in 328
    responses of 328, 334
    roundworms 330–331
    segmented 331–333, 334
    tapeworms 329–330
wrasse 381

X chromosome 121, 122
xylem 275, 279, 281, 283

yaks 423
Y chromosome 121, 122
yeast 70, 75, 238–239, 240
yellow fever 600
Yellowstone National Park 748, 776

Zeiss, Carl 31
zooflagellates 222
zygote 252, 253, 663–664, 669

Acknowledgments

Staff Credits

The people who made up the **Life, Earth, and Physical Science** team—representing design services, editorial, editorial services, electronic publishing technology, manufacturing & inventory planning, marketing, marketing services, market research, online services & multimedia development, production services, product planning, project office, publishing processes—are listed below. Bold type denotes core team members.

Carolyn Belanger, Barbara Bertell, Kristen Braghi, **Roger Calado, Jonathan Cheney, Lisa Clark,** Ed Cordero, Patricia Cully, Patricia Dambry, **Kathleen Dempsey,** Jim Fellows, Joel Gendler, Robert Graham, Joanne Hudson, Don Manning, Brent McKenzie, Paul W. Murphy, **Cindy Noftle,** Julia Osborne, **Caroline M. Power,** Shelley Ryan, **Robin Santel,** Helen Young

Additional Credits

Peggy Bliss, Barnard Gage, Julia Gecha, Adam Goldberg, Jessica Gould, Anne Jones, Dorothy Kavanaugh, Toby Klang, Jay Kulpan, Danny Marcus, Jeanne Maurand, Shilo McDonald, Carolyn McGuire, Tania Mlawer, Angela Sciaraffa

Illustrations

Alexander and Turner: 253, 287, 292, 293
Sally Bensusen: 343, 357
Suzanne Biron: 26, 43, 80, 92, 100, 152, 170, 212, 238, 260, 300
Phil & Jim Bliss: 1b, 1m
Annette Cable: 306–307
Carmella Clifford: 637, 641
Warren Cutler: 413
Bruce Day: 478,
David Fuller: 146–147
Andrea Golden: 179, 319, 682t
Biruta Hansen: 362, 398, 692–693
Floud E. Hosmer: 624
JB Woolsey Associates: xvii, 5, 7, 8, 8tl, 8tr, 20, 64t, 87, 92b, 93br, 96, 97, 99, 104, 119, 121, 123, 124, 135, 143, 162, 163, 166, 169, 174, 183, 187, 188, 207b, 227, 235t, 271t, 283, 290, 295, 300, 314, 317, 332, 348, 374, 380, 382, 390, 400, 416, 421, 444, 461, 520, 541, 567, 573, 619, 633, 639, 649, 651, 655, 668, 678, 681, 694, 698, 708, 719, 725b, 746, 753b, 792, 401
John Edwards & Associates: 45, 483, 625, 630, 722, 731, 744
Keith Kasnot: 37br, 40tr, 521, 523
MapQuest.com,Inc.: 155, 683tm, 683tr, 735, 736, 738
Martucci Studio: 75, 215, 245t, 303, 407, 503, 515, 563, 577, 594, 615, 705, 741, 753t, 796b, 797, 798
Matt Mayerchak: 47, 81, 14, 171, 213, 243, 335, 369, 459, 501, 531, 587, 617, 653, 679, 751, 794, 795b, 795m
Fran Milner: xii, xxi, 311, 351, 355, 385, 391b, 393, 528, 544, 550–51, 570
Karen Minot: 465, 466
Paul Mirocha: 447
Morgan Cain & Associates: 19b, 19t, 22, 23, 32, 49, 52, 57, 59, 68, 76–77, 78, 79, 105, 108, 109, 110, 160, 206b, 206t, 207t, 236, 245b, 271b, 279, 350, 371, 388, 429, 473, 496, 522, 539, 543, 549, 553, 589, 596, 600, 609, 626, 632, 662, 711, 713, 717, 749, 750, 788l, 788r, 789tl, 789tr
Ortelius Design: 189br, 198bl, 198t, 199b, 199t, 232, 456, 464–65, 602, 729
Stephanie Pershing: ix, 261
Judith Pinkham: 334, 345, 400, 414, 449, 493, 498, 524, 548, 575, 610, 627, 678, 694, 767
Matthew Pippin: 377, 724b
Pat Rossi: 208–209, 220b, 221b, 329, 375, 375r, 396, 426, 427, 445, 485bl, 485br, 485tl, 485tr
Richard Salzman-Walter Stuart: xviii, 404, 455
Sandra Sevigny: 475, 481
Walter Stuart: 538, 158tl, 234bl, 321, 367, 720, 257, 263
Cynthia Turner: 276b, 291

Photography

Photo Research Sharon Donahue, Sue McDermott, Paula Wehde
Cover image Steve Bloom/Masterfile

Front Matter: Page i, ii, Steve Bloom/Masterfile; **iiil,** Courtesy of Michael J. Padilla, Ph.D.; **iiir,** Courtesy of Martha Cyr, Ph.D. and Ioannis Miaoulis, Ph.D ; **viiit,** Fran Lanting/Minden Pictures; **viiib,** Dr. David Scott/CNRI/Phototake; **ixt,** Frans Lanting/Minden Pictures; **ixbm,** Ray Coleman/Photo Researchers; **ixbr,** Biozentrum, University of Basel/Science Photo Library/Photo Researchers; **xl,** Frans Lanting/Minden Pictures; **xm,** Belinda Wright/DRK Photo; **xr,** Fred Whitehead/Animals Animals; **xitl,** Renee Lynn/Tony Stone Images; **xibl,** Stuart Westmorland/Natural Selection; **xitr,** Robert Calentine/Visuals Unlimited; **xibr,** Joe McDonald/Tom Stack & Associates; **xiit,** Andrew Syred/Science Photo Library/ Photo Researchers; **xiib,** Bill Longcore/Science Source/Photo Researchers; **xiiit,** Pete Saloutos/The Stock Market; **xiiibl, bm,** Superstock; **xiiibr,** Salisbury District Hospital/Science Photo Library/Photo Researchers; **xivt,** David Lassman/The Image Works; **xivm,** David Liebman; **xivb,** Daryl Balfour/Tony Stone Images; **xv,** Richard Haynes; **xvi,** James L. Amos/Photo Researchers; **xvii, xviii,** Richard Haynes; **xviii inset,** Runk/Schoenberger/Grant Heilman Photography; **xixt,** Images International/Erwin C. Bud Nielsen/Visuals Unlimited; **xixb,** Richard Haynes; **xxt,** James Watt/Animals Animals; **xxb,** The Granger Collection, NY; **xxi,** Art Wolfe/Tony Stone Images; **xxii,** Courtesy of Cindy Friedman; **2,** Michael Dick/Animals Animals; **3l,** Courtesy of Cindy Friedman; **3r,** USDA/S.S./Photo Researchers.

Introduction to Life Science
Page 4, David Young-Wolff/PhotoEdit; **5,** Daniel J. Cox/Tony Stone Images; **6,** John Warden/Tony Stone Images; **7,** Bill Banaszewski/Visuals Unlimited; **9,** Roger Tully/Tony Stone Images; **10,** Photo Spin/Artville/PNI; **11,** Richard Haynes; **12t,** Charles Gupton/Tony Stone Images; **12m,** Nieto/Jerrican/Photo Researchers; **12b,** Douglas Faulkner/The Stock Market; **13tl,** Andrea Sacks/Tony Stone Images; **13bl,** Jeff Dunn/ IndexStock Imagery; **13tr,** Paula Lerner/IndexStock Imagery; **13br,** Tim Thompson/Tony Stone Images; **14,** David Young-Wolff/PhotoEdit.

Chapter 1
Pages 16–17, Joe McDonald/DRK Photo; **18t,** Russ Lappa; **18b,** Beatty/Visuals Unlimited; **19,** John Pontier/Animals Animals; **21,** Michael Quinton/Minden Pictures; **22, 23,** The Granger Collection, NY; **24l,** James Dell/Science Source/Photo Researchers; **24r,** Zig Leszcynski/Animals Animals; **25,** Jim Brandenburg/Minden Pictures; **27t,** Richard Haynes; **27b,** Joseph Nettis/Photo Researchers; **27 inset,** John Coletti/Stock Boston; **28, 29l,** The Granger Collection, NY; **29r,** Caroline Biological Supply Company/Phototake; **30 both,** The Granger Collection, NY.; **31t,** H.R. Bramaz/Peter Arnold; **31bl,** Corbis-Bettmann; **31br,** Lawrence Migdale/Stock Boston; **33,** CNRI/Science Photo Library/Photo Researchers; **34t,** Runk/Schoenberger/Grant Heilman Photography; **34b,** Doug Wilson/Westlight; **35l,** M. Abbey/Visuals Unlimited; **35r,** Runk/Schoenberger/ Grant Heilman Photography; **36,** Dr. Dennis Kunkel/Phototake; **37,** Bill Longcore/Photo Researchers; **40,** K.G. Murtis/Visuals Unlimited; **41,** John Cardamone/Tony Stone Images; **42l,** Dr. David Scott/CNRI/Phototake; **42r,** Dr. Dennis Kunkel/Phototake; **43,** Runk/ Schoenberger/Grant Heilman Photography; **44,** Russ Lappa; **46,** Biological Photo Service.

Chapter 2
Pages 50–51, Julie Habel/Westlight; **52,** Russ Lappa; **53,** Gary Bell/Masterfile; **54,** Okapia-Frankfurt/Photo Researchers; **54 inset,** Andrew Syred/Science Photo Library/Photo Researchers; **55,** Hans Blohm/Masterfile; **56,** NASA; **58l,** Stanley Flegler/Visuals Unlimited; **58m, 58r,** David M. Phillips/Visuals Unlimited; **60,** M. Abbey/Visuals Unlimited; **61t,** Russ Lappa; **61b,** Paul Barton/The Stock Market; **62,** Cosmo Condina/Tony Stone Images; **62 inset,** Biophoto Associates/Photo Researchers; **63t,** Russ Lappa; **63bl&br,** Dr. Jeremy Burgess/Science Photo Library/Photo Researchers; **65t,** Frans Lanting/Minden Pictures; **65b,** Tom J. Ulrich/Visuals Unlimited; **66,** William Johnson/Stock Boston; **67l,** Phil Dotson/Photo Researchers; **67r,** Stephen Dalton/Photo Researchers; **69,** Mark Newman/Visuals Unlimited; **70,** Terje Rakke/The Image Bank; **72t,** David Scharf/Peter Arnold; **72b,** Larry Lefever/Grant Heilman Photography; **73,** Art Wolfe/Tony Stone Images; **74,** Biophoto Associates/Science Source/Photo Researchers; **75b,** Roy Morso/The Stock Market; **76 all, 77 all,** M. Abbey/Photo Researchers; **80,** Robert Knauft/Biology Media.

Chapter 3

Pages 84–85, Ron Kimball; **86t,** Mike Rothwell/Tony Stone Images; **86b,** Corbis-Bettmann; **87,** Barry Runk/Grant Heilman Photography; **90 both,** Meinrad Faltner/The Stock Market; **91,** Inga Spence/Index Stock Imagery; **94–95,** Image Stop/Phototake; **98,** Hans Reinhard/Bruce Coleman; **101,** Richard Haynes; **102l,** David M. Phillips/Photo Researchers; **102r,** University "La Sapienza," Rome/Science Photo Library/Photo Researchers; **103l,** Jonathan D. Speer/Visuals Unlimited; **103r,** M. Abbey/Photo Researchers; **107,** AP/Wide World Photos; **112,** William E. Ferguson; **113,** Mike Rothwell/Tony Stone Images.

Chapter 4

Pages 116–117, Herb Snitzer/Stock Boston; **118,** Richard Haynes; **120,** Camille Tokerud/Tony Stone Images; **121 both,** Biophoto Associates/Science Source/Photo Researchers; **122,** Andrew McClenaghan/Science Photo Library/Photo Researchers; **124,** Superstock; **125t,** CNRI/Science Photo Library/Photo Researchers; **125b,** Lawrence Migdale/Tony Stone Images; **126t,** Simon Fraser/RVI, Newcastle-upon-TYNE/Science Photo Library/Photo Researchers; **126b,** Stanley Flegler/Visuals Unlimited; **127,** Corbis-Bettmann; **128,** Mugshots/The Stock Market, **128 inset,** CNRI/Science Photo Library/Photo Researchers; **129,** Will and Deni McIntyre/Photo Researchers Inc.; **130,** Richard Haynes; **132,** AP/Wide World Photos; **133,** Tim Barnwell/Stock Boston; **134,** Patricia J. Bruno/Positive Images; **135,** LeLand Bobbe/Tony Stone Images; **136,** Gary Wagner/Stock Boston; **137,** AP/Wide World Photos; **138,** U.S. Department of Energy/Human Genome Management Information System, Oak Ridge National Laboratory; **139,** Michael Newman/PhotoEdit; **140,** David Parker/Science Photo Library/Photo Researchers.

Chapter 5

Pages 144–145, Bill Varie/Westlight; **146t,** Portrait by George Richmond/Down House, Downe/The Bridgeman Art Library; **146b,** Corbis-Bettmann; **147t,** Tui De Roy/Minden Pictures; **147m,** Frans Lanting/Minden Pictures; **147b,** Tui De Roy/Minden Pictures; **148l,** Zig Leszczynski/Animals Animals; **148r,** Tui De Roy/Minden Pictures; **149,** Dr. Jeremy Burgess/Science Photo Library/Photo Researchers; **150,** Mitsuaki Iwago/Minden Pictures; **151,** Jeff Gnass Photography/The Stock Market; **153,** Richard Haynes; **154 both,** Breck P. Kent; **155 both,** Pat & Tom Leeson/Photo Researchers; **156t,** John Cancalosi/Tom Stack & Associates; **156b,** Tom McHugh/Photo Researchers; **157t,** James L. Amos/Photo Researchers; **157b,** Sinclair Stammers/Science Photo Library/Photo Researchers; **161,** Robert Landau/Westlight; **165,** Richard Haynes; **167l,** Keith Gillett/Animals Animals; **167m,** George Whiteley/Photo Researchers; **167r,** David Spears Ltd./Science Photo Library/Photo Researchers; **168l,** Gary Milburn/Tom Stack & Associates; **168r,** Daryl Balfour/Tony Stone Images; **174t,** Peter Cade/Tony Stone Images; **174m,** Tim Fitzharris/Minden Pictures; **174b,** Bridgeman Art Library; **175,** Ron Kimball; **176tr,** Charles Philip/Westlight; **176br,** Jack Daniels/Tony Stone Images; **176 the rest,** Corel Corp.; **177b,** C. Jeanne White/Photo Researchers; **177 the rest,** Corel Corp.; **178t,** Peter Cade/Tony Stone Images; **178–179b,** Nick Meers/Panoramic Images; **178 inset,** AP/ Wide World Photos.

Chapter 6

Pages 180–181, Institut Pasteur/CNRI/Phototake; **182t,** Russ Lappa; **182b,** Inga Spence/IndexStock Imagery; **184l,** Gerard Lacz/Animals Animals; **184m,** Tom Brakefield/DRK Photo; **184r,** Ron Kimball; **185,** J. Serrao/Visuals Unlimited; **186–187,** Thomas Kitchin/Tom Stack & Associates; **189,** Alan L. Detrick/Photo Researchers; **190t,** David M. Phillips/Photo Researchers; **190b,** Microfield Scientific Ltd/Science Photo Library/Photo Researchers; **191,** Ray Coleman/Photo Researchers; **192t,** Richard Haynes; **192b,** Science Photo Library/Photo Researchers; **193t,** Oliver Meckes/Photo Researchers; **193m,** David M. Phillips/Visuals Unlimited; **193b,** Scott Camazine/Photo Researchers; **194,** Dr. Rony Brain/Science Photo Library/Photo Researchers; **195,** Dr. K. S. Kim/Peter Arnold; **196,** Dr. Ennis Kunkel/Phototake; **197,** Alfred Pasieka/Peter Arnold; **198t,** PhotoDisc, Inc.; **198b,** Sally Ann Ullmann/FoodPix; **199t,** John Marshall/Tony Stone Images; **199b,** FoodPix; **200t,** E. Webben/Visuals Unlimited; **200b,** Ben Osborne/Tony Stone Images; **200 inset,** Michael Abbey/Photo Researchers; **203,** Richard Haynes; **204t,** Russ Lappa; **204bl,** Dr. Linda Stannard, UCT/Science Photo Library/Photo Researchers; **204bm,** Lee D. Simon/Science Source/Photo Researchers; **204br,** Dr. Brad Fute/Peter Arnold; **205m,** Tektoff-RM/CNRI/Science Photo Library/Photo Researchers; **205r,** CDC/Science Source/Photo Researchers; **208,** Biozentrum, University of Basel/Science Photo Library/Photo Researchers; **209,** Lee D. Simon/Science Source/Photo Researchers; **210,** James Darell/Tony Stone Images; **211,** David M. Dennis/Tom Stack & Associates; **212,** Custom Medical Stock; **213,** Biozentrum, University of Basel/Science Photo Library/Photo Researchers.

Chapter 7

Pages 216–217, David M. Dennis/Tom Stack & Associates; **218t,** Science VU/Visuals Unlimited; **218b,** Jan Hinsch/Science Photo Library/Photo Researchers; **219tl,** O.S.F./Animals Animals; **219tr,** A. Le Toquin/Photo Researchers; **219b,** Gregory G. Dimijian/Photo Researchers; **220,** Astrid & Hanns-Frieder Michler/Science Photo Library/Photo Researchers; **221,** Eric Grave/Science Source/Photo Researchers; **222,** Michael P. Gadomski/Photo Researchers; **222 inset,** Jerome Paulin/Visuals Unlimited; **223t,** Oliver Meckes/Photo Researchers; **223b,** Dwight R. Kuhn; **224 both,** David M. Dennis/Tom Stack & Associates; **225t,** Russ Lappa; **225b,** Sinclair Stammers Oxford Scientific Films; **226t,** David M. Phillips/Visuals Unlimited; **226bl,** D.P.Wilson/Eric & Daid Hosking/Photo Researchers; **226br,** Andrew Syred/Science Photo Library/Photo Researchers; **228t,** Richard Haynes; **228b,** Doug Perrine/Hawaii Whale Research Foundation - NMFS permit#882/Innerspace Visions; **229,** Sanford Berry/Visuals Unlimited; **230,** Kenneth H. Thomas/Photo Researchers; **232,** Robert P. Falls; **233t,** Russ Lappa; **233b,** Michael Fogden/Animals Animals; **234,** Fred Unverhau/Animals Animals/Earth Scenes; **235,** Nobel Proctor/Science Source/Photo Researchers; **236,** David Scharf/Peter Arnold; **237tl,** E.R. Degginger/Photo Researchers; **237bl,** Michael Fogden/Animals Animals/Earth Scenes; **237tr,** Rod Planck/Tom Stack & Associates; **237br,** Andrew McClenagham/Science Photo Library/Photo Researchers; **239,** Richard Haynes; **240,** David M. Dennis/Tom Stack & Associates; **241,** Rob Simpson/ Visuals Unlimited; **242l,** Rod Planck/Tom Stack & Associates; **242r,** Frans Lanting/Minden Pictures; **243,** Gregory G. Dimijian/Photo Researchers.

Chapter 8

Pages 246–247, J. Lotter Gurling/Tom Stack & Associates; **248,** Joanne Lotter/Tom Stack & Associates; **249,** Kjell B. Sandved/Photo Researchers; **250tl,** Richard J. Green/Photo Researchers; **250tr,** Brenda Tharp/Photo Researchers; **250m,** R. Van Nostrand/Photo Researchers; **250b,** Joe McDonald/Visuals Unlimited; **251tl,** Prenzel/Animals Animals/Earth Scenes; **251tr,** Frans Lanting/Minden Pictures; **251m,** Andrew J. Martinez/Photo Researchers; **251b,** Runk/Schoenberger/Grant Heilman Photography; **252,** Doug Wechsler/ Animals Animals/Earth Scenes; **254,** Richard Haynes; **255,** Images International/ Erwin C. Bud Nielsen/Visuals Unlimited; **256t,** Russ Lappa; **256b,** Christi Carter from Grant Heilman Photography; **257,** Runk/Schoenberger/Grant Heilman Photography; **258t,** Silkeborg Museum; **258b,** Farrell Grehan/Photo Researchers; **259l,** Runk/Schoenberger/Grant Heilman Photography; **259r,** William E. Ferguson; **260, 261,** Richard Haynes; **262,** Runk/Schoenberger/Grant Heilman Photography; **263,** Rod Planck/Tom Stack & Associates; **264t,** Milton Rand/Tom Stack & Associates; **264b,** Joanne Lotter/Tom Stack & Associates; **265l,** Frans Lanting/Minden Pictures; **265r,** Runk/Schoenberger/Grant Heilman Photography; **266,** Herve Donnezan/Photo Researchers; **267,** William James Warren/Westlight; **268,** Arthur C. Smith III/Grant Heilman Photography; **269,** Frans Lanting/Minden Pictures.

Chapter 9

Pages 272–273, E.R. Degginger; **274t,** Russ Lappa; **274b,** E. R. Degginger/Animals Animals/Earth Scenes; **275l,** Thomas Kitchin/Tom Stack & Associates; **275m,r,** Carr Clifton/Minden Pictures; **277tl,** D. Cavagnaro/Visuals Unlimited; **277bl,** E. R. Degginger; **277tr,** Frans Lanting/Minden Pictures; **277br,** William Harlow/Photo Researchers; **278 both,** Runk/Schoenberger/Grant Heilman Photography; **280,** Dani/Jeske Animals Animals/Earth Scenes; **282tl,** Runk/Schoenberger/Grant Heilman Photography; **282 the rest,** Robert Calentine/Visuals Unlimited; **284t,** Richard Haynes; **284b,** Bruce M. Herman/Photo Researchers; **285tl,** Ken Brate/Photo Researchers; **285tr,** Jim Strawser/Grant Heilman Photography; **285b,** Michael Fogden/Animals Animals/Earth Scenes; **286l,** Breck P. Kent/Animals Animals/Earth Scenes; **286r,** Breck P. Kent; **288,** C.J. Allen/Stock Boston; **289t,** Russ Lappa; **289b,** Jim Strawser/Grant Heilman Photography; **290,** E. R. Degginger; **291,** Private Collections/Art Resource; **294,** Richard Haynes; **296,** Alan Pitcairn/Grant Heilman Photography; **297,** William J. Weber/Visuals Unlimited; **298,** Porterfield-Chickering/Photo Researchers; **299tl,** E. R. Degginger; **299tr,** Mark E. Gibson/The Stock Market; **299b,** Larry Lefever/Grant Heilman Photography; **301,** Larry Lefever/Grant Heilman Photography; **304t,** Holt Studios International/Photo Researchers; **304b,** Andy Goodwin/Discover Magazine; **305t,** Courtesy of Rathin Datta; **305b,** Martin Bond/SDL/Photo Researchers; **306,** Paul Conklin/PhotoEdit.

Chapter 10

Pages 308–309, Hal Beral/Visuals Unlimited; **310t,** Richard Haynes; **310b,** Gary Bell/Masterfile; **312l,** Frans Lanting/Minden Pictures; **312r,** Oliver Strewe/Tony Stone Images; **313,** David & Tess Young/Tom Stack & Associates; **315,** Corel Corp.; **316,** William C. Jorgensen/Visuals Unlimited; **317l,** Daniel W. Gotshall/Visuals Unlimited; **317r,** Tim Davis/Tony Stone Images; **318,** Ted Kerasote/Photo Researchers; **320t,** Russ Lappa; **320b,** Gregory Ochocki/Photo Researchers;